CLASSICS IN EAST ASIAN BUDDHISM

Zen Evangelist

Shenhui, Sudden Enlightenment, and the Southern School of Chan Buddhism

JOHN R. McRAE

Edited by James Robson and Robert H. Sharf, with Fedde de Vries

A KURODA INSTITUTE BOOK
University of Hawai'i Press
Honolulu

© 2023 Kuroda Institute
All rights reserved
Printed in the United States of America

First printing, 2023

Library of Congress Cataloging-in-Publication Data

Names: McRae, John R., author. | Robson, James, editor. | Sharf, Robert H., editor. | De Vries, Fedde, editor. | Shenhui, 684-758. Works. Selections. English.
Title: Zen evangelist : Shenhui, sudden enlightenment, and the southern school of Chan Buddhism / John R. McRae ; edited by James Robson and Robert H. Sharf, with Fedde de Vries.
Other titles: Classics in East Asian Buddhism.
Description: Honolulu : University of Hawai'i Press, [2023] | Series: Classics in East Asian Buddhism | "A Kuroda Institute Book." | Includes bibliographical references and index.
Identifiers: LCCN 2022056042 (print) | LCCN 2022056043 (ebook) | ISBN 9780824895624 (hardback) | ISBN 9780824896461 (pdf) | ISBN 9780824896478 (epub) | ISBN 9780824896485 (kindle edition)
Subjects: LCSH: Shenhui, 684-758. | Zen Buddhism—China—Doctrines. | Buddhism—China—History—581-960.
Classification: LCC BQ9299.S547 M37 2023 (print) | LCC BQ9299.S547 (ebook) | DDC 294.3/9270951—dc23/eng/20221215
LC record available at https://lccn.loc.gov/2022056042
LC ebook record available at https://lccn.loc.gov/2022056043

The Kuroda Institute for the Study of Buddhism and Human Values is a nonprofit, educational corporation founded in 1976. One of its primary objectives is to promote scholarship on the historical, philosophical, and cultural ramifications of Buddhism. In association with the University of Hawai'i Press, the Institute also publishes Studies in East Asian Buddhism. To complement these scholarly studies, the Institute also makes available in the present series reliable translations of some of the major classics of East Asian Buddhism.

Cover art: Master Shenhui. Detail from the "Scroll of Buddhist Images" by Zhang Shengwen. Song Dynasty. Reproduced with the permission of the National Palace Museum, Taiwan.

University of Hawai'i Press books are printed on acid-free paper and meet the guidelines for permanence and durability of the Council on Library Resources.

Kuroda Institute
Classics in East Asian Buddhism

The Record of Tung-shan
William F. Powell

Tracing Back the Radiance: Chinul's Korean Way of Zen
Robert E. Buswell Jr.

The Great Calming and Contemplation: A Study and Annotated Translation of the First Chapter of Chih-i's Mo-ho chih-kuan
Neal Donner and Daniel Stevenson

Inquiry into the Origin of Humanity: An Annotated Translation of Tsung-mi's Yüan jen lun *with a Modern Commentary*
Peter N. Gregory

Zen in Medieval Vietnam: A Study and Translation of the Thiền Uyển Tập Anh
Cuong Tu Nguyen

Hōnen's Senchakushū: *Passages on the Selection of the Nembutsu in the Original Vow*
Senchakushū English Translation Project

The Origins of Buddhist Monastic Codes in China: An Annotated Translation and Study of the Changyuan qinggui
Yifa

The Scriptures of Wŏn Buddhism: A Translation of Wŏnbulgyo kyojŏn *with Introduction*
Bongkil Chung

Personal Salvation and Filial Piety: Two Precious Scroll Narratives of Guanyin and Her Acolytes
Wilt L. Idema

Signs from the Unseen Realm: Buddhist Miracle Tales from Early Medieval China
Robert Ford Campany

The Secrets of Buddhist Meditation: Visionary Meditation Texts from Early Medieval China
Eric M. Greene

Zen Evangelist: Shenhui, Sudden Enlightenment, and the Southern School of Chan Buddhism
John R. McRae
Edited by James Robson and Robert H. Sharf, with Fedde de Vries

Contents

Foreword by Peter N. Gregory — ix

Preface by James Robson and Robert H. Sharf — xiii

Abbreviations and Conventions — xxiii

Introduction: Shenhui and the Teaching of Sudden Enlightenment — 1

Part I. Texts — 43

Editor's Note by Fedde de Vries — 45

Platform Sermon — 47

Definition of the Truth — 72

Miscellaneous Dialogues — 129

Verses on the Five Watches — 221

Verses on Sudden Enlightenment, the Birthless, and *Prajñā* — 226

Part II. Shenhui and the Chan Tradition — 233

Religion as Revolution: Hu Shih on Shenhui's Role in Chan — 235

Shenhui as Evangelist: Re-envisioning the Identity of a Chinese Buddhist Monk — 275

APPENDIX: TEXTUAL SOURCES	301
BIBLIOGRAPHY	309
INDEX	323

Foreword

It is with great pleasure and deep satisfaction that the Kuroda Institute for the Study of Buddhism, in cooperation with the University of Hawai'i Press, is *finally* able to bring John McRae's unfinished manuscript on Shenhui to completion with this volume. Through the efforts and persistence of many colleagues and friends of John's, as Bob Sharf and James Robson detail in their preface, it represents the Kuroda Institute's continued commitment to publish major contributions to the study of East Asian Buddhism. John's work surely falls into that category of significance, and the result is something of which the Kuroda Institute is justly proud. The book also stands as a tribute to John as a colleague and friend. Even in its partially realized state, it is only fit that the Kuroda Institute should publish it, for John was a core member of the Institute through nearly the whole of his career, from 1980 to his untimely death in 2011—a period coinciding with Kuroda's emergence as a leading academic institution dedicated to the promotion of high-quality, cutting-edge research on East Asian Buddhism. John played a central role in this development over the course of three decades, thereby helping to establish the study of East Asian Buddhism as a vital area within the broader academic domains of Buddhist Studies and Asian Studies.

John was one of the original cohort of young scholars who gathered for the first Kuroda Institute conference, held at the Zen Center of Los Angeles in the spring of 1980, at which he presented a paper on the Oxhead school of early Chinese Chan (a revised version of which was subsequently published in the first Kuroda book in 1983).[1] This event was the catalyst for Kuroda's subsequent development as an academic enterprise, for the wealth of ideas generated by the synergy among the conference participants brought future conferences and publication possibilities into focus. The next conference, on the sudden and gradual polarity in Chinese thought, took place at the Kuroda Institute in Los Angeles in May 1981, with support from the American Council of Learned Societies.[2] At this conference, John presented a

---

1. *Studies in Ch'an and Hua-yen*, edited by Robert M. Gimello and Peter N. Gregory.
2. *Sudden and Gradual: Approaches to Enlightenment in Chinese Thought*, edited by Peter N. Gregory (1987).

paper on Shenhui and the sudden teaching, a revised version of which now serves as the introduction to this presentation of his Shenhui translations. Kuroda's third conference, assembling a different group of scholars to address the significance of the thirteenth-century Japanese Zen master Dōgen, was hosted by the Tassajara Zen Mountain Center in Big Sur in October of the same year.[3]

The success of these conferences and the sense of scholarly community they fostered among the participants brought the issue and necessity of publication to the fore. Since no viable venue for publishing conference volumes on these topics existed at the time, the Kuroda Institute invited the University of Hawai'i Press, a longtime publisher of books and texts in Asian Studies, to enter into a copublishing agreement for a series on East Asian Buddhism. Thus began a highly successful partnership that has lasted for four decades.[4] This volume marks the forty-third publication in our series, with future volumes currently in production, under revision, or under review.

John was a discussant in the fourth Kuroda conference, on traditions of meditation in East Asian Buddhism, held in May 1983. He also was an indispensable presence in a second Dōgen conference, held at both the Kuroda Institute and California State University, Los Angeles, in October 1983, which brought together three American scholars and four eminent Japanese colleagues, for whom John was a deft and indefatigable translator throughout the proceedings; moreover, he not only translated but presented the paper prepared by Takasaki Jikidō, who was unable to attend.[5] The sixth Kuroda conference, on Buddhist hermeneutics, was held at the Kuroda Institute in 1984, with support from the National Endowment for the Humanities. Although John was unable to attend, he had played a vital role in four of the first six Kuroda conferences.

At the Institute's next major event, a greatly expanded conference on Buddhist soteriology held at UCLA in 1988, John presented a paper on how encounter dialogue, so characteristic of the "classical" Chan discourse of the Song dynasty, reframed traditional notions of the Buddhist path to liberation. By this time, the Kuroda Institute had succeeded in establishing itself at the center of the burgeoning field of East Asian Buddhism, due in large part to its publications with the University of Hawai'i Press. Five of its early conferences had borne fruit in its Studies in East Asian Buddhism

---

3. The conference papers were subsequently published as *Dōgen Studies,* edited by William R. LaFleur (1985).

4. Here I would like to acknowledge the invaluable role that two superb editors at the press, Stuart Kiang and Patricia Crosby, played in launching, establishing, and building the series over the course of those forty years, a role that has continued to be played by their capable successor, Stephanie Chun. The overall success of the series owes much to their dedicated support.

5. Unfortunately, this was the only Kuroda conference out of the first six that did not make it to publication.

series.⁶ It had also published its first monograph by a single author, John's landmark study *The Northern School and the Formation of Early Ch'an Buddhism* (1986); on top of which, it had undertaken a second series with the University of Hawai'i Press, titled Classics in East Asian Buddhism, devoted to the publication of significant translations.⁷

The idea for the soteriology conference had first come up in the "what next?" discussion at the end of the second Kuroda conference, on the sudden/gradual polarity. It had resurfaced again at the end of the fourth conference, on traditions of meditation, as well as the sixth conference, on Buddhist hermeneutics. As a recurring topic in Kuroda board meetings, it gained traction when Rob Gimello and Robert Buswell, who had both been instrumental in getting the Kuroda Institute off the ground, proposed organizing a conference on Buddhist soteriology at UCLA, where Buswell had just been tenured. This was an opportunity to mount a conference on a much larger scale, bringing together a wide-ranging group of scholars with support from new and major sources, and it led to the publication of *Paths to Liberation: The Mārga and Its Transformations in Buddhist Thought*, edited by Gimello and Buswell, in 1992.

This UCLA conference brought to a close the first stage in the development of the Kuroda Institute. As the last Kuroda-inspired conference, it marked a transition to a new mode of operation in which the Institute would dedicate its main energies to its ongoing publication series. In response to new disciplinary approaches and areas of research, the Kuroda Institute's publications expanded in range over the course of the following years, and single-authored monographs came to predominate. As a member of the Kuroda board, John continued to play an invaluable role in that evolution, helping to guide the Institute's activities by reviewing and assessing manuscripts for publication, juggling finances to keep book production on track, and selecting future board members, not to mention a myriad of other tasks. It is thus with deep appreciation for all of John McRae's manifold contributions to Kuroda that the Institute publishes this volume.

Peter N. Gregory
Past Executive Director

---

6. The fifth volume in the series was *Buddhist Hermeneutics*, edited by Donald S. Lopez, Jr. (1988).

7. The first volume was *The Record of Tung-shan*, translated by William F. Powell (1986).

Preface

At the time of John R. McRae's untimely death in Bangkok on October 22, 2011, following a sixteen-month struggle with pancreatic cancer, he left behind a number of unfinished works, most notably a book-manuscript on the Chinese Chan master Shenhui 神會 (684–758), which included translations of Shenhui's writings and recorded lectures. McRae had been working on Shenhui off and on since the 1980s, and in 1999, at the prodding of Peter Gregory, he submitted a complete draft of his book on Shenhui to the board of the Kuroda Series (of which he was himself a member) to be reviewed for publication. The volume, entitled "Evangelical Zen: Shen-hui (684–758), the Sudden Teaching, and the Southern School of Chinese Ch'an Buddhism," received the enthusiastic support of the reviewers as well as from his colleagues on the Kuroda Board, and he was encouraged to ready the manuscript for publication.

But McRae was not forthcoming with his final revisions. He was a stickler, a perfectionist who felt there were still loose ends to be tied up. At the same time, he was becoming increasingly involved with the Bukkyō Dendō Kyōkai English translation series, translating five major texts for the series and serving as Publication Committee Chair for the project from 2006 until his death in 2011.[1] He was also engaged in writing an introductory book on Chan intended for a lay audience, and the finished book, *Seeing through Zen: Encounter, Transformation, and Genealogy in Chinese Chan Buddhism* (2003), incorporated some of the material from his Shenhui manuscript. His work on the Shenhui volume seems to have taken a back seat to these other projects through much of the 2000s.

In the meantime, the hard-copy facsimile of McRae's 1999 submission to Kuroda circulated among his colleagues. It was comprised of two parts, known as the "White Binder" and the "Blue Binder" from the colors of the three-ring binders used for the original submission. (The White Binder

---

1. McRae translated the *Questions of Mañjuśrī* (文殊師利問經, T 468); the *Vimalakīrti Sūtra* (維摩詰所說經, T 475); the *Śūramgama Samādhi Sūtra* (佛說首楞嚴三昧經, T 642); *Essentials of the Transmission of Mind* (黄檗山斷際禪師傳心法要, T 2012-A); and the *Platform Sūtra of the Sixth Patriarch* (六祖大師法寶壇經, T 2008). He was working on Jizang's *Commentary on the Meaning of the Lotus Sutra* (法華義疏, T 1721) at the time of his death.

xiii

contained McRae's extensive historical study of Shenhui's life and work, while the Blue Binder contained his translations of the Shenhui corpus along with a number of appendices.) After McRae's death, we asked his wife, the eminent Buddhist scholar Jan Nattier, if she might be able to retrieve the latest version of the Shenhui book manuscript from his hard drive so that we could finally publish it. It took a lot of fiddling, but we were eventually able to recover and convert the digital files into a readable format.

The conversion was not, however, easy. McRae was a bit of a computer geek, always experimenting with new character encoding and software technologies. He was among the first adopters of personal computers in our field and was once a proud owner of the first "portable" (or "luggable") computer: an Osborne that weighed *only* 25 pounds. (The Osborne, complete with built-in CRT monitor, was designed to travel under an airplane seat, which was unprecedented at the time.) Long after outgrowing his Osborne, McRae continued to keep abreast of the latest character-encoding, word-processing, and page-layout software. In the days before Unicode, it took considerable technical skill and ingenuity to manage both Sino-Japanese characters and Roman fonts with diacritics in one and the same file, and McRae experimented with a variety of approaches over the years. Moreover, he was intent on doing the page layout of his Shenhui volume by himself. All this meant that the project, which had been gestating over literally decades, had gone through innumerable digital-file conversions. The last iteration of his preface to his Shenhui manuscript, recovered from his computer, gives an idea of the state of the electronic files:

> In mid-July 2010, in need of an intellectual change of pace, I chanced upon a manuscript hidden in a leafy subdivision of my computer's file system. Named "000Shenhui.pdf," it contained a rather mangled draft of the book now before you. There were other files as well, with extensions leading back from INDD to RTF to XML to MIF and eventually FM, indicating a succession of conversion efforts from FrameMaker, that workhorse of desktop publishing packages abandoned (on the Macintosh) by Adobe, to the present InDesign format. Most of the intermediate files were garbled in major ways, with characters such as Ø, √, ¥, and ½ showing up in place of diacritically marked characters. Somehow, though, the Chinese and Japanese characters had made it through mostly unscathed.

So while we did manage to recover the files, they were in a version of InDesign that is no longer supported, and utilized a number of file extensions that are now obsolete. With the help of Alberto Todeschini, we were able convert the files to MS Word, giving us access to John's most up-to-date version of the manuscript.[2]

---

2. Among the files we recovered was the following draft of the acknowledgments for the volume: "The research and translations included in this volume have benefitted from a number

Preface

We discussed McRae's Shenhui project at a meeting of the Kuroda Institute board in the fall of 2014, following which we—James Robson and Robert Sharf—decided to conduct a cross-country graduate seminar that would focus on the Shenhui materials recovered from Dunhuang. The seminar, which used Skype to link our Harvard and Berkeley classrooms, gave us the opportunity to go through his translations and assess the current state of the volume. Among other things, the exercise reconfirmed our sense of the historical significance of the Shenhui corpus. Scholars of Chinese Buddhism often pay lip service to Shenhui's role as champion of Huineng and his Southern Chan, but apart from the pioneering work of Jacques Gernet that appeared some seventy years ago (1949, 1951) and McRae's own articles on the subject (see below), there are few Western-language studies of the Shenhui materials, much less translations of them into English. This is due, in part, to the fragmentary state and philological challenges of the surviving manuscripts.

Our joint graduate seminar also confirmed the quality of McRae's work on the subject: his exacting and copiously annotated translations, along with his critical historical reconstructions. However, we were dismayed to discover that, at the time of his passing, he had been in the midst of an extensive rewrite that involved the disassembly of virtually every chapter of the historical study in the White Binder. In his draft preface to the project, he writes:

> Although a lot of work was required merely to make the text readable once again, I came to enjoy adding to the work of the younger John McRae, the text's original author. In particular, I was able to make use of the excellent new resources now available to us electronically, not only the CBETA and SAT electronic editions of the Chinese Buddhist canon that have so wonderfully transformed our field, but the more recent Dharma Drum Buddhist College Buddhist Authority Database Project (authority.dila.edu.tw). Also, I have re-structured the book somewhat, making an entirely new chapter out of what had been two appendixes plus other material published and unpublished.

The new material that he was incorporating is indeed extensive and includes a newly discovered stele with more precise biographical data on Shenhui,

---

of sources. I am grateful to have received financial assistance from both the National Endowment for the Humanities of the United States and the Council for Cultural Planning and Development of the Republic of China; the Council for Cultural Planning and Development has also provided funds to help defray the costs of publication. Since I effectively stole time from another project to finish this book, I must also thank the Foundation for Scholarly Exchange (Fulbright Foundation) of Taipei for their support.... My deep gratitude is due to Rachel Teck, who found serving as research assistant preferable to enrolling in any of my courses, so much so that she continued in this role well past her graduation from Cornell. Finally, my thanks to Jan Nattier, who found the manuscript incomprehensible on first reading and covered the entirely revised version her first reaction necessitated with blue ink."

as well as new editions of the Shenhui documents by Asian scholars. But McRae was far from finished with his revisions, and the chapters we had at our disposal were in various states of repair and were littered with his notes about things to "GET," "CHECK," and so on.

In the end we decided it best to set aside the analytical chapters and focus instead on making his translations of the Shenhui corpus available. We hired Fedde de Vries, a graduate student at UC Berkeley who had been a participant in our graduate seminar, to go through the translations, notes, and bibliography, and ready the translations for publication. (Fedde's editorial note explains how he handled the textual issues.)

In place of the unfinished historical and analytical chapters in McRae's manuscript, we decided to include three of his previously published articles on Shenhui in this volume. These articles emerged from his ongoing engagement with Shenhui over many years, and cover much of what appears in the chapters we had to jettison. The first, "Shenhui and the Teaching of Sudden Enlightenment" (1987), is placed before the translations, as it serves as a cogent introduction to Shenhui and his writings. The other two essays—"Religion as Revolution: Hu Shih on Shenhui" (2001); and "Shenhui as Evangelist: Re-envisioning the Identity of a Chinese Buddhist Monk" (2002)—are included in the second part of this volume. We hired Guttorm Gundarsen, a graduate student at Harvard, to convert the files to an MS Word document, change all of the romanizations of Chinese terms to Pinyin, add in the Chinese characters for Chinese terms, and, very selectively, update a few of the footnotes. Finally, we would like to thank Stuart Kiang, who edited McRae's initial publications in the Kuroda series, for undertaking the daunting task of cleaning up the manuscript that had passed through so many hands.

McRae did his PhD in the Department of Religious Studies at Yale University, under the supervision of Stanley Weinstein (1929–2017). Weinstein was known for the rigorous philological training he gave to his students, based, in part, on Japanese models of textual scholarship. It was common for Weinstein's students to conduct their dissertation research in Japan, and McRae spent several years in Kyoto studying under Yanagida Seizan (1922–2006), perhaps the most accomplished and influential scholar of Chan and Zen in the twentieth century.

Yanagida worked in multiple areas of Chan and Zen scholarship, but his most important contribution may have been his work on the Dunhuang manuscripts related to the emergence of the Chan tradition in the seventh and eighth centuries. This large body of materials constitutes an enormous puzzle: the *Sitz im Leben* of many of the documents is uncertain, as the authorship, place, and date of composition are often missing or patently spurious; these uncertainties contribute to the challenges in deciphering these often-cryptic texts. Through years of meticulous detective work, Yanagida was able to organize the pieces of the puzzle into a coherent picture, rewriting the early history of Chan in the process.

McRae's PhD dissertation built upon Yanagida's work. The dissertation focused on the Dunhuang manuscripts associated with "East Mountain" or "Northern school" figures such as Daoxin (580–651), Hongren (606–674), Shenxiu (606?-706), and Puji (651–739). Prior to the discovery of the Dunhuang manuscripts in the early twentieth century, the writings of these masters had been all but lost to history, and their teachings known only through the voices of their detractors, namely, the professed heirs of Huineng's "Southern school." As such, later Chan writings—the "vulgate" Chan canon that emerged in the Song and was passed down to the present day—would denigrate the Northern teachings as "gradualist" and inferior to the "sudden" teachings of Southern Chan.

McRae's meticulous analysis of the Northern school materials reveals the distortions and biases of the received tradition. To pick a single example, McRae takes to task the standard narrative that Northern teachers advocated a gradual path—that they viewed Buddhist practice as constituting a step-by-step ascent toward awakening. Instead, McRae shows that Northern teachers taught something closer to "constant practice"—an approach that anticipates later Sōtō Zen teachings in Japan. For the Northern school, Chan practice was not a *means* to achieving liberation so much as a moment-to-moment re-cognition and affirmation of what is already the case, that is, of one's abiding *bodhi*.

McRae revised and published his dissertation under the title *The Northern School and the Formation of Early Ch'an Buddhism* (1986), and to this day the book remains one of the most comprehensive, authoritative, and significant studies of early Chan. But while the Northern lineage masters were undoubtedly key players in the rise of Chan, a full reconstruction of early Chan history must take into consideration the contributions of rival lineages as well. One such lineage is the Oxhead tradition, which, according to Yanagida, may have played a role in mediating the debates between Northern and Southern masters. (Yanagida suggests that the Dunhuang recension of the *Platform Sūtra* may have been compiled and edited by someone affiliated with the Oxhead line.) McRae completed a detailed analysis of the Oxhead materials while he was still at work on his dissertation; entitled "The Ox-Head School of Chinese Ch'an Buddhism: From Early Ch'an to the Golden Age," it appeared as a chapter in the first volume in the Kuroda Institute's Studies in East Asian Buddhism series, *Studies in Ch'an and Hua-yen*, edited by Robert M. Gimello and Peter N. Gregory (1983). McRae was also interested in the Hongzhou lineage associated with Mazu Daoyi (708–788); Mazu and his successors may have been instrumental in the development of Chan "encounter dialogue," a genre that would come to epitomize Chan wisdom later on. While still a student, McRae had published a translation of Yanagida's article, "The 'Recorded Saying' Texts of Chinese Ch'an Buddhism," which included a discussion of "encounter dialogue."[3] His own foray into this subject—a chapter titled "The Antecedents of Encounter Dialogue in Chinese Ch'an Buddhism"—appeared in the collection *The Kōan: Texts and Contexts in Zen Buddhism,* edited by Steven Heine and Dale S. Wright (2000).

McRae was, in short, interested in a comprehensive reconstruction of early Chan, in which Northern school, Oxhead, and Hongzhou teachers would all play major roles. But the narrative would not be complete without taking into account the contributions of Shenhui; indeed, the problematic shibboleths that came to be applied to the Northern school originated with Shenhui's critique, and arguably were amplified in the modern period through the early work on the Shenhui corpus by Hu Shih in China and D. T. Suzuki in Japan. It was only natural that McRae would turn his attentions to Shenhui following the publication of his *Northern School* tome. Indeed, he envisioned producing a trilogy on early Chan, in which his *Northern School* book would be the first volume, his book on Shenhui the second, and an unrealized volume on Mazu and the Hongzhou school the third.

Shenhui is renowned as a leading disciple and champion of Huineng and his Southern school; some scholars believe that Shenhui may have been instrumental in the compilation of the *Platform Sūtra,* a text designed in part to legitimize Huineng's status as Sixth Patriarch. But despite Shenhui's historical importance, his own lineage seems to have died out rather quickly, and records of his teachings had been few and far between until the discovery of the Dunhuang materials.

By placing the Dunhuang texts alongside other historical sources such as the writings of Zongmi (780–841), scholars have been able to reconstruct a general outline of Shenhui's life. Some seven years after his teacher Huineng's death in 720, Shenhui moved to Nanyang, near his birthplace and not far from the eastern capital Luoyang. Sometime around 732 he began to attack the Northern school teachers in what are called the Huatai debates. It was here that Shenhui emerged as a passionate and strident "evangelist" (to use the term McRae came to favor) for the Southern school. In 745, Shenhui moved to the Heze si in Luoyang, which gave him a larger and more politically powerful audience for his attacks on Northern lineage teachers. In 753, he was banished from Luoyang, apparently at the behest of Northern school partisans, and in the following year he took up residence in the Kaiyuan si in Jingzhou. In 755, with the breakout of the An Lushan rebellion, he was allowed back to the capital, where he assisted in a government campaign to raise much-needed funds to suppress the rebellion via the sale of monastic ordination certificates. (The possession of such a certificate rendered the holder exempt from taxes and corvée labor.) Shenhui died in 758 at the Kaiyuan si.

---

3. The translation appeared in Lai and Lancaster, *Early Ch'an in China and Tibet,* 183–205.

Of course, Shenhui is best known as an indefatigable evangelist—McRae also suggests using the term "apostle"—for Huineng's distinctive approach to Chan. The rubrics of "Southern versus Northern" and "sudden versus gradual," seem to have been concocted by Shenhui (or those in his circle) as rhetorical devices intended to elevate the teachings of his own lineage at the expense of his rivals. His success in this somewhat quixotic quest speaks to his abilities as a charismatic preacher who could appeal to a broad audience. But McRae's use of "evangelist" is intended to capture something more than Shenhui's skill as a public speaker; Shenhui's "crusade" (also a term used by McRae) sought to induce an immediate "transformative experience" in his rapt audience—an experience of *bodhicitta* ("mind of awakening") in the here and now. His skills as a proselytizer bringing the "good news" to the masses were duly recognized and exploited by the imperial authorities, who put those skills to work to raise government funds.

As mentioned above, McRae's research reveals the degree to which the received view of the Northern school teachings is a fiction created by Shenhui to score rhetorical points; McRae argues that Northern and Southern teachings may have been closer to each another than the canonical narrative would have us believe. He also argues that Shenhui was not particularly effective or even active as a meditation teacher or spiritual mentor; according to historical documents, Shenhui's own students were few and did not leave much of a legacy. Be that as it may, McRae credits Shenhui for his outsized role in shaping what would later emerge as "classical Chan," including (1) the Chan rhetoric of "suddenness"; (2) the rise of sectarian consciousness; (3) the evolution of "transmission of the lamp" ideology; (4) the adoption of the "rule of rhetorical purity"; and (5) the rise of a colloquial style of Chan dialogue.

McRae was attracted to Shenhui for the important part he played in the rise of Chan, both institutionally (in securing Huineng's lineage as the "orthodox" one), and doctrinally (in championing the Perfection of Wisdom literature and the rhetoric of suddenness). But in working on Shenhui over many years, McRae seems to have grown disheartened with Shenhui, notably with his overweening evangelism, and his shrill and self-aggrandizing tirades against rival teachers. The parallel McRae drew to the American "crusader" Billy Graham (1918–2018) was not intended to reflect well on Shenhui. Among other things, both Shenhui and Graham were known for consorting with powerful politicians, raising the specter of an unhealthy if not unholy alliance between religion and politics.

McRae was, accordingly, somewhat skeptical about the more glowing image of Shenhui left by Hu Shih and perpetuated by D. T. Suzuki, that is, of Shenhui as an inspired revolutionary who initiated a veritable "'Chinese renaissance' in which superstition and ritual were rejected in favor of a native Sinitic proto-rationalism."[4] While McRae deemed this evaluation to be "entirely

---

4. From the essay "Shenhui as Evangelist," included in this volume.

wrong," he was, at the same time, acutely aware that Hu Shih's reading of Shenhui reflected Hu Shih's own time, place, and intellectual commitments. That is, McRae was cognizant that he was himself subject to the same critique—that he too could not avoid imposing his own assumptions and preconceptions on his picture of Shenhui, including, perhaps, a certain distaste for more strident strands of contemporary evangelical Christianity.

While this volume is not exactly the book on Shenhui that McRae intended, the translations and historical essays collected here do represent his sustained efforts over many years to breath some life into Shenhui. In the end, McRae's stated hope was that making Shenhui's surviving writings accessible through his carefully annotated English translations would allow readers to form their own opinions. We are now happy to make these translations, together with his previously published articles on Shenhui, more widely available.

THE TRANSLATIONS

1. *Platform Sermon*
   This work contains a clear statement of Shenhui's ideas about the sudden teaching, including a criticism of improper attitudes toward meditation practice stated without explicit sectarian identification. It probably derives from the years 720–730, while Shenhui was living in Nanyang.
2. *Definition of the Truth*
   This work is an overtly polemical text, with somewhat limited doctrinal sophistication, containing Shenhui's attack on the so-called Northern school. It is based on public sermons (actually dramatically staged debates) that Shenhui gave in 730, 731, and 732, although the text was edited sometime during 744–749 and was further augmented either at the very end of Shenhui's life or after his death.
3. *Miscellaneous Dialogues*
   There are several quite different versions of this text, apparently edited after Shenhui's death. These texts contain various dialogues from throughout his career, many but not all of which parallel material in his other texts (particularly the Northern school critiques). This is a rich but sometimes intractable resource.
4. *Verses on the Five Watches*
   This title is used for two or three similar compositions that circulated under Shenhui's name, including *Cycle of the Five Watches of the Heze [Temple] Reverend [Shenhui]* and *Cycle of Five Watches on the Determination of the False and True in the Southern School*, in which his ideas are presented in a popular song format. They are interesting primarily for their sociological implications, although they do display one or two points of doctrinal interest.

5. *Verses on Sudden Enlightenment, the Birthless, and Prajñā*
    This work, apparently written sometime after 745, is a relatively polished essay containing the gist of the *Definition of the Truth*. Other versions of the text are also known as the *Treatise on the Manifestation of the Teaching*—the title of the excerpt in the *Record of the Mirror of Truth*—and the *Record of the Manifestation of the Teaching of Great Master [Shenhui] of Heze [Temple]*—the title used in the *Transmission of the Lamp*.

James Robson
Robert H. Sharf

Abbreviations and Conventions

A	Authority Database
J.	Japanese
Skt.	Sanskrit
T	Taishō shinshū daizōkyō
X	Xu zang jing
ZZ	Dai Nihon zoku Zōkyō

Authority Database citations [A000000] refer to the ID numbers of entries in the person database maintained by the Buddhist Studies Authority Database Project at https://authority.dila.edu.tw/person.

References to the Taishō edition include text number before a colon, followed by volume, page, register (a, b, or c), and line number(s).

Location markers in the translations, [HS000] and [DTS000], refer to Hu Shih's and D. T. Suzuki's editions of the texts, respectively. See the appendix on Textual Sources for details on existing editions of the Shenhui texts.

Introduction
Shenhui and the Teaching of Sudden Enlightenment

I. Prologue

A. The Understanding of Suddenness in Modern Chan Studies
The field of Chan 禪 studies has seen some very lively disputes over the course of the twentieth century, but there has been general agreement on the proposition that the doctrine of sudden enlightenment represents the highest expression of the doctrinal mainstream of early Chinese Chan Buddhism. Although there is some quibbling regarding details and specific interpretations, scholars working in this field often describe the history of the doctrine of sudden enlightenment within Chan in terms of three subjects: (1) Huineng's 慧能 doctrine of sudden enlightenment as shown in his "mind-verse" (*xinjie* 心偈) in the *Platform Sūtra of the Sixth Patriarch* (*Liuzu tanjing* 六祖壇經); (2) Shenhui's 神會 campaign in opposition to the gradual teaching of the Northern school and in support of the public recognition of Huineng as sixth patriarch; and (3) the continuation of the spirit of Huineng in the teachings and religious practice of Mazu 馬祖, Shitou 石頭, and the later Chan tradition.

Research done in recent years has shown that the traditional interpretations of these three subjects are all substantially incorrect, although the implications of these findings have not yet been fully realized. The history of early Chan is in the process of being thoroughly rewritten, but it is already clear that the doctrine of sudden enlightenment and the dispute between the sudden and gradual teachings should no longer be used as yardsticks by which the religious message of Chan and its widespread acceptance in Tang 唐 dynasty China are understood.

In the first place, we know now that it is impossible to describe the teachings of the historical figure Huineng (638–713) with any certainty whatsoever. The rather extensive works of Huineng's most active disciple, Shenhui[1]

This study originally appeared as "Shen-hui and the Teaching of Sudden Enlightenment in Early Ch'an Buddhism" in Gregory, *Sudden and Gradual: Approaches to Enlightenment in Chinese Thought*, 227–278.

1. This essay is the first in a set of studies on Shenhui. Also planned are an examination of Hu Shih's interpretation of Shenhui's historical significance, an investigation of the possible relationship between Nanyang Huizhong and Shenhui's lineage, and, ultimately, an annotated and copiously cross-referenced translation of the entire corpus of Shenhui's known works.

(684–758), never quote his master's sayings. Since Shenhui could have bolstered the legitimacy of his doctrinal claims by quoting Huineng, we may infer that Shenhui did not possess any record of Huineng's teachings.[2] An epitaph for Huineng written by the poet Wang Wei 王維 and commissioned by Shenhui or one of his followers contains a biographical statement but only vague allusions to his teachings.[3] Hence it is most reasonable to assume that Shenhui was guided only by his memory and not by any written transcript of Huineng's teachings, and that Shenhui's recollections regarding Huineng's teachings were not sharply distinguished from Shenhui's own teachings. The *Platform Sūtra*, which purports to record one of Huineng's sermons, is now known to have been written about the year 780 by a member of an early Chan faction known as the Oxhead school (*Niutou zong* 牛頭宗). The possibility that this text contains at least some kernel of Huineng's teachings is undercut both by the differences between the contents of this text and the doctrines of Shenhui and by the similarity between those contents and the known doctrines of the Oxhead school.[4] Huineng is extremely important as a legendary image, but the indications of any historical contributions by him are irretrievably lost.[5]

Thus the *Platform Sūtra*'s account of the exchange of mind-verses between Huineng and Shenxiu 神秀 (606?–706) of the Northern school, perhaps the most famous anecdote in Chan history, has been discovered to be a creative legend rather than a factual account. Although this is not to say that the legend was unimportant—far from it!—the ideas contained in these two verses should not be understood in terms of a simple opposition between

---

2. This point is made by Philip Yampolsky, *Platform Sutra*, 32. There is one possible exception, however: the sermon attributed to Shenhui in the *Transmission of the Lamp* (*Jingde chuandeng lu* 景德傳燈錄), fasc. 28, T 2076: 51.439b–440a, includes six questions and answers between Shenhui and the "sixth patriarch" (*liuzu* 六組). Yanagida Seizan, "Goroku no rekishi," 395, suggests that this is an excerpt from a very early text of Shenhui's, which does seem plausible from the contents. However, he also suggests that the term *liuzu* does not necessarily refer to Huineng. His point, I believe, is that the passage is so early that the teacher involved may have been Shenxiu, under whom Shenhui also studied. I can see no reason to disagree with Professor Yanagida's point, and a presentation of the contents of this text would add substance to my argument below regarding Shenhui's early teaching career. However, since doing so would be based solely on doctrinal grounds and would involve a considerable amount of supporting analysis, I have decided to keep to the general practice of using only contemporary materials. Incidentally, Robert Zeuschner has published a translation of the other material included here (i.e., Shenhui's address and not the dialogues) in "A Sermon by the Ch'an Master Ho-tse Shen-hui."

3. This epitaph is discussed in Yampolsky, *Platform Sutra*, 66–69. A liberally annotated edition may be found in Yanagida, *Shoki Zenshū shisho*, 539–558.

4. The Oxhead school authorship of the *Platform Sūtra* was the subject of an extensive argument in Yanagida, *Shoki Zenshū shisho*, 181–212. Although this argument is based largely on circumstantial evidence, to my knowledge it has not been challenged. In addition, I have found Yanagida's theory to conform well with other information regarding the Oxhead school. See McRae, "The Ox-head School of Chinese Buddhism," 218–232.

5. On the development of the legend of Huineng, see Yampolsky, *Platform Sutra*, especially 58–88.

the "gradual teaching" of Shenxiu and the "sudden teaching" of Huineng. Rather, the two verses constitute a single unit expressing a rarified understanding of the "perfect teaching" of constant bodhisattvic practice. That is, one should labor unceasingly to save all other sentient beings from suffering even as one remained constantly in meditation, but without ever conceptualizing sentient beings, salvific action, or meditation.[6]

In fact, in direct contrast to the traditional interpretation, Northern school ideas and terminology were used in the compilation of these famous verses. This is true not only of the basic metaphors, such as the mirror stand, the bodhi tree, and polishing, which one would expect to have had some association with Shenxiu. The most intriguing aspect of the verses is that the line "Fundamentally there is not a single thing," which occurs as the third line of "Huineng's" verse in all but the Dunhuang 敦煌 version of the text, itself is presaged by a line in a Northern school text. Perhaps more important, Northern school texts contain numerous discussions of the nonexistence of a "single thing." Therefore we must conclude that Northern school ideas were used in the compilation of the *Platform Sūtra* mind-verses.[7] As a result, what was once introduced as a very simple rubric for explaining the origins of the doctrine of sudden enlightenment in the Chan school must now be explained as the result of an extensive and even convoluted doctrinal progression. The traditional interpretation of the anecdote and verses as representing gradualist versus subitist positions must be discussed in the context of the mid-ninth century and beyond and should not be used to describe either the historical or doctrinal development of early Chan Buddhism.

The third subject listed above, the continuation of the early Chan doctrine of sudden enlightenment by Mazu Daoyi 馬祖道一 (709–788), Shitou Xiqian 石頭希遷 (700–790), and the later Chan tradition, also involves unsupportable assumptions. The relatively late provenance and the Oxhead school authorship of the *Platform Sūtra* clearly obviates the possibility of any direct succession from Huineng and/or Shenhui to Mazu et al., and the fictive nature of such a succession is corroborated by the biographical evidence.[8] Moreover, we should not be misled by the fact that the later Chan school adopted the name "Southern school," which was Shenhui's battle standard against the gradualists of the so-called Northern school. In fact, this continuity of sectarian labeling obscures the single most important distinction in eighth- and ninth-century Chan: that between the "early Chan" factions (the Northern, Southern, and Oxhead schools) and the "classical Chan" beginning with Mazu's Hongzhou 洪州 school.

---

6. See McRae, *Northern School*, 1–7 and 235–238, for a more extensive discussion of the mind-verses of the *Platform Sūtra*.

7. See McRae, *Northern School*, 237–238, for the specific references underlying this assertion. An additional supporting reference is mentioned in n. 80 below.

8. Judging from the biographical data, Mazu was most greatly indebted to masters of the Northern school and Sichuan faction lineages. See Nishiguchi Yoshio, "Baso no denki," 123–124.

Indeed, understanding the dynamics of the early-to-classical transition is one of the most important issues now facing Chan studies. This is because of the very distinct nature of the disconformity between the two, which is manifested in the marked differences in the textual legacies of early and classical Chan: classical Chan is distinguished by its almost total dedication to the practice of "encounter dialogue," the spontaneous and unstructured repartee between masters and students. Where early Chan texts contain a wide variety of doctrinal formulations, practical exhortations, and ritual procedures, the texts of classical Chan are more uniform in their dedication to the transcription of encounter dialogue incidents, and they delight in baffling paradoxes, patent absurdities, and instructive vignettes of nonconformist behavior. Where early Chan texts attempt to infuse new meanings and a new spirit of dedication into conventional Buddhist doctrines and practices, classical Chan texts reject or simply ignore traditional activities completely. And where early Chan texts are alternately charming, informative, and baffling in their varied attempts to enunciate the new message, classical Chan texts derive their power from vivid portrayals of specific living masters and students grappling with real spiritual problems.

For better or worse, the elucidation of the early-to-classical transition also involves some very difficult problems regarding the primary sources. Perhaps the most remarkable indication of the very existence of the discontinuity between early and classical Chan is that the texts of the classical phase—or at least the most distinctive texts, those containing transcripts of encounter dialogue—are uniformly absent from the finds at Dunhuang.[9] One reason for this absence, of course, is the great geographical distance between Dunhuang and south-central China, where Mazu and his Hongzhou school flourished. Also, the very close relationship between the encounter-dialogue practice of classical Chan and word play in oral Chinese must have left the Tibetans in Dunhuang and Tibet proper very much unmoved. It would be many years before Chan was transmitted (to any substantial degree) even to Korea and Japan, which imbibed much more heavily of Chinese language and culture. Either classical Chan was not considered an appropriate model for export to Dunhuang and Tibet, or the Buddhist community in Dunhuang was neither ready nor able to consider such a new type of religious practice.

The absence of classical texts from Dunhuang is not merely an indication of cultural and chronological disparity, for it means that we are left without any independent scale by which to understand the textual develop-

---

9. There are one or two texts attributed to classical Chan figures found at Dunhuang, but the texts themselves manifest none of the distinctive characteristics of classical Chan texts. The most prominent example is the *Guishan jingce* 溈山警策 (Guishan's Wakening Stick) attributed to Guishan Lingyou 溈山靈祐 (771–853), which occurs in a Dunhuang manuscript under the title *Dagui jingce* 大溈警策. This text, which is discussed by Tanaka Ryōshō in his *Tonkō Zenshū bunken,* 335–342, contains a very conventional message on monastic discipline. This work has been translated by Melvin Takemoto in his "*Kuei-shan ching-ts'e.*"

ment of classical Chan. We simply do not have any texts relevant to the earliest period of classical Chan that did not pass through the hands of Song dynasty editors, who either knowingly or unknowingly homogenized the editions they produced. Such problems are beyond the scope of this paper.[10]

What is striking about the emergence of encounter dialogue in south-central China is not merely that it occurred, but that it seems to have been the total focus of attention by the members of the Hongzhou school and the subsequent Chan tradition. In other words, although we can perceive in early Chan prototypic forms of encounter dialogue,[11] this was but one aspect of early Chan religious practice. On the other hand, although encounter dialogue may be interpreted in terms of doctrines and practices developed by the Northern, Southern, and Oxhead schools and the Sichuan factions, it received such a single-minded emphasis in the Hongzhou school and other classical Chan factions that their religious practice was fundamentally different from the pluralistic endeavors of early Chan. Hence the differences between early and classical Chan are both qualitative and quantitative, and at the very least it should be clear that we cannot march directly from Huineng to Mazu.[12]

So what, then, was the real impact of Shenhui and his doctrine of sudden enlightenment?

B. Shenhui and Modern Chan Studies

For a variety of reasons, it is perfectly understandable that Shenhui's life and teachings became a cynosure of scholarly interest during the twentieth century. Transcripts of his oral and written teachings are among the most interesting and thought-provoking of the many early Chan texts discovered at Dunhuang. Not only is it unusual for such texts to be specifically attributable to a single historical personage, but they seem to derive from different points throughout Shenhui's career and thus to allow consideration of the evolution of his positions, a unique opportunity within the context of early Chan studies. Even granting the apparent discontinuity between early and classical Chan, it is still the case that the labels "Southern school" and "sudden teaching" were accepted by the orthodox tradition as descriptions of the mainstream of Chinese Chan. Since it was indeed Shenhui who first championed the doctrine of sudden enlightenment and the cause of the Southern school, his career did have a much greater impact on the development of Chan than is apparent in the traditional literature.

In spite of this, I believe that modern scholarship overestimates Shenhui's significance and distorts the nature of his contributions. This misinterpretation

---

10. Professor Yanagida's recent "Goroku no rekishi" is a grand summation of his work on the history of Chan recorded sayings literature, from its beginnings up to Linji Yixuan 臨濟義玄.

11. See McRae, *Northern School*, 91–97.

12. My primary research at present concerns the Hongzhou school of Mazu and its relationship to early Chan.

of Shenhui's teachings and historical role devolves initially from the work of the noted Chinese scholar Hu Shih (1891–1962), who was the first to discover and study the Dunhuang manuscripts of Shenhui's teachings.[13] Briefly put, Hu Shih believed that Shenhui's career signaled the beginning of a major transformation, not only in Chinese Buddhism, but in Chinese intellectual and cultural history in general. Hu defined this transformation as the reassertion of native Chinese values and the rejection of the Buddhist ideas that were so popular during the Six Dynasties and early Tang dynasty periods. The mechanism by which Shenhui initiated this transformation was the teaching of sudden enlightenment, which Hu believed to be inherently Chinese in its essentially simple approach to the problem of religious cultivation.[14]

Hu Shih's basic work on Shenhui was widely accepted by other authorities, although usually without reference to his larger interpretive scheme. Not the least significant of these other scholars was D. T. Suzuki, whose distinctive interpretation of Chinese and Japanese Zen, especially Rinzai, inspired great interest in and significantly informed the modern understanding of the Chan/Zen tradition. Suzuki sharply criticized Hu's overly historical approach to Chan studies but did not fault his findings.[15] Suzuki agreed that Shenhui was responsible for the eventual success of the sudden teaching, but he tended to ignore the subject of Shenhui's historical contributions; in his interest to get at the heart of the Chan message, Suzuki was much more attracted to discussion of the original creative insight of Chan, which he attributed to Bodhidharma and Huineng. Suzuki did feel that the triumph of the message taught first by Bodhidharma and Huineng and later by Shenhui represented a major transformation in Chinese Buddhism, although in his mind this transformation was not the reemergence of native Chinese culture but rather the final elimination of extraneous intellectual baggage from a tradition destined to become the unalloyed expression of the "enlightenment experience."

Indeed, Shenhui *was* a major figure in the development of Chinese Chan Buddhism, although his contributions were quantitatively less significant

---

13. Hu Shih's biographical study of Shenhui was published in 1930. It is reprinted in his *Shenhui heshang yiji*, 3–90, as well as in Yanagida, *Ko Teki Zengaku an*, 99–142. The latter volume contains all of Hu Shih's published writings on Chan Buddhism, most of which concern Shenhui either directly or indirectly.

14. Hu Shih's comprehensive theory of Chinese history is stated in a number of works, the most concise statements occurring in his articles "Chinese Thought" and "Religion and Philosophy in Chinese History."

15. The disagreement between Hu and Suzuki, which led to a well-known exchange of articles in *Philosophy East and West*, is without question the most celebrated mismatch of modern Chan studies. Unfortunately, this exchange of articles occurred virtually at the end of their respective academic careers, decades after their most creative periods. Perhaps as a result of this, neither man seems to have had the interest or capacity to really consider the other's position, and no one since then has chosen to redefine and carry on their dialogue. See Hu's "Ch'an (Zen) Buddhism in China," and Suzuki's rejoinder, "Zen: A Reply to Hu Shih."

and qualitatively different from the manner in which they are described in most modern writings on Chan. Chan Buddhism did undergo a major transformation in the latter part of the eighth century (this is not quite the same as saying that the emergence of Chan per se represented a transformation in Chinese Buddhism or in Chinese intellectual history), but Shenhui was only one of a number of individuals involved in the process. The emergence of Chan was a major event in Chinese religious and intellectual history—an event that must be considered within the larger context of the transition from the medieval society of the Tang to the premodern society of the Song—but the teaching of sudden enlightenment was only one of the many relevant doctrinal and practical factors involved.

In the pages that follow I offer a preliminary re-evaluation of Shenhui's life and basic doctrines, especially his doctrine of sudden enlightenment, based in part on new epigraphic and textual evidence. This material has allowed me to develop a new chronology for Shenhui's life and a new interpretation of his early doctrinal development, both of which imply a much closer relationship between him and the Northern school than has previously been thought to have existed. The analysis of this relationship provides the basis for a hypothesis concerning the role of the doctrine of sudden enlightenment in Shenhui's life and thought and, to a lesser extent, in the subsequent Chan tradition.

II. Shenhui's Biography

Very recently, the study of Shenhui's biography[16] has been aided by the discovery of his stele and ritual implements at Longmen 龍門. Although the stele in question was crudely done and is very simple in content, it was erected in 765 and thus represents the earliest source for the dates of Shenhui's life. The major contribution of this new discovery is its statement that Shenhui died in 758 at the age of seventy-five and after fifty-four years as a monk. The revision of Shenhui's dates to 684–758 (the dates given previously were 670–762) clears up a controversy about his age at the time of his commencement of training under Huineng, although it makes his period of service to the Tang ruling house after the An Lushan rebellion remarkably brief. The newly discovered stele is also the earliest source to refer explicitly to Shenhui as the seventh patriarch of Chan. Along with the stele were discovered four artifacts connected with Shenhui that are exquisite examples of Tang craftsmanship: a reliquary bowl with cover in the shape of a stūpa (which contained ashes—probably Shenhui's—when it was discovered), a *kuṇḍika* water vessel, a long-handled censer, and a begging bowl. The first three items are

---

16. The first modern study of Shenhui's biography was that published in 1930 by Hu Shih, cited in n. 13 above. Hu's findings, including his more recent conclusions, are summarized by Yampolsky in his *Platform Sutra*, 23–38.

of gilt bronze, and the last was of very lightweight pottery lacquered to a highly reflective gloss.[17]

A. Shenhui's Early Training

Shenhui was born in 684 as a member of the Gao 高 family of Xiangyang 襄陽.[18] His biography in the *Song Biographies* (*Song gaoseng zhuan* 宋高僧傳) describes him in typical fashion as a gifted youth conversant in the *Laozi* 老子 and *Zhuangzi* 莊子 who discovered Buddhism while reading the *Hou Han shu* 後漢書 (Book of the Later Han [Dynasty]). He left home to become a monk under Dharma Master Haoyuan 顥元 of Guochang si 國昌寺 in Xiangyang, a figure who is otherwise unknown.[19] According to Zongmi 宗密 and the *Transmission of the Lamp* (*Jingde chuandeng lu* 景德傳燈錄), Shenhui first traveled to Caoqi 曹溪 (in modern Guangdong province) to study under Huineng at the age of 14.[20] Using the dates given in the newly discovered

---

17. The discovery of Shenhui's stele was announced by Wen Yucheng, a member of the Longmen museum staff in Henan. Wen's article, "Ji xin chutude Heze dashi Shenhui taming," describes the inscription and analyzes its historical significance. This article was subsequently summarized in Japanese, with substantial additional analysis and a transcription and Japanese translation of the inscription, in Takeuchi Kōdō, "Shinshutsu no Kataku Jinne tōmei." Shenhui's ritual implements appeared in an exhibition of artifacts from China that toured Japan in the summer of 1986; see the Tokyo National Museum's *Kōga bunmei tenran*, plates 110–113 and explanation on pp. 185–186 (Japanese) and 201 (English). Professor Yanagida informed me in a personal communication shortly after the exhibition of its inclusion of Shenhui's bowl and other artifacts; he seems willing to accept them as authentic. The occurrence of the begging bowl in Shenhui's grave corroborates the implication of written sources that he did not possess the legendary bowl of Bodhidharma—or at least that he did not pass it along to a disciple. The exhibition catalogue describes the bowl simply as a gilt bronze bowl with cover in the shape of a stūpa; the ash found within it is said to be from incense.

18. Shenhui's family name and place of birth are given in his biographies in both the *Song Biographies*, T 2061: 50.756c–757a, and the *Transmission of the Lamp*, T 2076: 51.245a–b. Hu, *Yiji*, 5, corrects the two variants given in Zongmi's works to Gao. Three of Zongmi's works contain biographical statements for Shenhui: the *Yuanjue jing dashu chao* 圓覺經大疏鈔, fasc. 3B, ZZ 1 / 14 / 3.277a–d; the *Yuanjue jing lueshu chao* 圓覺經略疏鈔, fasc. 4, ZZ 1 / 15 / 2.131a–d; and the *Zhonghua quan xindi chanmen shizi chengxi tu* 中華傳心地禪門師資承襲圖 or "Chan Chart," ZZ 2A / 15 / 5.433d–434a, or Kamata Shigeo, *Zengen shosenshū tojo*, 277. The *Dashu chao* and *Lueshu chao* accounts are identical, except that the former contains additional information given under Huineng's name. Below I will cite the *Lueshu chao* only where it differs from the other text. Part of the "Chan Chart" account is taken verbatim from the *Dashu chao*.

19. The *Continued Biographies*, T 2060: 50.587a, mentions a Dhyāna master Hao from Xiangyang who was the teacher of a monk who died in 632 at the age of 61. Although this is considerably before Shenhui was born, the coincidence of place and personal names suggests some kind of relationship between the two individuals.

20. Wang Wei's epitaph for Huineng states that Shenhui began his studies under Huineng when he (Shenhui, that is) was "middle-aged" (*zhongnian* 中年). Hu Shih and others have taken this to be more authoritative than the age followed here (see Yampolsky, *Platform Sutra*, 26n), but Takeuchi, "Shinshutsu no Kataku Jinne tōmei," 317, argues forcefully that the character *zhong* 中, "middle," should be read as *chong* 冲, meaning adolescence. The *Caoqi dashi zhuan* 曹溪大師傳, a biography of Huineng written about the same time as (but independently of) the *Platform Sūtra*, has the event occurring at Shenhui's age thirteen. See ZZ 2B / 19 / 5.485b, or *Enō kenkyū*, 42. Zongmi's *Dashu chao* gives his age as fourteen. Also, in the *Platform Sūtra*

stele inscription, this would have been in 697. It is not known exactly how long Shenhui stayed in Caoqi. Eventually, he traveled north and in 704 took the full ordination in Chang'an 長安.[21] He must have continued his religious training under northern master(s) at this time; Zongmi actually says that he studied under Shenxiu himself for three years.[22] In any case, according to Zongmi, after Shenhui returned to Caoqi sometime during the years 707–709, Huineng "recognized his pure maturity and silently transmitted the secret words" to him.[23] Shenhui no doubt stayed with Huineng until the latter's death in 713.

B. Shenhui's Teaching Career

It would be very interesting to know of Shenhui's activities during the years 713–720, immediately after Huineng's death. Although I will make some inferences regarding this period below, virtually no specific biographical data is available.[24] The *Song Biographies* says very tersely that after Huineng's death Shenhui "wandered about to famous sites." In 720 he took up residence at the Longxing si 龍興寺 in Nanyang 南陽, which was only a short distance north of Xiangyang, his native place, and not very far from the eastern capital of Luoyang 洛陽. Shenhui apparently began to focus his attentions on Luoyang during this period; the *Song Biographies* claims that his teachings started to become known at this time, even though the school of Puji 普寂 was still predominant.[25] Shenhui's works contain dialogues with prominent individuals identified with Nanyang, some of which may derive

---

Huineng addresses Shenhui as a "young monk." These details would seem to corroborate Takeuchi's interpretation.

21. The fact that Shenhui took his full ordination in Chang'an is stated in Zongmi's *Dashu chao* and in the *Transmission of the Lamp*, which also states that he returned to Caoqi in 707–709. The date 704 for Shenhui's ordination was determined by subtracting the length of Shenhui's career as a monk from his age at death as given in the stele.

22. This subject is discussed in Hu, *Yiji*, 7–8.

23. See the discussion in Takeuchi, "Shinshutsu no Kataku Jinne tōmei," 316–317.

24. Shenhui did have contact with a student named Shenying 神英 in the sixth month of 716, but only to suggest that the student go to Mount Wutai 五台. Their meeting may have taken place at Nanyue 南嶽, but this is uncertain. See Ui Hakuju, *Zenshūshi kenkyū*, 1:207 and 248–249. Ui, 207–208, criticizes Shenhui for taking a student so early in his career, but there is no evidence that the contact between the two was anything more than incidental. For a comprehensive treatment of Shenying, see "Shen-ying's Experiences on Mount Wu-t'ai" by Raoul Birnbaum. The encounter with Shenhui is mentioned on p. 121.

25. *Song Biographies*, T 2061: 50.756c.

from this period.[26] Shenhui's *Platform Sermon* probably also dates from this period, although the dating is uncertain.[27]

---

26. See Hu, *Yiji*, 13–14. Yampolsky, *Platform Sutra*, 24–25n, gives a very convenient résumé of the various manuscripts (and most of the editions) of Shenhui's various works. There are several manuscripts of the text containing Shenhui's miscellaneous dialogues. Two of these were circulated under the provisional title "Shenhui's Recorded Sayings" (*Shenhui yulu* 神會語錄 or *Shenhui lu* 神會錄), i.e., a fragment published by Hu Shih (Pelliot 3047 [part 1]; see the *Yiji*, 91–158, for Hu's editions, annotation, and commentary) and another owned by Ishii Mitsuo in Japan and published in facsimile in 1932 under the title *Tonkō shutsudo Jinne roku*, and two years later in an edited version by D. T. Suzuki and Kōda Rentarō, *Tonkō shutsudo Kataku Jinne zenji goroku*. In 1956, however, Iriya Yoshitaka discovered a third manuscript (Stein 6557) during an examination of Stein collection microfilms, which was published with an introduction and annotation by Hu Shih in 1960. (Hu's work was published in the *Zhongguo Zhongyang Yanjiuyuan Lishi Yuyan Yanjiusuo jikan* 中央研究院歷史語言研究所集刊, extra vol. 4, no. 1 [September 1960]: 1–31; I have consulted the reprinted version in Hu's *Yiji*, 401–452.) This third version bears the title *Nanyang heshang wenda za chengyi* 南陽和尚問答雜徵義, or "Dialogues on Miscellaneous Inquiries to the Reverend [Shenhui] of Nanyang." (Yanagida, "Goroku," 367–369, suggests that the character *cheng* 徵 refers to questions placed by a teacher to students, rather than vice versa; the interpretation is a problem because the character does not occur in the body of the text. I will cite the text below by the abbreviated title *Miscellaneous Dialogues*.) It includes a preface by one Liu Cheng 劉澄, who is identified in Ennin's 円仁 catalogue as the compiler of the text; see Yanagida, "Zenseki kaidai," 461. Paul Demiéville's "Deux documents de Touen-houang sur le Dhyāna chinois" contains a discussion of Stein 6557.

In addition to the text in the *Yiji*, the *Suzuki Daisetsu zenshū*, 3:236–288, contains a synoptic edition of Pelliot 3047 and the Ishii manuscript. Jacques Gernet, *Entretiens du Maître de Dhyāna Chenhouei*, contains translations of all of Shenhui's works found in the first edition of Hu Shih's *Yiji*, including the *Miscellaneous Dialogues*. Gernet's "Complément aux entretiens du Maître de Dhyāna Chen-houei," contains the balance from the Suzuki and Kōda edition of the Ishii manuscript.

No doubt drawing from Hu's analysis (*Yiji*, 415–421), Yanagida, "Goroku," 367 and 370–372, suggests that the different manuscripts for the *Miscellaneous Dialogues* derive from different points in Shenhui's career, with the manuscript bearing Liu Cheng's preface being the earliest and only containing material antedating Shenhui's move to Luoyang in 745. Pelliot 3047, however, includes some additional dialogues and refers to Shenhui as Heze heshang 荷澤和尚 (preceptor of Heze [si]), so it was compiled after 745. The Ishii manuscript is the latest of the three, since it manifests significant editing and contains material not found in the other two versions (some of the most interesting of which—biographies of the patriarchs, etc.—is omitted from the *Suzuki Daisetsu zenshū* edition and must be sought in Suzuki's 1934 publication of the text, a rare volume). The compiler Liu Cheng, incidentally, may have been related to several other men bearing the same surname known to have been close to various early Chan figures; see Yanagida, "Goroku," 377.

27. The full title of this work is *Nanyang heshang dunjiao jietuo chanmen zhi liaoxing tanyu* 南陽和上頓教解脫禪門直了性壇語 (Platform Sermon by the Preceptor of Nanyang on Directly Comprehending the Nature according to the Chan Doctrine of the Sudden Teaching and Emancipation). This is generally considered to be Shenhui's earliest extant work, dating from his residence at Nanyang beginning in 720, although there is no specific evidence pertaining to its date. Professor Tanaka, *Tonkō Zenshū bunken*, 254, dates the *Platform Sermon* as post-718. This is no doubt correct, but I have been unable to trace the reasoning or evidence involved. See Yanagida's characterization of this work summarized in n. 139 below.

The first manuscript of this work (Beijing *han*-81) was discovered and published by Suzuki; see his "Jinne oshō no dango to kangaubeki Tonkō shutsudo bon ni tsukite"; *Shōshitsu issho*, 37–55; and *Kōkan Shōshitsu issho*, 57–71 (text) and 50–68 (commentary). This material is reproduced in *Suzuki Daisetsu zenshū*, 3:290–317, with the commentary preceding the edited text. (There seems to have been only the most minor modifications to the *Zenshū* version.)

INTRODUCTION   11

In 730, 731, and 732, Shenhui lectured before public audiences of monks and laymen, openly and vociferously attacking the teachings and religious genealogy of Puji (651–739) and Xiangmo Zang 降魔藏 of the Northern school. The best-known of these public lectures occurred at the Dayun si 大雲寺 in Huatai 滑臺 (Hua xian 滑縣, Henan) on the fifteenth day of the first month of 732, the date that is often mistakenly given (rather than 730) for the initiation of Shenhui's anti-Northern school campaign. Zongmi states that Shenhui criticized the Northern school with regard to the transmission of Bodhidharma's robe in Luoyang while he was in Luoyang prior to 732, but this statement may not be chronologically rigorous.[28] Since Dharma masters from Fuxian si 福先寺 and Heze si 荷澤寺 in Luoyang supposedly took part in the 732 meeting, we may infer that Shenhui had already developed special relationships with these monasteries.[29] The location of the other meetings is not known. (I will discuss the possible reasons for Shenhui's choice of Huatai in section A of the conclusion to this essay.)

In 745 Shenhui formally took up residence at Heze si in Luoyang, which is the location with which he is most closely associated. The *Transmission of the Lamp* actually states that it was only after his move to Luoyang in 745 that Shenhui wrote the *Xianzong ji* 顯宗記 (Record of the Manifestation of the Teaching) and "defined the two schools," i.e., the "southern [Hui]neng sudden school and northern [Shen]xiu gradual teaching."[30] The *Definition*

The existence of another manuscript (Pelliot 2045 [part 2]) was first discovered by Wang Zhongmin and announced in Hu Shih's "Xin jiaoding de Dunhuang xieben Shenhui heshang yizhu liangzhong." (Also included in this manuscript [referred to as part 1] was Shenhui's *Definition of the Truth*.) This version is republished in Hu's *Yiji*, 225–252. Professor Iriya has also discovered two additional fragments (Stein 2492 and 6977).

Shinohara Hisao 篠原壽雄 used all the available versions of the text in preparing his edition and translation, "Kataku Jinne no kotoba." Certain errors in Shinohara's work were revised in Nakamura Shinkō's "*Nan'yō wajō tonkyō gedatsu zenmon jiki ryōshō dango* hon'yaku."

The *Platform Sermon* was translated into English by Walter Liebenthal as "The Sermon of Shen-hui" (1952). Liebenthal used only one manuscript, Pelliot 2045, although he was able to refer to Gernet's *Entretiens*.

28. See Ui, 212.
29. See Suzuki Tetsuo, "Kataku Jinne ron," 226.
30. T 2076: 51.245a. The title *Xianzong ji* 顯宗記 is used for the text in the *Transmission of the Lamp*, T 2076: 51.458c–459b. A similar title, *Xianzong lun* 顯宗論 (Treatise on the Manifestation of the Teaching), is used for the excerpt (matching the Dunhuang text) found in the *Zongjing lu* 宗鏡錄 (Record of the Mirror of Truth), T 2016: 48.949a–b. The original title is *Dunwu wusheng bore song* 頓悟無生般若頌 (Verses on Sudden Enlightenment, the Birthless, and *Prajñā*). This title occurs in Stein 468, an annotated edition of which may be found in Hu, *Yiji*, 193–199, with Hu's commentary following on 200–208. The Dunhuang version is said to be simpler than the text found in the *Transmission of the Lamp*, and lacks the statement of twenty-eight patriarchs attached to the latter. (Yanagida, *Shoki zenshū shisho*, 124, 324, and 365–380, has argued that the scheme of twenty-eight patriarchs was an innovation of the *Baolin zhuan* 寶林傳 and never suggested by Shenhui.) There is a second Dunhuang manuscript (Stein 296) of unknown length. The earliest notice of the Dunhuang version of this text (Stein 468) was in Yabuki Keiki, *Meisha yoin—Tonkō shutsudo miden koitsu Butten kaihō*. Robert B. Zeuschner has translated the text in "The *Hsien-tsung chi*: An Early Ch'an Text." This text is written in polished form and lacks the evangelical immediacy and polemical fire of the *Definition of the Truth*.

of the Truth, which was based primarily on the 732 Dayun si lecture, was also edited sometime during the years 744–749, probably shortly after Shenhui's move to Heze si in 745.[31] Tacitly admitting that Shenhui's activities at Huatai had not had much of an impact, Zongmi suggests that it was from the time of his move to Luoyang that the differences between the Northern and Southern schools became widely known.[32] The *Song Biographies* says that Shenhui established a hall at Heze si containing a likeness of Huineng, for which a layman named Song Ding 宋鼎 erected a stele. The newly discovered stele for Shenhui corroborates this in its vague statement that Song Ding (whom the stele identifies as a *bingbu shilang* 兵部侍郎 or vice minister of the ministry of war) "extended an invitation [to Shenhui to come to] Luoyang to expansively open the Dharma eye, erected an epitaph, and established a likeness."[33] Presumably both the epitaph and the likeness were Huineng's, the former probably being that written by Wang Wei.[34] The *Song Biographies*, again, reports that Shenhui also taught about the succession from Śākyamuni and the six Chinese patriarchs and had pictures painted of the latter, to which Fang Guan 房琯 added a preface.[35] About this time Shenhui was also involved in efforts to provide the third patriarch, Sengcan 僧璨, with a suitable biography.[36] (Sengcan had been the most obscure of the Chinese patriarchs ever since the formation of the theory of the transmission from Bodhidharma around the turn of the eighth century.)

Although Shenhui openly criticized the heterodox transmission and faulty teachings of the Northern school after his move to Heze si in 745, there is no specific record of any public lecturing by him there until 749. According to one sometimes unreliable text, beginning in this year Shenhui continued his public attack on the Northern school from the ordination

---

31. Suzuki Tetsuo has noticed that the text's reference to the date of the original Huatai debate is couched in terms of a usage that was instituted in 744. He also suggests that 749 is the terminus ad quem for the text since it does not mention the debate that occurred in that year, according to the *Records of the Transmission*. See "Kataku Jinne ron," 225–226 and 238 nn. 8–9. The *Records of the Transmission* citation occurs at T 2075: 51.185b, or see Yanagida Seizan, *Shoki no Zenshi 2*, 155.

There are three Dunhuang manuscripts for the *Definition of the Truth* (*Putidamo nanzong ding shifei lun* 菩提達摩南宗定是非論, Definition of the Truth [regarding] Bodhidharma's Southern School): Pelliot 2045 (pt. 1), 3047 (pt. 2), and 3488 (pt. 1). The text occurs in Hu, *Yiji*, 260–314. The discovery of the manuscripts of this text by Hu in Paris was the catalyst for his biographical study of Shenhui and, indeed, all of his subsequent work on Chinese Chan. Yanagida, "Goroku," 376, suggests that this text stands midway between the first and third versions of the *Miscellaneous Dialogues* in the development of Shenhui's teachings.

32. This comment is in all three of Zongmi's texts, as mentioned in Ui, 231. In the preceding pages, Ui emphasizes the lack of impact of Shenhui's campaign.

33. Takeuchi, "Shinshutsu no Kataku Jinne tōmei," 324.

34. As mentioned in Yampolsky, *Platform Sutra*, 66n, Jacques Gernet, in "Biographie du Maître Chen-houei," 48, has suggested on the basis of the title used to identify Wang Wei that the epitaph for Huineng was written after 739.

35. Ui, 210–211, points out that these refer to the material found only in the Suzuki / Kōda edition of the Ishii manuscript of the *Miscellaneous Dialogues*.

36. This is discussed in Matsuda Fumio 松田文雄, "Jinne no hōtōsetsu ni tsuite."

platform every month.³⁷ However, the variety of subjects discussed in Shenhui's *Miscellaneous Dialogues,* which contains exchanges with monks and laymen primarily from the Nanyang period of Shenhui's life, suggests that the anti-Northern school campaign was not his only concern.³⁸

C. Shenhui's Banishment and Reinstatement

In 753 Shenhui was banished from the capital at the instigation of a military official named Lu Yi 盧奕, who memorialized against the possible problems involved with Shenhui's large audiences. Lu Yi is said to have been guided in this matter by Puji, even though this influential Northern school monk had died almost a decade and a half earlier.³⁹ Zongmi points out that the religious leadership of the Northern school did not agree with Shenhui's banishment, which was the work of ignorant followers more given to a sense of competition. Actually, given the political climate in Chang'an in 753, it is quite possible that the mere fact of Shenhui's large audiences might have been as important in Shenhui's removal from the capital as any factional aggressiveness.⁴⁰

In any case, Shenhui's banishment seems to have been anything but severe. On the basis of Lu Yi's accusation, Shenhui was taken by two high-ranking ministers to meet Emperor Xuanzong 玄宗. A conversation in the emperor's bath house was followed by an edict "'demoting' Shenhui and relocating him to the provinces,"⁴¹ first to Yiyang 弋陽, Jiangxi, and then to Wudang 武當, Hubei. In 754 Shenhui was transferred by imperial order to Xiangyang. Finally, in the seventh month of 754, an imperial proclamation had him take up residence at the Kaiyuan si 開元寺 in Jingzhou 荊州. Of these locations, Xiangyang was Shenhui's native place, and Jingzhou was one of the most important centers of Buddhist activity in south-central China. In addition, Wudang was then the residence of Nanyang Huizhong

---

37. This is according to the sometimes unreliable *Records of the Transmission,* as mentioned in n. 130 below.

38. A reference in Zongmi's writings suggests that Shenhui also gained prominence through his explanation of the metaphor of the three carts in the *Lotus Sūtra;* Hu infers from the biography of the individual mentioned that this occurred around the end of the Kaiyuan period (713–741). The wording also implies that Shenhui was residing at the Longxing si in Nanyang at the time. See Ui, 209, citing Hu, *Yiji,* 14, and the text on 110–111. The inference regarding Shenhui's residence is from Ui, 230.

39. Actually, given the anachronistic references to Puji and Shenxiu in the biographies of late eighth-century figures, this may not be that great a problem; Lu Yi's guidance from Puji could have been through his own memory of the master or through some contemporaneous successor. See McRae, *Northern School,* 71 and 293–294n. The phrasing of the *Song Biographies* reference is also somewhat vague in saying that Lu Yi falsely memorialized against Shenhui to "curry favor" with (*o* 阿, also meaning to "fawn on" or "flatter") Puji.

40. Whatever the degree of Northern school involvement in Shenhui's removal from the capital, it is possible that he exaggerated the entire incident so as to incite his followers against the Northern school. In this case, there would be no reason to suppose that all of Shenhui's public lectures were virulent attacks on the Northern school; the polemical maneuver would have occurred after his expulsion from Luoyang.

41. This and the following information is according to Zongmi's *Dashu chao.* The term used is *chu* 處, which refers to a demotion and/or relocation.

(d. 775), who was to become famous after Shenhui's death. The two men must have met during this time, if not before, and it is my impression that Huizhong's later activities were in some sense a continuation of Shenhui's.[42] Zongmi, who is our source for the details of Shenhui's movements, says that the Northern school was present at all four locations. Far from being a "banishment," the impression given by the description of Shenhui's movements is that of an imperially sponsored regional lecture tour.

After the beginning of the An Lushan rebellion in 755, the central government found itself very short of funds, and it was soon suggested that ordination platforms be established in the major prefectures and aspirants allowed to become monks after the payment of "incense money" (*xiangshui qian* 香水錢). Theoretically, the ordinands had to be able to recite five hundred pages of scripture in order to be ordained; in fact, anyone willing to pay one hundred strings of cash was accepted.[43] The reason for paying such sums, of course, was that monks were exempt from further taxation. After two abortive attempts—in which Shenhui presumably did not participate[44]—in the fifth month of 757 an order was promulgated to carry out the plan throughout the entire country, beginning in Luoyang.[45]

Shenhui's former accuser Lu Yi had been killed by the rebels in the twelfth month of 755, so there was nothing to prevent Shenhui from being summoned back to the eastern capital to lead the sale of ordinations. Specifically, we are told that he built a temporary chapel and established a square ordination platform among the ruins of burned Buddhist monasteries. Shenhui seems to have begun his fundraising activities while the rebels were still in at least nominal control of the two capitals, since the *Song Biographies* says that he was greatly beneficial to the future emperor Daizong 代宗 (r. 762–779) and his general Guo Ziyi 郭子儀 when they retook Chang'an and Luoyang in the ninth and tenth months of 757, respectively. Because he was able to raise a great deal of money for the Tang government, Shenhui was summoned to the palace to receive offerings sometime after Emperor Suzong 肅宗 (r. 756–762) returned to Chang'an. The emperor also built a "Chan building" (*chanyu* 禪宇) for Shenhui at Heze si in recognition of his services to the state. It is interesting to note how brief was Shenhui's participation in this fundraising endeavor: from the promulgation of the order in the fifth month of 757 at the earliest until his death in the same month of the following year.[46]

---

42. I will document the reasons for this impression on a later occasion, but see n. 137 below.

43. Ui, 234.

44. According to Yamazaki Hiroshi, "Kataku Jinne zenji," this plan was first carried out by the infamous Yang Guozhong 楊國忠 in either Taiyuan 太原 or Hedong 河東. The same scheme was used after Yang's death, this time in Pengyuan 彭原.

45. The plan was initiated by an order issued from Emperor Suzong's camp at Fengxiang 鳳翔 (in modern Shaanxi) at the instigation of Pei Wan 裴冕 (d. 769).

46. Peterson, "Court and Province in Mid-and Late T'ang," 474, describes this year as being toward the end of a period of rebel ascendancy (July 756 to November 757) and immediately preceding a period of relative military inactivity (autumn 757 to autumn 758).

D. Shenhui's Death and Official Recognition

Shenhui died at the Kaiyuan si in Jingzhou on the thirteenth day of the fifth month of 758.[47] His death is described in typical Chan fashion: after commanding his students to ask him for the last time about the Dharma and repeatedly praising the "single unconditioned (or, inactive) Dharma" (*wuwei yi fa* 無為一法), he passed away in the middle of the night. According to Zongmi, that night the military governor of Shannan dong dao 山南東道, Li Guangzhu 李廣珠,[48] supposedly saw him passing through the air on his lecture seat. When Li went to inquire at Shenhui's monastery, it was discovered that the elderly monk had died.

There are minor discrepancies regarding Shenhui's stūpas. According to Zongmi, in 759 a stūpa was erected at Longmen, and in 763 the location of the stūpa was named Baoying si 寶應寺. The *Song Biographies*, on the other hand, suggests that the stūpa was moved to Baoying si in Luoyang in 763.[49] For whatever reason, in 765 the stūpa at Longmen was rebuilt and the newly discovered stele added. The relationship between this and the previous stūpa or stūpas is uncertain. However, the stele inscription does say that Li Si 李嗣, or Li Wangzai 李王再, probably the same individual who appears in the *Definition of the Truth* as Si Daowang 嗣道王, received Shenhui's remains for interment into the new stūpa.[50]

The stele inscription of 765 refers to Shenhui as "Seventh Patriarch and National Teacher," which were unofficial appellations used out of respect for a departed master.[51] In 770 there was an imperial bequest of a name tablet for his "patriarchal hall" (*zutang* 祖堂), which was called the Hall of the Transmission of the Dharma of the True School of Prajñā (*Zhenzong bore chuanfa zhi tang* 真宗般若傳法之堂). In 772 a similar bequest included a name tablet for his stūpa, which bore the title Stūpa of the Great Master of Prajñā (*Bore dashi zhi ta* 般若大師之塔).[52] Hence Shenhui is known by the posthumous titles

---

47. The specific date used here is that given in Shenhui's stele inscription. The *Dashu chao, Song Biographies*, and *Transmission of the Lamp* place Shenhui's death at the thirteenth day of the fifth month, although the years differ. Zongmi's text agrees with the stele in assigning the year 758 to Shenhui's death. The *Song Biographies* specifies a year in terms that do not match any legitimate year, although Hu Shih thought the year intended was 762. See Hu Shih, "Xin jiaoding de Dunhuang xieben," 875. The *Song Biographies* states that Shenhui lived to be ninety-three whereas the *Transmission of the Lamp* agrees with the stele in reporting his age at death to be seventy-five. Takeuchi, "Shinshutsu no Kataku Jinne tōmei," reviews these discrepancies on pp. 315–316. Ui, 235–236, notes that there is a discrepancy about the location where Shenhui died, either Kaiyuan si or Heze si. I have followed the stele and *Dashu chao* (see the following anecdote, which refers to Kaiyuan si), but note that this further reduces the length of time he was involved in fundraising on behalf of the government.

48. Otherwise unknown.

49. T 2061: 757a.

50. See Takeuchi, "Shinshutsu no Kataku Jinne tōmei," 324, and Suzuki Tetsuo, "Kataku Jinne ron," 320.

51. Takeuchi, "Shinshutsu no Kataku Jinne tōmei," 320, adduces evidence to show that "national teacher" was not used as an official title at the time, but rather as a generic term of reference for masters of great standing or national prominence.

52. See ibid.

"True School" and "Prajñā." In 796, according to Zongmi, Emperor Dezong ordered his crown prince to call an assembly of Chan masters, after which Shenhui was formally recognized as the seventh patriarch of Chan.[53]

III. Traces of Shenhui's Influence in Northern School Literature

A. The Problem of Shenhui's Early Teaching Career

Ironically, decades of study of the Chan materials from Dunhuang has resulted in the increased obscurity of an important part of Shenhui's religious development. Formerly, anyone interested in the early formation of Shenhui's personal philosophy could simply point to the teachings of his master Huineng as known through the *Platform Sūtra* and other works. However, the specific teachings of the historical Huineng—as opposed to the legendary personality depicted in the *Platform Sūtra* and elsewhere—are completely unknown. On the other hand, Zongmi explicitly refers to Shenhui's spiritual maturation around the time of his ordination in Chang'an, which implies that Shenhui was influenced by other teachers in addition to Huineng.

And what about the period after Huineng's death, when Shenhui supposedly traveled about to religious sites in different parts of China? Why did Shenhui wait for almost two decades after his master's death in 713 to initiate his campaign on behalf of Huineng's recognition as sixth patriarch and against the supposed errors of the Northern school? Once again, the absence of any direct quotations from Huineng's teachings in Shenhui's works renders uncertain the substance and extent of Shenhui's religious inheritance from his southern master, but it seems reasonable to suppose that Shenhui's ideas developed substantially in the north both at the time of his ordination and after Huineng's death.

In fact, it is not difficult to imagine that Shenhui's experience in the north was quite positive both before and after Huineng's death. As far as we can tell, cordial relations prevailed between Huineng and the members of what is now called the Northern school during the first two decades of the eighth century. During this time Huineng was perceived as a member in good standing, albeit far removed, of that loosely knit confraternity: he is included along with Shenxiu, Lao'an 老安, and others in the well-known list of Hongren's 弘忍 ten disciples that first occurs in Northern school texts, and his name also occurs in an obscure work found in one of the most important of Northern school Dunhuang manuscripts, in this case accompanied by such well-known names as Aśvaghoṣa, Huike 慧可, and Shenxiu.[54]

Moreover, at least three students are known to have studied under

---

53. Zongmi mentions this in his *Chan Chart*. See ZZ 2A / 15 / 5.434b, or Kamata, *Zengen shosenshū tojo*, 277. Ui, 237, points out that a similar resolution of conflict in the Vinaya school took place in 778.

54. The earliest work in which the list of Hongren's students occurs is the *Masters and Disciples of the Laṅkāvatāra*, which was composed in 713–716. The provenance of the second text is probably similar. See McRae, *Northern School*, 38–39 and 84.

Huineng and other Northern school masters. Other than Shenhui himself, the most interesting of these was a monk named Jingzang 淨藏 (675–746), who studied under the Northern school master Lao'an, then traveled south to meet Huineng, and ultimately returned to the north to maintain his first teacher's stūpa.[55] Although Shenhui's example should perhaps be excluded from consideration here on logical grounds (since the issue is the believability of his studies under Shenxiu), there is no a priori reason to reject the possibility that Shenxiu directed him to go to Caoqi to study under Huineng at the time of the former master's invitation to the imperial court. Although no one else is known to have accompanied Shenhui to Caoqi, the suggestion itself would not have been out of character for Shenxiu, who left other students behind in Jingzhou in an atmosphere more conducive to meditation than that at Luoyang and Chang'an.[56] The implication is that there is no reason to distinguish Huineng and his teachings from the rest of early Chan until the onset of Shenhui's propaganda drive.

B. The Texts

I will introduce below a partial translation of an early Chan text that sheds light on Shenhui's ideas and associations at a time when he was cooperating with Northern school figures, prior to the initiation of his anti-Northern school campaign. The text is known as the *Treatise on the True Principle* (*Dasheng kaixin xianxing dunwu zhenzong lun* 大乘開心顯性頓悟真宗論, Treatise on the True Principle of Opening the Mind and Manifesting the [Buddha-]Nature in Sudden Enlightenment [according to] the Mahāyāna).[57] Although Shenhui had some influence on the *Treatise on the True Principle*, the most intriguing aspect of the text is its obvious Northern school origin. First, both Shenhui and the Northern school master Lao'an are listed as the teachers of the text's author, Huiguang 慧光, who may have also studied

---

55. See McRae, *Northern School*, 58–59 and 291n.

56. This is known through a letter written by Shenxiu's sometime student Yixing 一行. See McRae, *Northern School*, 51 and 289n.

57. This text, the complete Dunhuang manuscript for which is Pelliot 2162, was first described in Yabuki's *Meisha yoin*, 538–540. The text may be found in T 2835: 85.1278a–1281c or the *Suzuki Daisetsu zenshū*, 3:318–330. Photocopies of a fragment, Stein 4286, which includes approximately the first third of the text but in a most disordered fashion, are reproduced at the end of Jao Tsung-I's "Shenhui menxia Moheyan zhi ruzang," following 178. Another printed version (based on the *Taishō* edition) occurs in Kim Kugyŏng's *Jiangyuan congshu*. For an analysis of the authorship and contents of this text, including the relationship between it and other Northern school literature, plus a comparison with the *Essential Determination*, see Tanaka Ryōshō, *Tonkō zenshū bunken no kenkyū*, 237–259. The partial translation included in this essay is based on the Suzuki edition, which I have checked against the photographs of Stein 4286, with reference to Tanaka, *Tonkō zenshū bunken*, 253–254, for comparison with the *Essential Determination*. Recently, J. C. Cleary has published a translation of the entire *Treatise on the True Principle* in *Zen Dawn*, 103–130. Cleary's translation is uneven in style but generally accurate, and his reading occasionally implies punctuation superior to that of the Suzuki edition. Unfortunately, he refrained from including any annotation or interpretation of the text, and he apparently used the outdated *Jiangyuan congshu* edition. See my review of *Zen Dawn* in *Eastern Buddhist* 19, no. 2 (1986): 138–146.

under Puji.[58] Second, the very structure of the text is closely modeled on a Northern school text known as the *Essential Determination* (*Dunwu zhenzong jingang bore xiuxing da bi'an famen yaojue* 頓悟真宗金剛般若修行達彼岸法門要訣, Essential Determination of the Doctrine of Attaining the Other Shore [of Nirvāṇa] by the Practice of Adamantine Wisdom [according to] the True Teaching of Sudden Enlightenment).[59]

The author of the *Essential Determination* was Zhida 智達 (d. 714), who is identified in the preface as a student of Lao'an and Shenxiu (as compared to Lao'an and Shenhui for the author of the *Treatise on the True Principle*). An epitaph discovered recently by Bernard Faure indicates that this monk (also known by the rare three-character surname and given name Houmochen Yanzhi 侯莫陳琰之) was a native of Chang'an who became a monk at age twenty, entered Mount Song 嵩 and studied first under Lao'an (given here as Ācārya An) and later under Shenxiu (Xiu heshang 秀和上). After more than twenty years of training he attained enlightenment, after which he changed his name to Zhida on the basis of Shenxiu's comment that his "wisdom and discrimination [were] unhindered" (*zhida biancai wuai* 智達辯才無礙). Afterwards he traveled about the Luoyang and Hebei 河北 areas teaching. He died on the tenth day of the sixth month of 714, although his age is not given. In addition to some interesting dialogue, Zhida's epitaph is notable for including the phrase "broadly opening (i.e., disseminating) the teaching of sudden enlightenment" (*dunwu zhi zong* 頓悟之宗) and references to "expedient means" (*fangbian* 方便) and "transmitting the lamp" (*chuandeng* 傳燈). Although this is substantially more detail than is given in the *Essential Determination*, text and epitaph are in complete agreement.[60]

---

58. A monk named Huiguang 慧光 who studied under Puji is known as the man who "discovered" the *Chanmen jing* 禪門經 or *Sūtra of Chan* around the year 720. See Yanagida's "Zenseki kaidai," 462, and "*Zenmonkyō* ni tsuite." Both Yanagida and Tanaka, *Tonkō Zenshū bunken*, 243–246, infer that these were two separate individuals. Tanaka, in fact, goes on to note the structual similarities between the *Treatise on the True Principle* and certain other early Chan texts and concludes by suggesting that the Huiguang of this text was a fictional personality. If he were a real individual, and taking the year 725 as a rough date for the composition of the *Treatise on the True Principle*, Huiguang would have been born around 680.

59. For a discussion and edition of this text, including a translation of the Tibetan version, see Ueyama Daishun, "*Tongo shinshū yōketsu*." Ueyama argues convincingly that the Tibetan translation of this text is more reliable than any of the Chinese manuscripts. Yanagida, "Zenseki kaidai," 458–459; Yanagida, "Hokushū-Zen no shisō," 80; and Tanaka, *Tonkō Zenshū bunken*, 251–256, describe this text as a later Northern school product.

60. See the *Liudu si Houmochen dashi shouta ming wen bing xu* 六度寺侯莫陳大師壽塔銘文並序 by Cui Kuan 崔寬, which occurs in the *Mangluo zhongmo yiwen sibian*, comp. Luo Zhenyu, *Shike shiliao xinbian*, 19:14263b–14264b. Faure has reported his findings in "Le maître de Dhyāna Chih-ta et le 'subitisme' de l'école du Nord." In addition to the information mentioned, the names of the half-dozen disciples responsible for constructing his stūpa are given, although none of them is immediately recognizable to me. According to the figures given in the epitaph, Zhida was at least forty years of age during Shenxiu's lifetime. Hence he must have been born sometime around or before (perhaps well before) 660. The epigrapher is mentioned briefly in the *Tang shu, Ershiwu shi*, Kaiming shudian ed., 3411c, in the context of

The *Essential Determination* and the *Treatise on the True Principle* are both presented as oral dialogues between a Chan master and a layman—but a close reading of the preface of each text reveals that teacher and interrogator are one and the same individual! Since the *Essential Determination* was written in 712 (while Shenhui was still with Huineng in Caoqi) and since it betrays no influence by Shenhui, we may infer that it was the model for the *Treatise on the True Principle*, rather than vice versa. This is in accord with the probable post-720 date of composition of the *Treatise on the True Principle*.[61] The efforts taken in these two texts to present their messages in dramatic form is a delightful innovation in the history of Chan literature, the power of which is only confirmed by its duplication.[62]

The modeling of one text on the other is not limited to overall structure, since a considerable portion of the prefaces of the two texts are identical. In the partial translation below, identical or closely similar passages are printed in italics. In addition, omissions (relative to the *Treatise on the True Principle*) are indicated by ellipses enclosed in square brackets. Finally, I have numbered the questions for the reader's convenience.

Treatise on the True Principle

Compiled and Explained by the Śramaṇa Dazhao 大照
and the Layman Huiguang[63]
[Preface]

In the melding of the mind in the great enlightenment (*dadao* 大道), it is the one true principle that is manifested. The former and later sages proceed only according to this teaching. To the enlightened, the triple realm is only the mind; the unenlightened are asleep within the false and the correct. The doctrine (*zong* 宗) of the Mahāyāna must manifest the true in relation

---

his older brother Cui Ning's 崔寧 biography and with regard to an incident in 767. Thus either the stele was erected quite some time after Zhida's death in 714 or the elaborate prestige titles by which Cui Kuan is identified (which identify him as rank 5a1 by Hucker's scheme) were added by the recorder of the epitaph. If the former alternative is the case, it is possible that the epitaph was written to corroborate the *Essential Determination*.

61. The *Treatise on the True Principle* shares a passage with the Northern school's *Masters and Disciples of the Laṅkāvatāra*, which was composed sometime during the years 713–716 far away from the two capitals. I suspect that the direction of borrowing was from this text to the *Treatise on the True Principle*, rather than vice versa. See sec. III.B.1 below. Also, the borrowing of the name of Huiguang (which even in the case of the *Chanmen jing* may be fictional) implies that the *Treatise on the True Principle* derives from sometime after 720, although once again the borrowing could have gone the other way.

62. The close relationship between these two texts has also been the subject of comments in Yanagida, "Hokushū-zen no shisō," 80. Both Ueyama, *"Tongo shinshū yōketsu,"* 67–68, and Tanaka, *Tonkō zenshū bunken no kenkyū*, 253–254, include synoptic presentations of the two prefaces.

63. The colophon of the *Essential Determination* reads "Chan Master Zhida's oral determination of the questions of Houmochen Yan, transcribed by the scribe Ying 縈."

to characteristics.[64] To comprehend the [Buddha-]nature (*liaoxing* 了性)[65] is to know the quiescence of all the dharmas: Phenomena are based on causes and conditions, and names (i.e., perceived identities) are created through the provisional conjunction [of individual elements]. To not comprehend [the Buddha-nature] is to be attached to names and fixated on words, to grasp at one's thoughts and [for one's mind] to race among the false.

If you wish to control the false and return to the true, making both defiled and pure universally same (*pingdeng* 平等), you must concentrate the will and contemplate the mind (*zhuyi guanxin* 注意觀心). Fundamental enlightenment will appear of itself. You should practice your mental contemplation (*yiguan* 意觀) with energy, but without interrupting your concentration[66] to think about reaching the "other shore" [of nirvāṇa]. Remain constantly immersed in profoundly deep meditation. Practice long, without cease, and matters will all come to their own natural conclusion (i.e., spiritual progress will occur automatically). If you persevere in contemplation, you will gradually progress toward the true.

If you let go of body and mind, their defects will be evaporated.[67] Your willful functions (*qizuo* 起作) are permanently serene; [your mind] illuminates without being conditioned[68] [by its objects]. Consign yourself freely to samādhi, [so that you may] incubate the way (*dao* 道) and nurture virtue (*de* 德), thus helping to create (*zicheng* 資成) the *dharmakāya*. Being enlightened to the mind-source, one is without obstruction and without hindrance, one is in essence like space: this is called the limitless samādhi. The mind is without exit and entrance (i.e., it does not enter and leave meditative or perceptual states): this is called the samādhi of no quiescence. To be pure and without seeking with respect to all the loci of being (*yousuo* 有所)[69] is called the inconceivable samādhi. For one's samādhi to be unobscured (*sanmei bu mei* 三昧不昧) and to not derive from conditions is called the samādhi of the dharma-nature.

---

64. Following Cleary, *Zen Dawn*, 105, I repunctuate Suzuki's edition to end the sentence after *zhen* 真, "true." Suzuki shows three missing characters just prior to *sheng* 乘, "vehicle," for which Stein 4286 has x*ie zheng da* 耶正大, "false (heterodox), correct, great." An attempt seems to have been made to delete the character *ding* 定, which I have interpreted as having the force of "must," from Stein 4286.

65. Stein 4286 has *xing* 性, "nature," instead of Suzuki's *wu* 悟, "enlightenment."

66. The character *yi* 意 is difficult to translate consistently. In Indian Buddhist philosophy it refers to *manas* and may be used as a synonym for consciousness in general, as a term for the sixth sensory faculty (the mind as the processor of data from the other senses), or, in Yogācāra, as the name of the seventh *vijñāna*. In Chinese the character also has the meaning of "will" or "intention." Hence the different translations here as "will," "mental," and "concentration."

67. "Evaporated" is a translation of *xuhuo* 虛豁, "[made] empty and expansive."

68. Stein 4286 has *yuan* 緣, "conditioned," rather than Suzuki's *xiang* 像, "modeled on."

69. "Realms of existence" might be a better translation here, except for the need for parallelism with *wusuo*, which occurs in the *Treatise on the True Principle*. See n. 81 below.

INTRODUCTION

All the students [nowadays] seek just for understanding, not for their own realization. You should definitely understand that it would be mistaken to attempt to cultivate the Mahāyāna without understanding pacification of the mind (*anxin* 安心).

At the time, there was a *layman of the surname* Li 李 *and name* Huiguang. *He was from Chang'an in Yongzhou* 雍州. *His religious name was* Dazhao.[70] *Unconcerned with fame and profit but wishing to seek* bodhi, [...][71] *he first studied under Ācārya* [*Lao*]*an and later under Preceptor* [Shen]hui.[72] *He intimately received oral determinations* [*of the teachings*] *from both of them; the doctrines* [*of Chan*] *were secretly transmitted to him. He thoroughly penetrated the fundamental source of the wondrous principle of the vital doctrine, and his exit from being and entrance into nonbeing were perfectly coalescent and free.*[73] [...][74] *During his time off from meditation, the layman lamented the* [*plight of*] *deluded* [*sentient beings*] *and has accordingly* manifested [...] the abstruse teaching of phenomena and principle. He explained the wondrous meaning and *revealed the essentials of the Dharma.* [...] [His teachings] *may be called a ship for crossing the ocean, by which one can "proceed directly to* bodhi.*" These words are worthy of trust.* Hopefully, those who are not now enlightened will become enlightened, those whose [minds] are not now pacified will become pacified, and those who are not emancipated will become emancipated.[75]

[Text]

1. The layman asked: "Buddhism is abstruse and mysterious, so that it is incomprehensible for the ordinary person. Its literature is vast and its doctrines

---

70. The *Essential Determination* identifies Houmochen's lay name as Yan 琰 (the epitaph has Yanzhi 琰之) and his religious title as Zhida.

71. Bracketed elisions indicate the occurrence of material in the *Essential Determination* that is not found in the *Treatise on the True Principle*. Here the former text states that Zhida stayed on Mount Song for more than twenty years.

72. Zhida, of course, was a student of Lao'an and Shenxiu.

73. I wonder if the phrase "exit from being and entrance into nonbeing" (*chuyou ruwu* 出有入無) is similar to the reflexive literary form known as *huwen* 互文, so that Huiguang was able to enter and exit both being and nonbeing.

74. Here the *Essential Determination* reads: "His accordance with the mysterious wisdom within the house (i.e., immanent in sentient beings) and attainment of the correct realization of cultivating the mind (*xiuxin*) were incomparable." The term *xiuxin* 修心, of course, recalls the title of the *Treatise on the Essentials of Cultivating the Mind* (*Xiuxin yao lun* 修心要論) attributed to Hongren.

75. For this paragraph, the *Essential Determination* has: "In his time off from contemplation, the layman lamented the [plight of] deluded [sentient beings] and eventually utilized their [errors] to formulate a dialogue whereby he could reveal the essentials of the Dharma. He may be called the 'dragon-and-elephant of the house of Śākya, the boat across the ocean [of ignorance].' A sūtra says: 'Go directly to *bodhi*.' These words are worthy of trust. Future students are thus fortunate to be able to maintain [awareness of the] mind (*shouxin* 守心) according to the text." Following this, the *Essential Determination* has: "Recorded by the prefect (*cishi* 刺史) of Dizhou 棣州 (Yangxin xian 陽信縣, Shandong) Liu Wude 劉無得 on the fifth day of the eleventh month of the first year of Xiantian 先天 (= December 8, 712)."

difficult to understand. I [would now] inquire of the dhyāna master [regarding] the essentials of the teaching. [...] Temporarily cease with expedient means and speak directly.[76] Do not forsake the common sort [of ignorant person such as myself], and please have no secrets."[77]

Dhyāna Master Dazhao answered: "Excellent! Excellent! From your question, I can see that you have the aptitude of a bodhisattva and wish to purify and develop yourself. In my forty-five years of life and over twenty years as a monk,[78] never has anyone asked me about this meaning (i.e., about the ultimate message of Buddhism). What problems do you have? What doubts can I settle? Ask directly and I will explain directly—do not bother with elaborate speech."

2. Question: "If one wishes to enter into enlightenment (*rudao* 入道), what dharma should one cultivate? What dharma should one view? What dharma should one realize? What dharma should one seek? To what dharma should one become enlightened? And what dharma should one attain, so as to proceed to *bodhi*?"

Answer: "You should not view a single dharma, and neither should you have any seeking. You should not realize a single dharma, and neither should you have any subsequent [attainment]. You should not become enlightened to a single dharma, and neither is there any enlightenment (*dao* 道) that can be cultivated. This is *bodhi*."

3. Question: "Since beginningless time this disciple has been floating along in the waves of saṃsāra, at odds with the [true] principle. Although I have heard the teaching of suddenness (*dunshuo* 頓說), I have been stupid and have not understood. My spirit (*shenshi* 神識) is obscured and I know not where it is—I am like a drunken man who cannot sober up. On behalf of deluded sentient beings, I beseech you to bestow the expedient means that are in accord with the truth [regarding] a few questions."

Question: "What is the true nature (*zhenxing* 真性)?"

Answer: "The nonactivated mind (*buqi xin* 不起心), which is constantly without characteristics and pure."

4. Question: "What are the self-natures (*zixing* 自性)?"

---

76. Stein 4286 has *zhenyan* 真言, "true words," instead of Suzuki's *zhiyan* 直言, "direct words," but note the *zhiwen zhishuo* 直問直說, "ask directly and I will explain directly," just below.

77. For this paragraph the *Essential Determination* has: "Yan inquired of Dhyāna Master Zhida, 'Buddhism is abstruse and...difficult to understand. I would like to inquire of the essential teaching of Chan—not in order to gain rebirth as a man or god, but to proceed directly to the "other shore" of *bodhi*. I request that in your compassion, you will not forsake the common sort...and please have no secrets. Refrain from discussing mundane paths. Please do not belabor your wisdom in regard to the conditioned [matters of] this world; I request that you favor me with the essential teaching of the unconditioned [matters of the] supramundane.'" (Elisions mark language identical to that in the *Treatise on the True Principle*.)

78. The *Essential Determination* has Zhida say he is fifty-three years old and had been a monk for thirty-two years.

Answer: "The perceptive capacities (*jianwen juezhi* 見聞覺知]), the four elements, and all dharmas each have their own self-natures."

5. Question: "From what are these self-natures generated?"

Answer: "They are generated from the false (i.e., the deluded) mind."

6. Question: "How can the self-natures be transcended (*li* 離)?"

Answer: "When the mind is not activated, they are transcended."

7. Question: "What is enlightenment (*dao*)? What is the principle (*li* 理)? What is the mind (*xin* 心)?"

Answer: "The mind is enlightenment. The mind is the principle. The principle[79] is the mind. Outside the mind there is no principle; outside the principle there is no mind. The capability of the mind to be universally same (*pingdeng*) is called the principle; the capability of the principle to illuminate brightly is called the mind. When mind and principle are universally same, they are called the Buddha-mind. He who attains this principle does not perceive [that there is any] saṃsāra.

There is no difference between ordinary people and sages; [perceptual] realm and wisdom are not distinct. Phenomena and principle are both melded [together]; defiled and pure are as one. That which illuminates truthfully as the principle cannot be other than enlightenment (*dao*). Self- and other-[natures] are both transcended—in all activities and at all times, there is neither any before or after, nor any intermediate. Bondage and emancipation [occur] spontaneously. This is called enlightenment."

1. The Northern School Character of the Essential Determination and Treatise on the True Principle

I have already mentioned the specific attribution of the *Essential Determination* to a Northern school figure, but it is still important to consider the doctrinal character of this text in order to gauge the nature of Shenhui's influence on the *Treatise on the True Principle*.

The Northern school character of the *Essential Determination* is apparent in several ways. First, the text pays attention to the "non-activation" (*buqi*) of the mind, which was a well-known catchword for Chan practitioners in the second decade of the eighth century.[80] Second, many of the doctrinal formulations found in the *Essential Determination* are done in a style known as "contemplative analysis" (*guanxin shi* 觀心釋, or *kanjin shaku* 観心釈 in

---

79. Stein 4286 has the character *li* here twice.

80. Sometime after his entry into Chang'an in 716, the esoteric master Śubhākarasiṃha critized Shenxiu's student Jingxian 景賢 (660–723) and other devotees of Chan for what he thought was self-defeating single-mindedness: "You beginners are [in such] great fear of activating the mind and mobilizing thoughts (*qixin dongnian* 起心動念) that you cease to make spiritual progress. In single-mindedly maintaining non-thought (*wunian* 無念) as the ultimate, the [longer you] search, the more unattainable [is your goal]" (T 18.945a). Hence *buqi* 不起, *wunian*, and, incidentally, *wu yi wu* 無一物, "not a single thing," which occurs on 945b, were well-known terms at the time.

Japanese) that typifies Northern school texts.[81] Third, the use of terms such as *shouxin*, "to maintain [awareness of] the mind," which is the key doctrine of an important text attributed to Hongren, indicates a close relationship with the Northern school.[82] Fourth, the text was circulated within the late Northern school corpus of material.[83]

One interesting feature of the *Essential Determination* is the manner in which it combines the rhetoric of "viewing the mind" with that of "seeing the [Buddha-]nature." The latter concept is in fact the very heart of one of the most important motifs of early Chan doctrine, but it was only with Shenhui that it became a well-known slogan. In fact, the *Essential Determination* cites the *Nirvāṇa Sūtra*, just as Shenhui was to do a few years later: "See the [Buddha-]nature and achieve the enlightenment of Buddhahood."[84]

Perhaps even more than the *Essential Determination*, the *Treatise on the True Principle* is clearly a Northern school text. The central theme is once again the contemplation of the mind, which this text also explicates in terms of "non-activation" or *buqi*. The text uses the term *li*, "to transcend" in a fashion similar to Northern school usage. Other similarities with known

---

81. The term "contemplative analysis" derives from the writings of Zhiyi 智顗 and refers to the explication of Buddhist terms and ideas by recourse to insights gained during meditation. Applied to early Chan texts, it refers to the sometimes bizarre and almost always forced reinterpretations of standard terminology in terms of the contemplation of the mind. Both the Northern and Oxhead schools are known for this practice. For a longer discussion of this practice, see McRae, *Northern School*, 198–207. The *Essential Determination* applies this style of interpretation to a famous line from the *Diamond Sūtra*: *ying wusuozhu er sheng qi xin* 應無所住而生其心:

"For all [moments of] consciousness to be nonexistent is called the 'locus of nonbeing' (*wusuo* 無所). To refrain from any further activation of consciousness (*bu qixin*) is called 'residing' (*zhu* 住). [In the phrase] 'generating consciousness' (*er sheng qi xin* 而生其心), 'should' (*ying* 應) means 'should' (*dang* 當) and to 'generate' (*sheng* 生) means to 'view' (*kan* 看). Thus 'should view the locus of nonbeing' is equivalent to [the phrase] 'generating consciousness….'"

Question: "What thing does one see?"
Answer: "The [*Nirvāṇa*] *Sūtra* says: 'See the [Buddha-]nature and achieve the enlightenment of buddhahood.'" (Ueyama, 96–97)

The *Nirvāṇa Sūtra* citation is actually a modified summary of material at T 374: 12.547a. For early occurrences of the term *wusuo*, see Yanagida, *Daruma no goroku*, 158n; Ogawa Kan'ichi, "Hannya haramitta shingyō kaidai," 83b; and Iriya Yoshitaka, *Denshin hōyō—Enryōroku*, 124n. Since the *Diamond Sūtra* line is quoted in at least one other text by a Northern school figure, its presence here cannot be used as evidence of influence from Huineng; see Yixing's 一行 (685–727) commentary on the *Dari jing* 大日經 (*Mahāvairocana Sūtra*), T 1796: 39.579b.

82. For two occurrences of *shouxin* in the *Essential Determination*, see nn. 74 and 75 above. For a discussion of the doctrine of *shouxin* in the *Treatise on the Essentials of Cultivating the Mind*, see McRae, *Northern School*, 136–138.

83. See Ueyama's description of the manuscripts for this text, "Tongo shinshū yōketsu," 34–36.

84. See n. 81 above.

Northern school literature are the use of the distinction between inner-directed and outer-directed wisdom and the use of a distinctive "contemplative analysis" style of doctrinal reinterpretation.[85] Also, the pairing of *shun* 順, "direct," and *wang* 妄, "false," is similar to the *shunguan* 順觀, "direct contemplation," and *niguan* 逆觀, "reverse contemplation," of the Northern school's *Treatise on Perfect Illumination* (*Yuanming lun* 圓明論), and the description of the *zixin* 自心, "self-mind," and *wangxin* 妄心, "false mind," resembles the dualism of Shenxiu's *Treatise on the Contemplation of the Mind* (*Guanxin lun* 觀心論).[86] Finally, at one point the *Treatise on the True Principle* shares a passage with the Northern school's *Masters and Disciples of the Laṅkāvatāra*, which was written sometime during the years 713–716, and at another point discusses an obscure scripture in a fashion similar to that in the *Treatise on the Contemplation of the Mind*.[87]

For the purposes of this discussion, however, it is also important to note the apparent indications of Shenhui's presence within the doctrines of the *Treatise on the True Principle*. The points that most clearly parallel his later doctrinal inclinations are the apophatic mood of some of the statements regarding the contemplation of the mind (evident to a certain extent in section 2 of the translation), occasional references to the doctrine of suddenness, and the use of the phrase "truly comprehend the [Buddha-]nature" (*zhen liaoxing* 真了性). This terminology figures prominently in the title of Shenhui's *Platform Sermon*.[88]

Before drawing any conclusions from this evidence, let me briefly discuss another relevant text.

2. The Evidence of the Treatise on the Dharma-nature

The *Essential Determination* and *Treatise on the True Principle* are not the only sources of evidence for Shenhui's early membership in the Northern school doctrinal community. Another interesting text found among the Dunhuang treasures is a short essay provisionally titled the *Treatise on the Dharma-nature* (*Faxing lun* 法性論), which contains terminology reminiscent of Shenhui's *Platform Sermon*. This treatise occurs in two out of eight or nine manuscripts devoted to a set anthology of Northern Chan material. The two manuscripts in question are the longest and most complete of the entire set, which includes the very important *Treatise on the Essentials of Cultivating the Mind* (*Xiuxin yao lun* 修心要論) attributed to Hongren, Shenxiu's *Treatise on the Contemplation of the Mind*, and other less well known East Mountain teaching and

---

85. See the *Suzuki Daisetsu zenshū*, 3:327, 326–327 and 329, respectively.
86. See ibid., 320. (*Zixin* is, however, an unusual term.)
87. See Tanaka, *Tonkō Zenshū bunken*, 247–250.
88. One apparently Northern school text bears the title *Liaoxing ju* 了性句 (Stanzas on Comprehending the Nature), but it does not contain the three-character phrase so characteristic of Shenhui. See *Suzuki Daisetsu zenshū*, 2:450–452.

Northern school texts.[89] Another interesting detail is that the last few lines of this treatise occur in one Dunhuang manuscript in conjunction with a verse by a Reverend Ji, presumably Puji of the Northern school.[90] Although it is impossible to identify the specific author of the *Treatise on the Dharma-nature,* the text obviously derives from an era when there was no explicit animosity between the groups now known as the Northern and Southern schools and when the teachings of Huineng and Shenhui were accepted as variations on the East Mountain teaching.

The *Treatise on the Dharma-nature*[91] exhibits a number of similarities with Shenhui's thought. First of all, of course, is the attention to the concept of "seeing the nature" or *jianxing* 見性 (*kenshō* in Japanese). Although both the concept and the specific terminology do occur in pre-Shenhui Northern school literature,[92] the term occurs in both the title and text of Shenhui's *Platform Sermon.* Hence it seems safe to suggest that this terminology and the associated ideas constitute an early trademark of Shenhui's religious philosophy. In addition, the *Treatise on the Dharma-nature* quotes a line from the *Vimalakīrti Sūtra* that also occurs in Shenhui's works—and in the *Treatise on the True Principle.*[93] Both Shenhui and the *Treatise on the Dharma-nature* make use of a metaphor involving gold and gangue in order to explain the existence of the Buddha-nature within sentient beings.[94] In a passage already mentioned above, both describe the relationship between meditation and wisdom as one of "equivalent functioning" (*ding hui deng yong* 定慧等用), and the character *jia* 家, normally meaning "house," occurs in this text exactly

---

89. I use the terms "East Mountain teaching" and "Northern school" to represent (1) the basic doctrines of early Chan generally attributed to Hongren and Daoxin 道信, and (2) the more complex ideas formulated by Shenxiu and his disciples. See McRae, *Northern School,* 8–10, for an explanation of this somewhat arbitrary but useful distinction. (Where the term Northern school occurs independently it may be used inclusive of the other term.) The anthology referred to here is described in ibid., 311–312n.

90. See *Suzuki Daisetsu zenshū,* 3:445, and *Kōkan Shōshitsu issho,* 89. The shared passage begins with a quotation from the *Nirvāṇa Sūtra* (actually a paraphrase of T 374: 12.547a) and continues in language that is very similar to that in the *Platform Sermon;* Hu, *Yiji,* 243. (See n. 81 above, and compare a passage attributed falsely to Nanyue Huisi 南嶽慧思 in the *Zongjing lu,* T 2016: 48.941a.) Taken by itself, this set of coincidences would not be particularly meaningful because of the haphazard nature of the Dunhuang manuscript transcriptions.

91. "Treatise on the Dharma-nature" is Suzuki's provisional title; the text itself does begin with a reference to *faxing* 法性 but later on reads: "Now, according to the true and comprehensive manifestations of the nature in the gateway of principle of the sudden teaching, the reference to 'seeing the nature' is to the Buddha-nature (*foxing* 佛性)." See *Suzuki Daisetsu zenshū,* 2:444.

92. See the *Treatise on the Essentials of Cultivating the Mind* in McRae, *Northern School,* 125 and 317n79.

93. See T 475: 14.554b; *Suzuki Daisetsu zenshū,* 2:445 and 3:322; and Hu, *Yiji,* 236. The implications of this coincidence need to be studied further. The line itself reads: "Constantly seek the practice of wisdom of the true characteristic of non-thought," but the Chan texts omit "practice."

94. *Suzuki Daisetsu zenshū,* 3:444 and 2:237 (*Miscellaneous Dialogues*).

as it does in Shenhui's *Platform Sermon* as a substitute for the grammatical particle *zhi* 之 (e.g., *guang zhi shi deng jia yong* 光之時燈家用).[95] Moreover, the text uses the terms *wuxiang* 無想 and *wunian*, both of which may be translated as "non-thought." This is significant because Shenhui laid great emphasis on *wunian*, which he contrasted with the *linian* 離念 or "transcendence of thoughts" of the Northern school. Taken collectively, these correspondences suggest a close relationship between the *Treatise on the Dharma-nature* and Shenhui's teachings as seen in his *Platform Sermon*.[96]

The doctrinal presence of Shenhui, and behind him Huineng, in the *Treatise on the True Principle* and the *Treatise on the Dharma-nature* seems to me to be beyond question. This doctrinal presence and the identification of the *Treatise on the Dharma-nature* with Caoqi would have been appropriate for an early stage in Shenhui's teaching career, when he wished to attribute his doctrines retrospectively to his master Huineng. At the stage when both this text and the *Treatise on the True Principle* were produced, probably during the 720s, Shenhui would still have perceived himself and would have been perceived as a member of the religious community that we now refer to as the "Northern school." At this point Shenhui's ideas were in perfect harmony with the overall framework of early Chan doctrine.[97]

IV. Shenhui's Teachings and the Doctrines of the Northern School

Actually, the close relationship between Shenhui's teachings and the doctrines of the Northern school does not end with these very early works. Professor Yanagida has suggested that the "Southern school" was predicated on the "Northern school," and indeed we can find evidence of this in Shenhui's writings.[98]

Our focus here will be on two texts, the *Platform Sermon* and the *Definition of the Truth*. Certain of Shenhui's other writings may contain passages representing his earlier teachings, but the identification of these passages depends on complex and sometimes subjective arguments. Actually, even the dates of these two texts are not certain: the *Platform Sermon* is generally considered to have been written sometime during the 720s, but there is no

---

95. See the passage that occurs in conjunction with the verse by Puji.

96. However, note that the *Treatise on the Dharma-nature* points out that attachment to *wunian* can also represent a serious spiritual problem, an awareness that seems to have escaped Shenhui.

97. This analysis differs from that of Yanagida and Tanaka, who feel that the *Essential Determination* is more advanced doctrinally than the *Treatise on the True Principle* and that both texts represent a Northern school response to Shenhui's doctrines. (See Tanaka summary, *Tonkō Zenshū bunken*, 255–256.) I believe that the revision offered here is a more reasonable interpretation of the evidence, not all of which was available when they were writing on the subject.

98. See Yanagida, *Shoki zenshū shisho*, 101.

specific textual evidence to support this supposition. True, it does lack the polemical vitriol of the *Definition of the Truth,* but it would be unreasonable to assume that Shenhui never abandoned his campaign against the Northern school, even temporarily. Close attention to the content and dating of Shenhui's dialogues with laymen whose biographies are known may eventually help us specify the date of composition of the *Platform Sermon,* but this is a task for the future. On the other hand, the *Definition of the Truth* may have undergone considerable editing between the public lecture of 732 on which it is primarily based and the final redaction of the text during 745– 749. However, although the *Definition of the Truth* is more primitive doctrinally than the *Platform Sermon,* there is no sharp divergence between the two. Given these uncertainties, at this stage we may consider evidence from both these texts at once.

First, it is relatively simple to identify Shenhui's criticisms of Northern school doctrines in these texts. The most obvious of these, of course, are the references to specific approaches to meditation, especially his well-known "four pronouncements" criticizing "freezing the mind to enter samādhi, stopping the mind to view purity, activating the mind for outward illumination, and concentrating the mind for inner realization." These occur in both the *Platform Sermon* and *Definition of the Truth,* although it is only in the latter text that they are specifically directed at the teachings of the Northern school.[99] There are also other less well known comments in a similar vein, including criticism of the tendency to "grasp purity" and a rejection of the "looking afar" practices (found in the Northern School's *Five Skillful Means*).[100] The contention that one must actually perceive or "see" the Buddha-nature rather than simply accept its presence within oneself may also be an implicit criticism of the *Treatise on the Essentials of Cultivating the Mind* attributed to Hongren.[101] I have detected at least two other implicit criticisms of Northern school doctrines, one a reference to realizing the *dharmadhātu* with the *dharmadhātu* and the other a denigration of the use of expedient means rather than the doctrine of suddenness.[102]

But Northern school texts also contain numerous warnings against meditative abuses. The most common such warning is against "blankness of mind" (*wuji* 無記), a dull state of consciousness in which the practitioner is entranced by or attached to his objects of perception. Such warnings occur in several Northern school texts.[103] The description found in the *Five Skillful Means* of Hīnayānists as being unable to hear while in meditation is in effect a criticism of "freezing the mind to enter samādhi," to borrow Shenhui's

---
99. *Definition of the Truth,* section 22.
100. *Platform Sermon,* sections 3 and 4.
101. *Platform Sermon,* section 6.
102. *Platform Sermon,* sections 3 and 7.
103. See, for example, the *Treatise on the Essentials of Cultivating the Mind,* in McRae, *Northern School,* 128.

INTRODUCTION

phrasing.[104] Also, a statement on meditation by Shenxiu exhibits a sharp awareness of the problems of mental blankness, dualistic conceptualization, and grasping for the fruit of enlightenment.[105]

The Northern school passage that contains sentiments most similar to Shenhui's criticisms, however, is found in the *Essential Determination*:[106]

> The minds of all sentient beings are all generated from the storehouse of the tathāgatas.
> If you wish to save the myriad living beings[107]
> You should clearly contemplate the recollections of the lion (i.e., the Tathāgata).[108]
>
> The mind comes from the locus of nonbeing.
> You must vow to forsake the myriad conditions
> If they occur (*lai* 來, "come") then view them with complete attention.[109]
> This is called the "uninterrupted dharma."
>
> The mind comes from the locus of nonbeing.
> With complete attention one views, and views again.
> Viewing, viewing, viewing without interruption.
> This is called "wisdom without impurity."
>
> The mind comes from the locus of nonbeing.
> When one craves understanding of the scriptures,
> One considers them occasionally and does not view everlastingly.
> This is called "craving worldly wisdom."
>
> The mind comes from the locus of nonbeing.
> When one craves the development of conditioned [abilities]

---

104. McRae, *Northern School*, 181–183. The *Treatise on Perfect Illumination* contains a critique of what it calls "reverse contemplation" (*niguan*), in which objects are analyzed down to their smallest constituent particles and then into nothingness. This seems to be directed at an older and already outmoded doctrinal position; whether or not anyone actually practiced according to this approach in the early eighth century is dubious. See McRae, *Northern School*, 213–215.

105. McRae, *Northern School*, 215–217.

106. The Chinese version used here is that which was first presented in Suzuki's *Shōshitsu issho*, but I have used Ueyama's edition, "*Tongo shinshū yōketsu*," 102–103. His translation of the corresponding Tibetan is on p. 88.

107. The term *youqing* 有清 here is synonymous with *zhongsheng* 眾生, "sentient beings."

108. Where the Chinese has *yi* 億, "recollection," Ueyama translates the Tibetan as *jūsho* 住處, "residence."

109. The Tibetan for the middle two lines of this stanza are somewhat different: "Other elements come in [each] moment. / When they come fix the mind and attention (*xin* and *yi*) [on them] and view."

One recollects emptily rather than viewing determinedly.
This is called the "heretical teaching."

The mind comes from the locus of nonbeing.
When one craves entry into the trance of empty tranquility,
One's mind is tranquil but one's consciousness sinks[110] into emptiness.
This is called the "difficulty of the auditor" (*śrāvaka*).[111]

The mind comes from the locus of nonbeing.
When one is constantly immersed in the purity of the locus of nonbeing
And does not emerge into the [phenomenal] world,
This is called the "fetters of the bodhisattva."

The mind comes from the locus of nonbeing.
When, in the locus of nonbeing, one is constantly pure
And emerges into the world with champaign sameness,
This is called the "emancipation of the bodhisattva."

The mind comes from the locus of nonbeing.
When purity is constantly immediately manifest
And one is unattached to all characteristics,
This is called the "realm of the buddhas."[112]

The mind comes from the locus of nonbeing.
The eastern quarter cannot be calculated,
And the four directions are likewise.
This is called "returning to the great house."[113]

It should be obvious that the "viewing the mind" practices of the Northern school were not exactly as Shenhui described them, but were instead free and easy exercises in the emulation of the expansive mind of the sage. More important in the present context, however, is the observation that the

---

110. The character *fan* 汎, "float," is presumably a mistake for *mo* 沒, "sink."
111. The Tibetan stanza reads:

The mind comes from the locus of nonbeing.
If one is attached to the attainment of empty immobility,
then understanding it by fixing the mind on it to understand it is an attachment to emptiness.
This is called the "teaching of the auditors."

112. The Tibetan version lacks this and the previous stanza.
113. The Tibetan has "returning to [one's] original house." The Chinese has the concluding line: "The other teachings also have four-line [verses], but they cannot be connected with (lit. 'attached' to) the larger topic of the treatise."

descriptions of these practices contained warnings against the same abuses Shenhui later descried so strongly.

In addition, the following statement attributed (no doubt falsely) to Daoxin indicates that the Northern school masters also instructed their students to refrain from "activating the mind for outward illumination": "If the mind activates (*qi* 起) its cognitive [functions] (*jue* 覺) in connection with some sense realm separate from itself, then contemplate the locus of that activation as ultimately nonactivating (*buqi*)."[114] "Daoxin" also describes meditation practice in an apophatic mode similar to that favored by Shenhui:

> Do not [practice] mindfulness of the Buddha, do not grasp the mind, do not view the mind, do not measure the mind, do not meditate, do not contemplate, and do not disrupt [the mind]. Just let it flow. Do not make it go and do not make it stay. Alone in a pure and ultimate location (i.e., the absolute), the mind will be naturally bright and pure.[115]

Although I could provide additional documentation to show that Shenhui's criticisms failed to portray the meditation practices of the Northern school fairly, accurately, or completely, his reportage is not really at issue here. It is possible, of course, that some of the members of the Northern school undertook practices that were not in accord with the highest understanding of their teachers' guidance, but this possibility too is beside the point at the moment. Instead the present concern is the lack of absolute originality of Shenhui's criticisms themselves within the context of the Chan tradition. The passages cited above indicate that there are numerous precedents within Northern school texts for those criticisms.

But there are two differences between the uses of such criticisms in Northern school works and by Shenhui. First, the Northern school texts address their comments to meditation practitioners in order that they might refine their spiritual endeavors to the highest possible degree. In the context of Shenhui's overall message, on the other hand, the criticisms seem to be used as a justification for the rejection of a certain approach to meditation, or even a total repudiation of meditation practice per se. Second, in the *Definition of the Truth*, of course, Shenhui applied his criticisms to the teachings of specifically named masters. Thus his innovative use of these criticisms involved not only the precipitation of these critical sentiments into a concise set of slogans but also the radical expansion of their interpretation and their use within a polemical context.

Shenhui's doctrines were of course not limited to the criticism of the Northern school. The following similarities between his doctrines and the ideas of that school have generally not been appreciated, however: Shenhui's

---

114. See Yanagida, *Shoki no Zenshi 1*, 249, or T 2837: 85.1288a.
115. See Yanagida, *Shoki no Zenshi 1*, 205, or T 2837: 85.1287b.

redefinition of *zuochan* 坐禪 or "seated meditation" is cast in the "contemplative analysis" style, in which nominally unacceptable correlations are made in order to jar the reader or listener to a new religious perspective. Thus the character *zuo* 坐, "to sit," becomes the "non-activation of thoughts," while *chan*, "meditation," becomes "seeing the original nature."[116] Although "seeing the nature" was one of Shenhui's most characteristic doctrines and was used without particular emphasis in earlier texts, the concept of "non-activation" was a very central concept in the teachings of the Northern school, as we have seen above. This term occurs repeatedly throughout Shenhui's writings.[117]

There are references in Shenhui's writings to the transcendence of the body, ego, and consciousness, and to the autonomy attained in the various sense capabilities and types of sensory data.[118] Exactly the same type of assertions vis-à-vis individual components of human existence are made almost ad nauseum in the *Five Skillful Means*. Shenhui also posits some distinctions very similar to the concepts of inner sageliness and outer wisdom, as well as those of fundamental and successive wisdom.[119] In addition, he makes references to space very similar to those in the *Five Skillful Means* and the *Treatise on Perfect Illumination*.[120] Finally, the very use of the concept of the Buddha-nature obscured by illusions harks back to Hongren's *Treatise on the Essentials of Cultivating the Mind,* even though the interpretation differs.[121]

V. Shenhui's Emphasis on Sudden Enlightenment

Although there is evidence of a core of shared ideas in the works I have discussed thus far, we should not lose sight of an important distinction. In the *Treatise on the True Principle* and the *Treatise on the Dharma-nature*, Shenhui's ideas appear to have been inserted into an identifiably Northern school message. In Shenhui's own works, however, the message is different, even though we can detect numerous similarities with earlier Northern school ideas.

The major impression one gets from reading Shenhui's works, of course, is the very concrete sense of his doctrine of sudden enlightenment. This

---

116. See the *Definition of the Truth* in Hu, *Yiji*, 287–288. Shenhui's formulation is carried a step further in the *Platform Sūtra*; see Yampolsky, *Platform Sutra*, 140.

117. Suzuki Tetsuo has pointed out a subtle difference in terminology between Shenhui's writings and the *Platform Sūtra*, in that the former exhort the reader to "see the [Buddha-]nature" (*busshō o miyo* 佛性を見よ) where the latter refers to "seeing the nature" (*kenshō*) as a bound form. See his "Kataku Jinne no ken no shisō" and "Kataku Jinne yori dankyō ni itaru kenshō no tenkai."

118. *Platform Sermon*, section 5.

119. Ibid.

120. *Platform Sermon*, sections 4 and 6.

121. *Platform Sermon*, section 2.

impression holds even in the case of the *Platform Sermon,* in which he hardly uses the term "sudden" (*dun* 頓) at all. It is abundantly clear in this text that Shenhui's intent was that those listening to him should generate *bodhicitta,* the aspiration to achieve enlightenment, even as they listened to his sermon. He appears to have been a consummate evangelist: although the ethical vows found at the beginning of the text were no doubt part of the conventional liturgical repertoire, Shenhui must have used them in order to lead his congregation to a more exalted frame of mind in which they would be more open to moments of inspiration. There is not however any real consideration of the practice of meditation after that first generation of *bodhicitta,* a term which he uses in a manner that is virtually tantamount to the final achievement of enlightenment. For example, Shenhui's *Definition of the Truth* contains the following verse in adulation of *bodhicitta:*

> Although *bodhicitta* and the ultimate [realization] are no different,
> Of the two [states of] mind, it is the first which is [more] difficult.
> With oneself still unsaved, to first save others—
> Thus do we reverence the initial [achievement of] *bodhicitta.*
>
> By this initial *bodhicitta* one becomes a teacher of humans and gods,
> Superior to the *śrāvakas* and *pratyekabuddhas.*
> With such a *bodhicitta,* one transcends the triple realm,
> Hence this is called the most insurpassable.[122]

Shenhui does not hedge on the issue of immediate inspiration by specifying some preliminary period of religious practice, however brief. His best-known metaphor for the relationship between the initial moment of enlightenment and the subsequent course of self-cultivation is that of childbirth, in which a baby is born suddenly but must mature gradually.[123] (I am always astounded by the monkish oversimplification of this metaphor!) Shenhui's prescriptions to be followed during the period of maturation are very general, however, and it seems likely that he was more adept at inspiring his listeners to that first moment of inspiration than at guiding practitioners throughout their careers.

The strongly propagandistic flavor of the *Definition of the Truth* leaves the very palpable sense that, in this case, Shenhui is more interested in winning converts to his faction—or at least in winning agreement with his positions—than in actually inspiring spiritual experiences in his listeners. We should not overlook the correlation with this more contentious atmosphere and the

---

122. *Definition of the Truth,* section 7. It is also possible that Shenhui purposely avoided specific statements regarding meditation practice so as not to invite criticisms of the type he addressed to the Northern school. See the conclusion of this essay.

123. *Definition of the Truth,* section 21.

much more numerous, if frequently unexplained, explicit references to suddenness. Nor should we overlook the fact that the only practical injunctions found in the *Definition of the Truth* enjoin the congregation to recite the *Diamond Sūtra* in order to achieve their first moment of insight. In the context of the developing Chan tradition, this was definitely a retrograde position.[124] In other words, Shenhui's polemical fervor correlates with doctrinal and practical superficiality.

VI. Conclusion

A. The Religious Context of Shenhui's Training

It is clear from the evidence that Shenhui began his religious career in a presectarian Northern school milieu. Please note that I use the term "Northern school" in a different manner than did Shenhui: for him, the term was polemical, an intentionally critical epithet applied to men who he felt were not privy to the spirit of Bodhidharma's teachings and hence should not be allowed to appropriate the term "Southern school." In my usage, on the other hand, the term "Northern school" refers to the informally organized group of masters and disciples who enunciated and disseminated the new message of Chan in the two capitals of Luoyang and Chang'an during the early decades of the eighth century. These men referred to their own teachings as the "East Mountain teaching," the "Laṅkāvatāra school," and even as the "Southern school," so that it is only out of deference to the conventions of the later Chan tradition that I use the originally pejorative term "Northern school" in this regard.

It is important to keep in mind the presectarian nature of this school; the Northern school masters represent the entirety of early Chan at the beginning of the eighth century. They were no doubt a diverse lot, with a multiplicity of interests and spheres of activity, but the extant sources allow us to detect only minor differences of style between specific historical figures. There were several attempts to formulate coherent and comprehensive expressions of the religious message of Chan, but it is difficult if not impossible from this vantage point to correlate these formulations with specific lineages. The overwhelming impression one gets from this early literature is that of an abundant religious vitality, the energy with which the growing Chan movement was striving to recognize and articulate its own self-understanding. Huineng was certainly a member of this somewhat amorphous religious community, as was Shenhui before—and perhaps even after—the initiation of his anti-Northern school campaign.

---

124. *Definition of the Truth*, sections 33–44. The *Treatise on Perfect Illumination* contains the line "You cannot understand the principle of this through an [insight] into a text [gained] through recitation." See McRae, *Northern School,* 159.

There is no doubt that Shenhui was motivated at least in part by a sincere disaffection with contemporary developments in the realm of Chan. He was not, in fact, the first to offer such criticisms. Paradoxically, the very text that Shenhui cites in his criticism of Puji, the *Annals of the Transmission* (*Chuan fabao ji* 傳法寶紀), sharply criticizes Hongren, Shenxiu, and, implicitly, even Puji for popularizing Chan among large numbers of persons unready or unable to comprehend its deeper meaning.[125] These criticisms were clearly elitist and in some ways diametrically opposed to those of Shenhui, who went further than anyone else to simplify his teachings for public consumption. Nevertheless, we can easily imagine that there were wide variations in how both masters and students interpreted the spiritual enterprise embodied in the new religious movement known as Chan. Since we are limited to textual archives preserved for the most part at Dunhuang on the outskirts of the Chinese cultural realm, it is quite reasonable that these texts do not provide specific details of any such excesses, distortions, or facile interpretations. It has already been shown that Shenhui's criticisms of Northern school doctrine are off the mark, but they may have been valid with regard to non-mainstream tendencies.[126] Nevertheless, Shenhui's delineation of a Northern school defined entirely in terms of these non-mainstream tendencies was an intentional polemical trope.

The specific catalyst that led Shenhui to initiate his anti-Northern school campaign remains obscure. Given the partisan vigor with which he carried out his chosen mission, it is likely that his own personal temperament had a great deal to do with the matter, but there are also some indications that his religious lineage may have been a factor. I am not thinking of Huineng, but rather of Lao'an, the Northern school figure most closely associated with Huineng and Shenhui. We have the names of two monks who studied under both Huineng and Lao'an, and we should not forget that Lao'an's name is listed in both the *Essential Determination* and the *Treatise on the True Principle*. In addition, the very choice of Huatai as the scene of Shenhui's early attack on the Northern school may be related to the fact that it was Lao'an's birthplace.[127] Most intriguing is the observation that Lao'an's biography shows a definite tendency to one-upmanship with regard to the charismatic centenarian Shenxiu: according to his epitaph, Lao'an is supposed

---

125. See McRae, *Northern School*, 268–269. Faru (638–689), an important figure not relevant to the present discussion, is also among those listed for criticism.

126. See Robert Zeuschner's "An Analysis of the Philosophical Criticisms of Northern Ch'an Buddhism." Although the Dunhuang texts do not explicitly describe the possible excesses, etc., of early Chan, some of the texts may provide examples of simplistic approaches. One such example might be the *Nan Tianzhuguo Putidamo chanshi guanmen* 南天竺國菩提達摩禪師觀門 (The Contemplation Teaching of Meditation Master Bodhidharma from South India), T 2832: 85.1270b–c, or *Suzuki Daisetsu zenshū*, 2:219–221.

127. It may have been at least equally important that the magistrate at the time was Li Yong 李邕, a layman usually associated with Puji.

to have begun his studies under Hongren earlier, to have cut a more exotic figure, and to have lived even longer than Shenxiu.[128] It may be this tendency to one-upmanship in Lao'an that was translated into a spirit of factional competitiveness in Shenhui.

B. Shenhui's Doctrine of Sudden Enlightenment

Judging from the evidence introduced here, it seems reasonable to accept the traditional interpretation that Shenhui inherited his emphasis on sudden enlightenment from Huineng. However, we lack any reliable description of Huineng's teachings and thus cannot tell whether his instructions on the matter of sudden enlightenment remained consistent in both nature and emphasis before and after Shenhui's trip north. The most likely alternatives are as follows: if Shenhui had achieved his own moment of sudden inspiration prior to his ordination and further training in Chang'an, Huineng's remarks on his return might refer to Shenhui's greater appreciation of the wider spiritual ramifications of that experience. Or, Shenhui's wider understanding after several years in the north might have finally made it possible for him to achieve that sudden enlightenment after his return to Caoqi for further instruction under Huineng.

Although it is impossible to tell which, if either, of these scenarios is correct, we can safely infer that during this very early period there was no apprehension of any conflict or incompatibility between the doctrine of sudden enlightenment and the teachings of the Northern school. There is certainly no indication in any of the texts discussed above in conjunction with Shenhui's early career of any internal conflict or tension between sudden enlightenment and the surrounding doctrinal framework. On the contrary, the real difficulty is ascertaining where Shenhui's ideas begin and where they leave off. And this shared doctrinal foundation is apparent throughout Shenhui's works.

The notion of sudden enlightenment was absolutely central to Shenhui's religious philosophy. In one sense, this was a direct continuation of the Northern school mission of eliciting conversions to its own interpretation of Buddhism, as demonstrated in works such as the *Treatise on the Essentials of Cultivating the Mind* attributed to Hongren and the *Treatise on the Contemplation of the Mind* by Shenxiu. These texts urged their readers to give up formalistic practices justified on the basis of the accrual of religious merit and to turn immediately to the practice of meditation and the pursuit of enlightenment in this very life. Shenhui made this message even more immediate in his public sermons by attempting to inspire his audiences to make this

---

128. See McRae, *Northern School*, 57–58. If we are to believe the epitaph, Lao'an began his studies under Hongren even before Daoxin's death, was singled out by Empress Wu for his composure (during an incident that occurred in the company of Shenxiu, who goes unmentioned), and lived to the age of 128!

decision even as they listened to him—to have them achieve a state of religious exaltation through the power of his own charismatic delivery.

In a more immediate sense, though, Shenhui's single-minded emphasis on sudden enlightenment represented a qualitative change from the positions of earlier Northern school texts.[129] This is true not because his message differed in any major way, but rather because of his chosen medium. The central thread that unites all of Shenhui's ideas and activities was his vocation of lecturing from the ordination platform,[130] and it is thoroughly understandable that his chosen role of inspiring conversion to the Buddhist spiritual quest was combined with an overriding concern with the initial moment of religious inspiration. To put it in the simplest of terms, there is an inextricable relationship between Shenhui's emphasis on sudden enlightenment and his proselytic, evangelical role, so much so that it is impossible to tell which was cause and which was effect. Shenhui espoused the doctrine of sudden enlightenment because he taught from the ordination platform, and he taught from the ordination platform because he espoused the doctrine of sudden enlightenment.

This interpretation helps us understand one of the more curious aspects of Shenhui's doctrines: his failure to consider post-inspiration cultivation in any serious fashion. Although he did grant that gradual cultivation would be required after the initial experience of awakening, much as a child is complete at birth but must grow into an adult, Shenhui was apparently totally unconcerned with the details and dynamics of this process of spiritual maturation. This is the reason Hu Shih was able to refer to Shenhui's teachings as a "new Ch'an which renounces *ch'an* itself and is therefore no *ch'an* at all."[131] As a missionary concerned only with increasing the size of the flock, Shenhui was probably not directly involved in the ongoing instruction of trainees engaged in meditation and the other activities of the Buddhist spiritual path. At least, there are no indications in any of the doctrinal and biographical sources pertaining to Shenhui and his disciples that suggest any ongoing regimen of training. This supposition is also corroborated by the relatively early demise of Shenhui's lineage, which was superseded in

---

129. Yanagida, "Goroku," 392–393, describes Shenhui's philosophy as a doctrine of *dunjiao* 頓教 or the "sudden teaching," whereas the Northern school described a doctrine of *dunwu* 頓悟 or "sudden enlightenment." Although we take different views regarding the provenance of the *Treatise on the True Principle*, the distinction still holds.

130. The *Records of the Transmission* says that Shenhui preached from the ordination platform every month, "destroying the Chan of purity and establishing the Chan of the tathāgatas." This seems to be a general statement about Shenhui's career, but it probably applies mainly to his later years. See T 2075: 51.185b or Yanagida, *Shoki no Zenshi 2*, 155. In "Goroku no rekishi," 404–409, Yanagida discusses the sequence of developments regarding ordination platforms in China from Daoxuan 道宣 to Huizhong.

131. Hu, "Ch'an (Zen) Buddhism in China," 7.

size, vitality, and longevity by that of Puji.[132] Puji was able to inspire greater personal loyalty because he participated actively in the training of his successors, rather than merely starting them off on their religious careers as Shenhui did.

This lack of involvement in meditation practice may be another reason why Shenhui could distort the Northern school doctrine of constant practice into gradualism—he did not really understand the kind of sensitivity that was needed in the context of ongoing spiritual training. The doctrine of *shouxin* (maintaining [awareness of] the mind) attributed to Hongren is a good example of an approach to meditation whose practical multivalence is very easily overlooked. In the *Treatise on the Essentials of Cultivating the Mind* there is a palpable sense that this formulation is used simultaneously to induce trainees to vigorous effort and to restrain them from grasping for the fruit of enlightenment.[133] This is a type of subtle formulation that is entirely absent from Shenhui's writings.

To go one step further, it may well be the case that Shenhui emphasized the doctrine of the equivalence of the "three learnings" of morality, meditation, and wisdom precisely because it undercut the rationale for extended meditation practice and, by implication, the traditional monastic regimen of self-control and spiritual cultivation. Certainly the caricatures of Northern school monks in Shenhui's texts and their emphasis on the primacy of meditation practice imply that hard work was not required, only the inspi-

---

132. Shenhui's lineage is considered to have lasted for five generations, until the great Guifeng Zongmi 圭峰宗密 (780–841), but the linkage between the third through fifth generations is suspect. Ui, 255–256, points out that Shenhui had about half as many (33) known students as Puji, and that the ages of the students in the two lineages were about the same (only three of Shenhui's lived past 800). The geographical distribution of the two groups was also about the same. But in the next period, Shenhui's Southern school faction becomes so small as not even to be comparable to the Northern school. On p. 258, Ui notes that Shenhui's lineage includes only 12–15 individuals in the second generation. (Of these, I accept only nine as legitimate students of Shenhui. The biographies of all these figures are unknown.) Hence at this point (the third generation of the Heze school, beginning with Shenhui) the strength of the faction suddenly dissipated. After the year 800, only Yuntan 雲坦 (d. 816) and Faru 法如 (d. 811) continued on. Faru's successor Nanyin 南印 continued on only ten years after this, and this was in far-off Sichuan (and I do not accept Nanyin as a legitimate successor to Shenhui).

Judging from the biographies, only two of Shenhui's students stayed with him for any length of time. The biographies are strikingly uniform in their lack of detail regarding the students' activities before and after meeting Shenhui. For several of them, the characteristic profile is as follows: the encounter with Shenhui occurred early in the student's career and was followed by the student's retreat to some remote location, often a return to the student's original temple or native place. At this remote location, the student took up residence in a rude hut—his presence there sometimes being credited with the subjugation of wild beasts in the area—and the hut was eventually transformed into an active training center by dint of the student's abilities. The locations mentioned in this regard include Nanyang and Chang'an, as well as references (for two students) to Mount Yangqi 楊岐, a place name associated in later years with a faction of the Linji school, and other locations around Lake Dongting.

133. See McRae, *Northern School*, 136–137.

ration that Shenhui set out to provide.[134] Although Shenhui's life work was carried out on the ordination platform, his teachings lightened the burden of being a Buddhist monk and removed the distinction between monks and laymen, thereby aiding the dissemination of Chan among the unordained. In this sense there is a direct continuity between Shenhui's teachings and the *Platform Sūtra,* as well as one of the keys to the subsequent popularity of Chinese Chan.

C. The Acceptance of the Doctrine of Sudden Enlightenment within the Chan School

Paradoxically, although Shenhui was unconcerned with the problems of ongoing spiritual cultivation, his doctrine of sudden enlightenment was accepted because it was very useful in this regard. This point requires careful explanation.

In espousing subitism and rejecting gradualism, Shenhui explicitly selected a doctrine that disallowed dualistic formulations. The very problem with the gradualistic approach (other than the superficial but unforgettable implication that it was incredibly time consuming) was that it postulated both a difference between ignorance and enlightenment and the possibility of transporting oneself from one state to the other. There was no difference, according to this approach, between meditation undertaken for spiritual self-improvement and the performance of good works undertaken for the accrual of religious merit. For example, Shenhui criticized the Northern school's use of the term *linian,* the "transcendence of thoughts," which he felt implied a purposive or intentional effort to achieve a state of liberation—which would be a contradiction in terms. His alternative was *wunian* or "non-thought," by which he meant a level of consciousness ontologically prior to the discrimination of individual thoughts, or the source of liberation already immanent in sentient beings. Although the terms *linian* and *wunian* differ very little in their original meanings, Shenhui favored the latter because it had the appearance of being less dualistic.

Now, the experience of nondualism may be an important psychological feature of sudden enlightenment, but it was also something more than this. In combination with his doctrine of subitism, the very heat of Shenhui's criticism of gradualism had a rhetorical impact of the highest significance: by publicly criticizing one faction's meditation teachings he made all the members of the growing Chan school more aware of the external expression—the packaging, if you will—of their ideas and modes of practice. After Shenhui, Chan masters learned to protect themselves from criticism by

---

134. Yamazaki, "Kataku Jinne zenji," 208–211, characterizes Shenhui's lay followers as being predominantly ambitious self-made men rather than members of old elite families. Although these men succeeded through their own efforts, the secular correlation with the religious work versus inspiration dichotomy would be that of aristocratic privilege versus success in civil service examinations or on the battlefield.

avoiding dualistic formulations. His campaign worried subsequent masters into avoiding even the hint of gradualism and the spectre of unilinear, goal-oriented logic in the presentation of their own ideas. This is obvious in the ploy taken in the *Platform Sūtra* and other Oxhead school works, which define an ideal of spiritual training only to follow it with an immediate rejection of that ideal on the basis of its underlying dualism, resulting in the specification of a higher and more subtly defined religious ideal. (This process is known as *zhiyang* 止揚, "stopping and lifting," in a Buddhist context, or *aufheben* in Western philosophy.) The imposition of this avoidance of dualistic formulations, which I call the rule of rhetorical purity, was one of Shenhui's most important areas of impact on Chinese Chan.

The doctrine of sudden enlightenment was universally accepted by the Chan tradition after Shenhui, but how significant was this contribution in doctrinal terms? The terms "sudden teaching" and "sudden enlightenment" had at least as much value as slogans or labels as they did as substantive doctrinal positions. This was certainly true in the case of Shenhui, whose emphasis on the idea of sudden enlightenment is greatest where his polemical tone is most strident and his overall practical and theoretical framework is most backward. We often see the term used in the titles of other, nonpolemical texts, even where the doctrine is hardly considered in any explicit fashion in the body of the text itself—examples include both the *Essential Determination and Treatise on the True Principle* discussed above and the well-known *Essential Teaching of Sudden Enlightenment* (*Dunwu yao men* 頓悟要門) attributed to Dazhu Huihai 大珠慧海.[135] My impression, in fact, is that the term occurs much more frequently as an identifying slogan than as a doctrine with explicit content. I believe that the concept of sudden enlightenment became widely accepted in part because it was attractive, flexible, and inoffensive as a slogan.

No doubt the ontological and practical implications of the idea of suddenness were momentous, but they were also malleable. In its most simple sense, the term denotes nothing more than a nondualistic realization of religious truth achieved in a single moment of insight. On this level, the term was attractive in two ways at once: first, it at least appeared to offer religious aspirants a key to quick and easy achievement of the ultimate goal (in contrast to lifetimes of self-cultivation), and second, its use allowed one to assume a posture of accordance with the post-Shenhui requirement of rhetorical purity. Since Chan masters were not inclined to a more profound specification of both the ontological and practical implications of the idea—this would have been to engage in pointless doctrinal speculation—they could and did describe any number of teachings as being "sudden," without being bound to uphold the doctrine in absolute terms. Even Shenhui miti-

---

135. This text has been translated into modern Japanese by Hirano Sōjō in *Tongo yōmon*. There are also two unsatisfactory English translations in Blofeld, *The Zen Teaching of Hui Hai on Sudden Illumination,* and Thomas E. Cleary, *Sayings and Doings of Pai-chang, Ch'an Master of Great Wisdom.*

gated the impact of his own teaching of suddenness by requiring (or allowing) a subsequent period of gradual cultivation.

The slogan of suddenness is bandied about rather freely in the titles of Chan texts, and its specific doctrinal implications were not of primary importance. However, this was not just an empty slogan. On the contrary, I believe that the most important aspect of this slogan was that it combined within a single term the very kind of sensitivity toward meditation practice mentioned above. That is, where meditation texts and instructors once had to concatenate exhortations to energetic endeavor and injunctions against grasping for the goal, the doctrine (or slogan) of sudden enlightenment incorporated this practical sensitivity within itself. The appeal of a rapid and complete transformation into the enlightened state worked as a carrot to induce students to energetic endeavor, while the explicit caution against gradualistic approaches worked as a brake against dualistic conceptualization of the goal. Since the slogan "sudden enlightenment" could be appended quite easily to any text or doctrine to communicate the importance of this sensitivity but without making any great demands on the specific content of the texts or doctrines themselves, it should not be surprising that suddenness should have been accepted as a slogan. Thus it was that sudden enlightenment became the watchword of the Chan tradition.

D. Shenhui's Historical Impact on Chan

Just because Chan enthusiastically embraced Shenhui's slogan of sudden enlightenment, we should not conclude that the same was true of his other positions. In fact, Shenhui's contributions to Chan were generally achieved through a process of negative impact. Shenhui created a crisis in early Chan with his factionalist anti-Northern school campaign, which led to creative growth in Chan only because of the efforts taken by the tradition to overcome the divisiveness of his attack. It is not even accurate to say that he caused the disappearance of the Northern school, since it never existed as an institutional entity to begin with, or the supersedure of the sudden teaching over the gradual teaching, since no one ever advocated the doctrinally backward position that he described and criticized. In fact, many of the contributions of the "Northern school" were maintained by the later Chan tradition, even though they were presented under the aegis of the Oxhead and Hongzhou schools. The Oxhead school, with the *Platform Sūtra,* and the Sichuan factions, with the *Records of the Transmission,* collectively installed many of Shenhui's innovations into the Chan tradition—with his authorship neatly obscured.[136] Certain sayings of Mazu and Huizhong also appear to criticize ideas of Shenhui's.[137]

---

136. On the *Records of the Transmission,* see Yanagida, *Shoki no Zenshi 2,* 3–35, or "The *Li-tai fa-pao chi* and the Ch'an Doctrine of Sudden Awakening," trans. Carl Bielefeldt, in Lai and Lancaster, *Early Ch'an in China and Tibet,* 13–49.

137. See Yanagida, "Goroku," 388, 393, 402, and 407–408. On 410, he suggests that the *Platform Sūtra* then in turn criticized Huizhong's ideas. (Yanagida also mentions criticisms by members of the Oxhead school and other figures.)

Just as Shenhui's major effort was propagandistic, his major impact lay in the realm of rhetoric and mythopoeia. In addition to establishing a standard of rhetorical purity, he is responsible for the addition of many new anecdotes regarding Bodhidharma and the early patriarchs to the early Chan library. In the process Shenhui helped make the theory of the transmission of the Dharma much more concrete and precise, even though he did not significantly alter the conceptual basis of the theory.[138] Coupled with his penchant for story-telling, this new attention to the form rather than only the substance of religious pronouncements may have helped bring about the emergence of encounter dialogue and the "recorded sayings" genre of Chan literature.[139] These changes may be formalistic, but they were of the highest significance to the development of the Chan tradition.

The real transformation that took place in Chan during the eighth century was the emergence of the practice of "encounter dialogue" in the Hongzhou school of Mazu Daoyi, which is the earliest faction of the classical phase of Chinese Chan Buddhism. The literature of encounter dialogue may be placed under the rubric of the sudden teaching, in the sense that it satisfies the twofold criteria mentioned above. Since the practitioners of encounter dialogue relentlessly attacked gradualistic formulations and exhorted students on to diligent endeavor, they could make effective use of the slogan of sudden enlightenment. In addition, since Shenhui's anti-Northern school campaign and the appearance of the *Platform Sūtra* had provided a legendary explanation of the sudden-gradual dichotomy that was convenient, instructive (in a very profound sense), and entertaining, the later Chan school adopted this legend as part of its own historical self-understanding. In contrast to the image presented in this legend, however, the sudden-gradual dichotomy was something of a false issue in the development of Chan. Although Shenhui contributed to the increasingly clear crystallization of Chan ideas and to the elaboration of its iconoclastic spirit, his career did not represent a fundamental break in the course of the school's development. Shenhui's teachings were extensions of, rather than radical alternatives to, Northern school doctrine, and his innovations only contributed to the emergence of classical Chan within the overall context of early Chan in general.

---

138. Professor Yanagida feels that throughout his life Shenhui maintained a chronologically absurd theory of eight Indian patriarchs between the Buddha and Bodhidharma. See *Shoki zenshū shisho*, 124.

139. In fact, Professor Yanagida describes Shenhui's *Platform Sermon* as having all the basic elements of the genre: it was compiled by a named individual, rather than anonymously; circulation was intended to be limited to those with affinities for Shenhui's teachings; Shenhui is treated with the respect due one's personal master; and, most important, the emphasis of the text is on the instruction of the people actually in Shenhui's audience at one specific time. See "Goroku no rekishi," 391–392 and 399, plus the related comments regarding the *Miscellaneous Dialogues* on 369 and 376.

PART I

Texts

Editor's Note

As John McRae explained in a preface he had begun to draft, he had been at work on translating the Shenhui texts in this volume off and on since 1985. Coming back to them in 2010, he observed that "although a lot of work was required merely to make the text readable once again," he had come to "enjoy adding to the work of the younger John McRae, the text's original author." He passed away not long after writing those words, and five years later, I was invited to prepare McRae's translations for publication. It was clear from the state of the document that McRae, with his characteristic attention to detail and precision, had relished reworking his translations and amplifying their annotation. In the translations, he was still deciding between different phrases: whether to go with "spiritual compatriots" or simply "friends" for *zhishi* 知識; "great worthies" or the Sanskrit *bhadāntas* for *dade* 大德; "heretics" or "non-Buddhists" for *waidao* 外道; and so on. In some of the notes, he had obviously used the most modern tools available; others had been left unaltered, representing research done before the advent of electronic text searches via the CBETA and SAT platforms.

Like McRae, I have enjoyed working on these texts. For a student of medieval Chinese Buddhism, the texts are themselves invaluable documents, and McRae's extensive and groundbreaking scholarship adds layers of depth and insight through his notes. But where McRae had been free to edit the work of his younger self, I was contemplating someone else's text—someone I could not consult about problematic passages or possible emendations. How could I make the text presentable to the public while at the same time honoring his authorship? Ultimately I chose a conservative approach: as much as I could, I held back from letting my own preferences creep into the work and simply aimed at consistency and completeness.

I also endeavored to keep my own voice out of the final text as much as possible. Only occasionally have I stepped in with an editorial note, sometimes offering a divergent translation, sometimes noting a parallel that McRae had not found. Small emendations have been made silently. For example, where McRae was still mulling over alternative translations for certain technical terms, as noted above, I was forced to make the choice for him. In the same vein, there are a number of sūtra citations that recur in the texts, and McRae's translations of these passages were not rendered consistently. In all such cases, I adopted what seemed to be McRae's most recent decisions.

Most of the work I needed to do lay in the notes. McRae had left many of them unfinished, as evidenced by the tags "GET," "CHECK," or "FIX," indicating either that he was unsure and wanted to recheck the information, or that there was information missing—anything from the year of publication to the location of a quotation from the canon. Occasionally, I had to correct McRae's citations. Similarly, he had begun his work using Wade-Giles to transcribe Chinese names and terms, and while he had switched to Pinyin along the way, the files still contained a layer of Wade-Giles (often marked with "FIX"). In completing these notes and correcting minor errors, I did my best to envisage what McRae would have done.

A larger editorial conundrum concerned when and how to include relevant historical material that McRae had originally provided in analytical chapters—unfinished material that was not included in this volume. The notes to the translations often referred the reader to this material, and so, where possible, I have transferred what seemed relevant in the abandoned chapters to the notes in question.

If this relatively conservative editorial approach honors John McRae as the author, it also has the drawback of leaving the translation feeling at times like a work-in-progress. He might well have been unsatisfied with the end result. I do believe, however, that making McRae's lifetime engagement with the Shenhui materials available to scholars and general readers alike is eminently worthwhile, and I'm grateful to have been entrusted with this project.

Fedde de Vries

Platform Sermon

A Platform Sermon by [Shenhui,] the Reverend of Nanyang, on Directly Comprehending the [Buddha-]Nature according to the Chan Doctrine of Sudden Teaching and Emancipation

Nanyang heshang dunjiao jietuo chanmen zhiliaoxing tanyu
南陽和上頓教解脫禪門直了性壇語

1

The unsurpassable Dharma of enlightenment, the buddhas have profoundly lamented, is inconceivable.[1]

Friends,[2] you have been able to come here so that you can all generate the unsurpassable *bodhicitta*.[3] It is extremely difficult to encounter the buddhas, bodhisattvas, and true spiritual compatriots. Today you are going to hear something you've never heard before. In the past you never encountered it, but today you have.

The *Nirvāṇa Sūtra* says, "The Buddha asked Kāśyapa, 'Would it be difficult to throw a mustard seed down from Tuṣita Heaven and hit the point of a needle on the earth below?' Bodhisattva Kāśyapa replied, 'It would be extremely difficult, World-honored One.' The Buddha told Kāśyapa, 'This

---

This work probably derives from the years 720–730 while Shenhui was living in Nanyang 南陽, Henan. It contains a clear statement of Shenhui's ideas about the sudden teaching, including a criticism of improper attitudes toward meditation practice stated without explicit sectarian identification.

1. Yanagida, "Goroku no rekishi," 394, suggests this opening, with its stress on the unsurpassable Dharma of enlightenment (*wushang puti fa* 無上菩提法), is based in spirit on the *Diamond Sūtra*.

2. Shenhui addresses his audience with the term *zhishi* 知識, "friends," no doubt with awareness of the term *shan zhishi* 善知識, *kalyāṇa-mitra*, or "spiritual compatriot." In translating, it is often difficult to choose whether to use "friends" or simply "you." I have used both alternatives as convenient, and when the reference is in the third person I have also used "spiritual compatriot(s)."

3. The term for "unsurpassable *bodhicitta*" here is *wushang puti xin* 無上菩提心. The sentiment that encountering the true teachings of Buddhism was a rare opportunity is often found in meditation texts. See, for example, the *Essentials of Cultivating the Mind*, sections O and P, in McRae, *Northern School*, 128 and 129. Shenhui, of course, is unique in being so explicit about the unique value of his own teaching.

is not difficult. For the correct cause and the correct condition to meet—this is what is difficult!' "[4]

What are the correct cause and the correct condition? Friends, your generation of the unsurpassable *bodhicitta* constitutes the correct cause.[5] For the buddhas, bodhisattvas, and true spiritual compatriots to cast this unsurpassable *bodhicitta* into your minds such that you achieve the ultimate emancipation constitutes the correct condition. For the two to meet is excellent.

Friends, in the mouths of ordinary persons there are immeasurable bad words, and in their minds there are immeasurable bad thoughts, so that they are forever lost in saṃsāra and do not achieve emancipation. Each and every one of you must generate *bodhicitta*! Let us all reverence the buddhas so as to repent your [past transgressions]:[6]

> We reverence all the buddhas of the entire past.
> We reverence all the buddhas of the entire future.
> We reverence all the buddhas of the entire present.
> We reverence the treasury of sūtras of the honored Dharma of *prajñā*.
> We reverence the great bodhisattvas and all the sagely monks.

You should each repent in full sincerity, so as to purify your three types of action:

> In complete sincerity, we now repent any of the four major transgressions[7] committed with body, speech, or mind during past, present, or future, and wish that such transgressions be eliminated, never to arise again.

---

4. See the *Nirvāṇa Sūtra*'s reference to hitting a needle with a mustard seed, T 374: 12.372c18, as well as T 374: 12.533b for the scripture's explanation that sentient beings cannot see the Buddha-nature because the correct cause and correct condition have not occurred together. Correct cause and correct condition are defined as the Buddha-nature and the generation of *bodhicitta*, respectively, through which one achieves perfect and unsurpassable enlightenment, "just as gold is produced from rock." The same general notion of enlightenment depending on the conjunction of conditions is expressed in the *Essentials of Cultivating the Mind*, section I; see McRae, *Northern School*, 124.

5. Liebenthal, "Sermon of Shen-hui," 140, notes with surprise the divergence from the *Nirvāṇa Sūtra*, pointing out that the original meaning of *zhengyin* 正因, often "primary cause" but here rendered as "correct cause," is completely lost. He compares *Platform Sūtra*, T 2008: 48.340c8. See Yampolsky, *Platform Sutra*, 152, for the earlier version of this passage. Probably more than other Chinese Buddhist texts, Chan texts frequently misquote or paraphrase the scriptures.

6. Yanagida, "Goroku," 394, observes that the following vows are written with fixed rhythmic phrasing, and he suggests that they were recited one by one, first by Shenhui and then in unison by his congregation, in the manner of bodhisattva precept rituals. The Dunhuang version of the *Platform Sūtra* has the direction "three recitations" (*sanchang* 三唱) written in small characters at a similar location; see also Yampolsky, *Platform Sutra*, 143 and 144.

7. These are the four *pārājika;* that is, engaging in sexual intercourse, theft, murder, and making false claims about one's spiritual attainments.

In complete sincerity, we now repent any of the five contrary transgressions[8] committed with body, speech, or mind during past, present, or future, and wish that such transgressions be eliminated, never to arise again.

In complete sincerity, we now repent any of the seven contrary transgressions[9] committed with body, speech, or mind during past, present, or future, and wish that such transgressions be eliminated, never to arise again.

In complete sincerity, we now repent any of the ten wrong transgressions[10] committed with body, speech, or mind during past, present, or future, and wish that such transgressions be eliminated, never to arise again.

In complete sincerity, we now repent any of the serious transgressions committed with body, speech, or mind during past, present, or future, and wish that such transgressions be eliminated, never to arise again.

In complete sincerity, we now repent any of all transgressions committed with body, speech, or mind during past, present, or future, and wish that such transgressions be eliminated, never to arise again.

Friends, now that you have been able to come to this place of enlightenment,[11] each and every one of you can generate the unsurpassable *bodhicitta* and seek the unsurpassable Dharma of *bodhi*!

If you are going to seek the unsurpassable *bodhi*, you must have faith in the words of the Buddha and depend on the Buddha's teachings. What words has the Buddha spoken? The sūtra says, "Do not perform wrong actions, but undertake good actions, and purify one's intentions. This is the teaching of the buddhas."[12] All the buddhas of the past have preached as follows: to not perform wrong actions is morality, to undertake good actions is wisdom,

---

8. The *wu ni* 五逆 or five *ānantarya*, "[transgressions involving] immediate [retribution]," namely, to kill one's father, to kill one's mother, to kill an arhat, to cause blood to flow from the body of a buddha, and to disrupt the saṅgha; see *Bukkyōgo daijiten*, 357a–b.

9. As given in the *Fanwang jing* 梵網經, T 1484: 24.1008c1–3, these are the previous five transgressions plus the murder of either a monk or a teacher.

10. These are killing, stealing, sexual misconduct, lying, flattery, slander, insincere speech, lust, anger, and false views.

11. This term *daochang* 道場 (Skt. *bodhimaṇḍa*) referred originally to the Buddha's seat under the bodhi tree.

12. This is a very simple and old-fashioned interpretation of the "three learnings." Yanagida, *Shoki Zenshū shisho*, 150–152, points out that this interpretation was labeled as being Shenxiu's and rejected in the *Platform Sūtra*. Liebenthal, "Sermon," 141, cites the original reference in the *Nirvāṇa Sūtra* (T 374: 12.451c11), which itself derives from *Aṅguttara nikāya* 1.

and to purify one's intentions is concentration. Friends, only when the [equivalence of the] three learnings is included can it be said to be the teaching of the buddhas.[13] What[14] is the equivalence of the three learnings? These are morality, concentration, and wisdom.[15] The non-activation of the false mind is morality; the absence of the false mind is concentration; and the knowledge of the mind's absence of falsity is wisdom. This is called the equivalence of the three learnings.[16]

You must each maintain [mental and physical] abstinence.[17] If you don't maintain this abstinence, you will never be able to generate the good dharmas. If you are going to seek the unsurpassable *bodhi*, you must first maintain this abstinence—only after doing so can you gain entry [into *bodhi*]. And if you fail to maintain this abstinence, you won't get even a mangy fox's[18] body [in your next life], so how can you possibly acquire the meritorious *dharmakāya* of a tathāgata? Friends, to study and attain the unsurpassable *bodhi* without purifying the three types of action and without maintaining abstinence—this is impossible!

You must depend on conditioned morality and conditioned wisdom to manifest the unconditioned [morality and unconditioned] wisdom.[19] Con-

---

13. Nakamura's translation, "Dango hon'yaku," 146n5, notes that the character *deng* 等, "equivalence," occurs at this point only in the Stein ms., not in the Pelliot or Beijing mss. Since the term does occur in the interrogatory sentence that follows and at the end of this paragraph, I believe it is appropriate to assume the occurrence of the character at this location as well. Nakamura implies that it also occurs a third time, at the end of the paragraph. My impression is that this explanation is very much like the Northern school practice of contemplative analysis, although it is characteristic of Shenhui that he ends up with a slogan; see *Shenhui and the Teaching of Sudden Enlightenment*, n. 81.

14. The Stein ms. begins here in earnest.

15. The terminology used here is *jie ding hui* 戒定慧; Skt. *śīla, samādhi, prajñā*. The term *śīla* would be better rendered as "the precepts," but I have used "morality" as a convenient shorthand for this broad category of monastic regulations. These "three learnings," *trīni śikṣāni* or *sanxue* 三學, represent one of the oldest and most fundamental teachings of Buddhism.

16. The critical terms here are *wangxin bu qi* 妄心不起, *wu wangxin* 無妄心, and *zhi xin wuwang* 知心無妄. Yanagida, *Shoki Zenshū shisho*, 149–151, includes a translation of this passage, beginning with "Friends, in the mouths of ordinary persons…" Yanagida, "Goroku," 394–395, includes a translation of the last two paragraphs, beginning with "Now." The ritual here should be compared to those in the *Five Skillful Means*, the *Platform Sūtra*, and other early Chan works.

17. Nakamura, "Dango hon'yaku," 448d, defines the term used here, *zhaijie* 齋戒, as the temperance or moderation of mind and body, with *zhai* referring to that of the mind and *jie* to that of the body. This is exactly the sort of bifurcated definition and usage favored in the texts of the early Chan school. However, Yanagida, *Shoki Zenshū shisho*, 160n7, suggests that the term refers merely to the lay precepts in general.

18. Literally, a wild fox with boils. Liebenthal, 141, has "scabby jackal." The Tōdai goroku kenkyūhan's "Hokō" (Supplementary Edition of the Platform Sermon), 40, corrects an editing error in Yang's *Chanhua lu*, 6, line 8.

19. Liebenthal, 141, cites his translation of the *Yongjia zhengdao ge* 永嘉證道歌, "Yung-chia's Song of Experiencing the Tao," 16. Liebenthal is apparently referring to the occurrence of the terms *youwei* 有為 and *wuwei* 無為, "conditioned" and "unconditioned," respectively.

centration is different—to cultivate conditioned concentration would be to stay within the realm of causality belonging to humans and gods,[20] and this would hardly correspond with the unsurpassable *bodhi*.

Friends, the reason you have been wandering about in saṃsāra for as many great eons as there are grains of sand in the River Ganges without attaining emancipation is that you have never generated the unsurpassable *bodhicitta* because you never encountered the buddhas, bodhisattvas, and true spiritual compatriots.[21] Even if you did meet the buddhas, bodhisattvas, and true spiritual compatriots, you were unable to generate the unsurpassable *bodhicitta*. This is why you have been wandering about in saṃsāra for as many great eons as there are grains of sand in the River Ganges without attaining emancipation.[22]

2

Furthermore, if you do generate *bodhicitta* but only generate a Hīnayānist aspiration [for rebirth in the realms of] humans and gods,[23] there will be no avoiding the downfall when your blessings on earth or in heaven are exhausted. The buddhas who have appeared in the world are as numerous as the grains of sand in the Ganges.[24] The great bodhisattvas who have appeared in the world are as numerous as the grains of sand in the Ganges. Each and every one of the buddhas, bodhisattvas, and spiritual compatriots has appeared in the world to save people as numerous as the grains of sand in the Ganges. So how can it be that you have never met one of the buddhas, bodhisattvas, and spiritual compatriots and have been wandering about in saṃsāra until now, without attaining emancipation?[25] It can only be because in the past company of those buddhas, bodhisattvas, and spiritual compatriots, the condition [necessary for your generation of] the unsurpassable

---

Although the terminology is somewhat different, compare the *wuxiang jie* 無相戒 or "precepts of formlessness" in the *Platform Sūtra* T 2008: 48.339a12; Yampolsky, *Platform Sutra*, 141.

20. That is, it would only be enough to merit a favorable rebirth.

21. This emphasis on the rarity of meeting buddhas, etc., or encountering the teachings of Buddhism continues in the section immediately following this and is shared with the *Essentials of Cultivating the Mind* and other early Chan texts.

22. Again, the injunction to transcend mundane advantage in pursuit of true spiritual liberation occurs also in the *Essentials of Cultivating the Mind*. Unlike that text and the *Treatise on the Contemplation of the Mind*, however, Shenhui emphasizes the negative. Is he effectively keeping his audience in suspense? Or is this simply a function of his anti-Northern-school position?

23. That is, *ersheng rentian xin* 二乘人天心. [One could also take these as two categories: the Hīnayānist aspiration to become an arhat or *pratyekabuddha* and the aspiration to be reborn as a human or god. This applies throughout this paragraph.—Ed.]

24. Here Tōdai goroku kenkyūhan, 40, corrects a minor editing error in Yang, 6, marked as line 14, but actually line 15.

25. Tōdai goroku kenkyūhan, 40, corrects the punctuation in Yang, 6, line 16.

bodhicitta[26] did not occur for even a single moment. Or, there may[27] have been spiritual compatriots who did not comprehend the Dharma of unsurpassable *bodhi* and taught you with the Hīnayānist Dharma of the *śrāvakas,* meant for humans and gods. This is like "putting defiled food into a precious dish."[28] What is the "precious dish"? Friends, your generation of the unsurpassable *bodhicitta* is the precious dish. What is "defiled food"? It is the Hīnayānist Dharma of humans and gods. Although you may obtain some good and acquire the blessing of being born in heaven, when [your blessings] are exhausted[29] you will revert to being an ordinary person like you are today.

Friends, the Dharma that you should be inspired to study corresponds to the perfection of wisdom.[30] It goes beyond that of the *śrāvakas* and *pratyekabuddhas* and is identical to the prediction conferred by Śākyamuni on Maitreya, without any difference.[31]

The Hīnayānists pass through eons while grasping at concentration. Stream-enterers remain in concentration for eighty thousand eons, once-returners remain in concentration for sixty thousand eons, non-returners remain in concentration for forty thousand eons, arhats remain in concentration for twenty thousand eons, and *pratyekabuddhas* remain in concentration for ten thousand eons.[32] Why? Only after remaining in concentration for a sufficient number of eons are the great bodhisattvas able to reach them with their preaching. Only then are they able to generate *bodhicitta*, at which point they are identical to you who are generating *bodhicitta* today, and no different. This is because when the Hīnayānists are in concentration, even if someone does preach the Dharma of the unsurpassable *bodhi* to them, they are unable to comprehend. The sūtra says, "The goddess said to Śāriputra, 'Ordinary persons may repay their gratitude for the Buddhist Dharma, but the *śrāvakas* cannot.' "[33]

---

26. Nakamura, 146n8, follows the Beijing ms., which has *puti* 菩提 rather than *pusa* 菩薩. The character *lai* 來, "come," is used here as a colloquial verb complement.
27. Tōdai goroku kenkyūhan, 40, corrects a trivial—questionable, even—editing error in Yang, 7, line 1.
28. This is from the *Vimalakīrti Sūtra*, T 475: 14.540c27.
29. Tōdai goroku kenkyūhan, 40, corrects a minor editing error in Yang, 7, line 2. Effectively, Yang followed Hu's edition (*Yiji,* 231) in privileging a four-character phrasing here, but Kinugawa and his research team have restored a more colloquial rendering.
30. "Correspond" renders *xiangying* 相應.
31. This prediction occurs in the *Pusa chu tai jing* 菩薩處胎經, T 384: 12.1025c. For a different translation of this paragraph (two sentences here), see Jorgensen, *Inventing Huineng,* 278.
32. Liebenthal, 142n23, refers to the *Nirvāṇa Sūtra*, T 374: 12.431c15–432a6, although this describes styles of practice and the lengths of time required to achieve perfect enlightenment. For an expression of the same sentiment given here but regarding only arhats and a somewhat shorter length of time (a mere thousand eons!), see the *Treatise on Perfect Illumination,* a text formerly thought to have been associated with Shenhui (McRae, *Northern School,* 209, 215; translated on pp. 149, 171).
33. See the *Vimalakīrti,* T 475: 14.549b22; cf. the translation in Lamotte, *Vimalakīrti,* 180.

Since you have already come to this ordination platform to study the perfection of wisdom, I want each and every one of you to generate, both mentally and orally, the unsurpassable *bodhicitta* and become enlightened to the cardinal meaning of the Middle Path in this very place![34]

If you seek emancipation, you must transcend body, mind, and consciousness; the five dharmas, the three self-natures, the eight consciousnesses, and the two selflessnesses;[35] and you must transcend internal and external views.[36] Also, [as is said in the *Vimalakīrti Sūtra*], "the non-manifestation of body and mind is sitting in repose."[37] If one sits in this fashion, the Buddha will thereupon certify one's [enlightenment]." The six generations of patriarchs have transmitted the mind with the mind because it transcends words. The transmission from before is like this.

Friends, each and every one of you possesses the Buddha-nature within yourself.[38] Spiritual compatriots cannot give you the Buddha's Dharma of *bodhi*, nor can they pacify your mind for you.[39] Why? The *Nirvāṇa Sūtra* says, "The prediction has already been conferred on you. All sentient beings are originally in nirvāṇa and inherently possess the undefiled wisdom-nature."[40] Why are you unable to see that you are currently wandering in saṃsāra and failing to attain emancipation?[41] This is because [the Buddha-nature within you] is obscured by afflictions, so you cannot see it.[42] Only upon instruction from a spiritual compatriot will you be able to see it, after which you will end your wandering in saṃsāra and attain emancipation.

Liebenthal, 142n24, points out this is actually said by Kāśyapa to Mañjuśrī. *Fanfu* 返覆 is defined in *Bukkyōgo daijiten*, 113b, in terms of the repayment of gratitude.

34. Although I agree with the translations of both Nakamura, 139, and Yanagida, "Goroku," 394, one could render *xinkou* 心口 as simply "in your minds." The question is whether *kou* functions here as a colloquial Chinese suffix. Although we cannot resolve the issue in the absence of any explication by Shenhui, the dualistic terminology "minds and mouths" is quite conceivable within an early Chan text.

35. The terms used here come from the *Laṅkāvatāra Sūtra*, and Shenhui's rejection of these terms may indicate a switch from this scripture to the *Diamond*, as noted by Nakamura in "Dango," 376n40; see T 671: 16.514c and 587b.

36. The logic of interior and exterior is stated in the *Vimalakīrti*, T 475: 14.539c23.

37. Here the term for seated meditation is that from the *Vimalakīrti*, *yanzuo* 宴坐 (T 475: 14.539c17f.). The term is also used in the *Miscellaneous Dialogues*, section 2. *Tōdai goroku kenkyūhan*, 40, corrects the punctuation in Yang, 7, line 10.

38. The idea is that of the Buddha-nature, but note that Shenhui continues in his negative tone.

39. The term rendered as "pacify the mind" is *anxin* 安心. Here *Tōdai goroku kenkyūhan*, 41, corrects a significant editing error in which Yang, 7, line 12, followed Hu, *Yiji*, 232–233, rather than Suzuki. The issue here is that *renzhe* 人者 or 仁者, is an honorific form of second-person address, well-attested in Chinese Buddhist translations.

40. Liebenthal, 144n32, points out that this whole passage is not found in the *Nirvāṇa Sūtra*; the first sentence is apparently additional.

41. *Tōdai goroku kenkyūhan*, 41, corrects the punctuation in Yang, 7, line 13.

42. The theoretical construct here is identical to that of the *Two Entrances and Four Practices* and *Essentials of Cultivating the Mind*, but the emphasis is on the concrete act of seeing. There is none of the "it's-all-right" assurance of the latter text, at any rate.

3

Friends, everything you've studied in the past should be eliminated—don't read it![43] Friends, if you've been studying Chan for five years, or more than ten years, or twenty years, you may be deeply shocked when you hear this. But saying "eliminate" means only to eliminate the false mind, not to eliminate the Dharma. The true Dharma cannot be eliminated even by the buddhas and tathāgatas[44] of all the ten directions, so how could I eliminate it now? Just as a person walking, standing still, sitting, or lying down in space is never apart from space, so too is the unsurpassable Dharma of *bodhi*: it cannot be eliminated, and all one's actions and activities are inseparable from the *dharmadhātu*. The sūtra says, "Just eliminate the illness, do not eliminate the Dharma."[45]

Friends, listen well, and I will explain the false mind to you. What is the false mind? The lust for wealth and sex and the longing for gardens and houses is "gross falsity"—when you come here you should be without such desires. But you don't yet know about the existence of "subtle falsity."[46] What is subtle falsity? When you hear an explanation of *bodhi* and activate the intention to grasp *bodhi*; when you hear an explanation of nirvāṇa and activate the intention to grasp nirvāṇa; when you hear an explanation of emptiness and activate the intention to grasp emptiness; when you hear an explanation of purity and activate the intention to grasp purity; when you hear an explanation of concentration and activate the intention to grasp concentration: these are all [examples of] the false mind, of being bound to the Dharma, of having mistaken views of the Dharma. If your mind functions like this, you will not attain emancipation; this is not your inherently serene and pure mind.[47] If you attempt[48] to reside in nirvāṇa, you will be bound by nirvāṇa; if you reside in purity, you will be bound by purity; if you reside in

---

43. See translations by Gómez, "Purifying Gold," 78, and Yanagida, "Goroku," 395. The verb complex *mo yong kan* 莫用看, "don't read it," reminds one of the compound *kanjing* 看經, "to read the scriptures." On p. 396 Yanagida points out that the same colloquialism also occurs in the miscellaneous material circulated with the *Two Entrances and Four Practices* attributed to Bodhidharma.

44. Following Shinohara's translation, "Kataku Jinne no kotoba," 13, I interpolate the character *ru* 如, to make the phrase *zhufo rulai* 諸佛如來. This is in accord with Tōdai goroku kenkyūhan, 41, which similarly amends Yang, 8, line 2. [Another solution is to read *lai* as a colloquial verbal complement, resulting in the rendering "if all the buddhas of the ten directions come to dispel it..."—Ed.]

45. See the *Vimalakīrti*, T 475: 14.545a16–17; cf. Lamotte, *Vimalakīrti*, 124. The beginning and end of this paragraph are translated in Yanagida, "Goroku no rekishi," 495.

46. Liebenthal, 144n39, cites the *Nirvāṇa Sūtra*, T 374: 12.387b20–c8, but the passage is not relevant.

47. The term used here is *benzi jijing xin* 本自寂静心.

48. The verb *zuo* 作 indicates the willful or intentional performance of an action. In the technical jargon of early Chan, to "intentionalize" (*zuoyi* 作意) one's actions is the fundamental error that separates the unenlightened from the enlightened.

emptiness, you will be bound by emptiness; if you reside in concentration, you will be bound by concentration. To intentionally have your mind function in any of these ways is to impede the Path of *bodhi*. The *Diamond Sūtra* says, "If the mind grasps characteristics, you will be attached to self, person, sentient being, and lifespan."[49] [Again,] "transcending all characteristics is called 'the buddhas,' "[50] who transcend the characteristics of all dharmas. The *Vimalakīrti Sūtra* says, "What is the source of the illness?[51] It is object perception.... How can one eradicate object perception? With the unattainable."[52] The unattainable constitutes the source of non-illness.[53] If those who study the Path do not understand subtle falsity, how will they be able to transcend the great ocean of saṃsāra?

Friends, you should all take care to listen carefully as I explain[54] the pure inherent mind.[55] When you hear an explanation of *bodhi*, don't create the intention to grasp *bodhi*; when you hear an explanation of nirvāṇa, don't create the intention to grasp nirvāṇa; when you hear an explanation of purity, don't create the intention to grasp purity; when you hear an explanation of emptiness, don't create the intention to grasp emptiness; when you hear an explanation of concentration, don't create the intention to grasp concentration: to have your mind function like this is quietistic nirvāṇa. The sūtra says, "The eradication of the afflictions is not called nirvāṇa. Only the non-generation of the afflictions is called nirvāṇa."[56] It is like a bird flying through space—if it tried to stand still in space it would necessarily suffer a fall.[57] If those who study the Path cultivate the non-abiding mind[58] and have their minds abide in the Dharma, this is the attachment of abiding, not emancipation. The sūtra says, "There is no other illness, just the illness of emptiness, but this illness of emptiness is also empty."[59] The sūtra says,

---

49. From the *Diamond Sūtra*, T 235: 8.749b6–7.
50. Also from the *Diamond*, 750b9.
51. "Illness" in this passage of the *Vimalakīrti* stands for ignorance and suffering.
52. See T 475: 14.545a17–20.
53. Or, following Nakamura, 140, "Given the unattainable, there is no source of illness."
54. *Liaojian* 聊簡 is used here and again at the very beginning of section 6.
55. The term here is *zi ben qingjing xin* 自本清淨心. Shinohara, "Kataku Jinne," 15n1, notes comparable usages in other texts, including the *Essentials of Cultivating the Mind*. Yanagida, "Goroku," 95, suggests that the material that follows is the very heart of the *Platform Sermon*.
56. The same idea is expressed in the *Treatise on Perfect Illumination* (McRae, *Northern School*, 163). Liebenthal, 145n45, cites the *Nirvāṇa Sūtra*, T 374: 12.514a17, but the passage is not relevant. Shinohara, 15n3, cites a passage a few lines later in the same sūtra that is relevant (514c).
57. See Shenxiu's "question about things" regarding the tracks of a bird through space in the *Masters and Disciples of the Laṅkāvatāra*. Tōdai goroku kenkyūhan, 41, corrects the punctuation here in Yang, 8, line 14.
58. The term *wuzhu* 無住 in translations from Sanskrit often renders *apratiṣṭhā*, which occurs in the *Vimalakīrti*, *Śikṣāsamuccaya*, and *Laṅkāvatāra*, as well as the *Diamond Sūtra*, for example. See *Bukkyōgo daijiten*, 1328c–d.
59. See the *Vimalakīrti Sūtra*, T 475: 14.545a12–13.

"Constantly seek the wisdom of the true characteristic of non-thought."[60] He who [attempts to] realize the *dharmadhātu* with the *dharmadhātu* is a person of great self-conceit.

4

Friends, don't think about good and wrong [actions] at all.[61] You should not freeze your mind and force it to abide.[62] You should also not use the mind to directly observe the mind,[63] or else you will fall into an abiding of direct observation,[64] which is useless. Nor should you lower the eyes in front—you will fall into a visual abiding, which is useless. You should not create the intention to concentrate the mind, and you should not look afar or look near.[65] These are all useless. The sūtra says, "Non-contemplation is *bodhi*, because it is without recollection."[66] This is the mind that is empty and serene in its inherent nature.[67]

[Question:] Are there affirmative and negative in the mind?
Answer: No.
[Question:] Is there abiding in the mind, or coming and going in the mind?[68]
Answer: No.
[Question:] Are there blue, yellow, red, and white in the mind?[69]
Answer: No.

---

60. This is from the *Vimalakīrti Sūtra*, T 475: 14.554b23–24. See also Suzuki, *Zenshū*, 2:445 and 3:322.

61. Yanagida, "Goroku," 396–397, suggests that underlying this injunction is the metaphor of the darkness and brightness of space and the equivalence of the afflictions and enlightenment. On this last topic, see section 6 below.

62. The rhetoric of making the mind "abide" (*zhu* 住, i.e., stand still, or be fixed on a certain spot) is a major part of Shenhui's thought.

63. The two references here are expanded toward the end of this section into Shenhui's "four pronouncements" against yogic meditation practices.

64. This term, *zhishi zhu* 直視住, is not repeated in Shenhui's corpus.

65. The term *yuankan jinkan* 遠看近看 is clearly that of the Northern school.

66. This is a conflation of the *Vimalakīrti* (T 475: 14.542b24–25): "Non-contemplation (*buguan* 不觀) is *bodhi*, since it transcends the conditions. Nonpractice is *bodhi*, because it is without recollection (*wu yinian* 無憶念)."

67. The term here is *zixing kongji xin* 自性空寂心. See a similar usage, *zhufa benxing kongji* 諸法本性空寂, in the *Nirvāṇa Sūtra*, T 374: 12.379a16. Yanagida, "Goroku," 395–396, suggests this passage was to become a basic theme of virtually all subsequent Chan literature and, more specifically, the origin of Huineng's question to Huiming about his "original face" in the Kōshōji 興聖寺 and later versions of the *Platform Sūtra*.

68. Hu, 237, interprets the first of these alternatives, *zhuchu* 住處, "location of abiding," as a mistaken interpolation. I have followed Yanagida, "Goroku," 398, in reading the text according to the original as we have it. Incidentally, the second alternative follows a similar form, *laiqu chu* 來去處, literally, "location(s) of coming and going."

69. References to this set of colors occur in the *Miscellaneous Dialogues*, sections 2 and 34.

PLATFORM SERMON

[Question:] Does the mind have a place of abiding?[70]
Answer: The mind is without any place of abiding.
His Reverence said: The mind is non-abiding. Do you understand (zhi 知) the mind's non-abiding?
Answer: We understand.
[Question:] Do you understand it or not?
Answer: We understand.[71]

I have now posited knowing (zhi 知) from non-abiding by inference (tui 推).[72] How is this? Non-abiding is quiescence, and the essence of quiescence is called concentration.[73] The natural wisdom (zhi 智) that occurs on the basis of[74] this essence, whereby one can know the inherently quiescent

---

70. Stein 6977 begins here (HS 237.3), or rather with a question and response not found in the other mss.: "Does [the mind] have limits (xianliang 限量)?" "No." This term also occurs above and in the *Definition of the Truth,* but still I wonder if it is an error for the modern homophone xianliang 現量, which is a standard rendering of the Skt. pratyakṣa.

71. There is some question as to who is asking and who answering the questions posed here, since the Chinese omits all reference to subject or object. Based on Stein 6977, which has "'No-mind being the locus of non-abiding, do you know the locus of the mind's non-abiding?' Answer: '[I/we] know [it].'" After his presentation of this dialogue in Japanese, Yanagida, "Goroku," 397–398, notes that this dialogue was initiated by a question from Shenhui, who was aware of the "questions about things" in the *Masters and Disciples of the Laṅkāvatāra.* I differ in my interpretation of the characters heshang yan 和上言, "His Reverence said," in the middle of the dialogue, but I feel the reading selected is more straightforward and still supports Yanagida's observations about Shenhui's use of questions to lead his followers on to greater understanding. However, where the character yan 言, "speak, say," is used in the *Miscellaneous Dialogues* it seems to be in the citation of someone else's speech rather than in direct quotation (see *Miscellaneous Dialogues,* section 12). There do not seem to be any comparable usages in the *Platform Sermon.* Yanagida argues, based in part on this section of the *Platform Sermon,* that one of Shenhui's most important innovations was his use of oral dialogue. However, since Shenhui's respondent(s) here are anonymous, I have interpreted this dialogue as being more liturgical than spontaneous, on the model of those in the *Five Skillful Means* and have therefore read the responses in the plural. See the similar but much shorter dialogue at the beginning of section 7 below, which, if not a purely literary device of the written treatise, seems clearly like Shenhui speaking in response with his entire congregation.

72. Nakamura, 141, includes this sentence with the preceding dialogue, then starts a new paragraph, whereas I have followed Hu's editing. See similar usages of tui 推, "infer," just below, at the end of this and the following paragraphs. Instead of this question, Stein 6977 reads "Question: 'Now where does the mind abide, that it reaches the locus of non-abiding? Based on what matter do you further posit knowing, that you [know] the mind is non-abiding?' 'If knowing is not posited, then when the mind is non-abiding it falls into a blank emptiness. Therefore knowing is posited.'"

73. Although zhi 智 and hui 慧, "wisdom" and "sagacity," are not specifically described as "function" here, the ti-yong 體用 or essence-function construct is assumed as a logical antecedent of the assertion of identity. See Shenhui's comments on the identity of concentration and wisdom above.

74. Shenhui uses the character shang 上, "on top of," or cong ti shang you ziran zhi 從體上有自然智, "wisdom that occurs naturally from on top of the essence." This strikes me as a very literalistic usage. Similar usages below ("activate illumination on the basis of serenity," and "activate knowing on the basis of this empty and serene essence").

essence, is called sagacity (*hui* 慧).[75] This is the equivalence of concentration and wisdom.[76] The sūtra says, "Activate illumination on the basis of serenity,"[77] and the meaning here is the same. The non-abiding mind does not transcend knowing, and knowing does not transcend non-abiding. If one knows the mind's non-abiding, there is nothing else to be known.[78] The *Nirvāṇa Sūtra* says, "For concentration to be great and wisdom little is to increase one's ignorance. For wisdom to be great and concentration little is to increase one's wrong views. For concentration and wisdom to be equivalent is called 'seeing the Buddha-nature.'"[79] I have now posited knowing by infer-

---

75. Where it is paired with *zhi* 智, "wisdom," I render *hui* 慧 as "sagacity." Otherwise, it is rendered as "wisdom."

76. The equivalence of concentration and wisdom is one of Shenhui's most important doctrines. Gernet's translation (*Entretiens*, 50n3) refers the reader to the definitions of correct concentration and wisdom in the *Nirvāṇa Sūtra,* T 374: 12.527c16–17, which although couched in terms of typically Mahāyāna rhetoric are still quite some distance from Shenhui's formulation: "To not see the characteristic[s] of mind is called correct concentration (*zhengding* 正定); to not seek for the natures and characteristics and causes and conditions of the dharmas is called correct wisdom (*zhenghui* 正慧)." In his annotation to the *Miscellaneous Dialogues,* section 43, Gernet, 64n9, cross-references the *Records of the Transmission*'s description of Shenhui teaching that "preaching correctly is the precepts; preaching correctly is concentration; preaching correctly is wisdom" (T 2075: 51.185b17–18; Yanagida, *Shoki no Zenshi 2,* 155). Gernet also points out that the *Platform Sūtra* describes the equivalence of concentration and wisdom in terms of an absence of opposition between the mind and words, between ecstasy and preaching (T 2008: 48.338b12–13). This connection with preaching also occurs in the *Miscellaneous Dialogues,* section 44, where Shenhui is quoted as saying, "Precisely at the time when I am talking to you, concentration and wisdom are equivalent." Finally, Gernet notes the relationship between this theme and the treatment of the *Laṅkāvatāra*'s distinction between the penetrations of preaching and the truth (Gernet refers to these as doctrinal and discursive comprehension) in the *Miscellaneous Dialogues,* section 57.

77. The phrase *ji shang qi zhao* 寂上起照 is unidentified.

78. From the third sentence of this paragraph, beginning with "Non-abiding is quiescence," Stein 6977 has: "Non-abiding is the essence of fundamental quiescence (*benjiti* 本寂體). Based on this essence of fundamental quiescence there is a fundamental wisdom. To know the pure essence of fundamental quiescence (*benji jingti* 本寂淨體) is called the equivalence of concentration and wisdom. The essence of fundamental quiescence has a self-nature of concentration and wisdom. The fundamental wisdom's ability to know is its function." This terminology is not used elsewhere in Shenhui's works, implying a transcriptional error.

79. Although Liebenthal, 147n58, cites the *Nirvāṇa Sūtra,* T 374: 14.547a7f, and Shinohara, 17n6, suggests either 534a or 580b, this line does not occur in any of these locations. This passage is quoted by Shenhui in the context of a dialogue with Wang Wei and others in the *Miscellaneous Dialogues*. Suzuki Tetsuo ("Kataku Jinne no eikyō," 93) suggests that Shenhui drew from two locations in the *Nirvāṇa Sūtra,* at T 375: 12.827c (which describes those who lack either faith or wisdom) and 792c (which describes those in whom meditation exceeds wisdom, or vice versa). Gernet, 64n10, also suggests that the *Nirvāṇa Sūtra* passage at T 374: 12.580b18–20 may have inspired Shenhui's construction: "If a person has faith but no wisdom, he will increase in ignorance; if a person has wisdom but no faith, he will increase in heterodox views." This attention to both poles foreshadows the *Platform Sūtra*'s treatment of "thirty-six responses," about which the text comments that "if attached to emptiness you will only increase your ignorance; if attached to characteristics you will only slander the sūtras with

ence from non-abiding.[80] To know the empty serenity of the mind is its function.[81]

This is identical to the *Lotus Sūtra* saying, "The knowing and seeing of the Tathāgata is great and profound."[82] The mind is without limit and is identical to the Buddha in its greatness. The mind is without limit and is identical to the Buddha in its profundity, with no difference between them. The Buddha can infer the nature of the bodhisattvas' illnesses by viewing them in their practice of the profound perfection of wisdom.[83] The *Diamond Sūtra* says, "The bodhisattva-mahāsattva should thus generate a pure mind: Not abiding in forms does he generate the mind; not abiding in sounds,

---

heterodox views" (T 2008: 48.343c5; *Enō kenkyū*, 373; Yampolsky, *Platform Sutra*, 172–173). Suzuki Tetsuo ("Kataku Jinne no eikyō," 91–92) points out that this passage is given in expanded and modified form in the *Essential Teaching of Sudden Enlightenment* (X 63.20b19–22). On p. 93, Suzuki argues that this passage proves that the *Essential Teaching of Sudden Enlightenment* borrowed from the *Miscellaneous Dialogues*, and not vice versa. And, since only the *Miscellaneous Dialogues* and not the *Platform Sermon* uses *ti-yong* rhetoric in this location, the *Essential Teaching of Sudden Enlightenment* borrowed from the former.

80. Compare Nakamura, 141: "I have now carried the discussion to the non-abiding of the mind to explain knowing, in order for you to understand that the mind is serene." Instead of this relatively simple statement and the following assertion about knowing the empty serenity of the mind, Stein 6977 has: "I have now inferred to the locus of non-abiding. Non-abiding is the fundamental quiescence of the self-nature (*ben zixing ji* 本自性寂). Knowing is the function. Quiescence is the essence of illumination, and illumination is the function of quiescence. Quiescence is the essence, the fundamental concentration of the self-nature; illumination is the [function], the fundamental wisdom of the self-nature. As with a lamp and its light, although there are two [separate] names the essences are not different. The lamp is the light, and the light is the lamp. Apart from the lamp there is no separate light, and apart from the light there is no separate lamp. The lamp is the essence of the light, and the light is the function of the lamp." Although worded differently, this material is similar in content to what is found below.

81. Literally, is the *yongchu* 用處, "location(s) of function." Yanagida, "Goroku," 397–398, includes a translation of the preceding dialogue.

82. See T 262: 9.5c4–5. The term for the Tathāgata's "knowing and seeing" is *zhijian* 知見, referring to the liberating insight realized by the Buddha in his great awakening under the bodhi tree, when he clearly knew and saw all things as they truly are (Skt. *yathā-bhūta-jñāna-darśana*). Although this term traces back to the early Buddhist canonical accounts of the Buddha's enlightenment, in Chinese Buddhism it is most often associated with the passage in the *Lotus Sūtra* in which the Buddha declares that the one great reason all buddhas past, present, and future appear in the world is to make known (*kai* 開) and to reveal (*shi* 示) the Tathāgata's knowing and seeing so as to enable sentient beings to apprehend (*wu* 悟) it and to enter into (*ru* 入) the path to it. See T 262: 9.7a21–c9.

83. Yanagida, "Goroku," 400, translates this quotation from the *Lotus* and Shenhui's commentary. Compare the use of *tui* 推, "infer," here, just below, and just above. Presumably, Shenhui is referring not only to the Buddha and celestial bodhisattvas, but to Chinese Chan masters and their students and, even more specifically, to his own teaching abilities. As noted by Yanagida, in this Shenhui anticipates a claim made explicitly in the *Linji lu*. Tōdai goroku kenkyūhan, 42, points out that the seven references to "perfection of wisdom" in the *Platform Sermon* all use *bore boluomi* 般若波羅蜜 without the final *duo* 多, which should be excised from Yang, 9, line 11.

fragrances, tastes, tangibles, or dharmas does he generate the mind. Without any abiding does he generate that mind."[84] I now infer that "without any abiding" is your non-abiding mind. "Does he generate the mind" is to know the mind's non-abiding.[85]

The original essence is empty and serene.[86] To activate[87] knowing on

---

84. This line, *ying wu suo zhu er sheng qi xin* 應無所住而生其心, which Shenhui and after him the *Platform Sūtra* made famous, is from the *Diamond Sūtra*, T 235: 8.749c22–23; also see the reprise at 750b23–23. It supposedly inspired Huineng's final enlightenment. However, the citation of this line does not occur in the Dunhuang version of the *Platform Sūtra*, but only beginning with the Daijō-ji and Kōshōji versions; see *Enō kenkyū*, 132 and 285. The line also occurs in the *Dunwu zhenzong yaojue* 頓悟真宗要訣, and in a commentary by Yixing, T 1796: 39.579b25–26; see McRae, *Northern School*, 321n118. The same passage (749c22–23) is cited in the *Miscellaneous Dialogues*, section 26. The terminology of the "pure mind" *qingjing xin* 清淨心 is not Shenhui's customary vocabulary. Yanagida's translation of this passage (from the *Prajñā Sūtra* quotation down to just prior to the *Nirvāṇa Sūtra* citation below, "Goroku," 400–401), renders this as [the bodhisattva] "should not generate the mind in abidance in form." This reading is grammatically acceptable but inappropriate in view of Shenhui's division of the phrase into two for explanation just below. Yanagida, "Goroku," 615n384, points out that the Dunhuang version of the *Platform Sūtra* (as well as the *Anthology of the Patriarchal Hall* and *Transmission of the Lamp*) has Huineng hearing the *Diamond* in Nanhai, after which he travels to Huangmei to study with Hongren, but it does not emphasize the line quoted here by Shenhui. The *Caoqi dashi (bie) zhuan* (曹溪大師[別]傳) does not mention the *Diamond* at all (X 86.49b8; this text is listed in Japanese pilgrims' catalogues with the additional character *bie* 別). The first text to say that Huineng heard this particular line in Nanhai is a Song dynasty transmission history, the *Tiansheng guangdeng lu* 天聖廣燈錄 (X 78.445c11).

85. Yanagida, "Goroku," 503, points out that the logic underlying this interpretation of the *Diamond* derives from the *Zhao lun* 肇論, which reads a line from the *Fangguang banruo jing* 放光般若經 (a Western Jin translation of the *Perfection of Wisdom*) as "not moving the true limit [of ultimate reality], yet becoming the locus of establishment of the myriad dharmas" (*budong zhenji wei zhufa lichu* 不動真際為諸法立處; T 1858: 45.153a3), rather than the scripture's intended assertion, "not moving in the dharmas of equivalent enlightenment and becoming the locus of establishment of the myriad dharmas" (*budong yu dengjue fa wei zhufa lichu* 不動於等覺法為諸法立處; T 221: 8.140c15). Yanagida, *Daruma no goroku*, 151, suggests that this represents a reinterpretation of the original to fit a basic Chinese theme, that one can remain in accord with ultimate reality while simultaneously being active in the world. He sees this theme as the extension of a native logic found in the *Daode jing* to Buddhism and the basis of recurrent expressions in the Perfection of Wisdom literature, including the *Vimalakīrti*, which refers to "not moving from equivalent enlightenment, yet establishing the myriad dharmas" and "not rejecting the Dharma of the Path while still manifesting the affairs of an ordinary [unenlightened] person." Finally, Yanagida finds here not only the background of Shenhui's notion of the equivalence of the afflictions and enlightenment, as well as the imagery of space and its brightness/darkness, but also the logic behind the positive appraisals of the ordinary mind by Mazu and Linji.

86. Here *Tōdai goroku kenkyūhan*, 42, corrects a minor editing error in Yang, 9, line 14.

87. This and the untraced scriptural citation just above are two of only three places in the Shenhui corpus where *qi* 起, "to activate," is used in a positive sense. It may be reasonable to say that this is a usage that Shenhui is careful to avoid in his later teaching. In the *Definition of the Truth* "activation" is used in a consistently negative sense: the character occurs several times in Shenhui's "four pronouncements"; in his redefinition of the first part of *zuochan* 坐禪, "sitting meditation," as "for thoughts to not be activated" (section 22); with regard to a stage

the basis of this empty and serene essence and to well discriminate the blue, yellow, red, and white[88] of this world is wisdom (*hui* 慧). To not activate [the mind] in consequence of this discrimination is concentration.

Thus if one freezes the mind to enter concentration, one will fall into a blank emptiness.[89] To activate the mind to discriminate all the conditioned [realities of this] world after arising from concentration, and to call this wisdom—in the sūtras this is called the false mind! This is to be without concentration during wisdom and to be without wisdom during concentration. If one's understanding is like this, one will never transcend the afflictions.

To freeze the mind to enter concentration, to fix the mind to view purity, to activate the mind to illuminate the external, and to concentrate the mind to realize the internal[90]—this is not an emancipated mind, but rather a mind that is bound to the Dharma. Don't do this! The *Nirvāṇa Sūtra* says, "The Buddha told Bodhisattva Brilliance-of-Lazuli, 'Good youth, you should not enter the concentration of profound emptiness. Why? Because it renders the great congregation [of ordinary followers] dull.'"[91] This is because, once you have entered concentration, you cannot know the perfection of wisdom.

Just know yourself that the inherent essence is quiescent,[92] empty and without attributes. It is without abiding or attachment and equivalent to space—there is nowhere it does not pervade: such is the body of the buddhas.[93] Suchness is the essence of non-thought. Because of this idea, I posit non-thought as my doctrine. If you see non-thought, you will be constantly empty and serene even while your perceptive functions are operating.[94] This is [what it means] for the three learnings of morality, concentration, and wisdom to be simultaneously equivalent, and to be possessed of all the ten

---

of illuminative cognition, the extinction of which constitutes non-thought (section 48); in a description of the sage as "consign[ing] himself to non-activation to accord with the sound [of an echo in a mountain valley]" (section 52); and in the rhetorical question, "If one activates the dharma of the existence of seeing, where will the mind of seeing exist within the dharma?" (also section 52). In the *Miscellaneous Dialogues*, there are numerous negative usages.

88. The Stein ms. ends here, after the character *bai* 白, "white."

89. Compare warnings against blankness of mind (*wuji* 無記, Skt. *avyākṛta*) in the *Essentials of Cultivating the Mind*, as well as in a statement on meditation by Shenxiu; see McRae, *Northern School*, 128 and 216, and 319n95. After this point, Stein 6977 ends after a few lacunae-filled phrases.

90. These are Shenhui's famous "four pronouncements," which in *the Definition of the Truth* are attributed specifically to the Northern school. See their occurrence in the *Definition of the Truth*, sections 20 and 22, and the *Miscellaneous Dialogues*, sections 28 and 34. Also see the non-formulaic statement in the *Miscellaneous Dialogues*, section 6. Note that the character *zhu* 住, here rendered as "to fix," elsewhere occurs in the term *wuzhu* 無住, "non-abiding," as in the non-abiding mind; see note above.

91. See the *Nirvāṇa Sūtra*, T 374: 12.490c4–5.

92. *Benti jijing* 本體寂靜.

93. *Zhufo zhenru shen* 諸佛真如身.

94. The term here is *jianwen juezhi* 見聞覺知; see the *Definition of the Truth*, section 33 (n. 297).

thousand practices. This is [what it means] to be equivalent to the knowing and seeing of the Tathāgata, great and profound.⁹⁵ Why is it profound? It is called profound by those who have not seen the nature. If one comprehensively sees the nature, there is no profundity.⁹⁶

5

Friends, you should each in complete sincerity attain the emancipation of sudden enlightenment.⁹⁷

When your eyes see forms, discriminate well all [the dharmas of] form.⁹⁸ Do not activate [the mind] in consequence of this discrimination, but attain autonomy within form, so that within form you attain completely to the samādhi of emancipated forms.⁹⁹

When your ears hear sounds, discriminate well all [the dharmas of] sound. Do not activate [the mind¹⁰⁰] in consequence of this discrimination, but attain autonomy within sound, so that within sound you attain completely to the samādhi of emancipated sounds.

When your nose smells odors, discriminate well all [the dharmas of] odor. Do not activate [the mind] in consequence of this discrimination, but attain autonomy within odor, so that within odor you attain completely to the samādhi of emancipated odors.

When your tongue detects tastes, discriminate well all [the dharmas of] taste. Do not activate [the mind] in consequence of this discrimination, but attain autonomy within taste, so that within taste you attain completely to the samādhi of emancipated tastes.

When your body experiences tactile sensations, discriminate well all [the dharmas of] tactile sensation. Do not activate [the mind] in consequence of this discrimination, but attain autonomy within tactile sensation, so that within it you attain completely to the samādhi of emancipated tactile sensations.

When your mind discriminates dharmas, discriminate well all the dharmas. Do not activate [the mind] in consequence of this discrimination,

---

95. *Zhijian* 知見; see n. 82 above.

96. To "comprehensively see the nature" is *liao jian xing* 了見性; without *liao*, simply "see the nature." See the *Nirvāṇa Sūtra*, T 374: 12.527c19–20, with discussion to 528a4.

97. Since the sentence has a causative *ling* 令, to be more precise it should read "with each of you being completely sincere, I [Shenhui] will cause you, friends, to attain the emancipation of sudden enlightenment."

98. The "divide-and-conquer" approach to the different sensory faculties is unmistakably reminiscent of the *Five Skillful Means*.

99. Compare Nakamura, 142: "you attain emancipation and the form samādhi is sufficient."

100. Nakamura, 146n17, indicates that the Stein mss. include *xin*, "mind," at a total of seven equivalent locations, in contrast to the Beijing and Pelliot mss.

but attain autonomy within dharmas, so that within dharmas you attain completely to the samādhi of emancipated dharmas.

When all your sensory faculties discriminate well in this fashion, this is the fundamental wisdom. When you do not activate [the mind] in consequence of this discrimination, this is the fundamental concentration.

The sūtra says, "Without discarding the Dharmas of the Path, one still manifests the affairs of an ordinary person: [this is sitting in repose]."[101] [To perform] the myriad activities and worldly [affairs] without generating thoughts about those affairs: this is the combined cultivation of concentration and wisdom, which cannot be separated. Concentration does not differ from wisdom, and wisdom does not differ from concentration, just as a lamp and its light cannot be separated. When we consider the lamp, it is [seen to be] the essence of the light; when we consider the light, it is [seen to be] the function of the lamp.[102] [Thus] when we consider the light, it does not differ from the lamp; when we consider the lamp, it does not differ from the light. When we consider the light, it is not separate from the lamp; when we consider the lamp, it is not separate from the light. When we consider the light, it is the lamp; when we consider the lamp, it is the light.[103] Concentration and wisdom are the same.[104] When we consider concentration, it is the essence of wisdom; when we consider wisdom, it is the function of concentration. When we consider wisdom, it does not differ from concentration; when we consider concentration, it does not differ from wisdom. When we consider wisdom, it is concentration; when we consider concentration, it is wisdom. When we consider wisdom, there is no wisdom; when we consider concentration, there is no concentration. This constitutes the combined cultivation of concentration and wisdom, which cannot be separated.

The last two lines are based on Vimalakīrti's silent "true entrance into the Dharma gate of nonduality."[105]

---

101. See the *Vimalakīrti Sūtra,* T 475: 14.539c22. Yanagida (1989: 156–157) translates and comments on this passage. The term "combined cultivation of concentration and wisdom" (*dinghui shuangxiu* 定慧雙修) occurs twice below in this paragraph.

102. On use of *jia* 家, "house," as equivalent to the connective *zhi* 之, see Ishii, "Shintai kan'yo bunken."

103. See the *Platform Sūtra,* T 2008: 48.338b27.

104. See the *Miscellaneous Dialogues,* sections 32 and 42–44; the *Platform Sūtra,* T 2008: 48.338b8; and Huiyuan's preface to the *Damoduoluo Chan jing,* T 2145: 55.65b27–30.

105. See the *Vimalakīrti Sūtra,* T 475: 14.551c23–24. The *Vimalakīrti* has *zhenru* 真入, "true entry," where Shenhui tends to use *zhiru* 直入, "direct entry." Suzuki edited the mss. at this point to read *zhiru*, a precedent that Hu and Nakamura have followed, the former explicitly because of Shenhui's emphasis on suddenness. However, at this point in the text (as also noted in Yang, 11, line 5), the manuscripts actually have *ruzhen* 入真 (Hu's *Dingben*) or *ruzhi* 入直 (Beijing). Tōdai goroku kenkyūhan, 42, notes these complications and suggests there is no reason to amend the original from "true" to "direct," especially since the preceding material does not discuss sudden enlightenment.

6

I will explain[106] for you the meaning of "the afflictions are *bodhi*"[107] using space as a metaphor. Space is fundamentally without motion and stillness (i.e., movement), so that when light comes [into space] it is a bright emptiness;[108] when darkness comes it is a dark emptiness. A dark emptiness does not differ from a light one; a bright emptiness does not differ from a dark one.[109] Light and darkness come and go in space of themselves, but space is fundamentally without movement. The meaning of the afflictions and of *bodhi* is the same. Although ignorance and enlightenment differ, the nature of *bodhi* fundamentally never changes.

The sūtra says, "Just as you contemplate the true characteristic of [your own] body, so should you contemplate the Buddha."[110] To know that the mind is non-abiding is contemplation.[111] The mind of all the buddhas of the past is identical to the non-abiding mind of you friends today, with no difference. The sūtra says, "When I contemplate the Tathāgata, he does not come from the past, does not go into the future, and does not abide in the present."[112]

"Those who seek the Dharma should not be attached to the Buddha in their seeking; they should not be attached to the Dharma in their seeking; they should not be attached to the Saṅgha in their seeking."[113] Why? Because there is a Buddha-nature within the mind of each and every sentient being.[114] Friends, to activate the mind to seek outside yourself is called false seeking.

The *Wisdom Sūtra of the Heavenly King Pravara* says, "[The Buddha said,] 'Great King, this is the real.' 'World-honored One, what is the real?' 'Great King, the unchanging [is the real].' 'World-honored One, what is the un-

---

106. The term used is *liaojian* 聊簡, which has occurred above in section 3.

107. Liebenthal, 149n76; cf. *Platform Sūtra*, 340a15. Shinohara, 23n1, cites a comparable passage in the *Two Entrances and Four Practices* material, and a passage on *yanzuo* 宴坐 from the *Vimalakīrti Sūtra* and a passage from the *Daji jing* 大集經.

108. The term used here is simply *kong* 空, presumably a contraction of *xukong* 虛空, often "space" or "sky," an ambivalence that is exploited throughout the passage.

109. The text actually has "Darkness is empty and does not differ from light; light is empty and does not differ from darkness." Nakamura, 143, favors the translation given, no doubt on the basis of the original citation, which I have not yet found; Nakamura has the interpretation in quotation marks.

110. See the *Vimalakīrti Sūtra*, T 475: 14.554c29–555a1. Hu, 126, explains that this is Tathāgata Chan. This line and the one to follow are cited in the *Miscellaneous Dialogues*, section 2.

111. This is an example of "contemplative analysis," resulting in the redefinition of *guan* 觀, "contemplation." Here Tōdai goroku kenkyūhan, 42, corrects a minor editing error in Yang, 11, line 9.

112. This is from the *Vimalakīrti Sūtra*, T 475: 14.555a1–2. Literally, the Buddha is "without abiding" (*wuzhu* 無住).

113. See the *Vimalakīrti Sūtra*, T 475: 14.546a11–12.

114. See the *Nirvāṇa Sūtra*, T 374: 12.405b9 and passim.

changing?' 'Great King, it is called suchness.' 'World-honored One, what is suchness?' 'Great King, it can be known by wisdom but cannot be explained with words.... It transcends characteristics and is without characteristics. It far transcends thought and passes beyond the realm of understanding.'"[115] It is thus that the bodhisattva comprehends the profound *dharmadhātu*, and this is identical to the knowing and seeing of a buddha.

Friends, there is a Buddha-nature within your body which you have not been able to see completely.[116] Why? It is as if each and every one of you imagined a house, with clothing, furniture, and all the various things in it, so [strongly] that you knew they all existed without any doubt. This is called knowing (*zhi* 知) but not seeing.[117] If you were to go into this house equipped with all the things I've just mentioned, then this would be called seeing, not knowing. What you understand now is entirely based on someone else's explanations, [so that] you know there is a Buddha-nature within your body. But you have not been able to comprehensively see it.

Just to not intentionalize, and for the mind to be without activation: this is true non-thought. Ultimately, [non-thought][118] is not separate from knowing, and knowing is not separate from seeing. All sentient beings are fundamentally without characteristics. What I now call characteristics are all [aspects of] the false mind. If the mind is without characteristics, it is the mind of a buddha. If you intentionally make your mind not activate, this is the concentration of consciousness. It is also called the concentration of mistaken views of the Dharma.[119] [On the contrary, the true] self-nature of the mind is concentration.

---

115. See T 231: 8.693c; cf. 694a9, 13, and 20.

116. Here again, we find the Buddha-nature construct, with a very concrete, specific emphasis on seeing. Also, in what follows, note the implicit contemplative analysis of *zhijian* 知見 by separating it into "knowing" and "seeing," a reflection of the Northern school practice of dividing binomials for explication; see "Shenhui and the Teaching of Sudden Enlightenment," n. 81 above.

117. In the sentence that follows this I have followed the editorial corrections in Tōdai goroku kenkyūhan, 42, relative to Yang, 12, lines 6–7.

118. The phrase "to not intentionalize" renders *bu zuoyi* 不作意. On the definition of *wunian* 無念, "non-thought," see the *Platform Sūtra* for comparison, T 2007: 48.338 c5–21; 340a23–26. Liebenthal, 136–137, defines *wuzhu* 無住 as "freedom from attachment," *bu zuoyi* as "living without a purpose," *wunian* as "freedom from illusion," and *jian* 見 as "vision," in opposition to *zhi* 知, "knowledge." These renderings are now out of date. After "Ultimately," Hu, 246, added the character *jian* 見, "seeing," in brackets as the subject of the sentence; this addition is followed in Yang, 12, line 9. Tōdai goroku kenkyūhan, 42, argues that the subject is actually non-thought. This is a difficult choice. Elsewhere the *Platform Sermon* has "non-abiding mind does not transcend knowing, and knowing does not transcend non-abiding," and although this is a parallel form, grammatically the first element is more similar to non-thought than to seeing. My editorial choice here is based on the principle that one should change the original text as little as possible, and although Hu's emendation makes sense, it is unnecessary.

119. Here Tōdai goroku kenkyūhan, 42, corrects a minor punctuation error in Yang, 12, line 10.

Aśvaghoṣa says [in the *Awakening of Faith*], "For a sentient being to contemplate non-thought is thus the wisdom of a buddha."[120] The perfection of wisdom that I have just explained [allows one to] suddenly enter the teaching of the absolute from the teaching of saṃsāra. [Such a sentient being] does not have any interest in illuminating in front and illuminating behind, or in looking afar and looking near—you will leap over all the [levels of spiritual progress] up to the seventh stage of the bodhisattva [when you understand the following]: just point at the buddha mind; the mind is buddha.[121]

7

The sūtra says, "One should teach according to the Dharma."[122] When one explains *bodhi* orally, one's mind should be non-abiding.[123] When one explains nirvāṇa[124] orally, one's mind should be serene. When one explains emancipation orally, one's mind should be without fetters.[125]

---

120. See the *Awakening of Faith*, T 1666: 32.576b26–27 (cf. the very different Śikṣānanda translation at T 1666: 32.585a22–23); this line occurs in the *Awakening of Faith* as an anonymous scriptural citation. Tōdai goroku kenkyūhan, 43, corrects an editing error in Yang, 12, line 10; also see Hu, 247, in which *gu* 故, normally "therefore" but used here only as an emphatic, is separated from its original inclusion in the *Awakening of Faith* passage. Note Shenhui's crucial omission of the characters *neng* 能, "able to," and *xiang* 向, "approach"; the original line reads: "For a sentient being to be able to contemplate non-thought is to approach the wisdom of a buddha."

121. Nakamura's later translation of this passage ("Dango," 109) is somewhat different. As noted by Yanagida, "Goroku," 402, this use of *ji xin shi fo* 即心是佛, "the mind is buddha," seems to be the earliest in all Chan literature. And the immediately preceding line, *wei zhi foxin* 唯指佛心, "just point at the buddha mind," is without question directed by Shenhui at his congregation, one of his basic stances being the affirmation that his audience of ordinary sentient beings possessed the Buddha-nature. (In the brief dialogue at the beginning of section 7, Shenhui refers back to his role in the original dialogue using the word *zhi* 指, "point.") Nanyang Huizhong was later to criticize unnamed Chan teachers of the South—presumably Shenhui—for holding such non-Buddhist ideas. Yanagida, "Goroku," 502, notes the relationship between the Confucian concept of *daotong* 道統 and Mazu's concept of the ordinary mind being buddha.

122. See the *Vimalakīrti Sūtra*, T 475: 14.540a4. See Nakamura's later translation ("Dango," 109), which refers to the "Dharma taught by the Tathāgata."

123. To be "without abiding" is *wu zhusuo* 無住所. See the comments about *xinkou* 心口 in n. 34 above.

124. Tōdai goroku kenkyūhan, 43, corrects a transcription error in Yang, 12, lines 12 and 16, and 13, line 15, in which the abbreviation for *niepan*, 卅卅, was mistaken for the abbreviation for *pusa*, which has only two vertical strokes in each character.

125. Note that this material should be included as support of his argument about the importance of oral instruction and dialogue in Shenhui's teachings. Yanagida, "Goroku," 402, notes that Shenhui's final comment is an implicit criticism of Northern school teachings, which discuss emancipation and fetters; Shenhui is suggesting that their ideas may be acceptable, but one has to behave according to those ideas while explaining them.

[Question:] A moment ago,[126] I pointed to your non-abiding mind. Do you understand?

Answer: We understand.[127]

The *Nirvāṇa Sūtra* says, "This[128] is the cardinal meaning of emptiness."[129] If the three locations [that is, interior, exterior, and intermediate] are all empty, then the fundamental essence is empty and serene. If there were only the Middle Path, it would not be in the middle—the meaning of the Middle Path can only be posited on the basis of the extremes.[130] It is like three fingers, all alike—you can only posit a middle finger on the basis of the two outer ones [lit., the "two extremes"]. If there were no outer ones, there would also be no middle finger. The sūtra says, "Space is without middle and extremes, and the bodies of the buddhas are likewise."[131] The emancipated *dharmakāyas* of the buddhas are like space in having no middle and no extremes.

Friends, you must always understand as follows. I am now imparting[132] the unsurpassed Dharma of enlightenment to you, and citing the scriptures as proof [of my interpretation].[133] If you understand what I say, the six perfections, merits as numerous as the sands of the Ganges, and the eighty-four thousand teachings of samādhi of the buddhas[134] will all be

---

126. I have rendered *xianglai* 向來, "previously," as "a moment ago" in order to fit the sense rather than the specific wording. Yanagida, "Goroku," 402–403, translates from here to "ten stages of faith of the Mahāyāna" below.

127. This seems to be a brief reprise of the dialogue in section 4 above.

128. That is, the Buddha-nature.

129. See the *Nirvāṇa Sūtra*, T 374: 14.523b12 and 524b8. Prior to this quotation, Stein 6977 (2) has "'non-abiding mind, do you know it?' 'The *Vimalakīrti Sūtra* says, "The mind does not reside within, does not reside without, and does not reside in the middle." Does [the mind] have any locus?' 'No.'" See T 475: 14.541b19–20. From the *Nirvāṇa Sūtra* quotation onward, Stein 6977 (2) contains a few character variants and several lacunae, which I will not note here.

130. Nakamura, 146n30, adds the character *yi* 義, "meaning," implying that it occurs in P2045 and the Beijing ms.

131. This is from the *Rulai zhuangyan zhihui guangming ru yiqie fo jingkie jing* 如來莊嚴智慧光明入一切佛境界經, T 357: 12.248a1. The same citation also occurs in the *Masters and Disciples of the Laṅkāvatāra*. See Yanagida, *Shoki no Zenshi 1*, 287, in the section devoted to Hongren. Yanagida, "Goroku," 402, points out that this and the other citations used just above and below were already known to his listeners from Northern school writings, which Shenhui used to support his own interpretations.

132. The Chinese used here is *fenfu* 分付, which has the nuance of "giving a piece" to each of the audience.

133. Here Hu, 248, has *yin jing* 引經 as characters occurring in both manuscripts, which he suggests are incorrectly interpolated. Although omitted from Nakamura, 144, Yanagida chooses to follow the original. Stein 6977 (2) has *yin jing zheng* 引經證, which makes the issue involved explicit. Incidentally, for "Dharma of enlightenment" most of the texts have *daofa* 道法, but Stein 6977 (2) has *putifa* 菩提法.

134. Stein 6977 (2) has the two characters *gongde* 功德 before the reference to the buddhas, a reading I have followed here.

simultaneously anointed into your bodies and minds.[135] The *Vimalakīrti Sūtra* says, "*Bodhi* cannot be attained with the body, and it cannot be attained with the mind. Extinction is *bodhi,* because of the extinction of the characteristics."[136] It "cannot be attained with the body," because the mind does not reside outside [the body]. It "cannot be attained with the mind," because the body does not reside within [the mind].[137] "Extinction is *bodhi,*" because there is no intermediate location. "Because of the extinction of characteristics" is because all the false thoughts are not generated. "The illuminating essence stands alone, divine and without location." Friends, you should function like this!

Those of superior ability and superior wisdom are able to understand as soon as they hear an explanation of the perfection of wisdom, and will practice as it has been explained. Those of intermediate abilities, although not understanding at first, are able to understand if they sincerely[138] inquire into it. Those of lower abilities can only achieve faith from which they will not regress, so that in a future [lifetime] they will be able to enter the ten stages of faith of the Mahāyāna.[139]

---

135. The usage *guanru* 灌入, "anoint/enter," is unique, but it is very significant that Shenhui is invoking the imagery of the initiation ceremony and its rite of baptism by water. Also, note that Shenhui immediately undercuts the apparently esoteric imagery and references to body and mind with apophatic language from the *Vimalakīrti.*

136. See the *Vimalakīrti Sūtra,* T 475: 14.542b22–24. The division of the topic into body and mind, internal and external, is very much like the *Five Skillful Means.* Here the tripartite division of the *Vimalakīrti Sūtra* passage into internal, external, and intermediate, resembles nothing so much as the *Five Skillful Means'* formulae on the benefit of self, others, and both.

137. Compare the discussions in the *Treatise on Perfect Illumination* (McRae, *Northern School,* 152 and 165) on the mind not knowing its own location and not being inside the body because it is unaware of the activities of the five organs. In Stein 6977 (2) the preceding quotation from the *Vimalakīrti* is presented in fractured form, and the following explanation (down to the end of the paragraph) reads as follows: "It 'cannot be attained with the mind,' because one does not concentrate the mind [lacuna of two characters] within the memory. 'Extinction is *bodhi,*' because there is no intermediate location. 'Because of the extinction of characteristics' is because all the false thoughts are not generated. In the past [Śā]kya[muni]'s prediction of enlightenment for the bodhisattvas was [based on] this doctrine. The sūtra says, 'Transcendence is *bodhi,* because of the transcendence of the false thoughts. Non-contemplation is *bodhi,* because it is without recollection.' Friends, it would be good for you to function like this." The scripture cited here is the *Vimalakīrti,* with the first assertion being accurate (T 475: 14.542b25–26). The second assertion is incorrect; the *Vimalakīrti* actually states (542b24), "Non-contemplation is *bodhi,* because it transcends the conditions." It is very unusual for Shenhui to be citing such a positive reference to *li* 離, given his criticism of Northern school members for their espousal of *linian* 離念, "transcending the mind."

138. Here Hu, 249, has *quan* 勸, "exhort"; and Yang, line 7, has *qin* 勤, "make effort." *Tōdai goroku kenkyūhan,* 43, points out that the correct character is *qin* 懃. (Suzuki, in *Zenshū,* 3:314, has the correct character.)

139. Instead of the ten stages of faith, Stein 6977 (2) states that those of lower abilities would be able to enter the "position of sagehood" (*shengwei* 聖位). This fragment skips the next paragraph, and the 60 or so characters from the paragraph after that onward contain numerous lacunae.

However, if trainees[140] reject the false and grasp the pure, this is a tainted purity and not the original purity.[141] The *Flower Garland Sūtra* says, "It is like a dirty cleaning rag. First one applies soap, then one washes it with clean water. Although it becomes clean, this is not called clean. Why? This purity was attained on the basis of the dirt, so it is still impure."[142] The *Vimalakīrti Sūtra* says, "The practice of nondefilement, the practice of nonpurity: this is the practice of a bodhisattva."[143]

Friends, if you are not careful[144] and the false [mind] becomes activated, so that your thoughts [stray] far and near, you should not [make the mind] come back into concentration. Why? To make the mind go out is illness, and to make it come back into concentration is also illness. Both making it go out and making it come back are illness. The sūtra says, "The dharmas are without coming and going."[145] "The dharma-nature pervades all locations,"[146] so that the dharmas are without going and coming. If one becomes aware of a false [thought] as soon as it arises, then it will disappear with that awareness [of it], and that is precisely [what is meant by] the non-abiding mind of one's original nature.[147]

With being and nonbeing both eliminated and the sensory realm and wisdom both destroyed, just[148] do not intentionalize and that is the self-existent enlightenment. If there is the slightest bit of mind, [*bodhi*] will not be able to function.[149] The fundamental essence empty and serene, without a single thing to be attained: this is called the unsurpassable *bodhi*. The *Vimalakīrti Sūtra* says, "On the basis of the non-abiding foundation are es-

---

140. This is *xuedao* or, in the Beijing ms., *xuedao ren* 學道人. See Tōdai goroku kenkyūhan, 43.

141. The term here is *benzijing* 本自淨.

142. Shinohara, 30n1, indicates this is drawn from the *Xianshou pusa pin* 賢首菩薩. Tōdai goroku kenkyūhan, 43, points out that Yang, line 9, unnecessarily adds the character *hou* 後.

143. See the *Vimalakīrti Sūtra*, T 475: 14.545b29–c1. Nakamura, 144, has "Neither the defiled practice nor the pure practice…"

144. Here *yongxin* 用心 merely means "[to make] mental effort"; elsewhere by extension it refers to "mental cultivation." Nakamura, 146n33, points out that Shenhui uses this term in both positive and negative fashions, unlike *qixin* 起心 and *zuoyi* 作意, "activate the mind" and "intentionalize," which are always negative.

145. The closest match is from the Buddhabhadra translation of the *Flower Garland Sūtra* (T 278: 9.584c9), which has "going and coming" rather than "coming and going."

146. This line evokes a statement that occurs twice in the Śikṣānanda translation of the *Flower Garland Sūtra* (T 279: 10.156c15 and c19). Shenhui, or a source that he used, seems to be reading the two translations against each other. Tōdai goroku kenkyūhan, 43–44, notes that this verse phrase is quoted in the *Zongjing lu* (T 2016: 48.483c8–9 and 928b26).

147. The Chinese is *jue* 覺. Nakamura, 146n35, identifies *jue* 覺 here with cognition (Skt. *vicāra*), a usage identical to that in the Oxhead school's *Treatise on the Transcendence of Cognition*.

148. Tōdai goroku kenkyūhan, 44, observes that at this location the Beijing ms. has *ju* 俱, "together with," which Suzuki (*Zenshū*, 3:314) has correctly emended to *dan* 但, "only." See Yang, 13, line 14, which omits this variant.

149. Nakamura, 144, has "Do not use even the slightest bit of [false] mind."

tablished all the dharmas."[150] The refulgence of nirvāṇa and the refulgence of the precepts are also likewise.[151] The self-natures are empty and serene and without the characteristics of form.

> Although *bodhicitta* and the ultimate [realization] are no different,
> Of the two [states of] mind, it is the first which is [more] difficult.
> With oneself still unsaved, to first save others—
> Thus do we reverence the initial [achievement of] *bodhicitta*.
>
> By this initial *bodhicitta* one becomes a teacher of humans and gods,
> Superior to the *śrāvakas* and *pratyekabuddhas*.
> With such a *bodhicitta*, one transcends the triple realm,
> Hence this is called the most unsurpassable.[152]

When other masters are asked about this teaching, they do not explain but keep it secret. I am completely different—whether to many persons or few, I always explain it to everyone. If you receive the teachings of Chan from some teacher, you should [strive to] understand by yourself what you are taught, so that you penetrate its spirit.[153] If you penetrate its spirit, there will be no doctrine in all the sūtras and *śāstras* that you do not understand.[154] Even when the Buddha was alive, sentient beings of superior, intermediate, and inferior [abilities] followed him and left home [to become monks]. The teachings of the buddhas of the past have all been directed at the eightfold congregation; there has been no private teaching, no secret teaching. It is like the sun at noontime—there is nowhere that is not illuminated[155]—or like the dragon king causing rain, which falls equally without distinction,

---

150. See the *Vimalakīrti Sūtra*, T 475: 14.547c22.

151. Nakamura, 146n36, points out that the Beijing ms. has *niepan guang* 涅槃光 while the Pelliot ms. has *pusa guang* 菩薩光 or "refulgence of the bodhisattvas." The Pelliot ms. abbreviation (essentially, two grass radicals) for *pusa* (bodhisattva) may also be used on occasion for *niepan* (nirvāṇa).

152. This is the last verse in the Bodhisattva Kāśyapa chapter of the *Nirvāṇa Sūtra*, T 374: 12.590a21–24. The verse also occurs in *Definition of the Truth*, section 52, and the same idea is mentioned in the *Miscellaneous Dialogues*, section 1, as well as in the bodhisattva precept texts of Huisi 慧思 (X 59.352b15) and Zhanran 湛然 (X 59.356b7–8). Yanagida, "Goroku," 391, also notes an occurrence in the *Putixin lun* 菩提心論 attributed to Nāgārjuna and translated by Amoghavajra, T 1665: 32.573c4–7. Since this passage also includes the lines "Adoration to Cunda!" (573b29) that Shenhui quotes from the *Nirvāṇa Sūtra*, Yanagida makes the very cogent observation that, in part, Shenhui and Amoghavajra shared the same religious background. The term "triple realm" refers to the worlds of desire, form, and formlessness.

153. Using *tongxin* 通心.

154. This sentiment is implicit in Shenxiu's status as the "verifier of the Chan meaning" of the sūtras and explicit in the description of Huineng in the *Platform Sūtra*. The seed of the idea may be found in the *Essentials of Cultivating the Mind*'s assertion that *shouxin* 守心 is the fundamental teaching of the entire Buddhist canon.

155. See the *Da zhidu lun* 大智度論, T 1509: 25.197c6–7.

so that all the plants receive nourishment according to their kind.[156] The buddhas' teaching is also like this: they have all taught in the spirit of universal sameness,[157] not with the mind of discrimination,[158] and the sentient beings of superior, intermediate, and inferior [capabilities] have all understood. The sūtra says, "The Buddha teaches the Dharma with one sound, and sentient beings understand according to their kind."[159]

Friends, if you wish to study the perfection of wisdom, you should read widely in the Mahāyāna scriptures.[160] But those who teach Chan without admitting of sudden enlightenment and [teach] that enlightenment is only possible through the use of skillful means—this is the [mistaken] view of the very lowest category [of sentient being]. [Just as] a bright mirror can be used to reflect one's face, the Mahāyāna sūtras can be used to rectify the mind. The primary [issue] is not to doubt, and to rely on the words of the Buddha. You should purify your three types of action—only after doing so will you be able to enter the Mahāyāna. This sudden teaching depends entirely on the teaching of the Tathāgata, and your practice [of it] must not be mistaken. Strive diligently. If there are any with doubts, come ask me about them.

Go well.

---

156. It is worth noting how this passage closely resembles a passage in the *Lotus Sūtra* (T 9.19a18ff.) and, even closer, a passage in the *Platform Sūtra* (T 2008: 48.340b2–4). The latter is specifically in reference to the teachings of the *Diamond Sūtra*.—Ed.

157. Using *pingdeng xin* 平等心.

158. Using *wu fenbie xin* 無分別心.

159. See the *Vimalakīrti Sūtra*, T 475: 14.538a2.

160. Liebenthal, 149n87, notes "This seems not to fit with the acknowledged hostility of Chan Buddhism to book reading." He is no doubt thinking of Shenhui's own comment in section 3.

Definition of the Truth

Putidamo nanzong ding shifei lun

菩提達摩南宗定是非論

TREATISE ON THE DEFINITION OF THE TRUTH REGARDING
THE SOUTHERN SCHOOL OF BODHIDHARMA, IN ONE FASCICLE,
WITH PREFACE

Compiled by Dugu Pei[1]

1 [Preface]

From beneath Reverend [Shen]hui's Dharma-seat I witnessed his discussions with Dharma Master Chongyuan, then compiled [a written record of the events] in one fascicle.[2] The texts of the eighteenth, nineteenth, and twentieth years of Kaiyuan[3] were not uniform, with the compilations incomplete and the discussions different. At present I have taken the text of the twentieth year[4] as the basis [of this edition]. Afterwards, there is a Trans-

---

This work is based on public sermons (actually dramatically staged debates) that Shenhui gave in 730, 731, and 732, although the text was edited sometime during 744–749 and was further augmented either at the very end of Shenhui's life or after his death. It is an overtly polemical text containing Shenhui's attack on the so-called Northern school, with somewhat limited doctrinal sophistication.

    1. Dugu Pei 獨孤沛 (d.u.), the editor of the *Definition of the Truth*, otherwise unidentifiable. Based on the surname, he was from a northern family and was perhaps related to the Dugu Ji 獨孤及 of Henan, who in 772 wrote an epitaph for Sengcan as part of a Northern school promotional campaign. Yanagida, "Goroku," 367–377, suggests that Dugu Pei and Liu Cheng, the author of the preface to one version of the *Miscellaneous Dialogues*, were from northern families.

    2. The Chinese used in this preface for "to compile, record," is *xiu* 修. The implication of the *bian xiu* 便修 that occurs here is that Dugu Pei recorded his accounts of the debates immediately after they occurred. Yang, *Chuanhua lu*, 22n2, points out that Hu Shih's edition (*Yiji*, 260) inadvertently omitted the characters *yi juan* 一卷, "one fascicle."

    3. 730, 731, and 732, respectively.

    4. That is, 732. Hu, 260, notes that the original manuscript (i.e., P2045) has "text of the twenty-first year" rather than "single text of the twentieth year," as does the second portion of the text (i.e., P3047). He thus prefers to have this reference conform to the immediately preceding reference to public debates in 730, 731, and 732, but not 733. Also, note that here Dugu Pei uses *zai* 載 rather than *nian* 年 for "year," reflecting a practice that began in the first month of 744 under Emperor Xuanzong, as Hu, 370, points out. Although this evidence is relatively weak, it is probably the case that the preface was written after this date.

mission of the Genealogy of Masters and Students, which is also in popular circulation.⁵

Take refuge in the ocean of the Three Jewels:⁶
The dharma-nature storehouse of suchness!
The true body and the response bodies,
How great the compassion by which they save the world!⁷

Proficiency in the doctrine and proficiency in preaching⁸
Are like the moon located in the empty sky.

---

5. The Chinese title is *Shizi xuemo zhuan* 師資血脈傳. This is one of the alternate titles of the *Records of the Transmission*, which also include *Tradition of the Definition of the Truth That Demolishes the Heterodox and Reveals the Correct and Destroys All [States of] Mind* (*Ding shifei cuixie xianzheng pohuai yiqie xin zhuan* 定是非摧邪顯正破壞一切心傳) and *Teaching of Sudden Enlightenment in the Supreme Vehicle* (*Zuishang sheng dunwu famen* 最上乘頓悟法門). These titles clearly indicate that the *Records of the Transmission* was intended to inherit and supersede the legacy of Shenhui. (See T 2075: 51.179a; Yanagida, *Shoki no zenshi 2*, 37; Adamek, *Mystique*, 463–464n4; and below for the use of the third title to refer to the latter portion of the *Definition of the Truth* itself.) For the preface of the *Definition of the Truth* to refer to the *Records of the Transmission*, however, would imply a very late compilation of the former text, so here the reference is generally considered to be to the biographies of the six generations of patriarchs appended to the *Miscellaneous Dialogues*. Tanaka and Okimoto (*Daijō Butten*, 418) note that the *Shizi xuemo zhuan* does not now exist in an independently circulated form. For an abbreviated statement of the genealogy, see section 16 below. Yanagida, "Goroku," 378, includes a Japanese translation (or, rather, *yomi-kudashi* rendering) of this section of Dugu Pei's preface.

6. Yang, 22n3, points out that Hu, 260, misread the original's *hai* 海, "ocean," as *fa* 法, "Dharma."

7. Tanaka and Okimoto, *Daijō Butten*, 418, point out that the last three lines of this quatrain refer to the Three Jewels in succession: Dharma, Buddha, and Saṅgha. (The order is nonstandard.) Their interpretation of *zang* 藏, the last character in the second line, as "to store" (the dharma-nature and suchness), is unacceptable under ordinary rules of Chinese grammar.

8. Presumably, these terms are veiled references to the pointless theoretical skill of Northern school masters. The text actually has *zongtong li zongtong* 宗通立宗通, "proficiency in the doctrine establishes proficiency in the doctrine." Since this makes little sense either conceptually or grammatically, Tanaka and Okimoto, 205, read an implicit *zongtong ji shuotong* 宗通及說通, "proficiency in the doctrine and proficiency in preaching." (The same emendation is suggested independently by Yang, 22n3.) Their emendation is based on the occurrence of a discussion of the two terms in the *Miscellaneous Dialogues* (see Hu, 147, and the line *shuotong ji xintong* 宗通及心通, "proficiency in preaching and proficiency in the mind," in the Dunhuang version of the *Platform Sūtra* (Yampolsky, *Platform Sutra*, 159; *Enō kenkyū*, 327). The term *zongtong*, "proficiency (literally, 'penetration') in teaching," used in the first line, derives from the *Laṅkāvatāra Sūtra*; its companion term *shuotong*, "proficiency in preaching," refers to the oral expression of that fundamental teaching. (The association between the Northern school and the *Laṅkāvatāra Sūtra* would not have been lost on Shenhui.) As *Bukkyōgo daijiten* (646b) notes, in Chan literature the first often refers to self-benefit, while the latter is for the benefit of others. For the occurrence of the term in the *Annals of the Transmission* and other references, see McRae, *Northern School*, 256, 304n14, and 347n5.

Transmit only the Dharma of the sudden teaching,
Appearing in the world to destroy the heterodox teachings![9]

2

Question: What are the reasons for compiling this treatise? [HS261]

Answer: I have heard that "when the mind is generated the various dharmas are generated, and when the mind is extinguished the various dharmas are extinguished."[10] Everything depends on oneself, and delusion regarding the self[11] makes one an ordinary [unenlightened] person. The ancient sages all [realized that] defilements are the result of discord,[12] but the sentient beings of this world chase after [their pitiful] clods of dirt, cultivating the birthless but residing [ever more firmly in] saṃsāra![13] Students are deluded as to the method [of spiritual training], desiring motionlessness but [merely] fluttering about! The banners of true and false compete in only... differing from or equivalence to the complete truth.[14]

---

9. Yanagida, "Goroku," 378 and 612–613n345, points out that such "refuge verses" are a standard feature of Mahāyāna scriptures that was adopted by early Chan texts such as the *Annals of the Transmission*, *Masters and Disciples of the Laṅkāvatāra*, and *Essential Teaching of Sudden Enlightenment*. He suggests a specific relationship between those texts both here and in the *Awakening of Faith*, and points out that this genre was continued in later recorded-sayings texts.

10. This pair of observations occurs (with a trivial difference) in Bodhiruci's translation of the *Laṅkāvatāra Sūtra* (*Ru lengqie jing* 入楞伽經, T 671: 16.568c12), and again (with another trivial variation) in the *Awakening of Faith* (T 1666: 32.577b22–23), as noted by Yanagida ("Goroku," 379). Shenhui's was the first Chan text to cite this line, but the use of the *Awakening of Faith* is of course a continuation of and reaction against the Northern school's emphasis on this text. This line occurs (in the same form it appears here) in the *Records of the Transmission*, T 2075: 51.189c14–15, 193b14–15, and 194b23–24.

11. The Chinese reads *wangji* 妄己, "to do the self falsely." In his translation of this section of the preface, Yanagida, "Goroku," 378–379, reads *wang* 忘 as "to forget."

12. Tanaka and Okimoto, 205, place this phrase, *ran bian zhengguo* 染便諍果, in quotation marks as if it were a commonly known saying. I have been unable to find it elsewhere, however.

13. Tanaka and Okimoto, 206, add the second character of *shengmie* 生滅, "generation and extinction," or *saṃsāra*.

14. There are about four characters missing from the middle of this sentence, which is therefore unclear. The manuscript itself is very good, although the photos I have consulted (at occasional points only) are bad; the first character of the lacuna seems to me to be *wei* 維, "only." Tanaka and Okimoto, 206, omit the 13 characters (including lacuna) after "flutter about" as undecipherable. "Complete truth" renders *liaoyi* 了議, a term usually applied to sūtras based on the Skt. *nītārtha*.

3

Our Reverend Shenhui of Xiangyang[15] is enlightened to the forbearance of the birthlessness of all dharmas,[16] has attained unhindered wisdom, and preaches the Dharma of the Supreme Vehicle. He leads the various sentient beings [on to enlightenment] and teaches sentient beings [the Buddhist doctrine].[17] Those who have changed their direction in life through his teachings are like the hundred rivers proceeding to the ocean.[18]

On the fifteenth day of the first month of the twentieth year of Kaiyuan (732),[19] an unrestricted great assembly[20] was held at the Dayun si in Huatai. [Shenhui] ascended the greatly decorated lion's seat and preached to students of the Path[21] from all over China.

[Shenhui preached:] The Brāhman monk[22] Bodhidharma of the Liang dynasty was the third son of the king of a country in southern India, who left home while young [to become a monk]. His wisdom was extremely profound, and he attained Tathāgata Chan within the various

---

15. It is intriguing that Shenhui is identified in this fashion rather than with Nanyang. The following passage, ending with the transmission from Bodhidharma to Huineng, is translated by Yanagida, *Shoki Zenshū shisho*, 103–104.

16. The achievement of *wushengfa ren* 無生法忍, Skt. *anutpattika-dharma-kṣānti*, "forbearance of the birthlessness of the dharmas," is considered one of the most important achievements of the bodhisattva; see *Bukkyōgo daijiten*, 1331a–b.

17. According to Yang, 22nn5–6, the Chinese text here is in question, although the meaning is not.

18. This is an unconventional reading for *huixiang* 迴向, often used to translate the Skt. *pariṇāma*, following Yanagida, *Shoki Zenshū shisho*, 104. The sentence could also be read (as Tanaka and Okimoto, 206, do): "The transference [of merit] through his teaching is like the hundred rivers proceeding to the ocean."

19. Hu, *Yiji*, 261, notes that both mss. (i.e., P2045 and P3047) have "twenty-second year," but that he has corrected the date given. See *Yiji*, 365–370 (summarized in Yang, 22–23n7), for his explanation of the evidence involved.

20. The Chinese is *wuzhe da hui* 無遮大會, sometimes given in other sources as *sibu wuzhe da hui* 四部無遮大會, "unrestricted great assembly for the fourfold [Saṅgha]."

21. Throughout this translation I render *dao* 道 as "Path" in deference to its use for the Skt. *mārga* and to allow the reader to distinguish the usage here from the Daoist usage. Often in Chinese Buddhist texts this character will refer to the consummation of the spiritual path, i.e., enlightenment.

22. The text has *sengxue* 僧學, "monk-scholar." This is an unusual compound, at least in this order (the usual form would be *xueseng*), and Bodhidharma is not generally referred to as a scholar monk. (See the roughly analogous term *shiseng* 師僧, "teacher monk," which appears below.) In what is a very reasonable emendation, Yanagida, "Goroku," 379, reads *xue* as *zi* 字, "was styled" (i.e., "named"). Instead of "Brāhman monk," Tanaka and Okimoto, 206, identify Bodhidharma as an "Indian monk," implying the recognition that the caste label was applied indiscriminately in China. Compare this brief biographical statement with the slightly more detailed version at the end of the *Miscellaneous Dialogues*, section 50.

samādhis.[23] Eventually, motivated by this Dharma,[24] he traveled far across the waves to meet Emperor Wu of the Liang. Emperor Wu asked the Dharma master,[25] "I have constructed monasteries and saved people,[26] constructed images and copied sūtras. How much merit is there in this?" Bodhidharma[27] replied, "[These actions are] without merit." [HS262] Emperor Wu, who was of ordinary [unenlightened] intelligence,[28] did not comprehend these words of Bodhidharma's and sent him away.[29]

---

23. Based on an occurrence in the *Laṅkāvatāra Sūtra,* the term "Tathāgata Chan" became an important slogan for Chan, emphasized by Zongmi in particular. See the *Chan Preface* (Kamata, *Zengen shosenshū tojo,* 23), where "pure Tathāgata Chan" (*rulai qingjing Chan* 如來清淨禪) is one of several terms used to identify Bodhidharma's Chan and distinguish it from previous meditation teachings. Kamata (n. 25) suggests that the term was coined in order to indicate a type of Chan that exceeded the bodhisattvas' Mahāyāna Chan; Tathāgata Chan was for buddhas. I find it intriguing that Bodhidharma is supposed to have discovered this in various Mahāyāna samādhis, but this may be an indication of the transitional nature of Shenhui's preaching, which in the balance of the *Definition of the Truth* strives to replace the Northern school emphasis on the *Laṅkāvatāra* with the use of the *Diamond* (which was also used by the Northern school, of course, but to a lesser degree; see Yanagida, "Goroku no rekishi," 380–381). However, as Yanagida, *Shoki Zenshū shisho,* 214, points out, it was Shenhui who identified the Chan of Bodhidharma with the Tathāgata Chan of the *Laṅkāvatāra Sūtra*—not any of the Northern school texts. In the *Records of the Transmission,* T 2075: 51.185b15–16, the terms "pure Chan" and "Tathāgata Chan" are differentiated, with Shenhui destroying the former and establishing the latter; see Yanagida, *Shoki no Zenshi 2,* 154 and 159. Yanagida, 160, mentions another occurrence of the term "Tathāgata Chan" in the *Baizhang guang lu* 百丈廣錄, based on a line from the *Vajrasamādhi Sūtra* that is quoted five times in the *Records of the Transmission.* Kamata also points out the occurrence of the term in a sermon attributed to Mazu in the *Transmission of the Lamp* 28, T 2076: 51.440b15–16: "You possess it fundamentally and you possess it now; it doesn't depend on cultivating the Path and sitting in meditation. Neither cultivating nor sitting, this is pure Tathāgata Chan." See the discussion of this and related matters in the *Miscellaneous Dialogues,* section 6, where Shenhui discusses notions of the inherent possession and temporal realization of the Buddha-nature.

24. The text has *cheng si fa* 乘斯法, which literally means "make a vehicle of this Dharma" or "ride this Dharma."

25. Although it seems unnatural to refer to Bodhidharma as a *fashi* 法師, "Dharma master," this is how he is introduced in the very first two characters of Tanlin's preface to the *Two Entrances and Four Practices;* see Yanagida, *Daruma no goroku,* 25, and Broughton, *Bodhidharma Anthology,* 68–74.

26. In this context the term *duren* 度人, "to save people," or, more fully, "to help people cross over to the other shore of nirvāṇa," may refer to the ordination of monks. However, as spoken by Huike with reference to Bodhidharma, just below, it refers to spiritual salvation.

27. Here and below, Bodhidharma is referred to simply as Dharma. I have used the longer form for convenience and clarity.

28. *Bukkyōgo daijiten,* 1268d, gives no early citations for *fanqing* 凡情, which he glosses as "the mental disposition of an ordinary [unenlightened] person." See, however, the use of the term in the *Essential Teaching of Sudden Enlightenment*'s definition of "insentient": "What I now refer to as 'insentient' (*wuqing* 無情) is the absence of ordinary intelligence, not the absence of sagely intelligence (*shengqing* 聖情). Question: What is ordinary intelligence, and what is sagely intelligence? Answer: If one activates the two natures, this is ordinary intelligence. [When one realizes that] the two natures are empty, then this is sagely intelligence." See X 63.20c13–15; Hirano, *Tongo yōmon,* 54.

29. Yanagida, "Goroku," 380, suggests a development from this dialogue to that between

[Bodhidharma then] went to the Wei dynasty, where he met Huike.[30] Huike was forty at the time,[31] of the lay surname Ji, and from Wulao.[32] Eventually he followed Bodhidharma[33] to Shaolin si on Mount Song, where Bodhidharma preached the inconceivable[34] Dharma and Huike remained standing outside the hall.[35] That night snow fell, reaching Huike's hips, but he stood still and did not move. Bodhidharma said to Huike, "Why are you standing there?" With anguished tears, Huike replied, "Your Reverence has come from the west to this distant [land] to preach the Dharma in order to save people. Without fear for myself, I earnestly seek the excellent Dharma. I only ask Your Reverence for your great compassion and empathy!" Bodhidharma said to Huike, "I have never seen anyone seeking the Dharma like this."

Then Huike took out a knife and cut off his own left arm, placing it before Bodhidharma.[36] [HS263] Seeing this, Bodhidharma [said], "You are

---

Huineng and the prefect Wei Qu 韋璩 in the *Platform Sūtra;* see Yampolsky, *Platform Sutra,* 155–156. He also suggests that the criticism of Emperor Wu was intended by Shenhui as a criticism of the Northern school. This legendary encounter is repeated in many sources, probably the earliest of which is the *Records of the Transmission;* see T 2075: 51.180c18–23; Kamata, *Zengen shosenshū tojo,* 68; and Adamek, *Mystique,* 144 ff., 311–312.

30. As Yang, 23n8, observes, Dunhuang mss. generally use the form *hui* 惠 instead of its modern homophone 慧. The latter is the character used in the *Continued Biographies* and elsewhere.

31. Hu, 262, has a long note pointing out that the text here actually has "thirty" rather than "forty." However, the *Continued Biographies* biography of Huike describes him as forty, as does the other text of the *Definition of the Truth,* the *Records of the Transmission,* and the biography at the end of the Ishii version of the *Miscellaneous Dialogues,* which was published only after the first edition of *Yiji;* see Yang, 18.

32. This is Hulao 虎牢, later called Chenggao 成皋, in the northwestern part of Rongyang 榮陽, Henan, given as Wulao 武牢 because of a Tang taboo.

33. In contrast to previous mentions where his name is abbreviated, here Bodhidharma is referred to with the complete form of his name. Perhaps this indicates a source for the information concerning Huike different from that involving Emperor Wu. However, immediately below, the short form Dharma is used once again, as well as throughout the remainder of the anecdote (and this segment of what presumably was first a lecture by Shenhui).

34. The term used is *bu siyi fa* 不思議法, the third character of which was added to the text by Hu Shih.

35. It is not specified whether this was the Buddha Hall or Lecture Hall. More significantly, note that the scene is not the cave of many later stories and illustrations.

36. The first source in which this version of the story occurs is the *Annals of the Transmission* of the Northern school, a text that Shenhui vigorously attacks later in the *Definition of the Truth.* The *Annals of the Transmission* account is very brief, but includes a note contradicting the validity of the *Continued Biographies* account of Huike's losing his arm to bandits or rebels; see Yanagida 1971: 355; McRae, *Northern School,* 259; and T 2060: 50.552b22ff. Incidentally, although these contextual clues are by no means infallible, the placement of the *Continued Biographies* account implies that Huike lost his arm to bandits well after Bodhidharma had already entered nirvāṇa.

capable."[37] Although his name previously had been Shenguang,[38] he was called Huike afterwards, because of this. His deep faith was firm and strong, and he was prepared to destroy his body or discard his life in his quest for the excellent Dharma, just as the acolyte Snowy Mountain[39] [was willing to] give up his life to hear half a verse [of the teachings].

Bodhidharma then revealed the knowing and seeing of the buddhas, which [Huike] secretly matched.[40] He also transmitted a robe to Huike as the Dharma proof.[41] Huike subsequently transmitted it to Sengcan,[42] Sengcan

---

37. The character is *ke* 可. This, of course, is a pun on the second character of Huike's name, or rather Shenhui's explanation of how Huike received that name.

38. The character *zi* 字, "style" or "name," is represented in the text by the modern homophone 自 meaning "self." Hu's emendation follows the Ishii ms. of "Shenhui's Recorded Sayings" (*Shenhui yulu*); see "Shenhui and the Teaching of Sudden Enlightenment," n. 26.

39. This was the name given to the future Buddha Śākyamuni in one of his former lives. According to the "Sagely Practice" chapter of the *Nirvāṇa Sūtra*, when the future Buddha was practicing in solitude deep in the mountains, he was unaware of the Mahāyāna scriptures, so Indra transformed himself into a *rakṣa* and appeared before the bodhisattva, uttering the couplet "All conditioned processes are impermanent, these are the dharmas of generation and extinction." Upon hearing that the *rakṣa* was starving and could only eat warm human flesh, the future Buddha had him utter the concluding couplet before casting his own body from a cliff for the demon to eat. "When generation and extinction have been extinguished, tranquility is bliss," the couplet ran. Of course, having accomplished his mission of alerting the future Buddha to the existence of the Mahāyāna truths, the demon transformed himself back into Indra and caught the future Buddha's body before it hit the ground; see T 374: 12.450a12–451b5 (the two couplets are at 450a16 and 451a1) and *Mochizuki*, 3:2934c–2935b. Both *Mochizuki* and *Bukkyōgo daijiten*, 828d, refrain from offering a reconstruction of the bodhisattva's name.

40. The point is that Bodhidharma revealed to Huike the way that a buddha's mind functions and induced him to bring his own mental activity into accord, achieving enlightenment. The term for "knowing and seeing" is *zhijian* 知見; see the *Platform Sermon*, n. 82. "Secretly match" renders *mi qi* 密契, with the connotation that Huike's mind became identical to that of Bodhidharma and the buddhas, just as one half of a tally matches the other half.

41. The term used here is *faxin* 法信, in which the second character normally means "faith" but here must be taken as a symbol or verification of validity. The later editions of the *Platform Sūtra* refer to the robe as the "embodiment of reliance," *xinti* 信體, and as "emblematic reliance," *biaoxin* 表信. (This last compound is used in Dugu Pei's postface to the *Definition of the Truth*.) The robe in question is the monk's mantle, the *kaṣāya*. Originally, *kaṣāya* referred to the nondescript garb of hunters, and was adopted by the Buddhist clergy as a general term for robes made of patched-together rags of indistinct color. In East Asia the term came to be applied to the uppermost monastic garment or surplice, which was transformed into a colorful and often richly woven ceremonial shawl; "robe" is used here for simplicity. See *Bukkyōgo daijiten*, 298b–d and 455c–456a. Tanaka and Okimoto, 419, point out that the concept of the transmission of the robe is distantly based on Śākyamuni's bequest of a *samghati* (*sengqieli* 僧伽梨) to Kāśyapa. They cite the *Za ahan jing* 雜阿含經 (T 99: 2.303a29), the *Ayuwang jing* 阿育王經 (T 2043: 50.154a28–29), and the *Fu fazang yinyuan zhuan* 付法藏因緣傳 (T 2058: 50.301a14).

42. Rather than the standard form of *can* 璨, the text has 璨, which Hu points out is often the case in Tang dynasty writings. (See *Morohashi*, 7.964b, identifying this as a vernacular equivalent of 璨.)

DEFINITION OF THE TRUTH

transmitted it to Daoxin, Daoxin transmitted it to Hongren, and Hongren transmitted it to Huineng. For six generations the robe was transmitted continuously, without interruption.

4

I have also witnessed Reverend Shenhui preach from the lion's seat:[43] "There is no one else in China[44] who understands the teaching of Bodhidharma's Southern school.[45] If there were someone who knew, I would never preach about it. I preach today in order to discriminate the [HS264] true and the false for Chinese students of the Path and to define the teachings for Chinese students of the Path."[46]

To witness such inconceivable events made me gaze upon [Shenhui] with awe. When the ruler is inspired, good portents come from all over [his reign];[47] when the correct Dharma is propagated, people will recognize that which is fundamental. Therefore I have compiled this treatise.[48]

5 [Main Text]

At the time there was present in the Dharma assembly a Dharma master named Chongyuan from that monastery whose fame had already spread to

---

43. The following is presumably from another sermon by Shenhui, probably from one of the occasions in the early 730s, but it occurs nowhere within the present texts of the *Definition of the Truth* and *Miscellaneous Dialogues*.

44. Literally, "under heaven."

45. The Chinese here is *Putidamo nanzong yimen* 菩提達摩南宗一門. I have discussed precedents for the term "Southern school" in McRae, *Northern School*, 63, 94, and 292n153A. Also, see the occurrence of the term "one-vehicle teaching of South India" (*nan Tianzhu yisheng zong* 南天竺一乘宗) in the entry for Fazhong in the *Continued Biographies*, T 2060: 50.666b5, and McRae, *Northern School*, 25. Yanagida, *Shoki Zenshū shisho*, 596, uses the term "Southern school" to refer to the *Laṅkāvatāra Sūtra* teaching of Guṇabhadra and Bodhidharma (which has a three-fold terminus in Shenxiu, Lao'an, and Xuanze), with a specific statement that it was based on the school's origins in southern India (Yanagida 1985: 378).

46. This is one of the passages from which the title of Shenhui's text is derived. "True and false" here is *shifei* 是非, which in my translation of the title is reduced to "truth" (just as *daxiao* 大小, literally "large and small," means "size"). "Teachings" here is *zongzhi* 宗旨, which refers to the central doctrines in a profound sense. Hu has edited this passage somewhat, following precedents in this and the second *Yiji* text, since it is garbled in the original.

47. Although this eight-character phrase is cited as though it might be a common saying, I have not located it elsewhere. Literally, it reads, "When the ruler [or emperor and feudal lords] have a stimulus, portents come from the separate points [of the realm]." The Chinese is *junwang you gan, yiduan lai xiang* 君王有感，異端來祥.

48. Tanaka and Okimoto, 208, add Dugu Pei's name here. This is the end of Hu Shi's section 1.

the two capitals and beyond the seas.⁴⁹ His words were like a bubbling spring, and his questions truly exhausted the origin [of things]. He was a worthy counterpart to the earlier [Ārya]deva.⁵⁰ His contemporaries called him Yuan of Shandong—and how could this be in error?⁵¹

On this day Dharma Master Chongyuan entered the assembly, raised his eyebrows, and lifted his voice in total dedication to victory in battle [over Shenhui].⁵² Then the attendants rolled up the screen, calling to the officials [HS265] present that they would serve them.⁵³ His Reverence said, "This

---

49. The Chinese is *haiwai zhiwen* 海外知聞, which might be read, "who was knowledgeable regarding things from beyond the seas." However, see the similar descriptions of Chongyuan in section 7 and Puji in section 27. Chongyuan's religious identity remains a mystery. He is only mentioned on one other occasion in Chinese sources, as one of the interrogators of a nun named Benjing 本淨 (667–761) sometime during the Tianbao period, and probably between 745 and 752. (My tentative dating of this incident is based on Shenhui's entry into Luoyang, although perhaps irrelevant, and the date of the stele celebrating Benjing's activities.) In the *Song Biographies,* Benjing is described as a student of Huineng's who resided at Sikong shan on Mount Nanyue 南嶽司空山; see T 2061: 50.758c18. In this case Chongyuan is identified as Reverend Yuan of Taiping si in Luoyang 太平寺遠法師; the temple in question, in the Chanhe Huizu district of Luoyang, is only mentioned one other time, in the *Song Biographies,* T 2061: 50.736a08, which speaks of its holdings of money, oil, and wheat—like Heze si, not a very illustrious monastic establishment, perhaps more known for commercial activities than anything else. We know nothing else about Chongyuan's religious identity or understanding of Buddhism and so are left with the impression that his career was defined by the role he played in the *Definition of the Truth.*

50. This is the general sense of the sentence, which literally reads: "After Deva, presumably [he] was one [of the successors]." Āryadeva was a famous Mādhyamika philosopher of about the middle of the third century, most widely known as the author of the *Bai lun* 百論, Skt. *Śata(ka)śāstra*. Along with two treatises by Nāgārjuna, this is one of the three basic texts of the Chinese Sanlun school; see *Mochizuki,* 4:3351b–3352a, and Ruegg 1981: 50–54. Known also as Kāṇadeva, "One-eye Deva," because, before his introduction to Buddhism, he had torn out one eye to replace an eye that he had removed from an image of the god Maheśvara (*Dazizai* 大自在), he is recognized as the fifteenth Indian patriarch in the Chan genealogy given in the *Baolin zhuan* 寶林傳 and later works. His initiation into Buddhism came upon meeting Nāgārjuna, who tested Deva by placing a begging bowl filled with water in front of him. Deva threw a needle into it in such a way that it did not spill, indicating the complete equivalence of the two men's levels of understanding. This legendary event is supposed to have happened in 6 BCE, after which Deva traveled through India establishing the teaching of emptiness and defeating heretics. It is perhaps significant that Deva is recognized as a Brāhman of southern India, like Bodhidharma; see *Zengaku daijiten,* 1:168b, citing the *Baolin zhuan* 寶林傳, *Anthology of the Patriarchal Hall,* and the *Transmission of the Lamp;* see also Young, *Indian Buddhist Patriarchs in China,* 265–282.

51. Although this sounds like a double entendre, the second meaning being "Shandong is far off," there may be a good reason why Shenhui would have picked a monk from this region as his adversary.

52. The Chinese is *yiyu zhansheng* 一欲戰勝, "completely wanting battle victory." This description of a monk prepared for Dharma combat is so exceptional as to suggest Chongyuan's identity as a stooge or patsy for Shenhui's propaganda. By the end of the treatise, of course, Chongyuan has completely acquiesced to the superiority of Shenhui's teachings.

53. Hu (*Yiji,* 265) notes that in his first edition of the text he was unable to read this passage, and that Gernet (*Entretiens,* 111–112) listed it as an erratum and amended it according to an inspection of the actual manuscript. (See *Yiji,* 162, where he uses five empty squares

screen is not the usual sort used at the gates of [people's] homes. Why is this place [of enlightenment] being destroyed only to allow officials in?"[54] Dharma Master Chongyuan then took Shenhui's hand and rebuked His Reverence by saying, "Do you[55] call this an ornament or not?" His Reverence replied, "It is." Dharma Master Chongyuan said, "The Tathāgata has preached that ornaments are not ornaments."[56]

6

His Reverence said, "What the sūtra preaches is, 'Do not exhaust the conditioned and do not abide in the unconditioned.' "[57]

The Dharma master asked once again, "What does it mean to 'not exhaust the conditioned and not abide in the unconditioned'?"

His Reverence replied, "To 'not exhaust the conditioned' means that from

---

to indicate missing characters.) Hu adopts Gernet's reading of the text, which includes a question mark after *ji shi* 即是, "then," and a missing character before *juan* 卷, "rolls up," but comments that he still finds the passage none too easy to understand. Yang, 19, reports that both microfilm copies he inspected were unclear and that he has thus followed the Gernet/Hu emendation, even though he finds it difficult to understand, with the addition of one character (*jiang* 將) as indicated by him in 23n9. The notion of screens that roll up seems to be part of the problem, and although the specific actions taken are unclear the point is presumably to describe the obsequious attentions paid to official guests in Chinese Buddhist meetings.

54. Tanaka and Okimoto, 209, interpret the first part of Shenhui's statement as "This screen is not the property of the monastery!" Note that the character *men* 門, "gate," is present in the earlier edition of the *Yiji* (1966), whereas in the 1968 edition (p. 163) it is circled in red with a heading annotation "J.G." (for Jacques Gernet), but omitted here. (It's missing in Yang's transcription as well.) I am interpreting *chang* 場, "place," as a contraction of *daochang* 道場, *bodhimaṇḍa*. The Chinese for "officials" in both occurrences is *guanke* 官客, literally, "guests who are officials."

55. It is interesting that Dugu Pei refers to Shenhui as *heshang* 和上, "Reverend" or "His Reverence," but Chongyuan refers to him here as *Chanshi* 禪師, "Chan master." The implication is presumably that both are of roughly equal stature, so Chongyuan would not pay undue respect to Shenhui.

56. This is a paraphrase of the *Diamond Sūtra*, T 235: 8.749c19–20 and 751b10–11. Tanaka and Okimoto, 420, point out that D. T. Suzuki took this passage as the quintessence of this scripture's unique logic of identity/nonidentity. This entire little incident is not very clear: Shenhui seems to be appalled at the favoritism shown the official guests, which might well be correlated with his iconoclastic story about Emperor Wu's donations being of no religious merit. There seems to be an editorial attempt to portray Chongyuan's response as a clumsy attempt at the logic of nonduality, with the following exchange on exhausting the conditioned dharmas, etc. (section 6), being Shenhui's winning rejoinder. Although the logical relationship between the two sections is not immediately clear, the beginning of section 7 is enough to show this is all one interconnected script. One problematic point is, why should Chongyuan hold Shenhui's hand in making his rebuke? The Chinese has *ti heshang shou* 提和上手, and I wonder if the middle two characters should be excised to leave "Chongyuan held up his hand [and pointed at the screen]"? However, the verb *ti* means to hold something hanging down from the hand. See the *Miscellaneous Dialogues*, section 1, for a different representation of this exchange between Shenhui and Chongyuan.

57. This is from the *Vimalakīrti Sūtra*, T 475: 14.554b6.

the first generation of *bodhicitta* up to achieving perfect enlightenment seated under the bodhi tree[58] and entering nirvāṇa between the two *sāla* trees, [HS266] one never discards any dharma.[59] This is to 'not exhaust the conditioned.' To 'not abide in the unconditioned' is to study emptiness without taking emptiness as one's realization, to study non-action[60] without taking non-action as one's realization. This is to 'not abide in the unconditioned.'"

7

The Dharma master was silent then, waiting for a while before speaking. He said, "Lust and anger are the Path, which is not in ornamentation."[61] His Reverence said, "Then ordinary people must have attained the Path." Dharma Master Chongyuan said, "Why do you suggest that ordinary people have attained the Path?" His Reverence said, "You have said that lust and anger are the [Path], and since ordinary people are those who practice lust and anger, why would they not have attained the Path?"

Dharma Master Chongyuan asked, "Do you understand or not?" His Reverence answered, "I understand." The Dharma master said, "Understanding is non-understanding." His Reverence said, "The *Lotus Sūtra* says, 'From the time of my attainment of buddhahood, I have passed through immeasurable and unlimited *asaṃkhyeya* eons.'[62] Indeed, [the Buddha] did not attain buddhahood. And indeed, he did not pass through immeasurable and unlimited *asaṃkhyeya* eons."[63]

---

58. The term here is *zhengdeng jue* 正等覺, "correct and equivalent enlightenment," Skt. *samyak-saṃbodhi;* see *Bukkyōgo daijiten,* 702d.

59. This is, of course, a quick précis of the Buddha's life. However, I believe Shenhui uses this as an ideal model of religious experience for all true Buddhists to follow. See the same passage in the *Miscellaneous Dialogues,* section 60.

60. The term used here is *wuzuo* 無作, "nondoing." The term "unconditioned" is the famous *wuwei* 無為, used here in a common Buddhist technical sense.

61. This too is presumably a scriptural citation, but the source is unknown. Also unclear is why only the first two of the three poisons are mentioned. The *Vimalakīrti Sūtra* does contain the following line, which parallels at least the first part of Chongyuan's statement: "For those who are without the self-aggrandizement [of Hīnayānists], the nature of lust, anger, and delusion are emancipation" (T 475: 14.548a17–18).

62. See the "Lifespan of the Tathāgata" chapter, T 262: 9.42b12, b25, and c19.

63. Hu, 266, and Yang, 20, take these two sentences as questions, while Tanaka and Okimoto, 210, interpret them as declarative statements. I have taken the latter interpretation; otherwise, there is no way to explain Chongyuan's response. The Chinese phrase rendered here as "indeed" is *ying shi* 應是, lit. "should be this." It is remotely possible that the pattern *ying shi… ying shi* might be used to pose a question involving two alternatives, one of which would be presumed to be correct, but that is not the case here. Shenhui's statements constitute a radical extension of the *Lotus Sūtra* doctrine of skillful means: at T 262: 9.42c, the Buddha points out that his life story is but a teaching device to entice foolish sentient beings onward to greater spiritual awareness, and at 42c23 the Buddha says he actually never enters nirvāṇa. The *Lotus Sūtra* never states that the Buddha's enlightenment was also a pious fiction, but the position is at least arguable.

Dharma Master Chongyuan said, "This is the preaching of Māra."[64] His Reverence said, "Monks and laypeople, listen all! This is Dharma Master Chongyuan, who is recognized[65] by everyone from Chang'an and Luoyang to the [farthest] corners of the oceans [HS267] for his brilliance in doctrinal exposition. He is one who has lectured on the sūtras and treatises of the Mahāyāna without error. On this day he is saying that the *Lotus Sūtra* is the preaching of Māra! What, I wonder, is the preaching of the Buddha?"

At this point the Dharma master realized that his error was egregious, and he appeared dazed before the assembly. After a little while he tried to speak again, but His Reverence said, "You've been pinned to the ground. Why do you need to get up again?"[66]

8

His Reverence said to the Dharma master, "My holding this unrestricted great assembly and ornamenting this place of enlightenment today has not been for [the accumulation of] merit, but in order to define the principle [of Chan] for the students of the Path in China and to distinguish the true and the false for the students of the Path in China."[67]

His Reverence said, "If I were studying under [the Dharma master, I would recognize his teachings] as the Dharma master's as soon as I examined the case.[68] If the Dharma master studied under me, he would pass through three great *asaṃkhyeya* eons without being able to achieve [buddhahood]." [HS268]

---

64. Since Shenhui's position is too radical for him, and presumably because he realizes it is not found explicitly within the *Lotus*, Chongyuan denigrates Shenhui's position. Shenhui's response, like that of any combative debater, is to distort his opponent's position just enough to make it seem illegitimate.

65. It is possible that *xu* 許, "permitted," hence "recognized," actually occurs in its meaning as "location," hence "all locations." However, the preceding character *jie* 皆, "all," is usually adverbial. In addition, later on Shenhui uses this term to indicate that Shenxiu, Puji, and others should not be permitted to represent Chan.

66. Literally, "your backbone is touching the ground," using a wrestling analogy. Certainly the sense of combat—and Shenhui's victory—is very strong in this exchange.

67. This is one of the lines underlying the title of the treatise. Note that in section 4, the same injunctions regarding students of the Path are given in reverse order. For "principle," the text has *zhi* 旨, which Hu, *Yiji*, 267, amends to *zongzhi* 宗旨, no doubt based on section 4. This statement is paraphrased in the postface in section 55.

68. The phrases "activities of ordinary people" and "indicate my error" represent four characters that are very much unclear in the original manuscript. Hu, 267–268, has a long note pointing out he originally read these as the two characters *lan ji* 濫機, the meaning of which is obscure, followed by two blanks. Gernet subsequently amended the two blanks to *gao bu* 告不, literally, "inform not." Hu felt that the result was quite incomprehensible and probably derived from some Tang colloquialism, now unrecoverable. Yang, 21 and 23n10, has emended the text to *lan ji'an [qing]* 覽机案[頃], which I have followed here. The usage *ji'an*, "case," refers to a judge's legal document, as in the "precedent anthologies" of the Song dynasty.

9

When His Reverence said this, [the Dharma master] became thoroughly ashamed and afraid, looking at [Shenhui] with his face pale. Although the two bodhisattvas were questioning each other, they were both standing up and had not yet sat [down on the lecture seat and chair, respectively]. What was said was subtle and had not yet exhausted the feelings [between the two men]. At this point, as soon as Dharma Master Qianguang, one of the elder monks there,[69] saw that Dharma Master Chongyuan was defeated in this [opening] debate but was going to continue to resist, he had someone[70] set out chairs.[71] He then requested that they reopen the discussion and explicate their doctrines again, and at last he got His Reverence and Dharma Master Chongyuan to sit down. [HS269] His Reverence usually [spent his time in] meditation and did not contest with other beings, and even when asked to debate he demurred for quite some time.[72]

10

At that time the Dharma masters of Fuxian si and Heze si in this prefecture [i.e., Luoyang],[73] as well as several tens of Dharma masters from other loca-

---

69. The text describes him as one of the *shiseng* 師僧 or "teacher monks." He is no doubt the same individual as the Dharma master Qianguang of Weizhou 魏州乾光 who occurs in sections 27 and 31 of the *Miscellaneous Dialogues*.

70. The text has *shi ren* 是人, "this person(s)," which Gernet (*Entretiens*, 90n42) reads as a scribal error for the modern homophone 侍人, meaning "attendant person(s)." Hu cites two examples from the text to suggest that Tang colloquial usage would use *shi ren* as written to mean "persons" in general. Although his examples both involve the compound *suoshi* 所是, which would seem to be a bound colloquial form meaning "some" or "all," it seems best to avoid altering the text if at all possible. Yang, 21, also disagrees with Gernet's editorial intervention.

71. Since Chongyuan sits on a chair and Shenhui takes the lecture seat, this may mean chairs for all the monks present.

72. The term used for meditation is *qingchan* 清禪, "clear *dhyāna*." The text describes Shenhui in this fashion to heighten the drama of the debate, which is thus between a major Buddhist theoretician and a humble meditator who has to be forced to take part. Shenhui had supposedly come to lecture and was persuaded to debate only through Chongyuan's ardor and Qianguang's mediation. Although the total fiction of this entire characterization is transparent, the same posture of only teaching in response to questions also occurs in sections 15 and 30 of the *Miscellaneous Dialogues*. Later, this posture is carried forward in the Oxhead school's *Treatise on the Transcendence of Cognition;* see McRae, "Ox-head School," 213, where Professor Enlightenment tells his student Conditionality that he is only responding according to the questions put to him. Also, as Gernet notes in his translation of the *Miscellaneous Dialogues,* a similar pose is attributed to the fictitious master described in the *Mouzi liluo lun* 牟子理惑論; see Pelliot 1918: 303.

73. Is this evidence that the text was at least edited after Shenhui's move to Luoyang? In this line, Hu's edition (*Yiji,* 269) misses a couple of characters that are clearly in the origi-

tions, called to Shenhui to sit down. They all said, "You should sit. Today is just the day for you[74] to discriminate the false and the correct and to define the truth! Here are more than forty Dharma masters and treatise masters of great virtue to act as judges!"[75]

Being unable to refuse, His Reverence ascended the lecture seat. Just as "the bright mirror is not wearied by its multitudinous illumination, how could the clear stream [of his wisdom] be tired by the violence of the wind?"[76] Although the winner [of the debate] was already known, the assembly's request could not be denied. His Reverence was without doubt, and it was proper that he should be benevolent [and not refuse] on this day.[77]

11

Dharma Master Chongyuan asked once again, "In your cultivation of the three categories of wisdom, the ten stages of sagehood, and the four types of fruits, what stage have you reached now?"[78] His Reverence said, "I have completed the tenth stage [of the bodhisattva]." Dharma Master Chongyuan said, "Bodhisattvas of the first stage can [manifest] multiple bodies in a

---

nal; the correct reading is *dang* (?) *fu Fuxian si fashi Heze si fashi* 當府福先寺師荷澤寺法師. The character *dang* 當, "this," is obscure; Yang, 21, reads the character as *Luo* 洛, i.e., Luoyang. Although this does not seem to be the character actually used here—and Yang places it in brackets—this is certainly the meaning. Presumably this is an editorial slip by Liu Cheng working in Luoyang after 745. Grammatically, the characters *dangfu*, or even *luofu*, should the latter be correct, might or might not include both Heze si and Fuxian si.

74. The Dunhuang Museum ms. begins from the reference to Shenhui (as *Chanshi* 禪師, "Chan master").

75. Yang, 23n13, notes that *lunshi* 論師, "treatise master," does not occur in the Dunhuang Museum ms. Tanaka and Okimoto, 420n20, point out that *zhengyi* 證義 refers to the act or role of judge at a debate. Indeed, this definition is given in *Morohashi*, 10.584a.

76. The verb in the second clause here should be *dan* 憚, usually meaning "hesitate, be afraid," but here meaning "become tired," rather than *chan* 禪, "meditation," as Hu, 269, has it. Tanaka and Okimoto, 420n21, point out that this saying is found in the *Shishuo xinyu* 世說新語 2, 90; for the context (and a slightly different translation) see Mather, *Tales of the World*, 71.

77. Hu finds this sentence to be incomplete as it stands and adds the characters *burang* 不讓, "not refuse." Yang, 24, seems to reject this reading, but Tanaka and Okimoto, 420–421n22, point out that this four-character phrase is borrowed from the section on Wei ling gong in Confucius' *Analects* (15.36).

78. The Chinese for these categories are simply *san xian, shi sheng, si guo ren* 三賢十聖四果人, "three wise ones, ten sages, and persons of the four fruits." The first two categories refer to subsets of the fifty-two levels of the bodhisattva's progress: omitting the Ten Degrees of Faith, the "three wise ones" are the Ten Abodes, Ten Degrees of Action, and the Ten Degrees of Diversion, while the "ten sages" refers to the following Ten Stages. I am using the translations established in Hurvitz, *Life and Ideas*, 3 and 363–367. The four fruits are the stages of perfection in Nikāya doctrine, from *śrotāpanna* to arhat; see Tanaka and Okimoto, 421n23. The *Records of the Transmission* contains an edited abstract of Shenhui's dialogue with Chongyuan, beginning with this exchange; see Yanagida, *Shoki no Zenshi 2*, 154–156; and Adamek, *Mystique*, 340–341. P2045 begins with this phrase.

hundred buddha [HS270] realms, bodhisattvas of the second stage can [manifest] multiple bodies in a thousand buddha realms, and bodhisattvas of the tenth stage can [manifest] multiple bodies in immeasurable and infinite billions of buddha realms.[79] You say you've completed the tenth stage, so please manifest a divine transformation for us now." Chongyuan wanted him to do this with a very deep longing. In particular, since [Shenhui's] experience of enlightenment was mysterious in the extreme, his elaboration [of the teachings] was like an echo.[80] [HS276]

12

His Reverence said, "The *Great Parinirvāṇa Sūtra* says, 'When the Tathāgata was in the world, he only recognized Cunda's mind as identical to the mind of the Tathāgata. Although [Cunda's] mind comprehended the permanence of the Tathāgata, [the Buddha] did not recognize [Cunda's] body as identical to the Tathāgata's body.'[81] The sūtra says, 'Adoration to Cunda! Adoration to Cunda! Although his body is the body of an ordinary [unenlightened] person, his mind is the mind of the Tathāgata's!'[82] When the Tathāgata was in the world, he only recognized that the comprehension of Cunda's mind was like that of the Tathāgata—he did not speak of realization in the body. For my body to be that of an ordinary person in this period of the Final

---

79. The English "can [manifest] multiple bodies" renders what is in Chinese merely *fenshen* 分身, "divide the body."

80. Recall the *Treatise on the Transcendence of Cognition* of the Oxhead school. The text portrays Chongyuan's desire to see Shenhui's manifestation of supernormal powers as both extremely strong and based on a profoundly ignorant attachment. This is immediately contrasted to the profundity of Shenhui's enlightenment, which was *zhixuan* 至玄, "mysterious in the extreme." The mysterious realm, *xuan*, is that darkly numinous level of nonbeing that underlies all manifest reality. The character *ru* 如 in "like an echo" is the end of Hu's "fascicle one," P3047. At this point the text overlaps with the beginning of Hu's "fascicle two," P2045.

81. Brief lacunae in the Pelliot ms. made this sentence impossible for Hu, 276, to decipher; the Dunhuang Museum manuscript (Yang, 24) has filled in the blanks. Although this sentence is presented as a scriptural quotation, it does not occur in the sūtra in this form. Judging from the similar material below, it is better to read this as Shenhui's interpretation or, at best, loose paraphrase.

82. The line most similar to this occurs at T 374: 12.372b26: "Adoration to Cunda! Although you have received a human body, your mind is like the mind of the Buddha. You, now, Cunda, are truly a son of the Buddha, just like Rāhula and the others. Like Rāhula, not different." The material that follows is based on the Dunhuang Museum ms.; Hu, 276–278 (i.e., P2045) has substantial lacunae. The very end of Stein 6977 (2) includes an apocryphal scriptural quotation before disintegrating: "The *Nirvāṇa Sūtra* says, 'His body appeared the body of a human, but his mind was identical to the mind of the Buddha." Jingying Huiyuan 淨影慧遠 discusses this line from the *Nirvāṇa Sūtra* in his *Dasheng yizhang* 大乘義章 (T 1851: 44.814b10–14), but his point is to show that the Buddha only manifested nirvāṇa as a skillful means of teaching.

DEFINITION OF THE TRUTH   87

Dharma, and yet to have achieved the tenth stage—why should this be considered strange!"[83]

Dharma Master Chongyuan was quiet and did not speak.[84] [HS277]

13

His Reverence asked [Dharma Master] Chongyuan, "Have you seen the Buddha-nature?"[85]

Dharma Master Chongyuan answered, "I have not seen the Buddha-nature."

His Reverence said, "If you have not seen the Buddha-nature, then you shouldn't lecture on the *Great Parinirvāṇa Sūtra*."

Dharma Master Chongyuan said, "Why can't I lecture on the *Great Parinirvāṇa Sūtra*?"

His Reverence said, "The chapter on the Lion's Roar says, 'You should realize that anyone who is able to consider and explain the meaning of the *Great Parinirvāṇa Sūtra* has seen the Buddha-nature.' Since you have not seen the Buddha-nature, I say you should not lecture [on this scripture]."[86]

Dharma Master Chongyuan asked, "Have you seen the Buddha-nature?"

His Reverence answered, "I have seen it."

Dharma Master Chongyuan asked, "Did you see it inferentially, or did you see it directly?"

---

83. This reference to the decline of the Buddhadharma is unusual in Chan texts, although elsewhere Shenhui describes Northern school activities in such terms. Yang, 46n3, points out that 31 characters (from "When the Tathāgata was in the world" to this point) have been drawn from the Dunhuang Museum ms.

84. By comparing himself to Cunda, Shenhui was released from the obligation to manifest supernormal abilities. Of course, to manifest such abilities would have been contrary to the Vinaya, which Chongyuan and the other monks present must have known. Thus, in wanting so strongly to see such an irrelevant display, Chongyuan has been compromised.

85. The term used is *jian foxing* 見佛性. Yanagida, "Goroku," 385 and 613n351, repeats an observation that he has made before in that the phrase *jianxing chengfo* 見性成佛, "see the nature and achieve Buddhahood," is based on the words of Sengliang 僧亮 in the *Niepan jing jijie* 涅槃經集解 (T 1763: 37.490c26). Dialogues on seeing the Buddha-nature may be found in section 51 below (although the Buddha-nature is not explicitly mentioned) and in the *Miscellaneous Dialogues*, sections 13, 17, and 34, only the last of which specifically cites the *Nirvāṇa Sūtra* phrase in question. Section 51 of this text represents a continuation or variation of this dialogue on the *Nirvāṇa Sūtra;* obviously, the editor has used this dialogue both to open and close the debate. The following material, from Shenhui's question here down to Chongyuan's "Have you seen the Buddha-nature?" is based on Yang, 25–26. The lacunae here in P2045 total some 68 characters.

86. See T 374: 12.526a28–b1, which differs from Shenhui's citation in only minor ways.

His Reverence answered, "I saw it inferentially."[87] Then [the Dharma master] admonished, "What is comparison, and what is estimation?" His Reverence answered, "That which is called 'comparison' is comparison to Cunda. That which is called 'estimation' is equivalence to Cunda."

Dharma Master Chongyuan said, "Did you definitely see it?"[88] His Reverence answered, "I definitely saw it." Dharma Master Chongyuan asked, "In what fashion did you see it?" His Reverence answered, "In no [describable] fashion."

Dharma Master Chongyuan was silent and did not speak. His Reverence saw that the other was silent because he hadn't understood what was said, and was not going to ask anything more.[89]

14

His Reverence said, "Now listen, all you monks and laypeople! I want Chongyuan to ask me about 'seeing' once again. The spiritual training[90] I have been studying for more than thirty years is all contained in the single word 'seeing.' When Chongyuan asked me about seeing just now, it was not in accord with my meaning. And when I answered him that I have seen [the Buddha-nature], that also was not exhaustive.[91] I want Chongyuan to ask me about seeing again."[92]

Dharma Master Chongyuan said, "I also want to [HS278] ask you, [when you say you have] seen [the Buddha-nature], did you see with your eyes, did you see with your ears, did you see with your nose, did you see with your

---

87. The question posed to Shenhui is whether he saw the Buddha-nature using inference, *biliang* 比量 or *anumāna*, or direct sensory cognition, *xianliang* 現量, the standard translation for Skt. *pratyakṣa*. Along with knowledge gained through the authority of the Buddha, these constitute the three sources of knowledge in Buddhist epistemology; see *Bukkyōgo daijiten*, 1120b, 1.340a–b, and 1.492c–493a. In the question that follows Chongyuan breaks down the term for inference into its component characters *bi* and *liang*, "comparison" and "estimation." It seems an extraordinary admission that Shenhui did not see the Buddha-nature directly.

88. The wording is *dingjian* 定見, which could be interpreted as "see it in concentration." However, such an interpretation does not fit Shenhui's overall style of expression and does not occur in the following discussion.

89. Note that *shi* 識, "recognize," is used with the meaning "understand." Also, the character *zheng* at the end of this section occurs in the compound *zhengwen* 徵問, meaning "to question." The occurrence of this character here and in section 25 is evidence for its understanding in the title of the *Miscellaneous Dialogues*.

90. The term used is *gongfu* 功夫, literally, "effort."

91. The term is *jinqing* 盡情, "exhaust the feelings" or "exhaust one's intelligence" on a subject.

92. From here to where "Chongyuan closed his mouth and was silent" on the following page I have followed the text in Yang, 26. According to Yang, 46n7, Hu's text omits 116 characters here (Hu, 278–280, has roughly 70 characters interspersed with long lacunae). For some reason, Hu, 280, begins his third section in the middle of this long lacuna!

body, or did you see with your mind?" His Reverence answered, "Seeing is without any such categorization." Dharma Master Chongyuan said, "You must see in the same way that space does."[93]

His Reverence said, "You should not slander the Mahāyāna sūtras and *śāstras,* which preach that space is without seeing."[94] Dharma Master Chongyuan said, "How can space be without seeing?" His Reverence said, "Precisely[95] because space is without *prajñā,* one cannot say it sees." Dharma Master Chongyuan said, "If that's the case, do you have seeing or not?"[96] His Reverence said, "From the buddhas above to all sentient beings below, all alike have seeing."

Dharma Master Chongyuan said, "Why do they all have seeing?" His Reverence [HS280] said, "It is precisely because sentient beings have *prajñā* that one can refer to their seeing. Precisely because space is without *prajñā,* one cannot say that it sees." Dharma Master Chongyuan said, "*Prajñā* is without knowing, so how can you refer to seeing?"[97] His Reverence said, "*Prajñā* is without knowing, and there is nothing that it does not know. It is precisely because there is nothing it does not know that one can refer to its seeing."

Dharma Master Chongyuan closed his mouth and was silent.

15

His Reverence said, "Up to now Dharma masters have said that Chan masters are ignorant, but today a Chan master says that a Dharma master is

---

93. Literally, "You must have been identical with the seeing of space." This is a deliberate evocation of Northern school references to the unrestricted nature of space and the cultivation of a boundless form of *jian* 見, "seeing." The Northern school text known as the *Treatise on Perfect Illumination* includes some unique remarks on space, including the assertion that space is the essence of samādhi (see McRae, *Northern School,* 156, 210, and 218), while the *Five Skillful Means* contains descriptions of what appear to be exercises in which the practitioner emulates the expansiveness of space (176 and 229). Although one metaphorical identification of space and the mind occurs in the latter text (p. 185), I know of no explicit assertions within Northern school literature to the effect that space "sees" in some fashion. This is another instance in which Shenhui distorts his opponent's viewpoint.

94. It is curious that this term, *wujian* 無見, did not become a slogan like *wunian* 無念, "non-thought," or *wuxin* 無心, "no-mind."

95. This represents the character *zhi* 致, which seems to function here and in Shenhui's statements below as an indicator of emphasis.

96. Note the colloquialism, *yimo shi* 異沒時, "at such a time."

97. This entire dialogue is a commentary on the famous phrase just uttered by Chongyuan, *Banruo wu zhi* 般若無知, which is the title of an essay by Sengzhao 僧肇; see T 1858: 45.153a-54c. A rather dated translation is available in Liebenthal, *Treatises of Seng-chao,* 64–80. Jingjue's 淨覺 commentary on the *Heart Sūtra* (see Yanagida, *Shoki Zenshū shisho,* 596) also mentions this concept, as does Shenhui's *Verses on Sudden Enlightenment, the Birthless, and Prajñā.* Yanagida, "Goroku," 385–386, presents the following material (including the first three exchanges of the next section) in Japanese translation, without noting any section break.

ignorant."[98] Dharma Master Chongyuan asked, "Why do you say I'm ignorant?" His Reverence said, "Only to deplore that you do not [know][99] the equivalent study of meditation and wisdom."[100]

[Chongyuan] asked again, "What is your 'equivalent study of meditation and wisdom'?" His Reverence answered, "That which is called meditation is of an essence that cannot be attained. That which is called wisdom is the ability to see that unattainable essence. Peaceful and constantly serene, and having functions as numerous as the sands of the River Ganges [HS281]—therefore it is called the equivalent study of meditation and wisdom."[101]

16

Dharma Master Chongyuan said, "You talk about the central principles of Bodhidharma, but I wonder whether this Chan teaching has a lineal transmission, and what kind of explanation you've received."[102]

His Reverence answered, "From the past there has always been a lineal transmission."

Chongyuan asked again, "Since [the beginning of] the transmission,[103] through how many generations has it passed?" His Reverence answered, "It has now passed through six generations." Dharma Master Chongyuan said,

---

98. The term rendered as "ignorant" is *wu suo zhi* 無所知, literally, "devoid of knowing." Tanaka and Okimoto, 216, render this as "fool." In addition to referring to himself and Chongyuan, Shenhui is also making a general statement about the differing qualifications and achievements of scholars and practitioners. This may represent an astute observation, or perhaps just a thinly veiled insult.

99. The character *zhi* 知 is added by Hu, 280.

100. This term, *dinghui deng xue* 定慧等學, does not mean that one should undertake a balanced study of both meditation and wisdom but rather the awareness that these two form a polarity wherein one is the 'essence' and the other is the 'function,' which is to say they are different aspects of one another.

101. Yanagida, "Goroku," 614n353, suggests this dialogue evolved from that with Wang Wei included in section 42 of the *Miscellaneous Dialogues*.

102. The critical terms here are *zongzhi* 宗旨 for "central principles," *Chanmen* 禪門 for "Chan teaching," and *xiangchuan fuzhu* 相傳付囑 for "lineal transmission," literally "transmission and deputation." This is transparently a setup question. If Chongyuan were an independent scholar of the scriptures, he would hardly be asking right off about the transmission. He might have asked how Chan justifies its own existence, since it has no one central scripture, to which Shenhui could reply with information about the transmission. As it stands, the question assumes such a transmission would be required, betraying the Chan bias.

103. Hu, 281, points out that this passage was originally included with the first section of the text, through a mistaken placement of the page, and that he has moved it to its present location. He estimates that there are probably about 560 characters missing. Yang, 46n8, states that from "Since [the beginning of] the transmission" to "only one person was allowed as a successor" below, 96 characters have been added from the Dunhuang Museum ms. Comparing the Dunhuang Museum ms. with those characters still present in P2045, there does not seem to be any textual development or difference between the two.

"Please explain who these six generations of *worthies* are, and also the basis of the transmission."[104]

His Reverence answered, "There was a Brāhman monk of Shaolin si on Mount Song in the Latter Wei [dynasty], named Bodhidharma.[105] On Mount Song, this patriarch[106] Bodhidharma bestowed the robe[107] on Chan Master Huike. On Mount Huan, Chan Master Huike of the Northern Qi bestowed the robe on Chan Master Sengcan. On Mount Sikong, Sengcan of the Sui dynasty[108] bestowed the robe on Chan Master Daoxin. On Mount Shuangfeng, Chan Master Daoxin of the Tang dynasty bestowed the robe on Chan Master Hongren. On East Mountain, Chan Master Hongren of the Tang dynasty bestowed the robe on Chan Master Huineng. [Thus the transmission has] passed through six generations.

"Internally the matching of the Dharma [of enlightenment] was transmitted to seal the realized mind; externally the robe was transmitted to define the central principle.[109] In this transmission from the past, Bodhidharma's robe was given as a proof [of the validity of the transmission] in each and every case. The robe is now at Shaozhou [HS282] and is not to be given to anyone else.[110] [Any suggestion that some] other thing has been transmitted is a lie.[111] Furthermore, in these six generations from the past

---

104. The same question and answer occurs toward the end of the *Miscellaneous Dialogues* (see section 63ff.) There, however, the response is given in greater detail and seems to correspond to the "transmission of the genealogy of masters and students" referred to in Dugu Pei's preface; see section 1 above.

105. Literally, "with the *zi* 字 (style) Bodhidharma."

106. The term is *zushi* 祖師, which seems to be reserved for Bodhidharma and Huineng. When Shenhui refers to all six generations of patriarchs the usage is strictly in terms of generation, i.e., *liu dai shu* 六代數, "six generation count."

107. The term is *jiasha* 袈裟, Skt. *kaṣāya*.

108. The lacuna here in P2045 is about 17 characters in length.

109. The first clause of this translation may be overly mechanical, but it includes an important technical term. The term *qi* 契, "to match," as one half of a torn tally exactly matches the other half, is often used in the *Platform Sūtra* to describe the achievement of enlightenment. The word *yin* 印, "seal," is used in the sense of "certify." Considering this shared terminology, it is noteworthy that Shenhui then describes the robe (technically, the *kaṣāya* or stole) as "defining the central principle" of Chan, *ding zongzhi* 定宗旨. He goes on to describe the robe as a sign or "proof" (*xin* 信, usually meaning "faith").

110. Here and in the sentence just above the general word *yu* 與 is used for "give," rather than the more technical *fuzhu* 付囑, "bestowed upon." This is the earliest appearance of the notion that Huineng did not transmit the robe onward. Note that in this text Huineng's monastery is always referred to as being in Shaozhou, not Caoqi, which might be a subtle clue as to the relative dating of the text.

111. It is possible that Shenhui is referring to Bodhidharma's supposed transmission of the *Laṅkāvatāra Sūtra* to Huike. Takeuchi Kōdō, "Shinshutsu no Kataku Jinne tōmei," 136, notes that this denial of any object of transmission other than the robe contradicts the assertion that Bodhidharma transmitted the *Diamond Sūtra*, which Takeuchi argues was made only after Shenhui's death. For the *Diamond Sūtra* transmission and its possible dating, see the *Miscellaneous Dialogues*, section 64, n. 536.

only a single person was allowed in each generation, never two. Even if there were a thousand or ten thousand followers, only one person was allowed as a successor."[112]

Dharma Master Chongyuan asked, "Why is only one successor allowed in each generation?" His Reverence answered, "It is like a country that can only have a single king; it would be impossible for there to be two. It is like a single world that can only have a single *cakravartin* king; it would be impossible for there to be two *cakravartin* kings. And it is like a single world system that can only have a single buddha appear; it would be impossible for there to be two buddhas appearing in the world."[113]

17

Dharma Master Chongyuan asked, "Should everyone then refrain from teaching Chan and saving sentient beings?"[114] His Reverence answered, "It is truly inconceivable [to imagine that] everyone's refraining from teaching Chan and saving sentient beings would generate in sentient beings even a single thought of good.[115] In the past, when the Tathāgata Śākyamuni was in the world the various bodhisattvas and *śrāvakas* all taught the Dharma and saved sentient beings, but not a single person [other than Śākyamuni] dared call himself the Buddha."[116]

---

112. This is clearly Shenhui's attempt to establish Huineng's singular identity in the face of the wide popularity of early Chan and the large number of its adherents and teachers. Specifically, he may be referring to the *Annals of the Transmission*, which he attacks later, because it refers to some twenty-four persons in six generations. Ironically, the *Annals* also criticized the popularization of Chan and identified its own subjects as the only true teachers.

113. The term first used for "world" here is *si tianxia* 四天下, "four all-under-heavens," referring to the four continents of Buddhist cosmology. The term "world system" is *shijie* 世界. Note Puji's similar expression of aspiration to the rulership of the spiritual imperium. Clearly, if we are all buddhas by virtue of the immanence of the Buddha-nature, Shenhui is setting up Huineng as *primus inter pares*, as the single buddha or ruler of the spiritual realm. Why should he have done this? That is, why the plea for the exclusivity of Huineng's status, if not for factional reasons? His suggestion that Huineng had some special status no other Chinese monk possessed is really extraordinary when considered in this light.

114. The phrasing implies that many people are teaching Chan, but that Shenhui might disapprove of all of them. Once again, we may justifiably suspect a setup question. Otherwise, why ask only about Chan adherents?

115. Tanaka and Okimoto, 219, interpret this as two sentences, with Shenhui saying that no one should teach Chan, etc., since the inspiration of sentient beings to generate good thoughts is an inconceivable matter. It is true that *bu siyi* 不思議, "inconceivable," is usually used in a positive sense, but this interpretation makes little sense given the subsequent statement.

116. Shenhui thus claims that Huineng had the status and authority of the Buddha. Although similar to statements made about Puji after his death, the hubris of this arrogation is palpable. In this dialogue about ten characters not in P2045 have been restored from the Dunhuang Museum ms.; see Yang, 28 and 47n9.

Dharma Master Chongyuan asked, "You have said that the transmission from the past went to Chan Master Huineng, and that in a single generation there can only be a single person who establishes the central principle and opens the Chan master's gate to teach people.[117] What about the several hundred or more teaching Chan in the various prefectures of China today, each of whom establishes his own teaching hall[118] and confuses everyone with their teaching? From whom do they [HS283] descend?"[119]

His Reverence answered, "They descend from Chan Master Shenxiu.[120] Indeed, there were more than twenty who preached Chan and taught people without having the lineal transmission that would allow them to do so.[121] Descending from them, there are several hundred or more[122] who preach Chan these days and teach others with no sense of how people differ or the proper relations between teacher and student,[123] everyone competing for fame and gain without the true succession.[124] They disrupt the correct Dharma and delude students of the Path, and this is how it is during the extinction of Buddhism.[125] Chan Master Huineng did receive the unilinear transmission,[126] but among his ordained and lay followers, numbering several tens of thousands and more, there is not a single one who has dared open the gate of Chan [to teach].

---

117. The critical terms here are *zongzhi* 宗旨, "central principle," and *kai Chanshi men* 開禪師門, "opens the gate of the Chan masters to teach people." It is possible that "Chan master" should be left in the singular to represent Bodhidharma, but Chinese is not so specific about number.

118. Literally, establishing their own doors, i.e., to the teaching hall.

119. Yang, 47n10, states that 28 characters are missing from the preceding dialogue. Hu, 282–283, estimated lacunae in P2045 of about 15, 4, 4, 1, and 5 characters.

120. There are numerous lacunae here in P2045, and they are rather more extensive than suggested in Hu, 283.

121. The term "lineal transmission" here is slightly different from that above: *chuanshou fuzhu* 傳授付囑. Presumably, Shenhui is speaking of Shenxiu's first generation of successors.

122. That is, second-generation disciples of Shenxiu.

123. The phrases here are *wu daxiao* 無大小, "without great and small," which must refer to the varying capacities of different individuals, and *wu shizi qing* 無師子情, "without feelings of teacher and student." Shenhui seems to be very much concerned with hierarchical distinctions, which is certainly not in keeping with the image of him as a populist.

124. Here the term used for "succession" is *lincheng* 稟承.

125. This is a rare reference to the decline of the Dharma, to be considered along with the allusion to the "time of the Final Dharma" above.

126. "Unilinear transmission" renders the Chinese *didi xiangchuan fuzhu* 的的相傳付囑. See a similar usage just below, differing only in the absence of the last two characters.

If there is anyone who has attained the transmission, he has not preached about it up to now.[127]

18

Dharma Master Chongyuan asked, "People consider Chan Master Shenxiu a person who has attained the inconceivable fruit of enlightenment. Why do you refuse to recognize Chan Master Shenxiu as the sixth generation [of the transmission]?"[128]

His Reverence replied, "Because Chan Master Hongren never bestowed the transmission on Chan Master Shenxiu. Even if he attained the fruit of enlightenment afterward, he still does not have the right to occupy the sixth generation.[129] Why? It cannot be allowed because Chan Master Hongren made no long-range prediction of [Shenxiu's] enlightenment."[130]

Dharma Master Chongyuan asked, "Chan Master Puji[131] refers to himself

---

127. This is an unusual argument. First, note that Huineng's followers here number in the "tens of thousands and more," significantly greater than Shenxiu's. This is in great contrast to other comparative discussions (for example in the *Platform Sūtra*) that tacitly admit Huineng was virtually unknown. May we use this as evidence of Shenhui's attempt to create a populist appeal? Second, Shenhui's reticence regarding Huineng's successor is curious. Is it due to his own lingering sense of modesty that he would claim the authority of the Buddha for his teacher and not for himself? It seems as though he is using the very absence of visibility of Huineng's successor as proof that he is that one viable successor, which would be a perverse sense of logic, if true. Or should we take seriously the distinction between inferential and direct perception of the Buddha-nature stated above, and infer that Shenhui was Huineng's publicist but not his primary successor? Third, this is the only occasion when Shenhui refers explicitly to Shenxiu. But could we not speculate that Shenhui's primary motivation was a sense of having been rejected by this very prestigious teacher? That is, instead of being taken along with Shenxiu to the capital in 700 / 701, Shenhui was sent to the very far south to study with the unknown Huineng. The contrast between the two cultural milieux would have been quite pronounced, perhaps great enough to shock Shenhui into a reactionary populism. In any case, the rest of his career could be interpreted as his personal struggle to regain access to the capitals, to erase the slight that he may have felt at Shenxiu's hands. Yang, 47n11, states that 24 characters have been restored from the Dunhuang Museum ms.; this is rather more than Hu, 283, had estimated.

128. Note that the text does not use the term "sixth patriarch" but rather deals in terms of generations as positions to be filled.

129. It may be an important admission that Shenxiu may have gained enlightenment sometime after Huineng did. This admission is at the very least a recognition of Shenxiu's stature.

130. The term *shouji* 授記, Skt. *vyākaraṇa*, refers to a prediction of the future achievement of Buddhahood usually made by a buddha with regard to a disciple or bodhisattva; see *Bukkyōgo daijiten,* 641b–c. "Long-range" renders the Chinese *yao* 遙, "far," referring presumably to an enlightenment that would have occurred after Shenxiu left Hongren's side.

131. Throughout virtually the entire text of the *Definition of the Truth,* Puji and other Northern school objects of Shenhui's criticisms are referred to using the full forms of their names. Since the individuals who actually appeared in the debates, Chongyuan and Shenhui, are referred to only once in full and thereafter in abbreviated form, this suggests an editorial (and perhaps even oral) distinction. Hence the reference, not to "Chan Master Puji" but to "Reverend [Pu]ji" (Ji heshang) in section 54 implies a separate provenance for the latter part of the text.

as the seventh generation. What about this?"[132] His Reverence answered, "Now, if for Chan Master Shenxiu [HS284] the unilinear transmission never took place, and he is therefore barred from occupying the sixth generation, then how much more [impossible would it be for] Chan Master Shenxiu's follower, Chan Master Puji, to have received the transmission and to occupy the seventh generation? At present the two worthies Chan Master Puji of the Middle Peak [Mount Song] and Chan Master Xiangmo Zang of the Eastern Peak [Mount Tai][133] say that Chan Master Shenxiu is their sixth generation. I wonder what their proof is that Chan Master Shenxiu occupies the sixth generation.

"In enumerating the generations from the past, our school of Shaozhou has always taken Bodhidharma's robe as the proof [of the transmission]. Now Chan Master Puji has erected a stele on Mount Song, established a Hall of the Seven Patriarchs, and written the *Annals of the Dharma-treasure*.[134] In counting his seven generations, what did he consider to be proof? The transmission of the Buddhadharma and its line of succession through the generations is certainly not subject to the wishes of Chan Master Shenxiu's followers. Why? Because [Shenxiu] lacked the transmission, he can never be allowed [to act as the sixth generation]."[135]

19

Dharma Master Chongyuan asked, "Chan Master Shenxiu was the Dharma chief of the two capitals and the teacher of three emperors.[136] On what

---

132. Note that Shenhui does not use any term for "patriarch" here, but says only that Puji identified himself as being in the seventh generation (*di qi dai* 第七代).

133. Xiangmo Zang is identified with this location in his *Song Biographies* biography (T 2061: 50.760a9–27); he supposedly went there after an encounter with Shenxiu, part of which is presented in McRae, *Northern School*, 63. Note that both figures are identified very explicitly with choronym, title, and both characters of their names. "At present" renders the Chinese *jian* 見, nominally "to see," here equivalent to *xian*, as in *xianzai* 現在.

134. Puji's establishment of a so-called *qizu tang* 七祖堂, which is not mentioned elsewhere, was an important precedent to Shenhui's creation of a similar hall celebrating Huineng. The full title of the text mentioned here is *Chuan fabao ji* 傳法寶紀, but Shenhui always refers it as *Fabao ji*. Also, he overlooks the distinction that it was written by Du Fei 杜朏 at the request of Puji and probably Yifu 義福 in order to honor their teacher Faru; see McRae, *Northern School*, 86–88 and 255–269. The assertions made here are repeated at somewhat greater length in section 24 below.

135. Yang, 47n12, states that 19 characters have been restored from the Dunhuang Museum ms.

136. The terminology used here is *liangjing fazhu, sandi menshi* 兩京法主，三帝門師. Essentially the same description (*liangjing fazhu, sandi guoshi* 國師, "...national teacher") is given in Shenxiu's epitaph by Zhang Yue (Yanagida, *Shoki Zenshū shisho*, 499 and 508n). The *Masters and Disciples of the Laṅkāvatāra* mentions the service of Shenxiu, Xuanze 玄賾, and Lao'an 老安 as teachers to three emperors, and the details leading to this description of Shenxiu are briefly rehearsed much later in the *Da Song seng shi lüe* 大宋僧史略 (T 2126: 54.244c8–9); see Yanagida, *Shoki no Zenshi 1*, 295.

ground is he disallowed from serving as the sixth generation?" His Reverence replied, "From Bodhidharma down to Reverend Huineng, not a single one of the six generations of great masters was a teacher of emperors."[137]

Dharma Master Chongyuan said, "I wonder if the Dharma can be contained in [Bodhidharma's] robe, and if the robe can be used to transmit the Dharma."[138] His Reverence answered, "Although the Dharma is not contained in the robe, it is used to symbolize the succession from generation to generation.[139] By using the transmission of the robe as a proof, those who disseminate the Dharma will be sure of the succession,[140] and students of the Path [HS285] will know the central principle[141] without error. The Tathāgata Śākyamuni's golden-threaded robe from the past is now at Cockfoot Mountain, where Kāśyapa keeps it in anticipation of the appearance of [the future Buddha] Maitreya in this world. He will give the robe [to Maitreya] to show that the Tathāgata Śākyamuni used the transmission of the robe as a proof.[142] Our patriarch of the sixth generation has done the same."[143]

20

Dharma Master Chongyuan said, "I wonder if the Chan masters Huineng and Shenxiu were fellow students [under Hongren]." [His Reverence] answered, "They were." [Chongyuan] asked, "If they were fellow students, wouldn't they have taught in the same way?" [His Reverence] answered, "[Their teachings] were not the same."

---

137. This is a strange argument, logically speaking. Shenhui, who later served the imperial court in a most obsequious fashion, is at this point suggesting that the role of patriarch precludes a close relationship with the throne. Of course, he is building on the supposed interview between Bodhidharma and Emperor Wu—or perhaps it is better to say that Huineng's lack of prominence was the reason Shenhui chose to tell (or retell) this story about Bodhidharma. In abstract terms, the implication seems to be that a Chan patriarch cannot be subservient to the imperial court; the civil and religious realms are completely distinct.

138. This is to forestall any criticism of attachment to the robe as a trivial physical form. This could have been put as a much stronger and more probing inquiry.

139. The term here is *biao daidai xiangcheng* 表代代相承. See similar sentiments expressed in the *Miscellaneous Dialogues*, section 69.

140. The term is *lincheng* 稟承.

141. As above, the term is *zongzhi* 宗旨.

142. The original location referred to here, known as *Kukkuṭapāda-giri* in Sanskrit, is in Magadha; see *Mochizuki*, 1:842c–843a. (One of the most important religious sites in Yunnan is Mount Jizu 雞足山, the Chinese equivalent.) For the story regarding Kāśyapa and Śākyamuni's robe, see the *Fu fazang yinyuan zhuan* 付法藏因緣傳, T 2058: 50.301a9–14. The description of the robe involved as being made with golden thread, which specifically identifies the robe received by Kāśyapa with the one left with Maitreya, occurs in the *Da Tang xiyou ji* 大唐西遊記, T 2087: 51.919c6.

143. Here the full term *wo liudai zushi* 我六代祖師 is used. It is uncertain whether Shenhui means Huineng as the sixth patriarch, or all six patriarchs from Bodhidharma to Huineng.

[Chongyuan] asked further, "Since they were fellow students, how could [their teachings] not be the same?"

[His Reverence] answered, "When I say that [their teachings] were not the same, it is because Chan Master Shenxiu taught people to 'freeze the mind to enter meditation, fix the mind to view purity, activate the mind to illuminate the external, and concentrate the mind to realize the internal.' That's why [the two men's teachings] were not the same."[144]

Dharma Master Chongyuan asked, "Why would Chan Master Huineng not [teach people to] 'freeze the mind to enter meditation, fix the mind to view purity, activate the mind to illuminate the external, and concentrate the mind to realize the internal'? [HS286] What was Chan Master Huineng's practice?"[145]

His Reverence replied, "That [practice, i.e., Shenxiu's] is the regulation of the mind."[146]

Dharma Master Chongyuan asked, "Why shouldn't one [regulate] the mind to realize the internal?"

His Reverence replied, "That is the teaching of fools! Chan Master Huineng's practice transcends the two Dharmas of regulating and not regulating. Therefore the text of the [*Vimalakīrti*] *Sūtra* [reads], 'The mind does not abide within, nor is it located without: this is sitting in meditation.... If one sits like this, the Buddha will [grant] the seal of certification.'[147] For the past six generations,[148] no one ever [taught people to] 'freeze the mind to enter meditation, fix the mind to view purity, activate the mind to illuminate

---

144. The characterizations just given are Shenhui's famous "four pronouncements" about Shenxiu's teachings, which occur in several places after this in the *Definition of the Truth*, and also in the *Platform Sermon* (section 4, with one phrase missing) and in the *Miscellaneous Dialogues* (sections 28 and 34). The Chinese is *ningxin ruding, zhuxin kanjing, qixin waizhao, shexin neizheng* 凝心入定, 住心看淨, 起心外照, 攝心內證. In other contexts, *zhuxin* may be rendered as "[make] the mind abide/reside." Hu notes that in P2045, which is being followed here, the character for "realize," *zheng* 證, is given consistently as the very similar *cheng* 澄, "to clarify." P3488 and P3047 just as consistently use *cheng*, which Hu feels is a better rhyme with *ding* and *jing*, which end the first two phrases. Yanagida, "Goroku," 386–387, presents the preceding material followed by section 21 in Japanese translation. He also notes that the four pronouncements are included in slightly different wording in the *Linji lu* 臨濟錄, T 1985: 47.499b15–16.

145. It is curious that Shenhui never answers this question about Huineng's practice. According to Hu, 285–286, the lacuna in P2045 is about two lines in length, with only a few characters legible in three locations. Yang, 47n13, states that 13 characters have been restored from the Dunhuang Museum ms.

146. The term is *tiaofu* 調伏, "regulate and subjugate," which is an often used descriptive of meditative discipline.

147. T 475: 14.539c23 and 25–26. The last term is *yinke* 印可, which became very important in later Chan.

148. This construction seems to imply that the patriarchal succession only refers to that which led up to, or somehow ceased with, Huineng.

the external, and concentrate the mind to realize the internal.' That's why [the teachings of Shenxiu and Huineng] are not the same."[149]

Dharma Master Chongyuan asked, "Is there anyone who has [received] the transmission [of the Dharma] after Chan Master Huineng?"[150] Answer: "There is." Another question: "Who is it that transmits [the Dharma]?" His Reverence answered, "You will come to know it by yourself later."[151]

21

Dharma Master Chongyuan asked, "How can this teaching [of Shenxiu's] be anything other than Buddhism? Why is he not allowed [to be the sixth generation]?"

His Reverence answered, "It is entirely [HS287] because the sudden and the gradual are not the same. The utterances of each one of the great masters in my [lineage] for the [past] six generations[152] was like the direct insertion of a knife blade that [made their students] directly and comprehensively see the nature.[153] They did not speak of stages or gradual [attainment]. Students of the Path should suddenly see the Buddha-nature, then gradually cultivate the causes and conditions.[154] They should attain emancipation in this very life.[155] It is like a mother suddenly giving birth to a child and then providing milk, from which [the child] gradually grows up and the child's wisdom naturally increases. Sudden enlightenment and seeing the Buddha-nature is also like this: one's wisdom naturally increases gradually. Therefore [Shenxiu's teaching] is not allowed."[156]

---

149. Yang, 47n14 (cf. 30), states that 34 characters have been restored from the Dunhuang Museum ms. in the preceding, replacing lacunae estimated by Hu to be about 25 and 7 characters in length.

150. Hu, 286, notes that P3488 begins here; cf. 175–186. Although not a clear break, this ms. begins about where the text becomes more interesting doctrinally.

151. "By yourself" here is *zi* 自, which also can mean "naturally, automatically."

152. Here as above, Shenhui uses *wo* 我 for "our."

153. The Chinese is *dandao zhiru, zhi liao jianxing* 單刀直入・直了見性. This became a popular slogan for the sudden teaching; cf. the full name of the *Platform Sermon*, and note similar terminology in the Kōshōji 興聖寺 text of the *Platform Sūtra* reproduced in *Enō kenkyū*.

154. Hu, 175, points out that P3488 has *dunwu jianxiu* 頓悟漸修, "sudden enlightenment and gradual cultivation," instead of the present *dun jian foxing* 頓見性, "suddenly see the Buddha-nature." Since "sudden enlightenment followed by gradual cultivation" is one of Shenhui's slogans and thus represents an increased level of textual rationalization, this might be an indication that P3488 is slightly later than P2045.

155. The Chinese is actually "without transcending this life."

156. Yanagida, "Goroku," 386–387, presents this section, preceded by the first part of section 20, in Japanese translation.

22

Dharma Master Chongyuan asked, "The two great worthies Chan Master Puji of Mount Song and Chan Master Xiangmo Zang of the Eastern Peak[157] teach people to sit in meditation and 'freeze the mind to enter meditation, fix the mind to view purity, activate the mind to illuminate the external, and concentrate the mind to realize the internal.' They declare that this is the teaching. Why do you preach Chan today without teaching people to sit and 'freeze the mind to enter meditation, fix the mind to view purity, activate the mind to illuminate the external, and concentrate the mind to realize the internal'? What is 'sitting in meditation'?"

His Reverence answered, "To teach people to sit and 'freeze the mind to enter meditation, fix [HS288] the mind to view purity, activate the mind to illuminate the external, and concentrate the mind to realize the internal' is to obstruct *bodhi*. When I say 'sit,' [I mean that] 'sitting' is for thoughts to not be activated. When I say 'meditation,' [I mean that] 'meditation' is to see the fundamental nature.[158] Therefore I do not teach people to have their bodies sit and their minds abide while entering into concentration. If it were correct to declare such a teaching, then Vimalakīrti would not have scolded Śāriputra for sitting in meditation."[159]

23

Dharma Master Chongyuan asked, "Why is it improper for Chan Master Puji to use the label 'Southern school'?"

His Reverence answered, "Because when Reverend Shenxiu was alive, every student of the Path in China referred to these great masters as 'Huineng of the South' and 'Shenxiu of the North.'[160] Everyone knew this, and it is because of those titles that we have the two schools of North and South. Chan Master Puji was actually a student of [Shenxiu of] Yuquan monastery—although he falsely mouths off about himself as the Southern school, he's never been to Shaozhou. For that reason it's improper."[161]

---

157. That is, Mount Tài.

158. The critical terms are *nian buqi wei zuo* 念不起為坐 and *jian benxing wei chan* 見本性為禪; see the *Miscellaneous Dialogues*, section 60.

159. See T 475: 14.539c, as well as the Dunhuang version of the *Platform Sūtra*, section 16 (*Enō kenkyū*, 293–294). Hu, 288, notes that P3488 is missing a page, beginning with the characters *ruo zhi* 若指, "if one indicated [i.e., declared]." Yanagida, "Goroku," 387, presents the preceding material on "sitting" and "meditation" in Japanese translation, with the comment that this redefinition was one of Shenhui's most epoch-making innovations.

160. Yang, 31, points out that the Dunhuang Museum ms. actually has *nan Xiu bei Neng* 南秀北能, rather than *nan Neng bei Xiu*.

161. "Falsely mouths off" renders *kou wang cheng* 口妄程, "falsely says with his mouth."

24

Dharma Master Chongyuan asked, "Why do you enjoin Chan Master Puji [from using the name 'Southern school']?"

His Reverence answered, "Although Chan Master Puji claims to be [HS289] the Southern school, his real intention is to destroy the Southern school."

Dharma Master Chongyuan asked, "How do you know his intention is to destroy the Southern school?"

His Reverence lamented, "What suffering, what suffering! How painful, how painful! My ears cannot bear to listen; my eyes to see! During the third month of the second year of Kaiyuan (714), [Puji] had Zhang Xingchang,[162] an assassin from Jingzhou, disguise himself as a monk to try to take Reverend Huineng's head. The great master's holy form[163] was cut three times by a knife![164] Then [he had] Sheng Xu's[165] epitaph [written for Huineng] obliterated twice, and he also sent his student Wu Pingyi[166] and others to eradicate the Great Worthy [Huineng] of Shaozhou's epitaph. He then wrote an announcement that was chiseled over Chan Master Huineng's[167] epitaph, establishing that the [patriarch of the] sixth generation[168] was Chan Master Shenxiu [and giving] an account of that master-disciple succession and transmission of the robe. And now Chan Master Puji has erected a stele on Mount Song, established a Hall of the Seven Patriarchs, and written the *Annals of the Dharma-treasure,* in which he lists seven [patriarchal] generations without mentioning Chan Master Huineng.[169]

"Chan Master Huineng was the person who received the lineal transmission,[170] as well as being the teacher of humans and gods. The entire country knew of him, but he is nowhere mentioned [in the *Annals of the*

---

162. Zhang Xingchang's 張行昌 identity is unknown.

163. The term used here is *lingzhi* 靈質, "numinous substance."

164. Presumably, the incident recounted here did not involve three assaults with the knife, and was thought of instead as one of the three occasions when Huineng's body was desecrated.

165. Hu, 289, suggests that Sheng Xu 盛續 might be an author's name. This is only a tentative reading, and no such individual has been identified.

166. Li Yong's 李邕 epitaph for Puji describes Wu as a vice director of the Bureau of Evaluations (*kaoqiao yuan wailang* 考巧員外郎); see Yanagida, *Shoki Zenshū shisho,* 111 and 116n14.

167. Note the various forms of reference for Huineng here, including Neng Heshang 能和上, Dashi 大師, Shaozhou dade 韶州大德, and Neng Chanshi 能禪師.

168. There is a lacuna here of about four characters in length in P2045.

169. See section 18 where this sentence has already occurred. Although Shenhui may have indeed uttered the same words on more than one occasion, one suspects this overlap to be the result of Dugu Pei's editing. As noted by Hu, 349, the epitaph referred to here is presumably Li Yong's Songyuesi bei 嵩岳寺碑 (*Complete Writings of the Tang* 262), which contains an enumeration of the transmission from Bodhidharma to Huike, etc., on to Shenxiu and Puji.

170. The Chinese is *de chuanshou fuzhu* 傳授付囑.

Definition of the Truth

Dharma-treasure]. Chan Master Faru[171] was a fellow student of Chan Master Shenxiu's, but he was not the person who received the lineal transmission, nor was he a teacher of humans and gods. No one in China has heard of him—what succession[172] did he have that makes him the sixth generation? When Chan Master Puji erected his epitaph for Reverend Shenxiu, he made Reverend Shenxiu the sixth generation. And yet he has now written the *Annals of the Dharma-treasure* making Chan Master Faru the sixth generation! [HS290] I wonder, if the two great worthies are both to be counted as the sixth generation, which one is true and which is false? I would like to ask Chan Master Puji to think about this in detail!"[173]

25

Dharma Master Chongyuan asked, "Chan Master Puji began to teach several or more decades ago. Why didn't you realize this and define the central teaching [of Chan] earlier?"[174]

His Reverence answered, "Those who study the Path in China all doubted him and wanted to ask about the true central teaching, but Chan Master Puji's powerful following sang [out his claims so strongly] they made [Huineng's] disciples retire [without asking].[175] Those who did have doubts dared not say, 'I wonder which is true and which is false.' In the past, when the Tathāgata Śākyamuni was alive, bodhisattvas and *śrāvakas* from other locations, as well as all the heretics, asked questions of the Tathāgata, and he answered each and every one of them well and completely. When our Great Master [Huineng] of Shaozhou[176] was alive, he too answered well and completely the questions of each and every person who came to him and inquired.[177] I wonder, on the basis of what scripture

---

171. For information on this important monk, see Yanagida, *Shoki Zenshū shisho*, 35–46, and McRae, *Northern School*, 43–44.

172. The Chinese here is *chenglin* 承禀.

173. This usage gives the impression that these words were spoken while Puji was still alive, i.e., during the Huatai meetings. Yang, 47n17 (cf. p. 32), states that six characters have been restored here from the Dunhuang Museum ms.

174. The Chinese is *ding qi zongzhi* 定其宗旨; Shenhui's answer below refers to the "true central teaching," *zhen zongzhi* 真宗旨. The implication is that Shenhui should have come forward much earlier.

175. The Chinese reads *chang shi mentu tuochu* 唱使門徒拖出. Yang, 32, corrects *chang* 唱, "sing," to *he* 喝, "shout," a usage that is distinctly preferable in section 26. Whichever the case in this instance, the unified voices of Puji's following caused the *mentu* or disciples of Huineng to *tuochu*, "pull out," or retire without asking the probing questions that they might have asked. Incidentally, I normally render *mentu* as "followers" (see with reference to Shenxiu, below), but I have used "disciples" here to avoid confusion with Puji's group.

176. This is one of the standard forms of reference for Huineng in this text: *wo Shaozhou dashi* 我韶州大師.

177. Note the use of the character *zheng* 徵, as in the title of the *Miscellaneous Dialogues*. The similar sounding *cheng* 呈 is used with roughly the same meaning in the previous sentence.

does Chan Master Puji not permit anyone to ask questions about what is true and false?[178]

"In the third year of Chang'an (703), when Reverend Shenxiu ascended the ordination platform at the Yunhua monastery in the capital, Vinaya masters Wen'gang and Dayi were in the assembly.[179] They asked Reverend Shenxiu, 'We have heard that a robe of Bodhidharma's [is used to] transmit the succession. Shouldn't you have it?'[180] Reverend Shenxiu said, 'The robe transmitting the Dharma of Great Master Hongren of Huangmei is now with Chan Master Huineng of Shaozhou.'[181] [HS291] [Thus] when Reverend Shenxiu was alive he indicated that the robe transmitting the Dharma to the sixth generation[182] was in Shaozhou, and he did not claim that he should be counted as the sixth generation.[183] Now, in his claim to be the seventh

---

178. Tanaka and Okimoto, 226, interpret this phrase—*shui zhi shifei* 誰知是非—as a rhetorical question meaning, roughly, "who knows why Puji does this?" Their interpretation of the question I have placed in single quotes earlier in the paragraph is similar. I have interpreted the phrase as invoking the title of the *Definition of the Truth*.

179. This anecdote suggests that ascending the ordination platform to give a sermon of some sort was not Shenhui's innovation but derived (at least proximately) from Shenxiu and perhaps Wen'gang and others. The Hu Shi text is missing the two characters *lüshi* 律師, "Vinaya master," here. Tanaka and Okimoto, 226, consider this a reference to only one monk, named Vinaya Master Gang, with the other four characters indecipherable. Yang, 32, presents the text as referring unequivocally to Vinaya Masters Gang and Dayi. Although the full name is not given, "Vinaya Master Gang" is almost certainly Wen'gang 文綱 (636–727). On this prominent Vinaya master, see T 2061: 50.791b15–792b24, and especially 792b16 and 18. Wen'gang's biography suggests a web of associations involving Shenhui, Shenxiu, the imperial court, and Huatai. Wen'gang was a student of Daoxuan's (T 2061: 50.791a25) known for his discovery of Aśokan relics and his transcription of up to six hundred fascicles of scriptures using his own blood. He edited a translation done by Yijing 義淨 in 680 (710c24) and was the teacher of the Vinaya master Hengjing 恒景 (634–712; see T 2061: 50.732b17), a native of Dangyang and later a resident of Yuquan si there—implying a possible source of a later connection with Shenxiu. In 708 Wen'gang spent an entire summer retreat in the palace of Emperor Zhongzong, teaching and bestowing the precepts. A monk named Shenhui from Chang'an, Jingzhao Shenhui 京兆神, is listed (792b16) as one of his disciples (even though the second character is written with a different character from that used in Heze Shenhui's name, at this point our Shenhui was not yet associated with Luoyang). It is also possible, but not likely, that the individual mentioned here is Daogang of Pingyuan si 平原寺道綱 (d.u.; the monastery was presumably in the area of Pingyuan county, Shandong province), who was a student of the famous Vinaya master Dao'an 道岸 (654–717); see T 2061: 50.793c20. The identity of Dayi 大儀 is less certain. Someone by the same name is mentioned as one of the editors (*zhengyi* 證義) who worked on translating scriptures with Yijing (T 2061: 50.710c3 and c8; also see 731c15) and was also associated with Fazang (732a20). See also the epitaph by Wei Chuhou 韋處厚 (773–828; *Complete Writings of the Tang* 715).

180. The Chinese for "transmit the succession" is *xiangchuan fuzhu* 相傳付囑; see n. 102 above. The connotation of the question, which is posed in the vernacular in spite of the presumed formality of the occasion, is that Shenxiu probably does not have the robe.

181. P3488 resumes again after the characters *jin jianzai* 今見在, "is now at [i.e., with]."

182. The Chinese is *liudai chuanfa jiasha* 六代傳法袈裟.

183. The Chinese is *kou bu zi cheng wei di liu dai shu* 口不自程為第六代數, "orally did not say he was the sixth-generation count." The use of *kou*, "mouth," emphasizes that this assertion is about Shenxiu himself. This character is absent in the sentence that follows about Puji, although it is used with regard to his supposed intention to destroy the Southern school above at the end of section 23.

generation, Chan Master Puji falsely sets up Reverend Shenxiu as the sixth generation. That cannot be allowed."

26

His Reverence then announced[184] to Dharma Master Chongyuan and everyone assembled, "Do not think this is strange! There are many who teach Chan in this world at present, confusing those who study the Path in the extreme. I'm afraid that Māra the Evil One,[185] along with some heretics, are in their midst, deluding those who study the Path and destroying the correct Dharma. That's the reason for this explanation.

"During the Jiushi period (700)[186] [Empress Wu] Zetian invited Reverend Shenxiu to enter the palace. When he was about to leave [for the capital], all the monks and laypeople[187] there did obeisance to His Reverence and asked, 'After Your Reverence leaves [Yuquan monastery] to go to the palace, how should your followers here practice? On whom should we rely [now]?' Reverend Shenxiu said, 'In Shaozhou there is a great spiritual compatriot who [received] Great Master Hongren's deputation at the outset, and he has the entire Buddhadharma.[188] If any of you are unable to resolve [HS292] your doubts, you can go to him to ask. [His answers] will certainly surpass [your] conception, since he understands the central principle of the Buddhadharma.'[189]

---

184. Hu, 291, notes that in P2045 the five characters *ershi heshang gao* 爾時和上告 occur as only *you yu* 又語, "also said." He has corrected the text on the basis of P3488. Yang's edition of the Dunhuang Museum text combines the language of the two sources (p. 32), a tactic of questionable methodological validity but without serious impact.

185. The text has *tianmo boxun* 天魔波旬. The first character means *deva*, while the last three transliterate "Māra Pāpīyān," the full name of Māra; see *Bukkyōgo daijiten*, 985b.

186. The Jiushi 久視 period began in the fifth month of 700, and the next period, Dazu 大足, began in the first month of 701. Previously I suggested that Shenxiu was invited to court in 700 but actually arrived in 701 (McRae, *Northern School*, 51–52); the difference seems trivial, but the quotation below is supposed to have taken place at Shenxiu's departure from Yuquan si for the capital.

187. The Chinese is *suoshi daosu* 所是道俗. The reference to "all [Shenxiu's] followers" just below also uses *suoshi*.

188. Literally, "The Buddhadharma is entirely in that location." The word *chu* 處, "location," is often used in this text to stand for a person.

189. The Chinese for the last phrase is *Fofa zongzhi* 佛法宗旨. We might assume that this speech is entirely fictional, since it would seem to be based on the letter from Yixing to Zhang Yue that explains how Shenxiu left some of his students behind in Yuquan si to continue their meditation practice. (See the letter in *Complete Writings of the Tang* 914:16b–17b, and discussion in McRae, *Northern School,* 51 and 289n123.) The existence (and preservation) of the letter may indicate that this step of Shenxiu's was in some way unusual; presumably other masters would have brought their students with them, and the students would have jumped at the chance to go to the capital. On the other hand, Shenhui may be recalling what Shenxiu actually said upon sending him to the far south, no doubt with significant embellishment and specific detail. It is of course odd that Shenhui uses Shenxiu as a source of justification, even while he attacks the older monk's authority as a religious teacher.

"Furthermore, Chan Master Puji's fellow student,[190] the monk Guangji of Qingchan si in Chang'an, went to Shaozhou in the eleventh month of the third year of Jinglong (709).[191] After ten days or so, he entered His Reverence's room in the middle of the night to take the robe that had been transmitted [to Huineng]. His Reverence cried out, and Masters Huida and Xuanwu, hearing him shout,[192] got up to look. When they got arrived at His Reverence's room, they saw Guangji [escaping]. Master [Huida] grabbed Master Xuanwu's hand to prevent him from making any noise,[193] and they entered His Reverence's room. His Reverence said, 'Someone in the room reached out his hand to take the robe.' That night the northern and southern monks and laypeople[194] all came to His Reverence's room to ask, 'Was the intruder a southerner or a northerner?' His Reverence said, 'I only saw a person come in; I don't know if it was a southerner or a northerner.' The people gathered then asked, 'Was it a monk or a layman?' [His Reverence answered,] 'I don't know whether it was a monk or a layman.' His Reverence [actually] knew quite clearly[195] [who it was] but feared they might hurt him; hence he spoke as he did.

"His Reverence [Huineng] also said, 'It was not just today. When Great Master Hongren had the robe [HS293] [attempts were made to] steal it three

---

190. Presumably Puji could not be responsible for actions taken by a fellow student, so that this represents either a careful avoidance of direct criticism of Shenxiu or the aggregation of all accusations against Puji—or both.

191. The monk Guangji of Qingchan si in Chang'an 西京清禪寺僧廣濟: a monk by this name is listed in the *Song Biographies* and identified in one location with Tiangong si 天宮寺 in Henan province, which suggests a distant association with Shenxiu, who was ordained and passed away at this temple (McRae, *Northern School*, 47). Qingchan si 清禪寺 was the scene of Śikṣānanda's translation efforts; see T 2061: 50.719a1 and 736b24. However, this Guangji is said to have participated in a translation effort of 795, which would make him a very unlikely cat burglar in 709 (T 2061: 50.721b27). Perhaps the name in the *Definition of the Truth* was selected with some intent to embarrass this Guangji, but even this seems unlikely. [It is noteworthy that unlike all the other references to monastics in this text, Guangji is given no honorific at all.—Ed.]

192. The Chinese for Huineng's shout is written as *chang* 唱, "sing," corrected to *he* 喝, "shout," without comment by Hu, 292. This usage may be one reason why the same editorial change was made in section 25 above. Masters Huida 惠達 and Xuanwu 玄悟 are not identifiable.

193. I have read the text differently from Hu, 292, and Yang, 33. They have Guangji holding Xuanwu's hand and restraining him from calling out, but Guangji is the culprit. The text must explain why Guangji was allowed to escape, and Huineng's two disciples are depicted as gifted enough to be in accord with their master's desire not to expose the culprit.

194. The usage is *suoshi nanbei daosu* 所是南北道俗. The distinction between northerners and southerners, later to be so famously deconstructed in the *Platform Sūtra*, is certainly clearly maintained in this account! On the other hand, Huineng's reply just below seems vaguely similar to the initial dialogue between Hongren and Huineng in the *Platform Sūtra*.

195. Hu, 292, points out that the three characters here, *didi zhi* 的的知, "know quite clearly," are in P3488 (Hu, 177), replaced by *shishi rufang ren* 實識入房人, "actually recognized the intruder." There are other trivial differences between the two versions.

times,[196] and Great Master Hongren himself said, "When Great Master Daoxin had the robe there was one [attempt to] steal it."' Every [attempt to] steal it has been unsuccessful. Therefore the monks and laypeople of the south and north have become extremely agitated over this robe, continually confronting each other with swords and staffs.' "[197]

27

Dharma Master Chongyuan said, "Chan Master Puji's fame is countrywide and everyone in China knows of him.[198] Everyone says that he surpasses all conception.[199] Why do you go to such lengths to denounce and expel him? Aren't you risking your life?"[200]

His Reverence replied, "Someone who reads this treatise without understanding its purport[201] might call this 'denouncing and expelling.'[202] There's a difference between Chan Master Puji and the Southern school, and I'm adjudicating the true and false and defining the central teaching.[203] My present purpose is to establish the correct Dharma and disseminate the Mahāyāna so that all sentient beings will know about it. Why should I worry about [my] life!" [HS294]

---

196. This number is accepted by the *Records of the Transmission* (see Yanagida, *Shoki no Zenshi 2*, 99, and Adamek, *Mystique*, 181, with translation on 323) and the *Caoqi dashi (bie) zhuan* (曹溪大師[別]傳; X 86.49; see *Enō kenkyū*, 49–50). (The latter example conjoins the notion of possession of the robe with murderous attacks.) Just as meditation specialists such as Bodhidharma and Huisi were supposedly the targets of poisoning attempts, so was the possessor of the robe in danger from jealous monks. Of course, paired with this danger is the miraculous quality of the robe, which is impossible to steal (or, in the anecdote involving Huiming in the received version of the *Platform Sūtra*, impossible to lift); see T 2008: 48.349b16–c4.

197. This paragraph could have been spoken by Huineng, but given the final remarks about enmity between south and north it might be better to interpret it as attributed directly to Shenhui. Incidentally, this passage contains several uses of *chu* 處, "location."

198. The phrase *zhiwen* 知聞 is used in this sense in Dugu Pei's preface.

199. The Chinese reads *zhongkou gong chuan [wei] bu ke siyi* 眾口共傳[為]不可思議. The use of *chuan* 傳, "transmit," is a colloquial usage referring to oral reportage rather than to the Chan transmission. Hu notes that P3488 lacked the character *wei*. For a different translation of this section, see Jorgensen, *Inventing Hui-neng*, 460.

200. The Chinese here, *qi bu yu shenming you chou* 豈不與身命有讎, literally means "won't you have to give up your life in repayment [for this aggressiveness]?" In P2045 the next page (31 lines), beginning with *yu shenming*, is accidentally placed two pages (62 lines) below. Hu, 293, has followed P3488; Yang, 33–35, gives no indication of the matter.

201. The Chinese is *lunyi* 論意, "thesis" or "intent of the treatise."

202. This is a remarkable statement, no doubt the detritus of a somewhat confused editor, for whom Chongyuan is a metaphor for readers in general. It is remarkable that Shenhui is portrayed as saying this to someone with whom he is supposed to be conversing, not communicating in writing.

203. This is a colloquial rendering of the ideas that went into the title of this treatise: *wo zi liaojian shifei, ding qi zongzhi* 我自料簡是非，定其宗旨.

28

Dharma Master Chongyuan asked, "Haven't you written this treatise to seek fame?"[204]

His Reverence answered, "If I could write this treatise without any concern for my own safety, why should I care about fame?"[205]

29

Dharma Master Chongyuan asked, "In China Bodhidharma is called the first [generation of Chan], but to whom did Bodhidharma succeed? And through how many generations did [the transmission] pass?"

His Reverence answered, "In India, Bodhidharma succeeded Saṅgharakṣa, Saṅgharakṣa succeeded Śubhamitra,[206] Śubhamitra succeeded Upagupta, [HS295] Upagupta succeeded Śanavāsa, Śanavāsa succeeded Madhyāntika, Madhyāntika succeeded Ānanda, Ānanda succeeded Kāśyapa, and Kāśyapa succeeded the deputation of the Tathāgata.[207] In China Bodhidharma is the first generation, while in India Bodhidharma is the eighth.[208] In India Prajñāmitra[209] succeeded Bodhidharma, while in China Chan Master Huike succeeded Bodhidharma.[210] Since the deputation of the Tathāgata, [the transmission] in India and China has passed through fourteen generations altogether.[211]

---

204. Not only does this contradict the notion that the dialogue is the transcript of an oral sermon, but both this question and the previous passage imply that it was Shenhui who wrote the *Definition of the Truth*, not the author of the preface, Dugu Pei.

205. Hu, 294, notes some minor textual problems, some of which involve literary polishing present in P3488, implying that this ms. is later than P2045.

206. Yampolsky (*Platform Sutra*, 30) points out that the *Definition of the Truth* inverts the first two characters of the name Vasumitra as given in the preface to the *Meditation Sūtra of Dharmatrāta*, implying Śubhamitra. The error was perpetuated in the Dunhuang version of the *Platform Sūtra* (section 51 of Yampolsky's text, 179; *Enō kenkyū*, 383) and the *Records of the Transmission* (Yanagida, *Shoki no Zenshi 2*, 59; Adamek, *Mystique*, 105; and T 2075: 51.180b13). Like Yang, 47n18, and contra Hu (*Yiji*, 294), I feel it is better not to "correct" Shenhui's text.

207. The Chinese is *rulai fu* 如來付.

208. P3488 omits ten characters here. Note the consistent use of generational references rather than the titles "patriarch Ānanda," etc.

209. Yampolsky (*Platform Sutra*, 29n92) suggests that Prajñāmitra might represent a miscopying of the name Puṇyamitra that is included in the preface to the *Meditation Sūtra of Dharmatrāta*, T 618: 15.301c9.

210. The primary text omits Bodhidharma's name here.

211. P2045 and apparently the Dunhuang Museum ms. have "fourteen generations," while the slightly more polished P3488 has "thirteen generations." Hu, 295, implies that the confusion presumably arose over whether or not to count Bodhidharma twice, once for India and once for China, but Tanaka and Okimoto, 425n49, make the better suggestion that the larger number includes Śākyamuni whereas the smaller number does not. Shenhui's conception of the transmission from India to China has been discussed by Yanagida, *Shoki Zenshū shisho*, 123–125. Note the difference between this brief presentation and the hagiographies

30

Dharma Master Chongyuan asked, "On what basis is it known that Bodhidharma was the eighth generation in India?"

His Reverence answered, "This is based on the explicit enumeration of the Indian generations in the preface to the *Meditation Sūtra*. Also, Chan Master Huike personally asked Bodhidharma about the Indian succession[212] at Shaolin si on Mount Song, and Bodhidharma answered, 'It is entirely as explained in the preface to the *Meditation Sūtra*.' "[213] [HS296]

31

Dharma Master Chongyuan asked, "Do they transmit a robe in India also?"
Answer: "In India they do not transmit a robe."
Question: "Why do they not transmit a robe in India?"
Answer: "Since there are many who have attained the fruit of sagehood in India, their minds are without deceit, so they only transmit the matching of the mind [in enlightenment].[214] In China there are many ordinary [unenlightened] persons who falsely[215] seek fame and gain and mix up true and false. Therefore the robe is transmitted in order to define the central teaching."[216]

32

Dharma Master Chongyuan asked, "What Dharma do you cultivate, and what practice do you practice?"[217]

---

of the six Chinese patriarchs presented in the *Miscellaneous Dialogues* (sections 64–69). Also, the format of this brief transmission statement is unique in its central focus on Bodhidharma, from which the text counts back to Śākyamuni and then forward to Huike and only implicitly to Huineng.

212. Here the term used is *xiangcheng* 相承.

213. As Hu, 295–296, points out, this assertion involves the (presumably intentional) confusion of Bodhidharma with the Dharmatrāta whose teachings appear in the *Meditation Sūtra of Dharmatrāta;* see McRae, *Northern School,* 80–82, and Hu, 24–33.

214. The Chinese is *wei chuan xinqi* 唯傳心契. Yang, 34, points out that the first of these four characters is missing in the Dunhuang Museum ms.

215. The Chinese is *gou* 苟, normally meaning "if." Tanaka and Okimoto, 230, read this as the Japanese *midari ni,* presumably as a mistake for *wang* 妄.

216. Once again, *ding qi zongzhi* 定其宗旨, the theme that lies behind the title of the treatise. For a different translation of this section, see Jorgensen, *Inventing Hui-neng,* 278.

217. Hu, 296, makes this the beginning of the fifth section of his edition. Indeed, there is a very sharp break in subject matter here, with the initial dialogue of section 32 serving as an introduction to a long monologue by Shenhui. Tanaka and Okimoto, 425n51, point out these changes and suggest that sections 32–50 represent a different source appended to the original text. Section 32 also occurs in the *Miscellaneous Dialogues,* section 61, which includes the citation from the *Wisdom Sūtra of Heavenly King Pravara* from section 33 below.

His Reverence replied, "I cultivate the Dharma of the perfection of wisdom, and I practice the practice of the perfection of wisdom."

Dharma Master Chongyuan asked, "Why don't you cultivate other Dharmas and practice other practices [HS297] instead of only cultivating the Dharma of the perfection of wisdom and practicing the practice of the perfection of wisdom?"[218]

His Reverence answered, "I cultivate the perfection of wisdom, which incorporates all Dharmas. I practice the practice of the perfection of wisdom, which is the fundamental source of all practices.

"The adamantine perfection of wisdom
Is the most honored, the most excellent, the most supreme.
Without generation, without extinction, without going and coming,
All the buddhas derive from this."[219]

33

His Reverence said:[220] Friends, let me tell you: if you want to comprehend the most profound *dharmadhātu* and enter directly into the Samādhi of the Single Practice, you must first recite the *Diamond Sūtra* and cultivate the Dharma of the perfection of wisdom.[221]

Why? You should understand that those who recite the *Diamond Sūtra* do not do so out of [any] lesser merit.[222] It is likened to an emperor procreating a prince, who is never like ordinary people.[223] Why? Because [the

---

218. P2045 and the Dunhuang Museum ms. drop six and seven characters, respectively, at this point.

219. Presumably, this verse is intoned at this point by Shenhui. It also occurs in the *Platform Sūtra* (T 2008: 48.340a16–17; see *Enō kenkyū*, 313; and Yampolsky, *Platform Sutra*, 148), where the first line reads "great *prajñā*" rather than "adamantine *prajñā*." The Dunhuang Museum ms. is missing one character in the third line.

220. Given the absence of dialogue in what follows, I am simplifying the format by suspending the use of quotation marks to indicate Shenhui's pronouncements until the dialogue with Chongyuan resumes in section 51 below.

221. On the Samādhi of the Single Practice (*yixing sanmei* 一行三昧), see Faure, "One-Practice Samādhi." I have used the title *Diamond Sūtra* throughout because of its recognition value in English. Literally, it is the *Sūtra of the Adamantine Perfection of Wisdom*. The reader is asked to recall that each time the sūtra is named the words "Adamantine Perfection of Wisdom" are repeated in the text, with something approaching mantric incessancy. The question posed here reappears in the *Miscellaneous Dialogues*, section 24. The material that follows is different, but in both cases the emphasis is on the merit of reciting the *Diamond Sūtra*.

222. Literally, their recitation "does not come from small merit." Below, Shenhui cites the *Diamond Sūtra* to the effect that those who recite this scripture in their present lifetimes do so out of the karmic rewards of honoring innumerable buddhas in their past lives. Ogawa ("Tonkōbon Rokuso dankyō," 21) suggests that this passage formed the basis of the *Platform Sūtra*'s similar injunction of that text, which does not however mention the Samādhi of the Single Practice (*Enō kenkyū*, 314; Yampolsky, *Platform Sutra*, 149). Also see sections 39–40 and just below.

223. Literally, the offspring is never "identical to ordinary examples" (*tong suli* 同俗例). Tanaka and Okimoto, 230, read this as: "It is likened to an emperor being [re]born as a prince,

prince] derives from those who are most honored and esteemed. Those who recite the *Diamond Sūtra* [HS298] are the same. Therefore the *Diamond Sūtra* says, "Rather than having planted good roots before a single buddha, or two buddhas, or three, four, or five buddhas, [such persons] will have planted good roots before an immeasurable ten million buddhas. Those who hear [even] a word (of this teaching) and generate even a single moment's pure faith, [Subhūti,] are all known and all seen by the Tathāgata."[224] How much more so those who copy [the sūtra], "maintain it, recite it, and preach it for others."[225]

The *Wisdom Sūtra of the Heavenly King Pravara* says, "'How does the bodhisattva-mahāsattva practice the perfection of wisdom so as to penetrate the most profound *dharmadhātu*?' The Buddha said to Heavenly King Pravara, 'Great King, according to reality.'[226] 'World-honored One, what is the real?' 'Great King, the unchanging [is the real].' 'World-honored One, what is the unchanging?' 'Great King, it is called suchness.' 'World-honored One, what is suchness?' 'Great King, it can be known by wisdom but cannot be explained with words. Why? It goes beyond words, and is without this and that. It transcends characteristics and is without characteristics. It far transcends thought and passes beyond the realm of understanding.'"[227] This is the bodhisattva's comprehensive penetration of the profound *dharmadhātu*. [HS299]

34

The *Wisdom Sūtra of the Heavenly King Pravara* says, "There is no Dharma that can be used as a metaphor for the perfection of wisdom."[228] Those good young men and women who faithfully accept the *Diamond Sūtra* will gain

---

which according to worldly examples is impossible." Whichever interpretation is correct, the implicit biological/sociological elitism is probably common folk wisdom. For another metaphor involving a princely son, see section 36. In any case, Shenhui's purpose is to suggest that the recitation of the *Diamond Sūtra* derives from an extraordinarily meritorious background and yields transcendent results.

224. T 235: 8.749b1–4. Words in parentheses represent characters found in Hu's (1968: 298) edition but not in the original scriptural passage.

225. Here evoking T 235: 8.750c11–12.

226. Or, "as it is."

227. This is abbreviated from the *Wisdom Sūtra of the Heavenly King Pravara*, T 231: 8.693c24–694a13. According to *Mochizuki*, 3:2698a–b, this work in seven fascicles was translated during the Chen dynasty and corresponds to fascicles 566–573 of Xuanzang's *Da banruo jing* 大般若經 (T 220: 5–7.1b8). The passage cited here has nothing to do with the merit accruing from reciting the *Diamond*, of course. The "realm of understanding" renders *jueguan jing* 覺觀境, in which the first two characters represent the Skt. *vitarka* and *vicāra*, two basic functions of mental understanding that are to be eliminated in *dhyāna* practice; see *Bukkyōgo daijiten*, 176a.

228. T 231: 8.716b7. As noted by Yang, 47n19 (cf. 35), Hu, 298, inappropriately removes the scriptural attribution. I have reluctantly followed the section divisions established in Tanaka and Okimoto, 232, although this sentence might better go with the material in section 33.

merit inconceivable.[229] If this merit had form and shape, it would not fit within the [entire] realm of space! "To see the perfection of wisdom according to reality is called 'realization.' To penetrate with wisdom is called 'arriving.' "[230] "Even if all the sentient beings resided on the tenth stage and entered the various samādhis to contemplate the Tathāgata's meditation, it would be impossible to appraise."[231]

35

Good friends, you must recite the *Diamond Sūtra*.[232] This sūtra is called the "mother of all the Buddhas," and also the "patriarch of all the Dharmas."[233] Samādhis as numerous as the sands of the River Ganges together with the eighty-four thousand perfections[234] are all generated from the perfection of wisdom.[235] You must recite and maintain this sūtra! Why? The perfection of wisdom is the fundament of all the Dharmas. It is likened to a great wish-bestowing pearl within the ocean. [HS300] All the pearls within the ocean grow and expand due to the power of the wish-bestowing pearl. Why? Because of the meritorious virtue of the great pearl.[236] To practice the per-

---

229. Hu, 299, notes minor textual problems and also indicates that the ending of the misplaced page of P2045 comes in this line. As Tanaka and Okimoto, 426n55, point out, Shenhui applies assertions originally stated about the perfection of wisdom in general to the *Diamond Sūtra*.

230. This is also a quotation from the *Wisdom Sūtra of the Heavenly King Pravara*, T 231: 8.694a26, where it follows the king's question, "How can one realize and arrive at this *dharmakāya*?" and the Buddha's answer, "One arrives by means of the nondiscriminating wisdom that comes after realization of the transmundane perfection of wisdom." The king then asks about the difference between realization (*zheng* 證) and arrival (*zhi* 至), yielding the response quoted.

231. This is another unattributed citation of the *Wisdom Sūtra of the Heavenly King Pravara*, T 231: 8.700a8. The unabbreviated original reads, "Even if the sentient beings of all the worlds all resided on the tenth stage and entered the various samādhis for a hundred thousand trillion eons to contemplate the Tathāgata's meditation, it would be impossible to appraise." Just as Shenhui read this scripture's general statements about the perfection of wisdom to apply specifically to the *Diamond Sūtra*, here we must assume that he applies this statement about the profundity of the Buddha's meditation to the merit that accrues from reciting the *Diamond*. Although Yang, 47n20 (cf. 35), is unaware of the scriptural citation here, he is correct in noting how Hu, 299, misunderstands the line.

232. P2045 and apparently the Dunhuang Museum ms. say only "this sūtra."

233. The Chinese, which is curious and unknown elsewhere, is *yiqie zhufa zushi* 一切諸法祖師.

234. Literally, the "gates of the eighty-four thousand perfections," meaning the teachings of or routes of access to the myriad perfections.

235. The reader may recall that the sūtra's full title is *Adamantine Sūtra of the Perfection of Wisdom*. General references to the perfection of wisdom in this context may also be to the sūtra itself.

236. The terms used here are *moni bao* 摩尼寶, literally, "maṇi," and simply "treasure." The underlying Sanskrit is *cintāmaṇi* or *maṇiratna*. The usage here implies that the growth of individual pearls was catalyzed through the existence of some master gem.

fection of wisdom is the same, because all wisdom grows due to the perfection of wisdom.[237]

36

To not recite the *Sūtra of the Perfection of Wisdom* is likened to a crown prince forsaking his father, the king, and trying to ascend to the throne somewhere else. This would be impossible![238] Therefore the *Short Version of the [Perfection of Wisdom] Sūtra* says, "Again, Subhūti, [through the other] sūtras one cannot attain omniscience. Bodhisattvas who [rely on other sūtras] are discarding the root and grasping at branches and leaves."[239] Therefore the *Wisdom Sūtra of the Heavenly King Pravara* says, "The Buddha said to Heavenly King Pravara, 'The single Dharma that a bodhisattva-mahāsattva studies in order to penetrate all the Dharmas is the perfection of wisdom.' "[240] The perfection of wisdom is also called the secret storehouse of all the buddhas; it is further called the *dhāraṇī* Dharma. It is the mantra of great wisdom, the unsurpassable mantra, [HS301] the unequaled mantra. It can eradicate all suffering and is true, not false. It is because all the buddhas of the three periods of time depend on the perfection of wisdom that they attain the unsurpassable perfect enlightenment.[241]

37

Therefore the *Diamond Sūtra* says, "If each grain of sand in the River Ganges itself represented as many grains of sand as there are in the River Ganges, and if one donated the seven precious things [to fill up] as many trichiliocosms as there are grains of sand in all those Rivers Ganges, it still would not equal [the merit] of maintaining even a single four-line verse of this sūtra."[242] The former merit compared to this merit would not amount to one part in a hundred, nor one part in a hundred thousand trillion, nor even one part in a number whose magnitude is beyond even metaphorical expression.

---

237. This kind of totalistic emphasis is not at all unusual in Chinese Buddhist texts, but it is notable that Shenhui uses such a "unitary key" to religious practice, just as he favors a unilinear transmission scheme.

238. This is a paraphrase of the *Wisdom Sūtra of the Heavenly King Pravara*, T 231: 8.704b21. See section 33 above for another metaphor involving a prince.

239. Hu, 300, notes minor textual problems. The *Short Version of the Sūtra* (*Xiaopin jing* 小品經) is Kumārajīva's translation of the *Aṣṭasāhasrikā* (T 227: 8.537a25f.). The term used for omniscience here is a transliteration of *sarvajña;* see T 227: 8.556a9.

240. T 231: 8.688a8.

241. This is an unattributed (and slightly re-ordered) citation of the *Heart Sūtra* (T 251: 8.848c13–16), which itself seems to reprise the *Aṣṭasāhasrikā* (T 227: 8.543b25f.).

242. This is a paraphrase of the *Diamond Sūtra* (T 235: 8.749c26–50a5). A similar usage occurs in section 38.

38

Those of you who practice the Path [should understand that] "the gods and asuras of all the worlds all make offerings according to the location" of the *Diamond Sūtra*.[243] Why? Because wherever this sūtra is, that place is a stūpa.[244] Why? Because those who recite the *Diamond Sūtra* "can achieve the Dharma that is the most supreme, the premier, the rare."[245] Wherever there is a fascicle of the *Diamond Sūtra* all the buddhas revere that fascicle of the *Diamond Sūtra*,[246] just as the disciples of the Buddha[247] [HS302] revere the Buddha. Why? The sūtra says, "The teacher of the buddhas is the Dharma. Because the Dharma is permanent, the buddhas too are permanent."[248] Therefore the *Diamond Sūtra* says, "If in the morning one donates one's body as many times as there are grains of sand in the Ganges, and if during midday one donates one's body as many times as there are grains of sand in the Ganges, and if at night one donates one's body as many times as there are grains of sand in the Ganges, then having donated one's body in this fashion for an innumerable hundred thousand trillion eons, [the merit accruing from this] would still not equal that of listening to this sūtra and having faith in one's mind, without a doubt. How much more so for those who copy it, maintain it, and explain it to others?"[249]

---

243. See T 235: 8.750a6 and 750c21, with the former being a little closer to Shenhui's phrasing. Note, however, that in both locations the sūtra compares the worship of its location to that of a stūpa, a point that Shenhui ignores. Although the "cult of the book" may have replaced or built off of that of the stūpa in India, as shown in the research of Gregory Schopen, the situation was different in China (Schopen, "Notes on the Cult of the Book"). Yang, 25, notes that the Dunhuang Museum ms. is missing the second of these four characters.

244. P3488 includes the reference to each location of the sūtra's preaching being like a stūpa, while the other two mss. say: "that place is honored; whoever has this sūtra, that person is esteemed." See Hu, 301, and Yang, 36.

245. See T 235: 8.750a9. At 750b5–6, the sūtra also says that those sentient beings who are able to hear, believe, and maintain it are the "premier, the rare."

246. Indian texts were not bound in fascicles, so this line indicates a certain limitation in the perspective of Tang Chinese monks. However, the sūtra says much the same about any location where even a four-line verse is preached, and Shenhui uses the sūtra's somewhat unusual phrasing (750c20) for "wherever there is" (*zaizai chuchu* 在在處處).

247. Yang, 25, notes that the Dunhuang Museum ms. is missing two characters here.

248. This citation is slightly abbreviated from the *Nirvāṇa Sūtra* (T 374: 12.387c15–16). It is stunning that Shenhui can insert such a substantialist expression in the middle of his encomium on the scriptures of profound emptiness.

249. See T 235: 8.750c7. Shenhui has modified the language slightly, but the meaning is unchanged. With the final sentence, is Shenhui suggesting how great his own merit is, as someone who explains the scripture for others?

39

Therefore the *Diamond Sūtra* "was preached by the Tathāgata for those who are inspired by the Great Vehicle, it was preached for those who are inspired by the Supreme Vehicle."[250] Why? It is likened to a great *nāga* who does not rain on Jambudvīpa. If he made it rain on Jambudvīpa, [everything] would be washed away, like leaves [in a flood]. Yet if he makes it rain on the ocean, the ocean neither increases nor decreases.[251] If one is of the Great Vehicle, of the Supreme Vehicle, one becomes neither shocked, nor afraid, nor frightened, nor doubtful when hearing the *Diamond Sūtra* explained. You should know that such a good young man or woman has for immeasurably long eons always made offerings to immeasurable buddhas and bodhisattvas and cultivated all the good Dharmas—and [thereby] on this day is able to hear the perfection of wisdom without becoming shocked or doubtful.[252] [HS303]

40

Therefore the *sūtra* says, "If one could fill up the great trichiliocosm as high as the Brahmā Heaven with stūpas made of all the precious things, [the merit accruing from this] would still not equal that of reciting the *Diamond Sūtra* and cultivating the perfection of wisdom."[253]

If one taught as many sentient beings as there are atoms in the great trichiliocosm so that all of them realized the fruit of the stream-enterer, it would not equal reciting the *Diamond Sūtra*.

If one taught as many sentient beings as there are atoms in the great trichiliocosm so that all of them realized the fruit of the once-returner, it would not equal reciting the *Diamond Sūtra*.

If one taught as many sentient beings as there are atoms in the great trichiliocosm so that all of them realized the fruit of the non-returner, it would not equal reciting the *Diamond Sūtra*.

If one taught as many sentient beings as there are atoms in the great

---

250. T 235: 8.750c13. Tanaka and Okimoto, 427n68, point out that although the terms Great Vehicle (*dasheng* 大乘) and Supreme Vehicle (*zuishang sheng* 最上乘) are equated here, they are differentiated in the *Miscellaneous Dialogues*, section 13, where the former is associated with bodhisattvas and the latter with buddhas.

251. This is a paraphrase of the *Siyi fantian suowen jing* 思益梵天所問經 (T 586: 15.57c4). This relatively obscure sūtra was used by the Northern school, in Puji's training regimen, and in the *Five Skillful Means;* see McRae, *Northern School,* 66, 192–193, and 219.

252. Ogawa ("Tonkō-bon Rokuso dankyō," 21) points out that this material is used in slightly amplified form in the *Platform Sūtra*, where it follows material from section 33 of the *Definition of the Truth*.

253. Material similar to this occurs four times in the *Diamond Sūtra* (T 235: 8.749b18, 749c29–50a5, 751c29–52a4, and 752b22), but nowhere with the wording that Shenhui uses.

trichiliocosm so that all of them realized the fruit of the arhat, it would not equal reciting the *Diamond Sūtra*.[254]

If one taught as many sentient beings as there are atoms in the great trichiliocosm so that all of them realized the fruit of the *pratyekabuddha*, it would not equal reciting the *Diamond Sūtra.*

If one taught as many sentient beings as there are atoms in the great trichiliocosm so that all of them realized the ten degrees of faith, realized the ten abodes of mind, realized the ten degrees of mind or ten degrees of diversion of mind,[255] it still is not equal to reciting the *Diamond Sūtra* and cultivating the perfection of wisdom.[256]

Why is this so? Because this sūtra possesses[257] inconceivable merit that is ineffable, inestimable, [HS304] and infinite, besides accomplishing the profound and unsurpassable wisdom of the buddhas!

41

Therefore I tell you, friends, [even] if you have committed the evil of all the serious transgressions [that lead to rebirth in] the Avīci Hell, with no prospect[258] of repenting and extinguishing [the karmic results accruing], you must recite the *Diamond Sūtra* and study the perfection of wisdom, realizing that the transgressions of those who do so will be extinguished. Why? It is likened to birds of infinitely variegated colors that fly beneath Mount Sumeru and become entirely[259] the same color as the mountain. Why? Because of the power of the mountain's virtue. The power of the virtue of reciting the *Diamond Sūtra* is like this.[260]

---

254. The 33 characters up to this point are omitted from P3844.

255. For the English names of these stages, I have followed Hurvitz, *Life and Ideas*, 363–365, the only change being the inclusion of "mind" where Shenhui includes the character *xin* 心.

256. The pattern on which the previous material is based occurs twice in the *Wisdom Sūtra of the Heavenly King Pravara*, at T 231: 8.706a18, but Shenhui has expanded it for formulaic repetition. Of course, in the original it refers not to the *Diamond Sūtra* specifically but to the perfection of wisdom in general. Yang, 48n21 (cf. 37), notes that both mss. include the phrase "cultivating the perfection of wisdom," but it was mistakenly omitted by Hu, 303.

257. P3488 comes to an end at this point.

258. Here the text has *wu chu* 無處 where it should have *wu suo* 無所.

259. Hu, 304, reads *faxin* 發心, "generate *bodhicitta*," with a subsequent character missing. Given the context, he must have misread the ms. I have followed Yang, 27, which reads *jie de* 皆得, "all attain," with no lacuna.

260. This metaphor is found in the *Pusa cong doushu tian jiangshen mutai shuo guangpu jing* 菩薩從兜術天降神母胎說廣普經 (T 384: 12.1042a25). This sūtra, the title of which might be rendered as the *Extensive Sūtra of the Bodhisattva Preached by His Spirit from His Mother's Womb upon Descent from the Tuṣita Heaven*, was translated by Zhu Fonian. I have drawn this citation from Tanaka and Okimoto, 428n74, with amazement that they ever found it. Shenhui may have seen this scripture, or he may have known the metaphor from intermediate sources.

42

Friends, if you recite the *Diamond Sūtra* without entering the Samādhi of the Single Practice, it is because of the karmic obstructions from serious transgressions in your previous lives. You must recite this sūtra. Because of the power of this sūtra's virtue, you will experience the disparagement of your contemporaries and belittlement in your present [life]. But because of this belittlement and disparagement, the karmic obstructions from serious transgressions in your previous lives will be extinguished. When they are extinguished, you will enter the Samādhi of the Single Practice.[261] [HS305]

43

Therefore the *Wisdom Sūtra of the Heavenly King Pravara* says, "The Buddha told Mañjuśrī, 'Suppose that the buddhas, the tathāgatas, were as numerous as all the atoms in the world and that an evil person killed them all. What do you think, Mañjuśrī, would that person's transgression be great?' Mañjuśrī Bodhisattva said to the Buddha, 'World-honored One, the transgression would be inaudible, incalculable, inconceivable!'[262] The Buddha told Mañjuśrī Bodhisattva, 'If someone were to hinder the *Diamond Sūtra* and revile it without faith, the former transgression would not amount to one part in a hundred, nor one part in a hundred thousand trillion, nor even one part in a number whose magnitude is beyond even metaphorical expression.'"[263]

44

Therefore the *Diamond Sūtra* says, "The Buddha said, 'I remember that, in the immeasurable *asaṃkhyeya* eons prior to [my encounter with] Buddha Dīpaṃkara, I had met with eight hundred and four thousand trillion *nayutas* of buddhas and disciples of the buddhas, making offerings to and serving each and every one of them without wasting a moment.'" But I did not receive

---

261. This is loosely based on the *Diamond Sūtra* (T 235: 8.750c24), where "perfect and complete enlightenment" (Skt. *anuttara-samyak-sambodhi*) is mentioned instead of the Samādhi of the Single Practice. This citation is discussed in the *Miscellaneous Dialogues*, section 31. The term *qingshou* 輕受, "light reception" or "belittling experience," is not listed in *Bukkyōgo daijiten*. It seems incredible for anyone to argue that because of a sūtra's power one will be persecuted, and that through that experience one's karmic obstacles will be eliminated. Yet the rhetoric of persecution is widely deployed within the Chan tradition to justify the supremacy of one's understanding or practice. In terms of Shenhui's personal situation, this may be an expression of a need for validation.

262. The phrase *bu ke wen* 不可聞, "inaudible," is unusual, although understandable in the Indian context.

263. See T 231: 8.722a11. Hu, 305, illegitimately changes the original's "*Diamond Sūtra*" to "this sūtra." This is noted by Yang, 48n24 (cf. 38), although he does not recognize that the line is from the *Diamond*.

any prediction [from them] of my future enlightenment. Why? Because I had achieved something [HS306] attainable. And afterward, when I received the prediction of my future enlightenment from Buddha Dīpaṃkara, it was because I had read and recited the *Diamond Sūtra,* had cultivated the perfection of wisdom, and had achieved the unattainable. [As a result,] I have achieved buddhahood and am called Śākyamuni. "If one compares the merit from making offerings to the buddhas to that of reciting this *Diamond Sūtra* and preaching it to others, [the former would] not amount to one part in a hundred, nor one part in a hundred thousand trillion, nor even one part in a number whose magnitude is beyond even metaphorical expression."[264]

45

Therefore the *Wisdom Sūtra of the Heavenly King Pravara* says, "[The Buddha said,] 'Great King, it is likened to the four elements being dependent on space while space is not dependent on anything else. The afflictions are likewise, being dependent on the dharma-nature while the dharma-nature is not dependent on anything else. Great King, a bodhisattva-mahāsattva's practice of the perfection of wisdom—in truth may it be contemplated and understood.' "[265]

46

The *Wisdom Sūtra of the Heavenly King Pravara* says, "[The Buddha said,] 'Suppose that as many atoms as there are in the immeasurable *asaṃkhyeya*[266] great trichiliocosm of worlds were each one a great trichiliocosm of worlds and that all those great trichiliocosms of worlds were filled with the seven precious things piled as high as the Akaniṣṭha Heaven,[267] to be donated to as many sages as there are atoms in the great trichiliocosm of worlds—would the merit of this be great?' Mañjuśrī [HS307] Bodhisattva said, 'World-honored One, the merit [you described] previously was inconceivable, and how much more so this merit!' " The Buddha told Mañjuśrī Bodhisattva,[268] "If a good young man or woman circulates this *Perfection of Wisdom Sūtra* and explains it to others, the merit of [that material donation] compared to this merit will not amount to one part in a hundred, nor one part in a hundred

---

264. The two quotations occur at T 235: 8.750c27–751a4; the intervening explanatory material was added by Shenhui. As Yang, 48n25 (cf. 38) notes, the number rendered here as "eight hundred and four thousand trillion *nayutas*" (*babaisiqian wanyi nayouta* 八百四千萬億那由他) follows Kumārajīva's translation exactly, so that the revision by Hu, 306, is unwarranted.

265. See T 231: 8.701a12. "Contemplated and understood" may be an overtranslation of *guanzhi* 觀知.

266. Yang, 29, follows the sūtra in omitting the character *jie* 劫, Skt. *kalpa*, "eon," found in Hu's edition.

267. This is the highest of the eighteen heavens of the *rūpadhātu*.

268. Hu, 307, points out that the preceding 62 lines, or two sheets, were out of place in the original manuscript. In addition, the one sheet of 31 lines following this actually belongs to Shenhui's *Platform Sermon*, to which Hu has returned it.

thousand trillion, nor even one part in a number whose magnitude is beyond even metaphorical expression."[269] [HS308]

47

Therefore the *Diamond Sūtra* says, "[The Buddha said,] 'Subhūti, if someone were to donate the seven precious things in sufficient quantity to fill the immeasurable *asaṃkhyeya* worlds, and if a good young man or woman were to generate *bodhicitta,* recite this sūtra, and explain it extensively to others, the merit of the latter would far exceed that of the former.'[270] What does explaining it extensively to others mean? It is to not be attached to characteristics."
[Question:] What is it to not be attached to characteristics?
[Answer:] It is called suchness.
[Question:] What is suchness?
[Answer:] It is called non-thought.
[Question:] What is non-thought?
[Answer:] It is called to not think of being and nonbeing, to not think of good and evil, to not think of that which has boundaries and that which is without boundaries, to not think of that which has limits and that which is without limits.[271] It is to not think of *bodhi* and to not take *bodhi* as a thought, to not think of nirvāṇa and to not take nirvāṇa as a thought. This nonthought is the perfection of wisdom, and the perfection of wisdom is the Samādhi of the Single Practice.

48

Friends, if one is at the stage of practicing [the Dharma], and if one shines the light of awareness on a thought as soon as arises, the activated mind will disappear, and it will naturally vanish in the light of awareness, and that is

---

269. Paraphrased from T 231: 8.721c8, with "this sūtra" changed to *Perfection of Wisdom Sūtra*.
270. See T 235: 8.752b22; see also the *Miscellaneous Dialogues,* section 24. Shenhui omits the *Diamond Sūtra*'s reference to maintaining even one four-line verse. Also, in the sūtra the transition to the discussion about not being attached to characteristics is perfectly natural, since the immediately preceding lines discussed the "characteristics of the dharmas" that the Buddha defines as "non-characteristics." The rest of the dialogue is not in the sūtra but is created by Shenhui as a bridge to his own ideas of non-thought, expressed in the next section. Note how far we have gone from the lively discussion with Chongyuan to unstated questions and answers crafted to lend scriptural authority to Shenhui's ideas!
271. The "boundaries" (*bianji* 邊際) referred to here are spatial, while the "limits" (*xianliang* 限量) are quantitative.

precisely [what is meant by] non-thought.[272] This[273] non-thought is the absence of [any] single realm. If a single realm exists, this is to not be in correspondence with non-thought. Therefore, friends, to see according to reality is to comprehend the extremely profound *dharmadhātu,* and is the Samādhi of the Single Practice.[274]

49

Therefore, in the *Short Version of the Perfection of Wisdom Sūtra* [the Buddha] says, "Gentlemen, this is the perfection of wisdom: it is that which is called 'being without thoughts with regard to the dharmas.' We [buddhas] reside within the Dharma of non-thought and [thereby] attain golden bodies with thirty-two characteristics and great refulgence and inconceivable wisdom such as this. The unsurpassable samādhis and unsurpassable wisdom of the buddhas exhaust the limits of all the various merits. The buddhas explain all these various merits as being inexhaustible, so how much less likely is it that the *śrāvakas* and *pratyekabuddhas* would be able to understand them?"[275]

To see non-thought is for the six senses to be without defilement. To see non-thought is to attain access to the buddhas' knowing and seeing.[276] To see non-thought is called things as they truly are. To see non-thought is the cardinal meaning of the Middle Path. To see non-thought is to be simultaneously equipped with merits as numerous as the sands of the River Ganges. To see non-thought is to be able to generate all the Dharmas. To see non-thought is to embody all the Dharmas.[277] [HS310]

50

His Reverence said in a loud voice from his Dharma-seat within the great assembly:

---

272. This section also occurs in the *Miscellaneous Dialogues,* as part of section 24. The Chinese is *xin ruo you nian qi, ji bian juezhao* 心若有念起，即便覺照, which could also be translated as "if thoughts arise within the mind, this is understanding/illumination." Tanaka and Okimoto, 240, interpret the last compound, which is not a standard Buddhist technical term, as the "coarse activity" (*arai hataraki*) of the mind, and although this fits Shenhui's ideas in general it is not implicit in the terminology.

273. Here Yang, 30, notes that the Dunhuang Museum ms. lacks three characters, which he has supplied from Hu's edition.

274. Note that sections 33 and 34 include references from the *Wisdom Sūtra of the Heavenly King Pravara* to comprehending the *dharmadhātu* and seeing the perfection of wisdom "according to reality."

275. See T 227: 8.581c19. The same quotation occurs in the Ishii ms. of the *Miscellaneous Dialogues,* section 24. [The beginning of this sentence might also be interpreted as: "If all the buddhas were to explain these, they would never finish..."—Ed.]

276. To attain *xiang fo zhijian* 向佛知見.

277. Shenhui must mean that seeing non-thought allows one insight into all aspects of reality and the ability to generate all the religious principles of Buddhism, not to generate the dharmas as elemental metaphysical units. Tanaka and Okimoto, 241, adopt the latter interpretation. This is the end of Hu's fifth section.

I[278] have now been able to comprehend the Tathāgata-nature;
Now the Tathāgata is within my very body.
There's no difference between me and the Tathāgata;
The Tathāgata is my ocean of suchness![279]

I express my reverence for the buddhas of the ten directions, the great bodhisattva-mahāsattvas, and all the sages: I have now devoted my life to the writing of this *Treatise on the Unsurpassable Vehicle of Sudden Enlightenment*,[280] because I vow that all sentient beings should hear the praises of the adamantine perfection of wisdom, have definitive profound faith, and withstand [the truth] without retrogression.

I have now devoted my life, I vow that throughout all the future eons I will praise the adamantine perfection of wisdom, and I vow that all sentient beings will hear the praises of the perfection of wisdom, so that they will be able to read, recite, and maintain it, and will [thereby] be able to withstand [the truth] without retrogression. [HS311]

I have now devoted my life, I vow that throughout all the future eons will be heard the praises of the adamantine perfection of wisdom, and I vow that all sentient beings will hear the praises of the perfection of wisdom, because they will be able to definitively cultivate the perfection of wisdom and will [thereby] be able to withstand [the truth] without retrogression.

I vow[281] that in all the future eons I will devote my life to making offerings to the adamantine perfection of wisdom; I vow to be able to become a master[282] of the perfection of wisdom, always preaching the adamantine perfection of wisdom for all sentient beings; and [I] vow that all sentient beings shall hear the preaching of the adamantine perfection of wisdom and achieve the unattainable.

I vow that, on behalf of all sentient beings and in all future eons I will always devote my life to protect the adamantine perfection of wisdom, and

---

278. Using *wo* 我. Given this pronominal usage, it is likely that Shenhui declaims this as a model for his listeners rather than as a description of his own accomplishments.

279. This verse also occurs in the *Miscellaneous Dialogues*, section 69, at the end of the biography of Huineng. "Tathāgata-nature" (*rulai xing* 如來性) occurs in a number of scriptural sources. The assertions made here deserve comparison with Shenhui's identification with Cunda.

280. Along with the references in sections 27 and 28 above, this passage constitutes definite internal evidence that Shenhui (or his followers acting in his place) wrote the *Definition of the Truth* rather than simply compiling it from transcriptions of the sermons of the 730s. Were it not for the reference to the text here, this entire section might be read in the plural as material to be intoned in unison, or at least to be intoned on behalf of the entire audience. Although I have found it convenient to use the singular first-person pronoun rather frequently in the translation, it does not occur in the original until the expression indicated in the following note.

281. Here the text reads *yuan wo* 願我, "vow I." The next incidence of "I vow" represents the same construction, whereas the "I" (*wo*) does not occur in the final clause. The structure of the next sentence is similar, with "I" (*wo*) occurring only in the first clause.

282. Using *zhu* 主, "host."

I vow that all sentient beings will achieve the unattainable and at one time achieve buddhahood by relying upon the perfection of wisdom![283]

51

His Reverence asked Dharma Master Chongyuan, "Have you lectured on the *Great Parinirvāṇa Sūtra?*"[284]

The Dharma master replied, "I have lectured on the *Great Parinirvāṇa Sūtra* dozens of times."

His Reverence said, "All the sūtras and treatises of the Mahāyāna and Hīnayāna explain that sentient beings are not emancipated because they possess the two minds of generation and extinction. Furthermore, the *Nirvāṇa Sūtra* says,

> All the processes [of life] are impermanent;
> They are the dharmas of generation and extinction.
> When generation and extinction are extinguished, [HS312]
> Serene extinction is bliss.[285]

I wonder, can generation and extinction be extinguished or not? Is extinction extinguished with generation, or is generation extinguished with extinction? Is generation able to extinguish generation itself, or is extinction able to extinguish extinction itself? I would like you to answer each of these [questions] for me in detail."

Dharma Master Chongyuan said, "I too have noticed that the various sūtras and treatises contain explanations such as this, but to this point I have never been able to comprehend their meaning. If you comprehend their meaning, please explain it to the assembly."

His Reverence said, "I cannot demur from explaining it to you, but I fear no one will understand."

The Dharma master said, "There are over ten thousand monks and laymen here.[286] Can it be that not a single one will understand?"

---

283. This section seems out of place in the text as it now exists, and it is not clear exactly what is happening. Rather than Shenhui supposedly reciting all of this himself, this seems to be a finale of group dedication used in conclusion to the section on the virtue of reciting the *Diamond Sūtra*. That we now return to a dialogue with Dharma Master Chongyuan constitutes more evidence of editorial cutting-and-pasting. This is the end of Hu's sixth section.

284. This passage also occurs in the *Records of the Transmission;* see Adamek, *Mystique,* 340.

285. This verse is given in divided form in the *Nirvāṇa Sūtra,* T 375: 12.692a13 and 693a1. It is also found in the *Mile da chengfo jing* 彌勒大成佛經, T 456: 14.430b24, and, according to Tanaka and Okimoto, 430n86, elsewhere throughout the canon. A reference to "dharmas of generation and extinction" occurs in the *Miscellaneous Dialogues,* section 8.

286. I agree with Tanaka and Okimoto, 244, that this reading is appropriate, but it is incredible to think Shenhui's editor meant to imply that ten thousand people were in attendance. Hu, 497n17, is adamant in dismissing such simplistic fabrications of Shenhui's texts.

His Reverence said, "Look. Do you see or not?"
The Dharma master said, "See what?"[287]
His Reverence said, "Obviously, you don't see."[288]

When the Dharma master heard this, he held his tongue and did not respond. To say nothing was equivalent to declaring his submission,[289] and his followers became increasingly disappointed. The victory being determined, the monks and laypeople sighed and dispersed.[290]

52 [Postface]

The waters of wisdom [that derive from] His Reverence's lake of meditation have long enriched his mind-source; the lamp of compassion of his storehouse of the precepts has illuminated perfectly the realm of his body.[291] [HS313] He imparted the inconceivable Dharma, doing yet not doing anything; he lauded the Dharma gate that transcends characteristics, explaining yet not explaining anything. The six mindfulnesses[292] and the nine successive [stages of meditation][293]—his mind has melded with the real principle; the three baskets and the five vehicles—his body understands true suchness.[294] Therefore, when he enters into debate[295] the banners of heterodoxy are definitively destroyed; when he defines the alternatives of right and wrong the banner of the superior [teaching] will long be established. As to that echo within the empty mountain valley, he consigns himself to non-activation to accord with the sound; the bright mirror discriminates forms, reflecting that which has form and revealing its characteristics.[296]

---

287. In response to Shenhui's question, *kan jian bu jian* 看見不見, the Chinese here is *jian shimo* 見是沒. This colloquialism is identical to the modern mandarin *jian shenme* 見甚麼.

288. This brief exchange, from Shenhui's "Look. Do you see or not?," seems very much like later encounter-dialogue exchanges.

289. Literally, *fei lun yi yi quci* 非論一己屈詞, "not to dispute at all was an expression of submission."

290. The sigh here denotes admiration and respect. At the end of this sentence Hu, 312, has changed *ran* 然, "in such a fashion," to *yan* 焉, "at that point."

291. This is the same type of analogy used so often in early Chan texts, including those of the "Northern school" and the *Platform Sūtra*. The term *shenyu* 身域, "body realm," is unique.

292. The *liu nian* or *liu nianchu* 六念處 are mindfulness of the Buddha, Dharma, Saṅgha, the precepts, charity, and heaven, the last being subject to different interpretations (*Bukkyōgo daijiten*, 1459b, citing the *Mohe zhiguan* 摩訶止觀, T 1911: 46.77c).

293. The text here has only *jiu ci* 九次, which is no doubt an abbreviation of *jiu cidi chanmen* 九次第禪門, or *jiu cidi ding* 九次第定, the four *dhyānas*, four formless attainments, and *nirodha-samāpatti*.

294. Note the consistent mind-body parallelism throughout this passage, recalling the *Five Skillful Means*. The five vehicles refer to humans, gods, *śrāvakas*, *pratyekabuddhas*, and bodhisattvas.

295. The Chinese is *jianglun chu* 講論處, "lecture-debate location."

296. The mention of valley echoes alludes to a famous line in Sengzhao's *Zhao lun* 肇論 (T 1858: 45.158b25). "Non-activation" renders *wuqi* 無起, while "consigns" renders *ren* 任, "to give oneself to," "let go in." This entire passage is a concatenation of conventional slogans.

I[297] have been obsequious toward scholar-monks and have aggravated the followers, not caring about my mediocrity and daring to disclose my stupidity.[298] Striving on the path year after year,[299] I wished for attainment but was increasingly unsuccessful. This teaching is attained, however, when one stops seeking.[300] According to the principle of non-abiding, the concept of abiding becomes self-evident.[301] If one activates the dharma of the existence of seeing, where will the mind of seeing exist within the dharma?[302] When one is deluded as to the joy [of this teaching], the suffering within that joy is of an earlier time; when one is enlightened to suffering, the joy within that suffering is today's. Always regretful that I did not encounter vigorous encouragement, and even falsely praised, I have carefully recorded what I have heard and stored it in a case.[303]

> Although *bodhicitta* and the ultimate [realization] are no different,
> Of the two [states of] mind, it is the first which is [more] difficult.
> With oneself still unsaved, to first save others—[HS314]
> Thus do we reverence the initial [achievement of] *bodhicitta*.
>
> By this initial *bodhicitta* one becomes a teacher of humans and gods,
> Superior to the *śrāvakas* and *pratyekabuddhas*.
> With such a *bodhicitta*, one transcends the triple realm,
> Hence this is called the most unsurpassable.[304]

---

297. Using the form *mouyi* 某乙, "someone." The next couple of sentences could refer to foolish monks, but it seems better to read them as Dugu Pei's own deprecatory self-description.

298. *Morohashi*, 2.1830c, defines *taopei* 叨陪 as "to excessively serve the worthy," hence the rendering "obsequious." Since neither *Morohashi* nor the *Xiandai hanyu sanyin cidian* lists *lan yu* 灆預, "chaotically prepare," as a compound, I have approximated the nuance of the line with "aggravated." (I wonder if the first character should be *lan* 濫.) Finally, *Morohashi*, 4.3991b, defines *yongxu* 庸虛 as "stupid and lacking ability," hence "mediocrity." I wonder if the scholar-monks, *xuelü* 學侶 (which really could be trainee-monks), and followers, *mentu* 門徒, refer to doctrinal specialists and Chan practitioners. Or do both terms refer to the latter?

299. The Chinese is *binian daoye* 比年道業, "every year path work."

300. Although this may be merely conventional self-deprecation, it seems significant that Dugu Pei presents himself as someone dedicated but unsuccessful at the ordinary sort of spiritual practice. Did Shenhui's doctrines appeal particularly well to the manifestly (and self-consciously) unenlightened?

301. Literally, the concept of abiding is "based on the principle, clear and distinct."

302. Hu, 313, makes two minor editorial changes to the original here, which are followed by Yang, 41. Although Tanaka and Okimoto, 245, interpret this as a declarative sentence, the sentence-final *anzai* 安在 usually occurs in this position as an interrogative (*Morohashi*, 3.915b). The "dharma of the existence of seeing" renders the Chinese *youjian zhi fa* 有見之法, while "mind of seeing" represents *jianxin* 見心. [The first clause could also be taken as "gives rise to dharmas of views regarding existence."—Ed.] Both the terminology and the overall construction of this and the following sentence are somewhat opaque, in part because they belong to that awful genre of Chan platitudes more appropriate in an epitaph than a treatise.

303. The compiler is relating his own role in recording Shenhui's teachings, using a curious sort of not-quite-polished literary language.

304. This verse from the *Nirvāṇa Sūtra* (T 374: 12.590a21–24) also occurs in the *Platform*

53

That which is called the *Treatise on the Definition of the Truth regarding the Southern School of Bodhidharma* relates the succession from master to master of the six generations of great worthies and the transmission of the Dharma seal.[305] In the succession of the generations the fundamental teaching has been without alternation.[306] Ever since Great Master Bodhidharma, only one person has been permitted in each generation.[307] To say there might be two or three intervening [figures] is a mistaken practice of the Buddhadharma. How much more so [the situation] nowadays, when those who teach Chan are innumerable while those who study Chan remain completely unknown. [Those teachers] all lack their succession, so on what do they base their teachings? Their followers have mistaken chickens for phoenixes, have been fooled into thinking cattails are dried meat, have taken fish eyes as gems, and consider the evening light to be a treasure!

Our Reverend,[308] when the correct Dharma was in decline and the heterodox Dharmas were confusing [everyone],[309] [HS315] knew that he would have to carry out the prescription of the [wise] later doctor [even after] rejecting the [same] elixir of the former doctor.[310] [He vowed] he would raise up once again the true teaching, putting an end to the [incorrect] versions of today.[311]

[You need to] understand that that which is modeled on the pearl is not the pearl, that you falsely seek for the moon in the water! I see that those

---

Sermon, section 7. Note how Dugu Pei's postface returns to the *Nirvāṇa* rather than the *Diamond Sūtra*.

305. The Chinese here is slightly different from elsewhere in the text: *liudai dade shishi xiangshou, fayin xiangchuan* 六代大德師師相承、法印相傳.

306. The point is intentionally paradoxical in form, though not in content: even though the patriarchs have succeeded one after the other, the fundamental teaching (*benzong* 本宗) has never changed.

307. Once again, the rhetoric of permission, *xu* 許.

308. The Chinese is *wo heshang* 我和上.

309. The decline referred to here seems to be that after Huineng's death and before the Huatai meetings.

310. The reference here is to a story in the *Nirvāṇa Sūtra*, T 375: 12.862b25. Of two doctors, the former is a quack who depends on a milk preparation, which the latter has the king suppress because of its poisonous tendencies. Then, when the king becomes ill, the gifted second doctor prescribes the same milk preparation, causing the king no little consternation. The point is that what is bad in one situation is good in another, or that the doctrine of self was anathema to those of Hīnayāna tendencies, but Mahāyānists should recognize that the problem was not the human self but the attribution of substantiality to all things. Dugu Pei is presumably drawn to this parable because it implicitly depicts Shenhui as being recognized by the king for his wisdom, but he has (no doubt inadvertently) implied that Shenhui's teachings were the same as those already known from "Northern school" authorities. Hu, 314, suggests a minor alteration here, which is rejected as unhelpful and inappropriate editorial intervention by Yang, 48n26; cf. 42.

311. The Chinese *yunyun* 云云 could mean "etcetera," but here it seems to refer to the various things people say in error about the Dharma.

who study the Path do not have the Path but pointlessly aim for the mountain of treasures! This is truly to belabor the form and disport with the shadow; it is really to lift up one's voice and hear the mind echo.

For that reason I have compiled this treatise to provide some small compass [for students] and to have the great Path enrich sentient beings[312] while the correct Dharma circulates in the world. The vigorous exchange of questions and answers recorded at the beginning of the treatise will enable students to distinguish the true principle;[313] when those with doubts see the explanation of the master-disciple succession related later [in the text], it will eradicate their doubts.[314] Examining this treatise in detail, how inconceivable it is! Those who heard it said it was something they had never heard before, and those who saw it said it was something they had never seen before. This is how the treasure storehouse within one's own home suddenly opens of itself, and the ford over the ocean of suffering is unexpectedly attained!

54

Ah! The proof of the transmission of the six generations is now in Shaozhou, and yet the four categories of followers pointlessly wander about Mount Song![315] It can be said, fish may swim in the water but they spread their nets on the mountain high!

At that time a fellow student asked, "Reverend Puji[316] of Mount Song is the one buddha appearing in the world and the teacher of emperors. Everyone under heaven reveres his virtue; all within the four seas take refuge in him. Who can say what is right? Who can say what is wrong?" [HS316]

Also among the fellow students was an elder who replied, "Cease! Matters such as this are not for you to understand; matters such as this are beyond your comprehension. You only know how to honor what you hear and denigrate what you see, to emphasize the past and belittle the present.[317] You

---

312. The word used for "enrich" here is *xia* 洽.

313. The Chinese here is *zhenzong* 真宗. Hu, 315, omits these characters.

314. It is noteworthy that Dugu Pei's list of topics omits any mention of the recitation of the *Diamond Sūtra*. Hu, 315, omits two additional characters from this sentence; see Yang, 48n27; cf. 43.

315. The Chinese for "proof of the transmission," which presumably refers to Bodhidharma's robe, is *liudai chuanxin* 六代傳信. The "four categories" of followers refers to ordained and lay men and women.

316. Here and below Puji is referred to as "Reverend" rather than "Chan master." The description of Puji here is also unique to the conclusion of this text: in section 19, Shenxiu is described as the teacher of three emperors, but nowhere before this is such a reference made about Puji. The description of Puji in this fashion is undeniably reminiscent of the passages from epitaphs for him quoted in McRae, *Northern School*, 65, which could not have been written until well after the Huatai debates.

317. How often are such sentiments expressed in Tang texts? Is this a radically anti-traditionalist viewpoint?

believe you know the little stream, but how can you understand the great ocean? Our Reverend has received the transmission from the sixth generation, and the deputation is clear.[318] Furthermore, in essence, the teaching that he has established is not commensurate with that of other authorities."[319]

The assembly all snapped their fingers and said, "Excellent! How are they different?"[320]

He answered, "Without going into details, the import of His Reverence's oral teaching is profound. It cannot be understood with wisdom or recognized with consciousness.[321] Who can distinguish the degrees [of attainment] of the three categories of wisdom and the ten stages of sagehood? [Even] the *śrāvakas* and *pratyekabuddhas* do not understand the distinctions between them."[322]

Formerly, on the fifteenth day of the first month of the twentieth year[323] of Kaiyuan (732), [Shenhui] debated Dharma Master Chongyuan, briefly revealing the mind-ground, mobilizing the pneuma to ascend beyond the clouds, and uttering words so as to astound the audience. Monks and laypeople said to each other that he was a reincarnation of Bodhidharma. I have therefore edited into a treatise his extensive elaborations in response to the questions posed.

---

318. The Chinese is *wo heshang cheng liudai zhi hou, fuzhu fenming* 我和上承六代之後，付囑分明. Although this phrasing is perfectly natural, this is the first time the text has used *fenming*, "clear," to describe the transmission. Since Shenhui did not include himself in his own pronouncements, this is also the first occasion in this text in which he is explicitly connected to the six-generation transmission.

319. The Chinese is *suo li zongti yü zhujia bu deng* 所立宗体與諸家不等. The *zongti* used here corresponds to the *zongzhi* 宗旨, "central principle," used earlier in the text. Although *jia*, "house," is used in later Chan texts with the meaning of "school," here it probably means individual teachers other than Shenhui. (The same usage occurs toward the end of the verses, with a stronger sense of sectarian groups rather than individuals.) The quotation of this elder is an interesting textual complexity; does it imply to some degree that Shenhui's followers were intimately involved in the creation of this text and in furthering his campaign?

320. Within the sūtras, to snap the fingers, *tanzhi* 彈指, was a sign of approval or joy (*Bukkyōgo daijiten*, 941a–b). Within later Chan texts various other meanings are also attached to this signal (*Zengaku daijiten*, 2:836c). Hu, 316, has *Chan* 禪 instead of *tan* 彈, but Yang, 43, has what must be the correct form.

321. The character *shi* 識, which often renders *vijñāna* in Buddhist contexts, is used for "recognize" and "consciousness" in this sentence.

322. Literally, the limits or boundaries between them. Hu, 316, has the quotation from the elder extend down to the reference to the editing of the treatise, but I believe it is better to close the quotation here. Although there is no way to be certain, the elder's comments have the feeling of a posthumous appraisal. Certainly, the desire to collect a master's sayings in written form after his death is a widespread practice in Chan, from the *Essentials of Cultivating the Mind* onward.

323. The text actually has the twelfth year, but Hu, 315, revised this on the basis of the preface; see section 1.

55

The treatise says, "My holding this unrestricted great assembly is not for [my own] merit, but in order to define the true and the false for the students of the Path in China, so that all those in China can carefully distinguish between the heterodox and the correct."[324] The true and the false, heterodox and correct, are both clarified within the text. It also relates the fundamental teaching and the later generations of the transmission.[325] Although Reverend Puji has extensively saved sentient beings in this world, he is not the equal of [Huineng of] Caoqi.[326] The Southern school has therefore been described in this treatise.[327] [HS317]

Since today it is rare to hear of these matters, [those who can hear] will jump for joy, rejoicing beyond measure. Based on my own meager explanation of the void, I have composed this encomium:

> At the beginning of this treatise is Great Master Bodhidharma,
> Whose correct teaching[328] is recounted with refulgent praise of the root and
>   branches.
> When the Liang regime flourished he had come from India in dignity,
> Leaving this prediction, "My Dharma will decline after six [generations]."[329]
> His Path was dark and mysterious, and people could not understand it.
> Today there is only our Reverend who practices it.

---

324. This is a paraphrase of language in section 8.

325. Using *benzong* 本宗, which does not occur in the body of the text, and *chuan zhi houdai* 傳之後代, which I take to refer specifically to Shenhui.

326. Here Puji is referred to more conventionally using only the second character of his name. Since everywhere before he is referred to both as Chan master and with both characters of his name, we may infer that this section of the text was a later addition. This is also supported by the fact that this is the one and only occurrence of the place name Caoqi in the *Definition of the Truth*.

327. The text has *zhong* 中, "middle," for what must be *zong* 宗, "school" or "teaching." Tanaka and Okimoto, 248, interpret this as a reference to the treatise's having been preached "within the south" (*nanzhong* 南中), but they note (431n92) that Huatai was not in the south and their reading is tentative.

328. The Chinese here is *zhengzong* 正宗; the same term is used a few stanzas below.

329. This is a reworking of a prediction made by Huike in reference to the *Laṅkāvatāra Sūtra* and recorded in the *Continued Biographies*, "[The understanding of] this sūtra will become superficial after four generations. How utterly lamentable!" (McRae, *Northern School*, 28, and T 2060: 50.552b29–c1). Here it is meant to relate to the temporary eclipse of Huineng's teaching, but it is very curious that there is no other such reference in the text. The *Definition of the Truth* is, however, very insistent on the category of the six generations of the patriarchate. The *Shin jigen*, 1072a, defines *lingchi* 陵遲 as "gradual decline." See the same term again in the third-to-last couplet of the text, and further comments on this post-Huineng eclipse below. On the decline after six generations, see the *Chan Chart* in Kamata, *Zengen shosenshū tojo*, 277 and notes.

The treatise describes the six generations, with one person in each
    generation
Matching with the mind, leaving no room for nepotism in the Dharma.[330]
There is only the great affair, the treasure of the four seas,
Always deputed onward with careful consideration,
The robe emblematic of the proof [of transmission] to end the world's river
    of doubts.[331]
Without comparison under heaven, who [is worthy to] stand beside it?

With the great treatise of the Great Vehicle circulating in every direction,
The banner of the Dharma is erected once again, and the sun of wisdom
    shines,
A raft over the river of attachment, a bridge over the ocean of suffering!
Those who hear it and see it are enlightened to the true and permanent,
    [HS318]
The practice of the great Path, the song of correct teaching,
Without self and without person, good and evil undestroyed.

In reverentially examining this treatise, [I see] it mysteriously penetrating
    the wondrous principle,
First describing the questions and answers, and then relating the correct
    teaching[332]
Without thought and without capability,[333] speaking of emptiness without
    making anything empty,
With neither form nor characteristics, without virtue and without merit.
He who penetrates will see, only those having [karmic] connections will
    encounter it.
This sudden teaching of Chan is not the same as that of other authorities.[334]

---

330. Tanaka and Okimoto, 249, interpret the second part of this line as "it is not related to [expositions of] the Dharma." However, this interpretation of *qin* 親, "relatives," is curious. I believe the line refers to the notion that one should not transmit the Dharma to those who are unworthy, even if they are relatives, and have paraphrased the original accordingly. Note the similar sentiments expressed in the line below: "He who penetrates will see, only those having [karmic] connections will encounter it."

331. Technically, *yijin* 疑津 is a "ford" of doubts. The Chinese term was obviously selected for its rhyme.

332. This line shows that these final verses were appended to the *Definition of the Truth* after the insertion of the material related to the *Diamond Sūtra* contained in sections 33–50. The term for the "correct teaching" here, as just above, is *zhengzong*.

333. Yang, 48n29 (cf. 45), amends this to "without thought but able to think" (*wunian neng nian* 無念能念), which is a reasonable suggestion. I have preferred to leave the text unchanged.

334. The Chinese is *Chanmen dunjiao, zhujia bu tong* 禪門頓教，諸家不同. On *jia*, see n. 319 above; here its pairing with *chanmen*, literally "gate of meditation," i.e., "Chan teaching," would certainly allow us to interpret them as references to sectarian groups rather than individuals. This example has been overlooked in the consideration of the evolution of Chan's sectarian identity in China; see Foulk, "Ch'an School," 134.

The origins of this treatise are in the twentieth [year of] Kaiyuan.
In gradual decline of late, this year the Dharma is reinstated,[335]
Fundamentally clear and pure from the start, unrelated to the accretions of cultivation,
Rising to a seat upon the other shore, suddenly entering the gate of Chan.
[Shenhui's] merit extends beyond Luoyang, his prestige flows to Chang'an,[336]
He is a bright moon suspended alone, unmatched by the congregation of stars.

Treatise on the Definition of the Truth regarding the Southern School of Bodhidharma, in one fascicle[337]

---

335. As Yinshun, *Zhongguo Chanzong shi*, 246, notes, these two lines show that the present text of the *Definition of the Truth* was distantly based on the 732 debate but actually compiled sometime after Shenhui's banishment and reinstatement. Since this verse also talks about a decline "after the sixth generation" and "since that day," it seems that the treatise attempts to place the decline between Huineng's death and the Huatai meetings but reveals that the actual end to the decline did not occur until 757; see also section 53. The term *lingchi* is also used in the first stanza above; see n. 329 above.

336. These cities are referred to, literally, as "Luo[yang] on the [Yellow] River" and the "capital city" (*heluo* 河洛 and *jingyi* 京邑). "Prestige" is literally "fragrance," *fang* 芳.

337. Yang, 48n30, points out that the Dunhuang Museum ms. has the characters *xieliao* 寫了, "written," at the very end of the text, as if written by the scribe.

Miscellaneous Dialogues
Wenda zazheng yi
問答雜徵義

Dialogues on Miscellaneous Inquiries to the Reverend [Shenhui] of Nanyang

[Preface][1]
[HS426]...the teaching would pervade the *dharmadhātu*. From the southern sky[2] came the mental correspondence that the eastern country[3] depends on for the correct teaching.[4] The Dharma is not transmitted falsely; there must be someone on whom it can be conferred.[5]

The Reverend [Shenhui] of Nanyang, is certainly the culmination. He follows after the sixth generation, who was his former teacher; as the seventh in number, he is the present instructor.[6] [People] direct their love to him as

---

There are several quite different versions of the Wenda zazheng yi, apparently edited after Shenhui's death. These texts contain various dialogues from throughout his career, many but not all of which parallel material in his other texts (particularly the Northern school critiques). This is a rich but sometimes intractable resource.

1. This fragmentary preface is from S6557 in Hu's *Yiji*, 426–427, with notes given on 491–492. Suzuki's edition, following Ishii, does not include the preface, and since Suzuki has placed sections 1–5, taken from P3047, before the material that follows this preface in S6557 (see n. 13 below), it seems reasonable that the preface should be placed at the very beginning. Liu Cheng's preface is translated, or rather presented in *yomi-kudashi* form, in Yanagida, "Goroku no rekishi," 366–367.

2. That is, India.

3. That is, China.

4. The terms used here are *xinqi* 心契, "mind-match" (see the *Definition of the Truth*, section 31), and *zhengzong* 正宗, which is the teaching at the center of the Chan tradition (and not, at this point, the Chan school itself). The references are obviously to Bodhidharma and his Chinese successors.

5. I interpret the character *ji* 寄 in the sense of "to confer, entrust," as given in the *Shin jigen*, 280.

6. It is not certain whether *liudai* 六代, "six generation(s)," refers to Huineng alone or the six patriarchs from Bodhidharma to Huineng; the same uncertainty also occurs regarding the usage *liudai zushi* 六代祖師 in the *Platform Sermon*. In the *Definition of the Truth*, sections 3, 16, 20, 53, and 55 *liudai* is plural; in sections 18, 21, and 24 it is singular; and in sections 19, 25, and perhaps 54 it occurs in both numbers. The Chinese for "seventh in number" is *qishu* 七數, lit. "seventh number," a less common usage.

if to their own parents; he was invited to confer with kings and lords.[7] When the bright mirror hangs on high, [it illuminates] even homely men; when the ocean is deep beyond measure, its floodwaters roil with clear ripples.[8] At the precious verses one [hears something] more wondrous than a strand of blossoms; at the clear song one suddenly [experiences] the perfect fruit.[9] Although there were inquiries [made to Shenhui] by rich and poor, many of the records have been forgotten. If I had not compiled [this anthology], I fear [Shenhui's teachings] would not have been committed to writing.[10] I have also visited those who acquired [other transcripts of Shenhui's teachings] [HS427] and append these at the end [of this text]. I have inscribed [Shenhui's teachings] into a single fascicle, named "Dialogues on Miscellaneous Inquiries."[11] I will select only my [spiritual] brethren and not give this to anyone else.

Compiled by the former scribe of Mount Tang, Liu Cheng[12]

---

7. The original has *dan* 淡, "pale" or, in some usages, "peaceful and without desire." Hu suggests that this seems to be in error, and I have substituted the very similar *tan* 談, "discuss" or "confer." Yanagida ("Goroku," 372) points out that the reference to conversations with dukes is justified by the status of Wang Ju 王琚, one of Shenhui's interlocutors, and I have translated the clause with this in mind. See the dialogue in section 10 below.

8. I do not understand the intent of this clumsy pair of metaphors. The euphemism used for "men" here is *xumei* 鬚眉, "beard and eyebrows." (Women plucked their eyebrows; see *Morohashi*, 12.654b.) Suzuki seems to be following Hu Shi in alluding to Shenhui as having had white hair and eyebrows.

9. I believe the import of this is that, upon hearing the chanted verses of the Dharma sung in such clear and beautiful tones, Shenhui's listeners were transported immediately as if to the final stage of buddhahood.

10. The terms used here are *jicheng* 集成, "collect and make" or "compile," and *yijian* 遺簡, "committed to writing" or literally "to commit to a letter."

11. This is no doubt the earliest title for this text.

12. Liu Cheng 劉澄 (d.u.), probably also known as Disciple Liu Xiangqian 劉相倩, Huicheng 慧澄, and Dharma Master Cheng 澄法師, also occurs in sections 17 and 42. Here, the editor of the *Miscellaneous Dialogues* describes himself as Liu Cheng, a former scribe of Tangshan county in the Hangzhou area 杭州唐山縣 of Zhejiang province. Yanagida ("Goroku," 375) has suggested the identification of these three individuals as one; if this is the case, the name "Liu Cheng" is a combination of lay surname and religious moniker, an uncommon but certainly not unprecedented usage. Liu Xiangqian narrates one of the most interesting dialogues in the text (section 42, with content overlapping that of section 17), involving Wang Wei and others, one of them the monk Huicheng, whose understanding of Buddhism is contrasted with Shenhui's in the dialogue. The apparent irony of a single individual being both participant and recorder was overcome by the use of different names, a format used in other contemporaneous Chan texts. Although the progression of this individual's life is not clearly stated, we may infer that he was once a government scribe, then left home as Huicheng, then met Shenhui. It is also possible that this was the Huicheng who compiled (or transcribed) the *Chan Sūtra* (*Chanmen jing* 禪門經), an apocryphal text that appeared sometime in the second or third decade of the eighth century. Huicheng's initial encounter with Shenhui occurred sometime before 740–742, but it was during these years that he came to accept the superiority of Shenhui's teachings (see below). It is not known how long the two men were together, but given his later role as editor, Huicheng probably traveled with Shenhui to Luoyang in 745 and stayed with him after that. Gernet (*Entretiens*, 34n1) suggests that it was this monk named Huicheng who convinced Empress Wu that the *Scripture of Laozi Converting the Barbarians* (*Laozi*

1 [Text][13]

Dharma Master [Chong]yuan asked,[14] "Do you call this an ornament [or not]?" His Reverence said, "What the sūtra preaches is, 'Do not exhaust the conditioned and do not abide in the unconditioned.'" [The Dharma master inquired once again, "What does it mean to 'not exhaust the conditioned and not abide in the unconditioned'?" His Reverence replied, "To 'not exhaust the conditioned' means that] from the first generation of *bodhicitta* up to achieving perfect enlightenment seated under the bodhi tree [and entering nirvāṇa between the two *sāla* trees, one never discards any dharma. This is to 'not] exhaust the conditioned.' To 'not abide in the unconditioned' is to study emptiness without taking emptiness as one's realization, to study non-action without taking non-action as one's realization. This is to 'not abide in the unconditioned.'"

[The Dharma master] was silent then, waiting for a while before speaking. "Your Reverence, lust and anger are the Path, [which is not in ornamentation." His Reverence said, "Then ordinary people must have attained] the Path." The Dharma master[15] said, "Why do you suggest that ordinary people must have attained the Path? His [Reverence said, "You have said that lust and anger are the [Path], and since ordinary people are those who practice lust and anger], why would they not have attained the Path?"

The Dharma master asked, "Do you understand or not?" His Reverence [answered, "I understand." The Dharma master said, "Understanding is non-understanding." His Reverence said, "The *Lotus Sūtra* says], 'From the

---

huahu jing 老子化胡經) should be destroyed. However, the identification is impossible: the event in question occurred in 696, while the editor of the *Miscellaneous Dialogues* lived past Shenhui's death in 758. In any case, as a scribe Liu Cheng was not that prominent. See Hu, 491–492n2, on the use of the name Tangshan xian 唐山縣 for a region in Hangzhou beginning in 705; see also *Zhongguo lishi ditu ji*, map 5:55–56 (4)5, and *Morohashi*, 2.1027c. The dating of Huicheng's interaction with Shenhui is based on (1) the dating of section 42 to sometime between 739 and 748; (2) the association of Liu Xiangqian as editor with only S6557; and (3) the identification of Shenhui with Nanyang in S6557, implying a pre-745 date.

13. The following material, beginning on p. 236 in Suzuki, is from P3047 only. Note that S6557 omits the first five sections, going on to the dialogue that begins section 6 after the preface.

14. The following dialogue also occurs in the *Definition of the Truth*, section 5, which has been used to fill in lacunae here. See that section for basic annotation; very minor differences between the two versions will not be noted. Suzuki (*Zenshū*, 3:236n1) points out that Hu's indications of lacunae in the text (see Hu, 97–98) do not indicate the estimated number of characters missing. The full form of Chongyuan's name does not occur in the *Miscellaneous Dialogues* but is found in the *Definition of the Truth*. Dialogues with a figure who must be Chongyuan occur in sections 16, 23, 60, 61, and 63. The Chan master Yuan of Mount Oxhead introduced in section 45 is a different individual.

15. Here only *fashi* 法師, "Dharma master," where the *Definition of the Truth* has Chongyuan's name.

time of my attainment of buddhahood, I have passed through immeasurable and unlimited *asaṃkhyeya* eons.'"[16]

2

The senior subaltern of Jiangling commandery[17] asked His Reverence, "Vimalakīrti reprimanded Śāriputra, '...[if one has] the body sit and makes the mind abide and grasps at concentration, this concentration is a concentration within the triple realm.'[18] Therefore Vimalakīrti reprimanded Śāriputra, '[if one does not arise from] the concentration of extinction and manifest the various deportments of extinction.'[19] If..."

Answer: "When those who study the Mahāyāna are in concentration...all the various deportments without failing in or disturbing one's concentrated mind, this is [DTS237] 'sitting in repose.'"[20]

Question: "In..., [wisdom] is to be able to discriminate the colors blue, yellow, red, and white. To not activate [the mind] in consequence of this discrimination is [concentration].[21]...attain autonomy. The [other] senses are also likewise. This is for the views[22] to be unmoving...to attain."

---

16. In the *Definition of the Truth*, the dialogue continues to escalate dramatically; see sections 7–9. Here the subject is dropped until section 60. The Chongyuan debate is thus "wrapped" around both the *Definition of the Truth* and the *Miscellaneous Dialogues*, and these sections may represent either a prototype version of or borrowing from the *Definition of the Truth*.

17. Jiangling commandery 江陵郡長吏 in Jingzhou 荊州, Hubei province: *Morohashi*, 6.931b, points out that Jiangling was changed from a *fu* 府 into a *jun* 郡, "commandery," at the beginning of Tianbao (742–756) and returned to its original name at the beginning of Qianyuan (758–760). Thus this part of the *Miscellaneous Dialogues* derives from 742 or after, which is in accord with Yanagida's theories of the provenance of P3047. Gernet (*Entretiens*, 5, citing Rotours) points out the title occurring here was used officially during the period 742–757 but also occurred unofficially throughout the Tang. Hucker (*Official Titles*, 110 #153) defines the title *zhangli* 長吏 as a "generic term referring vaguely to the higher grades of subofficial functionaries (*li* 吏), but it may be encountered as an equivalent of *zhangguan* 長官 (senior official)." Neither the title *zhangli* nor the place name Jiangling occurs elsewhere in Shenhui's writings, and the individual referred to here is unknown.

18. The term rendered as "concentration" is *ding* 定, which can be either samādhi, *dhyāna*, or a general term for meditative concentration. The triple realm, *sanjie* 三界, refers to the three realms of desire, form, and formlessness, but may be understood as a general reference to the entire universe.

19. T 475: 14.539c21–22. The characters *mieyi* 滅儀, although something Shenhui might have concocted, are probably a scribal error for *weiyi* 威儀, "deportments." In this case, they presumably refer to walking, standing still, sitting, and lying down. Gernet, 5n6, takes this latter interpretation.

20. This term for seated meditation, *yanzuo* 宴坐, is used in the *Vimalakīrti Sūtra*. See its use in the *Platform Sermon*, section 2. [It seems reasonable to assume that the lacuna originally said something to the effect of "they manifest (all the various deportments)."—Ed.]

21. I have interpolated "wisdom" and "concentration" here because the passage resembles the *Platform Sermon*, section 4.

22. The text has *zhujian* 諸見, "various views," implying the Skt. *dṛṣṭi*. However, judging from the context it might be better to read this as an error for something like "various senses."

Answer: "It is only enlightenment[23] that is attained; non-enlightenment is not attained.... practice is to attain emancipation."[24]

Question: "What about the Mahāyāna sūtras?"

Answer: "The Buddha... 'Just as one contemplates the true characteristic of one's own body, so should one contemplate the Buddha. When I contemplate the Tathāgata, he does not come from the past, [does not go into the future, and does not abide[25] in the present].'[26] ... characteristic. Those who study the perfection of wisdom today and merely attain nonabiding are identical [to all the buddhas of the past]. The *Vimalakīrti* [*Sūtra* says]..."[27]

3

"... the present monks and laypeople posit the Buddha-nature[28] as natural."[29]

Question: "What about ignorance?[30]..."

[Shenhui asked in turn: If] the Buddha-nature is natural, then what is ignorance generated from?" No one was able to answer.

[Someone asked], "O Great Worthy, what about [ignorance]?"[31]

[Answer: "Ignorance is] also natural."

Question: "How can ignorance be natural?"[32]

Answer: "Both ignorance and the Buddha-nature are naturally generated. Ignorance is dependent on the Buddha-nature, and the Buddha-nature is dependent on ignorance. The two are mutually dependent, so that if they exist they both exist simultaneously. To completely understand is the

---

23. The Chinese is *jue* 覺.
24. The rhetoric here of *bujue* 不覺, "non-enlightenment," is reminiscent of the *Awakening of Faith*, but the specific line does not occur anywhere in that text. The characters *bujue* 不覺 are used with a different meaning in section 18.
25. The Chinese is *wuzhu* 無住.
26. The quoted lines are from the *Vimalakīrti Sūtra*, T 475: 14.554c29–555a2, and reappear in sections 34 and 55 below. The material in brackets is supplied to complete the quotation.
27. With so many lacunae, it is impossible to know where to put quotation marks and other punctuation. However, this entire section is very closely related to section 6 of the *Platform Sermon*.
28. The term used is *foxing* 佛性.
29. The term used is *ziran* 自然. That is, they consider the Buddha-nature (and, just below, ignorance) as originally extant. (Throughout this translation I use "original" and "originally" for the character *ben* 本 when the context involves opposition to concepts of temporality, but there is no difference between this and other usages of "fundamental" and "fundamentally.") This seems to be part of a statement or response by Shenhui. Gernet, 7, reads "establish the nature of buddha is spontaneity," using an inappropriate philosophical Daoist definition for this term.
30. The term used is *wuming* 無明.
31. There is a lacuna here, but given the context it is clear that the question is about ignorance.
32. Gernet, 7, cites a passage in the *Nirvāṇa Sūtra* where the Buddha-nature and afflictions are described as mutually dependent (T 374: 12.571a29–c3 and c5–6).

Buddha-nature, and not to completely understand is ignorance.³³ The *Nirvāṇa Sūtra* says, 'It is like gold and gangue, which are generated simultaneously.'³⁴ When a goldsmith smelts and refines them, the gold and gangue are separated. If the gold is refined a hundred times it becomes a hundred times [more] pure, but if the gangue is refined repeatedly it changes to slag.³⁵ Gold is likened to the Buddha-nature, and gangue is likened to the afflictions. The afflictions and the Buddha-nature exist simultaneously. The buddhas and bodhisattvas and true spiritual compatriots instruct [sentient beings] to generate *bodhicitta* and cultivate [DTS238] the perfection of wisdom, and thus to attain emancipation."

Question: "If ignorance is natural, then how is this different from the 'naturalness' of the non-Buddhists?"³⁶

Answer: "It is identical with the naturalness of the [philosophical] Daoists,³⁷ but the understanding of it is different."

Question: "How is it different?"

Answer: "Within the teachings of Buddhism the Buddha-nature and ignorance are both natural. Why? Because the myriad dharmas all depend on the power of the Buddha-nature.³⁸ Therefore the dharmas all belong to the natural. With the naturalness of the Daoists, 'the Way generates the one, the one generates the two, the two generate the three, and the three generate the myriad things.'³⁹ From the one on down, the myriad things are all 'natural.' Consequently, the understandings are not identical."⁴⁰

4

Question: "[The *Flower Garland Sūtra* refers to] 'the one *dharmakāya* shared identically by all the tathāgatas of the ten directions,'⁴¹ but I wonder, are [their *dharmakāyas*] identical or different?"

---

33. The Chinese for "understand completely" here is *jueliao* 覺了.
34. This is a paraphrase of the *Nirvāṇa Sūtra;* see T 374: 12.423a5–6 and 414c18–19.
35. Although Gómez ("Purifying Gold," 76) reads this as "sand and ashes," presumably following the bifurcation of the term in *Morohashi*, 7.374c, I prefer a unitary reading. Indeed, I suspect that *huitu* 灰土 is a technical term referring to slag, the refuse produced in smelting; the term *kuang* 礦 is rendered as gangue, the mineral and rock matter in which the gold occurs. Gómez's translation is actually based on the next passage in which this metaphor occurs, section 8.
36. "Non-Buddhists" is better for *waidao* 外道 than "heretics," which implies mistaken orthodoxy.
37. The term used is *daojia* 道家.
38. It seems somehow very colloquial to refer to the "power" of the Buddha-nature, *foxing li* 佛性力.
39. This is a famous line from the *Daode jing,* section 42. Note that I will translate the character *dao* as "Way" in Daoist contexts and "Path" or "enlightenment" in Buddhist contexts.
40. Compare the dialogue with Ma Ze on Daoist and Buddhist viewpoints in section 51.
41. The Chinese is *shifang zhu rulai tong gongyi fashen* 十方諸如來同共一法身, a very similar form of which is found in the *Flower Garland Sūtra* (T 279: 10.250a9 and 301b26).

Answer: "They are both identical and different."

Question:[42] "How can they be [both] identical and different?"

Answer: "If you place ten lamps in a dark room, their light will be shared identically. This is the meaning of 'identical.' To explain the meaning of separateness, that the lamps[43] are each separate is the meaning of 'separate.' Thus the *dharmakāyas* of the buddhas are originally not separate, but each utilization by those of wisdom[44] is separate. Hence [the answer] 'both identical and different.'"

5

His Reverence said, "The mundane realm[45] has its inconceivabilities, and the transmundane realm also has its inconceivabilities. What is inconceivable in the mundane realm is to rise suddenly from a commoner to the rank of emperor;[46] what is inconceivable in the transmundane realm is that the ten stages of faith[47] and [even] the first moment of *bodhicitta* correspond to the attainment of enlightenment in a single moment. If there is correspondence [DTS239] [between mind and] principle,[48] how could there be anything strange about it? This explains the inconceivability of sudden enlightenment.[49] Therefore the [*Lotus*] *Sūtra* says, 'The non-regressing bodhisattvas are as numerous as the sands of the River Ganges, but even if they united their minds in a single conception they would be unable to understand this.' How much less would the *śrāvakas* and *pratyekabuddhas* be able to understand it!"[50]

---

42. Suzuki (*Zenshū*, 3:238) corrects the *da* 答, "answer," in the text to *wen* 問, "question."

43. In this sentence the text changes from *yi* 異, "be different from," to the synonym *bie* 別, "be separate from." Hu, 100, indicates that approximately one character is missing between *zhan* 盞, "small [lamp] dish," and *deng* 燈, "lamp." This is probably an inadvertent space in the manuscript, best ignored.

44. The Chinese is *zhizhe shouyong* 智者受用.

45. The Chinese is *shijian* 世間, recalling Skt. *laukika*, to complement the *chu shijian* 出世間, or *lokottara*, below.

46. The Chinese is *buyi dundeng jiuwu* 布衣頓登九五, literally, "one's cloth [i.e., not silk] robes suddenly ascend nine-five." The number nine stands for *yang* 陽, and in the enumeration of the six lines of the *qian* 乾 hexagram the *yang* or imperial position is in the fifth place from the bottom; see *Morohashi*, 1.367c, citing the *Yi jing xici* 易經繫辭.

47. As noted in the *Definition of Truth*, for the translation of bodhisattva stages I rely on Hurvitz.

48. That is, the *dharmadhātu*. [This phrase might also be interpreted as "Since this corresponds with principle..."—Ed.]

49. The term for sudden enlightenment here is *dunwu* 頓悟. In the preceding sentence, "a single moment of correspondence" is *yinian xiangying* 一念相應.

50. See T 262: 9.6a16–17.

6

His Reverence explained to the vice minister[51] on this day, "In the cultivation of one's own body and mind, one may be either identical in mind or not identical with the buddhas and bodhisattvas.[52] If one attains identity [in mind with them], then this is to attain a portion of the Buddhadharma within the Buddhadharma.[53] If one does not attain identity, this is for one's life to pass in vain."

Question: "How does one attain understanding?"

Answer: "Just attain non-thought, and this is understanding."

Question: "How does one generate this non-thought?"[54]

Answer: "To not intentionalize[55] is non-thought. Based on the essence of non-thought there naturally exists a wisdom mandate.[56] Fundamentally, the wisdom mandate is the true characteristic. The buddhas and bodhisatt-

---

51. The individual referred to here only as *shilang* 侍郎 is unidentified; he may or may not be identical to the Kaifu of Tuoba mentioned later in the section. This may refer to (1) Song Ding 宋鼎 (fl. at least to 797; on him, see below); (2) Su Jin, who appears in section 13; or (3) the vice minister Miao who appears in section 26. See Hucker, *Official Titles*, 427 #5278 (3), for the position *shilang* 侍郎, which he describes as the second executive post in each of the ministries. The same term *shilang*, translated separately by Hucker as "attendant gentleman," was also used from the Han to the Tang to refer to a "relatively lowly secretarial post in Princely Establishments" (Hucker, *Official Titles*, 426 #5278 [1]), and it is not certain which usage is intended here. The title *Libu shilang* 禮部侍郎, "vice minister of the Board of Rites," is applied to Su Jin in section 13, one of the most important dialogues in the entire text, and to the otherwise unidentified Miao Jinqing in section 26. I have therefore used the more prestigious term for simplicity. There is no apparent relationship between these three dialogues, hence no way to speculate on the identity for the anonymous individual here. Song Ding appears in a funerary inscription for Shenhui that was only discovered in 1983 at Longmen. Both the *Song Biographies* (T 2061: 50.755b11) and the inscription identify Song Ding as a vice minister of the Ministry of War (*bingbu shilang* 兵部侍郎); Wu, "Heze Shenhui zhuan yanjiu," 903, cites evidence that Song Ding held this position from 744 to 749 or slightly later; see Yanagida, *Shoki Zenshū shisho*, 49 (including n. 36) and 185, for more information on a stele erected by Song Ding. Yampolsky (*Platform Sutra*, 36n119) states that although Song Ding's biography is unknown, his name appears in the *History of the Tang*, 197:4a, and *New History of the Tang*, 222:14b. Ogawa ("Kataku Jinne," 55n20) points out that the Song Ding, a prefect of Manzhou 蠻州, tentatively identified as Shenhui's associate in Yamazaki, "Kataku Jinne zenji," is a different individual.

52. This could also read "identical with the mind of the buddhas and bodhisattvas." The immediate context does not provide any clues as to the correct reading.

53. The Chinese is *yu fofa zhong de fofa fen* 於佛法中得佛法分.

54. It is possible that the third character of *ruowei sheng* 若為生 is used colloquially, hence simply "how about" non-thought. I have chosen the substantive meaning, due to the reference to "activation" in the answer.

55. The Chinese is *bu zuoyi* 不作意. Hu, 101, includes a handwritten note on the occurrence of this term in a poem by Du Fu 杜甫.

56. Literally, "upon the essence of" (*ti shang* 體上) non-thought there is *zhiming* 智命, an unusual compound. (If this compound did not occur twice, I would suspect the second character to be in error.) Note the implicit (and Northern-school-like) dualism of ignorance and wisdom here, both originally extant entities.

vas use non-thought as their *dharmakāya* of emancipation. If one sees[57] this *dharmakāya*, then one is [thereby] equipped with samādhis [as numerous as] the sands of the River Ganges and all the perfections. You and I,[58] in our studies together today of the perfection of wisdom, will attain a [state of] mind that is no different from that of the buddhas and bodhisattvas. If one can now, from within the sea of saṃsāra, attain but a single moment of mental correspondence with the buddhas and bodhisattvas, then to cultivate in the locus of what is encompassed within that single moment of thought is to know the Path, see the Path, and attain the Path."[59]

The vice minister said, "This ordinary [unenlightened] person [before you] now is an official, so how can I do this?" [DTS240]

"Your question indicates that you[60] [have achieved] a conceptual understanding today but have not yet been able to cultivate. By attaining this understanding,[61] and through its long-term subtle influence,[62] all your dualistic thinking and false thoughts[63] and your heavy [karmic transgressions] will lighten naturally and gradually. I[64] have seen it said in the scriptures that Brilliant Refulgence King, Moon Refulgence King, Crown-born King, Sage of Saṃsāra King, and Lord of the Gods King Brahmā are replete in the five desires, far more so than [all] the hundred thousand trillion kings of the present day.[65] Even if you only have a conceptual understanding of the perfection of wisdom and use your intellectual mind to submit questions to the Buddha, the Buddha will bestow his seal of authorization on you.[66] If

---

57. The Chinese character is *jian* 見, "see," which might be best understood here as *xian* 現, "manifest." The two are almost interchangeable in such situations.

58. The terms here are "Shenhui" and *shilang*, which read like oral self-reference by the former.

59. The second of these three is identical to the Chinese translation of Skt. *darśanamārga*, although it is uncertain whether Shenhui had this connotation in mind.

60. Literally, "inquiring of the vice minister, [I] today accept." The question word used is *zi* 諮 (*Morohashi* 35728, 10.531a), which has the connotation of a superior inquiring of an inferior. The usage here might be more in the sense of the compound *ziyi* 諮議, to "explain in response to questioning [from a superior]." See *Shin jigen*, 938b.

61. In the preceding sentence the term used is *xuejie* 學解, "understanding [gained through] study" or simply "conceptual understanding"; here the term is the essentially identical *zhijie* 知解. Shenhui's doctrine of initial inspiration followed by gradual cultivation is here shown to be ideally suited to laypeople, who can put off the real work until later!

62. The term *xunxi* 薰習 recalls Skt. *vāsanā*, the "perfuming" affect of chronic contact.

63. The Chinese is *panyuan wangxiang* 攀緣妄想, the former compound meaning thought that arises in conjunction with an object (*Bukkyōgo daijiten*, 1116d–17a) and the latter any deluded thoughts.

64. Using the self-reference "Shenhui."

65. This list of kings is unknown from other sources; it is no doubt significant that five kings and five desires are mentioned. Shenhui seems to be saying that the five kings, each a paragon of virtue, possess greater stores of the five desires than all the kings of the mundane world put together. The five desires (*pañca kama-guṇāḥ*) are those associated with the five sensory organs (*Bukkyōgo daijiten*, 377b).

66. The Chinese here is *lingshou yinke* 領受印可. The term *yinke* also occurs in the *Definition of the Truth*, section 20.

you attain the Buddha's seal of authorization you will be able to eliminate the five desires and realize the consummation of the various stages of the bodhisattva path."[67]

[Shenhui], the Reverend of Heze [si], sent a letter to the commander of Tuoba,[68] [which went]: "To accomplish the perfection of charity is to adorn the *dhamakāya* of emancipation.[69] However, since this teaching points directly at matching with the essential,[70] I will not use ornate language. [The essential truth] is merely that the minds of all sentient beings are fundamentally without characteristics.[71] That which is called characteristics is

---

67. The term *zhengwei* 正位, "position proper," which refers to permanent and unchanging enlightenment, in which there are no more *kleśas*, is used in the *Vimalakīrti Sūtra*, T 475: 14.542b7, 545c3, and 553c9; see *Bukkyōgo daijiten*, 697a–b.

68. The title *kāifŭ* 開府 is translated here as "commander" on the basis of Hucker, *Official Titles*, 274–275 #3103, which gives a Han dynasty equivalent of "executive," an honorific title referring to someone who "opened an office" equal in prestige to the three dukes, and two military usages from the Northern and Southern dynasties period and the Sui. The occurrence of the term in Shenhui's text would seem to indicate an individual of high military status. Given the identification with Tuoba, the ruling family of the Wei 魏 dynasty, it may be that this individual was merely descended from an earlier military strongman and that this title was used as a term of respect or even self-aggrandizement. It is notable that many of the official titles used in Shenhui's text seem to be ambiguous, nonspecific, and not necessarily very eminent. Incidentally, the identification of Shenhui with Heze si implies a post-745 origin for this material (although of course the title could have been applied later). This is curious in terms of the relative backwardness of the content, given Shenhui's other positions elsewhere. Hu, 101, followed by Suzuki (*Zenshū*, 3:239), has moved this sentence from its original location at the beginning of section 6, but the editorial revision is unwarranted for the following reasons. First, the material immediately following this note marker is in question-and-answer form that seems unsuitable for a letter. Second, Shenhui is referred to as *heshang* or "reverend," which is not a term of self-reference. Third, removing the reference to the letter from its original location results in an abrupt change of subject from wisdom to charity (although Shenhui interprets both in terms of non-intentionalization). Fourth, given the difference in topics the unidentified vice minister at the beginning of the section is not necessarily identical to the "commander of Tuoba" here.

69. Shenhui seems to be answering an inquiry about the merits of religious donations, and his terminology is reminiscent of the dialogue involving ornamentation above (section 1) and in the *Definition of the Truth* (section 5). "*Dharmakāya* of emancipation" (*jietuo fashen* 解脫法身) is not a bound technical term.

70. The Chinese is *zhizhi qiyao* 直指契要. The third character, meaning "to match," as one half of a tally matches perfectly with the other half, is used in Shenhui's writings (see n. 4 above) and the *Platform Sūtra* with the meaning of matching one's mind perfectly with the ultimate truth.

71. The Chinese, which is *wuxiang* 無相, is parallel to the term *wunian* 無念 or "non-thought," even though here the character occurs without the mind-radical that would make the term mean "without thought." However, in reading the next few lines we should be sensitive to the possibility that Shenhui is making an implicit connection between the mental and physical realms. Also, note the significance of *dan* 但, "merely," here, in accordance with Yanagida's comments as presented in McRae, *Northern School*, 111. This observation is also applicable to the word "merely" at the beginning of the third English sentence down.

entirely the false mind.⁷² What is the false? To intentionalize and make the mind abide,⁷³ grasping at emptiness and grasping at purity, and to activate the mind to seek after realization of *bodhi* and nirvāṇa⁷⁴—all this belongs to the false. Merely do not intentionalize, and the mind will of itself be without any object.⁷⁵ The objectless mind is empty and serene in its inherent nature.⁷⁶ Based on the essence of this empty serenity there naturally exists a fundamental wisdom, [of which] it is said that knowing is its function of illumination.⁷⁷ Therefore, the *Diamond Sūtra* says, 'Generate the nonabiding mind.'⁷⁸ This 'non-abiding mind' in essence is fundamental serenity. To 'generate that mind' is the function of fundamental wisdom. Simply do not intentionalize, and you will naturally be enlightened into [this truth]. Make effort, make effort!"⁷⁹

---

72. That is, all things considered to be "characteristics" are false mental constructs. The Chinese here is *wangxin* 忘心, closely related to the *wangxiang* 妄想 or "false thoughts" that occurs shortly above. Presumably, Shenhui has the *Diamond Sūtra* in mind, which says that "All that has characteristics is completely false." This line, which occurs at T 235: 8.749a23, is quoted in the *Five Skillful Means* (McRae, *Northern School*, 172) and the *Platform Sūtra*, T 2008: 48.337c6–7; see Yampolsky, *Platform Sutra*, 130.

73. That is, to remain motionless.

74. This is a non-formulaic reference to a position stated elsewhere as four separate pronouncements; see further on in this text, sections 28 and 34; the *Platform Sermon*, section 4; and the *Definition of Truth*, section 20.

75. Literally, the mind will be without any "thing," *wu* 物. Just below, the text refers to "objectless mind," *wuwu xin* 無物心.

76. The Chinese is *zixing kongji* 自性空寂.

77. Material similar to this occurs in the *Platform Sermon* as well as in the *Zongjinglu* (T 2016: 48.781a12–14), where it is cited as the teaching of the "Southern school." The concepts "fundamental wisdom" (*benzhi* 本智) and "function of illumination" (*zhaoyong* 照用) are common in both Shenhui's texts and early Chan writings in general.

78. This line from the *Diamond Sūtra* is also cited above, section 26, and in the *Platform Sermon*, section 3.

79. The Chinese phrases used here to explain the line from the *Diamond* are *benji zhi ti* 本寂之體 and *benzhi zhi yong* 本智之用. This is the only occasion in all of Shenhui's writings when he exhorts his readers/listeners to make effort. (In section 5 of the *Platform Sermon* he recommends that everyone "apply yourselves totally," but this is in achieving a type of understanding, not exerting oneself in spiritual cultivation.) Indeed, although the subject is the famous line from the *Diamond*, this passage is not at all distinctive and could easily be transplanted into a Northern school text. That is, there is no effort to deny the dualism implicit in the substance / function dichotomy, and the equivalents posed for the two components of the scriptural citation accord well with the bifurcation of enlightenment in the *Five Skillful Means;* see McRae, *Northern School*, 225–228 and passim. Also, this passage focusing on the *Diamond* is distinctly different from the material that follows, which is based on the *Nirvāṇa Sūtra*. (This combination of scriptural sources is, however, one feature of the *Definition of the Truth*.)

7[80]

Dharma Master Zuoben asked about the meaning of the verse on existence and nonexistence:[81] " 'Originally existent and presently nonexistent, originally nonexistent and presently existent: such a situation does not exist for the conditioned dharmas of the triple realm.'[82] What is the meaning of this [verse]?"[83]

[Shenhui answered: "What you, Dharma Master, ask about is something I have doubts about too."

A further question: "What's your doubt about?"][84]

Answer: "Ever since the Buddhadharma was transmitted to the east, there have been various great worthies, and they have all taken the eradication of the afflictions as fundamental."

---

80. This section in S6557 is clearly a variation on this section, done in a more vivid dialogic form. Hu, 492n4, suggests that since Ishii is a complete text in itself, this current section must have been added later, but the logic of this assertion is questionable.

81. Hu, 492n3, suggests that this sentence is a heading added by the compilers of S6557, since it is the only case in which the name of Shenhui's interrogator as given here is not identical to his name in P3047. The monk Zuoben 作本, is unidentified. This name, which means "making the fundamental," seems so close to the subject matter that one wonders if it is a contrived name.

82. The discussion of "original existence and present nonexistence" (*benyou jinwu* 本有今無) here includes a long string of scriptural citations and arguments, a heavily documented position on a topic that must have been very important to Shenhui. His point throughout is that Buddha-nature is not brought into existence by the act of its realization by human practitioners, but that it is always present within humans, even before its presence is realized. The terminology of "originally" and "presently" existent or nonexistent is necessarily formal because of the style of the scriptural citations, but the reader should look beneath this superficial formality to Shenhui's very direct message. In addition, of course, the rhetoric of *you* and *wu* resonates with the "being" and "nonbeing" of earlier Chinese Buddhist philosophy, although the terms here are qualitatively different. (On my usage of "originally" or "original" and "fundamental" or "fundamentally," see note 30 above.) This verse is a major topic in the *Nirvāṇa Sūtra*, in which it occurs in several locations. In the Northern version (the original translation by Tanwuchen 曇無讖 or *Dharmakṣema [360–433] in 421 in Northern Liang 北涼 territory), see T 374: 12.422c15, 464c10, 524b23, 531a28–29 (where the order of the first two lines is reversed: "Originally nonexistent and presently existent, originally existent and presently nonexistent," etc.). In the Southern version, which was edited by Huiyan 慧嚴, Huiguan 慧觀, and Xie Lingyun 謝靈運, the verse occurs (always as Shenhui has it—this appears to be the version he used) at T 375: 12.664a1, 707a21, 769a6, and 776a12. For traditional interpretations of this verse, see the *Da niepan jing jijie* 大涅槃經集解 (*Great Collection of Interpretations of the Nirvāṇa Sūtra*), T 1763: 37.471c1–474a29.

83. A very similar question is repeated in the variant section below. The answer that follows here in P3047, either directly in this version or after an explanatory exchange in the other, does not seem related to the question. I suspect a lacuna in the original.

84. The exchange in brackets only occurs in S6557 (Hu, 428). The Chinese used here is the primitively written colloquialism *yi shi mo wu* 疑是沒勿. Hu's interlinear note gives several equivalents ending with the modern *shenme*. Similar forms occur below in section 15.

Question: "Upon what principle do they take the eradication of the afflictions as fundamental?"[85]

Answer: "Upon the *Nirvāṇa Sūtra,* which says, 'Mañjuśrī said, "Cunda had doubts in his mind regarding the permanent abiding of the Tathāgata. Because he [then] attained understanding of the power of the Buddha-nature, he attained doubtlessness.[86] If one sees the Buddha-nature as permanent,[87] then originally, before one understands [the Buddha-nature], it must be impermanent. If originally it is impermanent, afterwards it must remain likewise. Why? It is like the things of this world, which originally were nonexistent but now are existent and after [their period of] existence return to nonexistence. Things such as this are all entirely impermanent."'[88]

"When we consider this scriptural passage, the doubt of Cunda's which was mentioned[89] by Mañjuśrī is the doubt as to whether the Buddha-nature is an impermanently abiding dharma. He was not inquiring about the afflictions, [and] was not doubting why the great worthies of past and present have taken the eradication of the afflictions as original."[90]

8

Question: "What is the meaning of the verse about original existence and present nonexistence?"

---

85. As Suzuki notes, the negative *fei* 非 here is no doubt an error for the copula *wei* 未. Hu, 428, notes the difference between this version and P3047 and suggests that its original reading of "Upon what principle can eradication of the afflictions not be fundamental" (retaining *fei* rather than emending it to *wei*) has already undergone editing. This is in justification of his strong impression that the character *yi* 疑, "doubt," must be added as in the translation.

86. The phrase *bian de wuyi* 便得无疑, "thus attained [to] doubtlessness," does not occur in the original sūtra.

87. The sūtra original and S6557 (Hu, 428) have the character *er* 而, a weak particle, which is preferable to P3047's original *fei,* "not" (Hu, 103), which would yield, "see the Buddha-nature as other than permanent." Also, the sūtra and S6557 have *jian* 見, "see," instead of P3047's *zhi,* "understand."

88. T 374: 12.422c4–8.

89. The character used here is *teng* 騰, to "raise" or "ride." I am tentatively interpreting this as a colloquialism meaning to "bring up."

90. I have rendered this sentence as best I can, but it seems possible that it would more easily be rendered as a question to Shenhui, to the effect of "the passage you just cited refers to doubts about the impermanence of Buddha-nature, so how is it relevant to our discussion of the eradication of the afflictions?" This reading would require assuming that a question word had dropped out and that there is a lacuna between this sentence and the following question. Hu, 492n4, suggests that the issue here is Shenhui's worry that the sūtra might be construed to suggest that the *kleśas* were fundamental or original, rather than adventitious. In the material immediately following, Shenhui argues for the latter alternative (which, incidentally, differs from the position taken in the *Awakening of Faith* and Northern school teachings, a point that should not be overlooked). Grammatically, the implication is that Shenhui reads the statement about all the previous worthies as "taking the *kleśas* that are eradicated as original."

Answer: "The *Nirvāṇa Sūtra* says, 'That which is originally existent is the originally existent Buddha-nature. That which is presently nonexistent is the presently nonexistent Buddha-nature.'"[91]

Question: "If you speak of the originally existent Buddha-nature, why do you also refer to the presently nonexistent Buddha-nature?"

Answer: "The nonexistent Buddha-nature I spoke of just now is invisible because it is covered by the afflictions. Hence it is called nonexistent. The 'originally nonexistent' of 'originally nonexistent yet presently existent' [refers to] the originally nonexistent afflictions. 'Presently existent' refers to the occurrence of the afflictions in the present.[92] Even though they [derive from] great eons [as numerous as] the sands of the River Ganges, the afflictions are also 'presently existent.' [To say, 'Within] the conditioned dharmas of the three periods of time there is no such situation' is to say that the Buddha-nature does not continue [through] the three periods of time."[93]

---

91. This statement is not found in the immediate vicinity of the verse in the Northern version of the *Nirvāṇa Sūtra*. However, after the occurrence of the verse in the Southern version at T 375: 12.707a21, the Buddha expounds on several definitions of what is "originally existent" (*benyou* 本有) and "presently nonexistent" (*jinwu* 今無; see 707b1–c22). The answer given in Shenhui's text is probably his own, since it is not in the sūtra. Ogawa ("Kataku Jinne," 40–41) analyzes Shenhui's understanding of the Buddha-nature on the basis of this dialogue. Gernet's rendering of this question (p. 17) has a very personal sense: "If one says that the Buddha-nature is not in us, it is because men, being clouded by the passions, cannot see it, and because of this say that it does not exist."

92. The preceding two exchanges are translated by Iriya Yoshitaka (*Baso no goroku*, 46), because the same *Nirvāṇa Sūtra* verse is discussed in the *Mazu yulu* in a sermon also found in the *Transmission of the Lamp*, T 2076: 51.440b15–16: "You possess it fundamentally and you possess it now; it doesn't depend on cultivating the Path and sitting in meditation. Neither cultivating nor sitting, this is pure Tathāgata Chan." Iriya points out that this verse was the subject of considerable debate, including an entire treatise attributed to Vasubandhu and translated by Paramārtha, plus comments in such texts as the *Dasheng xuan lun* 大乘玄論 (T 1853: 45.15a10f.) and *Baozang lun* 寶藏論 (T 1857: 45.143b18f.). The treatise mentioned here is the rather short *Niepan jing benyou jinwu ji lun* 涅槃經本有今無偈論 in one fascicle (T 1528: 26.281–82c). (Translated in or around 550, the text was ignored until the beginning of the Sui.) It is just possible that Shenhui was inspired by this treatise, either by his own reading or indirectly through one of his teachers. This is because the treatise also discusses the Buddha's special attention to Cunda, whose doubts are described as those peculiar to one dedicated to the salvation of all sentient beings (281a12f.); defines saṃsāra and nirvāṇa as different based on whether one is *shun* 順, "in accord," or *ni* 逆, "contrary" (282a23); and suggests that the first bodhisattva stage is thus the last (282a24). (See McRae, *Northern School*, 213–215, for a discussion of *shun* and *ni* in the *Treatise on Perfect Illumination*.) References in other sources to the phrase *benyou jinwu* are plentiful: some that I have noticed are in Jizang's 吉藏 *Zhongguan lunshu* 中觀論疏 (T 1824: 42.30b3f. and 74a4); the same author's *Dasheng xuan lun* 大乘玄論 (T 1853: 45.40a8f., 76a10); the anonymous *Baozang lun* 寶藏論 (T 1857: 45.145c21; falsely attributed to Sengzhao; see Sharf, "Coming to Terms," for a discussion and annotated translation); and Huizhao's 慧沼 (650–714) *Neng xian zhongbian huiri lun* 能顯中邊慧日論 (T 1863: 45.439a21). None of these, nor the several other citations given in the Taishō indexes that I have examined, bear any similarity to Shenhui's treatment, let alone that of Mazu. Iriya suggests that Mazu's treatment was epochal in that it raised the discussion (*shiyo* 止揚, "aufheben") to the absolute affirmation of present phenomenal existence.

93. I have followed Hu, 429–430, in bracketing part of this sentence as a scriptural citation.

Question: "Why does the Buddha-nature not continue through the three periods of time?"

Answer: "Because the essence of the Buddha-nature is permanent, it is not a dharma of generation and extinction."[94]

Question: "What are 'generation and extinction'?"[95]

Answer: "The three periods of time are generation and extinction."

Question: "Are the Buddha-nature and the afflictions immanent or not?"[96]

Answer: "They are immanent. Although they are immanent, generation and extinction are transitory,[97] and the Buddha-nature is intransitory. This is because the Buddha is permanent, like space.[98] Although bright and dark are transitory, space is intransitory. This is because [space] is intransitory.[99] [In this] world there are no dharmas that are not [subject to] generation and extinction."

Question: "If the Buddha-nature and the afflictions are immanent, why are only the afflictions not fundamental?"

Answer: "'It is like gold and gangue, which are generated simultaneously.'[100] When a goldsmith smelts and refines them, the gold and gangue are separated. If the gold is refined a hundred times it becomes a hundred times [more] pure, but if the gangue is refined repeatedly it changes to slag. [In] the *Nirvāṇa Sūtra* gold is likened to the Buddha-nature, and gangue is likened to the afflictions. The Mahāyāna sūtras and treatises all explain that the afflictions are adventitious sensory data, and so they cannot be called 'fundamental.' The afflictions are darkness—how could they become bright? The *Nirvāṇa Sūtra* says, 'It is said only that brightness destroys darkness, not that darkness destroys brightness.'[101] If it were the case that darkness

---

94. That is, it is not a conditioned dharma. The Chinese at the beginning of the sentence is *foxing ti chang* 佛性體常; the second part of the sentence alludes to the *Nirvāṇa Sūtra*'s famous verse on impermanence, which is quoted in full in section 16. The term *shengmie* 生滅 is used repeatedly throughout Shenhui's dialogues. Although a more felicitous English equivalent might be selected to indicate the conditioned or causally related activity of saṃsāra, I have used "generation and extinction" throughout in order to make his permutations on the individual components of the compound more easily understood.

95. Note the use of the colloquial interrogative form, *shiwu shi* 是勿是, equivalent to the modern transcription *shenme shi* 甚麻事. Note, incidentally, that this manner of "chaining" questions to the final clause of a preceding answer is reminiscent of the *Essentials of Cultivating the Mind*.

96. Here the word *ju* 俱 refers to the innate provision of something within human beings.

97. Literally, "they have 'coming and going.'"

98. Suzuki (Ishii) and Hu (S6557) read *foxing* 佛性, "Buddha-nature," rather than *fo* 佛, "buddha," as given by Yang.

99. This sentence is clearly redundant as given.

100. This citation from the *Nirvāṇa Sūtra*, as well as the explanation to follow, was already given above in section 3. Other than very trivial differences in wording, Hu, 431, indicates S6557 has "Dharma-nature" rather than "Buddha-nature" just below.

101. The source of this citation, which does not occur in the *Nirvāṇa Sūtra*, remains unidentified.—Ed.

destroyed brightness, then this would be transmitted in all the sūtras and treatises. [But] the sūtras and treatises do not contain this. How could such a teaching be postulated? If the afflictions were fundamental,[102] one would not be able to eradicate the afflications and seek nirvāṇa."

Question: "Why does the sūtra say 'not eradicate the afflictions and enter nirvāṇa'?"[103]

Answer: "[Because this would be to] figure that the afflictions are fundamentally and by nature without eradication. To suggest that the afflictions were by nature equivalent to nirvāṇa would make it impossible to exhort sentient beings to cultivate the six perfections, to eradicate all evil and cultivate all good. If the afflictions were taken as fundamental, [sentient beings would abandon] the fundamental and follow the derivative.[104] The *Nirvāṇa Sūtra* says, 'All sentient beings are fundamentally [in] nirvāṇa, and the undefiled wisdom-nature is fundamentally and naturally complete [in them].'[105] Also, 'It is likened to the wood-nature and fire-nature.'[106] These were generated simultaneously, and it was only when [the legendary sage king] Suiren used friction [to light cooking fires for humankind] that the fire and the wood became separate.[107] The sūtra says, 'Wood is likened to the afflictions, and fire is likened to the Buddha-nature.'[108] The *Nirvāṇa Sūtra* says, 'With the fire of wisdom one burns the fuel of the afflictions.'[109] The sūtra says that wisdom is the Buddha-nature.[110] Therefore, you should know that the various sūtras [all] contain these lines and explain that the afflictions are [not] fundamental."[111]

Question: "Why does [the Buddha say in] chapter fifteen, "On Pure

---

102. This phrase, six characters in length, does not occur in P3047.

103. P3047 (and hence, Hu) does specify this as coming from a sūtra, but simply reads "Why does one not enter the afflictions and enter nirvāṇa?"

104. Hu, 431–432, has expended considerable energy in unraveling the confusion in the manuscripts in this question and answer, moving characters around slightly and accepting Suzuki's suggested interpolation of one character. I have chosen to follow Hu's lead.

105. Unidentified. Nothing like these phrases (*benlai niepan* 本來涅槃 and *bulou zhixing* 不漏智性) occurs in the *Nirvāṇa Sūtra*.

106. That is, the primordial elements of wood and fire. This and the following citation from the *Nirvāṇa Sūtra* regarding wood and fire are unidentified. That sūtra does contain a somewhat similar image where afflictions are likened to wood and nirvāṇa is likened to the ashes that remain after burning the wood (T 375: 12.813b18–19 and 627, c28–29). I have limited the supposed scriptural citation to this sentence, because of the indigenous Chinese reference to follow.

107. The reference to *Suiren* 燧人 is drawn from the *Han Feizi* 韓非子, in the *wudu* 五蠹 section; see *Shin jigen*, 629a.

108. Unidentified.

109. T 374: 12.586c16–17.

110. This equation (*zhihui ji foxing* 智慧即佛性) does not occur in the sūtra. As noted by Hu, 432, the preceding 14 characters occur only in P3047.

111. The negative is inserted by Suzuki, no doubt with reference to its occurrence in Ishii. In this section the argument does not clearly support the concept that the afflictions are not fundamental. If anything, the logic used is irrelevant.

Practice," of the *Nirvāṇa Sūtra,* 'When I speak of the originally existent [I mean] the originally existent afflictions, and [when I speak of] the presently nonexistent [I mean] the presently nonexistent afflictions.'[112] [Also, the sūtra says,] 'The originally nonexistent is the originally nonexistent great *prajñā,* and the presently existent is the presently existent afflictions.' "[113]

Answer: "The afflictions are explained as fundamental in order to counteract the form body of the five *skandhas.* Also, [the Buddha] says in the sūtra, 'I preach thus in order to transform and save sentient beings. I also preach thus on behalf of *śrāvakas* and *pratyekabuddhas.*'[114] Also, the thirty-sixth chapter, "Kauṇḍinya," of the [*Nirvāṇa*] *Sūtra* says, 'Pure Will asked the Buddha, "Which is prior, the body or the afflictions?" The Buddha said, "The body could not be prior, the afflictions could not be prior, and the body and the afflictions could not both be prior. It is necessarily the case that the body must exist dependent on the afflictions.'[115] On the basis of[116] this line from the sūtra, you should understand that the afflictions are fundamental with regard to the body, not with regard to the Buddha-nature.[117]

"Also, the [*Nirvāṇa*] *Sūtra* says, 'It is because of the existence of the Buddha-nature that one can speak of the permanent; it is because of the permanent that one can speak of the fundamental. It is not that it was originally nonexistent and presently existent.'[118] Also, in the fifteenth fascicle the sūtra says, 'The Buddha-nature is without attaining and without generation. Why? It is neither form nor not form, neither long nor short, neither high nor low, neither generated nor extinguished.'[119] Therefore 'one can speak of the permanent, and because of the permanent one can speak of the fundamental.'

---

112. Unidentified. The chapter identification occurs only in S6557; see Hu, 433.
113. Unidentified. The term used is *mohe banruo* 摩訶般若.
114. T 375: 12.707, a23–25.
115. This is a rather expanded paraphrase of a dialogue in the *Nirvāṇa Sūtra;* see T 375: 12.848a26–b9. P3047 does not contain the sūtra's chapter specification, a strong indication that it was an earlier ms. than Ishii and S6557. Indeed, there are numerous minor differences between P3047 and the other two mss. in this section, as indicated in Hu, 106–107.
116. This is the character *yan* 驗. It apparently is used when making a logical inference or deduction based on scriptural citations.
117. This is Shenhui's basic point, that the afflictions, even if of an ontological priority comparable to the body, are of a different order of reality from the Buddha-nature.
118. That is, it is not the case that it originally did not exist but does now. The first part of this citation does not occur in the *Nirvāṇa Sūtra,* T 375: 12.758c16–17; the final phrase occurs twice in the *Nirvāṇa Sūtra;* see T 375: 12.708a21–23 and 801b26–29. It is cited again below as part of the former passage in its context. Suzuki notes that there must be something missing from S6557 and P3047 at this point; I am omitting Suzuki's minor editorial modifications. S6557 and P3047 have "It is because of the existence of the Buddha-nature that one can speak of the permanent. Fundamentally, it is not the case that there is the fundamentally nonexistent and the presently existent."
119. This passage is a rough paraphrase of T 375: 12.708a21–23. Here and throughout this section, fascicle numbers and chapter titles from the original scripture are specified in S6557 and Ishii, indicating textual development beyond P3047. The Chinese of P3047 reads *wuwen wusheng* 無問無生, "without question and without generation." The character *wen* must be an error for *de* 得, "attain," as in Ishii, S6557, and the original passage in the *Nirvāṇa Sūtra.*

Also, the nineteenth fascicle of the sūtra says, 'It is as if there were the seven treasures in a dark room—people would not know they existed, since they would be invisible due to the darkness. The person with wisdom would light a great bright lamp and carry it in to illuminate [the room, whereby he would] see everything. This person would see the seven treasures without ever saying they [only] existed presently.[120] The Buddha-nature is likewise: it does not only begin to exist for the first time in the present [moment of illumination], but is invisible due to the afflictions.'[121] This is called fundamental nonexistence. It is also as if a blind person who could not [even] see the sun and moon were to obtain an excellent medicine and heal himself, so that he could see. Because of this he would say that the sun and moon were originally nonexistent but presently existent.[122] [But] it was because of his blindness that they were invisible; the sun and moon are originally and naturally existent. The twenty-fifth fascicle of the sūtra says, 'That all sentient beings will in the future definitely attain perfect enlightenment—this is called the Buddha-nature. All sentient beings are presently fettered by the afflictions and therefore cannot see [the Buddha-nature]—this is called the originally nonexistent.'[123] Also, the nineteenth fascicle of the sūtra says, 'Whether there is a buddha [in the world] or not, the natures and characteristics [of the buddhas] are permanently abiding. It is because they are blinded by the afflictions that sentient beings do not see nirvāṇa and say that it is nonexistent. You should understand that nirvāṇa is a permanently abiding dharma, not [something that was] originally nonexistent and presently [DTS245] existent.'[124] 'The nature of the buddha[125] is not *skandhas*, realms, and faculties,[126] it is not originally nonexistent and presently existent, and it is not [something] previously existent that returns to nonexistence. It is from the generation of good causes and conditions that sentient beings are able to see the Buddha-nature.'[127] Because of being able to see the Buddha-nature, one should understand that it is originally and naturally existent."[128]

Question: "You have said that it exists originally and naturally. Why does one not see it naturally, and does one have to rely on causes and conditions?"

Answer: "It is as if there were water underneath the ground—if one does

---

120. That is, at the moment he illuminated them.
121. T 375: 12.735b13–17.
122. This is a paraphrase of T 375: 12.735c3–4.
123. T 375: 12.769a9–11. After "therefore" the text deviates from the quote.
124. T 374: 12.492a17–21.
125. P3047 (Hu, 108), refers only to the Buddha, not the Buddha-nature as do the other manuscripts and the original passage in the *Nirvāṇa Sūtra*.
126. The last term is, literally, "entrances"; the equivalent Sanskrit here is *skandha-dhātu-āyatana*.
127. T 374: 12.526b2–4.
128. The last line can also be read with a more personal sense: "when you attain a vision of the Buddha-nature you will understand…"

not expend the effort to bore a well, one will never get [the water].[129] It is also like a maṇi jewel, which will never become bright and will not be called a jewel if it is not polished.[130] The *Nirvāṇa Sūtra* says, "If all the sentient beings did not depend on the skillful means[131] and instructions of the buddhas, bodhisattvas, and true spiritual compatriots, they would never attain [enlightenment]. They would never be able to see it by themselves.[132] Because they cannot see it, they say there originally is no Buddha-nature. The Buddha-nature is not originally nonexistent and presently existent."

9

Dharma Master Zhen[133] asked: "What is the meaning of 'permanence'?"

Answer: "Impermanence is the meaning of permanence."

Question: "I just asked you the meaning of permanence. Why do you answer saying that impermanence is the meaning of permanence?"

Answer: "It is only because impermanence exists that one can explain permanence. If there were no impermanence, the meaning of permanence would not occur. Because of this, it is called 'permanence.' Why? It is likened to the long being dependent on the short and the short being dependent on the long. If there were no long one could posit no short.[134] Since these matters are interdependent, how could their meanings be different? Also, the imperceptibility[135] of the essence of the dharma-natures is the meaning of permanence. Also, space is also the meaning of permanence."

Question: "Why is space the meaning of permanence?"[136]

Answer: "Space is without large and small and without middle and extremes, and hence it is called the meaning of permanence.[137] To say that the dharmas are in essence imperceptible—this is 'not existent.' To be able to see their imperceptible essences, peaceful and permanently serene—this is 'not nonexistent.' Therefore is it called the meaning of

---

129. T 374: 12.492b7–9.

130. T 374: 12.423b13–15. The story behind this metaphor is of a merchant who owned a valuable jewel but was laughed at for owning mere glass. The same metaphor is cited in section 36.

131. Here P3047 includes *fangbian* 方便, absent in the other mss.

132. T 374: 12.408a24–25 contains a similar idea, although not the same wording.

133. Unidentified. Dharma Master Zhen's name is not specific enough to allow identification through other sources.

134. Gernet, 23n4, refers to the *Dazhidulun* 大智度論, T 1509: 25.147c8–9; translated in Lamotte, *Traité de la grande vertu*, 2:727–728.

135. *Bukede* 不可得, lit. "unattainability."

136. The eight characters of this question occur only in P3047.

137. Gernet, 23n5, suggests that Shenhui might have been inspired by the *Nirvāṇa Sūtra* (cf. T 374: 12.581a10–11 for a similar idea, if different wording), which states that the permanent (Skt. *nitya*) is the nature of the Buddha-nature just as nonbeing (*abhāva*) is the nature of space.

[permanence].¹³⁸ To discuss this in terms of existence and nonexistence, it is like this. To [discuss the same issue] with regard to the essences of the dharmas, then nonexistence does not not exist, and existence does not exist. To be replete with meritorious roots [as numerous as the] sands of the River Ganges—this is the meaning of permanence. Also, [with regard to] neither large nor small being the meaning of permanence, it is said that space is without largeness, so it cannot be described as large. Space is without smallness, so it cannot be described as small. That it is called large at present is the largeness of the small-minded; that it is called small at present is the smallness of the large-minded.¹³⁹ Those who are uncomprehending always discuss this in terms of permanence and impermanence. [But] if one is to be in accord with the principle of the dharma-nature,¹⁴⁰ there is no permanence and no impermanence. Since there is no impermanence, [the dharma-nature] is called permanent."

10

The secretary of the gate Wang Zhaogong¹⁴¹ inquired in verse about the meaning of the three vehicles:

---

138. The character *chang* 常, "permanent," is actually missing at this point in the text. See Hu, 436, for the numerous minor differences between the three mss. at this point. I have followed his use of P3047 here.

139. Literally, "the large of the smallest" (*xiaojia zhi da* 小家之大), and "the small of the largest" (*dajia zhi xiao* 大家之小). Gernet, 24nn7–8, suggests Shenhui was influenced by Zhuangzi's relativism.

140. Hu, 437, suggests that *faxing li* 法性理 should be read *faxing ti* 法性體.

141. Shenhui's interrogator here is Wang Ju 王琚, already mentioned in n. 7 above. Wang Ju's biography may be found in the *New History of the Tang*, 121, and *History of the Tang*, 106; also see *Morohashi*, 7.826b; Yu, *Tang cishi kao*, 2.687 and 5.2290; and the handwritten summary of the *History of the Tang* biography in Hu, 110. Wang Ju took part in the defeat of the Taiping Princess 太平公主, as a result of which he received the post of minister in the Ministry of Revenue (*Hubu shangshu* 戶部尚書) and was enfeoffed as Zhaoguo gong in 712; he also received the title "Grand Councilor in the Palace" (Neizaixiang 內宰相), which Hucker, *Official Titles*, 353a #4274, describes as an "unofficial and no doubt sardonic reference to any high official who won unusual favor with the ruler." Gernet, 25n1, points out that during the years 713–742 he was prefect of fifteen prefectures and two commanderies; he was prefect in Huahou (Huatai) in about 719 or 720, which may be one of the links between Shenhui, Nanyang, and Huatai. His appointment as prefect of Dengzhou and five other prefectures occurred in Kaiyuan 22, or 734; Hu believes the appointment at Dengzhou, near Nanyang, might have been when he met Shenhui. Later, Wang Ju's involvement in an abortive political initiative aroused the enmity of Li Linfu 李林甫 (683–753), who forced him to commit suicide in 746. The *Song Biographies*, T 2061: 50.762b24, mentions Wang Ju as a Kaiyuan-period sponsor of Nanyang Huizhong, so he may have been an important link between Shenhui and Huizhong. It is possible that this man is identical to the Wang Youlin, adjutant of Runzhou, mentioned in section 39, who is otherwise unidentified. Ge (1994: 56) suggests that the dialogue in question occurred in 713 because it uses Wang's title from 712, but of course this title represents the pinnacle of his career and could have been used anytime thereafter. See also Yanagida, "Goroku," 372, where Wang Ju is described as friendly with Li Yong, who is known for his epitaphs for Northern school figures. In addition, Yanagida suggests that the use of Wang Ju's title should

Within the [burning] house there are no three vehicles,
And outside there is only the one.
I do not understand what use there is
Of talking of these three vehicles.

Answer:

The three vehicles [are said to] exist outside the gate,
But when spoken of are [immediately] inside the house.
When the children hear of them,
They get the three vehicles.[142]

The next inquiry:

Now, outside the house,
Before the vehicles have been produced,[143]
They get the vehicles within the house—
So why do they have to go outside for them? [DTS247]

Answer:

Although the children get them,
They don't understand that the vehicles are vehicles.
Because they don't realize this themselves,
They search for them outside the gate.

Question: "How[144] could someone attain the fruit of the Path and not know it oneself?"

---

remind us of the statement in Liu Cheng's preface that Shenhui "was invited to have discussions with kings and lords." Gernet, 26n8, suggests that the dialogue between Wang Ju and Shenhui occurred after rather than before the Huatai affairs. Ui, *Zenshūshi kenkyū*, 209, suggests that the dialogue and relationship with Wang Ju shows that Shenhui was virtually unknown at the time and only beginning to attract attention; although this inference is not logically rigorous, the dialogue in question considers none of Shenhui's most cherished ideas and could well have occurred before Shenhui really achieved his full stride as a polemicist. The combined implication, which is too tentative to be taken as certain, is that the polemical fervor of the *Definition of the Truth* as a text is more pronounced than the events themselves.

142. This line actually states that they get the three vehicles "completely," the nuance being that they acquire the three vehicles then and there and that's the end of it. Also, the term *de* 得, "to get," means acquire both as an object per se and as an object of perception, so that hearing of the vehicles is to "get" them.

143. In P3047 and Ishii, these first two lines are given as part of the previous verse and the question is only two lines; the translation here follows S6557.

144. Note that while Ishii and S6557 have *hechu* 何處, P3047 has *hejia* 何家. This is a very instructive indication of the grammatical value of *jia*.

Answer: "It is evident from the text below [which says] 'they still did not recognize[145] the merit they had attained.' "[146]

Question:

If the children do not recognize it themselves,
How could[147] they seek [for the vehicles] outside the gate?
The father must know what the children have attained,
So why must he give them vehicles in addition?

Answer:

It is because the children do not recognize [the merit of the father's gift] themselves
That they search outside the gate.
The father gives them the [one] vehicle then, and
He also gave them [the three vehicles] before.

Question:

The three vehicles are fundamentally unreal, and
[The father's] preaching is [only] a provisional convenience.
If what is given are only the old vehicles,
Why should they receive things that are false?

Answer:

The father's intention was on the one [vehicle], but[148]
Through skillful means he provisionally spoke of the three.
In the preceding explanation of the three vehicles,
The three vehicles are fundamentally the one.

Question:

If the one vehicle may be taken as the three and
The three vehicles may be taken as the one,
Why did he not originally explain the one, but
Troubled to explain the three vehicles?

---

145. "Recognize" for *zhi* 知.
146. T 262: 9.19b26, and Watson, *Lotus Sutra*, 99, which suggests that sentient beings are no more conscious of the Tathāgata's benefit than the plants and trees are conscious of the benefits of rain.
147. On this use of *rong* 容 as an interrogative, see *Shin jigen*, 280a.
148. The translation here follows S6557 and Ishii; in P3047 the first line of this verse reads: "Although these vehicles have different names…"

Answer:

When explaining this to deluded people
The three are taken as the three vehicles,
Whereas in the understanding of an enlightened person
The three are fundamentally one.

11

Duke Cui of Ji[149] asked: "When you do seated meditation, after entering concentration[150] when do you emerge from concentration?" [DTS248]

Answer: "Chan is without location, so how can there be concentration?"[151]

Question: "If you say there is no concentration, what do you call mental cultivation?"[152]

Answer: "I just refrained from positing even concentration. Who said anything about mental cultivation?"[153]

Question: "If mind and concentration are both eliminated, how does one achieve enlightenment?"

Answer: "In speaking of this enlightenment, there is no enlightenment of any kind."

Question: "But if there is 'no enlightenment of any kind,' how does one attain 'this enlightenment'?"

Answer: "The 'this enlightenment' you've just mentioned is an enlightenment of some kind. If I say there is no '[enlightenment] of any kind,' then 'this' one is also nonexistent!"

---

149. Duke Cui of Ji 崔齊公, probably Cui Zongzhi 崔宗之 (d.u.): this man's father had assisted in the elimination of both Empress Weishi 韋氏皇后 and the Taiping Princess and was given the title used here after the first endeavor; the son Zongzhi inherited the title and seems to have distinguished himself primarily by drinking. The poet Li Bai 李白 describes drinking with Cui Zongzhi when the latter was banished from / to his post in Jinling, and Du Fu 杜甫 includes him in his "Song of the Eight Immortals of Drink" (*Yingzhong ba xian ge* 飲中八仙歌), another member of whom was Su Jin, introduced just below (section 13). This encounter must have occurred after 722, when Chi Zongzhi inherited his father's title, but it probably happened a decade or two later, after he had built his own reputation as an aesthete.

150. Or, samādhi.

151. As noted by Gernet, 27n3, the word *ding* 定 means both "samādhi" and "fixed."

152. The compound *yongxin* 用心 literally means "use / function the mind" but is used here with the connotation of the mental endeavor involved in spiritual practice. As Gernet, 36n1, notes, this is a technical expression of the Chan school, or rather of the meditation tradition in general.

153. Throughout this exchange there is wordplay on the meanings of *dao* 道 as a verb "to speak" and as the nouns "enlightenment" and "path." Here Shenhui alludes to the famous first line of the *Daode jing*.

12

Dharma Master Jian of Mount Lu[154] asked: "What is the meaning of the Middle Path?"

Answer: "It is the extremes."

Question: "I just asked you about the meaning of the Middle Path. Why do you answer that it is the extremes?"

Answer: "The Middle Path you just mentioned is necessarily dependent on the meaning of the extremes. Without depending on the meaning of the extremes one cannot posit the Middle Path."[155]

13

Su Jin, vice minister of the Board of Rites,[156] asked: "What is the Great Vehicle, and what is the Supreme Vehicle?"[157]

Answer: "That of the bodhisattvas is the Great Vehicle, and that of the buddhas is the Supreme Vehicle."

Question: "What difference is there between the Great and the Supreme Vehicles?"

---

154. Unidentified. Dharma Master Jian of Mount Lu 廬山簡法師 in Jiangxi province reappears in sections 38 and 47 below.

155. Compare this with Shenhui's explanation of permanence and impermanence above; obviously, this was a standard format he used. Gernet, 27n2, infers that this conversation (together with those in sections 11 and 14) was not recorded on the spot, but reconstructed afterwards.

156. This encounter occurred sometime before Su Jin's death, which seems to have occurred after 741 (some sources say he died in 734, but there is evidence he lived past 741). Su Jin 蘇晉, like Cui Zongzhi (see n. 149 above), was also known as one of the "eight immortals of drink." Hu, 495n12, identifies Su Jin as the son of Su Xiang 蘇珦, with whom he shares a *History of the Tang* biography (fascicle 100). (Also see *New History of the Tang*, fascicle 128, f. 1a13–1b6.) Su Jin was a precocious youth who passed his *jinshi* 進士 examination at an early age and became a secretariat drafter (*Zhongshu sheren* 中書舍人) and simultaneously an academician of the Institute for the Veneration of Literature (Chongwenguan xueshi 崇文館學士). Emperor Xuanzong routinely had him and one other official write the drafts of his edicts. His biography recalls Su Jin's being vice minister of the Ministry of Revenue (*Hubu shilang* 戶部侍郎), then in 726 becoming vice minister of the Ministry of Personnel (*Libu shilang* 吏部侍郎), but does not refer to him as holding this position in the Ministry of Rites (*Libu shilang* 禮部侍郎). According to Ogawa ("Kataku Jinne," 34), he held this position until 741, when he became prefect of Ruhou 汝州 (Lin'an xian 臨安縣, Henan). Du Fu's "Song of the Eight Immortals of Drink" includes the line, "Su Jin fasted long before the embroidered Buddha, and while drunk he would often love to escape in meditation (*chan*)." Yanagida, "Goroku," 372, notes that (in addition to Su Jin and Cui Zongzhi), Li Shizhi 李適之 (d. 747), whose name is associated with the *Damo lun* 達摩論 (Treatise of Bodhidharma), was also one of the eight immortals. (For Du Fu's poem, see n. 140 above.) The post-741 date of Su Jin's demise fits better with his identity as one of these eight immortals.

157. Yanagida, *Shoki Zenshū shisho*, 270, notes the similarity between the subject matter discussed here and a dialogue in the *Platform Sūtra*, T 2008: 48.343a7–15.

Miscellaneous Dialogues   153

Answer: "In their practice of the perfection of charity, the bodhisattvas of the Great Vehicle contemplate the essential emptiness of the three things."[158] [Their practice of the other] five perfections is [DTS249] like this. Hence the name 'Great Vehicle.' In the Supreme Vehicle, one simply sees[159] that the fundamental natures are empty and tranquil. Realizing that the three things are fundamentally empty in their self-natures, one does not activate any further contemplation.[160] And the [rest of the] six perfections[161] are likewise. This is called the Supreme Vehicle."

Another question: "Do you postulate causality?"[162]

Answer: "I do not posit causality."[163]

Question: "If you do not posit causality, how can one attain knowing?"

Answer: "Upon the fundamentally empty and serene essence there naturally occurs the wisdom of *prajñā*, which is able to know[164]—because of this I do not posit causality. If one posited causality, then there would be gradations."[165]

Question: "If that is so, then is it also the case that you do not postulate the cultivation of all the practices?"[166]

Answer: "If one can see [the Buddha-nature] like this, then the myriad practices are all accomplished."[167]

---

158. The three things are the donor, recipient, and gift.

159. The character *jian* 見, "see," is missing from S6557 and P3047.

160. The term here, *bu fu qi guan* 不復起觀, uses basic early Chan jargon. Yanagida, "Goroku," 611n336, suggests that this is a development on the fourth practice of the *Two Entrances and Four Practices* attributed to Bodhidharma, the "practice of accordance with the Dharma."

161. In P3047 the character *chen* 塵, "dust" or "sensory datum," occurs instead of the similar graph *du* 度, "perfection."

162. The verb used is *jia* 假, which refers to a secondary level of meaning. "Causality" here renders *yuanqi* 緣起. Note that S6557 and Ishii make the interrogative sense more explicit by adding the question word *fou* 否 to the end of the sentence.

163. "Posit" here renders *li* 立, "to establish."

164. Yanagida, "Goroku," 611n336, suggests that this is the innovative part of Shenhui's teaching. Material similar to this occurs in section 6, and most of the first portion of this sentence, *wuzhu tishang zi you benzhi, benzhi neng zhi* 無住體上自有本智, 本智能知, also occurs in section 26. Also see Chengguan's 澄觀 *Huayan jing shu yanyi chao* 華嚴經疏演義鈔 21 (T 1736: 36.164c23–25), where this concept is used to explicate the difference between the positions of Shenxiu and Huineng as found in the *Platform Sūtra* mind-verses: "Wisdom is fundamental wisdom, i.e., upon the non-abiding essence there naturally occurs true knowing, not that there is a separate knowing that knows the essence of the mind."

165. The term *cidi* 次第 at the end of this sentence means "progressions" or "stages."

166. This question and the subsequent answer do not occur in Ishii and S6557. Although they do form an effective bridge from one topic to the next, note the complete change in vocabulary before and after this omission.

167. Were it not for the reference to *jianxing* or "seeing the nature" in the subsequent question, this answer should have properly been translated as "if one attains a view such as this" (see Gernet, 29). However, Shenhui would never advocate adopting a "view."

Question: "If someone who sees this nature activates ignorance, does it create karmic bonds?"[168]

Answer: "Although he may activate ignorance, karmic bonds are not created."

Question: "Why are they not created?"

Answer: "Merely see the fundamental nature, the clear and pure essence of which is imperceptible, and the karmic bonds are naturally nongenerated."[169]

14

Question:[170] "I have heard[171] that when a mountain monk[172] did obeisance to Chan Master [Lao]an of Mount Song, the master said 'A monk who's obsessed with food,' but when a monk from Shoujisi did obeisance to Chan Master An, the master said 'A monk who's stingy with food.'[173] I want to ask you about these two." [DTS250]

Answer: "Eliminate both of them."[174]

Question: "How does one eliminate them?"

Answer: "Just transcend them, and you've eliminated them."

Question: "How does one transcend them?"

Answer: "How one transcends them is by not having any kind of transcendence."

Question: "Is this transcendence in the mind or transcendence in the eye?"

Answer: "When I just now [said] 'how one transcends them,' [I meant] no transcendence of either mind or eye."

Question: "If both mind and eye are unseeing, this must be a blind man."

Answer: "Only the blind can sing about their own blindness. For others

---

168. For *yejie* 業結, the combination of bad karma (*jie*) and the afflictions (*jie*), see *Bukkyōgo daijiten*, 407b.

169. Ishii and S6557 leave out *qingjing* 清淨, "clear and pure," which allows Suzuki to read the sentence, "Just see the essential imperceptibility of the fundamental essence..."

170. In P3047 the question is anonymous, but in Ishii and S6557 the questioner is explicitly identified as Li Jun, prefect of Runzhou 潤州刺史李峻 in Jiangsu province; see Hu, 442. Because of the absence of a specific subject, Hu's original edition did not begin a new section here (Hu, 114, and DTS249). But since the topic is clearly different from the preceding material, I have marked it as a separate section. See section 39 below for a dialogue with another official from Runzhou, Wang Youlin. Gernet, 30n9, identifies this as a *gong'an* 公案 (J. *kōan*), a precedent for meditation, and he is certainly correct that the style of asking one master about something another master has said is one of the hallmarks of encounter dialogue.

171. The characters *jianyou* 見有 are colloquial usage for citing anonymous knowledge. This reference to oral tradition seems a fundamental part of Chan literature.

172. The connotation of this term is negative, meaning something like "coarse monk from the boondocks." Later it was used as a deprecatory form of self-reference.

173. The first phrase is *chenzhou daoren* 趁粥道人, lit. "a monk who runs after gruel"; the second, *xizhou daoren* 惜粥道人. Presumably these phrases were meant to describe or respond to the two monks in some fashion, but the context is unclear. On Lao'an, see McRae, *Northern School*, 56–59.

174. "To eliminate" (*qian* 遣) has the connotation of "to forget about."

MISCELLANEOUS DIALOGUES

who see, fundamentally there is no blindness. The sūtra says, 'This is the fault of the blind person, not the fault of the sun and moon.'"[175]

15

Duke Zhang of Yan[176] asked: "You always preach the Dharma of non-thought and exhort people to spiritual cultivation, yet I wonder whether the Dharma of non-thought is existent or nonexistent."

Answer: "Non-thought cannot be said to be existent and cannot be said to be nonexistent.[177] To call it existent would be to have it identical to worldly existence, and to call it nonexistent would be to have it identical to worldly nonexistence. Thus[178] non-thought is not identical to existence or nonexistence."

Question: "What does one call it?"[179]
Answer: "It's not called anything."
Question: "What is it like?"[180]
Answer: "It's also not like anything.[181] Hence non-thought cannot be explained. Just now, my saying 'explained' has to do with responses to

---

175. Actually, the *Vimalakīrti*, T 475: 14.520b28, has only the second clause given here. The reference to the "fault" (*guo* 過) of blindness labels it the result of karmic transgression, an idea reminiscent of both religious Daoism and the Buddhist concept of karma.

176. Zhang Yue (667–730) was known as Duke of Yan from at least the beginning of Kaiyuan (712–742); the dating of this exchange is based on Wu ("Heze Shenhui zhuan yanjiu," 906), who suggests that Shenhui's contact with Zhang Yue probably occurred sometime during the years 717–718, while the prominent Buddhist layman was administrator of Jingzhou. Gernet, 31n1, on the other hand, suggests that the dialogue should be dated to the period between Zhang Yue's return to Luoyang in 721 after military campaigns in the northern frontier and his death about a decade later; Jorgensen (*Inventing Hui-neng*, 394) follows Gernet and refers to Zhang Yue's "return from exile in 721." This latter scenario seems unlikely to me, since during the last decade of his life, Zhang Yue was far too heavily involved in central court politics to have time for meeting a promising young Buddhist teacher residing in the provinces. In either case, if it is not a complete fabrication, the dialogue took place prior to most or all of Shenhui's activities in Huatai.

177. After this first part of the answer, the manuscripts differ in their readings. The translation is based on P3047. In S6557 and Ishii, this answer is followed by the question, "Why cannot non-thought be called existent or nonexistent?" which is answered with: "[Even] if it were called existent, it would not be identical to worldly existence, and [even] if it were called nonexistent, it would not be identical to worldly nonexistence. Thus non-thought may not be called existent or nonexistent."

178. "Thus" renders the Chinese *shiyi* 是以, which occurs again just below in a passage where the rendering "thus" is not quite right.

179. Literally, "what thing do you call it?" The Chinese is *huan zuo shimo wu* 喚作是沒勿 in S6557 and *huan zuo shi wu* 喚作是物 in P3047 and Ishii. Minor differences continue throughout the rest of the dialogue.

180. The Chinese is *zuo wu sheng shi* 作勿生是, negated just below as *yi bu zuo wu sheng* 亦不作勿生. The first part of this question occurs only in Ishii and S6557. The colloquialism *yimo shi* 異沒時 could also be read as "at that time," referring to the time of seeing.

181. The Chinese *yi wu* 一物, "single thing," here makes one think once again of the *Five Skillful Means*. I wonder if the scribe did not misunderstand the colloquialism of the preceding question. This is a most interesting passage, especially for its linguistic and textual dating evidence.

questions. Unless given in response to a question, there would never be an oral explanation.[182] It is like a bright mirror: unless presented with an object, the mirror never manifests an image.[183] My saying 'manifests an image' just now [means that] the image is only manifested as the response to an object."[184]

Question: "Does it not illuminate when not responding to an image?"

Answer: "Saying[185] 'illuminate'[186] has little to do with responding or not responding [to objects]; in both cases [the mirror] always illuminates."

Question: "You have said that there is no object or image and also no oral explanation, and that all of existence and nonexistence is entirely beyond being posited.[187] Now you refer to illumination, but what kind of illumination is it?"

Answer: "My reference to 'illumination' means that all of this exists because of the brightness of the mirror. Because of the purity of mind of sentient beings, there naturally exists a refulgence of great wisdom, which illuminates the world without exception.[188]

Question: "How does one get to see a non-thing, and seeing a non-thing, then call it a thing?"[189]

---

182. This is reminiscent of the Oxhead school's *Treatise on the Transcendence of Cognition*, in which Professor Enlightenment says at one point that he's answered according to the way the questions were put rather than stating any doctrine of his own. The ensuing reference to the mirror is apt, since the impact of Shenhui's "rule of rhetorical purity" was to limit Chan instruction to reaction rather than the proactive creation of doctrinal formulations; see McRae, "Ox-head School, 255–259.

183. The Chinese word *xiang* 像 is used here for both "object" and "image."

184. The Chinese is *wu* 物, usually translated "thing" but often used in reference to sentient beings. The role of this sentence seems to be to eliminate the ambiguity of using *xiang* for both object and image.

185. This usage *jin yan* 今言, "now say," which occurs frequently in this passage, means "to say X in the present context."

186. Unlike Ishii and S6557, which simply read *zhao* 照, P3047 here has *duizhao* 對照, "response-illumination." The first character is out of place. Incidentally, Gernet, 32n3, very aptly notes that the multivalence of *zhao* makes translation difficult here: the term refers to the reflection of images, the illumination of objects, and the activity of *prajñā*. I would add that seeing with the eyes was understood according to the same metaphor.

187. The term for "object or image" is *xingxiang* 形像, and that for "cannot be posited" is *buke li* 不可立.

188. The refulgence of great wisdom is *da zhihui guang* 大智慧光.

189. This could be translated "How does one get to see the thing of nonbeing...?" Or, roughly as Gernet, 33, has it, "What does one call viewing the absence of things?" [At this point, the manuscripts diverge once again. McRae translates the text as it occurs in P3047. After this question, Ishii and S6557 continue as follows:

Answer: "One simply sees nonexistence."
　　Question: "[But,] if it is nonexistence, then one sees that as a thing."
　　Answer: "[No,] although one sees it, one does not call that a thing."
　　Question: "If it is not called a thing, then what is it that you call seeing?"
　　Answer: "The seeing that is not a thing—that is called true seeing, constant seeing."

The last line could also be read as "When one does not see a single thing..."—Ed.]

Answer: "One does not call it a thing." [DTS252]
Question: "Then if you do not call it a thing, what is the Buddha-nature?"
Answer: "To see and not see without any thing is true seeing, constant seeing."[190]

16[191]

His Reverence asked Dharma Master Chongyuan, "Have you lectured on the *Great Parinirvāṇa Sūtra?*"

Dharma Master Chongyuan said, "I have lectured on the *Great Parinirvāṇa Sūtra* dozens of times."

His Reverence then said, "All the sūtras and treatises of the Mahāyāna and Hīnayāna explain that sentient beings are not emancipated because they possess the two minds of generation and extinction. The *Nirvāṇa Sūtra* [says],

All the processes [of life] are impermanent;
They are the dharmas of generation and extinction.
When generation and extinction are extinguished,
Serene extinction is bliss.

I wonder, can generation and extinction be extinguished or not? Is extinction extinguished with generation, or is generation extinguished with extinction? Is generation able to extinguish generation itself, or is extinction able to extinguish extinction itself? I would like you to answer each of these [questions] for me in detail."

Dharma Master Chongyuan said, "I too have noticed that the various sūtras and treatises contain explanations such as this, but to this point I have never been able to comprehend their meaning. If you comprehend their meaning, please explain it to the assembly."

His Reverence said, "I cannot demur from explaining it to you, but I fear no one will understand."

The Dharma master said, "There are over ten thousand monks and laymen here. Can it be that not a single one will understand?"

His Reverence said, "Look. Do you see or not?"

The Dharma master said, "See what?"

His Reverence said, "Obviously, you don't see."

When the Dharma master heard this, he held his tongue and did not respond. To say nothing was equivalent to declaring his submission, [DTS253]

---

190. Here the language is unmistakably reminiscent of the *Five Skillful Means;* see McRae, *Northern School,* 173 and (for a reference to "true seeing") 192. At the very least, it is interesting that this language occurs here, with no apparent knowledge of the *Platform Sūtra* verses.

191. For annotation on this section, see the same dialogue in the *Definition of the Truth,* section 51. This and the following two sections (and, to a certain extent, section 24) have Shenhui posing the questions of (presumably Northern school) antagonists.

and his followers became increasingly disappointed. The victory being determined, the monks and laypeople sighed and dispersed.

17

His Reverence asked Dharma Master Huicheng,[192] "By the cultivation of what Dharma is one able to see the [Buddha-]nature?"[193]

Answer: "First one must practice sitting and cultivate concentration.[194] After attaining concentration[195] one generates wisdom on the basis of one's concentration, and on the basis of one's wisdom one is able to see the nature."[196]

Question: "When cultivating concentration, surely it must be that one intentionalizes?"[197]

Answer: "That is so."

Question: "But if one intentionalizes, then this is a conceptual [type of] concentration, so how could one be able to see [the nature]?"[198]

Answer: "What I am referring to here as [seeing][199] the nature necessarily depends on the cultivation of concentration. If one did not cultivate concentration, how could one see the nature?"

Question: "This cultivation of concentration is originally the deluded mind's cultivation of concentration, so how could one attain concentration [this way]?"

Answer: "This cultivation of concentration naturally includes the illumination of both interior and exterior. One is thus able to view purity. Because of the purity of the mind, one is able to see the nature."[200]

---

192. On Huicheng, see n. 12 above.

193. The term used is *jianxing* 見性.

194. What the text literally says (*xuezuo xiuding* 學坐修定) may be another reflection of the Northern school tendency to divide binomials for explication; see McRae, *Northern School*, 201–205 and 224. Shenhui does notice this distinction, which is continued in the *Platform Sūtra*, but interprets Dharma Master Huicheng as meaning simply to "cultivate samādhi by practicing seated concentration."

195. That is, samādhi.

196. This section is a good example of the difference between the Ishii manuscript on the one hand and P3047 and S6557 on the other. In addition to the specific passages included only in the former, its more polished nature is indicated by (1) the repetition of the name Chan Master Cheng in the first reply; (2) the use of the more complete forms *wenyue* 問曰, etc., rather than simply *wen*; the use of the correct character for *hui* 慧, "wisdom," rather than the very commonly used homonym 惠, "kindness"; and the more formal question word *fou* 否 rather than 不 at the end of the second question.

197. The term here is of course *zuoyi* 作意; Northern school texts also criticize "intentionalization" and advocate "non-activation" of the mind (*buqi* 不起). The grammatical structure here involves a rhetorical question that expects a negative reply; the English rendering is meant to capture the thrust of the inquiry.

198. Ishii and S6557 have the character *xing* 性, "nature," here.

199. Ishii and S6557 have the character *jian* 見, "see," here.

200. Ishii and S6557 have the slightly different and more explicit "When one attains concentration in this cultivation of concentration the illumination of interior and exterior are naturally included. Because of the illumination of interior and exterior, one is able to see

Question: "The nature is without interior and exterior. If you refer to illumination of interior and exterior, this is fundamentally[201] [a function of the] deluded mind, and how could one thereby see the nature? The sūtra says, 'If one studies the various samādhis, this is motion and not seated meditation.'[202] If the mind follows the flowing of the realms, how can this be called concentration?' If concentration were like this, Vimalakīrti would not have had to reprimand Śāriputra for sitting in meditation!"[203]

18

His Reverence asked those who trained in the Path, "When we say 'mental cultivation'[204] does this involve intentionalization or not? If there is no intentionalization, then one is [DTS254] no different than a deaf fool.[205] If there is intentionalization, then there is something to be attained—and because [having something that is attained][206] amounts to being fettered, how can one thereby attain emancipation?[207]

"When *śrāvakas* cultivate emptiness and reside in emptiness, they are fettered by emptiness. When they cultivate concentration and reside in concentration, they are fettered by concentration. When they cultivate tranquility and reside in tranquility, they are fettered by tranquility. When they cultivate serenity and reside in serenity, they are fettered by serenity.[208]

"Therefore, the *Diamond Sūtra* says, 'To grasp at the characteristics of the

---

purity. Because the mind is pure, this is to see the nature." P3047 lacks the character *xin* 心 at the end of this statement.

201. The Chinese is *yuan* 元, usually rendered "originally."

202. Vimalakīrti says no such thing in his criticism of Śāriputra's approach to meditation in the Chinese version translated by Kumārajīva. The only reference to motion there is to "remaining motionless with regard to views yet cultivating the thirty-seven constituents of enlightenment"; see T 475: 14.539c24. [Curiously, the citation does occur outside the *Vimalakīrti Sūtra*, but only in commentarial literature. Chengguan 澄觀, Yanshou 延壽, and Zongmi 宗密 cite these lines as coming from the Chinese *Dharmapada* (*Fajujing* 法句經), which, however, does not contain these lines. See T 1736: 36.50c18–21; T 2016: 48.615c10–12 (and, without reference, 301b15–16) and 682a2–3; and T 2015: 48.405b29–c1, respectively.—Ed.]

203. See *Vimalakīrti Sūtra*, T 475: 14.539c24. The *Platform Sūtra* includes virtually the same injunction: "If he had sat motionless, Vimalakīrti would not have reprimanded Śāriputra for sitting in meditation in the forest"; see T 2008: 48.338b22–23, *Enō kenkyū*, 294, and Yampolsky, *Platform Sutra*, 137.

204. For *yongxin* 用心, see n. 152 above and the *Platform Sermon*, n. 144. S6557 and P3047 are a bit garbled at this point, as Suzuki notes.

205. The term used here is *longsu* 聾俗, which the *Shinjigen*, 813b, defines as a deaf person with no power of discrimination.

206. Adding from the Ishii manuscript.

207. Gernet, 36n2, suggests that an analogous reasoning occurs in the *Vimalakīrti*, T 475: 14.541b1–3, but at this location the discussion concerns the nonduality of the characteristics of form rather than fetters and emancipation.

208. There is no difference between tranquility (*jing* 靜) and serenity (*ji* 寂) except in sometimes being presented in opposition to physical and mental activity, respectively.

dharmas is to be attached to self, person, sentient being, and lifespan.'[209] The *Vimalakīrti Sūtra* says, 'To subjugate the mind is the Dharma of the *śrāvakas*. To not subjugate the mind is the Dharma of the foolish.'[210] Good people, mental cultivation is subjugation—how could it be called emancipation? Stream-enterers also subjugate [the mind], once-returners also subjugate, non-returners[211] also subjugate, and the four sages and three wise ones[212] also all subjugate [the mind]. How can one discern any difference [between them]? Concentration such as this can never be true emancipation."

19

Master Shenzu[213] asked: "This fundamental mind is the essence of suchness. But if [suchness] has no characteristics of green and yellow,[214] how can it be recognized?"

Answer: "Our minds are fundamentally empty and serene, and we are not aware of the activation of false thoughts. If one becomes aware of a false thought as soon as it arises, then the false thought is naturally extinguished in that awareness. This is to recognize the mind.[215] This is to perceive the [fundamental] mind."

---

209. This is from the *Diamond Sūtra,* T 235: 8.749b7–8. Gernet, 36, translates "other" instead of "person," yielding a pair that is very appropriate in early Chan writings but not the distinction originally implied in the sūtra, nor the way the passage was apparently understood by Shenhui. For comparison, see Edward Conze's explanation of the Sanskrit text (not necessarily precisely the same as Kumārajīva's original) in Conze, *Buddhist Wisdom Books,* 33–35.

210. See T 475: 14.545b25–26, where the order of these two sentences is the opposite of that in Shenhui's text and the references are actually to residing in (*zhu* 住) the subjugation or non-subjugation of the mind.

211. At this point Ishii has "Non-returners and arhats also subjugate. [Those in] the samādhi of non-perception and the samādhi of not non-perception also subjugate. [Those in] the four *dhyānas* also subjugate [the mind]."

212. The four sages (*si sheng* 四聖) are the stream-enterer, once-returner, non-returner, and arhat of Abhidharma systems, so it is reasonable to interpret the three wise ones (*san xian* 三賢) also in terms of the Abhidharma category of those who had achieved mastery of the five types of inhibitory contemplation, mental concentration on a separate characteristic, and mental concentration on a general characteristic; see *Bukkyōgo daijiten,* 461c. Gernet, 36n7, identifies the three wise ones as those bodhisattvas residing at either the ten abidings, the ten practices, or the ten reversions, the first three sets of stages in the Mahāyāna system (also given in Nakamura). However, the locus classicus given by Nakamura for the latter category is very late, and the Abhidharma category seems more appropriate.

213. This unnamed master cannot be identified. His monastery, Shenzu si 神足寺, was in Nanyang. The only other reference to Shenzu si mentions a monk named Huitiao 慧眺 (d. 639), who was too early to be the teacher mentioned here; see the *Huayan jing zhuanji* 華嚴經傳記 (T 2073: 51.162a28–b19) and the *Zongjing lu* 宗鏡錄 (T 2016: 48.921b4–18).

214. That is, of color.

215. Although the term "non-enlightenment" occurs elsewhere in the *Miscellaneous Dialogues* (see section 2), here the same characters *bujue* 不覺 are not used as a bound form; hence, "do not cognize." Nevertheless, the terminology here is that of the *Awakening of Faith,* which resolutely contrasts the unchanging absolute or suchness (*zhenru* 真如) with the conditioned realm of generation and extinction, or saṃsāra. Gernet, 37n4, cites the *Wisdom Sūtra of Heav-*

MISCELLANEOUS DIALOGUES 161

Question: "Although there may be the light of awareness [in what you describe], this is still identical to generation and extinction.[216] What teaching would you now preach to attain the absence of generation and extinction?"[217]

Answer: "It is just because generation and extinction come into being with the activation of mind. If the activation of mind is extinguished, then generation and extinction cease of themselves, and there are no thoughts that can be apprehended. In provisionally speaking of the light of awareness, with the extinction [of the activated mind] in the light of awareness, generation and extinction naturally cease to exist, and generation and extinction at once are neither generated nor extinguished."[218] [DTS255]

20

The Bhikṣu disciple Wuxing[219] asked: "I once saw Dharma Master Jun[220] of Xiangyang and the other Dharma masters [DTS274] in the Reverend's Hall[221] debate 'Form does not differ from emptiness, and emptiness does not differ from form. Form is identical to emptiness, and emptiness is identical to form,'[222] as well as the dragon girl's generation of *bodhicitta* and

---

enly King Pravara, T 231: 8.710b7–9, in reference to Shenhui's answer below, but the passage is not relevant. The sense of *zi* 自, here and just below rendered "naturally," is that the development is automatic and immediate.

216. That is, to the conditioned activity of saṃsāra.

217. *Bu shengmie* 不生滅, literally, the "not generation-and-extinction," or nirvāṇa. The question poses the criticism that Shenhui's prescription is limited because it leads causally to realization, which would still lie within the realm of saṃsāra, rather than to a type of understanding that is beyond causation entirely. Elsewhere *juezhao* 覺照 might be rendered "illumination of enlightenment" or "illumination and enlightenment," but the first character is used here and below to refer to the basic cognitive capability of the mind, not enlightenment per se.

218. This passage is an interesting example of the difference between S6557 / P3047 and Ishii, illustrating the manner in which the former is an abbreviated transcript of oral discussion and the latter a more polished version, edited with an admixture of colloquialisms. The final answer of the dialogue, in fact, is written in such a shorthand manner in S6557 and P3047 that it would be very difficult to understand without reference to Ishii. The following is the same answer from Ishii: "Answer: It is only because of the activation of the mind that there is generation and extinction. If the activation of the mind is extinguished, then generation and extinction are automatically eliminated and there are no thoughts (or, 'characteristics') that can be attained. I provisionally teach the illuminative cognition, in that when the illuminative cognition is extinguished [DTS255] generation and extinction are automatically nonexistent, and the generation [to which I refer] is not [that of] generation-and-extinction."

219. Unidentified but apparently present in Nanyang and Huatai before and after 732, respectively; see also section 22. Note that this translation follows the placement of sections 20–22 in P3047, whereas Suzuki has moved these sections to a later location, placing them between sections 51 and 52 to maintain alignment with the parallel sections (91–93) in Ishii; see the appendix, table 3.

220. Unidentified. This might be the Xiongjun who appears in the *Records of the Transmission,* who also is unidentified.

221. Heshang Tang 和尚堂.

222. This is the famous line from the *Heart Sūtra,* T 251: 8.848c8–10.

instantaneous attainment of right enlightenment proper, together with other doctrines.[223] I have doubts regarding these."

His Reverence said, "What dialogue between the Dharma masters did you hear?"[224]

He said, "I heard Dharma Master Yan [ask][225] Dharma Master Jun and the others, 'What about this "form does not differ from emptiness, and emptiness does not differ from form"?' Dharma Master Jun [answered], 'The meaning of this may be explained with reference to[226] the Dharma master's [i.e., your] body. What is the Dharma master, and what is not the Dharma master? If we examine[227] your ears, nose, etc., none of this is the Dharma master. This is only a provisional name. If we seek for the Dharma master's body, we will never be able to perceive it.[228] This imperceptibility is emptiness. It is because of the existence of provisional conditions that it is form.'

"What I have doubts about is this interpretation by Dharma Master Jun. I humbly request that Your Reverence indicate the essential purport for me."

His Reverence said, "What the Dharma master has said makes a certain amount of sense, but it does not correspond to the intentions of the sūtras.[229] I would say that Dharma Master Jun's explanation analyzes things to explain emptiness. He does not understand that the realm of the mind is taller than Mount Sumeru. You should now listen well, and I will explain it to you briefly.

"Form exists because the mind is activated, and emptiness exists because [form][230] is imperceptible. I would also say, there is form because of the wondrous existence [based on] the dharma-nature, and because of the wondrous nonexistence of form there is emptiness.[231] When the sūtra says, 'Form does not differ from emptiness, and emptiness does not differ from form,' the meaning is like this. I would also say, seeing is form, and seeing that which cannot be seen is emptiness. The sūtra says, 'Form is identical to emptiness, and emptiness is identical to form. Sensation, concept, inclinations, and consciousness are also like this.'" [DTS275]

---

223. The dragon king's daughter from the *Lotus Sūtra* (T 262: 9.35c12–19) reappears in section 70 below.

224. Using *jian* 見, "see."

225. Dharma Master Yan 巖法師 is unidentified. The verb is added from Ishii, which also has Dharma Master Pin 品 instead of Yan.

226. Using *jie* 借, "borrow."

227. Using *jianze* 檢責, "examine and pursue." The second character is normally used with the sense of censuring someone's errors; see *Morohashi*, 6.583c.

228. Literally, "get it."

229. Literally, "makes a certain manner of sense" (*zi zuo yijia daoli* 自作一家道理), and "if one seeks the intentions of the sūtras, it does not correspond."

230. Once again, the explicit subject is added from Ishii.

231. Gernet, 39, has this as an unidentified quotation. I have not been able to find it as such, and it is probably Shenhui's own formulation.

21

Another question: "The afflictions are immeasurable and limitless, so that even though the buddhas and bodhisattvas undertake eons of self-cultivation they are still unable to attain [enlightenment]. How could the dragon girl generate *bodhicitta* and achieve enlightenment proper in an instant?"

His Reverence said, "In the generation of the intention to achieve enlightenment there are sudden and gradual, and in delusion and enlightenment there are slow and rapid. Delusion is for successive eons, while enlightenment is of an instant. This meaning is difficult to understand, so I will first use some metaphors for you and then explain their meaning. It may be that you will attain enlightened understanding this way. It is like a gauze of threads, their number immeasurable, which are joined into a rope and placed on a piece of wood. With one slice from a sharp sword, they will all be instantaneously severed. Although the threads are numerous, they are not superior to a single sword. The person who generates *bodhicitta* is like this. If you encounter a true spiritual compatriot who uses [clever][232] skillful means to directly manifest suchness, you will sever the afflictions of all the stages using the adamantine wisdom and attain a suddenly expansive enlightenment.[233] If you see for yourself that the dharma-nature is fundamentally empty and serene, that sharp wisdom and clear understanding will let you penetrate without hindrance. When such is your realization, the myriad conditions will all be eliminated. False thoughts as numerous as the sands of the River Ganges will in a single moment be suddenly exhausted, and you will at that moment be complete in all the limitless merits. Having generated the adamantine wisdom, how could one not achieve [all this]?"

Another question: "I heard Dharma Master Jun explain that 'the dragon girl's was a provisional [achievement] and she did not attain the real [enlightenment]. If it had been real, how could she, in the instant she generated *bodhicitta*, have severed the afflictions of all the stages?' I have heard Dharma Master Jun explain it, but I still have doubts. Would you please explain it for me again?"

His Reverence said, "You should be able to understand it completely according to the explanation I just gave using the metaphor of the threads—how can there possibly be any doubt?

"The *Flower Garland* [*Sūtra*] says, 'At the beginning of the ten stages of faith, one generates the adamantine wisdom and thus attains enlightenment proper.'[234] How can the Dharma of *bodhi* have any gradations? If one says that the dragon girl's [attainment] was only provisional, then what power

---

232. P3047 has a lacuna at this place; the word is added from Ishii.
233. The term used is *huoran xiaowu* 豁然曉悟.
234. Unidentified citation.

can there be in the inconceivable perfect and sudden meaning of the *Lotus*?"235[DTS276]

22

Wuxing further asked about the meaning of the five eyes. "When I heard Dharma Master Jun lecture on the 'five eyes of the Tathāgata' of the *Lotus Sūtra,* he said236 that 'to enter emptiness from the provisional is called the wisdom eye, to enter the provisional from emptiness is called the dharma eye, and neither empty nor provisional is called the Buddha eye.'237 At this, the monks and laymen of the capital all sighed, 'How inconceivable.' I have doubts about this, and I wonder if his explanation is correct or not."238

His Reverence said, "What is your doubt? Try to explain it to me."

"My doubt is about the saying in the sūtra that 'the heavenly eye of a tathāgata is always239 in samādhi and sees all the buddha lands without their having any differences in characteristics.'240 Why does the wisdom eye have to enter emptiness from the provisional? And how can the dharma eye enter the provisional from emptiness? If such were the case, they would both be [subject to] causes [born of] characteristics.241 If one depended on the provisional, one could hardly enter emptiness, and if one did not depend on emptiness one would not be able to enter the provisional. We're now to understand242 that having entered emptiness one is no longer [in] the provisional, and having entered the provisional one is no longer [in] the empty. The two paths of empty and provisional seem clearly distinguished in the wisdom of the Dharma. But in the true eye of the buddhas there cannot be any differentiation. That is my doubt—please favor me with your resolution of it."

His Reverence said, "[Just as] there are sharp and dull among people, there are sudden and gradual among teachings. The Dharma master's ex-

---

235. The "perfect and sudden" teaching (*yuandun jiao* 圓頓教) does not occur in the *Lotus* itself but rather in the writings of Zhiyi; see, for example, T 1777: 38.522b20. This term does not occur elsewhere in Shenhui's writings.

236. From here down to "always in samādhi" I am following Ishii, since this material is missing in P3047.

237. The question refers to five types of supernormal vision, but only three are mentioned.

238. The word rendered as "correct" here is *ding*, "settled, defined," as in the title of the *Definition of the Truth*. Although I have followed the grammar of the sentence as it exists, the intended meaning may have been to ask, "Would you settle/define this for me?"

239. P3047 picks up the dialogue from here.

240. That is, he sees them without differentiating between them in any way. [The source of this citation is unknown; it does not occur in the *Lotus Sūtra,* nor can it be found elsewhere.—Ed.]

241. The characters *xiangyin* 相因 could of course mean "characteristics and causes."

242. The phrase *dangzhi* 當知 is usually put in the mouth of those making explanations, not stating questions. Thus within the written text at least, the question is a prop to the explanation that follows.

planation was probably made for deluded people. If we were to discuss the tathāgatas' five eyes, it would surely not be like that. When a tathāgata has manifested his similarity with ordinary people, it is said that he has physical eyes. Although this is the case, his seeing is different from that of ordinary people."[243] [DTS277]

[Wuxing] again said to His Reverence, "I ask you to proffer your resolution [of my doubt]."

His Reverence said, "To see form as clear and pure is the physical eye. To see the essence of the clear and pure is called the heavenly eye. To see the essence of the clear and pure in the various samādhis and the eighty-four thousand perfections, and in this seeing to simultaneously activate the functions, is called the wisdom eye. To see the essence of the clear and pure with no seeing and no non-seeing is called the Dharma eye. For one's seeing to be neither quiescence nor illumination is called the Buddha eye."[244]

23

Dharma Master Chongyuan asked: "What about emptiness? If one says that emptiness exists, then emptiness is still material. If one says that emptiness does not exist, how can one take refuge in it?"

Answer: "It is [only] for those who have not yet seen their nature that one talks of emptiness. If one sees the fundamental nature, then emptiness will also be nonexistent. To see thus is called 'taking refuge.'"[245]

24[246]

His Reverence said: "Friends, if you want to comprehend the most profound *dharmadhātu* you should enter directly into the Samādhi of the Single

---

243. These two sentences follow Ishii, which is different in subtle orthographic and phraseological ways from P3047. The latter, more primitive text has: "The Tathāgata is not like ordinary [unenlightened] people. It is said that he has physical eyes, but his seeing is different from ordinary people." Shenhui apparently conceived of a buddha as fundamentally different from ordinary human beings.

244. P3047 has "neither quiescence nor not-illumination," but I think the extra negative (*fei* 非) is extraneous. This phrase also occurs in the *Transmission of the Lamp*; see T 2076: 51.307a23ff., with thanks to Peter Gregory for mentioning this. Suzuki Tetsuo ("Kataku Jinne no eikyō," 91–96, esp. the chart on 91–92), points out that this passage is similar to language in the *Essential Teaching of Sudden Enlightenment* (X 63.20b11–14; Hirano, *Tongo yōmon*, 49).

245. The word "only" in brackets occurs in Ishii as *zhi* 只. Although this dialogue is clearly left over from the debates that were edited into the *Definition of the Truth*, nothing like this occurs in that text. Although the notion of seeing the fundamental nature is used by Shenhui in his definition of "seated meditation" (see section 23 of the *Definition of the Truth*), there is no reference to "taking refuge" as discussed here. The rhetoric of "nonexistence" (*buyou* 不有) here is similar to that used in section 7 of this text and elsewhere.

246. This section does not occur in P3074.

Practice. If you wish to enter this samādhi, you must first recite the *Diamond Sūtra*[247] and cultivate the perfection of wisdom.[248]

"Therefore, the *Diamond Sūtra* says, 'If there is a good young man or woman who generates *bodhicitta* and, taking even a *gāthā* of four lines from this sūtra, recites it and explains it to others, the blessings will surpass [the donation of a quantity of the seven precious things sufficient to fill up an incalculable number of world systems]. How much more so if that person explains it to others without grasping characteristics!'[249] To not grasp characteristics is what is called suchness.[250] What is that which is called suchness? It is non-thought. What is non-thought? It is that which is called to not think of existence and nonexistence, to not think of good and evil, to not think of the limited and the limitless, to not think of the restricted and the unrestricted, to not think of enlightenment and to not take enlightenment as one's thoughts, to not think of nirvāṇa and to not take nirvāṇa as one's thoughts—this is non-thought. This non-thought is the perfection of wisdom, and the perfection of wisdom is the Samādhi of the Single Practice. [DTS256]

"Friends, if one is at the stage of practicing [the Dharma], and if, as soon as, a thought appears in the mind, one shines the light of awareness on it, then the activated mind will be extinguished, and the light of awareness will disappear of itself, and that is precisely [what is meant by] non-thought.[251] This non-thought is the absence of any single realm. If a single realm exists, this is to not be in correspondence with non-thought. Therefore, friends, to see according to reality is to comprehend the extremely profound *dharmadhātu*, and is the Samādhi of the Single Practice.

"Therefore, in the *Short Version of the Perfection of Wisdom Sūtra* [the Buddha] says, 'Gentlemen, this is the perfection of wisdom: it is that which is called "being without thoughts with regard to the dharmas." We [buddhas] reside within the Dharma of non-thought and [thereby] attain golden bodies with thirty-two characteristics and great refulgence and inconceivable wisdom such as this. The unsurpassable samādhis and unsurpassable wisdom of the buddhas exhaust the limits of all the various merits. The buddhas explain

---

247. As in the *Definition of the Truth*, the full title of the sūtra is given in the text but abbreviated in the translation.

248. This topic also occurs in the *Definition of the Truth*, section 33. Although the material here is different, in both cases the emphasis is on the merit of reciting the *Diamond Sūtra*.

249. S6557 stops at the end of this passage from the *Diamond*, which is found at T 235: 8.752b23–26. (The same theme also occurs at 749b21–23, 750a3–5, 750a24–26, and 752a1–3.) The original point of the last sentence is that one should preach without grasping characteristics, but Shenhui might have taken it to include his audience as well, i.e., one should preach the Dharma so that one's listeners do not grasp at characteristics. Just after this passage occurs the *Diamond*'s famous *gāthā*, which is discussed below in section 29.

250. The Chinese here is *ruru* 如如.

251. The material beginning with this sentence up to the end of section 25 also occurs in the *Definition of the Truth*, sections 48–49.

all these various merits as being inexhaustible, so how much less likely is it that the *śrāvakas* and *pratyekabuddhas* would be able to understand them?' "252

25

His Reverence said, "To see non-thought253 is for the six senses to be without defilement. To see non-thought is to attain access to the knowledge of the buddhas.254 To see non-thought is called things as they truly are. To see non-thought is the cardinal meaning of the Middle Path. To see non-thought is to be simultaneously equipped with merits as numerous as the sands of the River Ganges. To see non-thought is to be able to generate255 all the Dharmas. To see non-thought is to embody all the Dharmas."256

26

Vice Minister Miao257 asked: "How should one cultivate the Path so as to attain emancipation?"
　　Answer: "Attain the non-abiding mind, and this is to attain emancipation."258
　　The vice minister asked: "Excellent. What is non-abiding?"
　　Answer: "The *Diamond Sūtra* contains the text." [DTS257]
　　Another question: "What does the *Diamond Sūtra* say?"259

---

　　252. This sentence might also be translated as "If all the buddhas were to explain these they would never finish, so how much less can *śrāvakas* and *pratyekabuddhas* explain them?"—Ed.
　　253. Did Shenhui have a uniquely visual style of thinking? See another example of this usage of *jian* 見, "see," in section 33. Beginning with this statement, the rest of section 14 in Ishii occurs as Suzuki's section 20 from P3047.
　　254. *Xiang fo zhi* 向佛智
　　255. P3047 has the character *zhu* 主, "master," rather than Ishii's *sheng* 生, "generate." Since the first character does not function well as a transitive verb, I have followed Ishii. [A possible way of rendering the text according to P3047 would be to say that one becomes "sovereign among all Dharmas."—Ed.]
　　256. Similar sentiments are expressed in the *Platform Sūtra;* see T 2008: 48.340c24–26, *Enō kenkyū*, 318–319, and Yampolsky, *Platform Sutra*, 153.
　　257. Vice minister of personnel Miao Jinqing (*libu shilang* Miao Jinqing 吏部侍郎苗晉卿) (685–765): his dialogue with Shenhui probably occurred in 741, when he was appointed to and then demoted from a position in the Ministry of Personnel. Gernet, 44n1, suggests that Miao Shilang 苗侍郎 is probably Miao Jinqing 苗晉卿, who was named to the position stated in 741. In the same year he was demoted in connection with a case of exam falsification (the evidence was reported to the emperor by An Lushan) and became prefect, *taishou* 太守, of Ankang 安康 in Shanxi and, in the following year, imperial investigation commissioner of Hedong 河東 (the present Shanxi 山西). An excellent administrator, he gradually returned to favor and was offered the post of minister of law during the An Lushan rebellion, but he refused on account of age. See the *History of the Tang*, 113:1a9, and the *New History of the Tang*, 111:1b1–2a13.
　　258. Or, "Attain the non-abiding mind, and you will [thereby] obtain emancipation." For the term *wuzhu xin* 無住心, see the *Platform Sermon*, section 3.
　　259. Using the colloquial *dao mo yu* 道沒語.

Answer: "The sūtra says, 'Subhūti, the bodhisattva-mahāsattva should thus generate a pure mind: not abiding in forms does he generate the mind; not abiding in sounds, fragrances, tastes, tangibles, or dharmas does he generate the mind. Without any abiding does he generate that mind.'[260] Just attain the non-abiding mind, and this is to attain emancipation."

The vice minister asked: "In non-abiding, how does one perceive[261] non-abiding?"

Answer: "Based on the essence of non-abiding there exists a fundamental wisdom, and this fundamental wisdom is able to know it. Make the fundamental wisdom generate that mind."[262]

27

Dharma Master Qianguang[263] asked: "What is the mind of the buddhas, and what is the mind of sentient beings?"

Answer: "The mind of sentient beings is the mind of the buddhas, and the mind of the buddhas is the mind of sentient beings."

Question: "If there is no difference between the mind of sentient beings and the mind of the buddhas, then why are sentient beings not called buddhas?"

Answer: "It is uncomprehending people who say there are sentient beings and buddhas. For those who comprehend, sentient beings and buddhas are fundamentally not different."[264]

---

260. This line (T 235: 8.749c20–23) is discussed by Shenhui in the *Platform Sermon*, section 4.

261. *Zhijian* 知見.

262. The Chinese here is *wuzhu tishang (zi) you benzhi neng zhi, ming* (or: *Chang ling*) *benzhi sheng qixin* 無住體上[自]有本智,本智能知,命[常令]本智而生其心 (*zi* 自 and *Chang ling* 常令 occur only in Ishii; Suzuki's suggests that *ming* has to be *ling*; Hu's handwritten note replaces *ming* with *Chang ling*). The problem of how one perceives a characterless fundamental mind is discussed above in section 19.

263. Dharma Master Qianguang 乾光法師 is unidentified. This individual appears in section 9 of the *Definition of the Truth* as one of the *shiseng* 師僧, "teacher monks," who helps resolve the tension between Shenhui and Chongyuan at the beginning of their debate. Yanagida, "Goroku," 388, very reasonably suggests that the following dialogue derives from those debates; Gernet, 45n1, suggests that he was a disciple of Chongyuan in those debates, but this is not necessarily the case. He reappears as the Dharma master Qianguang of Weizhou in section 31 below.

264. Here again the character used is *yuan* 元, usually rendered "originally." A similar sentiment occurs in the *Platform Sūtra* (T 2008: 48.340b28–29; *Enō kenkyū*, 316; Yampolsky, *Platform Sutra*, 151).

28

Question: "I have always heard that your preaching of the Dharma is different from everyone else's. If the Buddhadharma is of [only] one type, then why should there be any difference?"

Answer: "It is truly the case that the Buddhadharma is fundamentally[265] not differentiated. The views of students nowadays are either shallow or profound, and therefore what we say is different."

Question: "Please explain for us the reason for this difference." [DTS258]

Answer: "The difference I am referring to is due to [instructions to] freeze the mind to grasp concentration, or fix the mind to view purity, or activate the mind to illuminate externally, or concentrate the mind to realize internally.[266] One may activate the mind to contemplate the mind and grasp at emptiness, or activate awareness[267] to extinguish the false, and with the false extinguished take residing in awareness as the ultimate. Or, one may activate the mind to make it identical to emptiness, or one may extinguish both awareness and the false, residing in blank emptiness without comprehending the fundamental nature.[268] Approaches such as these are too numerous to talk about.[269] People these days do not comprehend the principle of the emptiness of fundamental nature, and they just make up anything.[270] This is how I mean 'different.' I will not [even] discuss ordinary [unenlightened] people: the Tathāgata has preached the unconditioned single Dharma, but there are differences between all the sages and wise men.[271] How much more so all those who study the Path today—how could they ever be the same?"

---

265. Again using *yuan*.

266. These, again, are Shenhui's "four pronouncements" against yogic meditation. Their first occurrence is in the *Platform Sermon*, section 4.

267. *Jue* 覺 here means "to become aware of" or "awareness," as seen in the same pattern elsewhere.

268. As Gernet, 46n1, suggests, Shenhui is referring to the types of errors and the correct ideal mentioned in the *Vimalakīrti Sūtra*, T 475: 14.554b5–6 and 554c3–5.

269. Literally, "One could not even speak of the groups [of people who teach] like this."

270. The term *benxing xu zhi li* 本性虛之理 is unusual. The phrase *sui nian ji cheng* 隨念即成 means "accomplished according to [their momentary] thoughts," i.e., made up however they wish. Gernet's rendering (p. 46) that the principle is realized in each of our thoughts, misses the colloquial nuance.

271. As Gernet, 46n6, suggests, this is a paraphrase of the *Vimalakīrti*, T 475: 14.749b17–18.

29

Question: "What is the meaning of the four-line *gāthā* from the *Diamond Sūtra*?"[272]

Answer: "I observe[273] that the various Dharma masters explain the meaning of the four-line *gāthā* with either eight characters to a line, or thirty-two characters for four lines, or five characters to a line, or three characters to a line, or derive the meaning from only twelve characters. There are some who take the *gāthā* at the end of the sūtra beginning 'All the conditioned dharmas' as the four-line [verse in question].[274] There are some who grasp 'the characteristic of no-self, the characteristic of no-person, the characteristic of no-sentient being, and the characteristic of no-lifespan,'[275] and call these the meaning of the 'four lines.' Bodhisattva Asaṅga says, 'Vast, the primal permanence—the nonconfusion of their minds is the meaning of the single line.'[276]

"My present [explanation] is different. Why? It is only because there is a characteristic of self that they can refer to a characteristic of no-self. It is only because there is a characteristic of person that they can refer to a characteristic of no-person. It is only because there is a characteristic of sentient being that they can refer to a characteristic of no-sentient being. It is only because there is a characteristic of lifespan that they can refer to a characteristic of no-lifespan.

"The meaning [I am stating] now is different. Why? No characteristic

---

272. This verse (T 235: 8.752b27–28) reads as follows:

All conditioned dharmas
Are like dreams, phantasmagoria, bubbles, shadows,
Like dew and like lightning,
So should one contemplate [i.e., understand] them.

The references here and below to the "four-line *gāthā*" are generally considered to be related to this verse, although Shenhui does give alternate references. I have rendered *ju* 句, "phrase," corresponding to the Skt. *pada*, as "line." Incidentally, Jorgensen (*Inventing Hui-neng*, 608) suggests that Shenhui's comments are made "in reference to that critical passage in the *Vajracchedikā* that allows identification of the reciter with the Buddha or Dharmakāya. This no doubt permitted Shen-hui to adopt the hubris of the identification he made of himself with the Tathāgata at the assembly at Hua-t'ai." I do not understand how this verse can be interpreted in this fashion.

273. Using *jian* 見, "see," to indicate general knowledge of others' activities.

274. This is the famous verse alluded to in section 24 and presented in n. 272 just above.

275. In its positive formulation, this list occurs multiple times in the *Diamond Sūtra*; its negative formulation is found at T 235: 8.750b15–16 and b19–20.

276. This verse, up to "their minds," is found in the *Commentary on the Diamond Sūtra*, which, as it happens, is attributed to Vasubhandu rather than Asaṅga (*Jingang banruoboluomi jing lun* 金剛般若波羅蜜經論; T 1511: 25.781.c23).

Miscellaneous Dialogues

of no-self, [no characteristic of no-person,][277] no characteristic of no-sentient being, no characteristic of no-lifespan—this is the true meaning of the four lines. Now observe[278] of the *Great Treatise on the Perfection of Wisdom*, [DTS259] which cites the sūtra's 'The perfection of wisdom is likened to a mass of fire that cannot be grasped from [any of the] four directions, ungraspable and also ungrasped: this is true grasping.'[279] This is the true meaning of the four lines."

30

Zheng Jun[280] asked: "What is the Path?"[281]
Answer: "The Path is without name."
Question: "If the Path is without name, why is it called the Path?"
Answer: "The Path never speaks of itself. One speaks of the Path in response to questions."
Question: "If 'Path' is a provisional name, then is 'without name' the true one?"
Answer: "It also is not true."
Question: "If 'without name' is not true, why is [the Path] said to be 'without name'?"
Answer: "It is only because there are questions that explanations exist. If there were no questions, there would never be explanations."[282]

31

Dharma Master Qianguang of Weizhou[283] asked: "The *Diamond Sūtra* says, 'If gentlemen and ladies who maintain and recite this sūtra are belittled by others, even though their karmic transgressions from previous lives would

---

277. This phrase is inadvertently omitted from the P3047, although it is present in Ishii.
278. This is a rendering of *jin jian,* 今見, "now see."
279. See T 1509: 25.190c23–26; and Lamotte 1970: 1060–1065, where the text concludes, not that "this is true grasping" but that "this is called grasping." The citation is in fact Rāhulabhadra's verse in praise of Prajñāpāramitā.
280. There is no explicit way to date Zheng Jun's 鄭潘 (Ishii has Zheng Xuan 鄭璿) interaction with Shenhui, but the exchange in which he is involved is very similar to that involving Zhang Yue (section 15).
281. This dialogue obviously plays with the opening line of the *Daode jing.* Here, as in the Daoist classic, both *dao* 道 and *ming* 名, "name," may be either singular or plural.
282. In other words, the Path(s) is (are) only said to be "without name(s)" in response to a question from a student, in this case a layman. For the position that doctrines are only stated in response to questions, see section 15. Gernet, 48n2, suggests that a similar principle is expressed in the *Mouzi liluo lun* 牟子理惑論.
283. Qianguang of Weizhou 魏州 in Hubei province was introduced in section 27 above. The passage here overlaps with material in the *Jingang jing jieyi* 金剛經解義 attributed to Huineng; X 24.527a21–b6.

have them fall into the evil realms, since they are belittled by others in this life the karmic transgressions from previous lives are extinguished.'[284] What does this mean?" [DTS260]

Answer: "People who maintain the sūtra receive [in their] present [lives] all forms of reverence, offerings, and obeisance. Although in the present they maintain and recite the sūtra, before they adopted the sūtra they had [accumulated] layered obstacles of karmic transgression. When they experience[285] the belittling of others, the power of their present maintaining of the sūtra causes[286] the complete extinction of all their layers of karmic transgression. Because these obstacles are extinguished, they ultimately attain perfect and unsurpassable enlightenment.

"The meaning:[287] The karmic transgressions from previous lives are likened to the false activation of the mind in previous thoughts. Those people who do the belittling in the present represent the subsequent thought's being both realization and repentance. When the activation of the previous false thought is extinguished, the subsequent repentance is also extinguished. When the two thoughts are both nonexistent, then the merit of maintaining the sūtra is complete, and this is the perfect and unsurpassable enlightenment [*anuttara-samyak-sambodhi*].[288] How can realization be equivalent to belittling? When the previous thought is falsely activated, then the subsequent realization is also an activation of mind, and even though this is called realization it does not transcend the ordinary [unenlightened state of mind] and is therefore likened to the 'belittling by people in the present.'"[289]

---

284. It is worth mentioning that here the *Diamond* is cited without error; see T 235: 8.750c24–27.

285. The term used is *gan*, as in *ganying* 感應, "stimulus-response."

286. P3047 has *neng ling* 能令, "able to cause," while Ishii has the much more emphatic *beibei fu neng ling* 倍倍復能令, "doubly again able to cause."

287. P3047 has simply *yili* 義理, while Ishii has the more explicit *you you yili shi yun* 又有理義釋云, "also, the 'Explanation of Meanings' says." The latter seems to be a reference to the commentary on the *Diamond Sūtra* attributed to Huineng (X 24.527b3–6), or perhaps another book of explanatory notes used by Shenhui's disciples. Indeed, the text shifts here from the more-or-less straightforward interpretation to a contemplative-analysis mode, so that the existence of a teachers' notebook is not at all improbable. The *Five Skillful Means* presents its extensive contemplative-analysis material in the context of a teachers' handbook; see McRae, *Northern School*, 218. In the following material, the people and transgressions, etc., involved in the scriptural passage are reinterpreted in terms of previous and successive moments of thought (as in the phrase "false activation of previous thoughts," *qiannian wang qixin* 前念妄起心), the activation of the mind, etc. The *Five Skillful Means* also devotes some attention to "fundamental wisdom" and "successive wisdom" in ways that resemble Shenhui's interpretation; see McRae, *Northern School*, 185.

288. The extinction of both previous and subsequent moments of thought is a positive eventuality in terms of contemplative analysis and the apophatic logic of emptiness.

289. The version of this dialogue in Ishii is slightly different in wording, in ways that may imply Shenhui's editors were not overly familiar with the contemplative-analysis style

32

Dharma Master Zhe[290] asked: "What is the meaning of the equivalence of concentration and wisdom?"[291]

Answer: "For thoughts to not be activated, empty and without anything existent, is called correct concentration. The ability to see the non-activation of thoughts, empty and without anything existent, is called correct wisdom. When concentration [is the subject it] is the essence of wisdom, and when wisdom [is the subject it] is the function of concentration. When concentration [is the subject it] does not differ from wisdom, and when wisdom [is the subject it] does not differ from concentration. When concentration [is the subject it] is wisdom, and when wisdom [is the subject it] is concentration. Why? Because their natures are naturally suchlike. This is the learning of the equivalence of concentration and wisdom."[292]

---

of interpretation: "Also, the *Explanation of the Meaning* (*Liyi shi* 理義釋) says: 'The karmic transgressions from previous lives are likened to the activation of the false mind in previous thoughts. Those people who do the belittling in the present are likened to the subsequent thought's being equal to realization, to the subsequent realization's being repentant of the previous false mind. When the activation of the previous false thought is extinguished, the subsequent repentance is also extinguished. When the two thoughts are both extinguished and nonexistent, then the merit of maintaining the sūtra is complete, and this is the perfect and unsurpassable enlightenment.' [The same text] also says, 'For subsequent realization to be likened to belittling means that when the false mind is activated in a previous thought, if one activates subsequent realization this is also an activation of mind. Even though this is called "realization," this realization does not transcend the ordinary [unenlightened state of mind] and is therefore likened to the belittling by people in the present.'" Note that the term "equal" in "subsequent thought's being equal to realization" is the character *qi* 齊, rendered simply as "both" in the translation of P3047. The usage is uncertain.

290. Unidentified. There is a reference to a Zhe gong (Lord Zhe) of Baoshan si in Xiangyang 襄陽報善寺哲公; see T 2016: 48.921b5. This is perhaps the same figure mentioned elsewhere (T 2016: 48.921b11, T 2016: 49.685c5, T 2061: 50.732a1, and T 2073: 51.162a29) as a Mādhyamika teacher of some reputation. Unfortunately, no biographical information is available about the Mādhyamika teacher, and Zhe gong of Baoshan si was active in the early seventh century.

291. The equivalence of concentration and wisdom (*dinghui deng* 定慧等) is an important doctrine in Shenhui's thought; see, for example, the *Platform Sermon*, section 4.

292. Both Hu, 128, and Suzuki (*Zenshū*, 3:260) emend *jue* 覺, "realization," (as P3047 has it) to *xue* 學, "learning" or "study," based on the fact that this latter character is used in (1) Ishii here, (2) the question attributed to Wang Wei in section 43 below, and (3) the corresponding passage in the *Platform Sūtra*, for which see T 2008: 48.338b10f.; *Enō kenkyū*, 292; and Yampolsky, *Platform Sutra*, 135.

33

The circuit prince presumptive[293] asked: "Is the Dharma of non-thought to be cultivated by ordinary people, or is it to be cultivated by sages? If it is a Dharma of sages, why do you encourage ordinary people to cultivate the Dharma of non-thought?"

Answer: "The Dharma of non-thought is a Dharma of sages; when ordinary people cultivate the Dharma of non-thought, they are not ordinary people."[294]

Question: "What Dharma is being contradicted by 'non,' and what Dharma is being thought of by 'thought'?"

Answer: "The 'non' refers to nonexistence. 'Thought' is only to think of suchness."

Question: "Is there truly any difference between this 'thought' and suchness?"

Answer: "There is no difference."

Question: "If there is no difference, how can one say 'to think of suchness'?"

Answer: "The thought referred to here is the function of suchness. Suchness is the essence of thought. It is in this sense that I posit non-thought as my teaching.[295] If one sees non-thought,[296] although one may be replete with sensory and perceptual understanding, one is permanently empty and serene."[297]

---

293. This individual, whose personal name was Li Zilian 李子鍊, is mentioned in Shenhui's stūpa inscription. Based on the date of the title used here, this encounter occurred sometime after 737.

294. Gernet, 51n3, suggests that Shenhui only addressed his teachings to those with superior capabilities. I think, rather, that he identified those whom he addressed as persons of superior capabilities.

295. To "posit non-thought as my teaching" renders *li wunian wei zong* 立無念為宗. Suzuki Tetsuo ("Kataku Jinne no eikyō," 91–96, esp. the chart on 91–92) notes that similar language occurs in the *Essential Teaching of Sudden Enlightenment* (X 63.18c21–23).

296. Here Ishii has *yan* 言, "say," rather than P3047's *jian* 見, "see."

297. "Sensory and perceptual understanding" here renders *jianwen juezhi* 見聞覺知. See the *Platform Sermon*, n. 94, and a similar espousal of seeing non-thought and serenity within sensory/perceptual activity in the *Platform Sūtra*, T 2008: 48.338c19–21; *Enō kenkyū*, 297; and Yampolsky, *Platform Sutra*, 139. Gernet, 52n5, refers to La Vallee Poussin (*Abhidharmakośa*, 4:160) for an explanation of *dṛṣṭa-śruta-mata-vijñata*, a source that no doubt underlies Shenhui's use of the corresponding Chinese term for the functioning of the six senses. Although he might have studied the *Abhidharmakośa* in his youth, it seems unlikely Shenhui would have been quoting from it directly; *Bukkyōgo daijiten*, 323d, indicates that the term occurs in the *Laṅkāvatāra*, and it was no doubt used elsewhere as well.

34

Dharma Master Zhide[298] asked: "You now teach that sentient beings should only seek for sudden enlightenment. Why shouldn't they follow the gradual cultivation of the Hīnayāna? If one has not yet ascended the nine-storied tower, how could one climb it without the use of gradual steps?"

Answer: "[In that case] I fear that what is climbed is not a nine-storied tower. Instead, I suspect that one would only be climbing a stupid little grave mound.[299] [DTS262] To really climb the nine-storied tower is the meaning of sudden enlightenment. Now, even though one must use the gradual [approach of] stairs in climbing a nine-storied tower, within [the doctrine of] sudden enlightenment no meaning of gradualness is posited.[300] The joint explication of principle and wisdom[301] is called sudden enlightenment. For one's understanding to be natural without depending on gradual steps is the meaning of sudden enlightenment.

"That the mind has been empty and serene from the beginning is sudden enlightenment. For the mind to be without any place of abiding[302] is sudden enlightenment. To be enlightened to the mind in the midst of dharmas, so that the mind is without anything that is 'attained,'[303] is sudden enlightenment.

---

298. Dharma Master Zhide 志德, who also appears in section 59, might conceivably be the Zhide 智德 (note the different first character) listed in the *Records of the Transmission* as one of Hongren's ten disciples; see T 2075: 85.1289c14; Adamek, *Mystique*, 320; McRae, *Northern School*, 37. All we know of this monk is that he was Korean and resided in Yangzhou (Buswell, *Formation of Ch'an Ideology*, 165). More likely would be the Zhide 智德 (A010273, d.u.) known as a resident of Guangzhai si 光宅寺 in Shanxi province and student of Nanyang Huizhong (T 2061: 50.763b17). However, given the different character used in these monks' names, neither identification seems likely.

299. The Chinese is *duitu Huzhong* 堆土胡塚. The first character used here, *Morohashi* 5354, is somewhat unusual; it should be read as *dui* 堆, *Morohashi* 5211. Hu, 130, proposes to reverse the order from *duitu* to *tudui*. I have translated the colloquial modifier *Hu* (in other contexts the character means "barbarian") as "stupid," in the derogatory colloquial English sense.

300. For the first character of the sentence P3047 has *nian* 念, "thought," but the very similar *jin* 今, "now," that occurs in Ishii must be correct. The last phrase is written in P3047 as *bu xiang zhong er li jian yi* 不向中而立漸義 and in Ishii as *zhong bu xiang jian zhong er li jian yi* 終不向漸中而立漸義; there is no reason to have the character *jian*, "gradual," twice, but Ishii's initial *zhong* 終, "finally," adds an appropriate emphasis. This line suggests that at least on some occasions Shenhui's interpretation of sudden enlightenment was substantially different from Zongmi's. Indeed, in the *Platform Sermon* Shenhui talks about sudden enlightenment followed by gradual enlightenment, and it is unclear why there is an apparent difference here.

301. This phrase is *lizhi jian shi* 理智兼釋, although it is given as *lizhi jian yi* 理智兼懌 in P3047, which might be read as either "joint bliss of principle and wisdom" or "mutual following of principle and wisdom."

302. This phrase *xin wu suo zhu* 心無所住 alludes to the famous *Diamond Sūtra* line at T 235: 8.749c22–23; see the *Platform Sermon*, n. 84.

303. That is, perceived.

To know all the dharmas is sudden enlightenment. To hear someone preach of emptiness without becoming attached to emptiness, and to not be attached to non-emptiness, is sudden enlightenment. To hear someone preach of the self without becoming attached to the self, without becoming attached to no-self, is sudden enlightenment. To not reject saṃsāra while entering nirvāṇa is sudden enlightenment.[304]

"Therefore, the sūtra says, 'There is natural wisdom—wisdom [acquired] without a teacher.'[305] Those who begin from the principle[306] move quickly toward enlightenment; those who cultivate the externals move slowly toward enlightenment.[307]

"Those who hear explanations of the inconceivability of the transcendent may generate surprise and doubt. [This is even more the case with] suddenness as an inconceivability of the mundane—do you believe it?"

Question: "What is its meaning? Please indicate its essentials."[308]

Answer: "As the great lord of the Zhou [dynasty] Fu [Xi] said, 'All poles, hooks, boards, and earthen walls are understood in the imperial mind and accomplished by workers.'[309] How could suddenly climbing the tower not be an inconceivable matter of the mundane? The inconceivability of the transcendent is [actually] for a sentient being whose mind exemplifies [the state of] being replete with ignorance and desire to encounter a spiritual compatriot and, in a single moment of correspondence, [DTS263] to achieve correct enlightenment.[310] How could this not be an inconceivable matter of the transcendent?

"Furthermore, the sūtra says, 'Sentient beings see the [Buddha-]nature and achieve the enlightenment of buddhahood.'[311] Also, 'The dragon girl generated *bodhicitta* and in an instant achieved correct enlightenment.'[312] Also, 'He caused sentient beings to enter into the knowing and seeing of the buddhas.'[313] If it were not for sudden enlightenment, then the Tathāgata would have given an inequitable explanation of five [different] vehicles.

---

304. Suzuki Tetsuo ("Kataku Jinne no eikyō," 91–96, esp. the chart on 91–92) indicates that this last sentence is given in slightly expanded form in the *Essential Teaching of Sudden Enlightenment* (X 63.22c11).

305. This is from the *Lotus Sūtra*, T 262: 9.13b25–26.

306. That is, from a basis of understanding.

307. This is a clear example of the use of *dao* 道 to mean "enlightenment" rather than "path."

308. The second sentence only occurs in Ishii.

309. It is not clear on what source Shenhui is drawing for this statement about the Zhou *taigong* Fu Xi 周太公傅義: the interpretation is questionable, and why is he identified with the Zhou? The terms are not listed in *Morohashi* and the *Zengaku daijiten* and do not occur in the *Xinwang ming* 心王銘 attributed to Fu Xi.

310. The term *zhengjue* 正覺 refers to the accomplishment of complete buddhahood.

311. There is no scriptural source for the phrase used here, *jianxing cheng fodao* 見性成佛道.

312. This refers to the famous story from the *Lotus Sūtra*; T 9.35c6–26.

313. The Chinese here is *ru fo zhijian* 入佛知見. This is from the *Lotus*, T 262: 9.7a26–27, b18; see the *Platform Sermon*, n. 82.

Now, I do not speak of five vehicles but only describe entering into the knowing and seeing of the buddhas. According to the meaning of the sūtra, I only manifest the teaching of suddenness: if there only exists the correspondence of a single moment of thought, then there truly is no further reliance on graduated stages.[314]

"The meaning of 'correspondence' is to see non-thought, to comprehend the self-nature, to be without anything attained.[315] Since one is without anything attained, this is Tathāgata Chan. Vimalakīrti said, 'Just as one contemplates the true characteristic of one's own body, so should one contemplate the Buddha. When I contemplate the Tathāgata, he does not come from the past, does not go into the future, and does not abide in the present.'[316] Because of non-abiding, this is Tathāgata Chan.

"Furthermore, the sūtra says, 'Originally all sentient beings are fully endowed with the undefiled wisdom-nature of the fundamental nirvāṇa.'[317] If you wish to discriminate well the manifestation of correspondence between one's own mind and the [absolute] principle,[318] then you must transcend[319] mind, intention, and consciousness;[320] transcend the five dharmas and the three self-natures, the eight consciousnesses and the two types of selflessness;[321] transcend internal and external views; transcend the two Dharmas of existence and nonexistence; and [become identified with that which is] ultimately, universally the same—peaceful and permanently serene, vast without limit, and eternally unchanging. Why? Because the pure essence of the fundamental nature is unattainable.

"If one sees in this fashion, then this is to attain the fundamental nature.

---

314. The term for "sudden teaching" here is *dunmen* 頓門. "Correspondence of a single moment of thought" is *yinian xiangying* 一念相應.

315. This line effectively combines some of Shenhui's most cherished phrases: *wei jian wunian zhe, wei liao zixing zhe, wei wu suo de* 謂見無念者，謂了自性者，謂無所得.

316. See T 475: 14.554c29–555a2. The first sentence of this has already been cited in section 2, and the complete passage is cited again in section 55.

317. At the end of the sentence, "originally" renders *benzi* 本自, lit. "fundamentally and naturally," which reinforces the preceding "original nirvāṇa," *benlai niepan* 本來涅槃. I have not found any scriptural source for this citation, although the first part of it seems like material from the *Nirvāṇa Sūtra*. A similar (with *chengfo* 成佛, "accomplish buddhahood," rather than *niepan* 涅槃, "nirvāṇa") line is attributed to this scripture in the *Zhongjing lu* (T 2016: 48.505a5–6). Shenhui's usage may have been a common misquotation already in his day. A similar line also occurs, not as a citation, in Zongmi's commentary on the *Sūtra of Perfect Awakening*: "By means of the correct *prajñā* wisdom, one contemplates that all living beings are fundamentally and originally replete with the undefiled wisdom-nature of *bodhi* and nirvāṇa" (T 1795: 39.545a12–13).

318. The Chinese is *li* 理.

319. It is odd for Shenhui to use *li* 離, "transcend" or "separate from," as often as he does in this passage.

320. The Chinese is *xinyishi* 心意識.

321. These are terms used in the *Laṅkāvatāra Sūtra*, e.g., T 671: 16.511b26–27.

If one sees the fundamental nature, this is to sit in the [DTS264] stage[322] of the Tathāgata; it is to see the Tathāgata. To transcend all characteristics is called 'the buddhas.'[323] For one who sees in this fashion, false thoughts as numerous as the sands of the River Ganges all become serene in a single moment. For one who sees in this fashion, pure and wondrous merits as numerous as the sands of the River Ganges all become equally provided in a single moment. To see in this fashion is called 'undefiled wisdom'; to see in this fashion is called 'the Dharma gate of a single word.'[324] To see in this fashion is to be 'perfect and complete in the six perfections.' To see in this fashion is the 'purity of the eye of Dharma.' To see in this fashion is to be without anything attained and constitutes true emancipation. It is to be identical to the Tathāgata. This is because 'the knowing and seeing [of the Tathāgata] is great and profound, and entirely without any distinction.'[325] One with understanding[326] such as this is a tathāgata, an arhat, a perfectly enlightened one. To see in this fashion is said to 'disseminate great wisdom, the refulgence of which illuminates [all] the world without exception.'[327] Why is this? The 'world' is the mind. To refer to empty serenity[328] is to be without any remaining thought and is therefore to refer to illuminating [all] the world without exception.

"The minds of those who study the Path[329] are without blue, yellow, red, and white; without exiting and entering, going and coming, distant and close, before and behind; without intentionalization and without non-intentionalization. Such is 'correspondence.' If there is exiting from and entering into concentration, if there are all the realms, and disputative argumentation over good and evil, then this is to completely fail to transcend the false mind, to be with that which is attained, to be conditioned, and to be entirely without 'correspondence.'

"He who is determined to achieve realization will only see non-thought, and he will be adamantine[330] and totally unmoving even when he faces the three armies, the blade is about to descend, and the wind sword is cutting his body to pieces.[331] If he sees buddhas as numerous as the sands of the

---

322. One could also read this as "land," *di* 地.
323. This is a citation from the *Diamond Sūtra* (T 235: 8.750b9, with a few different characters); it also occurs in the *Platform Sermon*, section 3.
324. The Chinese is *yi zi famen* 一字法門.
325. A citation from the *Lotus Sūtra* (T 262: 9.5c4–5); it also occurs in the *Platform Sermon*, section 4 (see n. 82). Both the sūtra and S3074 lack the character *yi* 一, "one" or "entirely" that occurs in Ishii.
326. The Chinese is *zhi* 知.
327. For this line, see section 15.
328. The Chinese is *kongji* 空寂.
329. The Chinese is *xuedaozhe* 學道者.
330. That is, *jingang* 金綱, Skt. *vajra*.
331. A "white blade" (*bairen* 白刃) is an unsheathed sword (*Morohashi*, 8.19c), while a "wind sword" (*fengdao* 風刀) is the wind inside the body that dismembers one at the point of

River Ganges coming toward him, he is without a single thought of joy, and if he sees sentient beings as numerous as the sands of the River Ganges suddenly destroyed, he does not activate[332] a single thought of compassion. This is to be a great hero and to attain the universally same mind of emptiness.[333]
[DTS265]
"If one sits so as to 'freeze the mind to enter concentration, fix the mind to view purity, activate the mind to illuminate the external, and concentrate the mind to realize the internal,'[334] this is to obstruct *bodhi* and not to be in correspondence with *bodhi*. How can one attain emancipation? It is not in 'sitting.' If one takes sitting as [the key to emancipation], then Śāriputra would not have been reprimanded by Vimalakīrti for sitting in meditation in the forest.[335] [Vimalakīrti] reprimanded him, saying, 'To not manifest[336] the body and mind[337] within the three realms is "sitting in meditation."'[338] To merely be without thought at all times, not seeing the characteristic called 'body,' is 'correct concentration.'[339] To not see the characteristic of mind[340] is 'correct wisdom.'"[341]

35

Yuan Zhongzhi, the revenue manager of Changzhou,[342] asked: "What is emptiness, and what is non-emptiness?"
Answer: "The essence of suchness is imperceptible, and it is called emptiness. To be able to see that imperceptible essence, [which is] peaceful[343]

---

death and is therefore likened to a sword (*Bukkyōgo daijiten*, 1185d, citing the *Mohe zhiguan* 摩訶止觀, T 1911: 46.40a).
332. The term used is *qi* 起, "to generate."
333. The assertion that one would become a *dazhangfu* 大丈夫 and to attain the *kong pingdeng xin* 空平等心 seems like a scriptural citation, but no such original has been found.
334. These maxims are three of the four pronouncements previously stated in section 28 above and in the *Definition of the Truth*, sections 20 and 22.
335. Yanagida, "Goroku," 388, states incorrectly that this passage is exactly the same as the last part of section 22 of the *Definition of the Truth*. Although it is no doubt derived from the Huatai debates, the two passages are similar but not identical.
336. Ishii has *xian* 現, "manifest," as in the *Vimalakīrti* original, but P3047 has *guan* 觀, "contemplate."
337. The Chinese is *shenyi* 身意.
338. See T 475: 14.539c20–21. Although the rest of the paragraph seems very close in language and content, it is not found as a scriptural citation.
339. The Chinese is *zhengding* 正定.
340. The Chinese is *xinxiang* 心相.
341. The Chinese is *zhenghui* 正慧.
342. Revenue manager Yuan Zhongzhi of Changzhou 常州元忠直 in Jiangsu province (or, according to Ishii, Yuan Sizhi 元思直) is unidentified. On "revenue manager" (*sihu* 司戶), see Hucker, *Official Titles*, 448 #5643.
343. The Chinese is *zhanran* 湛然.

and permanently serene, possessing functions as numerous as the sands of the River Ganges, is called non-emptiness."[344]

36

Dharma Master Yi of Mount Jiang[345] asked: "All sentient beings possess the nature of suchness. Within [that group] there are those who see it and those who do not. What is the difference?"

Answer: "Although sentient beings possess the nature of suchness, it is just like the *maṇi* jewel, which, while possessing the nature of brilliance, is ultimately never bright and pure until polished. The characteristics that differentiate [the two groups] are also like this: all the sentient beings that do not encounter a buddha, bodhisattva, or spiritual compatriot who induces them to generate *bodhicitta* will never be able to see it."[346]

37

Dharma Master Yiyuan[347] asked: "Although you explain that suchness is without form or characteristics, how would you lead us[348] sentient beings [DTS266] to gain entry into it?"

Answer: "The characteristic of suchness is the fundamental mind. Although [there is] thought there is nothing that can be thought, and although [there is] explanation there is nothing that can be explained. This is called 'gaining entry into it.'"[349]

---

344. Shenhui seems to be building this distinction between *kong* 空 and *bukong* 不空 on the model of the *Awakening of Faith*'s "enlightenment" and "non-enlightenment," *jue* 覺 and *bujue* 不覺. Sections 35–41, although short dialogues with different individuals, seem to have been grouped together because they discuss similar issues of conditioned/unconditioned and the proper approach to cultivating the immanent Buddha-nature. The combination of material from the *Diamond* and *Nirvāṇa Sūtras* evident here is also a significant characteristic of the *Definition of the Truth*, and the use of essence/function (*ti-yong* 體用) rhetoric in section 39 is characteristic of early Chan thought in general.

345. Dharma Master Yi of Mount Jiang 蔣山義 near Nanjing in Jiangsu province is unidentified.

346. The same metaphor is used toward the end of section 8. The *Nirvāṇa Sūtra*, T 374: 12.408a24–25, contains the underlying concept: "All sentient beings are also like this: because they are not able to associate with spiritual compatriots, even though they possess the Buddha-nature they are all unable to see it."

347. This person is unidentified. Ishii has his name as Yiwen 義聞 rather than Yiyuan 義圓.

348. P3047 includes the character *wo* 我, "I," which implies Yiyuan identifies with unenlightened sentient beings rather than with the enlightened Chan masters. Gernet, 59n2, suggests that *shi* 使, "cause," is an unusual usage in the manner of *wei* 為, "on behalf of." However, because in the question it is clearly Shenhui who is to do the causing and his followers who are to gain entrance into suchness, I believe this is an ordinary causative usage of *shi*.

349. This exchange is too brief to be fully understandable. First, it is unclear whether

38

Dharma Master Jian of Mount Lu[350] asked: "Although one may practice seeing,[351] this is still identical to generation and extinction.[352] What Dharma should one cultivate now so as to attain that which is not generation and extinction?"[353]

Answer: "Although I refer to 'seeing,' it is fundamentally without generation and extinction. Your reference just now to generation and extinction is itself the view[354] of a person of generation and extinction.[355] To be without generation and extinction is that which is not generation and extinction."[356]

39

Wang Youlin, adjutant of Runzhou,[357] asked: "What about 'for there to be no Dharma that can be explained is called "explaining the Dharma"'?"[358]

Answer: "The essence of the perfection of wisdom is imperceptible, and this is 'for there to be no Dharma that can be explained.' The essence of the perfection of wisdom naturally possesses wisdom, by which it illuminates the imperceptible essence, peaceful and permanently serene. [For one's

---

Shenhui means the ordinary mind, as in Mazu's famous later usage. More likely, he is thinking of the underlying mind of non-thought, and indeed the term "fundamental mind" (*benxin* 本心) is more reminiscent of the *Essentials of Cultivating the Mind* than Mazu. See however the very end of section 6 of the *Platform Sermon*. Second, the latter part of the answer presumes an understood topic of thought (*nian* 念) and explanation (*shuo* 說) in the definition of "gaining entry" (*deru* 得入). In section 52 of the *Definition of the Truth*, Shenhui is lauded for "explaining yet not explaining anything," and Shenhui's emphasis on the *Diamond* makes the usage here unexceptional, but there is no specific counterpart elsewhere in his writings. The terms of this dialogue parallel some of the contents of section 34 above and anticipate the discussion in 39 just below.

350. This unidentified Dharma master also appears in sections 12 and 47.

351. Ishii expands the three characters of P3047, *jian sui xing* 見雖行, to the more explicit *jianjue suiran xing* 見覺雖然行.

352. That is, saṃsāra.

353. Gernet, 60, interprets this in terms of Dharma Master Jian's personal practice: "Although I've practiced seeing.... What Dharma should I cultivate...?" Since the Chinese does not indicate person, both readings are acceptable. For a discussion involving change and the changeless, see section 54.

354. The Chinese is *jian* 見.

355. That is, someone in saṃsāra.

356. This last line is virtually a tautology, but the negatives are different: to be without saṃsāra is not to create saṃsāra.

357. Wang Youlin, adjutant of Runzhou 潤州司馬王幼林[琳] (the variant is in Ishii) in Jiangsu province, is unidentified. For another dialogue possibly involving him, see section 14.

358. This is from the *Diamond Sūtra*, T 235: 8.751c14–15; also see 749b12–18.

wisdom to] have functions as numerous as the sands of the River Ganges is called 'explaining the Dharma.'"³⁵⁹

40

Chan Master Chong of Mount Oxhead³⁶⁰ asked: "Are transgressions extinguished with repentance?"

Answer: "If you see non-thought, karma is automatically not generated. Why would one try [to use] the false mind to repent in some other way? If you want to repent, repentance is generation."

Question: "What is generation?"

Answer: "Generation is to generate extinction."³⁶¹

41

Master Huadi of Luofu³⁶² asked: "If all sentient beings are fundamentally clear and pure, why are they tainted by the dharmas of birth and death and unable to transcend the triple realm?"³⁶³

---

359. The punctuation and logical sequence here are tentative.

360. Chan Master Chong of Mount Oxhead 牛頭山寵 near Nanjing in Jiangsu province remains unidentified.

361. P3047 has *zhu* 主, "master," instead of the very similar graph *sheng* 生, "generation." Gernet, 61, uses the former character, but the latter is clearly mandated by the immediate context. Ishii has the correct character, which expands P3047 somewhat.

362. Master Huaidi 懷迪 of Luofu 羅浮 (A001896, fl. early eighth c.): Huaidi was an avid student of Buddhist scriptures who came into frequent contact with foreign monks because of his coastal residence, and through this reputation he was invited by Bodhiruci to Chang'an to assist in the translation of the *Ratnakuṭa* (*Baoji jing* 寶集經) as doctrinal editor (*zhengyi* 證義, lit. "verifier of meanings"). After this project he returned to the south, where he was involved in the translation of the *Śūraṃgama Sūtra*. After this, sometime during the Kaiyuan period (713–741), he traveled again to Chang'an, where he stayed for a time and in 758 was associated with another translation project (aborted in the aftermath of the An Lushan rebellion). Shenhui and Huaidi may have met while the latter was in Chang'an during the years 706–713 and could have been drawn together by their travels between north and south. (Mount Luofu is not that far from Shaozhou.) They almost certainly knew of each other's existence after 745, when both were in the northern capitals.

363. The *Śūraṃgama* (T 945: 19.106b12) discusses the mind of sentient beings in terms resembling these, and the problem Huaidi poses is a basic one. We should recall that the *Śūraṃgama* is also associated with Shenxiu of the Northern school; see the *Song Biographies*, T 2061: 50.738c4–6, and McRae, *Northern School*, 52 and 290n130, where Shenxiu's explanation of the "Chan meaning" of newly translated scriptures no doubt refers to the *Śūraṃgama*. It would seem that Huaidi is being introduced here as a representative of the Northern school, but it might be that this dialogue derives from a period (or a mode of religious activity) that antedated (or otherwise stood outside of) Shenhui's attack on the Northern school. That is, in his response below Shenhui seems to advocate some form of *qi* 起, "activation [of the mind]," suggesting that his position on *buqi* 不起 or "non-activation" might not have crystallized when this dialogue occurred.

Answer: "If I were to talk of those who do not realize that their own essence is fundamentally empty and serene but instead follow the false to activate binding karma, experience birth, and create evil, I would not be able to explain them at all. [Many of] those who cultivate the Path are also deluded regarding the Dharma, and they only plant the causes and conditions of becoming humans and gods, rather than seeking the ultimate liberation. Without encountering the buddhas, bodhisattvas or true spiritual compatriots, how can they escape rebirth and other sufferings?"

Question: "If one activates serene extinction in successive moments of mind, or in thought after thought enters the flow of the Dharma, how can this be other than to put one's thoughts into motion?"[364]

Answer: "As the bodhisattva approaches enlightenment,[365] his mind is non-abiding in thought after thought. This is likened to the flame of a lamp that continues naturally without interruption and without the lamp creating the flame. Why? Because it is said that as the bodhisattva approaches enlightenment his thoughts continue without interruption."[366]

---

364. P3047 suffers from lacunae here, so I have followed Ishii. "Successive moments of mind" and "thought after thought" represent *xin xin* 心心 and *nian nian* 念念, respectively. It is not clear whether the two conditions stated are to be understood as alternatives or equivalents.

365. It would be overtranslating here to render *xiang puti dao* 向菩提道 as "approaching the Path of enlightenment" (although see the next note), since the last character has the meaning of enlightenment. Just below the text has simply *xiang puti*.

366. The point is that the bodhisattva's mind is always in motion yet fundamentally quiescent, because he does not willfully "activate" thoughts. Hence for the ordinary person, to attain the status of bodhisattva (or true practitioner) by seeing non-thought, i.e., by penetrating to the quiescent substratum, is different from intentionally activating thought or intentionalizing non-thought. The terms in which this answer is posed are strikingly reminiscent of the extended metaphor on the lamp found in Shenxiu's *Treatise on the Contemplation of the Mind* and discussed in McRae, *Northern School*, 235, as the key to understanding his doctrine of the "perfect teaching." It may be significant that Shenhui limits this description to bodhisattvas who are approaching the "Path of enlightenment" (*puti dao* 菩提道), indicating some differentiation from the Northern school teachings to which this passage is so clearly indebted. Note that the statement regarding the bodhisattva's thoughts continuing without interruption is attributed to Huineng in the *Platform Sūtra* (T 2008: 48.338c6–7; *Enō kenkyū*, 296; Yampolsky, *Platform Sutra*, 138).

42

The disciple Liu Xiangqian[367] said, "When Wang Wei, then attendant censor of Nanyang commandery,[368] was in Lintuan station[369] he submitted

---

367. For Yanagida's identification of Liu Xiangqian with Liu Cheng, or Huicheng, see n. 12 above. The name Liu Xiangqian 劉相倩 given here is from Ishii (P3047 is basically illegible at this point). This section is translated in Yanagida, "Goroku," 373–374. I have taken the entire passage as a quotation from Liu. The placement of certain clauses varies between P3047 and Ishii; I have followed the latter because it reads more smoothly and lacks the minor orthographic flaws of the former. Although minor editing has clearly taken place, there is no change in the substance of the exchange. Yanagida (374–375) points out that this passage is extremely similar to and no doubt derives from section 10 of S6557.

368. Shenhui met Wang Wei in spring 741 at Lintuan station 臨湍驛 and discussed the Dharma with him and several other officials. Presumably it was after this meeting that Wang Wei wrote an epitaph for Huineng at Shenhui's request. At this time in his life Wang Wei was already a devout Buddhist, having lived a life of celibate devotion after his wife died in 734 (Ch'en, *Chinese Transformation*, 182). When his mother died in 742, he converted his home into a monastery. At the end of the Tianbao era (756) Wang Wei served in government for a time, but after being captured and held by An Lushan he did not return to political favor until his brother Wang Jin 王縉 (701?–781) intervened during the reign of Emperor Suzong 肅宗 (r. 756–762). At some point Wang Wei also wrote an epitaph for the important Northern school author Jingjue 淨覺, whose death I estimate as having occurred around 750 (Yanagida, *Shoki Zenshū shisho*, 517–534, and McRae, *Northern School*, 88–89). Gernet ("Biographie," 48) points out that after his appointment as attendant censor (*shiyushi* 侍御史) in 739, Wang Wei had to go to Hubei, where he probably met Shenhui at Lintuan. (In this section, the poet-official is addressed using a common abbreviation of his title as Wang Shiyu 王侍御; Hucker, *Official Titles*, 431 #5346 and #5350). This is the ultimate source for earlier statements that Wang Wei and Shenhui met, and that the poet-official wrote the epitaph for Huineng, in 739 or thereafter. More recent research on Wang Wei's life allows us to be more precise than this. The most rigorously argued chronology for this period of Wang Wei's life is that given by Wang Huibin, which improves on the evidence given in Gernet's "Biographie." Based on Tang historical sources and the subject matter of the poet's works, Wang Huibin shows that Wang Wei's departure for the south (to select local talent for administrative positions, known as *zhi nanxuan* 知南選) began around the eighth month of Kaiyuan 28 (740) and ended in the second month of the following year, taking him through Qianzhou 黔州 and Yuzhou 渝州 near Chongqing. It was only following this that Wang Wei sailed down the Yangzi to Xiakou 夏口 in Hubei, then back on the Han through Xiangyang and eventually on to Chang'an (Wang, "Wang Wei Kaiyuan xingzong qiu shi"). Note that this interpretation of Wang Wei's movements contrasts with the usual view that he proceeded initially down the Yangzi to Xiangyang and then on to Sichuan; although I have chosen to follow Wang Huibin here, that the encounter might have occurred in the eighth month of 740 rather than the second month of 741 is inconsequential for our purposes. Part of Wang Huibin's argument is phrased as criticism of the position taken in Chen Tiemin's chronology of the poet's life, which he critiques in greater detail in "*Wang Wei nianpu* shangping." Wang Huibin's detailed investigation agrees with the position taken earlier in Chen Yunji's 陳允吉 study of Wang Wei's relationships with Chan monks of both Northern and Southern schools ("Wang Wei," esp. pp. 58–59), which is accepted in Ogawa, "Kataku Jinne," 55n12. Finally, Chen Tiemin's position was adopted in a recent English monograph on the Buddhist dimensions of Wang Wei's poetry (Yang 2007: 40). However, in a recent email communication (September 2010), the author Yang Jingqing suggested ambivalence toward Chen's dating and was kind enough to provide PDF copies of Wang Huibin's articles and other resources.

369. According to Gernet, 63n4, Lintuan station was about fifteen *li* northwest of the Deng district in Henan. Yanagida, *Shoki Zenshū shisho*, 194n15, has it about seventy *li* to the northwest.

MISCELLANEOUS DIALOGUES 185

himself[370] to Reverend [Shenhui] and Chan Master Huicheng[371] of the same monastery and talked with them for several days. He asked His Reverence, 'How does one cultivate the Path so as to attain emancipation?'[372]

"His Reverence answered, 'The minds of sentient beings are fundamentally and naturally pure. If they then try to activate the mind in cultivation, this is the false mind, and they will be unable to attain emancipation.'

"In surprise, Attendant Censor Wang said, 'How extraordinary! In the past I have heard all the great worthies' explanations, but none of them has ever explained the Dharma like this!' He then said to Prefect Kou, Administrative Aide Zhang, and Adjutant Yuan,[373] 'This Nanyang commandery has [DTS268] excellent great worthies, whose Buddhadharma is really inconceivable!'

"Duke Kou said, 'The interpretations of these two great worthies are not the same.' Attendant Censor Wang asked: 'How are they not the same?'

"His Reverence answered, 'His saying that they are not the same is because Chan Master [Hui]cheng requires one to first cultivate concentration,[374] and after attaining concentration to then generate wisdom. My teaching is not like this.[375] When I was talking with the attendant censor just now, [I said that] concentration and wisdom were to be equivalent. The *Nirvāṇa Sūtra* says, "For concentration to be great and wisdom little is to increase one's ignorance. For wisdom to be great and concentration little is to increase one's wrong views. For concentration and wisdom to be equivalent is called 'seeing the Buddha-nature.'"[376] Therefore I say that [the interpretations of Chan Master Huicheng and myself] are different.'

---

370. The Chinese is *qu* 屈; the usage indicates Wang Wei's reverential deference to the monks. Gernet, 63, has Wang Wei begging Shenhui and his associates for their teaching, also an appropriate reading.

371. See n. 12 above.

372. P3047 has the question, "If the fundamental nature is fundamentally [pure (?)], Reverend, how does one cultivate the Path so as to attain the purity of emancipation? Does one further activate the mind?" The final question demands a negative response; Ishii includes the reference to activating the mind into Shenhui's response, just below.

373. Prefect Kou 寇太守: This is presumably Kou Yang 寇洋 (665–748). Based on Kou's appointment as prefect of Nanyang sometime around the early 740s, his encounter with Shenhui occurred sometime during the years 740–748. The other two individuals, the administrative aide Zhang and the adjutant Yuan, are unidentified. Yu (*Tang cishi kao*, 5, 2291) estimates that Kou Yang was governor of Nanyang around the beginning of the Tianbao period, but this seems only a general estimate, since only one individual comes between him and the earlier appointee Wang Ju, who was appointed to the post in 734 and was also associated with Shenhui.

374. That is, samādhi.

375. Ishii reads *ji zhi buran* 即知不然, "you should know it is not like that," rather than P3074's *Hui ze buran* 會澤不然, lit. "as for my [Shenhui's teaching], it is not like that."

376. This line (which does not occur as such in the *Nirvāṇa Sūtra*) is cited in the *Platform Sermon*, section 4. It also occurs in the *Essentials of Cultivating the Mind* as a citation from the *Nirvāṇa Sūtra* (X 63.20b19–20).

43

"Attendant Censor Wang asked: 'What is this equivalence of concentration and wisdom?'[377]

"His Reverence answered, 'What I call concentration is for the essence [of the mind] to be imperceptible. What I call wisdom is the ability to see that imperceptible essence. For these to be peaceful and permanently serene but possessing functions as numerous as the sands of the River Ganges is the equivalent study of concentration and wisdom.'

44

"The assembly arose and stood outside the hall.[378] Chan Master Huicheng said to Attendant Censor Wang, 'I have only just realized that my [interpretation] and Master Shenhui's are not the same.'[379] Smiling, Attendant Censor Wang said to His Reverence, 'How are they different?'[380]

"His Reverence answered, 'I have said [our interpretations] are different because Chan Master Huicheng has one first cultivate and attain concentration, then generate wisdom. My [interpretation is] different.[381] Precisely at the time when I am talking to you, concentration and wisdom are equivalent.[382] Therefore my [interpretation is] different.'

"Attendant Censor [Wang] said, 'Are you only just saying your [interpretation is] different?'[383]

---

377. Since this section continues Liu Xiangqian's narration, it is placed in global quotation marks. The doctrine of the equivalence of concentration and wisdom was important to Shenhui; see section 32. Below, the text uses *dinghui dengxue dengxue* 定慧等學, "equivalent study (i.e., cultivation) of concentration and wisdom," which also occurs in section 32.

378. This sentence is absent from P3047.

379. This could be read, "It would seem that my [level of] realization and Master Shenhui's are not the same." Note that here and below Shenhui is referred to as an *ācārya*.

380. P3047 does not describe Wang Wei as being amused by Huicheng's statement, and the specific nuance of Ishii's usage is uncertain. Perhaps Wang Wei is supposed to have been pleased at Liu Xiangqian's newfound realization? Whatever the intended connotation, the addition of this descriptive and the "stage direction" just above is exactly the kind of editing change that goes into the creation of a full-fledged encounter dialogue text.

381. Here both texts have the same phrase, reading *huiji buran* 會即不然.

382. The implication seems to be, not only that Shenhui's ideas are different, but that the level of attainment he maintains even during dialogue is different from that of Huicheng.

383. Here Wang Wei refers to Shenhui as *ācārya*. I have presented the closing exchange as contained in Ishii. P3047 has the characters *keyu* 客語, "guest-words," where Ishii has the orthographically similar *rong* 容, "insert." The same exchange in P3047 (cf. Yanagida, "Goroku," 374) is as follows: "Censor [Wang] said, 'Are you only just saying this?' Answer: 'It is impossible to accept even [that part of] my counterpart's words [as small as] a dust mote the size of the tip of a hair.' 'Question: 'Why is it impossible to accept your counterpart's words?' Answer: 'It is because our [interpretations are] now actually different. If you recognize us as the same, this would be [to accept] my counterpart's words.'" "Guest-words" are simply someone else's

"Answer: 'A dust mote the size of the tip of a hair could not be inserted [between my concentration and wisdom].'

"Another question: 'Why could it not be inserted?'

"Answer: 'I now [say] our [interpretations are] truly different. If I said they were the same, this would be to say [a dust mote] could be inserted.'"

45

Chan Master Yuan of Mount Oxhead[384] asked: "The Buddha-nature is immanent in all sentient beings but not immanent in all insentient things.[385] I have heard a senior great worthy say, 'Azure green, the emerald bamboo—all is the *dharmakāya;* luxuriant, the yellow flowers—nothing is not *prajñā*.'[386] Why do you now say that it is immanent in all sentient beings but not immanent in all insentient things?"

Answer: "How could one equate 'Azure green, the emerald bamboo' with the meritorious *dharmakāya* and make 'luxuriant, the yellow flowers' equivalent to the wisdom of *prajñā*? If you say that green bamboo and yellow flowers are the same as the *dharmakāya* and *prajñā,* then in what sūtra did the Tathāgata confer the prediction of future enlightenment on them? To say that green bamboo and yellow flowers are identical to the *dharmakāya* and *prajñā* is the teaching of non-Buddhists.[387] Why? Because the *Nirvāṇa Sūtra* says, 'Without the Buddha-nature' refers to insentient things."[388]

---

comments; in later Chan texts these include comments quoted from someone else or spoken on someone else's behalf (*Zengaku daijiten*, 150d–151a).

384. Unidentified. Sections 45–48 involve figures and, to an extent, topics associated with southeastern China (although not as far south as Caoqi).

385. This was a topic of considerable discussion in the latter half of the eighth century; see Sharf, "Chan Gong'ans," on Zhaozhou's *wu*, the first precedent in the *Gateless Barrier* (*Wumen guan* 無門關). The English "immanent in" represents Chinese *bian* 遍, "pervade."

386. This line occurs in a number of places in Chan literature, sometimes associated (falsely, it appears) with Sengzhao; see McRae, "Chan Commentaries," 98, and Yanagida, *Shoki Zenshū shisho,* 170 and 179n20–22, for a discussion of various places where it is cited. See also Yanagida, *Sodōshū*, 98–101, which includes comments on the appearance of this line and excerpt translations from the *Anthology of the Patriarchal Hall* entry for Dongshan 洞山 and the present section from the *Miscellaneous Dialogues,* including the observations that (1) Shenhui rejected the Oxhead school position that insentient objects possess the Buddha-nature, as indicated in this passage and the *Treatise on the Transcendence of Cognition,* and (2) Nanyang Huizhong's adoption of this position was meant to supersede both Shenhui's and the Oxhead school's positions.

387. The term here is *waidao shuo* 外道說.

388. The *Nirvāṇa Sūtra* line (T 374: 12.581a23–23) is a bit longer and uses the negative *fei* 非 rather than *wu* 無: "[That which is] not the Buddha-nature are all insentient things [such as] walls, tiles, and rocks."

46

Tang Fatong, senior subaltern of Suzhou,[389] asked: "Is the Buddha-nature of sentient beings the same as or different from the Buddha-nature of the buddhas?"

Answer: "It is both same and different."

Question: "Why is it both same and different?"

Answer: "To say it is the same is to liken it to gold [which remains the same no matter how it is formed]. To say it is different is to liken it to cups, dishes, and other utensils [which differ even though made of the same material]."[390]

Question: "What thing is it like?"

Answer: "It is not like any thing."

Question: "If it is not like any thing, why is it called 'Buddha-nature'?"

Answer: "That which does not resemble any thing is called 'Buddha-nature.' If it was like any thing, it would not be called 'Buddha-nature.'"

47

Dharma Master Jian of Mount Lu[391] asked: "What about [the saying] 'the bright mirror on the high platform is able to illuminate, and the myriad images all appear within it'?"

Answer: "'The bright mirror on the high platform is able to illuminate, and the myriad images all appear within it': In the transmissions from ancient worthies, they have all praised this as wondrous. Now, within this teaching[392] I do not accept that this is wondrous. Why? 'The bright mirror is able to illuminate the myriad images, and the myriad images do not appear within it': this I take as wondrous. Why? The Tathāgata with his nondiscriminating wisdom is able to discriminate all things. How could one take the discriminating mind as discriminating all things?"[393]

---

389. The senior subaltern of Suzhou 蘇州長史唐法通 is unidentified.

390. The most famous discussion of the relationship between gold (or metal) and the objects made with it is in Fazang's *Essay on the Golden Lion* (*Jin shizi zhang* 金師子章, T 1881: 45.668a-670c). See the translation in de Bary, Chan, and Watson, *Sources of Chinese Tradition*, 329–333. Gernet, 67n3, compares the *Nirvāṇa Sūtra*, T 374: 12.422c18–28, which states that the buddhas, bodhisattvas, et al. are like cows of different colors who all produce white milk.

391. This unidentified Dharma master has appeared in sections 12 and 38. Yanagida, *Shoki Zenshū shisho*, 266n13, surmises, from the dialogues in which Jian is involved, that he was probably of the Sanlun 三論 or Chinese Mādhyamika tradition. Yanagida, *Shoki Zenshū shisho*, 262–263, further suggests that this otherwise unknown passage is the source from which the *Platform Sūtra*'s mind-verses developed; I find it effectively indistinguishable from other pre-*Platform Sūtra* passages referring to the mirror.

392. The word for "teaching" here is *men* 門.

393. In other words, only nondiscriminating wisdom can discriminate all things, precisely because it does not discriminate. The *Vajrasamādhi Sūtra* (*Jingangsanmei jing* 金剛三昧經), which Buswell argues is a Korean apocryphon, contains a line that he translates: "The nature

48

Wang Yi, senior subaltern of Yangzhou,[394] asked: "Is there a buddha in the world or not?"

Answer: "It is not certain that there is, and not certain that there is not."

Question: "Why do you say it is not certain that there is, and not certain that there is not?" [DTS271]

Answer: "It is not certain that there is [because] the *Wisdom Sūtra of Mañjuśrī* says, 'The perfection of wisdom is imperceptible, enlightenment and nirvāṇa are imperceptible, and Buddha is also imperceptible.'[395] Therefore I say it is not certain that there is [a buddha in the world]. It is not certain that there is not [because] the *Nirvāṇa Sūtra* says, 'Whether there are buddhas or no buddhas, their natures and characteristics are permanently abiding.... Hence sentient beings can through good causes and conditions and skillful means attain a vision of the Buddha-nature.'[396] Therefore I say it is not certain that there is not [any buddha in the world]."

49

Monastery patron Qi[397] asked: "What is the Mahāyāna?"

Answer: "It is the Hīnayāna."

Another question: "I just asked about the Mahāyāna. Why do you say it is the Hīnayāna?"

Answer: "It is only because there is a Small [Vehicle] that the Great [Vehicle] can be posited. If there were no small, from where would the great be generated? What I just[398] called 'great' is the great of the small. What I just called the Mahāyāna is empty and without anything existent, so it cannot be called either great or small. It is likened to space: space is without quantitative

---

of bodhi is in fact free from discrimination. The non-discriminative knowledge cannot be fathomed by discrimination" (T 273: 9.371c12–13; Buswell, *Formation of Ch'an Ideology*, 232).

394. It is likely that Shenhui met with Wang Yi 王怡 (d.u.) as early as 722, when the latter was a higher ranking sub-official functionary in Yangzhou—i.e., about the same staff level as Liu Cheng and Dugu Pei, as well as Tang Fatong. Wang Yi held this post in Yangzhou around the years 720–722, and was regent of Luoyang 東都留守 from about 722 to 723. One would think that the latter position, which included acting in place of the emperor when he was out of the capital, would have been more prestigious than the general term *changli* 長史 used here, which Hucker (*Official Titles*, 111 #153) describes as a "generic term referring vaguely to the higher grades of sub-official functionaries." Wang Yi also appears in section 58.

395. T 233: 8.737a13–16.

396. T 374: 12.492a17–18. I am following Ishii, which is a better representation of the scriptural passage.

397. Monastery patron Qi 齊寺主 is unidentified. Qi is probably the lay surname. The term *sizhu* originally rendered the Skt. *vihara-svamin* and referred to a government official who administered the affairs of a monastery (*Zengaku daijiten*, 433d; *Bukkyōgo daijiten*, 561a). It is not clear whether such officials were monks or laymen during the period in question.

398. This renders *jin* 今, "now."

limit, but cannot be called without limit. Space is without spatial boundaries[399] but cannot be called without spatial boundaries. The Mahāyāna is likewise. Therefore the sūtra says, 'Space is without middle and extremes. The bodies of the Buddhas are also likewise.'[400] You just asked about the Mahāyāna, so I said it was the Hīnayāna. The principle of this is extremely clear—why should this be odd?"

50

Vinaya Master Xing[401] asked: "What is it [to say that] 'experiencing the tactile sensations is like the realization of wisdom'?"

Answer: "Experiencing the tactile sensations is said to be fundamentally motionless. It is like the images in a mirror that are all manifested within the mirror. Because the mirror is motionless, the myriad images and various actions are experienced [like] sensations by the bright mirror mind. 'Like the realization of wisdom' is fundamentally [DTS272] the wisdom of enlightenment. The fundamental wisdom is able to know wondrous existence.[402] The fundamental enlightenment is the wisdom-nature and is therefore called 'wisdom realization.'[403] To use a cow's horn as a metaphor for its creation, when the horn is fully grown it may not be called an 'as one wishes,'[404] and when it is an 'as one wishes' it cannot be called a 'horn.'[405] Although the horn embodies the nature of an 'as one wishes,' before the horn is destroyed[406] it cannot be called an 'as one wishes.' Although the 'as one wishes' is made out of enlightenment, the 'as one wishes' itself cannot be called enlightenment.[407] Therefore the sūtra says, 'Destroy enlightenment and the Path is achieved.'[408] It also says, 'If one's seeing per-

---

399. *Bian* 邊, lit. "extremes."
400. T 357: 12.248a1–2.
401. Vinaya Master Xing 行律師 is unidentified.
402. "Wisdom of enlightenment" is *juezhi* 覺智. The sentence that follows is *benzhi neng zhi miaoyou* 本智能知妙有.
403. This sentence (which I punctuate differently from Hu Shi) is *benjue zhixing gu cheng zhizheng* 本覺智性故稱智證. Ishii's version of this entire section is different in several places; to this point we find: "Answer: Experiencing the various tactile sensations is said to be unmoving in its fundamental nature. If one takes the different sensations as suffering, then this is motion. It is likened to a mirror's responding to a person's various types of actions and movements in no-mind. The present [subject of] experiencing the various tactile sensations [272] is also likewise. The wisdom realization here is the wisdom of fundamental enlightenment (*benjue zhi zhi* 本覺之智). As to my saying 'wisdom realization' just now, because the wisdom of fundamental enlightenment is able to know, it is called 'wisdom realization.'"
404. *Ruyi* 如意, here meaning a ceremonial scepter.
405. The assumption of this passage seems to be that *ruyi* scepters are made of horn.—Ed.
406. That is, before it is cut off.
407. The word for "enlightenment" used in this sentence is *jue* 覺, a pun on the homophone 角, "horn."
408. This phrase *miejue daocheng* 滅覺道成 is used in the *Vimalakīrti Sūtra* (T 475:

MISCELLANEOUS DIALOGUES 191

vades, then neither enlightenment nor illumination can be posited.'[409] Now, if one has enlightenment and illumination as existent, this is the pervading of seeing and hearing. If one cuts off the clear and pure essence, how will one be enlightened, how will one illuminate?[410] People take the things of this world as existent, but I say the things of this world are nonexistent; people take space as nonexistent, but I take space as existent. Why? The things of this world cohere as the conjunction of conditions, and when the conditions disperse they separate: when they encounter fire they burn, when they encounter water they get wet, and eventually they are destroyed. Hence I call them nonexistent. Space cannot be burned by fire, cannot be moistened by water, and is not eventually destroyed. Hence I call it existent. I also call it permanent."

51

While at [the imperial court],[411] Ma Ze, the administrative aide of Xiangzhou,[412] stated: "None of the Buddhist monks and Daoist priests who respond to the imperial court from throughout the land have been able to resolve my questions. I wonder if you will resolve my questions."[413]

Answer: "I am certainly no worse than them—I wonder what questions you have."

The administrative aide said, "I would like to give voice to them now, but I fear that you will not be able to answer them completely."[414]

Answer: "Just go ahead and express yourself, so that I can know what you understand and what you do not. If you never speak, how will I be able to know?" At the time three people who were present, the administrative

---

14.537c17) to describe the Buddha's enlightenment under the bodhi tree subsequent to vanquishing Mara.

409. "Neither enlightenment nor illumination" could be rendered "illumination of enlightenment." I have not been able to locate this phrase, *jian bian, ji juezhao yi bu li* 見遍，即覺照亦不立.

410. Ishii and P3047 are identical here except for minor details. Whereas P3047 uses the pun between "horn" and "enlightenment" at the end of the topic, Ishii has the character for the latter earlier on. Finally, Ishii has *yue* 約, "according to," in place of P3047's *duan* 斷, "cuts off." This is much more appropriate language with regard to "the clear and pure essence."

411. There is a two-character lacuna in P3047, while Ishii specifies *chaoting* 朝庭, "imperial court."

412. Ma Ze 馬擇, administrative aide of Xiangzhou 相州別駕 in Henan province, is unidentified.

413. In P3047, Shenhui is addressed as "Chan master" and refers to himself just below as "Shenhui"; in Ishii his name is not used. P3047 has two separate lacunae here. I have followed Ishii, which has no lacunae. "Questions" represents *yi* 疑, "doubts."

414. The text from this question up to the next is only found in Ishii. I am taking *zeyi* 擇疑, "select doubts," at the end of the question, as an orthographic error for *shiyi* 釋疑, "explain doubts."

aide Su Cheng, the administrator Pei Wen, and the adjutant Yuan Guangshao, all said, "Speak up to the Chan master."[415]

Administrative Aide Ma then asked: "The monks who respond to the imperial court from throughout the land only speak of causes and conditions and do not speak of naturalness.[416] The Daoist priests from throughout the land only speak of naturalness without speaking of causes and conditions."[417]

Answer: "That the monks posit causes and conditions without positing naturalness is the monks' stupid error. That the priests just posit naturalness without positing causes and conditions is the priests' stupid error."

The administrative aide asked: "I can understand the causes and conditions of the Buddhists, but what would their naturalness be? I can understand the Daoists' naturalness, but what would their causes and conditions be?"

Answer: "The naturalness of the Buddhists is the fundamental nature of sentient beings. Furthermore, the 'natural wisdom and teacherless wisdom' that the sūtras speak of is what is called natural.[418] The Daoist priests' causes and conditions are that 'the Way gives birth to the one, the one gives birth to the two, the two gives birth to the three, and from the three are born the myriad things.'[419] They are born dependent on the Dao. If there were no Dao, the myriad things would not be born. What I refer to as 'myriad things' all belong to causes and conditions."[420]

52

Fang Guan, the supervising secretary,[421] asked: "What is the meaning of 'the afflictions are enlightenment'?"

---

415. It is likely that adjutant Yuan Guangshao is the same as the adjutant Yuan 袁司馬 who occurs in section 42. The rest of these are unidentified. It is likely that these figures are, like Ma Ze, based in Xiangzhou.

416. The Chinese is ziran 自然.

417. Compare the discussions of naturalness in sections 3 and 53.

418. The phrase occurs in the *Lotus Sūtra* (T 262: 9.13b25–26) and the *Wisdom Sūtra of Heavenly King Pravara* (T 231: 8.696a2), although the point there is not that living beings are fundamentally endowed with this wisdom. Rather, it is the wisdom that a bodhisattva wishes to attain.

419. A citation from section 42 of the *Daode jing*.

420. In addition to minor embellishments and expansions, Ishii has a slightly expanded closing here. After the quotation from the *Daode jing*, we read the following interesting but somewhat repetitive explanation: "From the Way on down, everything belongs to causes and conditions. If there were no Way, how could anything be born from the one? What is referred to as the one here is established (*li* 立) on the basis of the Way. If there were no Way, the myriad things would not be born. What are referred to here as the myriad things exist only because of the prior existence of the Way. If there were no Way, there would also be no myriad things. What are referred to here as the myriad things all belong to causes and conditions." Note that here (DTS273–277) Suzuki's edition includes sections 20–22, following the order of Ishii. I have returned these sections to their location in P3047 and S6557.

421. Fang Guan 房琯 (697–763): based on Fang's official title, this encounter happened in or after 746. If so, then the connection with Fang Guan may have played an important role

MISCELLANEOUS DIALOGUES 193

Answer: "Let me now use space as a metaphor. It is like space, which is without movement and stillness. It is not that brightness comes and space is bright, or that darkness comes and it is dark. Dark space is no different from bright space, and bright space is no different from dark space. Brightness and darkness come and go of themselves, but space is originally[422] without movement and stillness. The meaning of 'the afflictions are enlightenment' is also like this. Although delusion and enlightenment are different, the mind of enlightenment is originally unmoving."

Another question: "What afflictions might one have and still become enlightened?"[423]

Answer: "The sūtra says, 'The Buddha preaches the Dharmas of delusion and enlightenment for people of middling and lesser abilities, but not for people of superior abilities.'[424] The sūtra says, 'Enlightenment is without past, future, and present, and therefore there is no one who attains it.'[425] The meaning of this is no different from your[426] view. A view such as this is not the estimation of someone of middling or lesser abilities."[427]

53

Li Mian, the vice magistrate of Junyi county,[428] inquired about the meaning of "natural."[429] He asked: "In the very beginning, didn't the Buddha attain

---

in Shenhui's being requested to perform fundraising services for the imperiled Tang state in 757, a project in which Fang Guan was prominently involved. Yanagida, "Goroku," 371, notes that Fang Guan was the son of Fang Rong 房融, the primary recorder (bishouzhe 筆受者) of the Śūraṃgama Sūtra (Shoulengyan jing 首楞嚴經), widely thought to be an apocryphon (T 945: 19.106b–55b). Another participant in this supposed translation, Huaidi of Mount Luofu, also conversed with Shenhui (see section 41). Huaidi and Fang Rong were involved in the supposed translation of the Śūraṃgama Sūtra in the south, sometime after Huaidi's return to the south in 713. Yanagida, Shoki Zenshū shisho, 372, suggests that this dialogue was fabricated, to support the notion of Shenhui's involvement in the promotion movement for Sengcan Ogawa ("Kataku Jinne," 36–37 and 55–56n21) points out that the title used for Fang Guan here (jishizhong, 給事中; Hucker, Official Titles, 133 #587) was granted him in 746. He also provides good evidence to suggest that Fang Guan did indeed write the epitaph for Sengcan attributed to him and that the epitaph does manifest an acceptance of Shenhui's ideas.

422. That is, fundamentally.
423. The Chinese for the last phrase is geng yong wu 更用悟, literally, "still [make] function enlightenment."
424. Unidentified citation.
425. Unidentified citation.
426. Using the title supervising secretary, geishi 給事.
427. Shenhui seems to be toadying to his prestigious guest?
428. Li Mian [Yuan] 李勉〔冤〕of Junyi county 浚儀 in Henan province: based on an orthographical similarity, Yanagida has corrected the original Li Yuan (given in brackets here) to Li Mian, who was an official known for his scholarship and virtue under Emperors Suzong, Daizong, and Dezong (who together reigned from 756 to 805). Based on his biography, this encounter with Shenhui happened sometime in or after 756.
429. The Chinese is ziran 自然.

the path through causes? If you say he did not attain it through causes, then by what teaching did he attain buddhahood?"

Answer: "The buddhas of the past did not attain enlightenment through causes."

Another question: "What is the meaning of this?"

Answer: "Sentient beings fundamentally possess 'the teacherless wisdom, the natural wisdom.'[430] It is through their reception of this natural wisdom that sentient beings are able to attain buddhahood. The Buddha uses this Dharma to extend and evolve[431] his teaching and transformation of sentient beings, so that they can achieve equivalent and correct enlightenment."

Another question: "You just said that sentient beings can achieve buddhahood because they have natural wisdom. Since sentient beings are now possessed of the Buddha-nature, why do you say that they cannot achieve buddhahood without natural wisdom?"

Answer: "Although sentient beings possess the natural Buddha-nature, they are unenlightened because they are deluded. [Their Buddha-natures] are covered by the afflictions and they circulate through saṃsāra and are unable to achieve buddhahood."

Question: "If the fundamental nature[432] of sentient beings is pure, from whence are the afflictions generated?"

Answer: "The afflictions and the Buddha-nature exist simultaneously. If you encounter the teaching[433] of a true spiritual compatriot, you will be able to comprehend the nature and become enlightened to the path.[434] If you do not encounter a true spiritual compatriot, then you will create the various [types of] evil karma and will not be able to escape saṃsāra, and therefore you will not be able to achieve buddhahood. It is like gold and gangue: when they exist in mutual dependence before the encounter with a goldsmith, they can only be called 'gold and gangue' and they do not function like gold.[435] It is through the goldsmith's refining that it can function as gold. Just as the afflictions abide [within sentient beings] in dependence on the nature, so are the afflictions [realized to be] naturally nonexistent if one comprehends the fundamental nature."

His Reverence then asked, "How about worldly ritual—is it originally or temporally existent?"

---

430. See n. 418 above.
431. The Chinese is *zhanzhuan* 展轉.
432. The Chinese is *benzi xing* 本自性.
433. The Chinese is *zhishi* 指示; more literally, "indication."
434. The Chinese is *liaoxing wudao* 了性悟道.
435. Literally, only when a goldsmith is "encountered." Also, "function as gold" is a convenient rendering of *de jinyong* 得金用, "attain the function of gold." The structure of the next sentence is similar.

District defender Li[436] answered, "It is through human agency that ritual now exists." [DTS279]

His Reverence further asked, "If it were existent now only through human agency, [what of] the wild dog's veneration of its prey and the otter's veneration of its fish?[437] This is instinctive understanding—how could it depend on human agency? If you understand this principle, you will understand completely how [worldly human ritual] is previously existent.[438] The Buddha-nature of sentient beings is also like this: it is originally existent and not attained from some other [source]."

54

Zhang Wanqing, magistrate of Neixiang county,[439] asked: "What is suchness like?"[440]

Answer: "Recently all the great worthies have said that the unchangeable is suchness. I differ [in saying that] being without change is suchness.[441] Recently all the great worthies have said that two things resembling each other is suchness. I differ [in saying that] when no things resemble each other, this is suchness."[442]

Question: "Is the [Buddha-]nature existent or nonexistent?"

Answer: "The Buddha-nature has the meaning of the non-extremes."[443]

[Question: "What is this 'meaning of the non-extremes'?"][444]

Answer: "Not existence and not nonexistence, therefore it is the non-extremes."

---

436. Li Mian is referred to as a *shaofu* 少府, which is an unofficial reference for district defender (*xianwei* 縣尉), the title used here; see Hucker, *Official Titles,* 243 #2549 and 414–415 #5097.

437. This phrase refers to these predators' natural tendency to arrange their prey in rows, implying the intention of ritual veneration. See the Yueling section of the *Liji*, specifically nos. 77 and 2.

438. In other words, it is a natural phenomenon.

439. Zhang Wanqing 張萬頃, magistrate of Neixiang county 內鄉縣令, Henan: Since the title used here was bestowed on the basis of contributions to the suppression of the An Lushan rebellion, this encounter occurred sometime during or after 756. Given Zhang Wanqing's posting, we may assume that it took place in Shenhui's former long-term residence.

440. The Chinese is *zhenru si he wu* 真如似何物, literally, "what kind of thing does suchness resemble?"

441. The difference between the worthies' and Shenhui's positions must hinge on the difference in nuance between the negatives *bu* 不 and *wu* 無, the former a verbal negative meaning "do not do" and the latter meaning "without." For another discussion of the distinction between generation and extinction and that which is not generation and extinction, see section 38.

442. It is unclear what the two things referred to are.

443. That is, Buddha-nature cannot be defined according to the two extremes of being and nonbeing. Ishii adds, "so why ask about existence and nonexistence?"

444. Added from Ishii.

Question: "What is not existence, and what is not nonexistence?"

Answer: "Not existence is not spoken of as not existence. Not nonexistence is not spoken of as not nonexistence.[445] Therefore both are imperceptible, and therefore [the Buddha-nature] is called the meaning of the non-extremes."

55

The disciple Cai Hao[446] said, "I once saw Wu Jiao ask Chan Master Zhong[447] about the meaning of the Middle Path. He asked about [the line], 'If existence and nonexistence are both eliminated, the Middle Path is also abolished.'[448] He asked fifty or sixty questions like this, which Chan Master Zhong answered by saying, 'This is emptiness.' [Wu Jiao] then [DTS280] asked, 'What kind of thing is emptiness?' The answer was, 'In addition to characteristics and the not-characteristics, there is an innate awareness.'[449] I would like to ask you in turn about this answer by Chan Master Zhong and the question by [Wu] Jiao."[450]

His Reverence said, "When Wu Balang was here from the third to the tenth month he asked solely about this meaning. My present explanation is different from Chan Master Zhong's."

Wu Jiao asked, "How is it different?"

His Reverence said, "'If existence and nonexistence are both eliminated, the Middle Path is also abolished' is non-thought. Non-thought is the single thought. The single thought is omniscience.[451] Omniscience is the profound

---

445. This could be translated, "one does not speak about what does not exist." Note that Ishii changes the meaning significantly, reading: "'Not existence' is to not speak regarding existence. 'Not nonexistence' is to not speak regarding nonexistence."

446. Unidentified.

447. Wu Jiao, referred to just below as Wu Balang, is also unidentified. Chan Master Zhong might be Nanyang Huizhong 南陽慧忠 (d. 775; see the *Song Biographies*, T 2061: 50.762b11–763b21), or it might be the Chan master Zhong of Mount Oxhead 牛頭山忠禪師 who is known to have been teaching at Zhuangyan si in Jinling (Nanjing) around 766 (see T 2061: 50.893c27–28). However, given the prominence of these two individuals, it is unlikely that either one would have been named in the abbreviated form used here.

448. This line is unidentified. The Chinese is *youwu shuang qian, zhongdao yi wang* 有無雙遣，中道亦亡.

449. The term *jusheng* or *jusheng qi* 俱生起 means "simultaneously arising with birth" or, roughly, innate, instinctive (*Bukkyōgo daijiten*, 269b). The term *shi* 識 at the end of the sentence may imply that the Ishii revision of *xiang feixiang* 相非相 to the homonyms *xiang feixiang* 想非想, meaning "thoughts and not-thoughts," is more reasonable. Huizhong's line could be read, "Whether thoughts or non-thoughts, there is also an innate consciousness."

450. This is a remarkable segment in that it shows something that happened very often in later Chan texts, when students and masters repeat questions they have heard elsewhere. In this case, the questioners are presumed to be literati or official supporters, whereas later on monks are involved. It is interesting that Shenhui knows this style of second-generation questioning but does not practice true encounter dialogue.

451. The Chinese is *yiqie zhi* 一切智, often for the Skt. *sarvajñā*.

perfection of wisdom. The profound perfection of wisdom is Tathāgata Chan.[452] Therefore, the sūtra says, ' "Vimalakīrti, how should one contemplate the Tathāgata?" Vimalakīrti said, "Just as one contemplates the true characteristic of one's own body, so should one contemplate the Buddha. When I contemplate the Tathāgata, he does not come from the past, does not go into the future, and does not abide in the present." Because of nonabiding, this is Tathāgata Chan. Tathāgata Chan is emptiness in its ultimate sense. Emptiness in its ultimate sense is just like this. The bodhisattva-mahāsattva examines and contemplates like this, proceeding ever upward to his own enlightenment to the sagely wisdom.' "[453]

56

Xu E, magistrate of Luoyang county,[454] asked: "Every one of the sūtras says that it itself is the source of the Dharma of the buddhas' perfect and unsurpassable enlightenment. I wonder which is prior, the Buddha or the Dharma? If the Buddha is prior, then what teaching did the Buddha use to attain enlightenment?[455] If the Dharma is prior, what person would there have been to preach it?" [DTS281]

Answer: "If one is discussing the Dharma of words, then the Buddha is prior and the Dharma is next; if [one is discussing] the serene Dharma, then the Buddha is latter and the Dharma prior. The sūtra says, 'The teacher of the Buddhas is what is called the Dharma. Since the Dharma is permanent, the Buddhas are also permanent.'[456] If one is discussing the inner teaching,[457] the sūtra says, 'Sentient beings possess natural wisdom, teacherless wisdom.'[458] Just as sentient beings receive this natural wisdom, cultivate according to their opportunities, realize the Dharma of serene extinction and attain buddhahood, so do they then turn the wheel of Dharma to teach and save sentient beings, who receive the teaching of the Buddha and attain full enlightenment."[459]

---

452. The Chinese is *rulai Chan* 如來禪.
453. See the *Vimalakīrti*, T 475: 14.554c27–555a2. Although the text has the opening scriptural question addressed to "gentlemen," *shannanzi* 善男子, I have amended this to "Vimalakīrti" as in the original. I have followed Ishii here, since P3047 has evidently garbled the passage somewhat. See sections 2 and 34 above for other citations of parts of this passage.
454. Unidentified.
455. The Chinese is *chengdao* 成道.
456. This is from the *Nirvāṇa Sūtra*, T 374: 12.387c15–16.
457. The term *lijiao* 裏教 is otherwise unattested. Ishii has "As to the teaching upon which the Buddha relied to achieve the path," using a different character *li*.
458. See n. 419 in section 51.
459. The term for "receive" is the same in both cases, *cheng* 承. The Chinese for "full enlightenment" is *zhengjue* 正覺. [This could also be read as "When sentient beings receive this natural wisdom, cultivate naturally, realize the Dharma of serene extinction, and attain buddhahood, they too turn the wheel of Dharma to teach and save sentient beings, who receive the teaching of the Buddha and attain full enlightenment."—Ed.]

57

Wang Bi, prefect of Nanyang,[460] asked about the *Laṅkāvatāra Sūtra,* "[What is the] meaning of generation, abiding, differentiation, and extinction?"[461]

Answer: "There are two meanings."

Question: "What are they?"

Answer: "A person's accepting a womb is generation, his growth to [the age of] thirty is abiding, his hair whitening and face wrinkling is differentiation, and the arrival of impermanence[462] is extinction. Also, for a seed of grain to be planted in the earth embodies the meaning of generation. Generation is equivalent to differentiation, to abiding. The meaning of generation is that, being generated, it is differentiated. Before being generated is the meaning of differentiation, and the time of being generated also incorporates the meaning of extinction.[463] When bodhisattva-mahāsattvas generate the perfection-of-wisdom mind, they incorporate these four characteristics."

Another [question]: "Do you[464] use the penetration of the preaching, or the penetration of the truth?"[465]

Answer: "The preaching is penetrated, and the truth is also penetrated."[466]

Another question: "What is the penetration of the preaching, and how do you explain the penetration of the truth?"

Answer: "When the mouth speaks of enlightenment and the mind has[467] some place where it resides, when the mouth speaks of nirvāṇa and the mind has generation and extinction, when the mouth speaks of emancipation and the mind has fetters—this is the penetration of the preaching, but the truth is not penetrated."

---

460. The *New History of the Tang,* 72:16b7, mentions a Wang Bi 王弼 from Hedong in Shanxi who was assistant to the underprefect of Chang'an. Gernet, 76n2, indicates the interview must have taken place after 742 without giving any evidence for his assertion.

461. Gernet, 76n5, observes that the same question is placed by Lingyou 靈祐 (771–853) in his recorded sayings text, *Tanzhou Guishan Lingyou Chanshi yulu* 潭州潙山靈祐禪師語錄 (T 1989: 47.579b15ff.). Gernet also suggests that the *Laṅkāvatāra* actually lacks reference to all four of the phases from generation to extinction; see T 670: 16.483a10–13 and 593b12f.

462. That is, death.

463. Ishii is considerably more polished here, and the interpretation varies somewhat: "Also, when a seed of grain first incorporates its sprout, this is the meaning of birth. After it is born is abiding, and this is the meaning of abiding. Birth is different from the time prior to birth, and this is the meaning of differentiation. Birth incorporates extinction, and this is the meaning of extinction." In both cases, the somewhat awkward "seed of grain" represents *guzi* 穀子, literally, "grain-child." The same term (and metaphor) occurs in section 59.

464. Using *Chanshi* 禪師, "Chan master," as a form of reference.

465. These terms, *shuotong* 說通 and *zongtong* 宗通, are from the *Laṅkāvatāra;* see McRae, *Northern School,* 304n14.

466. Here is yet another example of P3047 as rough shorthand annotation of an oral exchange, and Ishii as reconstituted dialogue; the latter has: "In what I am preaching now, the preaching is penetrated and the truth is penetrated."

467. Both versions have *wu* 無, "is without," but I have changed this to fit with the rest of the passage.

Another question: "What is the penetration of the truth?"

Answer: "Just comprehend the empty quiescence of one's inherent nature and do not activate any additional contemplation—this is the penetration of the truth."

Question: "When one is preaching[468] can there fail to be generation and extinction?"

Answer: "The sūtra says, 'Able to distinguish well the various characteristics of the dharmas, yet unmoving with regard to the cardinal meaning.'"[469]

58

Wang Yi, administator of Yangzhou,[470] asked: "If the Buddha-nature is contained within the mind of sentient beings, then when one dies and enters the hells does the Buddha-nature enter there too?"

Answer: "The body is a false body, and the creation of karma leading to the hells is also a false creation."[471]

Question: "If it is a false creation, then how does one enter the hells?"

Answer: "Entering is also false entering."

Question: "If it is false entering, then where is the [Buddha-]nature?"

Answer: "The nature does not transcend the false."[472]

[Question:] "Then does it enter [the hells] or not?"

Answer: "Although it enters simultaneously [with the deceased] it does not experience[473] [the sufferings of the hells]."

Question: "If it does not transcend the false, why does it enter [the hells] without experiencing [suffering]?" [DTS283]

Answer: "It is likened to being hit within a dream: when one awakes one's body does not feel [the blow]. Although the Buddha-nature enters [the hells] simultaneously it is without experience [of them]. Therefore one should know that the creation of transgressions is false and the hells are false; the two are both false and the experience of the false. The false is delusion as to the true, and the nature is originally without experience."[474]

---

468. The Chinese is *zhengshuo zhi shi* 正說之時, "precisely at the time of preaching." See a similar usage in section 44.

469. A citation from the *Vimalakīrti Sūtra;* T 475: 14.537c13.

470. Wang Yi appeared in section 48.

471. Note the probable confusion in the previous line between mind, *xin* 心, and body, *shen* 身. The term for "false" here is *wang* 妄.

472. That is, it is not separate from the false.

473. The Chinese is *shou* 受.

474. Here the broader implication seems to be that the Buddha-nature is entirely without experience, not just of the hells. Is the overall implication of the passage that the Buddha-nature is rather like an *ātman*? Ogawa ("Kataku Jinne," 57n32) suggests that this implies a notion of the Buddha-nature as an immortal spirit separate from the body, an idea exceptional in the context of Shenhui's thought but apparently adopted by some of Shenhui's successors. In my reading of this passage, however, I do not see Shenhui ever admitting that the Buddha-nature is independent of the body—he only hypothetically accepts his questioner's premise, without indicating his specific understanding of death, or even of the relationship between Buddha-nature and body.

59

Dharma Master Zhide[475] asked: "What about generation, abiding, differentiation, and extinction?"

Answer: "Generation, abiding, differentiation, and extinction are actually one.[476] Because they are one, therefore they are four. Beginningless ignorance relies on the Tathāgata storehouse. Therefore, when a single thought is generated to the least degree, it pervades all locations. The creations of sentient beings in the six realms of existence,[477] unrealizing and unknowing, pervade everywhere. Also, unrealizing and unknowing, coming from somewhere and going somewhere—so do sentient beings experience the six realms of existence.[478] Why is it like this? Sentient beings also think about and know all the sufferings and joys of the six realms of existence. They know because they have experienced them in the past. In false consciousness[479] there exists generation, abiding, going, and coming.[480] True consciousness[481] is suchness and entirely without going, coming, generation, and extinction.[482] It is as if when a man's eyes sleep, his mind of ignorance pervades all locations. When he awakes there exists the coarse and the fine.[483] Therefore pervading and not pervading are like a seed of grain first incorporating its sprout. This is the meaning of generation. After it is generated, it abides in generation.[484] After it abides, this is different from when it had not been generated. Thus with generation is incorporated the meaning of extinction. This is the meaning of generation, abiding, differentiation, and extinction."[485]

60

Dharma Master Yuan asked: "What does it mean to 'not exhaust the conditioned and not abide in the unconditioned'?"[486]

Answer: "'To not exhaust the conditioned' means that from the first generation of *bodhicitta* up to achieving perfect enlightenment seated under

---

475. Zhide appeared in section 34.
476. The Chinese is *zheng yan yi* 正言一, "correctly called one."
477. The Chinese is *liudao* 六道.
478. This is how I understand the nuance of this line. "Experience" represents *tiyou* 體有.
479. The Chinese is *jiashi* 假識.
480. Note how the opening topic has changed to *sheng zhu qu lai* 生住去來.
481. The Chinese is *zhenshi* 真識.
482. Now we have *qu lai shengmie* 去來生滅.
483. The pair "coarse and fine," *cuxi* 粗細, seems to metonymically represent the material world.
484. That is, in being alive.
485. See section 57 above. The discussion here is similarly simplistic.
486. This is the subject of the very first dialogue of section 1, which is marred by lacunae. This dialogue corresponds to section 6 of the *Definition of the Truth*.

the bodhi tree and entering nirvāṇa between the two *sāla* trees—one never discards any dharma. This is to 'not exhaust the conditioned.' To 'not abide in the unconditioned' is to cultivate emptiness without taking emptiness as one's realization, to cultivate non-action without taking non-action as one's realization. This is to 'not abide in the unconditioned.' As for sitting [in meditation], for thoughts not to be activated is 'sitting,' and to see the fundamental nature is 'meditation.'"[487]

61[488]

Dharma Master Yuan asked, "What Dharma do you cultivate, and what practice do you practice?"

His Reverence answered, "I cultivate the Dharma of the perfection of wisdom, and I practice the practice of the perfection of wisdom."

Dharma Master Chongyuan asked, "Why don't you cultivate other Dharmas and practice other practices?"

His Reverence answered, "I cultivate the perfection of wisdom, which incorporates all Dharmas. I practice the practice of the Perfection of Wisdom, which is the fundamental source of all practices.

"Therefore the *Diamond Sūtra* [says]:

> The adamantine perfection of wisdom
> Is the most honored, the most excellent, the most supreme.
> Without generation, without extinction, without going and coming,
> All the buddhas derive from this."

The *Wisdom Sūtra of Heavenly King Pravara* says, "'How does the bodhisattva-mahāsattva practice the perfection of wisdom so as to penetrate the most profound *dharmadhātu*?' The Buddha said to Heavenly King Pravara, 'Great King, according to reality.' 'World-honored One, what is the real?' 'Great King, the unchanging [is the real].' 'World-honored One, what is the unchanging?' 'Great King, it is called suchness.' 'World-honored One, what is suchness?' 'Great King, it can be known by wisdom but cannot be explained with words. [Why? It goes beyond words, and is] without this and that. It

---

487. The character *zuo* 坐, "sit," at the beginning of this sentence should probably be omitted. See the same equations in the *Definition of the Truth*, section 22. As pointed out by Suzuki Tetsuo ("Kataku Jinne no eikyō," 91–96, esp. the chart on 91–92), this passage is imitated (i.e., with slight changes) in the *Essential Teaching of Sudden Enlightenment* (X 63.21b21–c2; Hirano, *Tongo yōmon*, 11).

488. Part of this section (down to but not including the paragraph before the quotations from the *Vajrasamādhi*) is included in the *Definition of the Truth*, sections 32–33; see the translation of that text for annotation. Again, to simplify the format, quotation marks to indicate Shenhui's speech are omitted in the quotations from the *Heavenly King Pravara* and *Vajrasamādhi*.

transcends characteristics and is without characteristics. It far transcends thought and passes beyond the realm of understanding.'"[489]

"In order to comprehend the profound *dharmadhātu*, one must generate *bodhicitta* so that the two are not discriminated. Thus of the two minds[490] the first is the difficult one, when one would first save others before being saved oneself. Therefore I pay obeisance to the bodhisattvas of the initial generation of *bodhicitta*."[491]

[*The Vajrasamādhi Sūtra* says],[492] "Bodhisattva Emancipation said, 'World-honored One, does the mind of non-generation grasp or reject anything, and does it abide in any characteristic of the dharmas?' The Buddha said, 'The mind of non-generation grasps and rejects nothing. It resides in the not-mind; it resides in the not-dharma.'"[493]

[Again]: "Bodhisattva Mind-king said, 'Honored One, the wisdom of non-generation neither abides in nor departs from any location. The mind is without any location of abiding, and there is no location where the mind can abide. Since there's no abiding and no mind, the mind does not generate any abiding, and the mind is thus non-generating. Honored One, that the mind is without the practice of generation, how inconceivable!'"[494]

[Again]: "Bodhisattva Mind-king said, 'To practice according to non-generation is for nature and characteristics to be empty and serene, without seeing and without hearing, without attainment and without loss, without words and without explanation, without knowing and without concepts, without grasping and without rejecting. How could one grasp at realization? If one grasped at realization this would be [the cause of] disputation. Only when there is no argumentation and no theorizing is it the practice of non-generation.'"[495]

[Again]: "A thousand thoughts and ten thousand wonderings do not benefit [one's understanding of] the principle of the Path.[496] [Through chaotic activity one loses the fundamental mind-king. If there is no thought and wondering,] then there is no generation and extinction. In truth, to

---

489. The material in brackets has been supplemented from the *Definition of the Truth*, section 33.
490. That is, of the first *bodhicitta* and final realization
491. I have broken up Suzuki's paragraph.
492. This title is added by Suzuki to what are clearly scriptural passages preferred by Shenhui and / or his editors. In preparing translations of the following passages, I have consulted Buswell, *Formation of Ch'an Ideology*. On the connection between the *Vajrasamādhi* and Shenhui, see Adamek, *Mystique*, 443–444n180.
493. See the *Vajrasamādhi*, T 273: 9.367a4–6; Buswell, *Formation of Ch'an Ideology*, 193. Buswell's translation differs slightly from mine: "Lord! To what does the mind that produces nothing cling? What does it reject? In what characteristic of dharma does it linger?"
494. See T 273: 9.368a18–21; Buswell, 200. Note that Shenhui's text omits one phrase from the original. The first part of this passage reads, literally, "the wisdom of non-generation does not abide in all locations and not apart from all locations."
495. See T 273: 9.367c21–24; Buswell, 198.
496. The Chinese is *daoli* 道理.

not activate the various consciousnesses and to pacify the flowings [of desire, existence, and ignorance] so they are not generated is to attain the purity of the Dharma eye. This is called the Mahāyāna."[497]

62

Kang Zhiyuan, disciple of the Brahman monk from central India, Tripiṭaka Master *Kālamitra,[498] asked, "Reverend, having karmic connections [with you] over many eons... .[499] The matter of birth and death is great; the more I think about impermanence, the more profound my doubts grow, day by day. Not daring to pose questions, I only wish that in your compassion you might allow me to relate to you my mental state."[500] [DTS286]

His Reverence answered, "If you have doubts, state your questions as you wish."

Zhiyuan asked, "Every sentient being talks about cultivating the Path, but I wonder whether those who cultivate the Path attain buddhahood in a single lifetime or not?"

His Reverence answered, "They can attain it."

Another question: "How can they attain it?"

Answer: "In the teaching of the Mahāyāna karmic obstacles as great as the sands of the River Ganges can be eliminated in a single thought. When the [Buddha-]nature experiences non-generation,[501] one achieves enlightenment in an instant. Why couldn't one attain this in a single lifetime?"

Another question: "How is it possible to cultivate for only a single moment and achieve buddhahood? Please eliminate my doubt regarding this."

Answer: "What is called cultivation are conditioned dharmas, which, as you know, must belong to impermanence. When impermanence is left [far] behind[502] one transcends birth and death."

Another question: "All the buddhas are complete in the fruits of cultivation and have attained the enlightenment of buddhahood, yet now you say they do not rely on cultivation. How can this be believed?"

Answer: "If we mean the cultivation of faith and practice,[503] this is not

---

497. See T 273: 9.366c21–23; Buswell, 192. Shenhui's text omits the passage about chaotic activity contained in brackets (without which the passage is difficult to interpret), and instead of the "purity of the eye of Dharma" it refers to the "purity of the five dharmas."

498. Both Kang Zhiyuan 康智圓 and *Kālamitra 伽羅蜜多 remain unidentified.

499. Gernet, 78n2, refers to corrections in Hu Shi's edition, while Hu's handwritten note on p. 148 refers to an emendation of Gernet's. I see no sound basis for selecting any particular solution here.

500. The Chinese is *xindi* 心地.

501. This phrase could also be read as "When the essential nature is without generation..."—Ed.

502. There is a lacuna of one character here followed by *li* 離, "to leave behind," "to transcend." I suspect that it read *yuanli* 遠離, hence "far" in brackets.—Ed.

503. The Chinese is *xinxing xiuxi* 信行修習.

separate from the realization of wisdom.[504] And if one has the realization of wisdom, then one has the function of illumination.[505] Thus cause and result are perfectly matched,[506] and since generation and extinction are originally nonexistent, why should one rely on cultivation?"

Another question: "All the buddhas have attained enlightenment on the basis of the realization of wisdom. Now [you refer to] transcending the realization of wisdom, so what enlightenment [is attained]?"

Answer: "Enlightenment is essentially without any thing. It is also without estimation, and without the realization of wisdom and the function of illumination, and [without] the dharmas of motion and rest. Mind and intention are not posited,[507] and there is also no going and coming, no interior, exterior, and intermediate, no location at all. It is not quiescent and not chaotic, it lacks empty names, and it is without characteristics. It is without thoughts and without thinking, and perceptual understanding cannot [DTS287] reach it. It is the unrealized—the nature of enlightenment is completely uncharacterizable."[508]

Another question: "If it is uncharacterizable and cannot be reached by perceptual understanding, how can one attain emancipation?"

Answer: "For the three matters to not be generated is emancipation."

Another question: "What does it mean for the three matters to not be generated?"

Answer: "For the mind to not be generated is non-thought, for wisdom to not be generated is non-knowing, and for sagacity to not be generated is non-seeing. To penetrate this principle is emancipation."[509]

Another question: "If there is nonwisdom[510] then how can one, without generating knowing and wisdom,[511] see non-thought?"

Answer: "I have referred to the mind being concentrated but not to someone concentrating [the mind]—this is non-thought. Concentration and wisdom are undifferentiated—this is nonwisdom. Given wisdom and concentration, for the various views to not be generated—this is non-

---

504. The Chinese is *zhijue* 智覺.
505. The Chinese is *zhaoyong* 照用.
506. The Chinese is *wanran* 宛然.
507. The Chinese is *bu li xindi yidi* 不立心地意地.
508. The Chinese is *daoxing ju wusuode* 道性俱無所得.
509. This is the distinction between wisdom and sagacity, *zhi* 智 and *hui* 慧, as found in the *Five Skillful Means*. This is perhaps the clearest example of the peculiarly formulaic style of Northern school contemplative analysis found in Shenhui's works. Note, however, that although his correlation of wisdom with knowing and sagacity with seeing parallels the *Five Skillful Means*, he uses a tripartite and implicitly Yogācāra division of consciousnesses (which is also found in the *Five Skillful Means*).
510. The Chinese is *wuzhi* 無智.
511. The Chinese is *zhizhi* 知智.

seeing.[512] These are not dharmas of causes and results.[513] When one penetrates no-self, one will clearly know that generation is false generation and extinction is false extinction."

Another question: "All the buddhas have attained the enlightenment of buddhahood on the basis of causes and results. Now you refer to dharmas not of causes and results—how can one achieve the transmission from teacher to teacher?"

Answer: "In the Mahāyāna one achieves enlightenment at a single word.[514] When one first generates the intention to achieve enlightenment, one leaps thereby to the stage of buddhahood. Without past, future, and present, this is the ultimate emancipation."

Question:[515] "What is the Mahāyāna [understanding of] concentration?"

Answer: "Mahāyāna concentration is to not make mental effort, [to not view the mind],[516] to not view purity, to not contemplate emptiness, to not make the mind abide, to not purify the mind, [DTS288] to not view afar, to not view close up, to be without the ten directions, to not subjugate, to be without fear, to be without discrimination, to not sink into emptiness, to not abide in serenity, and for all false characteristics to not be generated. This is Mahāyāna concentration."

Question: "What does it mean to not make mental effort?"[517]

Answer: "Mental effort is existent, and existence is generation and extinction. No-effort[518] is nonexistent, without generation and without extinction."

Question: "What does it mean to not view the mind?"[519]

Answer: "To view is false, and to be without the false is to be without viewing."[520]

Question: "What does it mean to not view purity?"[521]

Answer: "To be without defilement is [also] to be without purity. Purity is just another characteristic, and so one should not view it."

---

512. Note the double meaning of *jian* 見 as "views" (Skt. *dṛṣṭi*), and the sensory act of seeing. Shenhui may not always be aware of switching from one meaning to the other, but he certainly plays on the term's multivalence.
513. That is, causally produced dharmas, *yinyuan fa* 因緣法.
514. The Chinese here is *Dasheng yanxia wudao* 大乘言下悟道.
515. Is it significant, in terms of textual composition, that we switch back to simply *wen* 問, "question," rather than *you wen* 又問, "another question," at this point? That is, might this be another segment? Gernet, 80n10, compares this line to the *Platform Sūtra*, T 2008: 48.339a3–5, where a similarly markless meditation is discussed, although the wording has little in common.
516. Suzuki adds these on the basis of the dialogue that follows.
517. The Chinese is *bu yongxin* 不用心.
518. Or "no-functioning."
519. The Chinese is *bu kanxin* 不看心.
520. This entire passage clearly assumes prior knowledge of the *Five Skillful Means*, perhaps the only time in Shenhui's writings.
521. The Chinese is *bu kanjing* 不看心.

Question: "What does it mean to not make the mind abide?"[522]

Answer: "To make the mind abide is a false endeavor, and so one should not make it abide. The mind is without location.[523]

"Based on your questions, all those who cultivate the Path [will achieve] enlightenment simultaneously."[524]

63[525]

Dharma Master Chongyuan asked: "You[526] talk about the central principle of Bodhidharma,[527] but I wonder whether this Chan teaching has a lineal transmission.[528] [53] Explain it to us."

Answer: "From the past until now there has always[529] been a lineal transmission."

Another question: "Through how many generations has it passed?"

Answer: "It has now passed through six generations."

[Question:] "Please explain who these six generations of great worthies were, and also the circumstances of their succession."[530]

64

The first generation, at Shaolin si on Mount Song during the Latter Wei, was a Brahman monk by the name of Bodhidharma.[531] He was the third son of the king of a country in southern India. He left home while young and was enlightened to the supreme vehicle, realizing Tathāgata Chan while in various samādhis. Taking a boat he crossed the ocean, passing far across

---

522. The Chinese is *bu zhuxin* 不住心.

523. The Chinese is *xin wu chusuo* 心無處所. Although the context here does not call for it, this could be translated "the mind is the locus of nonbeing."

524. This does not fit with the immediately preceding material and seems like the end of a text segment or dialogue. The balance of the *Miscellaneous Dialogues* occurs only in Ishii, and since the Suzuki edition in the *Zenshū* includes only the first two exchanges, I am following the earlier edition by Suzuki and Kōda, *Tonkō shutsudo Kataku Jinne*, with in-text markers keyed to its page numbers.

525. The text from this section up to section 69 closely resembles the *Definition of the Truth* in its emphasis on transmission.

526. Using *Chanshi*, "Chan master."

527. The Chinese here is *Damo zongzhi* 達摩宗旨.

528. The term here is *Chanmen you xiangchuan fushu* 禪門有相傳附屬.

529. The Chinese here is *ju* 具, lit. "complete."

530. The Chinese here is *chuanshou* 傳授. It is curious that this text provides hagiographical information for the six Chinese patriarchs without mentioning the Indian ones at all, while the *Definition of the Truth*, section 29, gives a list of fourteen patriarchs from the Buddha Śākyamuni to Huineng.

531. For simplicity, quotation marks to indicate that this is Shenhui's oral response to the question posed by Chongyuan will be omitted throughout the following genealogy. For another translation of this section, see Jorgensen, *Inventing Hui-neng*, 126–128.

the sea to come to this Han domain,[532] where he then met Huike. Huike followed Bodhidharma[533] to Shaolin si on Mount Song, where he served the master and attended to his every need. One night, as he stood outside the hall where Bodhidharma [preached], snow continued to fall, reaching Huike's hips. But he stood still and did not move. When the great master [Bodhidharma] saw this, he said, "What are you doing standing in the snow?" Huike said to the great master, "Your Reverence has come here from far away in the west to preach the Dharma in order to save people. Without fear for myself, I earnestly seek the excellent Dharma. I only ask Your Reverence, in your great compassion and empathy, to relieve the suffering of sentient beings, remove their difficulties, and reveal the knowledge of the buddhas! This is what I wish." Great Master Bodhidharma said, "I have never seen anyone seeking the Dharma like this."

Then Huike [54] took out a knife and cut off his own left arm, placing it before Bodhidharma. Bodhidharma saw that Huike was prepared to destroy his body or discard his life in his quest for the excellent Dharma, just as the [acolyte] Snowy Mountain had thrown himself [from a cliff] to hear half a verse [of the teachings].[534] He said, "You are capable. Formerly your name was Shenguang, but you shall be called Huike, because of this."[535] Then, using the *Diamond Sūtra*, Great Master Bodhidharma explained the knowing and seeing of the Tathāgata, bestowing this on Huike.[536] The words bestowed on Huike were the matching tally of the Dharma,[537] and the robe transmitted was the proof of the Dharma. It was like the Buddha's bestowing the prediction [of future buddhahood][538] on the daughter of the dragon king Sāgara. The great master said, "This single fascicle of the *Diamond Sūtra* [teaches]

---

532. That is, China.
533. Here and below Bodhidharma is referred to simply as Damo 達摩, "Dharma."
534. See the *Definition of the Truth*.
535. Translated literally, the name means "wisdom capable."
536. Cf. the account of this transmission at the end of section 3 in the *Definition of the Truth*. Yanagida, "Goroku," 413, suggests that the addition of the *Diamond Sūtra* to the transmission of Bodhidharma's robe may have been done with knowledge of the *Records of the Transmission*, which if true would imply a post-772 date for Ishii. Since only the robe is mentioned in the *Definition of the Truth*, the sūtra transmission could have been added later to counter the suggestion in the *Records of the Transmission* that the robe had been transmitted to Zhixian 智詵 and thus to Wuzhu 無住; see the *Definition of the Truth*, section 16 (n. 111).
537. The term is *faqi* 法契, "Dharma tally." See the *Definition of the Truth*, nn. 41 and 111.
538. The term is *shouji* 授記 (corresponding to the Skt. *vyākaraṇa*), used in the scriptures to refer to a buddha's prediction of enlightenment for a given follower. Here it is used to refer euphemistically to the succession from one patriarch to the next, an indication that the terminology for this process was not yet regularized. It is used throughout the following stories. In fact, in the story about the dragon king's daughter, the Buddha does not make any prediction of her future enlightenment, since the whole point of the story is that she achieves buddhahood in an instant. It is also difficult to see how this incident is related to the bequest of the robe; the only connections are that Shenhui referred to this incident during his teaching efforts and that the Buddha's supposed bequest to her was to someone without the special physical and supernormal attainments of a bodhisattva.

the direct and comprehensive attainment of buddhahood. You and those who come after me should base your cultivation on the gate of contemplating *prajñā*.[539] To not attain a single dharma is nirvāṇa, to be unmoving in body and mind is to achieve the unsurpassable enlightenment."

Great Master Bodhidharma taught monks and laypeople for six years, at which time difficulties arose. Six times he was poisoned, and five times he consumed it and then spat it out into a hole in the earth.[540] He said to Huike, "My karmic connections with this domain of Han have been exhausted. Afterwards, you too will not escape difficulties like this. The lives of those who transmit [the teaching] will be [as precarious as] a hanging thread until after the sixth generation. Take care, all of you." When he finished speaking he passed away. He was buried on Mount Song.

At that time National Commissioner[541] Song Yun met a foreign monk on Mount Congling[542] who was wearing a shoe on one foot while the other foot was bare. He said to the national commissioner, "The emperor of you Han [55] people met with impermanence today." When Song Yun heard this, he was greatly astonished and took note of the day and month.[543] Song Yun had asked Great Master Bodhidharma, "In your activities in the Han realm, did you gain any followers?" and Great Master Bodhidharma had said, "Forty years after me there will be someone to spread my Dharma in the Han realm." When Song Yun returned to court to see the emperor, the emperor had already died. When he examined the date marked by the foreign monk, there was no discrepancy, and Song Yun reported this to the officials at court. At that time there were several tens of Bodhidharma's followers at court, and they said to each other, "How could [that monk] not have been our Reverend?" So they exhumed his grave and opened his coffin, but his Dharma body was not there. All that could be seen in the coffin was a single shoe. Only by this [sign] did the entire country know that he had been a sage.[544]

---

539. The term "gate of contemplating *prajñā*" (*banruo guanmen* 般若觀門) would be unusual for Shenhui, but perhaps not for the successors of his who compiled this section of the text. For the rest of this short homily attributed to Bodhidharma, the text works to identify him with the *Diamond* rather than the *Laṅkāvatāra*.

540. Literally, "each time he dug in the earth and threw it out."

541. The title *guoshi* 國使 does not occur in Hucker's *Official Titles,* and although one could easily render it "national ambassador," it seems better to render it according to the use of *shi* 使 alone, in keeping with the general Tang dynasty usage by which it was applied to special appointments (Hucker, 31).

542. Congling 蔥嶺 (given here as 葱嶺) is the Chinese name for the Pamir mountains in Tajikistan. The use of *Huseng* 胡僧 rather than *fanseng* 梵僧 might imply Central Asian rather than Indian provenance, but the usage here may not be rigorous; see Boucher, "On *Hu* and *Fan* Again."

543. The text has *jian* 見, "look, see," but Suzuki and Kōda, 55, suggest *ji* 記, "note," would be more appropriate.

544. The Chinese is *shengren* 聖人. Note that in this story validation of Bodhidharma's greatness is shown through events at court, which conforms with Shenhui's own style but conflicts in part with the other facets of Bodhidharma's rustic image.

The shoe is now at Shaolin si, where offerings are made to it. Emperor Wu of the Liang wrote the text of his epitaph, which is now at Shaolin si.

65

The second generation, Chan Master Huike of the Northern Qi, came after Great Master Bodhidharma. His lay surname was Zhou, and he was from Wuhan.[545] When he reached forty years of age he began to serve Bodhidharma. After nine years[546] he listened to [Bodhidharma's] explanation of the *Adamantine Perfection of Wisdom Sūtra* and, upon hearing the words, realized that for tathāgatas the true absence of any dharma was the Buddha, and that enlightenment transcending all dharmas was called "the buddhas."[547] After receiving the prediction of his future buddhahood, he encountered the [56] eradication of the Buddhadharma by Emperor Wu of the Zhou, so he went into hiding at Mount Xian in Shuzhou.[548] After Bodhidharma's death, more than forty years passed before he began to teach again to lead sentient beings [to salvation]. It was then that Chan Master Sengcan served him faithfully for six years. The master relied on the *Diamond Sūtra* to explain the knowing and seeing of the Tathāgata, and upon hearing these words [Sengcan] was enlightened. He silently acknowledged the unspoken words of the Tathāgata,[549] and recognizing [Sengcan's] realization of the Dharma,[550] [Huike] transmitted the robe to him as the Dharma proof.[551] It was like Mañjuśrī's giving the prediction of future buddhahood to Sudhana.[552] [Later] Great Master Huike said to Sengcan, "I am returning to Ye to repay my debt," and he left Mount Xian to go to Ye to preach the Dharma. He did not care where he preached, whether in the market or on a street corner or down an alley, and monks and laypeople came to listen in reverential numbers that could not be counted.[553] After eleven years he encountered a number of disasters, which [people seemed to] compete in fomenting, and he was slandered as a wraith who was falsely destroying the Buddhadharma.

---

545. On Huike's biography, see McRae, *Northern School*, 21–23, 278–279n30.

546. In other sources Huike is said to have studied with Bodhidharma for six years, but this text (or this portion of it) has a particular fascination with the number nine. In addition to this occurrence, Daoxin served Sengcan for nine years (section 66) and Shenhui was a boy of nine when he first sought the Dharma from Huineng (section 70).

547. Two very rough citations of the *Diamond Sūtra*, T 235: 8.749c8–9 and 750b9.

548. Mount Xian 峴山 (also known as Xianshou 峴首) in Xiangcheng district 襄城區, Hubei, is not otherwise known in Chan sources.

549. The Chinese is *mishou moyu* 密授默語. The manuscript unnecessarily repeats 16 characters here.

550. The Chinese is *faqi* 法契, lit. "Dharma tally."

551. The Chinese is *faxin* 法信.

552. Shancai tongzi 善財童子, Skt. Sudhana, is the protagonist of the *Avataṃsaka Sūtra*'s "Entering the Dharmadhātu" chapter (*Ru fajie pin* 入法界品; Skt. *Gaṇḍavyūha*).

553. A new element in the hagiography of Huike, possibly designed to provide background for Shenhui's style of public teaching.

Eventually he encountered Zhai Zhongkan, prefect of Cheng'an Xian,[554] who without knowing why had Huike beaten to death. On the next day he came to life once again. He was also poisoned, and this time he died. It is all related in fascicle 10 of Yang Lengqie's *Ancient Stories of Ye*.[555] [57]

66

The third generation, Chan Master Sengcan of the Sui, followed after Great Master Huike. His lay surname is unknown, as is his place of origin. After receiving his master's prediction of future buddhahood, he began to behave like a deranged person in the marketplace, so as to escape the persecutions, and then he took to the mountain forests to recover, secluding himself on Mount Sikong in Shuzhou.[556] During that period Chan Master Daoxin, from the age of thirteen, served him for nine years. The master relied on the *Diamond Sūtra* to explain the knowing and seeing of the Tathāgata, and upon hearing the words [Daoxin] realized that "there are no sentient beings to attain nirvāṇa."[557] [Sengcan] had bestowed the unspoken words verifying the Dharma, and he then transmitted the robe as the Dharma proof. It was as if the precious pearl, the bright moon, had appeared in the great ocean! When Great Master Sengcan, Chan Master Baoyue, and Dinggong[558] went together to Mount Luofu,[559] Chan Master Daoxin wanted to accompany Great Master Sengcan on that occasion, but he was told, "You must not go. In time you will greatly benefit [sentient beings]." Great Master Sengcan returned to Mount Xian after three years on Mount Luofu. Once, while passing a cluster of houses, he called out, "You people should all donate some food to make a meal for this monk." Since the clerics and laypeople [of the area] had all taken refuge in him, there were none who did not donate. They held the vegetarian feast, and after everyone had eaten, it was under a great tree at the center of the spot where the feast had been held that [Sengcan] stood with his palms together and died. He was buried behind Shangu si. In the monastery there is an epitaph and an image, to which offerings are still being made.[560] [58]

---

554. If this were a real individual (which seems unlikely), his name might have been Chu 瞿 rather than the unusual Zhai Zhongkan 翟仲侃.

555. A nonextant work; see Adamek, *Mystique*, 519n37.

556. Shuzhou 舒州 in Anhui province was the administrative jurisdiction that included Mount Sikong 司空山.

557. From the *Diamond Sūtra*, T 235: 8.749a9–10.

558. Chan Master Baoyue 寶月禪師 and Dinggong 定公 are mentioned in the *Annals of the Transmission;* see McRae, *Northern School*, 261.

559. Mount Luofu 羅浮山 is in what is now Boluo county, Guangdong.

560. Shangu si 山谷寺 (安徽省安慶市潛山縣) was within the jurisdiction of Shuzhou. This location is mentioned as Sengcan's residence in the *Masters and Disciples of the Laṅkāvatāra* (Yanagida, *Shoki no zenshi 1,* 371). The next known reference to this location and the earliest reference to an epitaph is Dugu Ji's 獨孤及 (A010960; 726–777) text for Sengcan (Shuzhou Shangu si Jueji ta Sui gu Jingzhi Chanshi beiming bing xu 舒州山谷寺覺寂塔隋故鏡智禪師碑

67

The fourth generation, Chan Master Daoxin of the Tang, came after Great Master Can. His lay surname was Sima, and he was from Henei.[561] After receiving the transmission [from Sengcan] he went to Jizhou.[562] The city had been under siege by crazed rebels for over one hundred days, and the wells and springs were all dry. When Chan Master Daoxin entered the city, he exhorted the monks and laypeople to recite the *Great Perfection of Wisdom*. The frenzied attackers retreated, the wells and springs bubbled forth, and the city became completely safe. He was ordained in Jizhou, having met a monk there who did that.[563] Then he went to the summit of Mount Lu, from which he looked out and saw a purple cloud forming above Mount Potou at Huangmei in Qizhou. [Going to] this mountain, he took up residence there and renamed it Mount Shuangfeng.[564] During this period Chan Master Hongren, from the age of seven, served him for over thirty years. [Daoxin] relied on the *Diamond Sūtra* to explain the knowing and seeing of the Tathāgata, and upon hearing these words [Hongren] was enlightened to the forbearance of serene extinction and the Dharma of the Supreme Vehicle. Acknowledging the unspoken words verifying the Dharma, he then [received from Daoxin] the transmission of the robe as the Dharma proof. It was like the acolyte Snowy Mountain's receipt of the wish-giving gem.[565] Once again Great Master Daoxin had opened the Dharma gate to lead sentient beings [to salvation]. The elite from all around, finding his teachings exquisite, took refuge in him,[566] and this went on for more than thirty years. In the eighth month of the second year of Yonghui (651), he suddenly

---

銘弁序; see Yanagida, *Shoki no Zenshi 2*, 86). Written in 773, this cannot be the epitaph referenced here.

561. Henei 河內 refers to that portion of Henan north of the Yellow River.

562. The story that follows about Daoxin in Jizhou 吉州 is drawn from the *Continued Biographies;* see McRae, *Northern School*, 31.

563. According to this, Daoxin was officially ordained (*duren* 渡人) only after the incident in Jizhou.

564. Mount Shuangfeng 雙峰山 (Twin Peaks) is the usual name for this location in Huangmei 黃梅 (or Qizhou 蘄州) in Hubei; I have not seen the name Potou shan 破頭山 (Broken Head Mountain) elsewhere.

565. There are certain minor textual problems with this account of the transmission. Suzuki and Kōda, 58, are no doubt correct in pointing out that the characters *mo shou yu* 默受語, "silently receiving words," should be in the order *shou moyu*, as above in section 65 (see n. 549). I have followed this order in the translation. Suzuki interprets the character *ren* 忍, "forbearance," just above this as referring to Hongren. However, nowhere else in this section is any of the patriarchs mentioned without use of the title Chan Master or Great Master. In addition, the four-character phrase *wu jimie ren* 悟寂滅忍, "be enlightened to the forbearance of extinction/nirvāṇa," seems better on both stylistic and doctrinal grounds than simply "be enlightened to extinction/nirvāṇa."

566. This is how I understand the text's "exhausted beauty and took refuge" (*jinmei guiyi* 盡美歸依).

commanded his disciple Yuanyi to build a stūpa on the side of the mountain. On the fourth day of the ninth intercalary month, he asked, "Is the stūpa finished yet?" and was told [59] that it was finished. Going to the site, he saw that the stūpa was done. Then he returned to his room and quietly passed away. The great master was seventy-two. On that day there was a great earthquake, the sun and moon went dark, and the trees in the forest all shuddered. A half-year after he was buried, the stūpa opened by itself, for no reason, and up to now it has not been closed. Du Zhenglun wrote the text of his epitaph, which now stands on the mountain.[567]

68

The fifth generation, Chan Master Hongren of the Tang, came after Great Master Daoxin.[568] His lay surname was Zhou, and he was from Huangmei. After receiving his teacher's conferral of the prediction of enlightenment, he took up residence on Mount Fengmu, which was the eastern part of Mount Shuangfeng. This is the reason his contemporaries referred to the East Mountain teaching.[569] At that time Chan Master Huineng offered his services for eight months and achieved realization upon hearing the master explain the knowing and seeing of the Tathāgata according to the *Diamond Sūtra*:[570] "If this mind possesses 'abiding,' then this is non-abiding."[571] [Hongren] silently bestowed the unspoken words verifying the Dharma and then transmitted the robe as the Dharma proof. It was like Śākyamuni's bestowal of the prediction of future enlightenment on Maitreya.

Great Master Hongren taught for thirty years, guiding both clerics and laypeople. [People from] the four quarters took refuge in him, racing [to his side and gathering] like clouds. In the [second] year of Shangyuan

---

567. Yuanyi 元一 is known solely as the disciple who built Daoxin's stūpa; the account given here is derived from the *Annals of the Transmission*. This includes the reference to Daoxin's epigrapher, Du Zhenglun 杜正倫; see McRae, *Northern School*, 35 and 263.

568. The brevity of this hagiography of Hongren is either accidental or, more likely, a reaction against this figure's importance to proponents of the East Mountain teaching, i.e., members of the "Northern school."

569. Mount Fengmu 馮墓山 is an alternate name for Mount Shuangfeng, the Huangmei location of the "East Mountain teaching" (*dongshan famen* 東山法門). Zongmi's *Yuanjue jing da shu shi yi chao* 圓覺經大疏釋義鈔 (X 245: 9.532b3–4) identifies this as the eastern peak to which Hongren moved after Daoxin's demise. The *Platform Sūtra* refers to this location as Eastern Mount Fengmu (*dong fenmaoshan* 東馮茂山; T 2008: 48.337a23; Yampolsky, *Platform Sutra*, 127).

570. Accepting Suzuki's editorial revision of *bu* 不 to *bian* 便.

571. This is from the *Diamond*, T 235: 8.754c9–10. Takeuchi, "Shinshutsu no Kataku Jinne tōmei," 137, points out that this line from the *Diamond* occurs just after the famous line "Generate the non-abiding mind" (754a4) that was later taken as central to Huineng's teachings. Takeuchi suggests, in fact, that the present citation is the first indication of any special focus on this part of the scripture, a focus that later germinated into discussions of the more famous line.

(675)[572] the great master was seventy-four. On the eleventh day of the second month of that year, he died peacefully while sitting. On that day, the mountains fell and the earth moved, and clouds and mists covered the sun and moon. Lüqiu Jun[573] [60] composed the text of his epitaph. The epitaph stands at Huangmei.

69

The sixth generation, Chan Master Huineng of the Tang, came after Great Master Hongren.[574] His lay surname was Lu and his ancestors were from Fanyang. Because his father's official duties took him beyond Lingnan, he resided at Xinzhou.[575] At age twenty-two, he [went to] East Mountain to worship Great Master Hongren. The great master said, "Where are you from, and why do you do obeisance to me? What are you after?" Chan Master Huineng said, "Your disciple has come from Xinzhou[576] in Lingnan on purpose to do obeisance to you. I only seek to achieve buddhahood, and seek nothing else." Great Master Hongren said, "As a barbarian hunter from Lingnan,[577] how can you achieve buddhahood?" Chan Master Huineng said, "What difference is there between the Buddha-nature of this barbarian

---

572. The editors suggest supplying the character *yuan*, to read "first year of Shangyuan" 上元元年, but see Yanagida, *Shoki Zenshū shisho*, 55–56, where all the versions that use the Shangyuan era name specify his death as having occurred in the second year of that era.

573. Lüqiu Jun 閭丘均 (d.u.) was a literatus from Chengdu, Sichuan, who became prominent after Chen Zi'ang's 陳子昂 death in 702. Lüqiu was favored by the Anle Princess, which proved his undoing: he died in banishment after her execution in 710. He left a literary collection in ten (or twenty or thirty) fascicles. Given his period of activity, it seems possible that Hongren's followers in the metropolitan area might have prevailed upon Lüqiu Jun to compose an epitaph, but it seems questionable. The text is mentioned in the *Records of the Transmission* (T 2075: 51.182b5) and *Song Biographies* (T 2061: 50.754b22), but the latter text gives the lie to the claim by pinpointing its composition in the Kaiyuan period (713–742), long after Lüqiu Jun had died.

574. See the translation of this section in Jorgensen, *Inventing Hui-neng*, 135–137.

575. This is the earliest reference to Huineng's surname Lu 盧 and connection with Fanyang 范陽 in Hebei. Lingnan dao 嶺南道 refers to the entire area of Guangdong, Guangxi, and northern Indochina, with its administrative center in Guangdong city; the phrasing here is Lingwai 嶺外, "outside of Ling[nan 南]," written from a central or north China perspective; see Yampolsky, *Platform Sutra*, 126.

576. The original has Xinshan, or "Mount Xin," obviously a scribal error.

577. The Liao 獠 migrated from the Guizhou plateau across the Yangzi from the fourth century onward, and by Shenhui's time they had spread so widely that the term was applied to various non-Han ethnic groups. This usage *geliao* 獦獠, followed by the same account in the *Platform Sūtra*, may be one of the earliest occurrences of the binomial, which appears more frequently from the Song onward. Certainly its use here appears to be a contemptuous racist insult. In a Buddhist context, of course, killing animals engendered bad karmic consequences, and Hongren is suggesting that Huineng could not attain buddhahood because of his bad karma; see von Glahn, *Country of Streams and Grottoes*, 20–21. For a good discussion of the geography and social resonances of Lingnan 嶺南 during the Tang, see Jorgensen, *Inventing Hui-neng*, 494–503.

hunter and Your Reverence's Buddha-nature?" Great Master Hongren considered this retort profoundly unusual and wanted to talk with [Huineng] further, but since there were people nearby he sent him away, assigning him to work with the rest of the community. Thus [Huineng] spent eight months treading the hulling pestle.[578]

When Great Master Hongren sought him out within the community, he saw him [working] on the pestle. Speaking with him, [Hongren] realized that he had truly and comprehensively seen the [Buddha-]nature. That night he secretly called [Huineng] to his room, where they continued talking for three days and nights. [This was when Huineng] comprehensively realized the knowing and seeing of the tathāgatas without any lingering doubt or hindrance. After completing the transmission, [Hongren] said, "You have connections in Lingnan; [61] go there quickly. When the community learns of this, they will certainly [try to] do you harm." Chan Master [Hui]neng said, "Your Reverence, which way should I go?" Great Master [Hong]ren said, "I will see you off." That night they went to Jiujiang station[579] and then took a boat across the [Yangzi] river. The great master saw him across the river and returned that night to his mountain without any of the community members knowing of it.

Three days later, Great Master [Hong]ren announced, "The members of this community should disperse—there is no Buddhadharma here on this mountain. The Buddhadharma has just been transmitted to[580] Lingnan." When the members of the community heard the great master say this, they were greatly shocked, everyone looking around with a blanched face and saying to each other, "Who is in Lingnan? We must go to him to inquire [into the Dharma]." Faru of Luzhou,[581] one of the community members, remembered: "That young Huineng is from there." Then they all chased after him. Within the community was a general of the fourth rank who had resigned his appointment in order to enter the Path. His lay surname was Chen and his given name Huiming.[582] He had studied under the great master

---

578. Huineng was engaged in separating rice grains (previously threshed from the stalks) from their hulls by means of a mortar and foot-driven pestle. He is often depicted thus in later Chinese and Japanese art.

579. This story, about Hongren's secretly seeing Huineng off from Jiujiang station 九江驛 (in Jiangxi province) and returning the same night, was clearly written by someone without basic knowledge of the area. The distance calculator provided by the National Weather Service (http://www.nhc.noaa.gov/gccalc.shtml) estimates the distance from Mount Shuangfeng to Jiujiang as approximately 46 kilometers, much too far for Hongren to have gone and returned in one night. In March 2010 I heard a brief presentation at the Academia Sinica in Nankang, Taiwan, in which a graduate student made this same GIS-based observation. Unfortunately, I lost track of his name and have been unable to identify who should receive the credit.

580. Literally, "flowed to."

581. Faru from Luzhou 潞州 in Shanxi province was Hongren's longest serving disciple; see McRae, *Northern School*, 43–44 and 264–265.

582. This account of Chen Huiming 陳慧明 is expanded in the *Platform Sūtra*, as is the rest of this entire account.

for a long time without being able to achieve enlightenment. After the great master made his announcement,[583] he pursued [Huineng] without cease, traveling day and night so that he could cover twice the distance. He finally caught up with [Huineng] at Dayuling.[584] Huineng had been in hurried flight, afraid for his life, and he offered to Huiming the *kaṣāya* robe he was carrying. Huiming said to Chan Master [Huineng], "Really, I'm not after the *kaṣāya*. When Great Master [Hongren] sent you off, he [must have] instructed you with his teachings. I would like [62] you to explain them to me." Chan Master Huineng then give him a detailed explanation of the correct Dharma.[585] After Chan Master [Hui]ming heard this explanation of the mind-Dharma, he held his palms together and did obeisance [to Huineng]. Then he sent him off across the mountain quickly, because there were so many people chasing him.

Chan Master Huineng crossed the mountain and went to Shaozhou, where he resided at Caoqi, staying there for forty years.[586] Relying on the *Diamond Sūtra*, he made known the knowledge and vision of the tathāgatas once again. Clerics and laypeople gathered around him from all quarters, like clouds and rain. He was like the moon suspended in space, suddenly illuminating the myriad images of [the world of] form. On top of that, he was like the moon on the fifteenth day of the autumn [months], which no sentient being can avoid looking up to see.

In the second year of Jingyun (711), he suddenly ordered his disciples Xuankai and Zhiben[587] to go to his old home on Longshan[588] in Xinzhou and build a stūpa. In the ninth month of the first year of Xiantian (712) [Huineng] went from Caoqi to Xinzhou. On the third day of the eighth month of the second year of Xiantian, he told his followers, "I am going on a great trip." The disciple monk Fahai[589] asked him, "Reverend[590] [Huineng], will there be a succession after you? Why haven't you transmitted the robe?" His Reverence said, "Don't ask me that now. There will be a lot of trouble afterwards. I almost lost my life several times because of this *kaṣāya*. You will

---

583. That is, that the Dharma was no longer in Huangmei.

584. Dayuling 大庾嶺 is a mountain range running northeast-southwest in Guangdong province, dividing Jiangxi from Guangdong.

585. Suzuki has a note that *zhengfa* 正法 may be an error for *xinfa* 心法, "mind-Dharma," probably because of the appearance of *xinfa* in the following line. My translation follows the text as written.

586. This represents the time from just before Hongren's death in 674 to Huineng's death in 713, an accurate calculation but one that does not have Huineng moving anywhere during this period.

587. Although Xuankai 玄楷 is unknown from other sources, Yanagida, *Shoki Zenshū shisho*, 372, notes that Zhiben's 智本 name also occurs in the *Baolin zhuan* 寶林傳.

588. Longshan 龍山 is in Xinxing county, Guangdong province.

589. Fahai 法海 is of course known as the editor of the *Platform Sūtra*.

590. As the editors note, here there occurs an extra character *yue* 曰, "said." Here and just below, Huineng is referred to as *Heshang*, whereas throughout the rest of the text he is called *Chanshi*, "Chan master."

be able to understand this forty or more years after my nirvāṇa, when someone will come to establish the principle [of the Chan teaching]."[591]

That night [Huineng] died peacefully while sitting. The great master was seventy-six. On that day the mountains fell and the earth convulsed, the sun and moon went dark, the wind-[driven] clouds lost their color, and the trees in the forest turned white. Also, there was a strange fragrance everywhere that remained for several days. The Caoqi creek stopped flowing, and the spring lake dried up for three days. That year they welcomed His Reverence's shrine at Guo'en si[592] in Xinzhou, and in the eleventh month he was buried in Caoqi. On that day the hundred birds cried in sorrow, and the beasts and insects all bellowed. In front of the dragon crypt a white light appeared that went straight up to the sky, and only after three days did the top of it begin to disperse. The text of his epitaph was written by the palace aide Wei Ju. In the seventh year of Kaiyuan (719) someone obliterated it and inscribed another text there, but it briefly related the succession of the masters and disciples of the six generations and the transmission of the *kaṣāya*. That epitaph can now be seen at Caoqi.[593]

A follower asked, "I wonder, was it that the Dharma was in the robe,[594] and that's why the robe was used to transmit the Dharma?" The great master said, "Although the Dharma was not in the robe, it was used to demonstrate the succession from generation to generation. The robe was transmitted as a proof [of the Dharma] so that the Buddhadharma will safeguard its transmission, and those who study the Path can know the principle [of the transmission][595] without error or mistake. How much more so, since the golden-threaded *kaṣāya* of the Tathāgata Śākyamuni is now at Cockfoot Mountain. Kāśyapa keeps this *kaṣāya* now[596] solely to await Maitreya's appearance in the world, at which time he will give him the robe to demonstrate that Śākyamuni Tathāgata transmitted it to serve as proof [of Maitreya's succession]. Our six generations of [Chinese] patriarchs were also like this.

> I have now been able to comprehend the Tathāgata-nature;
> Now the Tathāgata is within my very body.

---

591. Once again, this is a reasonably accurate calculation of the time from Huineng's death in 713 to the most famous of Shenhui's debates in 732.

592. The shrine at Guo'en si 國恩寺 is termed a *shenzuo* 神座, literally, a "spirit seat."

593. Thus, the text implies, the contents of palace aide (*dianzhong cheng* 殿中丞) Wei Ju's 韋據 epitaph are unknown. This is in contradiction to assertions that follow. As the editors note, the character *chu* 除, "eliminate," is presumably an error for *xu* 敘, "relate." Hucker (*Official Titles*, 502 #6557–#6566) has several terms using *dianzhong* 殿中 to indicate the palace, but not *dianzhong cheng*. For *cheng* as "aide," see Hucker, *Official Titles*, 125 #457.

594. Literally, "on" (*shang* 上) the robe. Note that a similar section, with Chongyuan as the interlocutor, occurs in the *Definition of the Truth*, section 17.

595. That is, its *zongzhi* 宗旨.

596. Twice here the text uses *xian* (normally *jian*) 見 in the sense of "present." See similar usages in section 64.

There's no difference between me and the Tathāgata;
The Tathāgata is my ocean of suchness!"[597]

70

Verses on the Sudden Enlightenment of the Mahāyāna, with preface

Preface: To enter the *dharmadhātu* is to comprehend the mind; to attain the fundamental source is to see the nature. When the nature is pure, the *dharmakāya* becomes manifest of itself; when the mind is suchlike, enlightenment is abiding in essence. Heaven and earth cannot change its permanence; obscure and bright cannot change its principle. How could ignorance be its good host? Lust, the king of tempters, relies on space to create its causes. The *skandhas* and sensory data labor in creating one's karma. Thereby one[598] is able to benefit things. The wondrous power is unlimited, extending throughout the eighty-four thousand points of the teachings. Opening the thirty-seven essential Dharmas,[599] one can therefore disclose ignorance and enlightenment, providing a guide to the sudden and gradual.[600] When one is enlightened, the afflictions are enlightenment; when deluded, one heads south in a cart facing north.[601] The gradual [path] takes incalculable eons of existing in saṃsāra. The sudden [path] is like ascending to wondrous enlightenment in the time it takes to straighten an elbow.

According to this, far is far off. Who can disseminate it? Our Reverend [Shenhui] [65] of Heze. Innately wise, his virtue is in accord with the Path. His aspiration was in accord with his years, and when he was a young child he wandered about searching for the Path. The great worthies he met at the various mountains, he asked them all about the meaning of nirvāṇa and its fundamental serenity. They all paused and did not answer, thinking him very strange. He went to Lingnan, where he met the Honored One of Caoqi. Before he had finished doing his obeisances he had already become enlightened to the master's words. The basis of non-abiding is achieved through being naturally compassionate.[602] The Honored One followed this according to [the saying], 'Although the gold given was slight, the pearl with which he was rewarded was momentous.'[603] The mind was transmitted when it

---

597. This verse also occurs in the *Definition of the Truth*, section 50, but here it is supposed to be Huineng speaking.

598. The editors suggest that *ren* 人, "person," is an error for the modern homophone 仁, meaning "benevolence."

599. This refers to the thirty-seven constituents of the path (Skt. *bodhyaṅga*).

600. As the editors note, there seems to be something missing from the text here. The translation is therefore tentative.

601. Literally, heading toward the southern state of Chu 楚 in a cart facing north. *Shin jigen*, 988a, defines this according to a *xin yuefu* 新樂府 poem by Bo Juyi 白居易 (772–846).

602. I am following the editors' suggestion to change *de* 德, "virtue," to the modern homophone 得, meaning "get, achieve."

603. I have not been able to trace this saying.

matched a single person; the Dharma was transmitted so that it ascended through six patriarchs.[604] In such a way was the compassionate mind disseminated, drawing deeply of human feeling. Formerly, when nine years old, he generated the great vow, "If I become enlightened I pledge to explain it openly." Now [the teaching] has been handed down, and he has exceeded his former intention. He has revealed the drunkard's pearl and opened the poor woman's storehouse suddenly. The web of doubts has been slashed with wisdom's sword; the ford of ignorance crossed with the raft of insight. Great and profound, the fundamental source—he made all become enlightened to it. Elucidating the four practices[605] to manifest the teaching, he made known the five forbearances to suffuse [sentient beings] with joy. With no hankering for patriarchship,[606] these are his words.[607]

> Though the mind is subject to generation and extinction,
> The Dharma is without going and coming.
> In non-thought, sensory realms and ratiocination are not generated;
> In nondoing, mental activity ceases of itself.
> Either with temporal enlightenment does one extinguish the false,
> Or with inherent enlightenment realizes the true.
> Emancipation is of an instant, [66]
> Transcending one's circulation through the triple realm.
> Even though the elder's son offered a canopy,[608]
> The dragon king's daughter offered the pearl;[609]
> Of the two, this is even faster than that.
> This is what is called transcending to the other shore
> Without disturbing the mind,[610]
> Or realizing nirvāṇa without giving up birth and death.
> To achieve sudden enlightenment—how could it be far off?
> The wonders of the teaching of the Śākya are entirely here.
> Thus did [everyone, including] the crowned officials within the palaces

---

604. The editors suggest reading *deng* as "lamp" 燈 rather than "ascend" 登, but this would destroy the parallelism.

605. Although it could refer to something else, this seems to be a very rare reference to Bodhidharma's "four practices" (*sixing* 四行) from the *Treatise on the Two Entrances and Four Practices*.

606. As a verb *gan* 乾 means "to lust for advantage," and is equivalent to *jian* 奸.

607. The preceding is thus a rather long preface to what follows, which are "verses" only in the same loose sense as Shenhui's *Verses on Sudden Enlightenment, the Birthless, and* Prajñā. There is no break indicated in the edited text.

608. A reference to the *Vimalakīrti*, T 475: 14.537b25–27. After this offering, the Buddha, in an instant, shows the purity of the Saha world.

609. A reference to the *Lotus Sūtra*, T 9.35c12–19. In the famous story about the dragon girl's instantaneous accomplishment of Buddhahood, the dragon girl says that her becoming a buddha is faster than if she were to offer a pearl to the Buddha.

610. The Chinese is *budong yinian* 不動一念, i.e., to not allow one's intellect/mind to move at all.

And the old people within the villages
Attain what they had never attained before, and
Hear what they had never heard before.
I suspect he was the reincarnation of Bodhidharma,
The single manifestation of the udumbara [flower].
His praises arising both far and near, with
Joy and wonder in the Dharma [filling] every street,
The great treasure of the medicine king
Has arrived of itself!
This disciple, blind to enlightenment and slow of learning,
Has happily received the recondite meaning.
Where formerly I ascended by a roundabout route and
Traveled a thousand *li* to go an extremely short distance,
Now I've been given the straight map and
Observe the entire wilderness in the glance of an eye.
I cannot express my feelings with brush and ink;
Even with my life, how could I ever repay this merit?
Forthwith I express myself in [the following] short verse,
Which is but a tiny knoll aiming to heighten
Mounts Peng and Ying.[611]
Even a student such as I
Has attained to this!
Dark, the essence of the Path;
Clear, the nature of the Dharma.
Comprehend the false, and firmly
Cultivate morality and concentration.
How is one to maintain morality?
By perceiving its fundamental nature.
How is one to cultivate concentration?
By purifying oneself in non-thought. [67]
Diligently utilize sagacity,
Only then may the Dharma-sickness be eliminated,
Empty reflections without exhaustion,
And no particle unreflected.
Bright, like the autumn moon,
Brilliant, like the bright mirror.
Not defiled by the six senses,
One ascends to the Eightfold Path.
The Great Path prefers the level [expanse],
While humans prefer the [narrow] byways.
My joy at having encountered this teaching
Has doubled my happiness.

---

611. Mounts Penglai 蓬萊 and Yingzhou 瀛洲 are legendary mountains in the eastern ocean, inhabited by transcendents.

> I bow my head to the ground in humble devotion,
> And extend my reverence with sincere heart.
> The wondrous teaching of sudden enlightenment
> Has achieved its zenith in this.

Finished by command before the end of the eighth year of Zhanyuan (792) of the Tang, by the *śramaṇera* Baozhen, together with the judge Zhao Kanlin, at the Northern Court, at the instruction of Zhang Dafu.[612] Transcribed on the twenty-first day of the tenth month of the winter of that year. [68]

Transcribed by this *bhikṣu* on the twenty-third day of the tenth month of the thirtieth year of the Tang.

---

612. Baozhen 寶珍, Judge Zhao Kanlin 趙看琳, and Zhang Dafu 張大夫, all of Dunhuang, are unidentified.

Verses on the Five Watches
Wugeng chuan
五更傳

Cycle of the Five Watches of the Heze Reverend

First watch—beginning:
Within the city of nirvāṇa, seeing true suchness.
False thoughts have it that this is empty and unreal.[1]
Don't say they exist,[2] don't say they don't.
Neither defiled nor pure,
Transcending space.
Don't intentionalize, and
You'll enter [nirvāṇa] without remainder!
Comprehend the nature, and know you'll be emancipated—
Why bother sitting in meditation and making effort?

Second watch—quickening:
To know the mind is without thought, this is the Tathāgata.
False thoughts have it that this is empty and unreal.
...onto the mountain, not bothering with the steps.
Suddenly seeing the realm [of enlightenment],
The buddhas' gate opens.
The bliss of serene extinction[3]—
This is *bodhi*.
...lamp, eternally and universally illuminates.
Comprehensively seeing the fragrance, not going anywhere.[4]

The title *Verses on the Five Watches* (*Wugeng chuan*) is used for two or three similar compositions that circulated under Shenhui's name, including *Cycle of the Five Watches of the Heze Reverend* [*Shenhui*] (*Heze heshang wugeng chuan* 荷澤[寺]和尚[神會]五更傳) and *Cycle of Five Watches on the Determination of the False and True in the Southern School* (*Nanzong ding xiezheng wugeng chuan* 南宗定邪正五更), in which his ideas are presented in a popular song format. They are interesting primarily for their sociological implications, although they do display one or two points of doctrinal interest.

1. This line could also be read "False thoughts have it that emptiness is non-existent and existence is real" or "false thoughts are empty and not real." The same line is repeated at the corresponding location in the second stanza.

2. Here Yang, *Chanhua lu*, 127, has *wei* 未 instead of the modern homophone 為, which would yield "don't say it's not [yet] extant and don't say it's non-extant." This does not make much sense.

3. That is, nirvāṇa.

4. I am interpreting the third character of *wu qu lai* 無去來 as a colloquial verbal suffix indicating (roughly) completion of action rather than a verb meaning "to go."

Third watch—deepening:
The birthless...seated meditation in the forest.
Inner, outer, and intermediate—there are no locations.
Māra's army defeats itself and does not come to attack.
Don't intentionalize,
Don't freeze the mind.
Reside[5] in autonomy,
Transcend mental seeking.
Prajñā is fundamentally without location.
If you intentionalize, when will you awake to the sound of the Dharma?

Fourth watch—blocked:
...
...together transmitting the unconditioned Dharma.
The fabrications of stupid people are of many[6] kinds.
Don't you see?
It's difficult...difficult.
...manifest,[7]
Fundamental Chan.
If one is enlightened,[8] in an instant one sees.
When ignorant, for eon after eon one peers in the dark.

Fifth watch—opening:
The pure essence comes from the person of no-self.
Black and white are perceived, but one is not defiled.
Such[9] blues and yellows—in serenity they won't be discussed.
Comprehensively see,
Plainly know the true.
In accordance with the formless,
Transcend conditions and causes.
At all times always emancipated.
Companion to the profane, the softened refulgence does not defile the dusts.[10]

---

5. Long, *Lun Dunhuang ciqu*, 1803, reads this character *ren* 任, "depute, rely on," instead of *zhu* 住, "reside, [make] abide."

6. Although Long, 1803, reads the last three characters of this line as *shuoshuoban* 數數般, Yang, 127, has the second character as a lacuna.

7. Long has a one-character lacuna and the characters *duishi* 役示 here, whereas both Hu (*Yiji*, 461) and Yang have all three as a lacuna

8. Long has *wu* 無, "not," where Yang has the modern homophone *wu* 悟, "awake, be enlightened." Obviously, the second alternative is preferable.

9. I am taking *zhemo* 遮莫 as a colloquial demonstrative pronoun, equivalent to the modern *zheme* 這麼.

10. This is of course borrowing a line ultimately from the *Daode jing* 4, which is used in Northern school texts (see McRae, *Northern School*, 183) but not elsewhere in Shenhui's corpus.

Cycle of Five Watches on the Determination of the False and True in the Southern School[11]

First watch—beginning:
False thoughts and suchness do not reside apart.
When deluded, suchness is a false thought.
When enlightened, false thoughts are suchness.
Thoughts not activated,
then it's [nirvāṇa] without remainder.[12]
Seeing the fundamental nature,
You're equivalent to the emptiness of space.[13]
When there are doing and seeking, this is not emancipation.
When there is no doing and no seeking, this is effort.[14]

Second watch—quickening:
The great round precious mirror is placed upon the platform.
Sentient beings do not comprehend, but take ill with groping and grasping.[15]
From this come obstructions, so that the mind does not open up.
If it is fundamentally naturally pure,
Then there is no defiling dust.[16]
If there is no defiling attachment,
Saṃsāra is cut off.
All processes are impermanent—this is generation and extinction.
Just contemplate the true characteristic and see the Tathāgata.

Third watch—deepening:
The wisdom of the Tathāgata is imperceptible and profound.

---

11. This is the second of the verses, as given in S6103 and S2679. The translation here is based on Yanagida, "Goroku no rekishi," 389. In my review of the mss. I have noted several discrepancies with Hu's edition (*Yiji*, 461–463; cf. Long, 1804).

12. This could simply mean "then there's nothing further," but note the allusion to entering [nirvāṇa] without remainder in much the same location in the first cycle above.

13. This last phrase is reminiscent of the *Treatise on Perfect Illumination;* see McRae, *Northern School,* 155, 159, and 167.

14. This seems like a modern use of *gongfu* 功夫, meaning the effort of spiritual or inner athletics.

15. The term here, *panyuan* 攀緣 (Long has it as 攀援), means to "scramble up," as at the side of a hill, hence to grope and grasp. This is a basic feature of ordinary people's dualistic thinking. Yang, 129n3, indicates that the extant manuscripts have either *bing* 病, "illness" (as in Hu, 462), *jing* 境, "[sensory] realm," or *jing* 鏡, "mirror." Although Yang prefers the second alternative, I have remained with the first.

16. This line is absent in the original and has been added by Hu, 462, from another version; the line is included by both Yang and Long. This line is distinctly reminiscent of the *Platform Sūtra*'s mind-verse attributed to Huineng.

Only buddha and buddha are able to see [each other].[17]
The *śrāvakas* and *pratyekabuddhas* don't get it.[18]
Located in mountain caves, residing in Chan monasteries,[19]
They enter into empty meditation[20]
And thereby freeze their minds.
For their entire lives—which might as well be
Eighty thousand eons— they only carry hemp
And never pick up gold.[21]

Fourth watch—blocked:
The essential nature of the *dharmakāya*—don't work to view it.
Viewing fixes the mind, so one intentionalizes.
The result is identical to a mass of false thoughts.
Let the limbs go,
Don't clamp [the body] down.[22]
Deputing [all things to] the fundamental nature,
One is one's own official.[23]

---

17. Following Yang, with *wei fo yu fo* 唯佛與佛, "from buddha to buddha." Long's reading, *wei fo yu fa* 唯佛與法, "only buddhas [can see] the Dharma," is presumably a careless error. Note that the phrase "from buddha to buddha" occurs in Shenhui's stūpa inscription.

18. The compound *zhiyin* 知音, literally to "know the sounds," is to be someone who truly understands another's musical performance, and hence the underlying message. The reference is based on the example of Zhong Ziqi 鍾子期, who understood the depths of Boya's 伯牙 mind from the way he played the zither.

19. The term here is *chanlin* 禪林, which might be rendered simply "monastery" or perhaps "public monastery," many of which were named *chansi* 禪寺.

20. Elsewhere it might be appropriate to translate *kongding* 空定 as "samādhi of emptiness," but the popular context and polemic intent make such a technical rendering inappropriate here.

21. The Chinese literally reads *bu chong jin* 不重金 "not again the gold." Hu, 459, points out that this usage occurs in the seventh sūtra of the *Chang ahan jing* 長阿含經 (roughly equivalent to the *Dīgha nikāya* in Pāli), the *Bisu jing* 弊宿經 (*Pāyāsi Sutta* in Pāli); see T 1: 1.45b1–c1; Walshe, *Thus Have I Heard*, 364–365. The story involves two men, one wise and one foolish, who travel about looking for things of value. First, they each pick up piles of hemp that had been discarded, then hemp thread, then cloth, and so forth through a sequence of commodities up to silver and finally gold. On each occasion the foolish person keeps his load of hemp and the wise one discards what he has in favor of the more valuable commodity, and the reception the two receive upon returning home is understandably different. This story is told by Kāśyapa to a group of Brahmins, with the conclusion that they should discard their worthless ideas and hold to Buddhism.

22. I am rendering *cuanwan* 攢抐, the two characters which mean "to collect" and "to decrease," as a colloquial reference to the practice (probably falsely) attributed to the Northern school of exerting physical and mental control over the body. However, the *Five Skillful Means* does contain characteristically dualistic language that correlates serenity with "unfolding" and illumination with "constriction." Although these seem like references to physical changes, they are in fact different modes of enlightenment; see McRae, *Northern School*, 178 and 336n242.

23. Long, 1804, has *guankan* 觀看, "contemplate/look," instead of *gongguan* 公官, "official." Yang, 130–131, omits this reading, which occurs in S4634 and the two Beijing Library

Not thinking about good and evil—this is no-thought.
No-thought, no-thinking—this is nirvāṇa.

Fifth watch—opening:
Bodhi is without abiding, as well as basis.
In the past you sacrificed your lives without getting that for which you
    sought.
Our teacher has manifested this for all, an unforgettable debt.[24]
Furnishing the medicine of Dharma,
He opens wide the gate,
Eliminating the tissue of impediments,
Floating clouds cleared away,
Opening the Buddha-eye for sentient beings
To see the nature and escape from drowning [in saṃsāra].

---

mss. The usage "official" here is presumably metaphoric, but it seems like nothing else in the Shenhui corpus.

24. Long, 1804, has *pu sui* 普遂, "universally accomplish" (meaning that Shenhui had realized a simple path available to all), but Yang, 128, has *pu shi* 普示, "universally manifest," with no note. As indicated by Yang, the character *wang* 忘, "forget," was changed by Hu from the original *wang* 望, "wish." The word *en* 恩 refers to moral obligation, but it may also be a euphemism for monetary payment, yielding something like "our teacher's done this for everyone—don't forget to pay him!" See a similar joke in the *Essentials of Cultivating the Mind* (see McRae, *Northern School,* 22).

Verses on Sudden Enlightenment, the Birthless, and *Prajñā*
Dunwu wusheng bore song
頓悟無生般若頌

Non-thought is the true emptiness of things as they truly are,[1]
The knowing and seeing[2] of the birthless *prajñā*.
Illuminating the true and attaining the profane,
In true emptiness principle and phenomena are equally suchlike.
This is the essence of the teaching.[3]

Suchness is without thought, so it is not knowable by thoughts and ideas.
The true characteristic is birthless, so how could one, generating mind, be able to see it?[4]
The thought in non-thought thinks of *dhāraṇī*.[5]
The birth in birthless gives birth to the true characteristic.
Non-abiding yet abiding, one abides permanently in nirvāṇa.
Non-practicing yet practicing, one transcends[6] to the other shore.
Suchlike and unmoving, the function of movement is never exhausted.
Thought after thought without seeking, one seeks the constant non-thought.
Bodhi is without attainment, yet one [attains] the Buddha's Dharma body.
Prajñā is without knowing,[7] yet one knows all the Dharmas.
Concentration is wisdom, and wisdom is birthless.
The birthless is the true emptiness of the true characteristic;

A relatively polished essay containing the gist of the *Definition of the Truth*, this text was apparently written sometime after 745. An excerpt titled *Treatise on the Manifestation of the Teaching* (*Xianzong lun* 顯宗論) appeared in the *Zongjing lu* 宗鏡錄, and a later, slightly different version of the text can be found in the *Transmission of the Lamp* under the title *Record of the Manifestation of the Teaching of Great Master [Shenhui] of Heze [Temple]* (*Heze dashi xianzong ji* 荷澤大師顯宗記). That version is included below.

1. In this translation, "true emptiness" renders *zhenkong* 真空, while "things as they truly are" or "true characteristic" renders *shixiang* 實相.
2. *Zhijian* 知見.
3. The Chinese is *zongben* 宗本.
4. While the Dunhuang text has *sheng* 生, "birth," Yang, *Chanhua lu*, 51n1, suggests that the *Transmission of the Lamp*'s *se* 色, "form," is better. I prefer to stay with the original.
5. *Zongchi* 總持.
6. The character used here is *chao* 超.
7. This invokes the title of one of Sengzhao's 僧肇 famous essays.

Nonpractice pervades the Dharma realm.
The six perfections are henceforth perfect and complete,
The [thirty-seven] factors of enlightenment are herewith flawless.
Self and dharmas are both empty, existence and nonexistence are both eradicated.
Neither arriving nor reaching, neither going nor coming,
In essence one is enlightened to the three wisdoms,[8] the mind penetrates the eight emancipations.[9]
One's accomplishments encompass the ten strengths,[10] one's blessings include the seven treasures,[11]
One enters the teaching of nonduality relying on the principle of the One Vehicle.[12]
Peaceful and always serene, there is no limitation to its responsive functioning.
Functioning yet always empty, empty yet always functioning,
Functioning while[13] not existent, it is true emptiness;
Empty yet not nonexistent, it is wondrous existence.
[Wondrous existence,] therefore great *prajñā;*
True emptiness is pure nirvāṇa.

---

8. *Bukkyōgo daijiten,* 491b, explains the *san ming* 三明, "three wisdoms," as three extraordinary abilities achieved by practitioners: knowledge of past lives, knowledge of future eventualities, and the cessation of defilements.

9. *Bukkyōgo daijiten,* 1102b–c, defines the *ba jie* 八解, "eight emancipations," as either the eight types of *dhyāna,* referred to in this fashion because they lead to emancipation, or the following set of eight: (1) elimination of desire with regard to objects; (2) mental concentration on a single object; (3) maintenance of the mind in equanimity, unaffected by external realms; (4) maintenance of both body and mind in a realm of purity; (5) single-minded concentration on limitless space, eliminating the differentiations of external realms; (6) achievement of unlimited realms of mental and physical abilities; (7) attainment of the fundamental source transcending space and mind; and (8) realization of a level in which the fundamental source is always manifest.

10. *Bukkyōgo daijiten,* 661c–662a, defines the *shi li* 十力, "ten strengths," as ten special types of wisdom possessed by a buddha. These are (1) understanding the difference between what makes sense and what does not; (2) knowing the relationship between specific actions and their karmic results; (3) knowing the various types of meditation; (4) knowing the varying capabilities of sentient beings; (5) knowing the various desires of sentient beings; (6) knowing the fundamental natures of both sentient beings and dharmas; (7) knowing the locations of individuals in the different modes of existence after their deaths; (8) recollecting events from past lives of oneself and others; (9) knowing where sentient beings will die and where they will be reborn; and (10) eliminating afflictions and knowing the methods for doing so.

11. The Dunhuang ms. has seven *cai* 財, "wealths"; Yang, 51n3, indicates the *Transmission of the Lamp* text has *zhen* 珍. *Bukkyōgo daijiten,* 585d, defines *qi zhen* 七珍 as equivalent to the *qi bao* 七寶, "seven treasures," and as referring in particular to the seven treasures of the *cakravartin,* also pointing out, on 587c–d, that there are several variations in the list of seven treasures, which are most often thought of as seven types of jewels and precious substances: gold, silver, lapis lazuli, crystal, emerald, red pearls, and coral.

12. The two doctrines mentioned here are most closely associated with the *Vimalakīrti* and *Lotus Sūtras.*

13. This is where Stein 296, i.e., S5619, leaves off and S468 begins.

Prajñā is the brilliance that penetrates the subtle mystery.
The true characteristic is the realm comprehending suchness.
Prajñā is without illumination, yet able to illuminate nirvāṇa,[14]
Nirvāṇa is the birthless, yet able to give birth to *prajñā*.
Nirvāṇa and *prajñā*—their names[15] differ but in essence they are identical,
The names posited according to meanings while the Dharma is without fixed characteristics.
Nirvāṇa is able to see *prajñā*, and incorporates Buddha, Dharma, and Saṅgha.[16]
Prajñā illuminates nirvāṇa perfectly, and is called the knowing and seeing of the Tathāgata.
Knowing is to know the constant empty quiescence,
Seeing is to directly see the birthless.
Knowing and seeing are clear and distinct, neither one nor different,
Activity and serenity are both wondrous, principle and phenomena entirely suchlike.
When principle is pure, one is situated in phenomena and able to penetrate,
Penetrating phenomena, the principle is penetrated without hindrance.
The six senses undefiled—this is the accomplishment of meditation and wisdom,
Ideas and thoughts unborn, the essence of suchness is pure.
When awareness[17] is extinguished, the mind is empty.
In the correspondence of a single moment's thought is the sudden leap from ordinary person to sage.
Nonexistence cannot be nonexistence, and existence cannot be existence.
In walking, standing still, sitting, and lying down, the mind is unmoving.
In all the periods of time, one is empty and without attainment.

The buddhas of the three periods of time teach that all is suchlike.[18]
The bodhisattvas in their great compassion transmit it one after the other.
Arriving at Bodhidharma, who came as the first [patriarch], it has been transmitted through the generations, unbroken until the present.
That which is transmitted is the secret teaching, its point being the recognition of the [right] person;

---

14. In place of the previous three lines, the *Transmission of the Lamp* text has the following two lines of seven characters and one of eight: "*Prajñā* is the cause of nirvāṇa; nirvāṇa is the result of *prajñā*. *Prajñā* is without seeing, yet is able to see nirvāṇa."

15. As Yang notes, the Dunhuang text has *wo* 我, "self," here, but the *Transmission of the Lamp*'s *ming* 名 is clearly preferable.

16. Although Yang prefers the *Transmission of the Lamp* version over this, his interlinear note on p. 50 indicates some hesitation, and I prefer to stay with the original. The *Transmission of the Lamp* reads: "and it incorporates the Buddha's *dharmakāya*."

17. Here *jue* 覺 is best rendered as "awareness" rather than "realization" or "enlightenment."

18. The original has *ruru* 如如, which Yang, 51, needlessly changes to *ru si* 如斯 to match the *Transmission of the Lamp* version.

As with the king's crowning pearl, it is never wrongly bestowed.
Adorned in two ways, with blessings and wisdom, and the correspondence of understanding and practice: only then will it be established.
The robe is the proof of the Dharma; the Dharma is the teaching of the robe.[19]
Only the robe and Dharma are transmitted, nothing else is bestowed.[20]
Without the robe, the Dharma would not be transmitted; without the Dharma, the robe would not be received.
The robe is the robe proving the Dharma; the Dharma is the Dharma of the birthless.
The birthless is to be without falsity—this is the mind of serene emptiness.[21]
To know serene emptiness is to comprehend the Dharma body—such is true emancipation.[22]

[End of the] Verses on Sudden Enlightenment, the Birthless, and *Prajñā*, in one fascicle

Addendum

Record of the Manifestation of the Teaching of Great Master [Shenhui] of Heze [Temple]

Heze dashi xianzong ji

荷澤大師顯宗記[23]

Non-thought is the doctrine, and non-action is the fundamental.
True emptiness is the essence, and wondrous existence is the function.
Suchness is without thought, so it is not knowable by thoughts and ideas.
The true characteristic is birthless, so how could it be seen as form or mind?

---

19. The terms used here are *faxin* 法信 and *yizong* 衣宗. Yang's edition (p. 51) indicates that the first occurrence of *faxin* is actually given in the Dunhuang text as *fayan* 法言, "Dharma words," which I am taking to be a scribal error. (This is one case in which Yang might profitably have altered the text by adopting the *Transmission of the Lamp* version.)

20. Yang, 51, points out that the *Transmission of the Lamp* version has *fa* 法, "Dharma," here instead of *fu* 付, "bestow."

21. As noted by Yang, 51n8, Hu Shih (*Yiji*, 195) changed the character *xin* 心, "mind," in the original to *shen* 身, "body." I agree with Yang that this is an unwarranted editorial intrusion.

22. Yang, 51 and 52n8, following the *Transmission of the Lamp* version, repeats a phrase in this line: "To know serene emptiness is to comprehend the Dharma body, and to comprehend the Dharma body is true emancipation."

23. This version of the *Verses on Sudden Enlightenment, the Birthless, and* Prajñā made its way into the Song dynasty *Transmission of the Lamp*, compiled some two and a half centuries after the original composition.

The thought in non-thought thinks of suchness,
The birth in birthless gives birth to the true characteristic.[24]
Non-abiding yet abiding, one abides permanently in nirvāṇa.
Nonpracticing yet practicing, one transcends to the other shore.
Suchlike and unmoving, the function of movement is never exhausted.
Thought after thought without seeking, one seeks the fundamental non-thought.
Bodhi is without attainment, yet [by it] one purifies the five eyes and comprehends the three bodies.
Prajñā is without knowing, yet one actuates the six supernormal penetrations and promulgates the four wisdoms.[25]
Know this: concentration is without concentration, sagacity is without sagacity, and practice is without practice.
The nature is equivalent to space, and the essence is identical to the *dharmadhātu*.
The six perfections are henceforth perfect and complete, and the [thirty-seven] factors of enlightenment are herewith flawless.
Know this: Both self and dharmas are in essence empty, and existence and non-existence are both eradicated.
The mind is fundamentally non-active, and the Path is always without thought.
Without thought and without thinking, there is nothing sought after that is not attained.
Neither that nor this, neither going nor coming.
In essence one is enlightened to the three wisdoms, the mind penetrates the eight emancipations.
One's accomplishments encompass the ten strengths, one's blessings include the seven treasures.
One enters the teaching of nonduality relying on the principle of the One Vehicle.
Wonder among wonders, this is the wondrous Dharma body.
Heaven among heavens, this is the adamantine sagacity.
Peaceful and always serene, there is no limitation to its responsive functioning.
Functioning yet always empty, empty yet always functioning.
Functioning while not existent, it is true emptiness;
Empty yet not 'nonexistent,' it is wondrous existence.
Wondrous existence, therefore great *prajñā*;
True emptiness is pure nirvāṇa.

---

24. An alternative rendering of these last two lines: "What one thinks of in non-thought is suchness; what one births in the birthless is the true characteristic."—Ed.

25. *Bukkyōgo daijiten*, 527c–d, gives three different lists of four wisdoms. The most likely referent here is that consisting of wisdom of the Dharma (or dharmas), undefiled wisdom of the form and formless realms, understanding the minds of others, and the wisdom of ordinary people.

Prajñā is the cause of nirvāṇa; nirvāṇa is the result of *prajñā*.
Prajñā is without seeing, yet is able to see nirvāṇa.[26]
Nirvāṇa is the birthless, yet it can give birth to *prajñā*.
Nirvāṇa and *prajñā*—their names differ but in essence they are identical.
The names are posited according to meanings, while the Dharma is without fixed characteristics.
Nirvāṇa is able to give birth to *prajñā*, and so it is named the Dharma body of the true Buddha.
Prajñā is able to establish[27] nirvāṇa, and it is called the knowing and seeing of the Tathāgata.
Knowing is to know the mind's serene emptiness.
Seeing is to see the birthlessness of the nature.
Knowing and seeing are clear and distinct, neither one nor different,
Activity and serenity are both wondrous, principle and phenomena entirely suchlike.
This is for one to be accomplished in all locations.
This is for principle and phenomena to be without hindrance.
The six senses undefiled—this is the accomplishment of meditation and sagacity.
The six consciousnesses are not born: this is the power of suchness.
The mind ceases in accordance with its realms; when the realms are extinguished the mind is empty.
Mind and realms are both eliminated, essence and function are not different.
True suchness is pure in nature; the mirror of sagacity is without limit.
Just as water can distinguish a thousand moons, so can one see, hear, be aware, and know.
Seeing, hearing, being aware, and knowing—yet the constantly serene emptiness.
Emptiness is without characteristics, serenity is without birth.
One is not cloven to by good and evil, one is not controlled by quiet and disturbance.
One does not detest saṃsāra; one does not enjoy nirvāṇa.
Nonexistence cannot make [things be] nonexistent, existence cannot make [things be] existent.
In walking, standing still, sitting, and lying down, the mind is unmoving.
In all the periods of time, one attains that which is without attainment.

The buddhas of the three periods of time all teach like this.
The bodhisattvas in their compassion transmit it one after the other.

---

26. In this line the construction *neng jian* 能見, "able to see," could also be considered as one member of a subject/object (*neng suo* 能所) opposition; hence "it is *prajñā* which sees nirvāṇa."

27. The word used is *jian* 建, which is somewhat unusual.

From the parinirvāṇa of the World-honored One, the twenty-eight patriarchs of India
Have all transmitted the mind of non-abiding, and they have all preached the Tathāgata's knowing and seeing.
Arriving at Bodhidharma, who came as the first [patriarch], it has been transmitted through the generations, unbroken until the present.
That which is transmitted is the secret teaching, which must be bestowed on the [right] person.
As with the king's crowning pearl, it is never wrongly bestowed.
Adorned in two ways, with blessings and wisdom, and the correspondence of understanding and practice: only then will it be established.

The robe is the proof of the Dharma; the Dharma is the teaching of the robe.
Only the robe and Dharma are transmitted; there is no other Dharma.
Internally, they transmit the mind-seal, which seals and matches the fundamental mind.[28]
Externally, they transmit the robe, in order to demonstrate[29] the teaching.
Without the robe, the Dharma would not be transmitted; without the Dharma, the robe would not be received.
The robe is the robe proving the Dharma; the Dharma is the Dharma of the birthless.
The birthless is to be without falsity—this is the mind of serene emptiness.
To know serene emptiness is to comprehend the Dharma body, and to comprehend the Dharma body is true emancipation.

---

28. The Chinese is *nei chuan xin yin, yinqi benxin* 內傳心印，印契本心. The second phrase could be rendered "the seal matches the fundamental mind."

29. In this case the term *biao* 表 means to manifest or demonstrate externally.

PART II

Shenhui and the Chan Tradition

Religion as Revolution
Hu Shih on Shenhui's Role in Chan

The widely shared understanding of the role of Buddhism in Chinese history harbors profound and substantial errors deriving from the work of Hu Shih 胡適 (1891–1962) on the monk Shenhui 神會 (684–758). Although Hu's research on Shenhui was crucially important to the study of the Chan or Zen tradition as that field developed over the twentieth century, its influence and even its importance within the context of Hu's overall agenda seems to be largely unrecognized by scholars of Chinese history in general. After introducing these contributions and analyzing Hu's misperception of Shenhui, I will undertake a very partial survey of the legacy of his ideas and then comment on the significance of these findings for the broader understanding of Buddhism in Chinese history, returning finally for a brief statement of my own re-evaluation of Shenhui's religious persona and historical role.

I. The Discovery of Shenhui as a Great Historical Figure

During the early years of this century, Shenhui was not considered a very important figure at all. Comprehensive histories of the Chan/Zen tradition by Chisan Kohō 智璨孤峰 and Nukariya Kaiten 忽滑谷快天, for example, do not pay him much attention, and D. T. Suzuki's *Essays in Zen Buddhism* (First Series) does not even mention him.[1] This evident lack of interest is actually quite reasonable, because Shenhui is not, in fact, a very prominent figure within the traditional annals of the Chinese Chan school. He appears only as a minor figure in the *Platform Sūtra,* one of the most enduring works of early Chinese Chan Buddhism. His name does not occur within any of the most famous "public cases" or precedents circulated during the peak of Chan activity during the Song dynasty, nor is the full scope of his historical role immediately apparent in the *Transmission of the Lamp* (*Jingde chuandeng lu* 景德傳燈錄), the most important "transmission" text of the orthodox tradition. Although his teacher Huineng 慧能 (638–713) was the legendary sixth patriarch of Chan, Shenhui's own lineage ended after only five generations and is not considered to have been the mainstream of that ortho-

---

This essay was first published as "Religion as Revolution in Chinese Historiography: Hu Shih (1891–1962) on Shen-hui (684–758)" in *Cahiers d'Extême-Asie* 12 (2001): 59–102.

  1. Nukariya's contribution is titled *Zengaku shisoshi* (1923). Suzuki's *Essays* was first published in London by Rider in 1949, but it includes a 1923 preface by the author.

dox tradition. Finally, even when references to his ideas occur in important texts such as the *Essential Teaching of Sudden Enlightenment* (*Dunwu yao men* 頓悟要門) and the *Records of Linji* (*Linji lu* 臨濟錄), Shenhui's name is left unmentioned.

Shenhui's discovery as a figure of great historical significance was effected by the Chinese intellectual and political figure Hu Shih, who is famous for his participation in the May Fourth movement as well as for his application of Western research methods to the study of Chinese thought and culture. After writing a ground-breaking dissertation at Columbia University on the patterns of thought shared by the ancient philosophers, Hu made plans to carry his project on through the medieval period as well. In the context of this larger agenda, he decided to write a history of the Chan school, which intrigued him as a native response to the introduction of Buddhism. It was at this juncture that he became puzzled by the example of Shenhui. As Hu himself describes it:

> In 1924, when I was trying to write the draft of a history of Chinese Chan, I developed extreme doubts when I came to Huineng; when I reached Shenhui I became unable to write. When I discovered the notice of Shenhui's attack on the Northern school in the *Song Biographies* (*Song gaoseng zhuan* 宋高僧傳) and that of Shenhui's imperial recognition as seventh patriarch, in 796, in Zongmi's 宗密 works, I decided that I must seek for historical data relating to Shenhui....
>
> Only where can we search for Tang dynasty primary source material? At the time I devised a plan to go look among the manuscripts from Dunhuang. The Dunhuang manuscripts date from the North and South dynasties to the beginning of the Song, from 500 to 1000 CE—exactly the period I was interested in. Even more, during the Tang dynasty Dunhuang was by no means the out-of-the-way place [that it is today]. The writings of the great masters of the Chan school from the two capitals (i.e., Chang'an and Luoyang) and all other locations must have circulated there.
>
> Fortunately, in 1926 I had an opportunity to travel to Europe, so I took a few reference materials with me in preparation for visits to the Dunhuang collections in London and Paris. In mid-September I discovered three versions of Shenhui's recorded sayings in Paris, and in November I discovered his *Xianzong ji* 顯宗記 (Record of the Manifestation of the Truth), also found in fascicle 30 of the *Transmission of the Lamp* (*Jingde chuandeng lu* 景德傳燈錄) in London. There was a small quantity of extremely valuable Chan school source materials in addition to this. That my working hypothesis would unexpectedly yield such an incredible result had been completely beyond my greatest expectations before leaving China.[2]

---

2. Hu Shih, *Shenhui heshang yiji*, 1–3. Hu Shih's biographical account of Shenhui, first published in 1930, was included in the *Yiji*, published in 1966; all citations in this book refer to the second edition (1968), which includes copious handwritten annotation by Hu repro-

Chinese Chan texts from Dunhuang had already been displayed in public in Japan by Yabuki Keiki 矢吹慶輝, so Hu's inspiration to search among the Paris and London collections was not entirely without precedent. Nevertheless, the prescience of his search for Shenhui's texts, as well as Hu's discovery and subsequent publication of them, along with a detailed study of Shenhui's biography, was a major stimulus in the emergence of an international field of Chan and Zen studies.[3] On his way back from Europe to China he stopped in Japan, where he met with Japanese scholars, apparently with the expectation that they would include his editions of Shenhui's texts in the edition of the Buddhist canon then being published (the *Taishō shinshū daizōkyō*). Although the texts Hu Shih discovered were not immediately published in the *Taishō* canon (they were eventually to appear in volume 85, complete with Hu Shih's emendations in red and green ink), his work on Shenhui was the catalyst for the discovery of similar material in both Beijing and Japan.[4]

The discovery of new Chan texts from within the Dunhuang collections was a pivotal event that quite literally made possible the enterprise of Chan studies as it was practiced for the balance of the twentieth century. Many more spectacular manuscripts relevant to Chan but long since lost both to scholarship and the living tradition were found in the ensuing decades, allowing us to examine the origins and early development of Chinese Buddhism in a manner never before possible. But almost as important for the course of modern Chan studies was the manner in which Hu Shih depicted Shenhui. The following passages effectively summarize Hu's understanding of his subject:

> Shenhui was the seventh patriarch of the Southern school, the commander-in-chief of the Southern school's northern assault, the founder of a new type of Chan, and the creator of the *Platform Sūtra*. There is no one else in

---

duced in black, red, and green. The second edition contains what at the time were complete versions of all Shenhui's known works, edited by Hu in part on the basis of newly discovered manuscripts received through the efforts of Suzuki and Gernet.

3. Yanagida Seizan, "Goroku no rekishi," 365, points out that, since none of the texts Hu discovered in the Paris and London collections included their opening sections and titles, it was perspicacious of him to have recognized them as Shenhui's writings.

4. In a letter written to Iriya Yoshitaka on May 30, 1959, Hu stated that he finished his *Shenhui heshang yiji* quickly so that it could be included in the *Taishō*. Although admitting that it probably arrived in Japan after the deadline, he also criticized the conservative attitude of Japanese scholars, particularly D. T. Suzuki and Ui Hakuju, for not accepting Shenhui's role as the sole founder of the Southern school. See *Hu Shih shougao* 8b, 442–443, or Yanagida Seizan, *Ko Teki zengaku an*, 561–562. (The *Zengaku an* reproduces all of Hu Shih's published writings on Chan Buddhism except for most of the material in the *Yiji*. It also contains a useful chronological table listing Hu Shih's contributions to Chan studies and an explanatory article by Professor Yanagida.) This passage from Hu's letter is mentioned in Yamaguchi Sakae, "Ko Teki no Chūgoku Zenshūshi." The same issue is also mentioned in Yanagida Seizan, "Ko Teki hakase to Chūgoku shoki Zenshūshi no kenkyū," 31. The discoveries made in the wake of Hu Shih's efforts include Suzuki's editions of the recorded sayings of Shenhui and the Kōshōji text of the *Platform Sūtra*.

the history of Chinese Buddhism who had an impact exceeding his in magnitude or profundity.[5]

We can imagine [Shenhui as] a white-eyebrowed old monk sitting on top of the "lion's seat" on a decorated platform and yelling out in a loud voice his attack... [which was] the harbinger of the destruction of the Northern school and simultaneously of a great revolution in the history of Chinese Buddhism.[6]

The weapon of this revolution was "sudden enlightenment."... **We must realize that the battle between sudden and gradual is a life-and-death matter for all religions, for when the theory of sudden enlightenment appeared all ritual, worship, repentance, scriptural recitation, contemplation of the Buddha, temples, images, monks, and Vinaya became completely worthless.**... The theory of sudden enlightenment was a seed sown by Daosheng 道生 [and, it is implied, nurtured by Shenhui] that would eventually unite all of Chinese Buddhism as the Sudden school.[7]

How utterly peculiar is Hu Shih's image of this Chinese Buddhist monk! His language abounds in martial terminology, with words such as commander-in-chief, northern assault, destruction, weapon, and battle peppered throughout these critical passages. Although I have chosen these passages for their concision and impact, they are representative of Hu Shih's approach to Shenhui. Through his research, the image of Shenhui as a militant, even rabidly aggressive, innovator and exponent of a new and widely influential teaching has come to dominate modern historical writing on Chan Buddhism.

The extraordinary claims to Shenhui's significance made in these passages are not based on any casual extravagance of language. On the contrary, Hu Shih made Shenhui the very key to his understanding of Chan Buddhism and the medieval transformation of Chinese culture, and he projected onto Shenhui all his aspirations for the independent re-evaluation of Chinese civilization. The full implications of his depiction of Shenhui can only be understood within the context of his broader historical theory of the "Chinese Renaissance" that began in the Tang and took hold during the Song, when China was able to divest itself of intellectual and religious domination by India and revert to the simple, humanistic rationalism of the native Chinese

---

5. This passage is from the preface (3–4) to the second edition (1968) of Hu Shih's *Yiji*, the one cited throughout this study. As Yanagida, "Goroku no rekishi," 365–366, points out, this second volume was the culmination of a second period of international scholarship on Shenhui and included the results of Hu's preceding thirty years of study. In evaluating the specific set of statements quoted here, Yanagida, "Goroku no rekishi," 358, retains as still valid only that Shenhui was founder of a new type of Chan.

6. "Heze dashi Shenhui zhuan" 荷澤大師神會禪師傳, *Yiji*, 22, or *Zengaku an*, 108.

7. *Yiji*, 39–40, or *Zengaku an*, 116–117; emphasis in original. The emphasis is from Hu's second edition, as in the *Yiji*. The last sentence actually refers to Daosheng's doctrine of sudden enlightenment, but Hu Shih believed in a continuity from Daosheng to Shenhui.

tradition.[8] Hu Shih ascribed to Shenhui a pivotal role in this process, for it was his espousal of sudden enlightenment during the eighth century that instigated the resurgence of native Chinese culture during the eleventh and twelfth.[9] Therefore, not only is Hu Shih's work important to our understanding of Chan, but the full implications of his theory of the Chinese Renaissance are elusive without an appreciation of his interpretation of Shenhui. I will discuss these broader issues in the conclusion; at this point let me restrict myself to Hu Shih's impact on the understanding of Chan.

Hu Shih possessed a considerable intellectual stature, and his use of historical methods was significantly more rigorous than that of his predecessors. As a result, his flamboyant depiction of Shenhui, his description of Shenhui in heroic military terms, and his lionization of Shenhui within the grandiose sweep of Chinese history represent the cornerstones upon which much of modern Chan studies has been constructed over the last few decades. The great Ui Hakuju was very critical of Shenhui's disrespect for his one-time teacher Shenxiu 神秀, but his image of Shenhui is otherwise much the same as Hu Shih's.[10] Even D. T. Suzuki, who engaged Hu Shih in a very spirited public debate on the nature of Chinese Chan, never voiced any basic disagreement about Shenhui's role.[11] Indeed, although Suzuki was highly critical of Hu Shih's interest in historical context, the dramatic flair of Hu's interpretation of Shenhui was no doubt stimulating to Suzuki and his fellow Chan scholars; other authors may avoid Hu Shih's vivid imagery and martial jargon, but the notion of Shenhui as the dogged and somewhat roguish protagonist in a long factional struggle remains dominant even today.[12]

---

8. Hu's best-known work on this subject is *The Chinese Renaissance*. The version of Hu's theory I will be dealing with here is developed most clearly in his "Religion and Philosophy in Chinese History," and "The Indianization of China: A Case Study in Cultural Borrowing." Lin Yusheng suggests that "The Indianization of China" was written in a mood of cultural nationalism, when Hu Shih tended to see the intrinsic cruelty of the Chinese people in terms of the influence of Indian Buddhism. See Lin's chapter on "The Pseudoreformism of Hu Shih" in his book *The Crisis of Chinese Consciousness*, 99.

9. It is curious that Hu would have lionized a figure so obviously roguish as Shenhui (Hu clearly recognized that Shenhui was prone to exaggerations and misstatements of the truth) and an idea so allegedly radical as that of sudden enlightenment. Jerome B. Grieder's excellent *Hu Shih and the Chinese Renaissance*, 127, describes Hu's early (ca. 1919) political philosophy as "gradualism: slow, undramatic, promising no startling results, yet for all its slowness an optimistic creed."

10. See Ui Hakuju, *Zenshūshi kenkyū*, 2:226–229. Yamazaki Hiroshi's "Kataku Jinne zenji," 205–208, reviews the differences between Hu's and Ui's interpretations.

11. See Hu's "Ch'an (Zen) Buddhism in China" and Suzuki's rejoinder, "Zen: A Reply to Hu Shih." In many ways, the mutual criticisms of Hu and Suzuki seem always to miss their targets, and the two men seem to have exposed rather than debated their basic differences.

12. Yamaguchi notes that Hu Shih never attempted to sanctify Shenhui in the manner of a traditional scholar of religion, i.e., he never lost sight of the roguish side of Shenhui's character. See Yamaguchi's "Ko Teki," 67 (using the more precise page numbers of the original publication), quoting Hu Shih's *Yiji*, 424–425.

II. Shenhui and the Transformation of Chan

The factional struggle in which Shenhui was involved, of course, was on behalf of his own teacher Huineng's (638–713) Southern school and in opposition to the so-called Northern school of the disciples of Shenxiu (606?-706). In a book devoted to the Northern school and the formation of early Chan, I found that the supposed "struggle" was a one-sided affair: not only did the figures associated with the Northern school fail to leave any record of arguing in opposition to Shenhui's ideas, they were never organized in such a way as to constitute an entity so cohesive as implied by the term "school."[13] Nevertheless, the notion of some doctrinal turning point, some critical change in the history of Chan that was effected by Shenhui's career, still weighs very heavily within modern writings on the early development of the school as a whole.

If the notion of the Northern and Southern schools as basic divisions in Chan is now defunct (and unfortunately not everyone would agree that it is), the natural tendency is simply to displace the disconformity by a few generations and locate it between the "early" and "classical" periods. At least, this has been my own tendency. Based in large part on the work of Yanagida Seizan, I have tended to see these two periods as fundamentally different and distinguished by the absence or presence of "encounter dialogue": Where early Chan texts contain a wide variety of doctrinal formulations, practical exhortations, and ritual procedures, the texts of classical Chan are more uniform in their dedication to the transcription of encounter dialogue incidents, and they delight in baffling paradoxes, patent absurdities, and instructive vignettes of nonconformist behavior. Where early Chan texts attempt to infuse new meanings and a new spirit of dedication into conventional Buddhist doctrines and practices, classical Chan texts reject or simply ignore traditional activities completely. And where early Chan texts are alternately charming, informative, and baffling in their varied attempts to enunciate the new message, classical Chan texts derive their power from vivid portrayals of specific living masters and students grappling with real spiritual problems.[14]

Although this may be a fair description of the difference between the images of early and classical Chan as presented in the literature, it is now apparent that there is a very serious problem with taking the image of classical Chan as it has been transmitted to us as a valid representation of how

---

13. See McRae, *Northern School,* 241 and 244. Of course, in at least one case a lay patron of the Northern school seems to have intentionally ignored Shenhui's campaign; see the epitaph written for the third patriarch Sengcan 僧璨 by Dugu Ji 獨孤皮 well after Shenhui's death, as discussed in Yang Hongfei, "Hatsugen sareta Zenshūshi no issetsu," 350–353. The text in question occurs in several locations, most conveniently *Fozu lidai tongzai,* 佛祖歷代通載, T 2036: 49.603.

14. The bulk of this paragraph is drawn from my essay "Shenhui and the Teaching of Sudden Enlightenment."

Chan was actually practiced during the years that would correspond to the classical period. I still prefer to identify the famous patriarchs of the Tang—Mazu 馬祖, Shitou 石頭, and their several generations of successors—as belonging to a classical phase of Chan. However, this is not to say that the historical figures Mazu, etc., actually behaved in the charmingly iconoclastic fashion described in orthodox Chan literature. I have been engaged in analyzing the sources available regarding Mazu and his successors for the past several years and, in part through the wise counsel and firm prodding of my colleagues,[15] have come to believe that the famous stories involving the classical Chan masters are not journalistically accurate accounts of actual words and events, but rather retrospective recreations of how those masters must have acted, composed essentially out of whole cloth by later generations. Those stories still represent a classical image, in the sense that it is the theoretical model which Chan practice of the tenth century onward attempted to emulate. The stories might also be said to represent a "golden age" of Chan, in the sense of an idealistically remembered past. But we would do well to remember, as recent writings have emphasized, that the Song dynasty was unquestionably the peak of Chan activity in China and thus better qualifies for the appellation "golden age."[16] The classical period associated with the ninth century is not an age which ever happened, and certainly not immediately after the "early Chan" of the eighth century.

III. The Impact of Hu Shih's Research on the History of Chinese Thought

A. His Contributions to Chan Studies

Near the beginning of this paper, I described Hu Shih's discovery of texts by Shenhui among the treasures from Dunhuang. The study of Shenhui's writings, biography, and contribution to the transformation of Chinese Chan Buddhism was the primary focus of Hu Shih's work in this field. His understanding of Chan was the lynchpin of his overall interpretation of Chinese intellectual history, an interpretation which has had a major, perhaps even determining, impact on the modern historiography of Chinese Buddhism. At this point, after presenting a thorough reinterpretation of Shenhui's personality, ideas, and significance, and before considering the implications of that reinterpretation, it is time to reevaluate Hu Shih's analysis and its impact on Chan studies and Chinese historiography in general.

Hu Shih was an able, thorough, and innovative scholar whose work did much to set the course of modern Chan studies. He approached his subject with a broader perspective than might a purely sectarian scholar, and he stood virtually alone in refraining from treating the history of Chan solely

---

15. See McRae, "Encounter Dialogue and the Transformation of the Spiritual Path in Chinese Chan."
16. See especially Gregory and Getz, *Buddhism in the Sung.*

as a succession of individual patriarchs and their teachings. His detailed discussions of the problems of textual and historical authenticity are still eminently useful, even after decades of work by other scholars. And, of course, his discovery of Shenhui's texts among the Dunhuang manuscripts was a major event that greatly stimulated interest in Chan studies in China, Japan, Europe, and the United States.[17]

Hu Shih's work on Chan Buddhism took place during two periods: the first, during the years 1924–1935, when he made his major discoveries and formulated his general theories and style of interpretation, and the second, in 1952–1962, when he incorporated the implications of newly discovered manuscripts into his earlier work. His initial interest in Chan was itself the outgrowth of a monumental project undertaken in the second decade of the twentieth century: a comprehensive history of Chinese philosophy done according to strictly modern methodological standards. Hu's 1917 Columbia University dissertation, "The Development of the Logical Method in Ancient China," was the first step taken toward this end,[18] and the development of his interests is apparent in the content of his lectures at Beijing University.[19] However, even though they were mindful of his contribution, some of Hu Shih's most important contemporary colleagues in the study

---

17. Lou Yulie has written a convenient summary of Hu Shih's contributions to Chan studies, which includes observations based on Hu's diaries (*Hu Shi riji*) and his marginal comments on Buddhist texts (the originals of which are held at the Beijing University Library), and on the *Ko Teki Zengaku an;* Lou uses both Hu's writing and Yanagida's analysis. Lou's "Hu Shi Chanzongshi yanjiu pingyi" (An Evaluation of Hu Shih's Studies of Chan School History) was published in Beijing and subsequently translated into Japanese by Ogawa Takashi under the same title, "Ko Teki Zenshūshi kenkyū heigi." (All page references to Lou's article here are to the Japanese translation, which includes useful supplementary notes by the translator.)

18. *The Development of the Logical Method in Ancient China* was printed in Shanghai in 1922. In 1921 it had appeared in expanded form, in Chinese, as the first volume of a projected multivolume work, called *Zhongguo zhexue shi dagang, juan shang* 中國哲學史大綱, 卷上 (Outline of Chinese Philosophy, Volume One), published by Shangwu yinshuguan 商務印書館 in Shanghai. This was the only volume to appear; Hu Shih was sometimes called "Professor Volume One" (*shangjuan xiansheng* 上卷先生) for his propensity to leave projects unfinished.

19. Lou, 2–3, points out that even before Hu's first article on Buddhist meditation was published in January 1925, he devoted some of his university course lectures to Buddhism. That is, in September to October 1921, he included Buddhism in his lectures on Chinese philosophical history, and in June 1922 he lectured on the history of Buddhism and Chan. See pp. 230, 231, 235, and 236; and 366, 375, 382, and 384 of *Hu Shi riji*.

At this point let me observe that Lou, 3, adduces two comments written by Hu Shih in the margins of his copy of the *Vimalakītrti Sūtra* (*Weimojie suoshuo jing*). In his first comment, written in 1920, he refers to it as "thoroughly fabricated fiction" and considers it amazing that anyone could believe in it; in his second comment, four years later, he admits that he had been greatly mistaken and notes the literary richness and explanatory efficacy of the text. However, he also refers to the *Vimalakīrti* and the *Lotus Sūtra* as "truly two great demonic forces, which cannot be minimized." First of all, this shows that Hu Shih was working on Buddhist literature as early as 1920. More significantly, it shows that he began with a very negative attitude toward Buddhism but was able to learn and change his mind.

of Chinese philosophy were critical of the injection of personal beliefs into his work.[20]

Hu's analysis of classical Chinese philosophy was important for his approach to the subject within its overall historical and social context, an undertaking that was largely unprecedented within the Chinese intellectual tradition. He was extremely skeptical of traditional legends and developed analytical methods based on a combination of traditional Chinese textual criticism and modern scientific procedures. He was also willing to offer fresh interpretations, such as his understanding of the Daoists as realists and champions of individual freedom rather than mystics.[21] These aspects of Hu's work on Chinese philosophy, that is, the comprehensive, critical, and imaginative facets of his approach, were carried over into his work on Chan.

In the 1920s and early 1930s Hu Shih wrote a dozen articles and letters relevant to the study of early Chan. These ranged from analyses of Buddhist meditation techniques prior to the advent of the Chan school, to textual and biographical studies, and to historical summaries of the development of early Chan. Specifically, these writings include an analysis of Buddhist meditation techniques as seen through Chinese translations (1925), a discussion of Bodhidharma's life and significance (1927), a summary of the lineages of Chan during the poet-official Bo Juyi's 白居易 lifetime (1928), an analysis of the meditation tradition prior to the advent of the Chan school (1928), a brief discussion of various aspects of early Chan contained in a response to a letter from Tang Yongtong 湯用彤 (1928), reflections on his earlier treatment of Bodhidharma (1929), a study of an early biography of Huineng and its relevance to the *Platform Sūtra* (1930), a preface to the *Masters and Disciples of the Laṅkāvatāra* (*Lengqie shizi ji* 楞伽師資記, 1931), an article in English on the development of early Chan (1932), a second article on the *Platform Sūtra* (1934), a Chinese version of his views on the development of

---

20. After the first volume of Feng Youlan's 馮友蘭 *Zhongguo zhexue shi* 中國哲學史 (History of Chinese Philosophy) was published in 1931, it was reviewed by Chen Yinke 陳寅恪 and Jin Yuelin 金岳霖 for inclusion in a Qinghua University series. The comments by Chen and Jin, which are reported with agreement by Feng, draw comparisons with Hu's earlier work. Chen suggests that, although Hu's subject was ostensibly ancient Chinese philosophy, he was really discussing his own ideas, and Jin remarks that Hu had unconsciously adopted optimistic American attitudes toward progress and results, thereby revealing his own discomfort with the ancient world. While Feng recognizes Hu's contribution in being the first to write a comprehensive study of Chinese philosophy, he also suggests that Hu made forced comparisons with Western philosophy due to his weakness in the latter area. All three criticize Hu for approaching his subject from a specific philosophical viewpoint rather than as an unbiased historian of philosophy. See Feng Youlan, *Sansong tang zixu,* 226–228. I am grateful to Ye Wenxin of the University of California, Berkeley, for informing me of these comments.

21. Wing-tsit Ch'an, "Hu Shih and Chinese Philosophy." One point that does not seem to have affected Hu Shih's work on Chan is the suggestion that the logical method was more important in Chinese philosophy than had previously been thought. That is, he did not struggle to discern underlying logical principles in Chan texts, but accepted the generalization that Chan language was frequently illogical. Presumably, he wanted to preserve the appellation logical for native Chinese modes of thought.

Chan (1934), and a study of what Hu called the "Laṅkāvatāra school" or Lengqie zong 楞伽宗 (1935).[22]

The political turmoil surrounding World War II and the continuing Chinese revolution kept Hu Shih away from serious scholarship on Chan for a decade and a half. In the last decade of his life, however, he wrote another dozen articles (including textual editions) and as many letters to Professors Iriya Yoshitaka (a specialist in Chinese colloquial literature) and Yanagida Seizan (then an emerging authority on Chinese Chan) in Japan. In July 1952 he wrote an article on Zhu Xi's 朱熹 discussion of Chan (he had drafted a textual history of the *Zhuzi yulei* 朱子語類 in January 1950), and in September 1952 he completed the draft of another article (his third) on the *Platform Sūtra*. In January 1953 he gave a lecture at Teachers University (Shifan Daxue 師範大學) in Taiwan on his "new approach to the history of the Chan school,"[23] in April of the same year his well-known critique of Suzuki's work was published (along with Suzuki's reply) in *Philosophy East and West*, and in June he drafted a study of Zongmi's biography of Shenhui. The draft of his study of two newly discovered manuscripts of Shenhui's works was finished in November of 1958. In 1959 Hu wrote seven separate letters to Professor Iriya, and in the last two months of the year he drafted two articles on subjects involving the *Baolin zhuan* 寶林傳 (a Chan lineage history written in 801). The year 1960 saw another three letters to Professor Iriya, the publication of an appeal for continued efforts in the search for primary Chan texts, the draft edition of another newly discovered manuscript of one of Shenhui's works, and the draft of an article on a text of the *Wudeng huiyuan* 五燈會元 (a late collection of Chan lineage texts). In 1961 Hu sent a letter to Professor Yanagida and drafted two articles on Zhu Xi and another on Pei Xiu's 裴休 epitaph for Zongmi. In addition to these published works and completed drafts (his work on Shenhui's texts was published in the posthumous second edition of his *Shenhui heshang yiji* in 1968), Hu Shih's papers contained a large number of notes and essays on subjects related to early Chan.[24]

---

22. The most convenient source for Hu Shih's writings is the *Ko Teki Zengaku an*. For the articles listed, see 197–214, 53–64, 94–97, 215–234, 62–64, 66–75, 143–152, 721–691 [sic], 76–92, 459–521, and 154–195, respectively. The *Zengaku an* incorrectly includes an unsigned review of D. T. Suzuki's *Studies in the Laṅkāvatāra Sūtra*, published August 25, 1927, in the *Times Literary Supplement*, 579, as Hu Shih's. This review was originally noticed by Timothy Barrett and supplied by him to Professor Yanagida in my presence in about 1974, with the suggestion that it had been written by Hu Shih; Barrett has now realized that it could only have been written by Arthur Waley, who was working on Dunhuang materials at the time.

23. The "new approach" that Hu describes is based on his understanding of modern historical research, not any change in his own position. Lou, 3, notes that there is no discernible difference in his own fundamental viewpoint between this lecture and one given at Beijing Teachers University nineteen years earlier.

24. See the citation in *Zengaku an*, 50; the "Zhu Zi yulei di lishi" 朱子語類的歷史 was published in a revised version in 1959 by Zhengzhong shuju 正中書局. For the "Liuzu tan jing yuanzuo 'tan jing' kao" 六祖壇經原作「壇經」考, see *Hu Shi shougao* 7a, 91–100. For the other

Taken as a whole, Hu's writings represent a remarkable productivity, especially for someone who was not primarily a specialist in Chinese Buddhism or Chan studies. I have included the preceding enumeration of his work in some detail for two reasons. First, I suspect that most scholars of modern Chinese intellectual history are unaware of the relative weight of his work on Chan within the overall context of his life. Second, I suspect that students of Chinese religions are similarly unaware of Hu's work on Chan, other than the famous *Philosophy East and West* exchange with D. T. Suzuki. Although I will not argue the point in detail here, I further suspect that Hu's work on Chan was deeply influential upon his overall view of Chinese intellectual history.

B. Hu Shih's Historiographical Agenda

Hu Shih's interests in Chinese history were remarkably broad, far transcending his work on Shenhui and early Chan. For example, he became involved in academic discussions concerning the relative dating of Laozi and Confucius, the meaning of the rise of Neo-Confucianism in the Song, and a comparison of the rise of empirical scholarship in both the Qing and the European Reformation. Some of the primary issues involved in these discussions were the primacy of the Confucian tradition, the distinction between the religious and humanistic aspects of Confucianism, and the capabilities of Chinese civilization to adapt to the modern world and to undertake the kinds of changes necessary for effective modernization.

Although Hu Shih was a historian, he was no mere antiquarian. Rather, in keeping with the pragmatist teachings of his mentor John Dewey, Hu Shih undertook the study of history for the explicit purpose of serving the present. According to an excellent article by Irene Eber,[25] Hu Shih was in fact an active proponent of the historiographic principle of the "reorganization of the national past" (*zhengli guogu* 整理國古).

In its narrowest sense, reorganizing the national past implied the use of rigorous methodologies and an inquisitive yet critical approach to primary sources. On a broader level, this slogan provided a justification for a two-pronged endeavor. On the one hand, the scholar—and indeed the educated person in general—was to use this process to come to terms with his or her own tradition, to understand the Chinese past and its transformations. On

---

items listed, see *Zengaku an*, 522–543; *Hu Shi shougao* 7b, 221–232; *Yiji*, 223–399; *Hu Shi shougao* 8c, 413–477; *Zengaku an*, 545–614; *Hu Shi shougao* 7c, 517–566 and 445–516, and 8c, 478–516, and *Zengaku an*, 51 and 614; *Zengaku an*, 667–659; *Yiji*, 401–500; *Hu Shi shougao* 8c; *Zengaku an*, 615–657; *Hu Shi shougao* 7c, 581–592; 7b, 275–350, and 9a. For Hu's unpublished drafts and essays, see *Hu Shi shougao* 7a, 1–21, 73–90, and 103–119; 7b, 257–274, 351–376, 377–396, 397–406, 419–425, 407–418; 7c, 427–444; 8c, 561–566; plus tangentially relevant material in volumes 8a and 8b. Lou, 5, points out that, including both short writings and incomplete and unpublished works, Hu wrote more than forty pieces on Chan during this period.

25. Irene Eber, "Hu Shih and Chinese History." I would like to thank Joshua Fogel for showing me this article, on which I rely heavily in the next few paragraphs.

the other hand, this endeavor was always to take place for the benefit of the present and, more specifically, on behalf of the successful modernization of China. The past was to be investigated for characteristics that stood the test of time, for developments and transformations that helped one generate a prognosis for China's modernization in the twentieth century.

From the very beginning, then, Hu Shih's approach to historical writing placed him in a very delicate, not to say tenuous, subjective position. He wished to do scientific research on the Chinese past, but only as it explicitly served China's present needs. The definition of those present needs would be created by historians in the course of their own work, which would in turn provide a richer comprehension of the present and the ability to make certain estimates about the future. Hu Shih's mentor John Dewey said that the "intelligent understanding of past history is to some extent a lever for moving the present into a certain kind of future." As Eber describes it, history is from this viewpoint "a kind of dynamic continuum, interpreted in the present but moving at the same time unceasingly toward the future."[26]

Hu Shih's first elaboration of the concept of the "reorganization of the national past" was written in November 1919, after he had completed his studies under John Dewey and returned to China:

> Toward the old learning and thought, we make positive only one proposal, which is "reorganize the national past."... Why must we reorganize? Because ancient learning and thought until now has not been organized, had no starting point, and had no system. Therefore, the first step is to organize a logical sequence. Because very few of the former scholars who studied the ancient books had held the outlook of historical evolution (*lishi jinhua* 歷史進化, i.e., the genetic theory of history), they were not at all particular about origins and learning and the causal relations of thought. Therefore, the second step is to find out how all learning and thought arose, and after arising, what influence and results it had.... The third step is to thoroughly verify, and to render intelligibly and lucidly the meanings of the ancients...the fourth step being to gather the research of the previous three steps.... This is called "reorganizing the national past."[27]

Thus Hu Shih's first step was inductive; the logical sequence of the events and ideas of the past was to be established prior to detailed investigation. The risk of error through prejudice or preconception is obvious, but there is no indication that Hu Shih was sensitive to the problem.[28]

---

26. Eber, "Hu Shih and Chinese History," 172.

27. Eber, 175–176; her translation, with minor changes. Eber points out that in 1917 Hu Shih had used the English word "systematize" as an equivalent for *zhengli*, but that she uses "reorganize" throughout.

28. Eber, 172, mentions Rudolf Bultmann as a contemporary figure who was deeply sensitive to the existential problems of doing history. The contrast with Hu Shih, who seems to have never discussed such matters explicitly, is great.

Gu Jiegang 顧頡剛 and other scholars who adopted Hu Shih's slogan in the ensuing years defined it in broader terms than he did, emphasizing its connections with trends such as the new literature movement. Hu Shih himself pointed out the democratizing effects of historical reorganization, which would make the past accessible to those who are not themselves intellectuals. This made historians the transmitters of the national past to the Chinese people in the present. Those advocating this position came under widespread criticism, their reaction to which was to further broaden the implications of their quest for the reorganization of the national past.[29]

In his early writings Hu Shih was largely critical toward Confucianism, but his attitude gradually changed, propelled chiefly by the growing realization that he could reject its religious dimension while rehabilitating its humanistic and rationalistic aspects.[30] Eventually Hu could announce that "probably I am a Confucianist—now that Confucianism is dead."[31] He had also changed his opinion regarding the relationship between Confucianism and modernization. In addition to arguing the mutual compatibility of Confucianism and scientific thinking,[32] Hu Shih pointed out the existence of Confucian institutions that had prepared China for modernization.[33] Eber concludes that Hu Shih increasingly came to consider Daoism and nonreligious Confucianism as the two main currents of the Chinese tradition. He was also moving toward a more positive appreciation of Daoism as a tradition conducive to modernization, although this position was only fully expressed in the 1950s.[34]

C. The Theory of the Chinese Renaissance

During the early 1930s, just after his major work on Shenhui was completed and at virtually the same time that he was re-evaluating the Confucian and Daoist traditions, Hu Shih also articulated a general theory of the periods of Chinese history. The hallmark of this theory was the identification of several particularly creative epochs that he referred to as periods of "renaissance." As I have already mentioned, Hu Shih's interests spanned the entire

---

29. Eber, 177–182.
30. Compare his statements on Confucianism in *Logical Method*, 7–9, 17, 56, and 69, and the article "Shuo Ru," esp. 68 and 75. Also see Eber, 187.
31. "The Task of Modern Religion," 104.
32. See his comments in Haydon, *Modern Trends in World Religions*, 46; cited in Eber, 188.
33. He mentioned the examination system, the abolishment of primogeniture, the censorial system, the concept of the goodness of human nature, and the rationale for rebellion against tyrannical government provided by the theory of the mandate of heaven. See Hu Shih, "Historical Foundations for a Democratic China."
34. See Eber, 199–202. It is significant that Hu Shih did not significantly alter his estimation of Buddhism and Shenhui's role during the 1950s, when he modified several other aspects of his interpretation of Chinese history. For Hu's description of the successes and failures of Chinese classical scholarship during the last three hundred years, as well as a more detailed statement of the methodology of "reorganizing the national past," see his "Systematic Study of China's Cultural Heritage," 80–87.

breadth of Chinese history, from the time of the classical philosophers in the Eastern Zhou to the intellectual developments of the early Qing, and he identified several such periods of creative renewal during the course of this long history: (1) the Tang dynasty emergence of great poets, a new prose literature, and the development of Chan Buddhism; (2) the Song dynasty reform movements and development of Neo-Confucianism; (3) the thirteenth-century rise of dramas and the later great novels; and (4) the seventeenth-century revolt against Song-Ming rational philosophy and the development of new techniques of scholarship.[35]

The periods of interest here, of course, are the Tang and Song, and especially the emergence of Chan and the development of neo-Confucianism, which Hu Shih saw as intimately related processes. To appreciate Hu's understanding of these processes, we must go back to the two periods before the Song dynasty renaissance occurred. Hu Shih posited three periods of Chinese thought, which he describes in different works as follows:

1. The ancient period or classical age, which ended about 200 BCE, or the Sinitic Age, which lasted until the initial ascendency of Buddhism in the fourth century CE.
2. The medieval period, from approximately 200 BCE to 1000 CE, or the Buddhist Age, from 300 to 1100 CE.
3. The modern period, or the Age of the Chinese Renaissance, from about 1000 or 1100 to the present, respectively.[36]

Let me now adumbrate Hu Shih's explanation of these three periods.

[1.] The first of the three periods was characterized by humanism, rationalism or intellectualism, and a spirit of freedom and democracy. Purely religious sensibilities, however, were not as well developed as other aspects of ancient Chinese society:

> [The Chinese people] had no time to indulge in speculating about the ways of the gods, or in effusive praises of the wonderful benevolence of heaven which they never enjoyed. They had a very simple religion consisting chiefly in a worship of their own ancestors, a belief in the spirits and the powers of the natural forces, a worship of a supreme God or heaven (which was probably evolved out of the worship of natural objects), and a belief in divination. To these they added a belief in the idea of retribution of good and evil. There was neither Hell nor Paradise; no life after death, only a firm belief in the importance of the perpetuation of the family line,

---

35. This list occurs in the lecture "The Chinese Renaissance" from the eponymous book *The Chinese Renaissance*, 44–45.

36. See Hu's "Chinese Thought" and "Religion and Philosophy in Chinese History," 32. Hu presented a similar periodization of medieval Chinese history in *Zhongguo zhonggu sixiang xiaoshi* 中國中古思想小史 (written 1932), as noted in Yamaguchi, "Ko Teki," 67. Yamaguchi, 64–65, notes Hu's indebtedness to the historical formulations of Liang Qichao 梁啟超.

> primarily for economic reasons. This was the original religion of the Chinese. The extreme simplicity of this racial religion was the most remarkable in the history of mankind. There was little mythology, and little elaborate ritualism. It never had a generic name, and I have elsewhere proposed to call it "Siniticism."[37]

Hu often refers to the philosophies of this early period, especially Daoism, as "naturalistic,"[38] by which he apparently means that they were concerned only with immediate phenomenal reality rather than metaphysical abstractions of other realms. His most common descriptive, however, is that of "simplicity," which is clearly emphasized in the passage just introduced. As we shall see below, native Chinese thought was inherently and quintessentially simple, in direct contrast with the fundamental complexity of Indian Buddhism.

[2.] The dominant factor during the medieval period of Chinese history, according to Hu, was the introduction of Buddhism and its near-total domination of Chinese intellectual and religious life. Buddhism presented a serious problem for rationality and humanism, which were almost "submerged by Indian thought and belief."[39] The Indian religion possessed "impressive images and grandiose rituals and unintelligible metaphysics and superstitious charms and spells."[40] Hu stresses the extreme nature of the religious zeal displayed by the Chinese while they were under the sway of Buddhism, particularly the "inhuman fanaticism" of self-mortification:

> All the religions and philosophies of ancient China were free from the fantastic imaginativeness and hair-splitting analysis and gigantic architectonic structure which characterize all religious and philosophical literature of India. When China was brought face to face with India, China was overwhelmed, dazzled and dumbfounded by the vast output of the religious zeal and genius of the Indian nation. China acknowledged its defeat and was completely conquered.[41]

Hu's descriptions of the originally Indian religion are generally couched in terms of its complexity, often in a manner that scarcely disguises his own contempt. For example, he dismisses Yogācāra idealism as a kind of hair-splitting that was both entirely inimical to the Chinese mentality and ultimately inexpressible in the Chinese language. His treatment of the great pilgrim, translator, and Yogācāra authority Xuanzang 玄奘 is typical, if

---

37. *The Chinese Renaissance*, 80–81; the allusion at the end of this passage is to Hu's "Religion and Philosophy in Chinese History."
38. See, for example, *Yiji*, 52. In his contribution to *Living Philosophies*, 248, Hu refers to the "naturalism of some of the ancient Chinese philosophers," i.e., the Daoists; see n. 67 below
39. "Chinese Thought," 227.
40. "Development of Zen Buddhism in China," 482 (*Zengaku an*, 714).
41. "Development of Zen Buddhism in China," 481–482 (*Zengaku an*, 715–714).

curious. Not satisfied with the "close-minded fabrications of Chinese monks," Xuanzang traveled to India at a time when "complex philosophy" was in its very heyday, along with idealism, logic, and many kinds of "meaningless *dhāraṇīs*" (i.e., spells):

> The great Xuanzang threw himself into the great spider's web and could not escape, so becoming a great believer and proselytizer of the Vijñānavādin school [sic]. At this, seventh century China was transformed into a great colony of India's complex philosophy.[42]

The projection of a modern concept of imperialism onto the past is obvious. Although the flood of strange Buddhist ideas and practices overwhelmed the Chinese people for several centuries, the sense of fascination was accompanied by a more fundamental feeling of revulsion:

> But the native rationalistic mentality of the Chinese intelligentsia gradually reasserted itself and revolted against this humiliating domination of the whole nation by a foreign religion which was opposed to all the best traditions of the native civilization. Its celibacy was fundamentally opposed to the Chinese society which emphasized the importance of continuation of the ancestral lineage. Its mendicant system was distasteful to the Chinese social and political thinker who was naturally alarmed by the presence of millions of monks and nuns living as parasites on society. Its austere forms of asceticism and self-sacrifice and suicide were fundamentally against the idea of filial piety which regarded the human body as a sacred inheritance from one's parents. And its wonderfully abstruse mythology and metaphysics, never ending in the most ingenious inventions of new gods and new titles of the gods, and never failing in the most hair-splitting differentiations and sub-differentiations, were most foreign to the simple and straightforward ways of thinking of the native tradition. And, most important of all, the whole scheme of salvation as taught in Buddhism seemed to the Chinese thinker as most selfish and anti-social. Each man endeavors to become an arahat [sic], a bodhisattva, or a buddha. But, the Chinese began to ask, for what end? What value is there in a salvation which must require the forsaking of the family and the desertion of all one's duties to the family and the state?[43]

---

42. *Yiji*, 42–43; emphasis added. Hu Shih also dismissed the Tiantai 天台 school as a form of complex philosophizing. At one point, he also notes with obvious contempt that Zhiyi 智顗 was the sort of scholar who took 100,000 characters to explicate the two-character term for meditation, *zhiguan* 止觀 (concentration and insight).

43. *Chinese Renaissance*, 85. In his distaste for superstition, Hu refers to Tantrism as one of the "worst features of Mahāyāna Buddhism"; see "Religion and Philosophy in Chinese History," 51. On another occasion he says with obvious relief that in spite of the careers of Amoghavajra and Vajrabodhi, two of the major translators of esoteric texts, China did not

Can there be any doubt that the long tradition of Confucian anti-Buddhist polemic thrives in Hu Shih's writings?

[3.] The innate revulsion supposedly felt by the Chinese people toward Buddhism reached its natural expression in the modern period, or the Age of the Chinese Renaissance. During this period China divested itself of intellectual domination by India and reverted to the simple, humanistic rationalism of the native Chinese tradition. Buddhism only disappeared from China when its contributions were appropriated by Chinese society as a whole. Thus in the third or modern phase of Chinese history China assimilated the

> more subtle elements of the Indian culture—the philosophy of the world and of life, the moral and social standards, the intellectual habits—things...which had required much intermediate work of sifting, discarding, distilling, and reinterpreting, before some of them were sufficiently domesticated to be unconsciously appropriated into the Chinese culture.[44]

The Chinese Renaissance thus involved four types of effort aimed at overcoming the "humiliating domination of the whole nation by a foreign religion which was opposed to all the best traditions of the native civilization."[45] These efforts included (a) imitation, as practiced by the Daoists in an attempt to supplant Buddhism; (b) persecution, the motive of which was nationalistic in nature; (c) internal revolt, the process of radical simplification that occurred within Chinese Buddhism, specifically, within the Chan school; and (d) philosophical secularization, as undertaken by the Neo-Confucians of the eleventh and twelfth centuries.[46] By these means Buddhism was integrated into Chinese society and allowed to disappear.[47]

IV. A Critique of Hu Shih's Scholarship

A. The Misperception of Shenhui

Hu Shih's understanding of Shenhui's role in the formation of Chan Buddhism was based on a straightforward combination of Shenhui's own writings and the *Platform Sūtra*. For the former, the text of Shenhui's that was the most revealing for Hu was the *Definition of the Truth*. With regard to the

---

"fall" into becoming an esoteric or lamaist state; see "Chanxue gushi kao" 禪學古史考, in *Zengaku an*, 215–234, 222.

44. "Indianization of China," 239.

45. *Chinese Renaissance*, 85.

46. Yamaguchi, "Ko Teki," 71, cites various passages to indicate Hu believed that the task of the Song and Ming dynasty Neo-Confucians was only completed by the scholars of the Qing.

47. My impression is that Hu thought Buddhism flooded China simply because it was complex and filled naive religious desires. Also, note his comment in "Indianization of China," 231, that after 1100 or so Buddhism simply failed to have influence in China—omitting mention of the decline of Buddhism in India and the loss of easy passage across Central Asia.

latter, as stated in the passage cited in the opening of this paper, Hu Shih thought that the *Platform Sūtra* was written by Shenhui or one of his followers and that it accurately represented the teachings of his teacher Huineng.[48] Hu was also aware of some of the literature associated with the Northern school, not to mention the texts of the orthodox Chan tradition, which he used to corroborate and underscore his findings. The interpretation that Hu derived from these works may be summarized by three points:

1. Huineng and Shenhui taught a teaching of sudden enlightenment, in contrast to the gradual teaching of the Northern school.
2. Shenhui's campaign to rehabilitate Huineng's status was the natural outcome of the difference between these two teachings, and the battle was hard fought on both sides.
3. The eventual victory of the sudden teaching represented a basic change in the Chan tradition—in fact, the only truly fundamental change in the entire history of Chinese Buddhism.

Unfortunately, advances in scholarship in the last two decades or so have rendered virtually every aspect of Hu Shih's interpretation incorrect in some way or another.[49] To recapitulate the three points just stated:

[1.] Huineng probably did emphasize the sudden experience of enlightenment in his own teaching, and this emphasis may have been imparted by him to Shenhui. However, this was by no means unique within the context of early Chan, and nothing of any significance may be said about the historical figure Huineng. The *Platform Sūtra* does not record the actual teachings of Huineng. Nor was it written by Shenhui or a member of his school, but rather by a member of a slightly later faction known as the Oxhead school; the text as we have it today is a splendid montage of early Chan teachings from a number of sources. Since the earliest text of the *Platform Sūtra* is now known to date from around 780, the legendary image of Huineng that appears in it must be clearly distinguished from the historical personage, and the teachings of this landmark scripture are significantly different from those of Shenhui and, by implication, the historical Huineng.

Just as modern scholarship has tended to push the historical Huineng further and further into the shadows, so has the impact of figures associ-

---

48. Hu Shih's misunderstanding was bolstered in part by the misreading of a line in an epitaph by Wei Chuhou 韋處厚 (773–828) for Mazu's student Dayi 大義 (746–818) to read that Shenhui's students had composed the *Platform Sūtra*, whereas the line actually suggests that Shenhui's students had switched from an emphasis on the *Diamond Sūtra* to the use of the *Platform Sūtra*. See Lou, 9–10 (citing *Quan Tang wen* 全唐文 715.22, line 9) and the translator's n. 7 on p. 17, which refers to the analysis of this line (which I have followed here) by Lü Cheng, *Zhongguo Foxue yuanliu lüejiang*, 231 ff. The translator, Ogawa Takashi, also notes that Hu Shih later marked out part of his original misunderstanding in red ink, as shown in the *Yiji*, 75.

49. The discussion that follows here is summarized from my essay "Shenhui and the Teaching of Sudden Enlightenment."

ated with the so-called Northern school become increasingly clear. In fact, as already discussed above, Shenhui operated in an essentially Northern school milieu during his training and early teaching career.[50] There are pronounced similarities between his teachings and those of his predecessors in the Northern school: Shenhui's emphasis on sudden enlightenment was unusually thoroughgoing, for example, but it was a natural extension of tendencies exhibited in early Chan literature.

What was idiosyncratic in Shenhui's style of teaching was his consistent, even relentless, emphasis on the first moment of religious inspiration, or *bodhicitta* (which technically refers to the first experience of the urge to achieve enlightenment on behalf of all sentient beings). This emphasis may be correlated with Shenhui's vocation as an evangelist, seeking to inspire those in his congregations to achieve *bodhicitta* even as they listened to him, in a kind of conversion experience. The reason Hu Shih could describe Shenhui's teachings as a "new Chan which renounces *chan* itself and is therefore no *chan* at all"[51] was not because Shenhui forever banished the notion of meditation practice from the Chan tradition, but because Shenhui himself was not involved in the ongoing training of religious aspirants.

Shenhui's focus on the sudden teaching had one other important benefit: It allowed him to maintain a rhetorically unassailable stance, avoiding any semblance of dualistic conceptualization, even as he criticized the Northern school for a goal-oriented approach to meditation. Paradoxically, whereas for Shenhui the slogan of sudden enlightenment was a convenient polemical device that allowed him to avoid any real consideration of the problems of ongoing religious training, it was popular among later Chan masters for precisely the opposite reason. That is, sudden enlightenment was a flexible and positive label that implied just the sort of delicacy and sophistication required in Chan practice. The appellation "sudden" could be applied to a wide range of specific approaches, but in all cases it combined, first, an implied exhortation to drop all extraneous endeavors and focus on the very crux of the spiritual dilemma with, second, a strong warning against conceptualization and goal-oriented striving.

To Hu Shih, the two teachings of sudden and gradual represented fundamentally different motifs of primary importance in the history of Chinese Buddhism. It would be better to interpret them as dialectically inseparable motifs within the context of Buddhist spiritual training and doctrinal discourse.[52]

---

50. In this statement the term Northern school is used in the nonpejorative sense defined in McRae, *Northern School*, 8–10. The point is that the early Chan religious community in northern China was an essentially undifferentiated confraternity prior to the initiation of Shenhui's campaign against two of its major figures, whom he described as the heirs of a "Northern school" defined in pejorative terms.

51. "Chan (Zen) Buddhism in China," 7, repeated in brief on 17 and 20 (*Zengaku an*, 685, 675, and 672).

52. On the inseparability of the two motifs of sudden and gradual, see Faure, *Rhetoric of Immediacy*, 32–52.

[2.] Nor was the interplay between sudden and gradual a battle that ground inexorably on to the victory of the Southern school. Shenhui probably did carry out his campaign against the Northern school over the course of many years, beginning in 730 and reaching a peak in 745–749 and shortly thereafter. Even though this campaign was the hallmark of his career, we have no way to estimate how energetically or single-mindedly he pursued his mission. The *Miscellaneous Dialogues* includes exchanges not related to the campaign, and it seems best to understand him primarily as an evangelist whose proselyte style involved factionalist advocacy, rather than primarily as a factionalist advocate who spread his ideas from the ordination platform. As a public figure—even something of a popular religious entertainer, the Oral Roberts of eighth-century Luoyang—Shenhui must have varied his message from time to time.

Even more important, the battle was notably one-sided. Shenhui was banished for a time, and the explanation for this in the primary sources includes a reference to Puji 普寂 of the Northern school. There is some reason to doubt this reference, and to focus on Northern school pressure as the underlying cause of Shenhui's banishment is to ignore the main argument given: that Shenhui's large audiences represented a potentially dangerous situation in the sensitive political atmosphere of the second capital at Luoyang. And Shenhui's treatment at the hands of imperial officials was not at all severe. He was taken first to Chang'an for an audience with Emperor Xuanzong, then "demoted to the provinces," moving in fairly rapid succession to four very favorable locations. Since these locations are described as centers of Northern school activity, Shenhui's peregrinations seem more than anything else to resemble an imperially sponsored lecture tour. There is no evidence of any other direct response by the Northern school.[53]

And not only was the battle one-sided, from one standpoint it was a battle lost. Shenhui's campaign did decrease the luster of the Northern school, but it did not effect that school's destruction: the lineages of Shenxiu and Puji continued until at least the beginning of the tenth century, well after that of Shenhui himself.[54] In fact, Shenhui's lineage lasted only five generations, and the biographical links between the last few figures in his lineage are problematic. Although the name of Shenhui's faction, "Southern school," was adopted by the mainstream of the subsequent Chan tradition, the two were not identical.

Finally, the response of the later Chan tradition to Shenhui's campaign

---

53. It is significant that Northern school texts contain no reference to or refutation of Shenhui's positions. On Shenhui's banishment see McRae, *Northern School*, 241–242. Hu Shih seems always to have conceived of the Northern and Southern schools as discrete units locked in competition. In a July 1928 letter to Tang Yongtong, he refers to the repressive nature of the exile forced on Shenhui by the Northern school and to Shenhui's overthrowing of the Northern school after the An Lushan rebellion. See *Zengaku an*, 237.

54. See McRae, *Northern School*, 70. Hu Shih was well aware of the relatively early demise of Shenhui's faction.

was by no means as positive as Hu Shih has said. True, the slogan of suddenness and the banner of the Southern school were universally accepted, but these were pyrrhic victories. Shenhui may have been recognized by an imperial commission as seventh patriarch of Chan, but he was not treated so favorably in orthodox Chan historical works. As Hu Shih implicitly recognizes in the preface quoted above, Shenhui's role is ignored or at least severely downplayed in such texts. In fact, it is fair to say that Shenhui's factionalism created a crisis in Chan that his later contemporaries struggled to overcome. Thus we find a number of statements expressing an aversion to the sectarian distinction between North and South. Even more important, the *Platform Sūtra* may be viewed as an elaborate and exquisitely crafted effort at incorporating Shenhui's innovations into the developing Chan orthodoxy without reference to Shenhui himself.[55]

[3.] The gradual / sudden dichotomy was important in the early Chan tradition, but it does not circumscribe the most basic transformation in Chan. In spite of the distinctions between them, the early Chan factions known as the Northern school, Southern school (i.e., that of Shenhui), Oxhead school, and the Baotang 保唐 and Jingzhong 淨眾 schools of Sichuan all share a common mode of discourse.[56] Beginning with the Hongzhou 洪州 school of Mazu Daoyi 馬祖道一 (709–788), however, Chan undergoes a fundamental change. There are still important continuities between the classical Chan of Mazu and the earlier factions, but there is a more basic difference. Gone are the curious accoutrements of Chan's emergence from the broader Chinese Buddhist doctrinal and practical tradition—the radical redefinition of traditional Buddhist jargon in the process known as "contemplative analysis," the multifarious formulations of the "contemplation of the mind," and the adumbration of sometimes bizarre approaches to meditation practice. In their place is a single-minded emphasis on dropping all conceptualization and realizing the fundamental mind, as well as the emergence of a widespread devotion to religious practice in the context of personal interaction between masters and students. The emergent form of Chan practice is represented in "encounter dialogue," the sometimes enigmatic repartee found in most Chan literature.[57]

---

55. See McRae, "Ox-head School of Chinese Buddhism," especially 218–232.

56. Even the sources of the supposed conflict between the Northern and Southern schools lay not in the differences between them but in their similarities. Note the following propositions from Lewis Coser's *The Functions of Social Conflict* as quoted in John Gager's *Kingdom and Community*, 80–87: "conflict is a form of socialization"; "groups require disharmony as well as harmony"; and "far from being necessarily dysfunctional, a certain degree of conflict is an essential element in group formation and the persistence of group life." Just as Coser's propositions "bear directly on the question of orthodoxy and heresy in early Christianity" (Gager, 80), so do they bear on the conflict within early Chan.

57. It is this new style of spiritual training that constitutes a new paradigm for religious practice in China, for which the sudden / gradual dichotomy is insufficient as an explanatory device. See n. 91 below. The term "encounter dialogue" is a rendering of *kien mondō* 機緣問答; see Yanagida Seizan, "The 'Recorded Sayings' Texts of Chinese Chan Buddhism."

In addition to these three major points, recent scholarship has also undercut some of the minor details of Hu Shih's image of Shenhui. At the beginning of this paper I cited Hu's description of Shenhui as a "white-eyebrowed old monk," and although the color of Shenhui's eyebrows is unknown it is now clear that he was not as long-lived as we once believed. Shenhui's stele was recently discovered in China and reveals that his dates were not 668–760 or 670–762, as Hu Shih had established from other evidence, but 684–758. The new stele alters somewhat the chronology of Shenhui's early years, making his training in the North (probably under Shenxiu himself) more significant.

B. A Fundamentally Flawed Appreciation of Chan

Obviously, we cannot fault Hu Shih for not possessing the clairvoyant "heavenly eye" of Buddhist hagiography. However, even though decades of scholarship went into the explanation just given, it is still possible to criticize Hu Shih for what he did with the evidence that he knew.

The most fundamental problem in Hu Shih's work on Chan is his incredible inability to understand the nature of Buddhist spiritual training. His explanation of Chan religious practice is so superficial it is ludicrous. He describes Chan practice as having two phases: In the first phase, the master deliberately misleads and confuses his students by answering their questions with incomplete or illogical statements. When a student is thoroughly frustrated, he moves into the second phase, which is that of wandering. After traveling about for a time, studying under the great masters of the day, experiencing life's hardships and sharing his problems with kindred spirits, some random event triggers an experience of realization:

> Then, some day, he hears a chance remark of a charwoman, or a frivolous song of a dancing girl, or the chirping of a bird on yonder tree, or he smells the fragrance of a nameless flower,— and he suddenly understands! All his previous inquiries and searches and experiences become correlated somehow, and the problem seems so clear and the solution so evident! The miracle has happened and he attains his Sudden Enlightenment.[58]

And this is all. There is nothing manifestly wrong with Hu's description of the practice of wandering and the power of seemingly trivial perceptions. But what was it that the student studied under the "various great masters" of the day, and how did he study it? What solution was it that became "so evident" at the point of sudden enlightenment?

---

58. "The Development of Zen Buddhism in China," 505 (*Zengaku an*, 691). For comparison, also see his 1953 article "Chan (Zen) Buddhism in China," 23 (*Zengaku an*, 669). The only changes in the later article, other than slight changes in wording, are Hu's citations of the Neo-Confucian scholar Zhu Xi (see 22–23, or *Zengaku an*, 670–669). Of course, Zhu Xi is far from a reliable source on the subject of Chan.

Whatever the validity or superficiality of Hu's interpretation of sudden enlightenment, it is not relevant to Shenhui, whose works never allude to anything like the process of wandering and discovery Hu describes. It is unclear how much of the above description Hu would have applied to Shenhui, but he did misread the impact of Shenhui's non-practical approach to Buddhist evangelism so as to miss entirely the place of meditation in Chinese Chan training centers.[59] Hu Shih's appreciation of the transformation of meditation technique was also done entirely within the framework of the parameters simpler and complex, resulting in coverage that is itself simplistic and incomplete.[60] And it is inconceivable that the only role played by Chan masters in the process of training was the obfuscation of truth. Although Suzuki's rejoinder to Hu's criticism of him in 1953 is characteristically incoherent in its own way, his comment that Hu lacked an appreciation of the "enlightenment experience" of Zen was right on the mark:

> Hu Shih, as a historian, knows Zen in its historical setting, but not Zen in itself. It is likely that he does not recognize that Zen has its own life independent of history.[61]

Tu Weiming has mentioned to me (personal communication) that Suzuki and his followers in Japan were simply unable to accept that Hu's interpretation of Chan training could be as superficial as it seemed and hence did not respond to its naivete in writing. In fact, I believe that Hu Shih's understanding of Chan was not only superficial but fundamentally flawed: when we consider the overall fabric of his interpretation of the role of Chan in Chinese history, it becomes apparent that he applauded Shenhui solely for instigating the excision of Buddhism from the mainstream of Chinese culture and the subsequent reemergence of the naturalistic and rationalistic aspects of the native "Sinitic" tradition. Therefore, Hu Shih's use of the phrase "a *chan* that was no *chan* at all" was tantamount to describing Chinese Chan as a religion that was without religion, i.e., without

---

59. For an excellent discussion of the reticence of Chan literature on the subject of meditation practice, see Carl Bielefeldt, *Dogen's Manuals of Zen Meditation*.

60. Hu describes Indian Buddhist meditation practice in terms of its fundamental complexity and dedication to gradualistic schema of self-perfection. In one article, Hu offers a chart that marks a "trend of increasing complexity" from Yoga to Yogācāra and esoteric Buddhism and a countervailing "trend of increasing simplicity" from Buddhist meditation to Chinese Chan. See "Chanxue gushi kao," 262 (*Zengaku an*, 222). Hu's study of pre-Chan Indian Buddhist meditation theory seems to have been limited to the classification of different schools and teachers in terms of simplicity and complexity, suddenness and gradualness. (See "Chanxue gushi kao," 267; *Zengaku an*, 227.) His remarks reveal a certain ambiguity about the partially sudden and partially gradualistic nature of Bodhidharma's teachings, but he is unequivocal in describing the gradualism and complexity of the teachings of Shenxiu and the Northern school. It was against this devotion to gradualism and complexity that Shenhui led his momentous revolt.

61. "Zen: A Reply to Hu Shih," 26.

superstitious elements as Hu Shih defined them. For Hu Shih the achievement of enlightenment was therefore not a religious experience, not a cathartic moment of insight into the vibrant numinosity of all things, but rather a resigned acceptance that the world was exactly as the senses presented it. Rather than "seeing the Buddha-nature" and gaining entry into an ineffable truth, Shenhui's sudden enlightenment was an unencumbered experience of the simple rationalism of the naturalistic Chinese tradition and at the same time, to Hu Shih, a precursor of modern scientific thinking. No wonder Suzuki was unable to respond!

Not only did Hu fail to resonate with the spirituality of Chan, his very dedication to history led to distorted historical judgments. He was openly cynical of the educational level of the Chinese Buddhist clergy, more than once referring to their ignorance of Sanskrit and inability to understand history.[62] Both of these criteria are irrelevant to spirituality and the religious life, and the second places a distinctly anachronistic requirement on the shoulders of medieval monastics, who could hardly be expected to think of past and present in Hu Shih's terms. Hu complemented the author of the *Masters and Disciples of the Laṅkāvatāra* for his critical attitude much as he might any modern scholar, completely failing to consider that the text was not written in a modern historiographical context.[63] Hu's distaste for historical inaccuracy led him to disregard any source that did not pass his criteria of authenticity—at one point he dismissed the entire body of Chan recorded sayings literature as "99% false."[64] It should go without saying that the value of that literature does not lie in its potential use as journalistic record, so that in naively seeking out historically reliable information Hu failed to perceive the very dynamism of the Chan tradition.

No doubt Hu Shih's rejection of the fabrications of Chan literature was a function of his basic drive to replace the legendary fabrications of Chinese history and philosophy with systematic interpretations, but in this case why was Hu Shih not more suspicious of the legendary aspects of the *Platform Sūtra*? Here he accepted the traditional account of the orthodox Chan histories virtually in its entirety, modifying it only to indicate Shenhui's role. He could have noticed, for example, that Shenhui never quoted Huineng and that the Dunhuang manuscript of the *Platform Sūtra* belittles Shenhui,

---

62. For example, Hu refers to Shenhui and his contemporaries in the Chan school in this way; see *Yiji*, 27.

63. See "Lengqie zong kao" 楞伽宗考, 227 (*Zengaku an*, 187). The point in question is whether the fifth patriarch Hongren 弘忍 (Shenhui's second-generation predecessor) produced any written works. The position taken by the *Masters and Disciples of the Laṅkāvatāra* (*Lengqie shizi ji* 楞伽師資記), that Hongren did not, was not devoid of sectarian implications. See McRae, *Northern School*, 91. The error Hu Shih committed here is the so-called historians' fallacy, or "the error of assuming that a man who has a given historical experience knows it, when he has it, to be all that a historian would know it to be, with the advantage of historical perspective." See Fischer, *Historians' Fallacies*, 209.

64. "Chanzong shi diyi xin kanfa" 禪宗史第一新看法, 170 (*Zengaku an*, 542).

details which suggest that the text was written after Shenhui's death and by someone outside his school.[65]

Hu Shih focused almost entirely on Shenhui and the historical development of early Chan, but he failed to appreciate the substantial differences between early and classical Chan. His only characterization of Chan Buddhism after the great Linji Yixuan 臨濟義玄 (Rinzai Gigen in Japanese; d. 867) is that Chan masters learned to speak more and more in riddles and meaningless statements in order to hide the truth from their students. Nor did he ever express interest in the precedent anthologies (*gong'an ji* 公案集, or *kōan shū* in Japanese) of the Song dynasty—the *Blue Cliff Record* (*Biyan lu* 碧嚴錄) and the *Gateless Barrier* (*Wumen guan* 無門關)—a failure that is surprising in view of his deep interest in colloquial literature.[66]

In fact, one of the easiest ways to appreciate Hu Shih's limitations as a scholar of Chinese Chan is to take note of the vast array of subjects he chose *not* to study: he never wrote a single article on any subject in Chinese Buddhism other than Chan and the earlier meditation tradition. The Pure Land school would have been an excellent subject by which to study the sinification of Indian Buddhism, and esoteric Buddhism might have afforded interesting insights into the role of ritual in the adoption of a very complex "Indian" style of religious practice. In other words, both of these traditions might have presented interesting possibilities for Hu Shih to explore the ramifications of legitimate interests in the diffusion and transformation of culture.

Given the depth and extent of the errors in Hu Shih's work on Shenhui, it is reasonable to wonder what other forces might have motivated him to devote so much energy to the subject. That is, to what extent were his misperceptions informed by an underlying agenda not made explicit in his writings on Chan? For this, we must turn again to his general theory of Chinese history and his work on the Chinese Renaissance.

C. The Pragmatic Intentions of Hu Shih's Historiography

Why did Hu Shih so fundamentally misperceive Shenhui? And why was he content with such a superficial appreciation of Chinese spirituality? The answers to these questions become apparent when we consider the pragmatic goals of his historiographical mission. I submit that Hu Shih's historical theories on Shenhui, Chan, and Chinese history were fundamentally flawed by his naively pragmatic historical perspective. This perspective was expressed in his dedication to the reorganization of the Chinese past, which in Hu Shih's mind involved the following basic assumptions:

---

65. See Yampolsky, *Platform Sutra*, 32, 93, 97–98, and 169–170. Yanagida, *Shoki Zenshū shisho*, 148–161, has also noticed significant doctrinal differences between Shenhui's writings and the *Platform Sūtra*.

66. See Hu's *Baihua wenxue shi*.

1. Superstitious religiosity is bad, and scientific naturalism is good.
2. Chinese history should be investigated to reveal the progressive ascension of scientific naturalism over superstitious religiosity.
3. The results of this investigation will determine the prospects for and the modes of China's success in the modernization of economic, social, and political institutions.

Hu Shih's strong predisposition against all forms of superstition and religion was a constant throughout his life. As a child, he was repulsed by his mother's faith in Buddhism and took refuge in the Neo-Confucian ideology of his late father.[67] His feelings toward Buddhism should be obvious in the passages quoted above—let there be no mistake, he despised the religion. Needless to say, Hu Shih's thorough distaste for Buddhism was inherently incompatible with his own dedication to scientific accuracy, since it rendered him a far from dispassionate observer. Hu Shih's work on Chan could remain superficial because he had no underlying empathy with religious experience and because of his simplistic dichotomy between science and superstition. Needless to say, recent work on the relationship between science, superstition, magic, and religion reveal these to be overlapping categories with rich varieties of meaning.

Hu Shih used historical research to reveal a preconceived evolution of Chinese culture. Hu Shih is surprisingly explicit on this point: in his own description of the task of reorganizing the Chinese past, the first step to be taken was to "organize a logical sequence." The ultimate risk of this approach, of course, is that his work becomes entirely derived from his first a priori assumptions. It is interesting to compare Hu Shih's preconceptions with those of D. T. Suzuki. Where Hu defined the primary thrust of Chan as good, because it was intrinsically Chinese and thus neither Indian nor Buddhist, Suzuki embraced the enlightenment experience because it was the ultimate message of Buddhism and the heart of Japanese culture. I find

---

67. In his contribution (generally referred to in secondary literature as "My Credo and Its Evolution," a title that does not appear in the original) to *Living Philosophies*, a collection of individual statements by Albert Einstein and other great minds of the early twentieth century, 235–263, Hu Shih describes his father as "strongly opposed to Buddhism and Taoism" (241). After his father's death, however, his mother brought him up in an "idolatrous environment," against which he revolted through reading the anti-Buddhist polemic of Fan Zhen 范縝 (243). Hu writes gleefully of one occasion when he scandalized his family by suggesting that the images at a local shrine be desecrated (245–246). See Hu's "Cong baishen dao wushen" (From Reverence to Atheism), dated Christmas day, 1930. These matters are summarized succinctly by Min-chih Chou, *Hu Shih and Intellectual Choice in Modern China*, 4–5. On pp. 11–13, Chou describes the discrediting of Buddhism as one of Hu's major concerns during his early years in Shanghai at the beginning of the twentieth century, a concern fueled both by his Neo-Confucian training and the iconoclastic spirit of contemporary Chinese modernism. In 1911, while in America, Hu's identification of Christianity with superior Western culture led to an uncritical—and temporary—conversion (see 41–42). In 1912 he remarked that Catholic liturgy was "just like the repulsive Buddhist ceremonies" (44).

the irony almost overwhelming in both cases: Hu Shih claimed to be a scientific observer and was not, and Suzuki rigidly clung to the claim that Chan spontaneity freed one from preconception. In any case, Hu Shih's understanding of science was simplistic and his self-portrayal as a scientific historian verged on the hypocritical.

This is not to say that Hu Shih's interpretation of Chinese history did not change over time, only that his research served to explicate and reinforce his basic philosophical approach. Thus his increasing tendency to view Confucianism positively as time went on does not reflect a fundamental change, but only the growing conviction that the rationalistic and religious aspects of the tradition could be treated separately. Similarly, Hu Shih was able to create a similar differential reappraisal of the role of Daoism because he no longer needed to balance the entire Daoist and Confucian traditions against each other. With regard to Chan, it is remarkable how little his ideas changed between his two periods of work in the field—even the language used in articles from the 1930s and 1950s remains essentially unchanged.[68]

The distorting impact of Hu Shih's pragmatic agenda is also expressed in his very decision to focus on Chan. Indeed, those who know his work in other areas of Chinese philosophy and literature have occasionally expressed surprise to me that he devoted so much energy to the study of Chan Buddhism. Hu Shih focused on this subject not because he saw Chan as a significant Buddhist school, nor even as an intrinsically interesting religious phenomenon. Instead, he selected it as an object of study because it could be interpreted as the key to the rejection of Buddhism by Chinese culture and thus the key to the eviction of all forms of unscientific superstition from modern China. His motivation to study Buddhism was thus analogous to a missionary's interest in local folk religion, the study of which provides the basis for the conversion of the heathen: he only studied Chan in order to show how its rise led to the decline of Buddhism in general and the renascence of indigenous Chinese culture. The study of Chan was for Hu Shih precisely Dewey's "lever for moving the present into a certain kind of future."

D. Projecting the Present onto the Past

Hu Shih's discovery and study of Shenhui's works took place after he had embraced the mission to reorganize China's national past, and his work on Chan in general took place at roughly the same time that he was developing his theory of the Chinese Renaissance. Although I have no direct evidence of the relationship, it seems likely that Hu Shih's work in Chan studies helped change his attitude toward Confucianism. That is, through his identification of Chan as an antiritualist and hence antireligious trend in Chinese religion, Hu Shih came to distinguish between the humanistic and religious aspects

---

68. See n. 58 above. The only change in Hu Shih's ideas on Chan that I have detected is the admission that one of Shenhui's followers rather than Shenhui himself was the author of the *Platform Sūtra*.

of the Confucian tradition. Hence the identification of Buddhism as the root cause of China's problems and Shenhui as providing the beginning of China's solution allowed Hu Shih to describe the Neo-Confucian revival of the Song in terms of its success in secularizing the Indian religion.

Earlier in his career, Hu Shih had been tempted to reject Confucianism entirely because of its religious dimension, which he later came to feel was adopted (unfortunately) from Buddhism. The Neo-Confucian secularization of Buddhism was one step forward in Hu's eyes, but the task of subsequent centuries was to overcome the religious legacy of an Indianized Neo-Confucianism. His efforts in this regard, i.e., his study of the rejection of Neo-Confucianism by Qing scholars, are beyond the scope of this paper, but we may note Eber's conclusion that during the 1930s Hu Shih "increasingly tended to see logical continuity—rather than discontinuity—leading from past events to present modernization. In other words, the present was not to be built on the dead ashes of the past, but on viable tradition."[69]

I believe that Hu Shih's work on Chan was profoundly influenced by his desire for the independence and well-being of modern China. According to this hypothesis, his interest in Shenhui and his interpretation of the heroic qualities of Shenhui's mission were a projection of his wish for the salvation of the Chinese people from the tribulations of modernization. It is even possible that Hu Shih's concern for the unfairness of history to men such as Shenhui was a reaction to his own status in the turbulent politics of the 1920s. In any case, it is only by this hypothesis that we can understand Hu's repeated references to Shenhui as a product of an age in which men were thinking "dangerous thoughts," by which he apparently means politically subversive or culturally destructive ideas.

We should also note that the selection of Shenhui as a champion of a new interpretation of Chinese history followed a strategy evinced in Hu Shih's other writings. Paul Cohen has commented to me that Hu had a tendency to study previously unrecognized subtraditions, to rehabilitate them from the obscurity of the past.[70] Joshua Fogel's paper on the "rediscovery" of Cui Shu 崔述 and other Qing dynasty figures points out that the mere fact of having been forgotten by the Chinese mainstream cloaked them in a sort of charisma for Hu and his followers. Fogel also suggests that Hu similarly "prided himself on the distance he maintained from political affairs," the implication being that Hu Shih was setting himself up for a similar "re-

---

69. Eber, "Hu Shih and Chinese History," 196.
70. This comment occurred in the discussion after a presentation of this material at the Fairbank Center at Harvard University. One such example is detailed in Fogel, "On the 'Rediscovery' of the Chinese Past," in which the nationalistic component of the rediscovery of Cui Shu is unmistakably related to Hu's work on Shenhui; even the lament "That such a great scholar with such impressive writings should have been buried for a hundred years [sic] is indeed a great shame to the Chinese intellectual community" (229) follows the same form as Hu's laments regarding Shenhui.

discovery" and elevation to sage status sometime in the future.[71] Even more significant than this wish for personal redemption is that by rediscovering Shenhui and other figures from the Chinese past, Hu Shih could write into Chinese history the resources he deemed necessary for China's survival as a modern culture without falling captive to the attractive but menacing power of the West.[72]

There is also a remarkable congruence between Hu Shih's own prescription for positive change in modern China and the characteristics of Shenhui's teachings that he found most interesting. According to Jerome Grieder, Hu Shih "assign[ed] primacy to intellectual reform as a first step toward the creation of a new political and social order."[73] Hu Shih maintained that

> thought and literature are of first importance. The sickness of our country is not rooted in the behavior of warlords and bureaucrats but in our mental laziness, superficial ideas, superstition in placing all our reliance on heaven, and lack of public spirit. These evils are our real enemies—they are the forebears of corrupt politics.... To overthrow the corrupt politics of today needs our common effort; but to destroy the forebears of corrupt politics— the "ghosts" of thought and literature of the last two thousand years— requires more work![74]

Indeed, Hu Shih made individual liberation a prior condition of political liberation, saying that "the salvation of the nation must begin with the salvation of you yourself!"[75] Beyond this, Hu Shih attributed to movements of individual redemption (Shenhui's Chan Buddhism and Hu's own liberal message) the capability of instigating political revolution, in spite of their failure to address systems of political power.[76] Hu Shih specifically compared periods of renaissance in traditional China with the modern effort to generate a new colloquial literature, and we may infer that he studied the back-

---

71. Fogel, 232. The inference drawn here is mine.
72. This inference is based in part on Chou, *Hu Shih and Intellectual Choice,* 56.
73. Grieder, *Hu Shih and the Chinese Renaissance,* 327, discusses Neo-Confucianism and Buddhism in terms that clearly reflect Hu's ideas (14–17), summarizes "Hu's theory of the evolution of rationalism in Chinese thought" (164–168), and discusses the modern renaissance in his final chapter. However, I find it curious that all this is done without explicit reference to Hu's historical theory. (Indeed, other than a few sentences quoted from Hu Shih on p. 318, the term "renaissance" never appears in any quotation from any Chinese source in Grieder's book; the early twentieth-century discussion of the fate of modern China was couched more in terms of revolution than renaissance.) Grieder's book is well written, extremely useful, and soundly researched, but he might have done well to consider the contents of *The Chinese Renaissance* for its relevance to Hu's political thought, in particular his espousal of *wuwei* as an approach to government. (See Grieder, 261–264.)
74. "Wo di qilu" 我的歧路, in *Hu Shi wencun* 3, 108, as translated by Lin Yusheng, "Pseudo-reformism," 86–87.
75. Grieder, *Hu Shih and the Chinese Renaissance,* 215.
76. Benjamin Schwartz pointed out to me (private communication) that Hu generally failed to consider issues of power relationships.

ground of the Song dynasty renaissance in order to comprehend his own role in the one he perceived in twentieth-century China.[77]

Certainly Hu Shih could have foreseen no better eventuality for modern China than to imitate and incorporate the lessons of the West while still retaining an inherently "Sinitic" nature. Nowhere is the relationship between Hu Shih's scholarship and value system more apparent than in his comments on the subject of naturalism, which was for him almost an absolute principle to be associated with scientific rationalism. The third item in his "Naturalistic Conception of Life and the Universe" reads:

> On the basis of all our verifiable scientific knowledge, we should recognize that the universe and everything in it follow natural laws of movement and change—"natural" in the Chinese sense of "being so of themselves"—and that there is no need for the concept of a supernatural Ruler or Creator.[78]

Hu's further comments indicate his firm belief in the progression from primitive superstition to the conscious cooperation of modern man in "reducing the brutality and wastefulness of the natural struggles."[79] One important corollary of these beliefs is that the naturalism of classical Chinese philosophy represented a significant contribution by China to world civilization. Hu also believed that modern China could benefit through the application of Daoist ideas on governance.[80]

There is a clear congruence between Hu's interpretation of Shenhui and his modern insistence on "the values of individual dignity and intellectual independence which were, in his [i.e., Hu's] view, the indispensable components of national and cultural regeneration."[81] That is, Shenhui's importance was in re-appropriating from a basically Indian worldview the Chinese right to "individual dignity and intellectual independence." It should not be too harsh to conclude that his interpretation of Shenhui said more about Hu Shih than it did about eighth-century Chan Buddhism.[82]

---

77. In *The Chinese Renaissance*, 44–45, Hu states that the periods of renaissance in traditional China differed from the twentieth-century renaissance only in the "absence of a conscious recognition of their historical mission." That modern renaissance, he writes, was aimed at producing a new literature (in colloquial Chinese) and at emancipating individual Chinese from the forces of tradition. "It was a movement of reason versus tradition, freedom versus authority, and glorification of life and human values versus their suppression." Finally, the modern renaissance was humanist in the sense that it was led by men who attempted to study the Chinese cultural heritage by means of new methods of historical criticism and research.

78. Einstein et al., *Living Philosophies*, 260–261.

79. Ibid., 263.

80. See the reference to *wuwei* in n. 73 above.

81. Grieder, *Hu Shih and the Chinese Renaissance*, 322. Also see Grieder's summary of Hu's system of beliefs on 325–326.

82. Hu Shih clearly opposed Indian superstition and Chinese naturalism, while in the modern context he wanted to wed Western science with that native sensibility. However, there are conceptual similarities between the "complexity" of the Indian religion and the rational

Why did Hu Shih study Shenhui? Far from being an incidental or peripheral concern in his life, the study of early Chan and the figure of Shenhui represented an enterprise that was uniquely suited to Hu Shih's broader interests and deepest inclinations.[83] Hu explicitly stated that he studied the glories of the Chinese past in order to release himself from direct contact with the miseries of the Chinese present, and he openly advocated this avocation to his fellow students and countrymen. The study of early Chan was for him a particularly soothing escape, for by rediscovering Shenhui he could rewrite history into a kind of past that would allow China to face its modern challenges. By identifying Chan with the revival of protoscientific Chinese naturalism, Hu Shih provided China with both the intellectual resources and the humanistic model for its modern salvation.[84] A humanist who worshipped the salvific efficacy of modern science, Hu Shih was racked by an awareness of his own inability to change China directly. And, of course, he was incensed with the stupefying role of the Chinese tradition, especially the superstition that he perceived in his mother's Buddhist faith. The result was integral to his very existence: Hu Shih made Shenhui into someone he was not and Chan into something it was not, all because Hu Shih himself was not the someone he would have been and China was not the realm he would have had it be.

V. Chan and the Chinese Renaissance in Contemporary Historiography

A. On Hu Shih and the Study of Chinese Buddhism

Even though Hu Shih's work on Chan and the Chinese Renaissance has not received prominent explicit attention, my impression is that it has been widely influential, or at least that it exemplifies the dominant approach of modern historiography on medieval and premodern China. In this sense his impact resembles that in another area, for as Joshua Fogel remarks about the "rediscovery" of Qing intellectuals by Hu Shih and others,

---

principles of modern science. It is too bad Hu Shih was not aware of the modern dialogue on whether or not primitive superstitious thought constitutes proto-science.

83. Min-chih Chou has commented perceptively on Hu Shih's advocacy of the literary revolution, his attitudes toward Chinese culture, and his dedication to classical scholarship. See his *Hu Shih and Intellectual Choice,* 149–200. In particular, Chou's analysis of the differences between Hu Shih's writings in Chinese and English and between his scholarly and popular writings evokes the full dimensions of the pain in Hu Shih's soul. Although Hu's writings on Chan vary little depending on whether they are in Chinese or English (those in Chinese are more often given to scholarly detail), his feelings of alienation and defensiveness are frequently just below the surface.

84. Lin Yusheng suggests, in overstated terms, that for Hu Shih the idea of progress was an unambiguous movement toward Dewey's instrumentalism, and that Hu's intellectual agenda was to make "Chinese culture a scientistic one in which everything—including ethics—was to be arbitrated by science and the Deweyan method of science." See Lin, "Pseudoreformism," 83n and 91.

this revival project in the hands of Hu Shih and his colleagues has virtually provided us with our present curriculum for the study of modern Chinese intellectual history. One would like to know why, for example, the cluster of eighteenth-century figures we read about is always the same.... Largely responsible for this, I believe, is the work of Liang Ch'i-ch'ao (and K'ang Yu-wei before him), Hu Shih, the early Ku Chieh-kang, Ch'ien Mu, William Hung, and a handful of other towering intellects who in the late Ch'ing and early Republic did an enormous service to our field in bringing into popular focus a number of men forgotten or ignored by earlier generations of Chinese. As scholars, however, it is our responsibility not merely to accept this legacy, but to criticize it vigorously and point to its flaws.[85]

Hu Shih's work on Chan Buddhism and the Chinese Renaissance embodies the following systemic errors:

1. A strong prejudice against Buddhism and religion in general, which was equated with superstition.
2. The implication that Buddhism first succeeded in penetrating China because of the cultural weakness and malaise of the Six Dynasties period, coupled with the converse assertion that the decline of Chinese Buddhism began with the transformation of Chinese society in the late Tang.
3. The correlation of the emergence of Chan with the transformation of Chinese society and the decline of other forms of Buddhism, coupled with a focus on the emergence of Chan to the exclusion of other facets, schools, and contributions of Buddhism, even including later periods of Chan.
4. The uncritical use of historical research in service of the needs of the present.

[1.] There is little reason to consider the first point. Hu Shih's prejudice against Buddhism was extreme and debilitating, to a degree that does not obtain in later scholars working in this area.[86] His beliefs regarding the identity of religion and superstition and the fundamental difference between superstition and science were unsophisticated even for his day, and they do not merit serious consideration now. However, even though we may have rid ourselves of overt prejudice, it is still important to understand and undergo "consciousness raising" concerning our own preconceptions.[87] That is, in

---

85. Fogel, "'Rediscovery' of the Chinese Past," 234.
86. This is certainly not the only field to suffer from a strong dose of prejudice; cf. Edward Said's *Orientalism* and the discussion it has generated.
87. In n. 28 above Eber notes Bultmann's sensitivity to the problems implicit in writing history to show the comparison with Hu Shih. The choice is apt, especially since Bultmann explicitly noted the difference between prejudice and preconception. See his "Is Exegesis without Presuppositions Possible?" from a selection of essays originally published in German in 1957.

what ways does the conventional interpretation of the role of Buddhism in Chinese history reflect problematic preconceptions?

[2.] It is undeniably true that the diffusion of Buddhism to China was aided by the apparent conceptual congruence between it and philosophical Daoism. It is also true that some of the trends in philosophical and alchemical Daoism in South China during the early part of the Six Dynasties period may be characterized as being in part functions of a cultural malaise. I would suggest, however, that Chinese cultural weakness and malaise cannot be accepted as primary reasons for the Buddhist "conquest" of China. Certainly the bare fact of disunity and the control of northern China by non-Chinese rulers were important factors that influenced the identity of Buddhism as it developed in China, but the religion spread in different ways throughout the northern and southern portions of the country. Indeed, the historiographical problem here is typified by the term "country": even granting the contemporary urge to reunify China, it is problematic to conceive of Six Dynasties China as a single state undergoing a temporary, non-normative period of disunion; we cannot suspend our knowledge of the later series of unified regimes, but we must resist predicating unification as an inevitable event already embodied in embryo form in Six Dynasties China. It has been said that European scientific and philosophical innovations were made possible by the many different political units there and by the absence of a single monolithic regime, and we may approach the diversity of the Six Dynasties in a similarly positive vein. That is, rather than focus on the weakness of the disrupted unity we would do well to focus on the potential for creative growth.

The problematic nature of the "weakness and malaise" explanation of Buddhism's initial acceptance by the peoples of China is put into stark relief when we consider the implicit corollary: that when Chinese society became strong and healthy once again it rejected Buddhism as useless foreign superstition. Thus it is generally said that Buddhism began to decline in China about the time that Chinese society underwent the major social changes associated with the Tang/Song transition.

We should reconsider what we mean when we talk of the "decline" of Chinese Buddhism. It may well be true that certain of the more prominent forms of elite Buddhist activity largely disappeared or were severely curtailed, among them translations from Sanskrit, the formation of new schools, and the composition of systematic Buddhist theory. We have long known that conventional Buddhist sources from the Six Dynasties and Sui/Tang periods place a great emphasis on literary endeavors and historical writing. These were by no means the only facets of the religion, however, and it is incorrect to suppose that significant changes in the composition of systematic doctrinal expositions—even the complete disappearance of the practice—is necessarily correlated with comprehensive and systemic decline.

There are several reasons why we are inclined to think of post-Tang Chinese Buddhism in terms of decline and decay. One major factor has been the legacy of Japanese scholarship on Chinese Buddhism. The fact of Ennin's

圓仁 presence in China during one of the worst persecutions of Buddhism there may have helped fix the notion of the post-Tang decline in the Japanese mind,[88] and the traditional tendency of Japanese Buddhist studies has been to postulate "schools" of Chinese Buddhism paralleling the institutional identities of the schools of Nara Japan.[89] Since such schools did not arise in China and were not transmitted to Japan following the Tang (the transmission of Zen and Pure Land Buddhism to Japan are taken as qualitatively different phenomena), we have naturally—and mistakenly, I believe—tended to view post-Tang Chinese Buddhism in terms of its inevitable "decline."

The widespread acceptance of the Naitō hypothesis, which takes the transformation of Chinese society during the Tang as a major watershed in Chinese history, has led scholars to homologize the various religious developments of the post-Tang dynasties under the general rubric of popular religion. Since Buddhism flourished within the medieval culture of the Tang and earlier dynasties, it is natural that scholars would think that it would assume the alternate state, i.e., decline, in the premodern culture of the Song and beyond. And the very term "popular religion" carries the connotation that Buddhism was no longer a vital part of elite culture. Chinese Buddhism did experience a fundamental change after the events of 755 (the An Lushan rebellion), 845 (the Huichang persecution), and 875 (the Huang Chao rebellion), but even a radical decrease in the number of new innovations in systematic Buddhist doctrine is not equivalent to the absence of all innovation.[90]

However, the judgment that post-Tang Chinese Buddhism was in decline—or at least largely irrelevant—is in large part the legacy of orthodox Chinese scholarship. The work of Hu Shih, which revels in the Neo-

---

88. Reischauer, *Ennin's Travels in Tang China*, 35–37, deals only briefly with Ennin's impact on Japanese Buddhism. On this subject see Weinstein, "The Beginnings of Esoteric Buddhism in Japan: The Neglected Tendai Tradition." With regard to de Bary's assertions about this important pilgrim, I disagree with the characterization of him as a "last great figure" in the Sino-Japanese Buddhist tradition. Also, there were a great number of subsequent pilgrims, especially those associated with the Zen school, who moved between China, Korea, and Japan, and who did more to transmit Buddhism to Japan than merely function as a "neutral excipient" for the transmission of Neo-Confucianism.

89. This tendency has long been recognized and is being changed. For example, Sekiguchi Shindai's 関口真大 documentation that the "five periods and eight teachings" of the Tiantai school has led to a re-evaluation of the manner in which systematic Buddhist doctrine was formulated at different points in the Chinese tradition. One example of such innovative research is that by Peter N. Gregory on the differing hermeneutical goals of "doctrinal categorization" (*panjiao* 判教) in the Huayan tradition; see Gregory's *Tsung-mi and the Sinification of Chinese Buddhism*. However, it is important to realize that Chinese Buddhist "schools" do not share the peculiar institutional identities of the Japanese denominations that developed in the Tokugawa period.

90. On the relative impact of the Huichang persecution and Huang Chao rebellion, see Weinstein, *Buddhism under the T'ang*, 147.

Confucian "renaissance" that began in the Song, has been a very prominent model.

[3.] I am perfectly ready to accept the assertion that the rise of Chan Buddhism was roughly contemporaneous with major changes in Chinese society. I am also willing—even eager—to argue that the emergence of Chan represented an important facet of the transformation of Chinese religion to match the transformation of Chinese society.[91] But should we necessarily correlate these social and religious changes with religious decline? In addition, since the social changes involved the decentralization and fragmentation of political power (at least until the founding of the Song), we are in fact faced with a resounding contradiction: that both the initial acceptance and growth of Buddhism and its eventual decline were caused by essentially identical forces. Although this is not an entirely inconceivable paradox, we should be prepared to reexamine this double-edged use of a single argument.[92]

Indeed, if we accept the possibility of the transformation of Chinese Buddhism concurrent with the transformation of Chinese society, we should expect that the older standards for gauging the level of religious fervor should no longer apply. From the perspective of Chan studies it seems foolish to conceive of Buddhism during the Song as being in a state of decline. By many potentially measurable indicators, in fact, I would suspect that Buddhism was at least as successful then as during any other period of Chinese history. The composition of systematic doctrinal and historical texts may have largely come to an end during the Song, but we need to reassess the writings of the Song in terms of a more sophisticated appreciation of the "schools" of Chinese Buddhism. In any case, in addition to the previously important categories of temple construction, ordination of monks, and imperial support, we should consider the widespread activities of the various Chan factions, as indicated

---

91. Where Hu Shih focused on the doctrine of sudden enlightenment, I have developed an interpretation of the transformation of Chinese Chan in terms of its generation of a new paradigm for religious practice. (See my essay "Encounter Dialogue and the Transformation of the Spiritual Path in Chinese Chan" for an initial statement.) Hopefully, this interpretation will allow us greater insight into the events of the past without committing the same methodological transgressions as those I attribute to Hu Shih. In the first place, Hu Shih interpreted the doctrine of sudden enlightenment as something of a universal switch that completely transformed all of Chinese Buddhism. Unidimensional, omnipotent mechanisms such as this are hardly possible and should be avoided. Second, we will have to modify the assumption that Chinese culture and the Buddhist religion were separate systems that can be discussed and analyzed separately. Especially during the periods under consideration here, it is valid to consider Buddhism a foreign religion only insofar as the concept of "foreign religion" was operant within Chinese culture.

92. One obvious change was that the force of cultural diffusion from India had declined by the ninth century. Slightly before this time we begin to see diffusion from east to west along the Silk Road, a function of the strength and vitality of the Tang. Although the influx of Buddhism from India and Central Asia to China did not abate entirely, around the time of the reestablishment of central political administration under the Song, Islam more than Buddhism was moving across the same critical area.

by vigorous growth of Chan training centers and the dynamic evolution and large-scale publication of Chan literature.[93]

I find it significant how little attention Song dynasty Chan has received in the scholarly literature, at least until the past few years. The study of *early* Chan has been an exciting enterprise, one in which I have enjoyed taking part. However, the very extent to which attention has been focused on the emergence of Chan to the exclusion of other subjects is a function of the disposition to treat Chinese Buddhism in the same terms as those defined by Hu Shih. Far from being irrelevant, the development of Chan after the Tang is of immense importance in the history of Chinese Buddhism and of Chinese culture in general. The trajectory of Chan Buddhism in China must take it into the Song, when it flourished on a national scale and when it institutionalized the new paradigm initially generated by classical Chan in the late eighth and early ninth centuries. It is not a problem at all for Chan to be reaching its peak at the same time that Neo-Confucianism arose; in fact, I would much rather have us approach Chinese history in terms of multiple, chronologically overlapping trends rather than the totalistic binary switches implicit in Hu Shih's scheme of periodization.

We have seen some research in Chinese Pure Land Buddhism, but there could certainly be more. There has been virtually no research in Chinese esoteric Buddhism, which arrived in China in the eighth century and was extremely popular through the Song. Since esoteric Buddhism in many ways represents a counter-example to that of Chan, research in this subject has great potential for challenging and substantiating generalizations about Chinese Buddhism developed through the study of Chan. Chinese esoteric Buddhism is *the* least well-studied tradition of East Asian religions.

[4.] Ultimately, all the problems in Hu Shih's work derive from a single point: his dedication to the pragmatic use of history. Hu Shih wanted to expel superstition in favor of science in modern China, and he longed for the intellectual transformation that would make this possible. Thus he lionized Shenhui, the Buddhist monk who performed the distinctly anti-Buddhist service of undercutting all religious practice with a revolutionary doctrinal innovation. His interpretive structure simply overwhelmed the evidence.

B. On the Legacy of Hu Shih's Approach

Although it may be impossible to detect the specific influence of Hu Shih at every turn, it is not difficult to find interpretations that closely parallel his throughout English-language writings on Chan Buddhism.

Arthur F. Wright's *Buddhism in Chinese History*, still an eminently readable volume more than four decades after its publication, cites Hu Shih and

---

93. In a study of Chan-related commentaries on the *Heart Sūtra*, I have tentatively concluded that there were important continuities from the Tang to the Song and again from the Ming onward. See McRae, "Chan Commentaries on the *Heart Sūtra*." The reaction to the repressive nature of the Yuan dynasty and the idiosyncratic approach to Buddhism of the founding emperor of the Ming might be considered keys to changes in Chinese Buddhism just as fundamental as those of the late Tang.

utilizes his concept of the appropriation of various facets of Buddhism by the native Chinese tradition after the end of the Tang. However, Wright refrains from importing the most characteristic elements of Hu's overall theory into his work.

Kenneth K. S. Ch'en takes almost the opposite approach in *Buddhism in China: A Historical Survey*, by depicting Buddhism after the Tang in terms of its overall decline. Although this depiction is neither entirely inaccurate nor entirely dependent on Hu Shih's theory, the correlation is likely; Ch'en was at least familiar with Hu's interpretation of the role of Buddhism in Chinese society.[94] In his later work, *The Chinese Transformation of Buddhism*, Ch'en explicitly refers to Hu's ideas on the Indianization of China, but only as a foil for his own elaboration of the converse effect, the Sinification of Buddhism.[95]

The most striking example of the influence of Hu Shih's theories may be found in Jacques Gernet's magnum opus, the very impressive work entitled *A History of Chinese Civilization*. Gernet's description of innovations in Chinese society around the year 1000 and his justification of the term "Renaissance" are especially reminiscent of Hu Shih.[96] Not only does Gernet describe the fate of Buddhism after the Tang in terms of a general decline in religious enthusiasm, he describes the Chan school as "more Chinese than Buddhist" and castigates the literature of Chan and other Buddhist writers during the Song dynasty as an unimaginative "balance sheet of the past."[97]

Finally, many of the criticisms stated above with regard to Hu Shih could be applied, with significant but not fundamental alteration, to the work of William T. de Bary. It goes without saying, of course, that de Bary's work lacks even a hint of the gauche and simplistic prejudice that was a constant in Hu Shih's writing. However, the two scholars' schemes of periodization are virtually identical: Where the Chinese scholar used three major periods, the American uses four, the only difference being the bifurcation of Hu's modern age into de Bary's Neo-Confucian and modern ages. Otherwise, even the dates and names given are similar.[98] In discussing the Buddhist

---

94. See Ch'en, *Buddhism in China*, 207.

95. Ch'en, *Chinese Transformation*, 3–5. Ch'en also mentions, on 5n, *The Indianization of China and of South-East Asia* by H. G. Quaritch Wales (London: Bernard Quaritch, 1967), a volume I have not been able to consult.

96. Gernet, *History of Chinese Civilization*, 298.

97. Cf. ibid., 295–296.

98. Professor de Bary's four lectures were on the Classical Age, also called the Formative Stage (roughly 11th cent. BCE through the 2nd cent. CE), the Buddhist Age (3rd to 10th cent.), the Neo-Confucian Age (11th to 19th cent.), and the Modern Age (19th cent. to the present). Hu Shih's scheme of three major periods of Chinese history is reminiscent of the thesis-antithesis-synthesis model of German philosophy. This impression is of course lessened in de Bary's approach, but in either case I wonder how history can be compartmentalized so easily. What factors differentiate the ages from each other, and what are the mechanisms and dynamics of change? I suspect that the entire notion of such macro-level periods reflects a type of prospective analysis. That is, were de Bary's four ages chosen through an overly strong influence of modernization theory, where the past is examined not for its own sake but in order to explain how it moved into the present? To the extent that this is true there is an underlying congruence with Hu Shih's goals.

Age, Professor de Bary too implies that Buddhism first succeeded in penetrating China because of the cultural weakness and malaise of the Six Dynasties period, and he concentrates on precisely the same period of early Chan as that studied so intensively by Hu Shih. Where Hu Shih emphasized the importance of Shenhui, de Bary focuses on the legendary sixth patriarch Huineng as depicted in the *Platform Sūtra*. And where Hu Shih perceived Shenhui as a revolutionary figure, de Bary describes Huineng as "a new model of direct and sudden enlightenment for Everyman" and "the personification of the Chinese egalitarian ideal." Obviously, these are terms that resonate with de Bary's postulation of a liberal tradition in China.[99]

My point is not that Wright, Ch'en, Gernet, and de Bary should be castigated for the errors of their ways, but that the dominant approach to the role of Buddhism in Chinese history needs to be revised. Indeed, de Bary's extremely productive and influential career provides a useful model for the realignment and promotion of Buddhist studies in this country. Just as the research he has performed and sponsored has transformed our understanding of Neo-Confucianism from that of an unimaginative and sterile political ideology into that of a dynamic and rich humanistic tradition, so should those of us in Buddhist studies work to transform the frequent misunderstanding of our subject from that of an irrelevant digression from the true course of Chinese history to that of a vital and creative religious system. This will be to the benefit of not merely those in Chan studies[100] or even Buddhist studies in general, but to all of us who study East Asian civilizations.

VI. Shenhui and the Role of Chan Buddhism in Chinese History

Just because Chinese Chan enthusiastically embraced Shenhui's slogan of sudden enlightenment, we should not conclude that the same was true of

---

99. The inference that de Bary's treatment correlates with his interest in the Chinese "liberal tradition" is mine; he does not use the term in his lecture in this context. Perhaps not coincidentally, Hu Shih also used the term liberal to describe Chinese Confucianism.

100. Where Neo-Confucianism was once perceived as dull and lifeless, the critical assessment of Chan Buddhism in Western writings on traditional China has been held hostage to the image of the religion as a popular modern social phenomenon. The energetic missionary activities of D. T. Suzuki were effective in opening our eyes to the incredible treasures of East Asian civilization—an accomplishment for which everyone engaged in the humanistic study of world civilizations, both east and west, should be grateful—but they also succeeded in fixing a very distinctive image in our minds: Chan (or Zen) was unique, personal, ahistorical, transcendent, ineffable, irrational, even mystical. To Suzuki, the only feature of Chan worth considering was its central religious message, which he referred to as the "enlightenment experience." Even where he was involved in the discovery and publication of primary texts relevant to the origins of Chan, Suzuki did his best to read them so as to support his own very traditionalistic yet idiosyncratic interpretation of the intuitive brilliance of Bodhidharma and Huineng. The rigidity of Suzuki's historical prejudice was a supreme irony in view of his position that the Chan enlightenment experience freed one from dogmatic preconceptions. On the occidentalist agenda at the foundations of Suzuki's career, see Sharf, "The Zen of Japanese Nationalism."

his other positions. In fact, Shenhui's contributions to Chan were generally achieved through a process of negative impact. Shenhui created a crisis in early Chan with his factionalist anti-Northern school campaign, which led to creative growth in Chan only because of the efforts taken by the tradition to overcome the divisiveness of his attack. It is not even accurate to say that he caused the disappearance of the Northern school, since it never existed as an institutional entity to begin with, or the superseding of the gradual teaching by the sudden teaching, since no one ever advocated the doctrinally backward position that he described and criticized. In fact, many of the contributions of the "Northern school" were maintained by the later Chan tradition, even though they were presented under the aegis of the Oxhead and Hongzhou schools. The Oxhead school, with the *Platform Sūtra*, and the Sichuan factions, with the *Records of the Transmission* (*Lidai fabao ji* 歷代法寶記), collectively installed many of Shenhui's innovations into the Chan tradition—with his authorship neatly obscured. Certain sayings of Mazu and Huizhong also appear to criticize ideas of Shenhui's.[101]

Just as Shenhui's major effort was propagandistic, his major impact lay in the realm of rhetoric and mythopoeia. In addition to establishing a standard of rhetorical purity, he is responsible for the addition of many new anecdotes regarding Bodhidharma and the early patriarchs to the early Chan repertoire. In the process Shenhui helped make the theory of the transmission of the Dharma much more concrete and precise, even though he did not significantly alter the conceptual basis of the theory.[102] Coupled with his penchant for storytelling, this new attention to the form rather than only the substance of religious pronouncements may have helped bring about the emergence of encounter dialogue and the "recorded sayings" genre of Chan literature.[103] These changes may be formalistic, but they were of the highest significance to the development of the Chan tradition.

The real transformation that took place in Chan during the eighth century was the emergence of the practice of "encounter dialogue" in the Hongzhou school of Mazu Daoyi, which is the earliest faction of the classical phase of Chinese Chan Buddhism. The literature of encounter dialogue may be placed under the rubric of the sudden teaching, in the sense that it satisfies the twofold criteria mentioned above. Since the practitioners of

---

101. See Yanagida, "Goroku no rekishi," 388, 393, 402, and 407–408. On p. 410, he suggests that the *Platform Sūtra* then in turn criticized Huizhong's ideas. (Yanagida also mentions criticism by members of the Oxhead school and other figures.)

102. Yanagida argues that throughout his life Shenhui maintained a chronologically absurd theory of eight Indian patriarchs between the Buddha and Bodhidharma. See Yanagida, *Shoki Zenshū shisho*, 124.

103. In fact, Yanagida describes Shenhui's *Platform Sermon* as having all the basic elements of the genre: it was compiled by a named individual rather than anonymously; circulation was intended to be limited to those with affinities for Shenhui's teachings; and, most important, the emphasis of the text is on the instruction of the people actually in Shenhui's audience at one specific time. See Yanagida, "Goroku no rekishi," 391–392 and 399, plus the related comments regarding the *Miscellaneous Dialogues* on 369 and 376.

encounter dialogue relentlessly attacked gradualistic formulations and exhorted students on to diligent endeavor, they could make effective use of the slogan of sudden enlightenment. In addition, since Shenhui's anti-Northern school campaign and the appearance of the *Platform Sūtra* had provided a legendary explanation of the sudden / gradual dichotomy that was convenient, instructive (in a very profound sense), and entertaining, the later Chan school adopted this legend as part of its own historical self-understanding. In contrast to the image presented in this legend, however, the sudden / gradual dichotomy was something of a false issue in the development of Chan. Although Shenhui contributed to the increasingly clear crystallization of Chan ideas and to the elaboration of its iconoclastic spirit, his career did not represent a fundamental break in the course of the school's development. Shenhui's teachings were extensions of, rather than radical alternatives to, Northern school doctrine, and his innovations only contributed to the emergence of classical Chan within the overall context of early Chan in general.

Shenhui as Evangelist
Re-envisioning the Identity of a Chinese Buddhist Monk

Speaking of Zen Masters

Zen masters are not all the same. That is, we have become accustomed to thinking of Chan or Zen teachers as belonging to an ideal type known as "Zen master," each one the specific iteration of a generalized model. There is a certain range of variation within the genre, to be sure: each individual teacher has his own unique identity, involving personal temperament, teaching style, and doctrinal perspective. In spite of these differences, though, we tend to conceive of Chan masters as all performing a single function, the instruction of students in the process of spiritual self-cultivation. Exactly what this process involves, how different masters collaborate in the guidance of their students, as well as what precisely constitutes the Chan master's contribution to the students' lives—and why the Chan master's identity is so overwhelmingly masculine, even for female teachers—are very difficult to explain, of course. Nevertheless, there is an unspoken agreement that the performance of this role constitutes the sine qua non of being considered a legitimate contributor to the Chan tradition. In spite of these difficulties, or perhaps precisely because of them, our shared understanding of "Zen master" stands artificially separate from the vicissitudes of history and outside of perceived variations in human culture.

I do not mean to claim that this shared understanding constitutes a psychological archetype, nor that the contemporary Japanese understanding is identical to the contemporary American one, for example. And, of course, there are no doubt substantial differences between our various contemporary understandings and those of medieval and premodern Chinese, Koreans, or other East Asians. In spite of these differences, when we read and write about Chan Buddhism, of whatever time period and cultural setting, we tend to imagine the principal actors in terms of some monolithic image of Zen

---

This paper first appeared in Japanese in a festschrift volume for Professor Tanaka Ryōshō 田中良昭 of Komazawa University, *Zengaku kenkyū no shosō: Tanaka Ryōshō hakushi koki kinen ronshū*, 1–26 (from the back of the book). It was reprinted, in English, in the *Journal of Chinese Religions* 30 (2002): 123–148. The author would like to thank Stephen R. Bokenkamp and Robert F. Campany for comments on an earlier draft, as well as colleagues at the University of Toronto, Indiana University, and the University of California at Berkeley for the helpful suggestions after oral presentations at those institutions.

masters interacting with their students. I suggest that this tendency limits our ability to appreciate the cultural dynamics of the historical evolution of Chan, that it leads us to conceive of the tradition in intellectually unhealthy terms as composed of a succession of essentially and typologically identical, if temperamentally distinct, figures who stand outside of time and culture.

Of course, many written and oral pronouncements of the Chan tradition are aimed at convincing us that this is precisely the case: that the lineage of patriarchs represents a succession of enlightened individuals who all performed essentially the same functions of teaching and transmission. Part of my goal in writing this essay is to argue that, no matter how profoundly influential this construct may be in the context of individual religious training in the Chan tradition, to use it in unchallenged fashion as a template for our understanding of the historical evolution of the school is intellectually indefensible. In the following pages I will show how breaking free from the Zen-master stereotype can open up new possibilities for the understanding of Chan's evolution as a phenomenon of human culture.

The specific case to be considered here is the Chinese Chan monk Heze Shenhui 荷澤神會 (684–758), who is widely known as the first proponent of Huineng's 慧能 (638–713) status as "sixth patriarch" and advocate for the teaching of sudden enlightenment within the Southern school. To put it most concisely, in this essay I will show that (1) Shenhui was not a "Zen master" at all, but a man whose primary religious vocation was that of evangelist; (2) appreciating Shenhui's identity in this fashion is theoretically elegant, in the sense that it allows a straightforward and comprehensive interpretation of his life and teachings; and (3) the resulting reinterpretation has significant ramifications for the understanding of Chan and Chinese Buddhism as a whole. In other words, the payoff for using the example of Shenhui to deconstruct the shared understanding of Zen master is both substantial and multidimensional.

Shenhui as Factionalist Campaigner

Shenhui is best known for the campaign he undertook on behalf of the Southern school and his teacher Huineng and in opposition to advocates of a so-called Northern school who were students of Shenxiu 神秀 (606?–706). Shenhui initiated this campaign in 730, 731, and 732 in a series of public events that were staged as debates between himself and another monk standing in for the Northern school and held at Huatai 滑台 (Hua xian, Henan 河南省滑縣), about two hundred kilometers east-northeast of Luoyang along the Yellow River. After moving into the capital city of Luoyang in 745, Shenhui continued his campaign on a monthly basis, at least until his banishment from the city in 753. Although we must admit the likelihood that other concerns also occupied Shenhui's attentions during those nearly twenty years—i.e., that his involvement in the campaign may have been episodic or discontinuous—there is an obvious overall contour of acceleration and crescendo to this aspect of his life. Overall, his sphere of activities moved from geographical periphery to imperial center, where he gathered increasing attention until the time of his banishment.

One reason for Shenhui's success in this campaign must have been the histrionic manner in which he pursued it. Near the beginning of the edited transcript of the "debate" of 732, a text known as the *Definition of the Truth*,[1] it is said that Shenhui's adversary "raised his eyebrows and lifted his voice in total dedication to victory in battle" over Shenhui. Shenhui wins their brief initial verbal skirmish (as he does all the others, too!), after which his opponent "realized that his error was egregious, and he appeared dazed before the assembly. After a little while, he tried to speak again, but Shenhui said, 'You've been pinned to the ground. Why do you need to get up again?'"[2] And, just a few lines later, Shenhui and his adversary stand facing each other in anger, "their faces pale."[3] All of this shows that the notion of a conflict between the Northern and Southern "schools" of Chan was created initially through the medium of staged theatrics and their literary representation in Shenhui's written texts.

Shenhui's substantive criticisms of the "Northern school" (a name that he devised and applied for the first time to Shenxiu and his students) were twofold: that Shenxiu had not received the direct transmission of Buddhism from Bodhidharma and that the Northern school understanding of Buddhism was inferior. At this point I would like to focus only on the latter point, which is epitomized in Shenhui's criticisms of alleged Northern school meditation practices. In particular, he is famous for the denunciation of instructions to "freeze the mind to enter concentration, fix the mind to view purity, activate the mind for external illumination, and concentrate the mind for internal realization."[4] These "four pronouncements" are actually a major cornerstone of Shenhui's teachings; they are repeated several times as anonymous criticisms of contemporary practices in his earliest text, the *Platform Sermon* (which probably antedates the anti-Northern school campaign), while in the *Definition of the Truth* they are applied specifically to members of the Northern school. Simply put, these four pronouncements represent a rejection of a yogic approach to meditation practice, one in which individual practitioners cultivate different states of consciousness as a form of mental calisthenics. The alternative, of course, was to practice in such a way as to achieve "sudden enlightenment" (*dunwu* 頓悟), an

---

1. Here I use an abbreviated title, the full form being *Putidamo nanzong ding shifei lun* 菩提達摩南宗定是非論 (Definition of the Truth [regarding] Bodhidharma's Southern School). For passages cited from this text, see Hu Shih, *Shenhui heshang yiji*, 260–316, and my translation in this volume (cited as *Definition of the Truth*). This text was edited after 745 and again after Shenhui's death; hence it does not constitute a perfect transcript of the 732 event.

2. Literally, "your backbone is touching the ground," using a wrestling analogy. Certainly, the sense of combat—and Shenhui's victory—is very strong in this exchange; see *Definition of the Truth*, section 7.

3. *Definition of the Truth*, section 9.

4. The Chinese is 凝心入定，住心看淨，起心外照，攝心內證.

instantaneous transformation from the unenlightened to the enlightened state. (This brief description will have to do for the moment; we will come back to the subject of sudden enlightenment below.)

Hu Shih 胡適 (1891–1962) has taken Shenhui's pronouncements to represent a veritable revolution in Chinese Buddhism, the beginning of a "Chinese renaissance" in which superstition and ritual were rejected in favor of a native Sinitic proto-rationalism. To him, Shenhui's teaching of sudden enlightenment thus represented the weapon by which Chinese culture began to throw off the yoke of Indian domination. Hu describes the entire situation in terms that are unmistakably redolent of the political travails of China in the early twentieth century, when he was writing. Within this context, he uses the memorable phrase "a new Chan that was no *chan* at all" to suggest that Shenhui had founded a new type of Chan Buddhism entirely divorced from the practice of *dhyāna* or meditation practice per se.[5]

In view of the subsequent evolution of Chan and Chinese Buddhism as a whole, it is obvious that Hu Shih was entirely wrong in his historical analysis. Simply put, neither Chinese Buddhism nor the Chinese Chan school eliminated the practices of meditation and ritual, as Hu suggested they did on the basis of Shenhui's impact. I have published a global critique of Hu's misinterpretation of Shenhui's life and teachings elsewhere;[6] at this point we need to focus solely on the following question: What role did the denunciation of yogic meditation practice play in Shenhui's own life and teachings? That is, even though Shenhui's denunciation of yogic meditation did not lead to a thorough rejection of meditation practice in all subsequent Chinese Buddhism, how did it fit within Shenhui's life and teachings as a whole?

In answering this question, let us notice two items about Shenhui. First, there is no evidence that he ever gave serious attention to the problems students face in the ongoing practice of meditation. Nothing in any of his texts ever suggests a sensitivity to the problems of spiritual maturation that occur after one has started on the path. There is no nuanced description of how to seek earnestly and energetically for the goal, even while refraining from positing enlightenment as an essentialized "goal," for example—as was done in texts of earlier Chan teachers.[7] This is of course an argument from silence, but given the volume of information we have about Shenhui—we have more

---

5. The name "Chan" was originally a Chinese transliteration of the Skt. *dhyāna* or Prakrit *jhāna*), meaning "concentration meditation," an important aspect of Indian Buddhist religious practice. Hu's catchword phrase, which he repeats often for increased impact, thus relies on the dual meaning of the term as the name of a religious movement or school and a term for meditation practice.

6. See "Religion as Revolution: Hu Shih on Shenhui's Role in Chan," reprinted in this volume.

7. The primary example here is of course the *Treatise on the Essentials of Cultivating the Mind* (*Xiuxin yao lun* 修心要論) attributed to Hongren (601–674), but the various passages on meditation practice attributed to Shenxiu and other Northern school figures, or circulated anonymously, might also be adduced here.

extensive documentation for him than for any other early Chan monk—the silence speaks volumes.

Second, the evidence concerning Shenhui's contacts with students and potential students indicates a consistent pattern: he was an inspiring figure to many, but the long-standing mentor of none. The following are all the contacts for which relevant biographical information is known:[8]

1. Sometime before 707 Shenhui met **Huilang** 慧朗 (662–725) at a location in what is now Zhejiang province. Shenhui refused Huilang's request to be the latter's teacher, since the much older prospective student had already "long accumulated pure karma," and he directed Huilang to Mount Tiantai 天台山. Along the way Huilang encountered a mysterious monk who inspired him to achieve an expansive enlightenment experience by pointing out that traveling afar was not necessary for understanding the eternally serene Dharma. Following this, Huilang returned to a temple in his native place. Huilang's biography continues on with a reference to Cunda that is reminiscent of the Southern school master's ideas, implying that whatever might have actually transpired between Huilang and Shenhui was edited with knowledge of Shenhui's later teachings.[9]

---

8. The discussion here is limited to information bearing on the given student's relationship with Shenhui. Oddly, with one minor exception none of the monks mentioned by name in Shenhui's writings are known from other biographical sources. (That exception is Chongyuan 崇遠, his debate opponent, whom I will not discuss here.) In addition, I have been unable to consult the epitaph for Huijian 慧堅 (d. 806), mentioned in n. 27 below. On Shenhui's disciples in general, see Ui Hakuju, *Zenshūshi kenkyū*, 238–255, and Wu Qiyu, "Heze Shenhui zhuan yanjiu," esp. 911–912. The major primary source used here is the *Song Biographies* (*Song gaoseng zhuan*, T 2061), but a list of disciples occurs in the *Transmission of the Lamp* (*Jingde chuandeng lu*), T 2076: 51.301a28–b10. One possible successor to Shenhui for whom no such information is available is Moheyan 摩和衍 (fl. 794), who defended the doctrine of sudden enlightenment in debates with Kamalaśīla at bSamyas monastery near Lhasa in 794. I will not discuss Nanyin 南印 here because the *Song Biographies* (T 2061: 50.772b4) identifies him as a student of Jingzhong Shenhui 淨眾神會 (720–794), not Heze Shenhui. See n. 13 below.

9. See *Song Biographies*, T 2061: 50.758c28–759a1. Huilang is not mentioned by Ui, but see Yanagida Seizan, *Shoki Zenshū shisho no kenkyū*, 198 and 200. The encounter occurred at North Mountain in Quzhou 衢州, just south of Huilang's native place, Xinding Sui'an 新定遂安, in Chun'an xian 淳安縣, Zhejiang. Judging from context, the encounter between Shenhui and Huilang occurred before 707, when the former might well have been wandering about to different Buddhist sites and teachers. Given the two men's ages, it is also possible that Huilang influenced Shenhui. That is, in 716 Huilang established an ordination platform on Dragon Mountain at Muzhou 睦州龍山 (just to the west of Xinding Sui'an), anticipating Shenhui's later activities. According to the biography, it was only here that Huilang took the full precepts himself, and Yanagida notes that his long-term status as layman resembles the life of Huineng. Huilang's biography in the *Song Biographies* includes several odd stories, casting him in both occultish and iconoclastic form. A foreign monk named Cunda was active in north China (including Mount Wutai) at about this time (see *Song Biographies*, T 2061: 50.844a5 and 890c23–891a6) but I believe the reference in the *Song Biographies* entry for Huilang is to the Indian figure. On Shenhui's self-identification with Cunda, see the *Definition of the Truth*, section 12.

2. Perhaps a decade later Shenhui met a monk named **Shenying** 神英, whom he advised to go to Mount Wutai 五台山 and worship Mañjuśrī Bodhisattva. Proceeding there in the sixth month of 716, Shenying had a visionary experience.[10]
3. **Jinping** 進平 (699–779), from Chang'an, was originally a commentator on the sūtras and treatises. When he turned to the practice of meditation and encountered Shenhui (identified here with Luoyang), he said, "Incredible! As to that which is not known from outside oneself—how could it be difficult?" Jinping then moved to a mountain probably located about 60 kilometers east-southeast of Nanyang. Later, during the period 756–758 (one wonders if this actually occurred after Shenhui's death in 758) Shenhui dispatched Jinping to deliver an ivory ritual scepter with handle to Huineng's stūpa; given the probable location of Jinping's residence he and Shenhui may have kept up contact, but there is no specific evidence of their relationship.[11]
4. It was only through wandering that **Daoyin** 道隱 (707–778) attained Shenhui's sudden illumination of the essence of the mind. After doing so he was called back to his native place in Ningzhou 寧州, (Qingyang xian 慶陽縣, Gansu) by lay supporters, where eventually his own body and that of a disciple were interred in undecayed form in Two Sages Chapel 二聖院.[12]

---

10. See Ui, *Zenshūshi kenkyū*, 207 and 248–249. Ui criticizes Shenhui for taking a student so early in his career, but there is no evidence that the contact between the two was anything more than incidental. For a comprehensive treatment of Shenying, see Raoul Birnbaum, "Manifestation of a Monastery." The encounter with Shenhui is mentioned on p. 121; the *Song Biographies* account occurs at T 2061: 50.843a11. Their meeting may have taken place at Nanyue 南岳, but this is uncertain. Incidentally, the encounter between Shenhui and Shenying resembles that between Shenxiu and Xiangmo Zang 降魔藏; see *Song Biographies*, T 2061: 50.760a9–28.

11. See *Song Biographies*, T 2061: 50.891a28–b5. Zongmi's *Chan Chart* (the *Zhonghua chuan xindi chanmen shizi chengxi tu* 中華傳心地禪門師資承襲圖) lists a Jinping which Ui, 244, identifies as this monk. Jinping's residence was at Xiyin shan in Tangzhou 唐州西隱山; Tangzhou was at the modem Piyuan xian 沘源縣 in Henan province. There is some confusion about Jinping's location of residence. The *Song Biographies* and *Transmission of the Lamp* identify him as a resident of Xiyin shan in Huai'an jun 懷安郡, corresponding to Xuanhua xian 宣化縣 in Hebei province. Neither Xiyin shan nor Huai'an jun are otherwise known (with regard to Chinese Buddhist monks, at any rate), and the Tangzhou location seems much more likely. Also, the reading of the gifts presented to Huineng's stūpa as an ivory ritual scepter and handle is speculative; the *Song Biographies* entry for Huineng reads *yayang he yi bing* 牙癢和一柄 (T 2061: 50.755b22–23). *Morohashi*, 7:609a, defines *yayang* only as "to gnash the teeth," based on the *Dream of the Red Chamber;* no other reference work I have consulted includes the term, which does not occur elsewhere in the *Taishō*. My reading is based on an analogy with the ritual scepters known as *ruyi* 如意, on which see *Bukkyōgo daijiten*, 1059d–1060a, and *Zengaku daijiten*, 988d–989a (which also gives the intriguing synonym *wayōshi* 和痒子, also not found elsewhere). Finally, note that Yuanzhen 圓震 (see item no. 10 below) lived even closer to Shenhui, on a mountain in Nanyang.

12. See *Song Biographies*, T 2061: 50.891b6–19. An explicit comparison is made to the alchemical refinement of cinnabar. For geographical identifications I have used county designations given by *Morohashi*, while consulting the historical atlas *Zhongguo lishi ditu ji*.

5. According to his biography in the *Song Biographies*, **Weizhong** 惟忠 (705–782) studied Buddhism from a young age under an otherwise unknown Chan master, presumably in Weizhong's native Chengdu. Later, during his wanderings Weizhong met Shenhui on Mount Song (a location with which Shenhui is not otherwise associated), cutting off his doubts in silence. Realizing through his investigations the exceptional qualities of Mount Huanglong 黃龍山, Weizhong constructed a thatched hut there, pacifying the mountain's poisonous dragons.[13]

6. **Haoyu** 皓玉 (703–784), originally from Shangdang 上黨 (Changzhi xian 長治縣, Shanxi) "greatly illuminated the mind-seal" under Shenhui—then entered a temple at Nanyue to "cultivate the way" (*yangdao* 養道).[14]

7. **Guangfu** 廣敷 (695–785), a resident of Nanyan 南燕 (Yanjin xian 延津縣, Henan), about 60 kilometers southeast of Huatai, was ordained and then wandered to Shaolin si 少林寺 and the two capitals. Encountering Shenhui and "greatly illuminating the mysterious principle" (*da ming xuanzhi* 大明玄旨), he took up residence at Mount Yangqi 陽岐山 in Yichun xian 宜春縣, Jiangxi, where he became renowned for interacting with Daoist immortals.[15]

8. **Fulin's** 福琳 (704–785) biography in the *Song Biographies* is appended to that of the poet-monk Jiaoran 皎然 (d.u.), whose epitaph Fulin wrote. Fulin was a native of Jingzhou 荊州, an important Buddhist location associated with Tiantai Zhiyi 天台智顗 (538–597) and Shenxiu, and his father was supervisor of the office (a minor clerical position) at the Jingzhou administrative headquarters in Xiangyang, Hubei, Shenhui's native place. After taking full ordination Fulin went to Luoyang to pay reverence to Shenhui, "matching the true mind" under him. After this Fulin proceeded to Huangpo 黃陂 (north of Hankou 漢口), where he built a thatched hut that developed into an active meditation center.[16]

---

13. See *Song Biographies*, T 2061: 50.763c8–20. The Chan master mentioned here was named Daoyuan 道願. Ui, 53–54, points out that the Mount Huanglong on the border of Jiangxi, Hubei, and Hunan was later an important Chan location and might be the one indicated here. In this entry Weizhong is identified with the surname Tong 童; other sources refer to a Weizhong by the surname Zhang 張. Zhang Weizhong is identified by Zongmi as the same individual as Nanyin (d. 821). This allowed Zongmi to claim descendance from Heze Shenhui, when his actual lineage derived from Jingzhong Shenhui. See Gregory, *Tsung-mi*, 35–37, including 36n33, and *Song Biographies*, T 2061: 50.772b2–12, for Nanyin.

14. See *Song Biographies*, T 2061: 50.893a14–18.

15. *Song Biographies*, T 2061: 50.838b15–25. In his youth Guangfu studied with Sihao 思浩 of Chang'an (otherwise unknown).

16. *Song Biographies*, T 2061: 50.892b22–28. Also see the *Transmission of the Lamp*, T 2076: 51.305b19–24, and Ui, 246. Fulin is identified as residing at Dashi shan in Huangzhou 黃州 大石山, some 50 kilometers east-southeast of Huangpo (Xinzhou xian 新洲縣). Fulin's epitaph for Jiaoran may be found in *Quan Tang wen* 全唐文, j. 919.

9. **Zhiman** 志滿 (705–785), from Luoyang, heard of the success of Shenhui's preaching in Luoyang after becoming ordained at the Longxing si in Yingchuan 潁川龍興寺 (Xuchang 許昌, Henan), about 150 kilometers southeast of Luoyang. After "attaining the essence of the mind" (*de liao xinyao* 得了心要) from Shenhui, Zhiman traveled south to Lingtang Spring at Mount Huang 黃山靈湯泉 in She xian 歙縣, Anhui, where he built a hut. After taming the tigers in the area, his residence became a major Chan (or meditation) chapel.[17]

10. **Yuanzhen** 圓震 (705–790), the son of a military functionary from Zhongshan 中山 (location unknown), loved to study as a youth but suddenly gave up Confucianism for Buddhism, traveling to Mount Baici 白磁山 (location unknown) to study under a monk there. Later he encountered Shenhui and "attained the Dharma" (*de fa* 得法), after which he secreted himself at Mount Wuya in Nanyang 南陽烏牙山. There he pacified the giant snakes and poisonous dragons with the "teaching of no-mind and the cultivation that cuts off thought" (*wuxin zhi hua, juelü zhi xiu* 無心之化絕慮之修).[18]

11. **Wuming** 無名 (722–793), whose family lived in Luoyang, left home at age twenty-eight (by the Chinese reckoning, in 749) and took up residence at Tongde si 同德寺 in Luoyang. After a period of Vinaya study he heard of the Chan teaching (*Chanzong* 禪宗) and traveled about, then received the "mind-seal" (*fushou xinyin* 付授心印) bestowal from Shenhui. After Shenhui gave him the name "no-name" because of the namelessness of his (i.e., Shenhui's) teaching, Wuming went on an extensive pilgrimage to the five peaks and a long list of other Buddhist mountains. He passed away while sitting at Mount Wutai, where he had arrived three years earlier; when his body was

---

17. *Song Biographies*, T 2061: 50.766c19–28. The printed *Taishō* text and the electronic CBETA version have slightly different misprints for the first character of Yingchuan 潁川, which is a Sui-dynasty place name equivalent to the Tang Xuzhou 許州. Assuming that the reference to Longxing si is not anachronistic, this would imply that Zhiman was ordained sometime after 738, when the temple system of this name was established. This fits well with Zhiman's encounter with Shenhui's teaching in Luoyang, presumably after 745. Zhiman is identified in the *Song Biographies* with Lingtang (Spring) in Xuanzhou 宣州, Anhui, but his temple was actually on Mount Huang, on the border between Xuanzhou and Xizhou. After building his hut, Zhiman is welcomed to the Lingtang Spring area by locals who collect *huanglian* 黃連 (coptis root, a medicinal) there. For the identification of *huanglian*, see Campany, *To Live as Long as Heaven and Earth*, 149.

18. *Song Biographies*, T 2061: 50.838c3–15. Yuanzhen's teacher at Mount Baici was Zhiyou 智幽 (otherwise unknown). Mount Wuya is also associated with Dengzhou 鄧州, Henan, implying that it is to the south of Nanyang along the border between the two prefectures. After his death, Yuanzhen's disciples interred his body into a stūpa without cremation, implying a form of mummification.

cremated two years later a full *sheng* (about 0.6 liters) of *śarīra* was obtained from his ashes.[19]

12. **Huiyan** 慧演 (718–797), son of a minor functionary from Xiangyang, lived at the Kaiyuan si there and became ordained under a monk who taught the *Nirvāṇa Sūtra*. After mastering this he led a group of compatriots wandering, during which time he met Shenhui at Luoyang and "penetrated the great contemplation" (*tongda daguan* 通達大觀). Afterwards he entered Nanyue and later resided in Liyang 澧陽 (Li xian 澧縣), Hunan), where he enlightened many students from the southern Yangzi region.[20]

13. **Shengguang** 乘廣 (717–798) is the subject of an epitaph written by Liu Yuxi 劉禹錫 (772–842), an eminent scholar-official who also wrote a preface for the *Platform Sūtra*. At age seven the future Shengguang demonstrated an aptitude for the study of Confucian texts, and at age thirteen he turned his aspirations to Buddhism. His first discipleship was under a teacher in Hengyang (Hengyang xian 衡陽縣, Hunan), following which he went to Luoyang to rely on Shenhui, under whom he "matched the true vehicle" (*qi zhensheng* 契眞乘). He then built a hut on Mount Yangqi (also the residence of Guangfu, n. 7 above); when he was cremated nearly a hundred pearl-like *śarīra* were found in his ashes.[21]

14. After becoming ordained, while in Luoyang **Xingjue** 行覺 (708–799) encountered Shenhui and "became enlightened to the mysterious

---

19. *Song Biographies*, T 2061: 50.817a18–b9, with some additional information in the *Guang Qingliang zhuan* 廣清涼傳, T 2099: 51.1121a15–24. Sometime during Emperor Dezong's reign (780–804) Wuming is supposed to have submitted a memorial that thwarted a recommendation by the official Hu Huan 狐峘 to reduce the number of Buddhist clergy. In addition to his Vinaya and Chan studies, Wuming was supposedly a gifted writer, to whom (according to the *Song Biographies*) there was attributed a commentary on the *Sūtra of Amitābha* 阿彌陀經. Wuming is also remembered within the Huayan tradition as a teacher of Chengguan (738–839); see the concise summary of the evidence regarding this in Gregory, *Tsung-mi*, 64 and 64–65n150. Ui, 241–242, infers that Chengguan studied with Wuming in Luoyang prior to 776, and Gregory states that this would have happened between 757 and 775, if it occurred at all. On p. 44 (n. 66), Gregory mistakes an Indian monk named Wangming (亡名 in Chinese) with Wuming.

20. *Song Biographies*, T 2061: 50.892c25–893a3. Although Huiyan is described as being from Xiangyang, his father was a minor functionary of some sort in Dongping 東平絲曹, corresponding to the modem Dongping county in Shandong province, which during the Tang was part of Yanzhou 兗州; the bureaucratic term *toucao* 絲曹, literally "yellow-cord section [clerk]," is otherwise unknown. Huiyan's ordination master was Bianzhang 辯章 (unidentified). Shenhui is referred to here as the "patriarch of Heze" (*Heze zushi* 荷澤祖師).

21. See *Yuanzhou Piangxiang xian Yangqi shan gu Guang chanshi bei* 袁州萍鄉縣楊岐山古廣禪師碑, *Quan Tang wen* 全唐文, 610.6a–8b (7825–7826). Shengguang's first teacher is identified as Tianzhu Xiang gong 天住想公, otherwise unknown. In this case Tianzhu must refer to another Mount Heng (also known as Mount Huo 霍山) in Anhui province (see *Morohashi*, 3:503a). One of Shengguang's students, Zhenshu 甄叔 (d. 820), is known as a successor to Mazu Daoyi 馬祖道一 (709–788) through the *Song Biographies* and references in two other epitaphs; see Ui, 253, for references.

principle, resolvedly correcting his behavior." After this experience he wandered about the Yangzi region and took up residence in a deserted temple.[22]

15. After becoming ordained, **Guangyao** 光瑤 (or **Guangbao** 光寶; 716–807), originally of Taiyuan 太原, forsook the study of Sūtra and Vinaya in favor of meditation practice. He visited many Chan masters before meeting Shenhui, who "scooped the gold dust out of his eyes" so that he "saw clearly in all ten directions." He then moved to Mount Meng in Yizhou 沂州蒙山 (Linyi xian 臨沂縣, Shandong), where he built a thatched hut and practiced meditation. Attracting the attention first of local residents and then the prefect of neighboring Yanzhou 兗州 (Ziyang xian 嶧陽縣, Shandong), he was installed in a temple there and developed a large following.[23]

16. Sometime after **Faru** 法如 (or **Zhiru** 智如; 723–811) entered the Dharma and was ordained, Shenhui inspired him by "conferring his oral instructions of mind" (*shou qi xinjue* 授其心訣) on him. This occurred in Luoyang, after which Faru ascended Mount Taihang 太行山 (which lies along the borders of Henan, Shanxi, and Hebei provinces), where he built a hut below Horsehead Peak 馬頭峰. The hut was eventually expanded into a conventional temple (identified by Zongmi as Faguan si in Cizhou 磁州法觀寺, Hebei, his native place), but when a local prefect invited him to take residence in the prefectural city Faru declined and then "manifested serenity," i.e., died.[24]

17. Both the epitaph and the *Song Biographies* entry for **Lingtan** 靈坦 give his dates as 709–816, but it seems more reasonable that he was born around 726. He was obviously a highly esteemed—and, even at an age of about ninety, quite venerable—monk at the time of his death, and there are reasons to suspect that the two sources are not very reliable about the early part of his life. He is described as a descendant of Empress Wu's whose father had been prefect of Luoyang. A precocious youth, he held an official position as tutor to a prince (汰子通事舍人) at the age of thirteen. Then he encountered Shenhui's teaching in Luoyang, which was "just beginning to obstruct the brilliance of Puji and gradually eliminate the way of Shenxiu." According to the epitaph, Lingtan stayed with Shenhui for eight or nine years, receiv-

---

22. See *Song Biographies*, T 2061: 50.893a4–14. Xingjue is associated with Guochang si in Jingzhou 唐荊州國昌寺. The text's description of Shenhui's teaching impact here is 開悟玄理，乘心矯跡, literally, "opening into enlightenment to the mysterious principle and firm maintenance of the mind [against] distorted traces."

23. See *Song Biographies*, T 2061: 50.766c29–767a8. The Chinese character interpreted as gold "dust" here is problematic. The description of enlightenment as allowing one to see in all ten directions is reminiscent of early Chan expressions.

24. See *Song Biographies*, T 2061: 50.893c15–22. The name Zhiru is listed in Zongmi's works as one of Shenhui's successors and as the third-generation progenitor of Zongmi. See Ui, 239–240.

ing a silent transmission from him just before the master was exiled in 753. After this, Lingtan moved to Floating Log Temple on Mount Lu 盧山浮槎寺 to study the canon, then in 770 went to the capital to pay his respects to National Teacher Nanyang Huizhong 南陽慧忠國師 (d. 775). According to the *Song Biographies,* when Lingtan requested permission to leave Chang'an three years later, Huizhong memorialized to the throne on his behalf, describing him as a "fellow student" (*tongmen* 同門) of his and a disciple of Shenhui's, and requested the bestowal of an official title. The *Song Biographies* is particularly detailed about Lingtan's subsequent places of residence and activities, which several times included the pacification of poisonous snakes and turtles. From 810 he resided at Hualin si in Yangzhou 揚州華林寺 (near Jiangdu xian 江都縣, Jiangsu). In 815 two monks arrived from Kucha, requesting that he come there to teach. After holding a memorial service on the thirteenth day of the fifth month of 816, the fifty-ninth anniversary of his master Shenhui's death, Lingtan announced to the assembly that he was accepting the foreign monks' invitation. He became ill during the seventh month of that year and, according to his own prediction, died on the eighth day of the ninth month.[25]

The preceding examples establish a strikingly consistent pattern: In all but one of these cases Shenhui is depicted as an inspiring individual who had no involvement in the ongoing training of students—that is, the monks in question were enlightened by Shenhui but then went off somewhere else to continue their training. Many of the students thus inspired went off to practice meditation in rustic locations that eventually grew into active temples. In two cases Shenhui is depicted as explicitly demurring from the role of instructor (perhaps simply because he was too young). And, in a

---

25. See *Song Biographies,* T 2061: 50.767a15–b28. The *Shenseng zhuan* 神僧傳 (T 2064: 50.1002c24) states that Lingtan studied under Shenhui for a long time, but this seems only a summation of the other sources. The epitaph for Lingtan by Jia Su 賈餗 (d. 835) is entitled *Yangzhou Hualin si Dabei chanshi beiming bing xu* 揚州華林寺大悲禪師碑銘並序; it occurs in *Tang Wencui* 唐文粹, *j.* 64, and *Quan Tang wen* 全唐文, *j.* 731. The *Song Biographies* entry, which postdates the epitaph, contains colorful material and details not found in the earlier source. For example, according to the *Song Biographies* the transmission to Lingtan occurred in 745, not 753. I am suspicious of the veracity of any relationship between Shenhui and Lingtan because of the latter's age at the time of his death, which at 108 years was extreme in length and auspicious in number. In addition, various elements of the epitaph adopt ideas that only became current after Shenhui's death, such as the notion of twenty-eight patriarchs from Śākyamuni to Bodhidharma (rather than Shenhui's thirteen). In other words, it is probable that he was born significantly after 709 and was perhaps just entering his maturity at the time of Shenhui's death in 758. In spite of these reflections, the epitaph is an interesting document, which contains perhaps one of the earliest statements of the genealogy of the "transmission of the lamp" (*chuandeng* 傳燈), a term it uses. For the interpretation of *fucha* 浮槎 as "floating log," see Huilin's 慧琳 *Yiqie jing yinyi* 一切經音義, T 2128: 54.820b6.

distinct pattern not manifest in other similar materials,[26] there is no clear record of any monk training under Shenhui. The only exception to this pattern is Lingtan, who supposedly studied under Shenhui for eight or nine years, precisely during his Luoyang period. Even if we accept this as factual, Lingtan's experience with Shenhui was exceptional in another way: after separating from the master in 753, Lingtan devoted himself not to the practice of meditation but to reading the Buddhist canon, quite unlike Shenhui's other students. Although his epitaph and the *Song Biographies* depict Lingtan as a holy figure, there is no explicit reference to meditation practice. This reticence is not significant in the context of the biographies of Chan masters in general, but it does conform with the general pattern involving Shenhui and his students.

Therefore, we may conclude that Hu Shih was correct in describing Shenhui's teachings as a "new Ch'an that was no *ch'an* at all"—but only with regard to Shenhui himself. In other words, although Shenhui did constitute an inspiring presence to a significant number of students, he does not match our generalized image of what a Zen master is because he did not teach the practice of meditation or guide students in the ongoing process of spiritual cultivation.[27] In other words, Shenhui was not a "Zen master."

---

26. One of those in attendance for a presentation of this paper on March 19, 2002, at the University of California, Berkeley, made the perceptive suggestion that the pattern depicted for Shenhui's students might be a motif of literary expression rather than a shared biographical feature. To test this possibility I have explored entries in the *Song Biographies* in the two subchapters following Shenhui's entry (part of the section on meditators). Without attempting a comprehensive analysis, it seems that there may be an association between teachers identified with sudden enlightenment and short training tenures; the most obvious example is the legendary Xuanjue 玄覺, who supposedly stayed with Huineng for only a single night. That this story was remembered suggests that the brief term of training was surprising, but the pattern of inspiration followed by departure (at least in the *Song Biographies* text) also occurs for Huineng's student Xingsi 行思 (T 2061: 50.760c4–5), a semi-legendary figure. Some of the monks who studied under Mazu Daoyi also demonstrate the inspiration-and-departure format; see T 2061: 50.767c28–29, 768a17–18, and 768b5–6. However, there are several who do not; see T. 2061: 50.766c9–11, 768b22–26, 768c23, and 769a27. Northern and Oxhead monks also demonstrate both patterns; those depicted as being inspired and departing occur at T. 2061: 50.757c5–7, 759c10, 761b17–18, 762b13–14, 765a20–21, 765b13–14, and 765c26–27, while those described as having longer training tenures may be seen at T. 2061: 50.759b21, 759c26–27, 760c13, 761c23, 764b22–26, and 767c8–9. Many of the entries are difficult to categorize, but it seems clear that the *Song Biographies* demonstrates no structure patterning regarding meditation specialists from these lineages.

27. This pattern is reinforced by a statement found in the epitaph for a student of Shenhui's named Huijian 慧堅, who died in 806: "When teaching, suddenness and not gradualism should be used. In the process of self-cultivation, purification occurs gradually and not suddenly." I have been unable to check the epitaph for Huijian, by Xu Dai 徐岱 and entitled *Tang gu Zhaosheng si dade Huijian chanshi bei* 唐古招聖寺大德慧堅禪師碑, which occurs in Nishikawa Yasushi, *Sei'an hirin*, plate 103, and Tsukada Yasunobu, *Sei'an hirin no kenkyū*, 123ff.

Shenhui as Fundraiser

The second widely known aspect of Shenhui's life is his activity as a fundraiser on behalf of the Tang ruling house after the An Lushan rebellion of 755. In order to help pay for the military campaign, Shenhui was asked to organize a program to ordain men as Buddhist monks. This provided emergency economic relief, but at a profound long-term expense: the ordinands paid a hefty fee to the government for the right to become monks (the specific amount paid is unknown[28]), but they received a lifetime tax exemption in return! The practice was not limited to the royal house, however, since part of the evidence for its use is the existence of a gold ingot (weighing about three-quarters of a kilogram) inscribed to indicate that it derived from ordination fees paid to the rebel side. Shenhui's participation in this program of ordinations seems to have taken place for no more than a year at the very end of his life, and he probably carried out his role in Jingzhou or other provincial locations rather than Luoyang itself (which at the time his involvement began was still in rebel hands).

Why would Shenhui have been called on by the government for this type of service? One reason, of course, was presumably that he already had a reputation for assistance in ordaining monks. Although there is little we can say about his activities in this regard, it seems that he was not directly involved in the administration of the precepts themselves. None of the students listed above were ordained under him, and one student (Huijian) actually left Shenhui's side to go get ordained somewhere else.[29] Shenhui never mentions the mechanics of Buddhist ordination, and it seems unlikely that he had the temperament to attend to training students in the details of monastic regulations and ritual deportment. Our only clue is that Shenhui's earliest text is known as the *Platform Sermon* (*Tan yu* 壇語) in which the "platform" involved was presumably the ordination platform. This suggests that Shenhui was participating in what might be called the "ordination platform movement" initiated by the great biographer, Vinaya specialist, and visionary Daoxuan 道宣 (596–667) in the very last year of his life. However, the evidence for this movement, if such it was, does not immediately bear on Shenhui's religious identity, so I will defer discussion of it until another occasion.[30]

The primary reason Shenhui was tapped for this form of government service must have been that he had already established himself as an effective fundraiser. Actually, the "debates" of 730, 731, and 732 with which Shenhui initiated his anti-Northern school campaign were actually large fundraising events, of a type known as *wuzhe da hui* 無遮大會 or "unrestricted

---

28. Ui, 234, but without citing any source. I have not been able to find any contemporary source that specifies the amount paid.
29. This fact has previously been noticed by Ge Zhaoguang, "Heze zong kao," 65.
30. I have summarized the issues involved in McRae, "Daoxuan's Vision of Jetavana."

great assemblies."[31] A better appreciation of the background and religious identity of these meetings will help us in understanding Shenhui's career as a fundraiser.

In the original usage these assemblies were supposedly held every five years[32] at the sponsorship of the king, and all people regardless of class or religious status were invited to receive the dual donations of material wealth and the Dharma. Said to have been initiated by Aśoka, the practice was observed by Xuanzang 玄奘 (600?-664) in India on several occasions; his descriptions involve sometimes annual observances of up to twenty-one days in length in which kings made extensive donations to the fourfold Saṅgha.[33] The practice first became popular in China during the Liang: Emperor Wu of that dynasty (who is often said to have modeled his actions on the legend of Aśoka) held one such assembly in 519, another in 529 with some fifty thousand people in attendance, another in 533 with supposedly more than three hundred thousand people in attendance, and others in 535, 536, and 547. Similar assemblies were held by Emperor Jianwen of the Liang, probably in 550,[34] Emperor Wu of the Chen in 557 and 558,[35] Crown Prince Yang Guang (the eventual Emperor Yang) of the Sui in 582,[36] Emperor Wen of the Sui in 601,[37] Emperor Yang of the Sui in 606,[38] Emperor Gaozu of the

---

31. Sometimes given in other sources as *sibu wuzhe da hui* 四部無遮大會 or "unrestricted great assembly for the fourfold [Saṅgha]" and other similar terms.

32. Hence the Skt. *pañca-vārṣikā-pariṣad*, which was known to Chinese writers through a transliteration but does not correspond precisely to the term used in China. One etymology of the term derives it from an event that took place when the future Buddha was five years old; see *Mochizuki Bukkyō daijiten*, 5:4547b.

33. See *Da Tang Daci'en si sanzang fashi zhuan* 大唐大慈恩寺三藏法師傳, T 2053: 50.233b19, 243b2, 248b17, and 249c14; and *Da Tang xiyu ji* 大唐西域記, T 2087: 51.873b19, 894c4, and 935c20, as well as, in a text translated by Xuanzang, *Da aluohan Nantimiduoluo suo shuo fa zhuji* 大阿羅漢難提蜜多羅所說法住記, T 2030: 49.13b19. Also see *Guang Hongming ji* 廣弘明集, T 2103: 52.271b4–5.

34. *Fozu tongji* 佛祖統紀, T 2035: 49.450c9.

35. *Fozu tongji*, T 2035: 49.352b8 and 352b11; and *Shishi jigu lüe* 釋氏稽古略, T 2037: 49.802c17. A text written by Emperor Wen of the Chen associated with a repentance rite also refers to an "unhindered (*wu'ai* 無礙) great assembly"; see *Guang Hongming ji*, T 2103: 52.334c7–28, esp. c18. Another text by the same ruler derives from an unhindered great assembly in which he "donated his body" to the Saṅgha on behalf of his empress; see 334c29–335a25. Finally, a general reference to such assemblies as part of the Buddhist activities of the Chen occurs at *Bianzheng lun* 辯正論, T 2110: 52.503c29.

36. *Fozu tongji*, T 2035: 49.353b9; T 2036: 49.558b9; and *Shishi jigu lüe*, T 2037: 49.807c14.

37. *Shishi jigu lüe*, T 2037: 49.809c11. This event is mentioned also at *Guang Hongming ji*, T 2103: 52.217a23, as one of the observances held in conjunction with the establishment of stūpas throughout the country, which is the subject of this entire fascicle of Daoxuan's *Guang hongming ji*.

38. *Shishi jigu lüe*, T 2037: 49.811a4. A general reference to such assemblies as part of Emperor Yang's Buddhist activities occurs at *Bianzheng lun*, T 2110: 52.509c1.

Tang in 618,[39] and Emperor Zhongzong of the Tang in 709 or 710.[40] In virtually all cases, the unrestricted great assemblies held under imperial sponsorship occurred in the very last year or the first year of reign periods, so that it is reasonable to infer that they were used as major ritual events to mark an auspicious change of era.

During the Tang such assemblies no longer remained the province of emperors, but were sponsored by individual monks as well. We know of such events sponsored by Fazhen 法珍 of Wutai Shan (d. 593);[41] Fachang 法常 (567–645);[42] the Huayan specialist Fazang 法藏 (643–712);[43] Xuanyan 玄儼 (655–742);[44] and the Vinaya master and missionary to Japan Jianzhen 鑑眞 (J. Ganjin; 687–763).[45] Thus the meetings held by Shenhui occurred within a particular social and liturgical context that was widely understood by his contemporaries.

We may thus make the following inferences about Shenhui's sponsorship of such meetings. First, these were large, even spectacular events. The Buddhist community would have been aware in general terms of the tradition of such meetings from Emperor Wu of the Liang onward, and in the early 730s there would still have been fresh memories of the more recent meeting sponsored by Emperor Zhongzong. In addition to large numbers of monks, nuns, laymen, and laywomen, a broad cross-section of the local community would have been in attendance, with a natural emphasis on members of government and elite families. Second, we may correlate Shenhui's participation in such assemblies with his abilities as a public sermonizer. Judging from the biographies of monks roughly his contemporaries who participated in similar events, the most important prerequisites seem to have been philosophical sophistication, a gift for public speaking, or a dedication to fundraising on behalf of the Buddhist Saṅgha.[46]

---

39. *Shishi jigu lüe*, T 2037: 49.812b26, with further description at *Bianzheng lun*, T 2110: 52.511b12–20.

40. *Fozu tongji*, T 2035: 49.372c21 and 451a19. Also see the chronological table in *Mochizuki Bukkyō daijiten*, 6:163, which cites the *Jiu Tang shu* 舊唐書 on this event.

41. *Guang Qingliang zhuan* 廣清涼傳, T 2099: 51.1118a15. In the following enumeration I have included only those events which took place before or during Shenhui's life.

42. *Continued Biographies*, T 2060: 50.541b11.

43. *Dafangguang fo huayan jing ganying zhuan* 大方廣佛華嚴經感應傳, T 2074: 51.175c13.

44. *Song Biographies*, T 2061: 50.795c24.

45. In addition to the meetings listed here, there were several held later during the Tang. On Jianchen, see Ishida Mizumaro, *Ganjin*, 48 and 311. Jianzhen (Ganjin) also held unrestricted offering services on behalf of foreign monks in Japan, who lacked the familial connections that were the underlying bases of most monks' living expenses; see 124–125 and 140.

46. Incidentally, although Shenhui and his contemporaries might not have recognized it, their participation in these great donative assemblies was roughly simultaneous with the end of imperial sponsorship for such assemblies. This was a symptom of the growing regionalization of Chinese Buddhism. As is apparent in the Hongzhou school of Mazu, Chinese Buddhism was moving toward the greater attention to local elite society that would characterize the Song.

Given this background, the very first passage attributed to Shenhui in the edited text of the *Definition of the Truth* is significant:

> The Brāhman monk Bodhidharma of the Liang dynasty was the third son of the king of a country in southern India, who left home while young to become a monk. His wisdom was extremely profound, and he attained Tathāgata Chan (*rulai chan* 如來禪) within the various samādhis. Eventually, motivated by this Dharma,[47] he traveled far across the waves to meet Emperor Wu of the Liang. Emperor Wu asked the Dharma master,[48] "I have constructed monasteries and saved people, constructed images and copied sūtras. How much merit is there in this?" Bodhidharma replied, "These actions are without merit." Emperor Wu, who was of ordinary [unenlightened] intelligence, did not comprehend these words of Bodhidharma's, and sent him away.[49]

In other words, at the very beginning of his fundraising assembly, Shenhui recounted a story about one of the most famous sponsors of such assemblies that seemed to undercut the very concept of making donations on behalf of the saṅgha! This is a consistent pose throughout the text, by the way, for a bit below we read Shenhui's statement:

> I preach today in order to discriminate the true and the false for Chinese students of the Path and to define the teachings for Chinese students of the Path.[50]

That Shenhui presented himself as not being interested in donations, but rather in disseminating the teaching of Chan—how are we to evaluate this public stance? He may have been sincerely disinterested in collecting donations, just as he may have been genuinely surprised in his success as a fundraiser. Nevertheless, the record shows that he was extraordinarily successful—so much so as to eventually be recognized by the Tang ruling house!

On further consideration, it seems likely that Shenhui's very posture of disinterest in donations was an effective fundraising technique. Chinese audiences must have long since become tired of straightforward petitions from saṅgha members for financial support, and Shenhui's iconoclastic teachings would have appeared as a breath of fresh air. Perhaps even more, the histrionics of the "debates" he staged—which were obviously highly en-

---

47. The text has *cheng si fa* 乘斯法, which literally means "make a vehicle of this Dharma" or "ride this Dharma."

48. Although it seems unnatural to refer to Bodhidharma as a *fashi* 法師, or Dharma master, this is how he is introduced in Tanlin's 曇林 preface to the *Two Entrances and Four Practices*. See Yanagida, *Daruma no goroku*, 25.

49. See the *Definition of the Truth*, section 30.

50. *Definition of the Truth*, section 4. This is one of the lines underlying the title of the treatise.

tertaining as religious performance—must have packed in crowds of the curious, intent on enjoying the spectacle involved. Therefore, the very disavowal of interest in monetary donations—as depicted in the encounter between Emperor Wu and Bodhidharma—seems to have had a paradoxical effect of stimulating even greater levels of donations.

I suggest that this actually represented an important building block of a general fundraising strategy adopted by the Chinese Chan school, one which stated to the lay public: "As Chan monks we would rather be meditating somewhere, and we recognize that your financial support is of only limited religious value. The only endeavor of real religious benefit is what we stand for, the practice of meditation and spiritual cultivation." The unspoken message that accompanied this public posture was, "Since we are fundamentally disinterested in fame and gain, as well as personal position, we are the best candidates for running the monastery." And this is precisely what happened: when the dust cleared after the fall of the Tang and the passage of the Five Dynasties, Chan monks were the abbots—and thus chief fundraisers for—over nine-tenths of the largest monasteries in the land. It was an impressive administrative takeover![51]

To fully understand Shenhui's role in all this, we have to look behind his identity as factionalist campaigner and fundraiser, to the religious vocation that defined all of his teachings and activities: that as evangelist.

Shenhui as Evangelist

The term "evangelist" (ad. L. *evangelista*, ad. Gr. *euaggelisthj, euaggelos*) derives of course from biblical usages, where it refers to those who bring the "good news" of the Christian message to the uninitiated. The following is from the *Oxford English Dictionary:*

> In the primitive Church, the designation given to a certain class of teachers, mentioned in *Eph.* iv. 11 after 'apostles' and 'prophets', and presumably having the function of preaching the gospel to the unconverted. The title has at various periods been revived, usually denoting an itinerant preacher having no fixed pastoral charge. At present, in the usage of various Protestant denominations, it means chiefly a layman commissioned to perform home missionary work.[52]

The purported authors of the four gospels of the New Testament are sometimes referred to as evangelists, but the earliest evangelist for whom we have any significant biographical information is the figure known as Philip the Evangelist (b. first century). Philip was one of seven deacons who tended the Christian community of Jerusalem, thereby leaving the Apostles free to

---
51. I consider this subject at greater length in McRae, *Seeing through Zen*.
52. *Oxford English Dictionary,* 2nd ed., s.v. "evangelist."

carry out their missions. The title "evangelist" derives from his energetic preaching style, which he used in missions to various locations.[53]

Jumping to modern times, Billy Graham's (b. 1918) identity as an evangelist derives from his charismatic preaching of the Christian gospel at large "crusades" held in many American cities.[54] In modern religious studies evangelistic zeal of this kind is generally seen as a trait not just of individual preachers but of a set of religious movements that emerged in Europe and America during the eighteenth century. The subsequent popular success of these evangelical movements has brought about a shift in usage, defined as follows in the *Encyclopedia of Religion:*

> The term evangelicalism usually refers to a largely Protestant movement that emphasizes (1) the Bible as authoritative and reliable; (2) eternal salvation as possible only by regeneration (being "born again"), involving personal trust in Christ and in his atoning work; and (3) a spiritually transformed life marked by moral conduct, personal devotion such as Bible reading and prayer, and zeal for evangelism and missions.[55]

The question is, how could such a definition apply to Shenhui? In the present case, we are dealing solely with one historical figure: although we might consider the early Chinese Chan movement as a revitalization movement, or even a sort of fundamentalist "return to origins" (to perceived origins, of course!), I have no intention of discussing the entire movement in terms of any "evangelical" religious identity. That being said, the itinerant aspect of Shenhui's life may match that of Christian evangelists, but it hardly seems distinctive in the context of medieval Chinese Buddhism.

In order to convert the question into something useful for our purposes, let us modify the *Encyclopedia of Religion* definition as follows:

> A Chinese Buddhist monk might be considered "evangelistic" if he (1) emphasized a specific source of absolute religious authority; (2) taught that ultimate liberation was possible only through the transformative experience of the inspiration to achieve enlightenment on behalf of all living beings (*bodhicitta*); and (3) worked to make that transformative experience available to as many people as possible.

These are the terms in which Shenhui may be considered to have had a religious vocation as an evangelist. Let us see how each different aspect worked out in his life.

---

53. *Encyclopædia Britannica*, s.v. "Philip the Evangelist," http://www.britannica.com/biography/Saint-Philip-the-Evangelist.

54. *Encyclopædia Britannica*, s.v. "Billy Graham," http://www.britannica.com/biography/Billy-Graham.

55. Marsden, "Evangelical and Fundamental Christianity," 5:190b.

First, the specific source of religious authority on which Shenhui based his teaching activities was not the Buddhist canon per se, although he certainly approached the sūtras with no less an attitude of devotional acceptance than that with which modern evangelical Christians approach the Bible. In his case the primary source of religious legitimation was not the scriptures, but rather the lineage of buddhas and patriarchs that extended from Śākyamuni down through Bodhidharma and the other Chinese patriarchs to Huineng and then Shenhui himself. For Shenhui the Chan lineage was not just an abstract issue of doctrine, but a necessary component of his religious identity and the very source of his own authority as a teacher. Remember that his very first words in the preface to the *Definition of the Truth* recount the story of Bodhidharma's encounters with Emperor Wu and then with Huike, and then go on to enumerate the succession of masters from Bodhidharma to Huineng. The same succession is described with much greater detail at the end of Shenhui's text, and it looms in the background throughout. Hence this lineage schema is not merely the basis of a factional dispute with those who traced their spiritual heritage through Shenxiu rather than Huineng, but rather the very source of his religious authority as the legitimate bearer of the Buddha's teachings.

Two other strategies are used in the *Definition of the Truth* to bolster Shenhui's religious authority. First, his amanuensis and editor Dugu Pei 獨孤沛 (d.u.) describes his master in glowing terms, identifying him as uniquely qualified to preach the Dharma:

> Our Reverend Shenhui of Xiangyang is enlightened to the forbearance of the birthlessness of all dharmas, has attained unhindered wisdom, and preaches the Dharma of the Supreme Vehicle. He leads the various sentient beings [on to enlightenment] and teaches sentient beings [the Buddhist doctrine]. Those who have changed their direction in life through his teachings are like the hundred rivers proceeding to the ocean.[56]

Dugu Pei also uses a combination of quotation and description:

> I have also witnessed Reverend Shenhui preach from the lion's seat: "There is no one else in China who understands the teaching of Bodhidharma's Southern school.[57] If there were someone who knew, I would never preach about it. I preach today in order to discriminate the true and the false for Chinese students of the Path and to define the teachings for Chinese students of the Path."

---

56. *Definition of the Truth*, section 3.
57. The Chinese here is *Putidamo nanzong yimen* 菩提達摩南宗一門. I have discussed precedents for the term "Southern school" in *Northern School*, 63, 94, and 292n153A. Also see *Continued Biographies*, T 2060: 50.666b5, and McRae, *Northern School*, 25; and Yanagida, *Shoki Zenshū shisho*, 596, and Yanagida, "Goroku no rekishi," 378.

To witness such inconceivable events made me gaze upon [Shenhui] with awe. When the ruler stimulates [the cosmos], good portents come from all over [his reign]; when the correct Dharma is propagated, people will recognize that which is fundamental.[58]

Second, Shenhui describes himself as having the spiritual understanding of a bodhisattva at the tenth stage—or at a level of enlightenment penultimate to that of buddhahood. This is an astonishing claim, which contravened the spirit if not necessarily the strict letter of Chinese monastic discipline, and his debate opponent asks in amazement:

"Bodhisattvas of the first stage can manifest multiple bodies in a hundred buddha realms, bodhisattvas of the second stage can manifest multiple bodies in a thousand buddha realms, and bodhisattvas of the tenth stage can manifest multiple bodies in immeasurable and infinite billions of buddha realms. You say you've completed the tenth stage, so please manifest a divine transformation for us now."[59]

This is an eminently reasonable challenge, in effect to say, "You claim to be an enlightened bodhisattva, so show us what you can do!"

Shenhui responds by describing himself as being like Cunda, the layman who gave the Buddha his last meal. Now, it is a curious feature of Buddhist hagiography that Cunda was not excoriated for giving the Buddha a meal that made him get sick and die; on the contrary, he is considered to have played a necessary and honored role in the final episode of the Buddha's teaching career. Hence Shenhui paraphrases (actually, misquotes) scripture to define his own religious identity:

The *Great Parinirvāṇa Sūtra* says, "When the Tathāgata was in the world, he only recognized Cunda's mind as identical to the mind of the Tathāgata. Although Cunda's mind comprehended the permanence of the Tathāgata, the Buddha did not recognize Cunda's body as identical to the Tathāgata's body." The sūtra says, "Adoration to Cunda! Adoration to Cunda! Although his body is the body of an ordinary unenlightened person, his mind is the mind of the Tathāgata's!"[60]

[Shenhui continued]: When the Tathāgata was in the world, he only recognized that the comprehension of Cunda's mind was like that of the Tathāgata—he did not speak of realization in the body. For my body to be

---

58. *Definition of the Truth*, section 4.
59. *Definition of the Truth*, section 11.
60. The line most similar to this in the *Nirvāṇa Sūtra* occurs at T 374: 12.372b26: "Adoration to Cunda! Although you have received a human body, your mind is like the mind of the Buddha. You, now, Cunda, are truly a son of the Buddha. Like Rahula, you are equivalent [to the Buddha] and not different."

that of an ordinary person in this period of the Final Dharma, and yet to have achieved the tenth stage—why should this be considered strange![61]

This bit of doctrinal sophistry allows Shenhui to negotiate a very important point for Chinese Buddhists. We have to remember that medieval Chinese did not conceive of the "historical Buddha" in the same humanistic terms we use today. Rather than imagining a gifted human being who lived at a critical juncture in human cultural history, they believed in superhuman buddhas with golden sixteen-foot-tall bodies that were endowed with numerous extraordinary characteristics. The buddhas and bodhisattvas of medieval Chinese belief were not merely able to levitate and read minds—such mundane superhuman powers!—but were also capable of manifesting whole world systems in the palms of their hands, or illuminating all the heavens and hells with beams of light from their foreheads. In other words, the buddhas and bodhisattvas functioned on a scale of power and grandeur quite beyond the comprehension of ordinary human beings. We may presume that Shenhui was incapable of such feats.

It certainly must have been shocking to Shenhui's audiences to hear him claim to have the enlightenment of a tenth-stage bodhisattva, but his identification with Cunda was a key to making Shenhui's Chan transmission schema effective. In other words, by the combination of the transmission schema and the model of Cunda, "our own Chinese" teacher Shenhui gave himself the authority to teach in place of the Buddha himself.[62] In other words, Shenhui had devised a way to argue that Chinese Chan teachers had the same religious authority as the Buddha himself. Although the specific argument was never used again, as far as I know,[63] this was a culturally liberating innovation.

The second aspect of the definition of Shenhui as an evangelist given above is that he taught a promise of ultimate liberation through the transformative experience of the inspiration to achieve enlightenment on behalf of all living beings (*bodhicitta*). This is of course precisely what Shenhui taught his audiences, the very climax of his sermons. The major impression one gets from reading Shenhui's works, in fact, is the very concrete sense of his doctrine of sudden enlightenment. This impression holds even in the case of the *Platform Sermon,* in which he hardly uses the term "sudden" (*dun* 頓) at all.[64] The most enduring impression of this text, indeed, is that Shenhui expected the members of his audience to attain an experience of *bodhicitta*

---

61. *Definition of the Truth,* section 12.
62. In addition, his adoption of the ordination platform may have strengthened this sense of religious authority, to the extent that such platforms were conceived of as stūpa forms at which the Buddha was present.
63. There are ten or so references to Cunda in the Chan texts for which electronic versions are now available; none of them involve any claim or even reference to Shenhui's notion, a version of "enlightenment in this very body."
64. The term *dun* 頓 occurs only three times in this text.

right then and there, while listening to him. The following are some of the more explicit indications of this expectation:

> Friends, you have all been able to come here so that you can all generate the unsurpassable *bodhicitta*. It is extremely difficult to encounter the buddhas, bodhisattvas, and true spiritual compatriots. Today you are going to hear something you've never heard before. In the past you never encountered it, but today you have....
>
> Friends, your generation of the unsurpassable *bodhicitta* constitutes the correct cause. For the buddhas, bodhisattvas, and true spiritual compatriots to cast this unsurpassable *bodhicitta* into your minds such that you achieve the ultimate emancipation constitutes the correct condition. For the two to meet is excellent....
>
> You must each and every one of you generate *bodhicitta*!...
>
> Now, friends, now that you have been able to come to this place of enlightenment (*daochang* 道場, Skt. *bodhimanda*), you can each and every one generate the unsurpassable *bodhicitta* and seek the unsurpassable Dharma of *bodhi*!...
>
> Since you have already come to this ordination platform (*tanchang* 壇場) to study the perfection of wisdom, I want each and every one of you to generate, both mentally and orally, the unsurpassable *bodhicitta* and become enlightened to the cardinal meaning of the Middle Path in this very place![65]

Also contained in the *Definition of the Truth* is the following verse in adulation of *bodhicitta*:

> Although *bodhicitta* and the ultimate [realization] are no different,
> Of the two [states of] mind, it is the first which is [more] difficult.
> With oneself still unsaved, to first save others—
> Thus do we reverence the initial [achievement of] *bodhicitta*.
>
> By this initial *bodhicitta* one becomes a teacher of humans and gods,
> superior to the *śrāvakas* and *pratyekabuddhas*.
> With such a *bodhicitta*, one transcends the triple realm,
> Hence this is called the most unsurpassable.[66]

Shenhui does not hedge on the issue of immediate inspiration by specifying some preliminary period of religious practice, however brief. His most well-known metaphor for the relationship between the initial moment of enlight-

---

65. This is abbreviated from the *Platform Sermon*, sections 1–2.
66. *Definition of the Truth*, section 7. It is also possible that Shenhui purposely avoided specific statements regarding meditation practice so as not to invite criticisms of the type he addressed to the Northern school.

enment and the subsequent course of self-cultivation is that of childbirth, in which a baby is born suddenly but must mature gradually.[67]

The third characteristic of Shenhui's evangelistic identity as posited above is his activism in bringing the "good news" of Chan to others. Given Shenhui's activity on the ordination platform, we may grant this point without further discussion.

Conclusion: Re-imagining Chan

Our understanding of the historical evolution of Chinese Chan Buddhism evolved over the course of the twentieth century through an international scholarly initiative of textual discovery and analysis. The contour of this initiative can be described through a series of landmark events: Hu Shih's discovery of Shenhui's writings in 1926, D. T. Suzuki's editions of the *Platform Sūtra* and other early Chan texts in the 1930s, the correspondence between Iriya Yoshitaka and Hu in the 1950s, Yanagida Seizan's historical study of early Chan and Philip Yampolsky's English translation of the *Platform Sūtra* in 1967, and Tanaka Ryōshō's comprehensive textual analyses of the 1970s and 1980s. There has been an obvious process of sequential development involved in all this, in which each scholar's work incorporates and moves beyond the contributions of his predecessors.

Our task, at the beginning of the twenty-first century, should be to reconceptualize the understanding of Chan historical development using the best analytical tools available to us. It seems unlikely that this century will witness the same explosion of primary source materials that was occasioned by the Dunhuang cave manuscript finds, although of course only time will tell. Whatever new treasures the future brings, we should undertake our own researches not merely as one more step in the sequential process outlined just above, but rather as a comprehensive reformulation of all the evidence available to us. In order to undertake this reformulation we need to pay attention not only to the primary evidence, but also to the more elusive features of our own roles as analysts. Instead of assuming that we occupy an uncompromised analytical perspective hovering somewhere above and outside our subject matter (Thomas Nagel's "view from nowhere"), we should pay careful attention to how the construction of our own intellectual identities alters our very perception of the primary evidence. We can learn more about our chosen subject matter by deconstructing our own projections and expectations regarding it, by playing those projections and expectations off against each other and observing what subset relationships and interference patterns develop.

This paper constitutes one small step in this process of reformulation. The evidence contained in it has been known, for the most part, for many years; it is the global reconfiguration that is new. My contention is that there

---

67. *Definition of the Truth*, section 21.

has been a feedback relationship between our shared image of the Zen master and our interpretations of Chinese Chan. This feedback relationship can be broken—or at least dissected—by considering how a monk who was not primarily a meditation teacher or spiritual instructor made epochal contributions to the historical evolution of Chan. By analyzing the life and teachings of Heze Shenhui with a conscious bracketing of the Zen-master typology, we gain a more nuanced appreciation for the cultural dynamics involved in the creation of Chinese Chan. In addition, by using this one example to free ourselves from (at least this one form of) stereotypical thinking, there is the promise of even more substantial rewards, in the form of inferences and analyses not yet imagined, in the foreseeable future.

Specifically, there are three different categories of conclusions that may be drawn from this inquiry:

1. Participant Roles and the Complexity of Chinese Chan

Shenhui's case adds texture to our understanding of Chinese Chan. It suggests that other distinctive roles within the movement may also be identified with further research, and it implies that complex relationships probably also existed between those performing different roles, or in the lives of those performing different roles at different times. That is, by liberating this one historical figure from the constraints of the fixed Zen-master typology, we have hopefully become sensitive to the ways and extents to which others who contributed substantially to the evolution of Chan as a set of cultural processes may have deviated from the standard image in their own distinctive manners. Hence, not every person who is known by the label "Zen master" should be considered a variant of a single type or genre. On the contrary, in medieval China at least, the title may indicate little more than shared general participation in the set of cultural vectors referred to collectively as "Chan."

2. Multiple Contexts in the Evolution of Chan

This study shows how important Chan doctrines and slogans may derive from religious contexts—legitimate religious contexts—other than the imagined meditation hall community. Specifically, if we dispense with the image of Shenhui as Zen master, then his apophatic references to meditation practice have different implications. We must reject Hu Shih's characterization of his teachings as "a new Chan that was no *chan* at all," or at the very least limit the relevance of this characterization to the individual example of Shenhui. In addition, it is only by approaching Shenhui's life based on his identity as an evangelist that we can achieve a synthetic and comprehensive appreciation of his conception of sudden enlightenment. Finally, by appreciating the social context in which the anecdote of the encounter between Bodhidharma and Emperor Wu of the Liang was first presented, we can develop a better understanding of the impact of the story's apparent iconoclasm. This leads to an entirely different appreciation for the role of fundraising in the lives of Chan masters, as well as an entirely new approach to conceptualizing the transformation of Chinese Chan from the Tang to the Song.

Just as we may gain a new sensitivity to the role these various ideas and motifs played in Shenhui's life and teachings, we may also become more sensitive to the manner in which the very same ideas and motifs performed very different roles in the lives and activities of subsequent Chan figures. Thus we see, in very stark terms, how Buddhist doctrine does not necessarily flow out of meditative experience, as is often argued. On the contrary, religious doctrine grows out of a complex interplay of rhetorical forces, in which ideas about (one might also say mythologies of) meditation may be just as important as meditation practice itself.

3. The Contextualized Location of Chan within Chinese Culture

The result of these inferences is the de-stabilization of simplistic models of a "pure Chan" that exists within a more-or-less defiled cultural context, or of a central core of authentic religious behavior surrounded by peripheries of less-enlightened activity. Thus the Chan tradition should not be conceived of simply in terms of a central community of meditation specialists (with "meditation" here defined broadly so as to include the endeavors of interpersonal dialogue and precedent introspection, etc.) surrounded by other communities of laypeople and monastics not directly, or not single-mindedly, involved in the same pursuit. Instead, we should recognize that the image of the central community of meditation specialists, consisting of one or more Chan masters and a number of students, is itself a construct generated through the medium of the Chan tradition.

Thus, recognizing Shenhui's religious identity as evangelist makes possible both a different appreciation for his historical contributions and a more nuanced understanding of the Chan tradition as a whole.

APPENDIX

Textual Sources

Platform Sermon

The first manuscript discovered (1934) was the Beijing *han*-81, reproduced in Suzuki's *Zenshū*, 3:290–317. Hu Shih's edition (*Yiji*, 225–252) is based on Pelliot 2045. The fragments Stein 2492 and 6977, and Dx. 942 and Dx. 1920+1921 from the Leningrad collection, are represented in the Tōdai goroku kenkyūhan's supplementary edition of the *Platform Sermon* (1998). In addition to the Chinese versions, a partial Tibetan translation of the *Platform Sermon* is included in Pelliot tib. 116, 183.3–186.2; see Macdonald and Yoshiro, *Documents tibetains*, plates 112–113. Shinohara Hisao used the Beijing manuscript, Pelliot 2045, and Stein 2492 and 6977 in preparing his edition and translation, published in "Kataku Jinne no kotoba." Certain errors in Shinohara's work were revised (although not all the faulty citations were indicated) in Nakamura Nobuyuki's "Nan'yō wajō tonkyō." I have verified Nakamura's revisions by checking them against the original manuscripts, and I have found his Japanese translation to be much more sensitive to colloquial Chinese usages. Hence I have noted the few occasions when our interpretations differ. A more polished version of this translation, but with streamlined annotation, can be found in Tanaka and Okimoto, *Daijō Butten*, 87–114.

Yang Zenwen's *Chanhua lu* contains the most widely available reproduction of the *Platform Sermon*, as well as Shenhui's other works. Errors in the editing of the *Platform Sermon* in Yang's edition have been corrected in the Tōdai goroku kenkyūhan's supplementary edition. Spearheaded by Kinugawa Kenji 衣川賢次, this "Research Group for Tang-Dynasty Recorded Sayings" in Kyoto, including Nishiguchi Yoshio 西口芳男, Yukiko Macadam, and others, considered all the Chinese manuscripts mentioned above—with the Dunhuang Museum materials identified as separate manuscripts (Dx. 942 and Dx. 1920+1921)—as well as six different previous editions. Although some of their corrections may be trivial, others have important implications regarding the meaning and punctuation of the text.

The *Platform Sermon* was translated into English by Walter Liebenthal in "The Sermon of Shen-hui" (1952), which also includes the *Verses on the Five Watches*. Liebenthal based his work on the manuscript introduced to him by Wang Chongmin, Pelliot 2045, although he followed Suzuki's edition for part of his translation while also referring to Jacques Gernet's *Entretiens du Maître de Dhyâna Chen-hoei* (1949), a French translation of about two-thirds of the text. Much of Liebenthal's commentary is acceptable in terms of Indian or fifth-century Chinese Buddhism, but it is not specific to Shenhui or even to Chan. I have referred to his translation extensively and have corrected many of his citations.

A short time ago, a modern Chinese translation was published in Xing Dongfeng's "Shenhui yulu" (1996). This translation appeared too recently to be of use in my own work, and I have found nothing in its annotation that is not better represented elsewhere.

My translation uses the section divisions initiated in the Hu edition, which are of course not indicated in the original. I have not used the much shorter subdivisions of Suzuki's edition, nor have I chosen to present the text without any section divisions, as has Yang. Table 1 correlates the sectional divisions presented here with the pagination of the Suzuki, Hu, and Yang editions.

Definition of the Truth

There are four Dunhuang manuscripts for the *Definition of the Truth*, three from the Pelliot collection discovered (or rather recognized) by Hu Shih (nos. 3047 and 3488) and D. T. Suzuki (no. 2045) and one held by the Dunhuang Prefectural Museum (part of text no. 77), which was brought to my attention by Yang Zengwen.

Editions of the text are available in Hu, 260–316, and Yang, 17–48. (The earlier version in Hu, on pages 225–252, is based solely on Pelliot 3047, which only represents part of the text.) A French translation of the text can be found in Gernet, *Entretiens*.

Table 1. *Platform Sermon:* Text alignment with manuscript editions

Sec.	Suzuki	Hu	Yang
1	308	225	4
2	309	230	6
3	310	233	7
4	311	236	9
5	312	241	10
6	313	244	11
7	314	247	13

Appendix

In presenting this translation, I have followed the section divisions adopted by Tanaka and Okimoto and have included markers in the text, in square brackets, keyed to the pagination of the Hu edition, using the form [HS###]. Table 2 aligns the section divisions with the pagination of the Hu and Yang editions.

Table 2. *Definition of the Truth:* **Text alignment with manuscript editions**

Section	Hu	Yang	Section	Hu	Yang
1	260	17	29	294	33
2	260	17	30	295	34
3	261	17	31	296	34
4	263	19	32	296	34
5	264	19	33	297	35
6	265	19	34	299	35
7	266	20	35	299	35
8	267	21	36	300	36
9	268	21	37	301	36
10	269	21	38	301	36
11	269	24	39	302	36
12	276	24	40	303	37
13	277	24	41	304	37
14	277	26	42	304	37
15	280	26	43	305	38
16	281	27	44	305	38
17	282	28	45	306	38
18	283	28	46	306	38
19	284	29	47	308	39
20	285	29	48	308	39
21	286	30	49	309	39
22	287	30	50	310	40
23	288	31	51	311	40
24	288	31	52	312	41
25	290	32	53	314	42
26	291	32	54	315	43
27	293	33	55	316	43
28	294	33			

Miscellaneous Dialogues

Three manuscripts of the *Miscellaneous Dialogues* are known: Pelliot 3047, Stein 6557, and Ishii. The latter, named after its owner, Ishii Mitsuo 石井光雄, is the most polished of the three. An edition of this manuscript was published by Suzuki Daisetsu and Kōda Rentarō in 1934. Hu's *Yiji* includes two recensions of the text, one based on Pelliot 3047 (p. 97 ff.) and the other on Stein 6557 (p. 426 ff.), although Hu's (often handwritten) notes refer to all three manuscripts. The text in Suzuki's *Zenshū*, 3:236–238, is a synoptic edition combining part of P3047 with the Ishii manuscript. (Note that Suzuki's edition does not include the last seven sections, which are present in Ishii.) Yang's edition (p. 57 ff.) includes material from all three manuscripts but is based primarily on the Ishii manuscript, especially in the order of presentation: sections that do not occur in Ishii, including the first seven sections following the preface, are given at the end. A French translation of the text is available in Gernet's *Entretiens*.

Table 3 aligns the section divisions in the text (as represented in the translation) with the pagination of the manuscript editions. Since Suzuki's edition uses a "Hu Shih" text—in effect, a reprint of Hu's recension of P3047 (Hu-1 in the table)—to fill in the missing sections from Ishii, these page locations in Suzuki are given in parentheses. Passages that do not occur in P3047 are indicated with blank spaces under Hu-1. Note that the section

Table 3. *Miscellaneous Dialogues:* **Text alignment with manuscript editions**

Section	Suzuki (Ishii+)	Hu-1 (P3047)	Hu-2 (S6557)	Yang (Ishii+)
Preface	-	-	426	57
1	(236)	97	-	115
2	(236)	97	-	116
3	(237)	98	-	117
4	(238)	100	-	118
5	(238)	100	-	118
6	(239)	101	-	118
7	(240)	103	427	57/120
8	241	103	429	60
9	245	108	435	63
10	246	110	437	65
11	247	111	439	66

Section	Suzuki (Ishii+)	Hu-1 (P3047)	Hu-2 (S6557)	Yang (Ishii+)
12	248	112	440	66
13	248	112	440	67
14	249	114	442	68
15	250	115	443	68
16	252	-	446	70
17	253	116	448	71
18	253	118	449	72
19	254	118	450	72
20	273	119	-	91
21	275	120	-	92
22	276	122	-	93
23	255	123	451	73
24	255	-	451	73
25	256	123	-	74
26	256	123	-	74
27	257	124	-	75
28	257	125	-	76
29	258	126	-	76
30	259	127	-	77
31	259	127	-	78
32	260	128	-	79
33	261	129	-	79
34	261	130	-	80
35	265	134	-	82
36	265	134	-	82
37	265	135	-	83
38	266	135	-	83
39	266	135	-	84
40	266	135	-	84
41	267	136	-	84

(continued)

Table 3. *Miscellaneous Dialogues:* **Text alignment with manuscript editions**
(*continued*)

Section	Suzuki (Ishii+)	Hu-1 (P3047)	Hu-2 (S6557)	Yang (Ishii+)
42	267	137	-	85
43	268	138	-	85
44	268	138	-	86
45	269	139	-	86
46	269	140	-	87
47	270	140	-	88
48	270	141	-	88
49	271	-	-	89
50	271	141	-	89
51	272	142	-	90
52	277	-	-	94
53	277	-	-	95
54	279	144	-	96
55	279	145	-	97
56	280	146	-	98
57	281	146	-	98
58	282	-	-	99
59	283	-	-	100
60	283	-	-	101
61	284	-	-	101
62	(285)	148	-	121
63	288	-	-	103
64		-	-	103
65		-	-	105
66		-	-	106
67		-	-	107
68		-	-	108
69		-	-	109
70		-	-	112

APPENDIX 307

divisions in the translation and in the various editions do not exactly coincide, and occasionally one edition might group passages together that in another are given as separate sections. In the translation, text markers in square brackets—[HS###] and [DTS###]—indicate the corresponding locations in the Hu and Suzuki editions.

Verses on the Five Watches

There are three editions of the *Verses on the Five Watches:* Hu, 452–477; Yang, 126–129; and Long, in "Lun Dunhuang ciqu"—the former two being of higher quality. As mentioned above, the verses were translated by Liebenthal in 1952.

Verses on Sudden Enlightenment, the Birthless, and *Prajñā*

The most complete Dunhuang version of this text is Stein 468. The earliest annotated edition may be found in Hu, 193–199, with commentary on 200–208. Another manuscript, Stein 5619, consists of only the first twenty lines (reproduced in Yabuki, *Meisha yoin kaisetsu*). The text also occurs in the *Transmission of the Lamp,* where it has the title *Heze dashi xianzong ji* 荷澤大師顯宗記 (Record of the Manifestation of the Teaching of Great Master [Shenhui] of Heze [Temple]) (T 2076: 51.458c25–459b6). A similar title, *Xianzong lun* 現宗論 (Treatise on the Manifestation of the Teaching), is used for an excerpt of the verse found in the *Zongjing lu* 宗鏡錄 (T 48.949a–b). Yang, 49–53, has compared both Dunhuang manuscripts with Hu's edition for his own version of the text, and he has included the entire text as it occurs in the *Transmission of the Lamp* as well. Yang's edition is flawed in minor ways by his use of the latter version to emend the text, although it is superior to Hu's in that it uses both available Dunhuang mss. For my translation I have used the editions by both Hu and Yang, with reference to the Stein manuscript and the versions found in the *Transmission of the Lamp* and the *Zongjing lu*. For reference, I have also appended, as an addendum to the translation, the version of the text found in the *Transmission of the Lamp*.

Bibliography

Primary Texts, Collections, and Reference Works

Annals of the Transmission (*Chuan fabao ji* 傳法寶紀, Annals of the Transmission of the Dharma-treasure). In Yanagida, *Shoki no zenshi 1*, 327–435; English translation in McRae, *Northern School*, 255–269.

Anthology of the Patriarchal Hall (*Zutang ji* 祖堂集). See Yanagida, *Sodōshū*.

Authority Database. See Buddhist Studies Authority Database Project.

Awakening of Faith (*Dasheng qi xin lun* 大乘起信論). T 1666: 32.575b9–583b17.

Bainaben ershisi shi 百衲本二十四史 (Twenty-four Histories from Various Publications). Taibei: Taiwan Shangwu yinshu guan, 1967.

Buddhist Studies Authority Database Project. Dharma Drum Institute of Liberal Arts. http://authority.dila.edu.tw/.

Bukkyōgo daijiten 仏教語大辞典 (Encyclopedia of Buddhist Terms). By Nakamura Hajime 中村元. 3 vols. Tokyo: Tokyo shoseki, 1975.

Complete Writings of the Tang (*Qinding quan Tang wen* 欽定全唐文, Imperially Determined Complete Writings of the Tang). Edited by Dong Gao 董誥 et al. 1841. Reprint, Taibei: Hualian chubanshe, 1965.

Continued Biographies (*Xu gaoseng zhuan* 續高僧傳, Continued Biographies of Eminent Monks). T 2060: 50.425c20–707a27.

Dai kanwa jiten 大漢和辞典 (Great Chinese-Japanese Dictionary). Compiled by Morohashi Tetsuji 諸橋轍次. 13 vols. Tokyo: Taishukan shoten, 1955–1960.

Dai Nihon zoku Zōkyō. 150 vols. Kyoto: Zōkyō shoin, 1905–1912. See also *Xu zang jing*.

Diamond Sūtra (*Jingang bore boluomi jing* 金剛般若波羅蜜經, Skt. *Vajracchedikā-prajñāpāramitā-sūtra*, Diamond Wisdom Sūtra). Translated by Kumārajīva. T 235: 8.748c–752c.

Enō kenkyū—Enō no denki to shiryō ni kan suru kisoteki kenkyū—恵能研究—恵能の伝記と資料に関する基礎的研究 (Studies on Huineng: Fundamental Studies on Huineng's Biography and Source Materials). Compiled by Komazawa Daigaku Zenshū Kenkyūkai 駒沢大学禅宗研究会. Tokyo: Daishukan shoten, 1978.

Essential Determination (*Dunwu zhenzong jingang bore xiuxing da bi'an famen yaojue* 頓悟真宗金剛般若修行達彼岸法門要訣, Essential Determination of the Doctrine of Attaining the Other Shore [of Nirvāṇa] by the Practice of Adamantine Wisdom [according to] the True Teaching of Sudden Enlightenment). In Ueyama Daishun, "*Tongo shinshū yōketsu*."

309

Essential Teaching of Sudden Enlightenment (*Dunwu rudao yaomen lun* 頓悟入道要門論). X 63.18a6–24a24.

Five Skillful Means (*Wu fangbian* 五方便). English translation in McRae, *Northern School*, 171–196; textual sources, 327–330n161.

History of the Tang (*Tang shu* 唐書). In *Bainaben ershisi shi*.

Kadokawa shin jigen 角川新字源 (Kadokawa New Character Etymology Dictionary). By Ogawa Tamaki, Nishida Taichirō, and Akatsuka Kiyoshi. Tokyo: Kadokawa Shoten, 1970.

Lotus Sūtra (*Miaofa lianhua jing* 妙法蓮華經, Skt. *Saddharma-puṇḍarīka-sūtra*, Sūtra on the Lotus of the Wondrous Dharma). Translated by Kumārajīva. T 262: 9.1c–62b.

Masters and Disciples of the Laṅkāvatāra (*Lengqie shizi ji* 楞伽師資記, Records of the Masters and Disciples of the Laṅkā[vatāra]). T 2837: 85.1283a5–1290c26.

Mochizuki Bukkyō daijiten 望月仏教大辞典 (Mochizuki Encyclopedia of Buddhism). Edited by Mochizuki Shinkō 望月信亨. 10 vols. Tokyo: Sekai seiten kankō kyōkai, 1933–1936.

Morohashi. See *Dai kanwa jiten*.

New History of the Tang (*Xin Tang shu* 新唐書). In *Bainaben ershisi shi*.

Nirvāṇa Sūtra (*Da banniepan jing* 大般涅槃經, Skt. *Mahāparinirvāṇa sūtra*). Translated by Dharmakṣema ("Northern" edition). T 374: 12.365c–603c. Translated by Huiyan ("Southern" edition). T 375: 12.605a–852b.

Platform Sūtra (*Liuzu tan jing* 六祖壇經, Platform Sūtra of the Sixth Patriarch). T 2008: 48.337a–345b. All citations are from the Dunhuang version. English translation in Yampolsky, *Platform Sutra of the Sixth Patriarch*.

Quan Tang wen. See *Complete Writings of the Tang*.

Records of the Transmission (*Lidai fabao ji* 歷代法寶記, Records of the [Transmission of the] Dharma-treasure through the Generations). T 2075: 51.179a–196b. English translation in Adamek, *Mystique of Transmission*, 297–405.

Shin jigen. See *Kadokawa shin jigen*.

Song Biographies (*Song gaoseng zhuan* 宋高僧傳, Biographies of Eminent Monks [Compiled during the] Song Dynasty). T 2061: 50.710b8–899c24.

Taishō shinshū daizōkyō 大正大藏經. Edited by Takakusu Junjirō 高楠順次郎 and Watanabe Kaigyoku 渡邊海旭. 100 vols. Tokyo: Taishō issaikyō kankōkai, 1924–1932.

Transmission of the Lamp (*Jingde chuandeng lu* 景德傳燈錄, Record of the Transmission of the Lamp [Compiled during the] Jingde Era). T 2076: 51.196b9–467a28.

Transmission of the Treasure Grove (*Baolin zhuan* 寶林傳). In Yanagida, *Sōzōichin Hōrinden*.

Treatise on Perfect Illumination (*Yuanming lun* 圓明論). In McRae, *Northern School*, following 394; English translation, 149–171.

Treatise on the Contemplation of the Mind (*Guanxin lun* 觀心論). T 85.1270c10–1273b04.

Treatise on the Essentials of Cultivating the Mind (*Xiuxin yaolun* 修心要論). In McRae, *Northern School*, following 394; English translation, 121–132.

Treatise on the Transcendence of Cognition (*Jueguan lun* 絕觀論). In Yanagida and Tokiwa, *Zekkanron;* partial English translation in McRae, "Ox-head School of Chinese Buddhism," 211–215.

Treatise on the True Principle (*Dasheng kaixin xianxing dunwu zhenzong lun* 大乘開心顯性頓悟真宗論, Treatise on the True Principle of Opening the Mind and Manifesting the [Buddha-]Nature in Sudden Enlightenment [according to] the Mahāyāna). T 2835: 85.1278a–1281c. Also in *Suzuki Daisetsu zenshū*, 3:318–330.

Two Entrances and Four Practices (*Erru sixing lun* 二入四行論, Treatise on the Two Entrances and Four Practices). In *Transmission of the Lamp,* T 2076: 51.458b21–c24; English translation in McRae, *Northern School,* 102–106.
Vimalakīrti Sūtra (*Weimojie suoshuo jing* 維摩詰所說經, Skt. Vimalakīrti-nirdeśa-sūtra). Translated by Kumārajīva. T 475: 14.537a–557b.
Wisdom Sūtra of the Heavenly King Pravara (*Shengtianwang bore boluomi jing* 勝天王般若波羅蜜經, Skt. *Suvikrāntavikrāmi-paripṛcchā-prajñāpāramitā-sūtra*). Translated by *Upaśūnya. T 231: 8.687a–726a.
Xiandai hanyu sanyinci cidian 现代汉语三音词词典 (Comprehensive Chinese Dictionary). Beijing: Yuwen chubanshe, 2005.
Xu zang jing 續藏經. 150 vols. Taibei: Xinwenfeng chubanshe, 1968–1970. Reprint of *Dai Nihon zoku Zōkyō.*
Zengaku daijiten 禅学大辞典 (Encyclopedia of Zen Studies). Edited by Zengaku Daijiten Hensanjo hen 禪學大辭典編纂所編. Tokyo: Komazawa University, 1978.
Zhongguo lishi ditu ji 中國歷史地圖集 (Historical Atlas of China). Edited by Tan Qixiang 譚其驤. Hong Kong: Joint Publishing, 1992.
Zongjing lu 宗鏡錄 (Record of the Mirror of Truth). T 2016: 48.415a–957b.

Secondary Sources

Adamek, Wendi L. *The Mystique of Transmission: On an Early Chan History and Its Contexts.* New York: Columbia University Press, 2007.
Bielefeldt, Carl. *Dogen's Manuals of Zen Meditation.* Berkeley: University of California Press, 1988.
Birnbaum, Raoul. "The Manifestation of a Monastery: Shen-ying's Experiences on Mount Wu-t'ai in T'ang Context." *Journal of the American Oriental Society* 106, no. 1 (1986): 119-137.
Blofeld, John. *The Zen Teaching of Hui Hai on Sudden Illumination.* London: Rider & Company, 1962.
Boucher, Daniel. "On *Hu* and *Fan* Again: The Transmission of 'Barbarian' Manuscripts to China." *Journal of the International Association of Buddhist Studies* 23, no. 1 (2000): 7–28.
Broughton, Jeffrey L. *The Bodhidharma Anthology: The Earliest Records of Zen.* Berkeley: University of California Press, 1999.
Bultmann, Rudolf. "Is Exegesis without Presuppositions Possible?" In *Existence and Faith: Shorter Writings of Rudolf Bultmann,* translated by Schubert M. Ogden, 289–296. New York: Meridian Books, 1968.
Buswell, Robert E., Jr. *The Formation of Ch'an Ideology in China and Korea: The Vajrasamādhi-Sūtra, a Buddhist Apocryphon.* Princeton, NJ: Princeton University Press, 1989.
Campany, Robert F. *To Live as Long as Heaven and Earth: A Translation and Study of Ge Hong's Traditions of Divine Transcendents.* Berkeley: University of California Press, 2001.
Ch'an, Wing-tsit. "Hu Shih and Chinese Philosophy." *Philosophy East and West* 6, no. 1 (April 1956): 3–12.
Ch'en, Kenneth K. S. *Buddhism in China: A Historical Survey.* Princeton, NJ: Princeton University Press, 1964.
———. *The Chinese Transformation of Buddhism.* Princeton, NJ: Princeton University Press, 1973.

Chen Yunji 陳允吉. "Wang Wei yu Nan Bei Zong Chanseng guanxi kaolüe" 王维与南北宗禅僧关系考略 (An Exploration of the Relations between Wang Wei and Monks of the Northern and Southern Chan Schools). *Zhongwen shehui kexue yinwen suoyin* 中文社会 科学引文索引 2 (1981): 60–65.

Chou, Min-chih. *Hu Shih and Intellectual Choice in Modern China*. Ann Arbor: University of Michigan Press, 1984.

Cleary, J. C. *Zen Dawn: Early Zen Texts from Tun Huang*. Boston: Shambhala, 1986.

Cleary, Thomas E. *Sayings and Doings of Pai-chang, Ch'an Master of Great Wisdom*. Los Angeles: Center Publications, 1978.

Conze, Edward. *Buddhist Wisdom Books: Containing the Diamond Sutra and the Heart Sutra*. London: Allen & Unwin, 1966.

Coser, Lewis. *The Functions of Social Conflict*. New York: Free Press, 1956.

Cultural Artifacts Working Team of Luoyang City (Luoyang shi wenwu gongzuodui 洛陽市文物工作隊), Yu Fuwei 余扶危, and Xing Jianluo 邢建洛 (lead authors). "Luoyang Tang Shenhui heshang shenta taji qingli" 洛陽唐神會和尚身塔塔基清理 (Arrangement of the Stūpa Base for the Burial Stūpa for Reverend Shenhui of the Tang [Discovered in] Luoyang). *Wenwu* 430, no. 3 (1992): 64–67 and 75.

De Bary, Wm. Theodore, Wing-tsit Chan, and Burton Watson. *Sources of Chinese Tradition*. New York: Columbia University Press, 1960.

Demiéville, Paul. "Deux documents de Touen-houang sur le Dhyāna chinois." In *Essays on the History of Buddhism Presented to Professor Tsukamoto Zenryū*, 1–14 (from the back). Kyoto: Research Institute for Humanistic Studies, Kyoto University, 1961.

Eber, Irene. "Hu Shih and Chinese History: The Problem of Cheng-li kuo-ku." *Monumenta Serica* 27 (1968): 169–207.

Einstein, Albert, et al. *Living Philosophies*. New York: Simon and Schuster, 1931.

Faure, Bernard. "The Concept of One-Practice Samādhi in Early Ch'an." In Gregory, *Traditions of Meditation in Chinese Buddhism*, 99–128.

———. "Le maître de Dhyāna Chih-ta et le 'subitisme' de l'école du Nord." Cahiers d'Extrême-Asie 2, 123–132. Kyoto: École française d'Extrême-Orient, Section de Kyōto, 1986.

———. *The Rhetoric of Immediacy: A Cultural Critique of Chan/Zen Buddhism*. Princeton, NJ: Princeton University Press, 1991.

Feng Youlan. *Sansong tang zixu* 三松堂自序 (Author's Preface to the Hall of Three Pines). Beijing: Xinhua shudian, 1984.

Fischer, David Hackett. *Historians' Fallacies: Toward a Logic of Historical Thought*. New York: Harper Torchbooks, 1970.

Fogel, Joshua A. "On the 'Rediscovery' of the Chinese Past: Ts'ui Shu and Related Cases." In *Perspectives on a Changing China: Essays in Honor of Professor C. Martin Wilbur on the Occasion of His Retirement*, edited by Joshua A. Fogel and William T. Rowe, 219–235. Boulder, CO: Westview Press, 1979.

Foulk, T. Griffith. "The 'Ch'an' School and Its Place in the Buddhist Monastic Tradition." PhD diss., University of Michigan, 1987.

Funayama Tōru 船山徹, ed. *Shintai sanzō kenkyū ronshū*. 真諦三藏研究論集 (Studies of the Works and Influence of Paramartha). Kyoto: Kyōto daigaku jinbun kagaku kenkyūjo/Institute for Research in Humanities, Kyoto University, 2012.

Furth, Charlotte, Judith Zeitlin, and Ping-chen Hsiung, eds. *Thinking with Cases: Specialized Knowledge in Chinese Cultural History*. Honolulu: University of Hawai'i Press, 2007.

Gager, John G. *Kingdom and Community*. Englewood Cliffs, NJ: Prentice-Hall, 1975.

Gernet, Jacques. "Biographie du Maître Chen-houei du Ho-tsö." *Journal Asiatique* 239 (1951): 29–68.

———. "Complément aux entretiens du Maître de Dhyāna Chen-houei." *Bulletin de l'Ecole française d'Extrême-Orient* 44, no. 2 (1954): 453–466.

———. *Entretiens du Maître de Dhyâna Chen-hoei de Ho-tsö (668–760)*. Publications de l'école française d'Extrême-Orient 31. Hanoi: École française d'Extrême-Orient, 1949.

———. *A History of Chinese Civilization*. Translated by J. R. Foster. Cambridge: Cambridge University Press, 1982.

Ge Zhaoguang 葛兆光. "Heze zong kao" 荷澤宗考 (A Consideration of Shenhui's School). *Xin Shixue* 新史學 5, no. 4 (1994): 51–78.

Gimello, Robert M., and Peter N. Gregory, eds. *Studies in Ch'an and Hua-yen*. Studies in East Asian Buddhism 1. Honolulu: University of Hawai'i Press, 1983.

Gómez, Luis O. "Purifying Gold: The Metaphor of Effort and Intuition in Buddhist Thought and Practice." In Gregory, *Sudden and Gradual: Approaches to Enlightenment in Chinese Thought*, 67–165.

Gregory, Peter, ed. *Sudden and Gradual: Approaches to Enlightenment in Chinese Thought*. Studies in East Asian Buddhism 5. Honolulu: University of Hawai'i Press, 1987.

———, ed. *Traditions of Meditation in Chinese Buddhism*. Studies in East Asian Buddhism 4. Honolulu: University of Hawai'i Press, 1986.

———. *Tsung-mi and the Sinification of Buddhism*. Princeton, NJ: Princeton University Press, 1991.

Gregory, Peter, and Daniel A. Getz, Jr., eds. *Buddhism in the Sung*, Studies in East Asian Buddhism 13. Honolulu: University of Hawai'i Press, 1999.

Grieder, Jerome B. *Hu Shih and the Chinese Renaissance: Liberalism in the Chinese Revolution, 1911–1937*. Cambridge, MA: Harvard University Press, 1970.

Haydon, Albert E., ed. *Modern Trends in World Religions*. Chicago: University of Chicago Press, 1934.

Hirano Sōjō 平野宗浄. *Tongo yōmon* 頓悟要論門 (Treatise on the Essentials of Sudden Enlightenment). Zen no goroku 禅の語録 6. Tokyo: Chikuma shobō, 1969.

Hucker, Charles O. *A Dictionary of Official Titles in Imperial China*. Stanford, CA: Stanford University Press, 1985.

Hurvitz, Leon. *Chih-I (538–597): An Introduction to the Life and Ideas of a Chinese Buddhist Monk*. Mélanges chinois et bouddhiques 12. Brussels: Institut belge des hautes études chinoises, 1980.

Hu Shih 胡適. *Baihua wenxue shi—shang juan* 白話文學史—上卷 (History of Vernacular Literature: Volume One). Shanghai: Xinxue shudian 新學書店, 1928.

———, "Ch'an (Zen) Buddhism in China: Its History and Method." *Philosophy East and West* 3, no. 1 (April 1953): 3–24.

———. *The Chinese Renaissance: The Haskell Lectures, 1933*. Chicago: University of Chicago, 1934. Reprinted with a new introduction, New York: Paragon Book Reprint Corp., 1963.

———. "Chinese Thought." In *China*, edited by Harley Farnsworth MacNair, 221–230. Berkeley: University of California Press, 1951.

———. *The Development of the Logical Method in Ancient China*. Shanghai: Oriental Book Co., 1922. Reprint, New York: Paragon Book Reprint Corp., 1963.

———. "Development of Zen Buddhism in China." *Chinese Social and Political Science Review* 15, no. 4 (1932): 475–505.

———. *Hu Shi riji* 胡適日記 (Hu Shih's Diary). Beijing: Xinhua shuju, 1985.

---. *Hu Shi shougao* 胡适手稿 (Hu Shih's Manuscripts). 10 vols. Taibei: Hu Shi Jinianguan, 1966.

---. "The Indianization of China: A Case Study in Cultural Borrowing." In *Independence, Convergence, and Borrowing in Institutions, Thought, and Art*, 219–247. Harvard Tercentenary Publications. Cambridge, MA: Harvard University Press, 1937.

---. "Religion and Philosophy in Chinese History." In *Symposium on Chinese Culture*, edited by Sophia H. Chen Zen (Ch'en Heng-che), 31–58. Shanghai: China Institute of Pacific Relations, 1931.

---. *Shenhui heshang yiji—fu Hu xiansheng zuihou de yanjiu* 神會和尚遺集—付胡先生最後的研究 (Anthology of the Extant Works of Reverend Shenhui—With Hu's Latest Researches). Taibei: Hu Shi jinian guan, 1966. Reprinted with handwritten annotation by Hu, 1968. Page references are to the 1968 edition.

---. "Shuo Ru" 說儒 (On Ru). *Hu Shi wencun* 胡適文存 4, no. 1 (1953): 1–103.

---. "A Systematic Study of China's Cultural Heritage." *Chinese Studies in History* 14, no. 3 (Spring 1981): 80–87.

---. "The Task of Modern Religion." *Journal of Religion* 14, no. 1 (January 1934).

---. "Xin jiaoding de Dunhuang xieben Shenhui heshang yizhu liangzhong" 新校定的敦煌寫本神會和尚遺著兩種 (Two Newly Edited Texts of Reverend Shenhui from the Pelliot Collection of Dunhuang Manuscripts). *Zhongguo Zhongyang Yanjiuyuan Lishi Yuyan Yanjiusuo jikan* 29, no. 2 (February 1958): 827–882.

Iriya Yoshitaka 入矢義高. *Baso no goroku* 馬祖の語錄 (Recorded Sayings of Mazu). Kyoto: Zen Bunka Kenkyūjo, 1984.

---. *Denshin hōyō—Enryōroku* (Essentials of the Transmission of Mind: Wanling Records). Zen no goroku 禅の語録 8. Tokyo: Chikuma shobō, 1969.

Ishida Mizumaro 石田瑞麿. *Ganjin—sono kairitsu shisō* 鑑眞—その戒律思想一 (Ganjin: His Thoughts on Precepts and Vinaya). Daizō sensho 大藏選書, no. 10. Tokyo: Daizō shuppan, 1974.

Ishii Kōsei 石井公成. "Shintai kan'yo bunken no yōgo to gohō: NGSM ni yoru hikaku bunseki." 真諦關與文獻の用語と語法 NGSMによる比較分析 (The Vocabulary and Syntax of Paramārthan Texts: A Comparative Analysis Using NGSM). In Funayama, *Shintai sanzō kenkyū ronshū*, 87–120.

Jao Tsung-I 饒宗頤. "Shenhui menxia Moheyan zhi ruzang, jian lun Chanmen nanbei zong zhi tiaohe wenti" 神會門下摩訶衍之入藏，兼論禪門南北宗之調和問題 (The Entry of Shenhui's Disciple Moheyan into Tibet and the Question of the Reconciliation of the Northern and Southern Schools of Chan). In *Xianggang Daxue wushi zhounian jinian lunwen ji* 香港大學五十週年紀念論文集, vol. 1. Hong Kong: University of Hong Kong, 1964.

Jorgensen, John. *Inventing Hui-neng, the Sixth Patriarch: Hagiography and Biography in Early Ch'an*. Leiden: Brill, 2005.

Kamata Shigeo 鎌田茂雄. *Zengen shosenshū tojo* 禅源諸詮集都序 (Comprehensive Preface to the Interpretations of the Source of Chan). Zen no goroku 禅の語録 9. Tōkyō: Chikuma shobō, 1971.

Kim Kugyŏng (Jin Jiujing) 金九經. *Jiangyuan congshu* 姜園叢書 (Jiangyuan Collectanea). Shenyang, 1934.

Lai, Whalen, and Lewis R. Lancaster, eds. *Early Ch'an in China and Tibet*. Berkeley Buddhist Studies Series, no. 5. Berkeley: Asian Humanities Press, 1983.

Lamotte, Étienne, trans. *The Teaching of Vimalakīrti (Vimalakīrtinirdeśa)*. Translated by Sara Boin. London: Pali Text Society, 1976. Originally published as *L'Enseignement de Vimalakīrti* (Louvain: Bibliothèque du Muséon, 1962).

———, trans. *Le traité de la grande vertu de sagesse de Nāgārjuna (Mahāprajñāpāramitāśāstra)*. Vol. 2. Louvain-la-Neuve: Publications de l'Institut orientaliste de Louvain, 1949.

———, trans. *Le traité de la grande vertu de sagesse de Nāgārjuna (Mahāprajñāpāramitāśāstra)*. Vol. 3. Louvain-la-Neuve: Publications de l'Institut orientaliste de Louvain, 1970.

La Vallée Poussin, Louis de. *Abhidharmakośa: Traduit et annoté par Louis de La Vallée Poussin*. 6 vols. Paris: P. Geuthner, 1923–1931.

Liebenthal, Walter. *Chao Lun: The Treatises of Seng-chao*. Hong Kong: Hong Kong University Press, 1968.

———. "The Sermon of Shen-hui." *Asia Major*, n.s. 3, no. 2 (1952): 132–155.

———. "Yung-Chia Cheng-Tao-Ko 永嘉證道歌 or Yung-chia's Song of Experiencing the Tao." *Monumenta Serica* 6, nos. 1–2 (1941): 1–39.

Lin Yusheng. "The Pseudoreformism of Hu Shih." In *The Crisis of Chinese Consciousness: Radical Antitraditionalism in the May Fourth Era*. Madison: University of Wisconsin Press, 1979.

Li Xueqin 李學勤. "Chanzong zaoqi wenwu de zhongyao faxian" 禪宗早期文物旳重要發現 (Important Discoveries of Early Chan School Artifacts). *Wenwu* 430, no. 3 (1992): 71–75.

———. "The Sermon of Shen-hui." *Asia Major*, n.s. 3, no. 2 (1952): 132–155.

Long Hui 龍晦. "Lun Dunhuang ciqu suo jian zhi Chanzong yu Jingtu zong" 論敦煌詞曲所見之禪宗與淨土宗 (On the Chan and Pure Land Schools Apparent in Dunhuang Verses). In *Dunhuang geci zongbian* 敦煌歌辭總編 (Comprehensive Edition of Dunhuang Songs), edited by Ren Bantang 任半塘, 1801–1818. Shanghai: Shanghai guji chubanshe, 1987.

Lou Yulie 樓宇烈. "Ko Teki Zenshūshi kenkyū heigi" 胡適禪宗史研究評議 (An Appraisal of Hu Shih's Research of Chan Buddhist History). Translated by Ogawa Takashi 小川隆. *Komazawa Daigaku Sōtōshū Shūgaku Kenkyūjo kiyō* 駒澤大學曹洞宗宗學研究所紀要 1 (March 1988): 1–18. First published as "Hu Shi Chanzongshi yanjiu pingyi" 胡適禪宗史研究評議 (An Evaluation of Hu Shih's Studies of Chan School History). *Beijing Daxue xuebao* 北京大學學報 3 (March 1987): n.p.

Lü Cheng 呂澂. *Zhongguo Foxue yuanliu lüejiang* 中國佛學源流略講 (Brief Lectures on the Origin and Development of Chinese Buddhism). Beijing: Zhonghua shuju, 1979.

Luo Zhenyu 羅振玉. *Shike shiliao xinbian* 石刻史料新編 (New Edition of Historical Materials Carved on Stone). Series 1. Taipei: Xin wenfeng chuban gongsi, 1977.

Macdonald, Ariane, and Yoshiro Imaeda [今枝由郎]. *Choix de documents tibetains conserves a la Bibliotheque nationale: complete par quelques manuscrits de l'India office et du British Museum*. Vol. 1. Paris: Bibliotheque nationale, 1978.

Marsden, George M. "Evangelical and Fundamental Christianity." In *Encyclopedia of Religion*. edited by Mircea Eliade. New York: Macmillan, 1987.

Mather, Richard B., trans. *A New Account of Tales of the World*. Minneapolis: University of Minnesota Press, 1976.

Matsuda Fumio 松田文雄. "Jinne no hōtōsetsu ni tsuite – toku ni sanzo kenshō mondai –" 神會の法統説について―特に三祖顯彰問題 (On Shenhui's Transmission Lineage: Especially the Question of the Third Patriarch). *Indogaku Bukkyōgaku kenkyū* 印度學佛教學研究 6, no. 2 (12 March 1958): 221–224 (532–535).

McRae, John R. "The Antecedents of Encounter Dialogue in Chinese Ch'an

Buddhism." In *The Kōan: Texts and Contexts in Zen Buddhism*, edited by Steven Heine and Dale S. Wright, 46–74. New York: Oxford University Press, 2000.

———. "Chan Commentaries on the *Heart Sūtra*." *Journal of the International Association of Buddhist Studies* 11, no. 2 (1988): 87–115.

———. "Daoxuan's Vision of Jetavana and the Ordination Platform Movement in Medieval Chinese Buddhism." In *Going Forth: Visions of Buddhist Vinaya: Essays Presented in Honor of Professor Stanley Weinstein*, edited by William M. Bodiford, 68–100. Studies in East Asian Buddhism 18. Honolulu: University of Hawai'i Press, 2005.

———. "Encounter Dialogue and the Transformation of the Spiritual Path in Chinese Chan." In *Paths to Liberation: The Mārga and Its Transformations in Buddhist Thought*, edited by Robert E. Buswell, Jr., and Robert M. Gimello, 339–369. Studies in East Asian Buddhism 7. Honolulu: University of Hawai'i Press, 1992.

———. *The Northern School and the Formation of Early Ch'an Buddhism*. Studies in East Asian Buddhism 3. Honolulu: University of Hawai'i Press, 1986.

———. "The Ox-head School of Chinese Buddhism: From Early Ch'an to the Golden Age." In Gimello and Gregory, *Studies in Ch'an and Hua-yen*, 169–263.

———. *Seeing through Zen: Encounter, Transformation, and Genealogy in Chinese Chan Buddhism*. Berkeley: University of California Press, 2003.

———. "Shen-hui and the Teaching of Sudden Enlightenment in Early Ch'an Buddhism." In Gregory, *Sudden and Gradual: Approaches to Enlightenment in Chinese Thought*.

Nakamura Nobuyuki 中村信幸. "Nan'yō wajō tonkyō gedatsu zenmon jiki ryōshō dango" 南陽和上頓教解脱禪門直了性壇語 (The Platform Sermon by the Reverend of Nanyang on Directly Comprehending the Nature according to the Chan Doctrine of the Sudden Teaching and Emancipation). In Tanaka, Okimoto, et al., *Daijō Butten*, 87–114.

———. "Nan'yō wajō tonkyō gedatsu zenmon jiki ryōshō dango hon'yaku" 南陽和上頓教解脱禪門直了性壇語翻訳 (A Translation of the Platform Sermon by the Reverend of Nanyang on Directly Comprehending the Nature according to the Chan Doctrine of the Sudden Teaching and Emancipation). *Komazawa Daigaku Bukkyōgaku kenkyūkai nempō* 8 (1974): 137–146.

Nishiguchi Yoshio 西口芳男. "Baso no denki" 馬祖の伝記 (The Biography of Mazu). *Zengaku kenkyū* 禅学研究 63 (1984): 111–146.

———. "Zengaku tenbyō (hachi): Jinne ni kakawaru Tonkō shahon no ichi danpen" 禅学点描（八）：神会にかかわる敦煌写本の一断片 (A Bit of Zen studies (8): A Dunhuang Manuscript Fragment Pertaining to Shenhui). *Zen bunka* 165 (1997): 119–122.

Nishikawa Yasushi 西川寧. *Sei'an hirin* 西安碑林 (The Forest of Stele in Xi'an). Tokyo: Kōdansha, 1966.

Nishitani Keiji 西谷啓司 and Yanagida Seizan 柳田聖山, eds. *Zenke goroku* 禅家語録 (Zen Recorded Sayings), vol. 2. *Sekai koten bungaku zenshū* 世界古典文学全集 36B. Tokyo: Chikuma shobō, 1974.

Nukariya Kaiten 忽滑谷快天. *Zengaku shisoshi* 禪學思想史 (A History of Chan Thought). Vol. 1. Tokyo: Genkōsha, 1923.

Ogawa Kan'ichi 小川貫弌. "*Hannya haramitta shingyō* kaidai" 般若波羅蜜多心經解題 (A Guide to the *Mahā-prajñāpāramitā-hṛdaya-sūtra*). Seiiki bunka kenkyū 西域文化研究, vol. 1. *Tonkō Bukkyō shiryō* 敦煌佛教資料. Kyoto: Hōzōkan, 1958.

Ogawa Takashi 小川隆. "Kataku Jinne no hito to shisō" 荷沢神会の人と思想 (Heze Shenhui's Personal Identity and Thought). *Zengaku kenkyū* 69 (1991): 20–59.

———. "Tonkō-bon Rokuso dankyō no seiritsu ni tsuite" 敦煌本六祖壇経の成立について (On the Formation of the Dunhuang Text of the Platform Sūtra). *Komazawa Daigaku Bukkyō kenkyūkai nempō* 20 (1987): 20–27.

Pelliot, Paul. "Meou-Tseu Ou Les Doutes Levés." In *T'oung Pao,* 2nd ser. 19, no. 5 (1918): 255–433.

Peterson, C. A. "Court and Province in Mid- and Late T'ang." In *Sui and T'ang China, 589–906,* pt. 1, edited by Denis Twitchett. Vol. 3 of *The Cambridge History of China.* Cambridge: Cambridge University Press, 1979.

Reischauer, Edwin O. *Ennin's Travels in Tang China.* New York: Ronald Press, 1955.

Ren Bantang 任半塘. Dunhuang geci zongbian 敦煌歌辭總編 (Comprehensive Edition of Dunhuang Songs). 3 vols. Shanghai: Shanghai hai guji chubanshe, 1987.

Schopen, Gregory. "The Phrase 'sa prthivīpradeśaś caityabhūto bhavet' in the Vajracchedikā: Notes on the Cult of the Book in Mahāyāna." *Indo-Iranian Journal* 17 (1975): 147–181.

Sharf, Robert H. *Coming to Terms with Chinese Buddhism: A Reading of the Treasure Store Treatise.* Studies in East Asian Buddhism 14. Honolulu: University of Hawai'i Press, 2002.

———. "How to Think with Chan Gong'ans." In Furth, Zeitlin, and Hsiung, *Thinking with Cases,* 205–243.

———. "The Zen of Japanese Nationalism." In Donald S. Lopez, Jr., ed., *Curators of the Buddha: The Study of Buddhism under Colonialism,* 107–160. Chicago: University of Chicago Press, 1995.

Shinohara Hisao 篠原寿雄. "Kataku Jinne no kotoba—Yakuchū Nan'yō wajō tonkyō gedatsu zenmon jiki ryōshō dango" 荷澤神會のことば：訳注『南陽和上頓教解脱禅門直了性壇語. (The Words of Heze Shenhui: An Annotated Translation of the Platform Sermon by the Reverend of Nanyang on Directly Comprehending the (Buddha-)Nature according to the Chan Doctrine of Sudden Teaching and Emancipation). *Komazawa Daigaku Bungakubu kenkyū kiyō* 31 (1973): 1–33.

Suzuki Daisetsu [D. T. Suzuki] 鈴木大拙. "Jinne oshō no dango to kangaubeki Tonkō shutsudo bon ni tsukite" 神会和尚の『壇語』と考ふべき敦煌出土本につきて. *Ōtani gakuhō* 大谷學報 16, no. 4 (December 1935): 1–30.

———. *Kōkan Shōshitsu issho oyobi kaisetsu* 校刊少室逸書及解說 (Notes on Lost Writings from Shaoshi). Osaka: Ataka Bukkyō bunko, 1936.

———. *Shōshitsu issho* 少室逸書. Osaka: Ataka Bukkyō bunko, 1935.

———. *Suzuki Daisetsu zenshū* 鈴木大拙全集 (Complete Works of D. T. Suzuki). 32 vols. Tokyo: Iwanami shoten, 1968.

———. "Zen: A Reply to Hu Shih." *Philosophy East and West* 3, no. 1 (April 1953): 25–46.

Suzuki Daisetsu and Kōda Rentarō 公田連太郎. *Tonkō shutsudo Kataku Jinne zenji goroku.* 敦煌出土荷澤神會禪師語録 (The Recorded Sayings of Chan Master Shenhui Discovered in Dunhuang). Tokyo: Morie shoten, 1934.

Suzuki Tetsuo 鈴木哲雄. "Kataku Jinne no ken no shiso" 荷澤神会の見の思想 (Heze Shenhui's Thoughts on "Seeing"). *Indogaku Bukkyōgaku kenkyū* 印度學佛教學研究 16, no. 1 (31; December 1967): 132–133.

———. "Kataku Jinne ron" 荷沢神会論 (An Essay on Heze Shenhui). *Bukkō shigakkai* 14, no. 4 (November 1969): 36–53.

———. "Kataku Jinne yori dankyō ni itaru kenshō no tenkai" 荷澤神会より壇經に至る見性の展開 (The Development of Seeing Into One's Nature from Heze Shenhui to the *Platform Sūtra*). *Indogaku Bukkyōgaku kenkyū* 印度學佛教學研究 17, no. 1 (33; December 1968): 302–304.

———. "'Tongo nyūdō yōmon ron' ni mirareru Kataku Jinne no eikyō" 『頓悟入道要論』にみられる荷沢神会の影響 (Heze Shenhui's Influence on the "Dunwu rudao yaomen lun"). *Shūgaku kenkyū* 12 (1970): 91–96.

Takemoto, Melvin Masa. "The *Kuei-shan ching-ts'e*: Morality and the Hung-chou School of Ch'an." MA thesis, University of Hawaii, 1983.

Takeuchi Kōdō 竹内弘道. "Shinshutsu no Kataku Jinne tōmei ni tsuite" 新出の荷沢神会塔銘について (On the Newly Discovered Stūpa Inscription for Heze Shenhui). *Shūgaku kenkyū* 27 (1985): 313–325.

Tanaka Ryōshō 田中良昭. *Tonkō Zenshū bunken no kenkyū* 敦煌禪宗文獻の研究 (Research on Dunhuang Chan Literature). Tokyo: Daitō shuppansha, 1983.

Tanaka Ryōshō 田中良昭 and Okimoto Katsumi 沖本克己. *Daijō Butten: Chūgoku—Nihon hen: Tonkō II*. 大乗仏典. 中国・日本篇：敦煌 II (Mahāyāna Buddhist Scriptures, China and Japan: Dunhuang Part 2). Tokyo: Chūō kōronsha, 1989.

Tanaka Ryōshō Hakushi Koki Kinen Ronshū Kankōkai 田中良昭博士古稀記念論集刊行会. *Zengaku kenkyū no shosō : Tanaka Ryōshō Hakushi koki kinen ronshū* 禅学研究の諸相：田中良昭博士古稀記念論集 (Various Aspects of Research on Chan: A Collection of Essays Celebrating Professor Tanaka Ryōshō's Seventieth Birthday). Tokyo: Daitō shuppansha, 2003.

Tōdai goroku kenkyūhan 唐代語録研究班 (Tang Dynasty Recorded Sayings Research Group). "Nan'yō wajō tonkyō gedatsu zenmon jiki ryōshō dango hokō" 《南陽和尚頓教解脱禅門直了性壇語》補校 (Supplementary Edition of the Platform Sermon by the Reverend of Nanyang on Directly Comprehending the Nature according to the Chan Doctrine of the Sudden Teaching and Emancipation). *Zoku gogen kenkyū* 俗語言研究 5 (1998): 39–46.

Tōkyō Kokuritsu Hakubutsukan. *Kōga bunmei tenran* 黄河文明展覧 (Exhibition on the Civilization of the Yellow River). Tokyo: Chūnichi shimbun sha, 1986.

Tsukada Yasunobu 塚田康信. *Sei'an hirin no kenkyū* 西安碑林の研究 (Research on the Forest of Stele in Xi'an). Tokyo: Tōhō shoten, 1983.

Ueyama Daishun 上山大俊. "Chibetto-yaku *Tongo shinshū yōketsu* no kenkyū" チベット譯「頓悟眞宗要決」の研究 (A Study of the Tibetan Translation of the *Essential Teachings according to the True Principle of Sudden Awakening*). *Zenbunka Kenkyūjo kiyō* 禅文化研究所紀要 8 (1976): 33–103.

Ui Hakuju 宇井伯寿. *Zenshūshi kenkyū* 禅宗史研究 (Studies in the History of the Chan School). Vol. 1. Tokyo: Iwanami shoten, 1939.

von Glahn, Richard. *The Country of Streams and Grottoes: Expansion, Settlement, and the Civilizing of the Sichuan Frontier in Song Times*. Cambridge, MA: Council on East Asian Studies, 1987.

Walshe, Maurice, trans. *Thus Have I Heard: The Long Discourses of the Buddha, Dīgha Nikāya*. London: Wisdom Publications, 1987.

Wang Huibin 王輝斌. "Chen Tiemin *Wang Wei nianpu* shangping" 陈铁民《王维年谱》商评 (A Criticism of Chen Tiemin's *Annals of Wang Wei*). *Xiangfan xueyuan xuebao* 1 (2007): 45–50.

———. 2003. "Wang Wei Kaiyuan xingzong qiu shi" 王维开元行踪求是 (Wang Wei's Travels during the Kaiyuan Period). *Shanxi daxue xue bao* 26, no. 4 (2003): 64–68.

Bibliography

Watson, Burton, trans. *The Lotus Sutra*. New York: Columbia University Press, 1994.
Weinstein, Stanley. "The Beginnings of Esoteric Buddhism in Japan: The Neglected Tendai Tradition." *Journal of Asian Studies* 34, no. 1 (November 1974): 177–191.
———. *Buddhism under the T'ang*. Cambridge: Cambridge University Press, 1987.
Wen Yucheng 溫玉成. "Ji xin chutude Heze dashi Shenhui taming" 記新出土的荷澤大師神會塔銘 (On the Great Master Heze Shenhui's Newly Discovered Stele Inscription). *Shijie zongjiao yanjiu* 世界宗教研究, no. 2 (1984): 78–79.
Wright, Arthur F. *Buddhism in Chinese History*. Stanford, CA: Stanford University Press, 1959. Reprint, New York: Atheneum, 1965.
Wu Qiyu 吳其昱. "Heze Shenhui zhuan yanjiu" 荷澤神會傳研究 (Research on Heze Shenhui's Biography). *Zhongyang Yanjiu Yuan Li-shi Yuyan Yanjiusuo jikan* 中研究院歷史語言研究所集刊 59, no. 4 (December 1988): 899–912.
Xing Dongfeng 邢東風. "Shenhui yulu" 神會語錄 (Shenhui's Recorded Sayings). *Zhongguo Fojiao jingdian baozang jingxuan baihua ban* 23 (1996): 187–227.
Yabuki Keiki 矢吹慶輝, ed. *Meisha yoin kaisetsu: Tonkō shutsudo miden koitsu butten kaihō*. 鳴沙餘韻解說：燉煌出土未傳古逸佛典開寶 (Rare and Unknown Chinese Manuscript Remains of Buddhist Literature Discovered in Dunhuang Collected by Sir Aurel Stein and Preserved in the British Museum). Tokyo: Iwanami Shoten, 1933.
Yamaguchi Sakae 山口栄. "Ko Teki no Chūgoku Zenshūshi ni tsuite" 胡適の中國禅宗史に就いて (On Hu Shih's History of Chinese Chan Buddhism). *Junsei Tanki Daigaku kenkyū kiyō* 順正短期大學研究紀要 3 (1973): 63–76. Reprinted in *Chūgoku kankei ronsetsu shiryō* 中國関係論説資料 15 (1973), sec. 1, no. 1 (Philosophy and Religion), 49–56.
Yamazaki Hiroshi 山崎宏. "Kataku Jinne zenji" 荷沢神会禅師 (The Chan Master Heze Shenhui). In *Zuitō Bukkyōshi no kenkyū* 隋唐仏教史の研究 (A Study of Sui-Tang Buddhism), 203–221. Kyoto: Hōzōkan, 1967.
Yampolsky, Philip B. *The Platform Sutra of the Sixth Patriarch: The Text of the Tun-huang Manuscript with Translation, Introduction, and Notes*. New York and London: Columbia University Press, 1967.
Yanagida Seizan 柳田聖山. *Daruma no goroku—Ninyū shigyō ron* 達摩の語錄—二入四行論 (Bodhidharma's Recorded Sayings—Treatise on Two Entrances and Four Practices). Zen no goroku 禅の語錄 1. Tokyo: Chikuma shobō, 1969.
———. "Goroku no rekishi—Zen bunken no seiritsushiteki kenkyū" 語錄の歴史—禅文献の成立史的研究 (The History of Recorded Sayings—A Study of the Historical Formation of Chan Literature; original English title: A Historical Survey of the Recorded Sayings of Chan Masters in View of the Formation of Chan Literature). *Tōhō gakuhō* 57 (1985): 211–663. Reprinted in Yanagida, *Yanagida Seizan shū*, 3–526.
———. "Hokushū-Zen no shisō" 北宗禪の思想 (The Thought of Northern School Chan). *Zenbunka Kenkyūjo kiyō* 禅文化研究所紀要 6 (1974): 67–104.
———. "Ko Teki hakase to Chūgoku shoki Zenshūshi no kenkyū" 胡適博士と中国初期禪宗史の研究 (On Professor Hu Shih's Research on Early Chinese Chan Buddhist History). *Mondai to kenkyū* 問題と研究 4, no. 5 (February 1975).
———, ed. *Ko Teki Zengaku an* 胡適禅学案 (Hu Shih's Studies on Chan). Kyoto: Chūbun shuppansha, 1975.
———. "The 'Recorded Sayings' Texts of Chinese Chan Buddhism." Translated by John R. McRae. In Lai and Lancaster, *Early Ch'an in China and Tibet*, 185–205.

---. *Shoki no Zenshi, 1—Ryoga shiji ki—Den'hōbō ki* 初期の 禪史, 1—楞伽師資記・伝法宝紀 (Early Chan History 1: Records of the Masters and Students of the Laṅkā(vatāra) and Annals of the Transmission of the Dharma-treasure). Zen no goroku 禅の語録 2. Tokyo: Chikuma shobō, 1971.

---. *Shoki no Zenshi, 2—Rekidai hōbō ki* 歷代法宝記 (Early Chan History 2: Records of the Transmission of the Dharma-treasure through the Generations). Zen no goroku 禅の語録 3. Tokyo: Chikuma shobō, 1976.

---. *Shoki Zenshū shisho no kenkyū* 初期禪宗史書の研究 (Studies in the Historical Works of Early Chan). Kyoto: Hōzōkan, 1967.

---. *Sodōshū* 祖堂集 (Anthology of the Patriarchal Hall). Zengaku Sōsho 禪學叢書 4. Kyoto: Chūmon Shuppansha, 1984.

---. *Sōzōichin Hōrinden, Dentō gyokueishū.* 宋蔵遺珍寶林傳, 傳燈玉英集 (The Remaining/Inherited Treasures of the Song Canon: The Transmissions of the Baolin [Temple] and Collection of Jade Heroes who Transmitted the Lamp). Kyoto: Chūbun shuppansha, 1975.

---. *Yanagida Seizan shū, dai-ni kan: Zen bunken no kenkyū jō* 柳田聖山集 第二巻 : 禅文献の研究上 (Complete Works of Yanagida Seizan, Vol. 2, Studies in Zen Texts 1). Kyōto: Hōzōkan, 1999.

---. *Zengo yoteki* 禅語余滴 (Drippings of Zen Language). Kyoto: Zen Bunka Kenkyūjo, 1989.

---. "*Zenmonkyō ni tsuite*" 禅門經について (On the *Sūtra of Chan*). In *Tsukamoto hakase shōju kinen Bukkyō shigaku ronshū* 塚本博士頌壽記念佛教史學論集, 869–882. Tokyo: Tsukamoto hakase shōju kinen kai, 1961.

---. "*Zenseki kaidai*" 禅籍解題 (A Guide to Chan Texts). In Nishitani and Yanagida, *Zenke goroku*, 445–514.

Yanagida Seizan 柳田聖山 and Tokiwa Gishin 常盤義伸. *Zekkanron: Eibun yakuchū, gembun kōtei, kokuyaku.* 絶觀論 : 英文訳注, 原文校定, 国訳 (Treatise on the Contemplation-Extinguished: A Translation Based on Professor Yanagida Seizan's Modern Japanese Translation and Consultations with Professor Iriya Yoshitaka). Kyoto: Zen Bunka Kenkyūjo, Chūgoku zenroku kenkyūban, 1976.

Yang Hongfei 楊鴻飛. "Zui ko Kyōchi zenji himei narabini jo ni hatsugen sareta Zenshūshi no issetsu" 隋故鏡智禪師碑銘并序に發現された禪宗史の一節 (A Moment in the History of the Chan School Revealed in the "Epitaph for the Late Jingzhi Chan Master of the Sui (Dynasty), with Preface"). *Indogaku Bukkyōgaku kenkyū* 印度學佛教研究 15, no. 1 (29; December 1966): 350–353.

Yang Jingqing, *The Chan Interpretations of Wang Wei's Poetry: A Critical Review.* Hong Kong: Chinese University of Hong Kong Press, 2007.

Yang Zengwen 楊曾文. *Shenhui heshang Chanhua lu* 神會和尚禪話錄 (Records of the Chan Sayings of Reverend Shenhui). Zhongguo Fojiao dianji xuankan 中國佛教典籍選刊 (Selected Chinese Buddhist Scriptures). Beijing: Zhonghua shuju, 1996.

Yinshun 印順. *Zhongguo Chanzong shi* 中国禅宗史 (A History of the Chan School in China). Nanchang: Jiangxi renmin chubanshe, 1999.

Young, Stuart. *Conceiving the Indian Buddhist Patriarchs in China.* Studies in East Asian Buddhism 24. Honolulu: University of Hawaiʻi Press, 2015.

Yu Xianhao 郁賢皓. *Tang cishi kao* 唐刺史考 (A Consideration of Tang Dynasty Prefects). Shanghai: Jiangsu guji chubanshe, 1987.

Zen Bunka Kenkyūjo Tōdai Goroku Kenkyuhan. *Jinne no goroku: dango* 神会の語錄 : 檀語 (The Collected Sayings of Shenhui: The Platform Sermon). Kyoto: Zen Bunka Kenkyūjo, 2006.

Zeuschner, Robert B. "An Analysis of the Philosophical Criticisms of Northern Ch'an Buddhism." PhD diss., University of Hawaii, 1977.

———, "The *Hsien-tsung chi:* An Early Ch'an Text." *Journal of Chinese Philosophy* 3 (1976): 253–268.

———. "A Sermon by the Ch'an Master Ho-tse Shen-hui." *Middle Way* 49, no. 3 (November 1974): 45–47.

Zhang Yihua 張翊華. "Xi Jiangxi Ruichang faxian de Tangdai Foju" 析江西瑞昌發現的唐代佛具 (Analysis of Buddhist Implements Discovered at Ruichang in Jiangxi). *Wenwu* 430, no. 3 (1992): 68–70.

Index

abstinence, 50
"activating the mind" (*qixin*): in *Definition of the Truth*, 97–99, 117; in *Miscellaneous Dialogues*, 161, 166, 169, 172, 179, 185; in Northern school works, 22–24, 31–32; in *Platform Sermon*, 54, 60–65, 69
afflictions, 64–66, 134, 141–145, 192–194, 217
An Lushan rebellion, xviii, 7, 14, 268, 287
Annals of the Transmission (*Chuan fabao ji*), 35
Aśvaghoṣa, 16, 66
Awakening of Faith (*Dasheng qi xin lun*), 66
"awareness of the mind" (*shouxin*), 24, 38

Baolin zhuan (*Transmission of the Treasure Grove*), 244
Baotang, 255
Baoying si, 15
Baoyue, Master, 210
Baozhen, 220
begging bowl, 7–8
Biyan lu (*Blue Cliff Record*), 259
blankness of mind (*wuji*), 28
Blue Cliff Record (*Biyan lu*), 259
bodhicitta (mind of awakening), xix, 253, 295; in *Definition of the Truth*, 33, 117, 122, 295–296; in *Miscellaneous Dialogues*, 131, 163, 166, 176, 180, 200, 202; in *Platform Sermon*, 33, 47–53, 70
Bodhidharma: encounter with Emperor Wu, 75–76, 290–291, 298; encounter with Huike, 77–79, 106–107, 207–210, 293; Hu's work on, 243; lineage, 11–12, 90–98, 106–107, 206–209; Shenhui's view of, 34, 42, 273, 277, 293; Suzuki's work on, 6
bodhisattva: Chinese concept of, 295; Shenhui's identification as, 294–295

Bo Juyi, 243
Buddha-nature of the insentient, 187–188
buddhas: Chinese concept of, 295; rarity of meeting, 51–52, 189
buqi xin ("non-activated mind"), 22–24, 31–32, 50–51, 61–65, 121, 132, 173

Cai Hao, 196
Caoqi, 8–9, 17, 19, 27, 36, 215–217
causes/conditions, 48, 192, 296
censer, 7–8
Chan Buddhism, classical: colloquial style of dialogue, xix; contemporary analysis of, 265–274; creative legend in, 2–3, 16, 42, 241, 252, 258–259, 272–274; decline in China, 251, 261–262, 266–269, 271; distinction between laymen and monks, 23, 39, 82–83, 131, 165, 168, 174; doctrinal development of, 3–5; Hu's history of, 236–245; in Japan, 268; lack of primary sources, 4–5; lineages, 35–36, 78–79, 90–107, 206–217, 254; misperceptions in, 256–260, 266–269; ordination program, xviii, 14, 287–290, 297; reconceptualization of, 297–299; role in Chinese history, 235–239, 266–270, 272–274, 299; and Shenhui, 37, 235, 254–255, 293; Shenhui's role in shaping, xix, 41–42; transformation in, 6–7, 39, 240–241, 255, 268–269, 273–274; unrestricted great assemblies, 75, 83, 126, 288–290; versus early Chan, 4–5, 41–42, 240–241, 255, 259, 270, 274; Zen masters, 275–276, 286, 298. *See also* factionalist campaign; Hu Shih; India; *specific doctrine; specific person;* sudden enlightenment

323

Chang'an: political climate in, 13–14; Shenhui's ordination in, 9, 16, 36. *See* Northern school
Ch'en, Kenneth K. S., 271–272
childbirth metaphor, 33, 37, 98, 297
Chinese history: contemporary work on, 265–274; disappearance of Buddhism, 251, 261–262; Hu's interest in, 245–247, 259–261; role of Buddhism in, 235–239, 266–270, 272–274, 299. *See also* Hu Shih
Chinese philosophy: Hu's analysis of, 243, 248–251
Chinese Renaissance, 271; contemporary work on, 265–274; Hu's work on, 238–239, 247–251, 261–265
Chisan Kohō, 235
Chong, Master, 182
Chongyuan: in *Miscellaneous Dialogues*, 157, 165, 201, 206; Shenhui's debate with. See also *Definition of the Truth*
Christian evangelists, xix–xx, 291–293
Chuan fabao ji (*Annals of the Transmission*), 35
classical Chan: lack of primary sources, 4–5; Shenhui's role in shaping, xix, 41–42; versus early Chan, 4–5, 41–42, 240–241, 255, 259, 270, 274
Cohen, Paul, 262
concentration. *See* meditation
conditioned (*youwei*), 15, 50–51, 81–82, 131, 170, 200–201
Confucianism, 245, 247, 251, 261–262
constant practice, xvii, 38
contemplative analysis (*guanxin shi* or *kanjin shaku*), 23–25, 32, 255
Cui, Duke, 151
Cui Shu, 262
Cunda, 86–88, 141, 279, 294

Daizong, 14
Daoism, 192, 247, 249, 251, 261, 264, 267
Daosheng, 238
Daoxin, xvii, 31, 79, 89, 91, 105, 210–212
Daoxuan, 287
Daoyin, 280
Dasheng kaixin xianxing dunwu zhenzong lun. See *Treatise on the True Principle*
Dasheng qi xin lun (*Awakening of Faith*), 66
Dayi, 102
Dayun si, 11–12, 75
Dazhu Huihai, 40
de Bary, William T., 271–272
Definition of the Truth (*Putidamo nanzong ding shifei lun*): about, xx, 11–12, 72, 277;

dating of, 28, 72; fundraising role of, 289–299; Hu's work on, 251–252; main text, 79–121; Northern school doctrine in, 27–32; postface, 121–128; preface, 72–79; religious authority in, 292–296; suddenness in, 33–34; textual sources, 300–301; translation, 72–128
Dewey, John, 245, 246, 261
Dezong, Emperor, 16
Dharma: transmission of, 42, 66–71, 169, 181–183, 197, 273
dharmadhātu, 28
Diamond Sūtra: in *Definition of the Truth*, 34, 108–117; in *Miscellaneous Dialogues*, 139, 159–160, 166–167, 170–172, 201, 207, 209–212, 215; in *Platform Sermon*, 55, 59
Dinggong, 210
ding hui deng yong (equivalent functioning of meditation and wisdom), 26
Dīpaṃkara, 115–116
direct (*shun*), 25
direct contemplation (*shunguan*), 25
dragon girl, 163, 176
Dugu Pei, 72, 293
Dunhuang manuscripts: absence of classical texts from, 4–5; Hu's work on, 236–237, 242; McRae's dissertation on, xvii; Yanagida's work on, xvi–xvii. *See also* Hu Shih
Dunwu rudao yaomen lun (*Essential Teaching of Sudden Enlightenment*), 40, 236
Dunwu wusheng bore song. See *Verses on Sudden Enlightenment, the Birthless, and Prajñā*
Dunwu zhenzong jingang bore xiuxing da bi'an famen yqojue (*Essential Determination*), 18–19, 21–25, 29–30, 35, 40

early Chan: doctrinal development of, 3–5; versus classical Chan, 4–5, 41–42, 240–241, 255, 259, 270, 274. See also *specific doctrine*
East Mountain teaching. *See* Northern school
Eber, Irene, 245–247, 262
emptiness: in *Definition of the Truth*, 82, 127; in *Miscellaneous Dialogues*, 131, 159, 161–165, 169, 176, 179–180, 196–197, 201, 205; in *Platform Sermon*, 54–55, 61, 64, 67; in *Verses*, 223, 226–232
encounter dialogue, x, xvii–xviii, 4–5, 42, 240, 255, 273–274

Ennin, 267–268
equivalence: doctrine of, 38–39, 50–51, 58, 90, 173, 185–186
equivalent functioning of meditation and wisdom (*ding hui deng yong*), 26
esoteric Buddhism, 259, 270
Essential Determination (*Dunwu zhenzong jingang bore xiuxing da bi'an famen yqojue*), 18–19, 21–25, 29–30, 35, 40
Essential Teaching of Sudden Enlightenment (*Dunwu rudao yaomen lun*), 40, 236
evangelist(s): Christian, xix–xx, 291–293; definition of, 291–293; emphasis on suddenness, 33, 37, 253, 295–296, 298; Huatai debates, xviii, 11–12, 35, 276–277, 290–291; McRae's use of term, xviii–xix; Shenhui as, 275, 291–297, 299
existence, 140–142, 146–148, 155–156, 162, 166, 177, 195–196, 200, 227–231
extinction: in *Definition of the Truth*, 108, 120; in *Miscellaneous Dialogues*, 132, 143, 157, 161, 181–182, 198–206, 218; in *Platform Sermon*, 68; in *Verses*, 223
eyes, 164–165

Fachang, 289
factionalist campaign: about, 11–13, 276–286; catalyst for, 35–36; doctrinal turning point, 41–42, 240–241, 255, 273–274; evidence in Shenhui's works, 27–32, 253, 274; Hu's depiction of, 252–253; McRae's dissertation on, xvii–xix; as rhetorical device, xix; as sectarian labeling, 3–4, 240–241, 255. See also *Definition of the Truth*
"false mind" (*wangxin*), 25, 50–51, 54–55, 61, 65, 139, 178, 182, 185
Fang Guan, 12, 192
Faru (Zhiru), 101, 214, 284
Faure, Bernard, 18
Faxing lun (*Treatise on the Dharma-nature*), 5–27, 32
Fazang, 289
Fazhen, 289
Five Skillful Means (*Wufang bian*), 28, 32
Flower Garland Sūtra, 69, 134, 163
Fogel, Joshua, 262, 265
"four pronouncements" (Shenhui), 28–29, 56–62, 97–99, 169, 179, 277
"freezing the mind," 28–29, 56–62, 97–99, 169, 179, 277
Fulin, 281
fundamental mind, 160, 180, 255

fundraising, xviii, 14, 287–291, 299
Fuxian si, 11, 84

gangue-gold metaphor, 26, 134, 143, 188
Gao (family name), 8
Gateless Barrier (*Wumen guan*), 259
generation: in *Definition of the Truth*, 108, 120; in *Miscellaneous Dialogues*, 143, 157, 161, 181–182, 198–206, 218; in *Verses*, 223
Gernet, Jacques, xv, 271–272
gradualism versus suddenness. *See* sudden-gradual dispute
Graham, Billy, xix, 292
Great Parinirvāṇa Sūtra, 86–87, 120, 157
Grieder, Jerome, 263
Guangfu, 283
Guangji, 104
Guangyao (Guangbao), 284
Guanxin lun (*Treatise on the Contemplation of the Mind*), 25, 36
guanxin shi (contemplative analysis), 23–25, 32, 255
Guifeng Zongmi, xviii, 8–16, 236, 244
Gu Jiegang, 247
Guo Ziyi, 14

Hall of the Transmission of the Dharma of the True School of Prajñā (*Zhenzong bore chuanfa zhi tang*), 15
Haoyu, 281
Haoyuan, 8
hells, 199
Heze dashi xianzong ji (*Record of the Manifestation of the Teaching*), 11
Heze Shenhui. *See* Shenhui
Heze si (Luoyang), xviii, 11–14, 84
Hongren: about, 212–213; criticism of, 35; doctrines attributed to, 24; lineage, 79, 91, 94–95, 102, 105, 211; McRae's dissertation on, xvii; teaching career, 16, 96, 212–215; *Treatise on the Essentials of Cultivating the Mind*, 25, 28, 32, 36, 38
Hongzhou school, 3–5, 41, 42, 255, 273
Houmochen Yanzhi, 18
"house" (*jia*), 26
Huadi, Master, 182
Huang Chao rebellion, 268
Huatai debates, xviii, 11–12, 35, 276–277, 290–291
Hubei, 13
Huichang persecution, 268
Huida, 104

Huiguang, 17, 19, 21
Huijian, 287
Huike, 16, 77–79, 91, 106–107, 207–210, 293
Huilang, 279
Huineng: about, 213; de Bary's depiction of, 272; as disciple of Hongren, 16, 213–216; lack of historical records on, 1–2, 16, 36, 252; lineage, 91–105; as member of Northern school, 34; in *Platform Sūtra*, 2–3; Shenhui as champion of, xviii, xix, 1, 16, 92–103, 252; Shenhui's study under, 8–9, 17, 235; stela, 12, 100–103; teaching career, 16–17. See also factionalist campaign; *Platform Sūtra of the Sixth Patriarch*; sudden-gradual dispute
Huiyan, 283
Huizhong, 13–14, 41, 273, 285
Hu Shih: about, xviii, xxiii, 6, 235; contributions to Chan studies, 241–245, 298; debate with Suzuki, 239, 244–245, 257–261; depiction of Shenhui as historical figure, 235–239; dislike of Buddhism, 260, 265, 266–267; historiographical agenda, 245–247, 259–266, 270; image of Shenhui, 238, 256; legacy of, 270–272; McRae's scepticism about, xix–xx; misperceptions of Chan Buddhism, 256–261, 266–267; misperceptions of Shenhui, 235, 251–256, 278–286; motivation to study Shenhui, 265; "new *chan* that was no *chan* at all," 37, 253, 257, 278, 286, 298; PhD dissertation, 242; on Shenhui's teaching career, 37, 253, 285–286; on transformation of Chan, 240–241, 255

ignorance, 39, 64, 133–134, 154, 200, 217
impermanence, 147–148, 203
"incense money" (*xiangshui qian*), 14. See also ordination program
India: great assemblies in, 288; Hu's work on, 249–250, 259, 264, 271, 278; lineage in, 106–107
inspiration-and-departure format, 285–286
Iriya Yoshitaka, 244, 297

Japan: Buddhism in, 268
jia ("house"), 26
Jian, Master, 152, 181, 188
Jiangxi, 13
jianxing ("seeing the Buddha-nature"), 24, 26, 32, 87–89, 98, 133–134, 141, 157–158, 258

Jianzhen, 289
Jiaoran, 281
Jingde chuandeng lu. See *Transmission of the Lamp*
Jingzang, 17
Jingzhong, 255
Jingzhou, xviii, 13, 15, 17, 287
Jinping, 280
Jun, Master, 161, 163–164

Kaiyuan si (Jingzhou), xviii, 13, 15, 17, 72
Kang Zhiyuan, 203
kanjin shaku ("contemplative analysis"), 23–25, 32, 255
kanxin ("viewing the mind"), 24, 30
karmic bonds, 154
Kiang, Stuart, xvi
kuṇḍika water vessel, 7–8

Laṅkāvatāra school. See Northern school
Laṅkāvatāra Sūtra, 198
Lao'an, 16–18, 35–36
Lenggie shizi ji (*Masters and Disciples of the Laṅkāvatāra*), 25, 243, 258
Lidai fabao ji (*Records of the Transmission*), 41, 273
Li Guangzhu, 15
Li Mian, 193
Lingtan, 284–286
Linji lu (*Records of Linji*), 236
Linji Yixuan (Rinzai Gigen), 259
Li Si, 15
Liu Cheng, 130
Liu Xiangqian, 184
Liu Yuxi, 283
Liuzu tan jing. See *Platform Sūtra of the Sixth Patriarch*
Li Wangzai, 15
Longmen, 7, 15
Longxing si, 9
"looking afar" practices, 28, 66
Lotus Sūtra, 59, 82, 83, 131–132, 135, 164
Luoyang: Shenhui in, xviii, 9, 11–15, 84, 276, 286; Shenhui's banishment from, xviii, 13–14, 254. See also Northern school
Lu Yi, 13–14

Maitreya, 52, 96, 212, 216
Mañjuśrī, 42, 116, 141, 189, 209
Masters and Disciples of the Laṅkāvatāra (*Lenggie shizi ji*), 25, 243, 258
Ma Ze, 191
Mazu Daoyi: criticism of Shenhui, 41, 273; Hongzhou school, 3–5, 41, 42, 255,

273; lineage, xvii, 1, 241; sudden enlightenment doctrine, 3
meditation: doctrine of equivalence, 38–39, 50–51, 58, 90, 173, 185–186; Hu's misperceptions of, 257; Northern school practices, 3, 28–32, 38–39, 253, 255, 278–286; seated, 32, 53, 63, 97, 99, 132, 151, 158–159, 179, 201; Shenhui's approach to, xix, 28–33, 38, 41, 253, 255, 278–286, 299; in "three learnings," 38–39, 49–52, 61. See also *Platform Sermon*
Meditation Sūtra of Dharmatrāta, 107
mental cultivation, 151, 159–160
Miao, Vice Minister, 167
Middle Path, 53, 67, 118, 152, 167, 196
"mind of awakening." See *bodhicitta*
Miscellaneous Dialogues (*Wenda zazheng yi*): about, xx, 13, 254; textual sources, 302–305; translation, 129–220
monastic ordination program, xviii, 14, 287–291, 296–297
monks: distinction between laymen and, 23, 39, 82–83, 131, 165, 168, 174; unrestricted great assemblies sponsored by, 75, 83, 126, 287–290. See also *specific person*

Naitō hypothesis, 268
Nanyang, xviii, xx, 9–10, 13, 47
Nanyang heshang dunjiao jietuo chanmen zhiliaoxing tanyu. See *Platform Sermon*
Nanyang Huizhong, 13–14, 41, 273, 285
naturalism, 260, 264–265
naturalness, 57, 98, 133–134, 139, 146, 176, 192–197
Neo-Confucianism, 245, 248, 251, 260, 262, 270–272
"new *chan* that was no *chan* at all" (Hu), 37, 253, 257, 278, 286, 298
niguan ("reverse contemplation"), 25
nirvāṇa, 53–55, 144–146, 177
Nirvāṇa Sūtra: in *Definition of the Truth*, 120; in *Essential Determination*, 24; in *Miscellaneous Dialogues*, 134, 141–147, 157, 185, 187, 189; in *Platform Sermon*, 47–48, 53, 58, 61, 67
"non-abiding mind" (*wuzhu xin*), 55–64, 67, 69, 122, 139, 167–168, 197, 212, 217
"non-activated mind" (*buqi xin*), 22–24, 31–32, 50–51, 61–65, 121, 132, 173
nondualism, 39–41
nonexistence, 140–142, 146–148, 155–156, 162, 166, 177, 195–196, 200, 227–231

"non-thought" (*wuxiang* or *wunian*): about, 27, 39; in *Definition of the Truth*, 117–118; in *Miscellaneous Dialogues*, 136–137, 155, 166–167, 174, 177–178, 182, 196, 204; in *Platform Sermon*, 56, 61, 65–66; in *Verses*, 226, 229–230
Northern school, doctrines of: Shenhui's teachings and, 27–32, 36–39, 42, 253, 274; versus Southern school, 41–42, 240–241, 255
Northern school, literature of: McRae's dissertation on, xvii–xix; meditation practices, 28–32, 38–39, 253, 255, 278–287; in *Platform Sūtra*, 3; presectarian nature of, 34; traces of Shenhui's influence in, 16–27. See also factionalist campaign
Nukariya Kaiten, 235

ordination program, xviii, 14, 287–291, 296–297
Oxhead school: authorship of *Platform Sūtra*, xvii, 2–3, 40–41, 252, 273; doctrines and practices, 5, 40–41; McRae's work on, xvii, xviii; role in factionalism, 255, 273

the Path, 171
"patriarchal hall" (*zutang*), 15
Pei Xiu, 244
perfection of wisdom: in *Definition of the Truth*, 108–119; in *Miscellaneous Dialogues*, 133–134, 137, 166, 171, 181, 189–191, 197, 201–203; in *Platform Sermon*, 52–53, 59–61, 66–68, 71
Perfection of Wisdom Sūtra, 111, 116–118, 166, 171, 201, 209, 211
"perfect teaching" (*yuanjiao*), 3
permanence, 147–148, 203
Philip the Evangelist, 291
Platform Sermon (*Nanyang heshang dunjiao jietuo chanmen zhiliaoxing tanyu*): about, xx, 47, 277; dating of, 10, 27–28, 47; Northern school doctrine in, 27–32; Northern school terminology in, 25–27; ordination platform in, 287; sudden enlightenment in, 33, 274, 296; textual sources, 301–302; translation, 47–71
Platform Sūtra of the Sixth Patriarch (*Liuzu tan jing*): continuity between Shenhui's teachings and, 39–41; creative legend in, 2–3, 16, 42, 241, 252, 258–259, 272–274; dating of, 2, 252; de Bary's

work on, 272; Hu's work on, 243–244, 251–252, 255, 258–259; Oxhead authorship, xvii, 2–3, 40–41, 252, 273; Shenhui's appearance in, 235; Shenhui as compiler of, xviii, 237; sudden enlightenment in, 1, 42; translations of, 297
"Prajñā" (posthumous title), 16
Puji: lineage, 94–95; McRae's dissertation on, xvii; as Reverend Ji, 26; role in Shenhui's banishment, 13, 254; school of, 9, 18, 38; Shenhui's criticism of, 11, 35, 99–100, 105, 124–125
Pure Land school, 259, 268, 270
purity: grasp for, 28, 54–55; rhetorical, xix, 40, 42, 273
Putidamo nanzong ding shifei lun. See *Definition of the Truth*

Qianguang, 84, 168, 171
Qingchan si, 104
qixin. See "activating the mind"

"recorded sayings" (*yulu*), 42, 258, 273
Record of the Manifestation of the Teaching (*Heze dashi xianzong ji*), 11
Records of Linji (*Linji lu*), 236
Records of the Transmission (*Lidai fabao ji*), 41, 273
religious authority: source of, 292–296
religious lineages, 35–36, 78–79, 90–107, 206–217, 254; Shenhui, 37, 235, 254–255, 295
reliquary bowl, 7–8
"reorganization of the national past" (*zhengli guogu*), 245–247, 259–260
repentance, 48–49, 114–115, 172–173, 182
"reverse contemplation" (*niguan*), 25
rhetorical purity, xix, 40, 42, 273
Rinzai Gigen (Linji Yixuan), 259
ritual implements, 7–8

sagacity. *See* wisdom
Śākyamuni, 12, 52, 92, 96, 101, 116, 212, 216
Śāriputra, 52, 99, 132, 159, 179
"seated meditation" (*zuochan*), 32, 53, 63, 97, 99, 132, 151, 158–159, 179, 201
"seeing the Buddha-nature" (*jianxing*), 24, 26, 32, 87–89, 98, 133–134, 141, 157–158, 258
"self-mind" (*zixin*), 25
Sengcan, 12, 78, 91, 209–211
sensory discrimination, 32, 62–63, 190

Shaolin si, 209
Shaozhou school, 91, 95, 99, 102–104, 124, 215
Shengguang, 283
Sheng Xu, 100
Shenhui: biography of, xviii, 7–16; banishment and reinstatement, xviii, 13–14, 254; as champion of Huineng, xviii, xix, 1, 16, 92–103, 252; death and official recognition, 15–16; disciples, 279–286; discovery as historical figure, 235–239; doctrine of sudden enlightenment, 32–34, 36–39, 253, 295–296, 298; early training, 8–9, 17, 34–36, 253, 256; emphasis on suddenness, 33, 37, 253; as evangelist, 275, 291–297, 298; as fundraiser, xviii, 14, 287–291, 299; Huatai debates, xviii, 11–12, 35, 276–277, 290–291; influence on Chan Buddhism, xviii, xix, 5–7, 41–42, 273–274, 298–299; lineage, 37, 235, 254–255, 293; Northern school doctrines and, 27–32, 36–39, 42, 253, 274; Northern school literature and, 16–27; religious authority, 292–296; ritual implements, 7–8; stele, 9, 12, 15, 256; teaching career, xix, 9–13, 16–17, 37, 253, 279–286. See also *Definition of the Truth;* Huineng; Hu Shih; *Platform Sermon; specific work*
Shenxiu: as disciple of Hongren, 16; lineage, 93–98, 102–103, 254, 293; McRae's dissertation on, xvii; meditation practices, 29; in *Platform Sūtra*, 2–3; rivalry with Lao'an, 35–36; Shenhui's criticism of, 35, 239–240, 276–277; teaching career, 9, 17, 18, 256; *Treatise on the Contemplation of the Mind*, 25, 36. *See also* Northern school
Shenying, 280
Shenzu, Master, 160
Shitou Xiqian, 1, 3, 241
shouxin ("awareness of the mind"), 24, 38
shun ("direct"), 25
shunguan ("direct contemplation"), 25
Sichuan schools, 5, 41, 255, 273
Si Daowang, 15
Song Biographies (*Song gaoseng zhuan*): Shenhui in, 8–9, 12–15, 236; Shenhui's disciples in, 279–289
Song Ding, 12
Song dynasty, 269–271
Song gaoseng zhuan. See *Song Biographies*

Song Yun, 208
Southern school, versus Northern school. *See* factionalist campaign
space metaphor, 64–66, 147, 189–190, 193, 223
spiritual maturation: Shenhui's lack of concern for, 37, 253, 278, 285–286
Śramaṇa Dazhao, 19
"stopping and lifting" (*zhiyang*), 40
suchness: in *Definition of the Truth*, 109, 117, 121; in *Miscellaneous Dialogues*, 160, 166, 174, 179–180, 195, 200–201; in *Platform Sermon*, 61, 65; in *Verses*, 223, 226–232
sudden enlightenment (*dunwu*): about, 1–5, 277–278; acceptance in Chan school, 39–41; role in Chinese Buddhism, 6–7, 39; Shenhui's doctrine of, 32–34, 36–39, 253, 295–296, 298; as slogan, 40–42, 253, 255, 272, 274. See also *Platform Sermon;* sudden-gradual dispute
sudden-gradual dispute: Hu's depiction of, 252–255, 258; in *Miscellaneous Dialogues*, 163–165, 175–179; revised understanding of, 1–3, 274; as rhetorical device, xix, 98; Shenhui's influence on, 39–41, 274
Su Jin, 152
Suzong, Emperor, 14
Suzuki Daisetsu (D. T.): debate with Hu, 239, 244–245, 257–261; *Essays in Zen Buddhism*, 235

Tanaka Ryōshō, 275, 297
Tang Fatong, 188
Tang Yongtong, 243
"three learnings," 38–39, 49–52, 61; doctrine of equivalence, 38–39, 50–51, 58, 90, 173, 185–186
transcendence, 24, 27, 32, 39, 154
transgressions, 48–49, 114–115, 171–172, 182
Transmission of the Lamp (Jingde chuandeng lu): Shenhui's death, 15; Shenhui's early training, 8–9; Shenhui as historical figure, 235, 236; Shenhui's work, 11
Transmission of the Treasure Grove (Baolin zhuan), 244
Treatise on the Contemplation of the Mind (Guanxin lun), 25, 36
Treatise on the Dharma-nature (Faxing lun), 25–27, 32

Treatise on the Essentials of Cultivating the Mind (Xiuxin yao lun), 25, 28, 32, 36, 38
Treatise on Perfect Illumination (Yuanming lun), 25, 32
Treatise on the True Principle (Dasheng kaixin xianxing dunwu zhenzong lun): commentary on, 17–19, 23–27, 32, 35, 40; translation, 19–23
"True School" (*zhenzong*): as posthumous title, 16
"truly comprehend the Buddha-nature" (*zhen liaoxing*), 25
Tu Weiming, 257

Ui Hakuju, 239
"unconditioned" (*wuwei*), 15, 50–51, 81–82, 131, 200–201
"unrestricted great assemblies" (*wuzhe da hui*), 75, 83, 126, 287–290

Vajrasamādhi Sūtra, 202
vehicles, 148–153, 189–190
Verses on the Five Watches (Wugeng chuan): about, xx; textual sources, 305; translation, 221–225
Verses on Sudden Enlightenment, the Birthless, and Prajñā (Dunwu wusheng bore song): about, xxi; textual sources, 305; translation, 226–232
"viewing the mind" (*kanxin*), 24, 30
Vimalakīrti, 63, 99, 132, 159, 179, 197
Vimalakīrti Sūtra, 26, 53, 55, 68, 69, 97, 133, 160

Wang Bi, 198
Wang Wei, 2, 12, 184–186
wangxin ("false mind"), 25, 50–51, 54–55, 61, 65, 139, 178, 182, 185
Wang Yi, 189, 199
Wang Youlin, 181
Wang Zhaogong, 148
Weizhong, 281
Wenda zazheng yi. See *Miscellaneous Dialogues*
Wen'gang, 102
Wisdom Sūtra of the Heavenly King Pravara, 64–65, 109–111, 115–116, 201
Wisdom Sūtra of Mañjuśrī, 189
Wright, Arthur F., 270–272
Wu, Emperor, 75–76, 209, 288–291, 298
Wudang, 13
Wudeng huiyuan, 244
Wufang bian (Five Skillful Means), 28, 32
Wugeng chuan. See *Verses on the Five Watches*

wuji ("blankness of mind"), 28
Wu Jiao, 196
Wumen guan (*Gateless Barrier*), 259
Wuming, 283
wunian. See "non-thought"
Wu Pingyi, 100
wuwei ("unconditioned"), 15, 50–51, 81–82, 131, 200–201
wuxiang. See "non-thought"
Wuxing, 161, 164–165
wuzhe da hui ("unrestricted great assemblies"), 75, 83, 126, 288–291
wuzhu xin ("non-abiding mind"), 55–64, 67, 69, 122, 139, 167–168, 197, 212, 217

Xiangmo Zang, 11, 95, 99
xiangshui qian ("incense money"), 14. *See also* ordination program
Xiangyang, 8, 9, 13
Xing, Master, 190
Xingjue, 283
Xiuxin yao lun (*Treatise on the Essentials of Cultivating the Mind*), 25, 28, 32, 36, 38
Xuanwu, 104
Xuanyan, 289
Xuanzang, 249–250, 288
Xuanzong, Emperor, 13, 254
Xue E, 197

Yabuki Keiki, 237
Yampolsky, Philip, 297
Yanagida Seizan, 297; on factionalism, 27; Hu Shih's work with, 244; McRae's study under, xvi–xvii, 240
Yi, Master, 180
Yiyang, 13
Yiyuan, Master, 180
Yogācāra, 249–250
youwei ("conditioned"), 15, 50–51, 81–82, 131, 170, 200–201
Yuan, Master, 187, 200–201

yuanjiao ("perfect teaching"), 3
Yuanming lun (*Treatise on Perfect Illumination*), 25, 32
Yuanyi, 212
Yuanzhen, 282
Yuan Zhongzhi, 179
yulu ("recorded sayings"), 42, 258, 273

Zen masters, 275–276, 286, 298
Zhai Zhongkan, 210
Zhang, Duke, 155
Zhang Dafu, 220
Zhang Wanqing, 195
Zhang Xingchang, 100
Zhao Kanlin, 220
Zhe, Master, 173
zhengli guogu ("reorganization of the national past"), 245–247, 259–260
zhen liaoxing ("truly comprehend the Buddha-nature"), 25
zhenzong ("True School"): as posthumous title, 16
Zhenzong bore chuanfa zhi tang (Hall of the Transmission of the Dharma of the True School of Prajñā), 15
Zhida, 18
Zhide, Master, 175, 200
Zhiman, 282
Zhiru (Faru), 101, 214, 284
zhiyang ("stopping and lifting"), 40
Zhiyi, 281
Zhong, Master, 196
Zhu Xi, 244
Zhuzi yulei, 244
zixin ("self-mind"), 25
Zongmi, xviii, 8–16, 236, 244
Zuoben, Master, 140
zuochan ("seated meditation"), 32, 53, 63, 97, 99, 132, 151, 158–159, 179, 201
zutang ("patriarchal hall"), 15

About the Author

John R. McRae (1947–2011) was a preeminent scholar of Chinese Buddhism who specialized in the rise of Chan (Zen) during the Tang dynasty. McRae studied under Stanley Weinstein at Yale University as well as with Yanagida Seizan and Iriya Yoshitaka in Kyoto and held positions at Cornell University and Indiana University before moving to Komazawa University. In addition to numerous articles and book chapters, he is author of *The Northern School and the Formation of Early Ch'an Buddhism; Seeing through Zen: Encounter, Transformation, and Genealogy in Chinese Chan Buddhism; East Asian Buddhism: A Survey;* and *Buddhism across Boundaries: The Interplay of Indian, Chinese, and Central Asian Source Materials* (co-edited with Jan Nattier). He also completed four translations of major Chinese Buddhist texts for Bukkyō Dendō Kyōkai's English translation series.